No Shame for the Sun

Gender, Culture, and Politics in the Middle East
Leila Ahmed, miriam cooke, Simona Sharoni, and Suad Joseph, *Series Editors*

No Shame for the Sun

• • •

Lives of Professional Pakistani Women

Shahla Haeri

Syracuse University Press

First Edition 2002

02 03 04 05 06 07   6 5 4 3 2 1

Mohamad El-Hindi Books on Arab Culture and Islamic Civilization are published with the assistance of a grant from Ahmad El-Hindi.

The paper used in this publication meets the minimum requirements of American National Standard for Information Sciences—Permanence of Paper for Printed Library Materials, ANSI Z39.48–1984.∞™

Library of Congress Cataloging-in-Publication Data

Haeri, Shahla.
No shame for the sun : lives of professional Pakistani women / Shahla Haeri.
p. cm.—(Gender, culture, and politics in the Middle East)
Includes bibliographical references.
ISBN 0-8156-2960-5 (cloth : alk. paper)—ISBN 0-8156-2979-6 (pbk. : alk. paper)
1. Women in the professions—Pakistan—Biography. I. Title. II. Series.
HD6054.2.P18 H34 2002
331.4'092'25491—dc21
2002010304

Manufactured in the United States of America

Az siday-i sukhan-i ishq nadidam khushtar
Yadigari keh dar in gunbad-i davvar bemaand

(Of all souvenirs beneath this revolving dome
none gives me more pleasure than the music
in the discourse of love)

—*Hafiz*

In fond memory of
Baji—Begum Kishwar Abid Hussain,
Appi—Begum Khurshid Merza,
and
Jahanara Akhlaq
To
Janu—Begum Soraya Alam
and
To the remarkable women of Pakistan
with love

SHAHLA HAERI is the director of the Women's Studies Program at Boston University. She has published numerous articles and books, including *Law of Desire: Temporary Marriage in Shi'i Iran*, also published by Syracuse University Press.

Contents

Preface

IN THE FIFTEENTH CENTURY, the Persian Sufi poet Jami (d. 1492) is reported to have recited a poem in praise of the Arab mystic Rabi'a (d. 801)— a slave girl who achieved mystical immanence and universal fame.[1] Were all women like Rabi'a, Jami declares, they would be shining like the sun—brilliantly and publicly visible. The title of this book, *No Shame for the Sun*, is inspired by this poem, in which the sun refers to Rabi'a. In Persian and Arabic mythology (and language), the sun is feminine. Jami seems to be saying that women such as Rabi'a should not be hidden either by their own veils or by their societies.

Since Rabi'a's time, many thousands of women in Muslim societies such as Pakistan have occupied a variety of public spaces through their professions and engagements with the state and civil society. But where are they in the social science literature on women from the Muslim world? The women portrayed in the growing feminist literature on Muslim societies seem to lead lives very distant from the lives of the authors who write about them. In this literature, one sees veiled women, peasant women, tribal women, urban poor women, but very few middle-class, educated, professional women, despite the latter's visible national profiles. Their stark invisibility took a larger theoretical significance for me when, perplexed by Western stereotypes that seem to "veil" professional Muslim women, I examined several bodies of literature in the course of conducting the research for this book. It is paradoxical that precisely women who have managed to move into the public space and to "shine"

---

1. For the English translation, see Schimmel 1986, 435. The original version of this poem is credited to Abu Abd al-Rahman al Sulami (d. 1021), from whose book *Classes of Sufis* and his chapter on Sufi women Abd al-Rahman Jami (1957 [1336], 615) reportedly took this poem. I am grateful to Jamileh Azamian for providing me with this information. On Rabi'a, see Smith 2001; and on the reference to Jami's praise of Rabi'a, see Smith 2001, 9–10.

in their own societies have been rendered invisible in academic and cultural portrayal in the West. To make them visible outside of their own communities is the purpose of this book.

Why, I ask, have professional Muslim women in their diversity remained invisible to a vast majority of anthropologists? Is it more difficult or discombobulating to write about those with whom one can identify more easily—those who are more like ourselves? What historical forces and theoretical rationales have contributed to the silence on this highly visible category of women in Pakistan and in the rest of the Muslim world? How is it that the cultural discourse of this politically significant—if small—segment has been heard so rarely outside of their own societies?

The case of women of Afghanistan dramatizes the invisibility and voicelessness of the educated professional Muslim women outside their own societies. For years, the dominant image of Afghan women, when they were in the news and at the center of attention, was that of faceless mobile objects, wrapped in blue *burqas*. The violence of forced veiling is obvious and should not be taken lightly, but neither should the symbolic "violence" of indifference and othering. Because women wear *burqa*—by force or by choice—does not mean that they stop being actors in their families and communities and lose their moral courage. It took a tragedy of the magnitude of September 11 to lift—ever so slightly—the "veil" of Afghan women's facelessness and to bring into the public's attention the extent of social involvement, the diversity and complexity of their lives and experiences. And then the White House discovered women very different from those seen on the print and electronic media, women who all along have been struggling against the successive oppressive regimes in their society (Benard 2002). Whether for political expediency or with a genuine desire for finding common grounds, First Lady Laura Bush extended an invitation to professional and unveiled Afghan women to the White House. The First Lady's public acknowledgment underscores the significance of understanding the diversity of women's lives and experiences, regardless of their religious or cultural backgrounds, in order to gain a more accurate knowledge of the other.

Aware of the gap between what I as an educated Muslim woman have experienced and observed in Iran and Pakistan and the representations of "Muslim women" outside of the Muslim world—for example, the case of Afghan women—I adopted a different approach. Heeding anthropologist Laura Nader's (1974) admonition to "study up," I shifted my attention away from the lives of the downtrodden and the subaltern, currently the dominant anthropo-logical focus, to conduct research among educated, skilled, middle-class, and upper-middle-class Pakistani women. I contend that educated, professional Muslim women's efforts to claim the public domain parallel the experiences of professional women in the rest of the world, where modernity has thrown into confusion gender sensibilities and relationships, dislocated masculine tradi-tional privileges and power, and disrupted religious and political institutions. Like professional women in most other societies, professional Pakistani women have power *and* agency, operating within both the domestic *and* public domains. Their efforts to reach their individual or collective goals often come into conflict with the objectives of their community, their male counterparts and kin, their friends and colleagues.

This book is an "ethnography" of six educated, middle-class and upper-middle-class, and professional Pakistani women, who, while challenging the status quo and traditional male hierarchy, have achieved a degree of success. It would be erroneous, however, to understand their success primarily in a tradi-tional masculine sense. Unlike men, they have had to struggle on several fronts simultaneously to reach their goals and to establish themselves as pro-fessionals. Through their struggles, these women have become aware of their own and other women's lives and situations in their society. They exercise power and authority in their chosen fields, and, perhaps because they do so, their status is often contested locally. These women's lives provide examples of ways of resolving particular religious, cultural, and political conflicts. The resolution of these conflicts, successful or problematic, challenges the notion of a "hegemonic" and monolithic Islam that victimizes Muslim women. Pak-istani women's narratives foreground the diversity and uniqueness of individu-als' experiences within a particular Muslim society.

Conducting research among equals was a novel experience for me—differ-ent from my previous research on temporary marriage among marginalized women in Iran in the late 1970s and early 1980s. Not only did Pakistani pro-fessional women's interests in social and political issues overlap with mine, but some had conducted research themselves and with similar critical awareness of social issues and cultural problems. Their lifelong experiences and struggles in both the private and the public domains provided them with the expertise to look at their society critically and to discuss issues of justice and gender, marriage and divorce, death and widowhood, honor and shame, feminism and fundamentalism, religion and politics. Astute observers, they discussed how

their identities were shaped and their experiences were framed by the structures of authority, power, and gender hierarchy in their society. Through their
confrontation with multiple conflicts and their experiences of success and defeat, they slowly but surely are changing their society's concept of gender, of
male and female roles and reciprocal responsibilities, and of religious hierarchies and political order.

I resisted the temptation to focus on the lives of public figures in order to
avoid questions of exceptionality. Except for one of them, a well-known poet,
I chose my "informants" from among ordinary people and eventually focused
on the lives of six of them in particular. I found their life stories compelling,
their determination to change their lives and surroundings inspiring, and their
critical reflections on their society informative. The women of this book are
highly articulate and vocal in their communities and represent their own
points of view eloquently. They can and do speak for themselves. What
emerges from professional Pakistani women's analyses of and reflections on
their society and from my dialogues with them is a collaborative effort. This is
not an ethnography in its traditional and usual sense, but a shared creation, a
"shared ethnography" in which women close to the author in terms of their education and profession embark on the task of reflecting, representing, and
reinterpreting.

I have avoided what seems to be the current tendency to portray women as
either obedient or rebellious. I find such dichotomization inadequate to the
task of describing or dealing with the complexity of women's responses to oppression and injustice. Professional Pakistani women's responses to the realities of their lives are clearly more diverse, complex, multilayered, and
ambivalent.

Acknowledgments

DURING THE RAGING WAR between Iran and Iraq in the 1980s, I seriously considered going somewhere else, such as Cairo, Egypt, for ethnographic research. But Dr. Ali Banuazizi, my friend of many years, said, "Go east, young woman [I was, then], go east." I did and am all the richer for it. Thank you, Dr. Banuazizi.

But then it took me almost ten years to complete this book. Along this long journey, many people, more than I can remember and thank properly, helped me. I would like to thank them from the bottom of my heart, and I pray that I have not left out any names inadvertently.

To all my Pakistani *rishteh dar*s: thank you.

Initial support came from the Social Science Research Council (SSRC, 1987–88), to whom I owe a much-belated thanks. I also owe thanks to the Berkeley Urdu Language Program in Pakistan for a fellowship (1988–89), the Chicago-based Fundamentalism Project (1990) for a short-term grant, and the American Institute of Pakistan Studies (AIPS) and its director, Charles Kennedy, for funding the major part of research for this book (1991–92). I also would like to acknowledge a second short-term AIPS postdoctoral grant (1997–98).

Among those who helped me in Pakistan, thanks go to Dr. Peter Dodd, the director of the Fulbright program and the United States Educational Foundation in Pakistan (USEFP) in Islamabad; Erica Dodd; the staff of USEFP, in particular Nargis Tajik, the Fulbright coordinator; and Afak Haidar and Nadeem Akbar of AIPS.

Lahore was our home, and the Alams our family. I do not know how to thank the Alam family for adopting me effortlessly as a member of their family. My profound appreciation, love, and thanks to Mr. Mahmoud Alam (Mian Jaan); Mrs. Soraya Alam (Janu); Scheherezade, the master potter, whom I

never cease to admire; the late Zahoor (*jaan*) ul-Alkhlaq; and Asad Alam for
making reservations for us at the beautiful Sindh Club in Karachi at the drop
of a hat. My gratitude also goes to the late Dr. Afzal Iqbal, the scholar-
diplomat; his wife, Dr. Zarina Salamat; and Mobaraka Salamat.

My husband and I were lucky to be adopted by another Pakistani family.
Our landlords and neighbors, Noreen (Ruby) and Ejaz Malik, were the best
landlords any tenants would pray to have. Nay, they were not just our landlords, but our best friends, companions, and, for me, often the best "informants." I am grateful for their continued love and friendship. I would also like to
acknowledge our neighbors to the left, the wonderful mother and daughter,
Jamila Apa and Naveed Anwar, whose reading of Urdu literature with me I
particularly cherish.

I am equally grateful to have had the good fortune to meet and befriend a
famous mother and daughter: the late Baji (Begum Kishwar Abid Hussain)—
whose house was a magnet for indigenous and foreign scholars, intellectuals
and diplomats—and Chandi (Begum Abida Hussain), the career diplomat and
politician.

In Lahore, I also met an Iranian scholar of Iqbal, Dr. Shahin Moghadam-
Safiari, whose untimely death I deeply mourn. I shall treasure the memories of
our *ziarat*s to Data Sahib. To the Kazim family, specifically Lubna Kazim,
whose home in the beautiful Mayo Garden was my first place of residence in
Lahore, I offer my special thanks. I am also grateful to Mrs. Noor Hamiddudin
for setting up my initial contact in Lahore and to Afroz Muhammad for introducing me to the Kazim family.

In Karachi, we were blessed with another set of friends: Begum Ghamar Es-
pahani, the Iranian wife of the first Pakistani ambassador to the United States;
the British general-consul Patrick Wogan and his vivacious Iranian wife, Afsaneh Khalatbari-Wogan, who insisted that I stay with them at the British
compound in Karachi; and Maryluz Schloeter, the subhead at the office for
United Nations High Commissioner for Refugees.

The lovely Masuma and Javid Lotia and Ammiji opened their home to us
and lavished us with their hospitality every time we went to Karachi. Mrs.
Doreen Rizvi also welcomed me into her home in Karachi, and Kishwar Rizvi
made the initial invitation. I thank both of them warmly. To the Belgrami family and to my cousin Muna Haeri Belgrami, whom I met for the first time in
Karachi, I would like to give a special tribute.

Among those in New Delhi, India, first and foremost I would like to extend my especial thanks to Shehla Haidar, at whose home I lived during my first trip to India and who introduced me to her extensive networks of family and friends everywhere I traveled in North India. The young and dynamic Iranian couple, Dr. Ranjbaran and his gracious wife, Goli, incorporated me into their family from the first day I arrived in New Delhi. It is with deep sorrow that I recall Dr. Ranjbaran's heart attack and sudden death during the same year.

I would like to thank Mr. V. S. Varma and his late wife, as well as their son, Virat Varma, and his wife, Pompush, for their hospitality in Srinager, Kashmir. I also am grateful to Indian scholars Beena Agarwal and Leela Dube. And I especially thank Dr. Christian Troll—Jesuit priest, scholar of Islam, and fellow seeker.

In Aligarh, I was fortunate to make the acquaintance of Nazir Ahmad, a renowned scholar of Persian literature; Samiuddin Ahmad, the chairman of the Department of Persian Literature at the university; Nahid Safavi; Shehnaz Hashmi; and Anwar Rizvi. I am grateful to Dr. Zakiyya Siddique, the principal of the Women's College in Aligarh, who gave a detailed tour of the college and invited me to share the Founder's Day with them. I also would like to thank the staff of the Abul Kalam Azad Library in Aligarh and of the Khuda Bakhsh Oriental Library in Patna, in particular its then director, Dr. Abid Reza Bedar.

In Pakistan, I owe a debt of gratitude to the scholars and academicians who befriended me, included me in their networks, and facilitated my entry into various institutions. In particular, I would like to thank Nighat Said Khan, the director of Applied Socioeconomic Resource and the founder of the Women's Studies Institute in Lahore; Beena Sarwar, the renowned journalist, who responded to my e-mail requests speedily and efficiently; Ahmad Rashid, another internationally acclaimed journalist; Negar Ahmed, the founder and director of the Aurat Foundation; Asma Jahangir, the indomitable lawyer and director of the Human Rights Commission of Pakistan, for inviting me to go with her to the Lahore High Court; Hina Jilani, another equally impressive human rights advocate; Farida Shaheed and Casandra Balchin, of Lahore's Shirkat Gah; Neelam Hussain and Farida Sher of Seamorgh; and Begum Bushra Rahman. I also am grateful to Dr. Haroon Ahmed, his wife, Anis Haroon, and the advocate Khalid Ishaq—all in Karachi; Shaheen Sardar Ali and Professor Farzand Durani in Peshawar; and Nageen Hayat, in Islamabad.

My colleagues and friends in the United States have been constant sources of intellectual enrichment and emotional support. I specifically would like to thank Ayesha Jalal, Karen Leonard, Mary Hegland, Rita Wright, Wendy Doniger, and Lila Abu-Lughod for reading various chapters of this manuscript and for providing invaluable comments and suggestions. I am deeply grateful to Leila Ahmed, who has been a continued source of support and inspiration; to Lois Beck, whose discerning comments polished my manuscript and with whom I share an interest in the anthropology of Iran; and to Irene Gendzier, a wonderful friend and a significant interlocutor at Boston University.

My deep appreciation and love go to Farzaneh Milani for reading my manuscript in its entirety and for her sustained emotional and intellectual support, as well as to Kaveh Safa, whose translation of Hafiz appears in the dedication—my intellectual debt to him is enormous; he is my *makhzanul akhbar,* "treasure mind." I would like to pay special tribute to Professor Seyyed Hossein Nasr; to Seyyed Vali Reza Nasr, with whom I share interests in and exchange ideas about Pakistan and Iran; and to John Esposito.

My great appreciation and love go to Tanvir (*meri behen*) and Masood (*jaan*) Ahmed Khan. I am particularly grateful to Tanvir *behen* for her continued help with the translations of Urdu passages and poetry and for patiently double-checking my frequent inquiries on Pakistan.

Angelic help arrived from two special women whose expert input I would like to acknowledge particularly and whom I thank enthusiastically: Margaret Studier, a longtime friend and colleague who transcribed all my tapes with speed and efficiency but with little financial reward; and Susan Husserl-Kapit, who edited my manuscript professionally and promptly, but also inexpensively. Mary Selden Evans at Syracuse University Press is a dream editor, and I would like to express my deep appreciation to her as well as to my copy editor, Annie Barva, whose meticulous editing much improved my manuscript.

I would like to express my heartfelt gratitude to Chancellor John Silber and Provost Dennis Berkey for making it possible for me to continue my association with Boston University; to Dean Susan Jackson for being a lightening rod for the Women's Studies Program; and to colleagues and friends, Professors Herbert Mason, Parker Shipton, and Robert Hefner.

Without the active and enthusiastic cooperation and collaboration of the women who tell their stories here, there would be, of course, no book. To all of you—Nilofar Ahmed, Quratul Ain Bakhteari, Sajida Mokarram Shah, Kishwar Naheed, Ayesha Siddiqa Agha, and Rahila Tiwana—a deeply heartfelt thanks.

The vital source of sustenance in my life continues to be my family. My parents, Jamal and Behjat, are the light of my eyes. My sisters—Shirin, Shokoofeh, and Niloofar—and my brother—Mohammad Reza—are the loves of my life. And my husband, Walter (Rusty) Crump, whose beautiful double exposure of Nageen Hayat and the green fields of northern Pakistan adorns the book cover, is the *color* of my life.

Abbreviations

ACBAR	Agency Coordinating Body for Afghan Relief
ANP	Awami National Party
ASR	Applied Socioeconomic Resource
CIA	Crime Investigation Agency
CIDA	Canadian International Development Agency
DOI	Daughters of Islam
HRCP	Human Rights Commission of Pakistan
JI	Jama'at-i Islami
MQM	Muhajir Qaumi Movement
NGO	nongovernmental organization
PML	Pakistan Muslim League
PPP	Pakistan People's Party
PSF	People's Student Federation
PTSH	posttraumatic syndrome hysteria
UNHCR	United Nations High Commissioner for Refugees
UNICEF	United Nations Children's Fund
USIS	United States Information Services
WAF	Women's Action Forum
WAR	Women Against Rape

Introduction

A FEW YEARS AGO I met a woman professor at a university faculty party in the eastern United States. In the course of our conversation, she learned that I had just returned from Pakistan, where Benazir Bhutto had been democratically elected prime minister for the second time (1993).[1] She asked, rather incredulously, "How is that possible? Isn't she a woman? Isn't Pakistan a Muslim society?"

"Yes, she is a woman," I said. "And yes, Pakistan is a Muslim society." It does not automatically follow that because Pakistan is a Muslim society, *no* woman can be elected a prime minister or that *no* Muslim man will ever vote for a Muslim woman.

What is culturally and historically specific to Pakistan that made it possible for a young Muslim woman to be elected prime minister, not only once but twice? Is women's leadership incompatible with Islam?[2]

In the late 1980s, as a human rights activist was interviewing me on the status of "Muslim women," he used the term *Muslim women* frequently, generally, and indiscriminately. It seemed as if he did not see me as an Iranian Muslim woman belonging to a particular society with a particular history and coming from a particular class, educational, and professional background. Which Muslim women was he talking about? He seemed profoundly innocent of the actual geographical, historical, cultural, and ethnic boundaries within and

1. One may note an ironic situation here. Benazir Bhutto covered her hair, was elected, and became the prime minister of a Muslim state. Hillary Rodham Clinton was put in her "proper place" during her husband's first presidential campaign when she asserted her difference by objecting to baking cookies.

2. Regarding the controversy surrounding Benazir Bhutto's leadership and for a historical study of Muslim women leaders, see Mernissi 1994; I. Malik 1997, 294 n. 50; and Shaheed 1990, 10.

among Muslim societies. Did he think Iranian women, diverse though they are in class, education, and ethnic identity, are really the same as Pakistani women or, for that matter, Saudi Arabian, Algerian, Afghani, or Malaysian women? How could the realities of the everyday lives of such a vast and diverse group of women, within and across the Muslim world, be viewed so uniformly and understood so unproblematically?[3] I asked him whether he would use such an essentialized—and meaningless at this level of generality—term when speaking, say, about Latin American women. Would he feel just as knowing and comfortable in referring to them as "Christian women"?

"No," he said.

"Why not?" I asked.

"Because, uh. . . ," he said. "Well, there is something peculiar about Islam!"

Is there something peculiar about Islam? Is Islam the leveler of diversity and difference that he perceived it to be? Islam is, of course, a world religion that transcends many cultural boundaries and territorial borders. But can one begin to understand different cultures merely by looking at their shared religion? Islam is declared constitutionally to be the state religion of both Pakistan and Iran. Are there no differences between Islam as practiced in Iran and Islam as practiced in Pakistan? Is there all religion and no culture in Muslim societies? What is the underlying power mechanism that gives an apparently rational observer the right to claim such categorical knowledge of the "other"?

When Sajida Mokarram Shah, a woman whose story is included here, lost her young husband in a tragic car accident in 1983, she and her four young children were expected to move into her brother-in-law's house and live under his supervision. The well-established tradition of levirate or widow inheritance among the Pathans/Pakhtun in Peshawar dictated this move.[4] Although social custom has long endorsed levirate and legitimized it in the name of religion, Islam does condemn the custom and instructs Muslims to avoid "inheriting" widows against their will (Qur'an 4:19). Educated and from an upper-middle-class background, Sajida resisted family pressure—from both her own family and her husband's family—and adamantly refused to allow her

---

3. See also Kahf 1999, 3, and L. Ahmed 1992.

4. *Pathan* is a Hindi term adopted by the British from the original *Pukhtun*, who claim descent to Afghan tribes. The language is called Pushto (Spain 1957, 135–53). See also Moorhouse 1984, 183, and A. Ahmed 1977, 112.

husband's brother to take control of her and her children. By going against the custom and asserting her autonomy, she threatened both her affinal relations and her own kin with the prospect of dishonor, although she had the explicit support of religious doctrine. Among the Pathans, whose identity is "defined explicitly in terms of marriage and control of women" and where women have "so little autonomy or control over their lives" (Tapper 1991, 207), her behavior was perceived as scandalous, indeed subversive. Her family, most pointedly her father, shunned her.

One may ask how it was possible for Sajida to defy cultural tradition in a society where "nothing is stronger than custom" (Cherry Lindholm 1996, 25; Tapper 1991). Conversely, if religion is the all-powerful source of the sociomoral order, how could such clear Islamic injunction be rejected in favor of social custom? Why is there so much resistance to women's autonomy and independence? Are contestory elements built into religion that in fact can be empowering to Muslim women?

I am always taken aback when, despite my efforts to explain the "phenomenon" of hopelessly passive, veiled Muslim women, a majority of my students retain their stereotypical images and beliefs of women in the Muslim world. The sensitivity they—and many scholars—show regarding the differences of race, class, and ethnicity in their own communities does not seem to extend to their views of their Muslim sisters. The cultural and historical diversity of Muslim women's lives and the specificity of their experiences and activities escape them, even as I—an unveiled, educated, professional woman—stand before them.[5] Somehow they do not seem to hear or see me as a reality different from their tenacious image of "Muslim women" as passive, victimized, and veiled, if at times sympathetic. I have wondered how analytically and politically useful this megacategory of obedient "Muslim woman" is, how it was created historically, and how it has been sustained popularly for so long, so stubbornly. How is it that my students, colleagues, and many others in the larger society seem to ignore my presence and that of many other women in my situation and so resolutely hold on to images of women they have never actually met? How did I become invisible? I have puzzled over the management and dissemination of knowledge in the West and the apparent resistance to learning about the dif-

5. See also Najmabadi (1997) for her resistance to being pigeonholed into preconceived categories.

ferences and similarities among and within Muslim societies and Muslim women. To understand this puzzle, I finally decided that the anomaly of educated, professional Muslim women needed to be addressed.

Popular perceptions become particularly difficult to dislodge because some Muslim states themselves—such as Saudi Arabia, Iran, Afghanistan, Pakistan, and Algeria—have produced enough news to encourage images of brutalizing Islam and of victimized Muslim women abroad. These states enforce and propagate their own unitary image of "the Muslim woman." Caught in the clashing multiple demands of modernity, nation-state building, and religious awakening, they appear to be wobbling constantly between granting women certain citizenship rights—initially often under international pressures—and withholding effective implementation—often under more conservative and religious pressures.

Muslim states are, of course, not uniform in their approach to addressing and redressing the legal, political, and social inequalities of their women citizens.[6] These states more often than not are contested entities in the Muslim world, hardly representing a democratic and majority point of view. The harsh measures taken by the Taliban in the name of Islam in Afghanistan ironically seemed to alert the Iranian Islamic Republic to its own puritanical absolutism and to its untenable claim to the "truth" of Islam. Ayatollah Khamenei, Iran's spiritual leader since 1989, has condemned the Taliban for its anti- and un-Islamic behavior, in particular its attitudes toward women.

Many Muslim women undoubtedly have been victimized (as is more or less true in most societies) and veiled, a fact that should not be trivialized. But the institution of veiling, purdah (as it is known in South Asia), though dominant in Muslim societies, is neither the source of women's victimization in the Muslim world nor exclusively a Muslim institution.[7] The custom of sex segregation or purdah is a well-established tradition in northern India and is prevalent among both Muslims and Hindus.[8]

6. See the series of articles in Kandiyoti 1991.

7. "Although Islam helped to institutionalize and perpetuate modesty and seclusion practices by endowing them with the aura of religious sanctity, these practices did not originate with Islam; they were well established in Byzantine and Syriac Christian and pre-Christian societies of the Mediterranean, Mesopotamia, and Persia before the coming of Islam" (Dumato 1995, 19–20). See also Shaheed 1989.

8. I am referring to the practice of sex segregation and not necessarily to the veil itself. For an interesting visual representation of purdah among the Hindus in Rajistan, India, see the doc-

But the symbolism of the veil, the motivations for wearing it, its styles and gradations—from a loosely draped scarf to a complete cover—vary tremendously within and across Muslim societies. Some women wear a veil to demonstrate religious conviction, some to be distinguished as respectable, others to remain anonymous or safe, and still others to cover their poverty. Some wear a veil out of respect for local custom, and still others are forced to do so under the threat of punishment. Veiling is also primarily an urban phenomenon, and many peasant and tribal women, though modestly dressed, do not wear a veil.[9]

That women are veiled does not necessarily mean that they are miserable, victimized, or inactive, though of course some may very well be. This stereotype is called objectively into question by the fact that in the late twentieth century many Muslim middle-class professional women chose to veil themselves, particularly in Egypt and Malaysia.[10] More challenging is the presence of veiled Iranian women leaders in the Parliament, who observe veiling more and more strictly the closer they are to the foci of power (Gerami 1996, 125–50). Although Iranian women have been forced to wear "Islamic veiling" in public since the establishment of the Islamic Republic of Iran in 1979—and many resent having to do so—they are participating more than ever in their own society's political and social life. The active presence of Iranian women in the public space is not, I must say, because of gender-friendly policies of the Islamic regime, but because of women's own determination and sustained challenges to the regime to respect its own rhetoric and to fulfill its promises of gender parity. Gender parity is still a distant dream for Iranian Muslim women,

umentary *Zenana: Scenes and Recollections* (Documentary Educational Resource, 1982, thirty-six minutes), directed by Roger Sandall and Jayasinhjii Jhala. For a series of interesting and detailed descriptions of similarities and differences between the veil and veiling in South Asia, see Papanek and Minault 1982.

9. In a review of the edited volume *Muslim Women's Choices* (El-Solh and Mabro 1994), Sandra Hale observes, "What is also *not* new [in the book] is the iconography: black *chadur*-wearing women on the cover and veiled faces on the back! Sometimes this can be an ironic statement, as in ironic juxtaposition, but I am not sure that that is what was intended here. Perhaps we should remind each other about the relatively low percentage of women, until very recently, who wore anything we could refer to as a 'veil' " (1996, 2).

10. For a detail analysis of veil and veiling, see El Guindi 1999. See also the video documentary *Veiled Revolution* (First Run Features Distributors, 1982, twenty-six minutes), directed by Elizabeth W. Fernea and Marilyn Gaunt.

but many of them have turned the veiling requirement into a license to appear in public, to resume professional careers, and to demand changes in personal laws and in political and professional institutions. Even in such situations, however, a professional woman's choice to veil is perceived as a further confirmation of passivity of women and oppression of religion or as an anomaly and a paradox, rather than as an empowering act. Indeed, women's choices to veil are seldom understood as individual or collective strategies used by some working women to legitimate their presence in the public domain and to assume a profession. The activities of both unveiled and veiled professional women continue to go unnoticed in the West.[11]

It would be too simple to blame the problem solely on my students' and colleagues' naïveté and inability to see the cultural specificity of Muslim societies and the diversity of Muslim women's roles, statuses, worldviews, and activities. The problem is owing in part to the unrelenting media fascination with and fear of veiling and veiled women—its automatic equation of veiling, oppression, female passivity, and, occasionally, eroticism—and in part to what is available for the public to read or to see in the form of films, ethnographies, and documentaries.[12]

There are, I believe, historical and theoretical rationales for the persistence of such outsider perceptions and stereotypes. The problem historically stems from the two dominant and formative discourses of the past century that merged into powerful frameworks for determining funding, study, and research in the Muslim world. By far the most important was the Orientalism discourse and the Orientalist textualist approach to the study of Muslim societies, notwithstanding ongoing academic and political debates and disputes. The other discourse involved early anthropological attempts to construct an anthropological canon of the Middle East. Whereas the first drew on the "high tradition," using the Scripture as the blueprint for understanding the Muslim world, the other identified the village or tribe as the "unit" of analysis, general-

11. I am aware of the multiplicity of cultures that constitute the Western world and hence the problems of using terms such as *the West* and *Western* categorically. I use these terms loosely and generally, meaning the dominant perception and representation of women and Islam in European and North American literature and media.

12. In the same vein, Dumato writes, "To what extent . . . is the industry of writing and teaching about Muslim women actually promoting a homogenized, problem-beset vision of reality, instead of one that reflects the experience of only some Muslim women at some particular time?" (1996, 13).

izing it to the entire Middle East (Eickelman 1989; Gilsenan 1990, 231; Street 1990; Breckenridge and van der Veer 1993). In both cases, the Middle East as a society and Islam as a religion were analyzed within the current theories of modernity, sovereignty, and social change; both society and its religion were presumed to be authoritarian, monolithic, and resistant to change (Breckenridge and van der Veer 1993, 7–8; Hefner 1998).

The dearth of literature, media reports, and visual portrayals of the social and political activities of professional women from the Muslim world is a puzzle until we consider these frames of reference. Why has this category of Muslim women who are accessible and visible in their own society—and often contested because of it—remained invisible in the West? How is it that their discourse has been heard so rarely outside of their own societies? Why have middle-class urban professional Muslim women failed to capture the imagination of anthropologists, the media, and the public, as their veiled sisters seem to have done so completely?

The evolving global power structure has confronted Muslim states with the daunting tasks of economic reconstruction and democracy, sovereignty and citizenship, religious revivalism and xenophobia, human rights and gender equity. Against this background, social analysis is challenged to breathe fresh perspectives into the research epistemologies of the Muslim world. In this book, I question both the trendy and the traditional approaches to knowing "Muslim women" and Islam and suggest a shift of focus, perspective, and approach to the changing configurations of female agency and structures of power and authority in Pakistan and, by implication, in the Muslim world.

In the past one hundred years or so, the Western literature and public media have represented Islam primarily as ahistorical, monolithic,[13] omnipotent, and, in that sense, "exceptional"—that is, different from other world religions (Hefner 1998). Embedded in such representation are the assumption of victimization of Muslim women (K. Ahmed 1992; Kahf 1999, 1–2) and a gradual amnesia regarding the history of the diversity of women's experiences in the Muslim world prior to the Enlightenment (Kahf 1999, 111). In particular,

---

13. The catastrophic events of September 11, 2001, and the subsequent distinctions President George W. Bush made between "good" Islam and "bad" Islam, one that members of his administration consistently underlined, seem effectively to have ushered in a change in the popularly held unitary image of Islam. The "Islamic monolith" has been at long last fractured publicly.

women's agency is denied, and religion is perceived to be the major if not the only *cause* of the oppression and victimization of Muslim women.

In this work, I try to decenter the dominant methodological and epistemological tendencies that portray the Muslim world as village or tribe and Islam as the hegemonic sociomoral order in the Muslim world. I suggest we approach religion as only partially hegemonic (Ortner 1996, 18) and in tight embrace with culture, particularly with the deeply entrenched moral code of honor, *izzat,* in Pakistan. Further, I suggest we should pay equal attention to the life and experiences of people like ourselves and conduct research among equals in the face of global sociohistorical currents that have demanded greater similarities and uniformity in the midst of claims to national sovereignty, ethnic diversity, and plurality. From this perspective, anthropologists are challenged to renegotiate critically the nuances of similarities between the "self" and the "other," rather than primarily to focus on the differences.

To understand the often paradoxical and ambivalent responses to social change in the Muslim world, I contend that we ought to document, demonstrate, and analyze the impact women have had on their societies, just as we have done regarding the impact of women in the Western world—for example, in work on the suffragette movement. If one were to compare the literature on Muslim women with the writing on women in the United States, it becomes clear that the women who are the subject of the latter study are for the most part middle class and educated.[14] One might ask, Why the difference? In Talal Asad's view, because of the anthropologists' use of "dual modality of historical time" when evaluating social change in the Muslim world (1993, 22). Such an epistemological approach has "enabled [anthropologists] to represent events as at once contemporaneous and noncontemporaneous . . . and thus some conditions as more progressive than others" (23).

I do not intend to be an apologist for misogynous practices that continue to oppress women in the Muslim world, but I also find it problematic to single out Islam as the champion of world oppression of women. Here lies a dilemma I have had to contend with, one that I think is the source of both my personal vulnerability and my professional strength. As a "translator" of Pakistani and Iranian cultures and as a Muslim feminist anthropologist, I find myself in the unenviable position of fighting on two or more fronts simultaneously: being critical of social injustice and violence against women "back home" while try-

14. I am grateful to Irene Gendzier for bringing this point to my attention.

ing to cut through layers of entrenched misunderstandings, misconceptions, and stereotypes abroad.

As professional women become active players in Pakistan and in much of the Muslim world, the contestations over who has the legitimacy to define, interpret, and control the sacred text and cultural traditions have intensified. Although relatively small in numbers and diverse in their professional pursuits, these women are involved in politics, are knowledgeable about their society, and are aware of the contested discourse of religious legitimacy and political alliances nationally and of the rapidly changing configurations of gender, power, and knowledge internationally.

In this book, I present the life experiences of six educated middle- and upper-class professional Pakistani women who reflect critically on various sociopolitical issues in their society as well as on the personal issues of identity, marriage, and sexuality. They also discuss their religion and culture and situate their lives within the existing structures of authority, power, and gender hierarchy. The women's stories of their struggles reveal their inner strength and moral courage. By challenging laws and conventions—often at a cost—they have raised questions about the legitimacy or morality of those laws and conventions. Professional and educated Pakistani women, and many others in similar situations, have been effective in raising social consciousness and sometimes in transforming the rules themselves.

Making Professional Pakistani Women Visible

Being a working woman in Pakistan almost by definition involves some kind of conflict with one's family, husband, lineage, and various social institutions.[15] In the words of Samina Matin, a female Pakistani psychiatrist, "In our society it is assumed that if there were any respectability in the family, women would not go out to work" (qtd. in Shah 1994a, 34).[16]

Because of the ethnic diversity in Pakistan, I planned to interview women

15. In 1983, the commission on the status of women in Pakistan reported, "Female employment is still taboo for most men in Pakistan and in the name of *izzat* (honor) women, both educated and uneducated, are precluded from becoming paid workers" (qtd. in I. Malik 1997, 154; see also Williams 1999, 209).

16. Based on a study of women industrial workers in Pakistan, Bano and Fahim (1995, 108–11) point to this and other problems for working and professional women.

from the four major provinces of Pakistan, each of which has its own distinct language, culture, and history: Punjab Province, the largest and politically most dominant; Sindh Province; North-West Frontier Province; and Baluchistan Province. I traveled extensively within these provinces, except Baluchistan, met many people, and interviewed some women formally and informally. The day before I planned to travel to Baluchistan and interview an educator, she telephoned to inform me that the state was under a local curfew and that it was not a good time for me to go there. By the time the curfew was lifted, she had gone abroad, and I was not able to contact her again.

I interviewed Kishwar Naheed and Ayesha Siddiqa in Lahore, the capital of Punjab. I met and interviewed Sajida Mokarram Shah in Peshawar, the capital of the North-West Frontier Province, and Rahila Tiwana in Karachi, the capital of Sindh. I conducted these interviews in 1992–93. I interviewed Nilofar Ahmed and Quratul Ain Bakhteari in the summer of 1998 in Karachi. Part of the reason for the time gap is that I later decided to go back to Pakistan to collect more data and to interview a professional woman with a religious background.[17] I initially planned to limit my book to five women, but when I went to Pakistan in the summer of 1998, some friends told me that I must meet Qurat, as she is popularly known, and interview her for my book. They were quite right, and I am thankful for their suggestion.

Our professional and intellectual compatibility as well as our cultural and religious affinity made our meetings and conversations all the more intimate and meaningful both for them and for me. They were as interested and passionate about social and political issues as I was. We talked for long hours—discussed, debated, and disputed political, religious, and feminist issues. They wanted to know about me, Iran, and my project in Pakistan. We shared personal stories, compared, contrasted, and discussed traditions, beliefs, and rituals in Iran and in Pakistan. Because of the individualistic nature of our conversations, we did not follow a set format, nor did I ask them to follow the traditional life-cycle approach to their lives. Each woman largely determined the form of her own narrative, and in retelling their life stories I have remained

---

17. I originally had interviewed Appa Nisar Fatima, a member of the Parliament and a former member of Jama'at-i Islami. She had left the party discretely and formed her own organization. I attended some of her talks and party gatherings. She unfortunately died of cancer in 1992, and my interviews with her remained unfinished. I have incorporated some of her comments and ideas in this book.

faithful to the style and manner in which they chose to share them with me. With the exception of Qurat, who took a chronological approach, almost all of them began by talking, often passionately—a passion sadly flattened in the text—about one or another major conflict and challenge that created a new awareness of themselves and often marked a turning point in their lives.

Methodological Reflections

In her book *Writing a Woman's Life*, Carolyn Heilbrun argues that anonymity historically has been "the proper tradition of women" (1988, 12). Anthropologists also traditionally have kept the identity of their informants anonymous, but their objective generally has been to protect them. I could not follow the anthropological tradition of masking the identity of my informants, not because I wanted to make them vulnerable, but because this anonymity would have been contrary to my effort to "unveil" them and to make them visible. Like Jami, the fourteenth-century Persian Sufi, I felt it would be a shame to keep professional Pakistani women's identity hidden and their contributions to the changing configuration of gender, power, and knowledge in their society disguised. Like Rabi'a, their ninth-century Arab mystic sister, Pakistani women are impressive and active in public and hence are "no shame for the sun." As if in spiritual agreement with Jami, not a single one asked to remain anonymous. They know about my project and are aware that stories of their lives will appear in this book. I have remained in touch with most of them, except for Sajida—for reasons that will become clear.

The fact that they are not anonymous potentially might involve ethical problems, as Laura Nader (1974) predicted, because some of their associates, friends, and foes still live in Pakistan. Much has changed both in their lives since I interviewed them in 1992–93 and in Pakistan, particularly since the September 11, 2001, tragedy. Some topics they discussed with me then potentially might be politically problematic now. In follow-up e-mail exchanges I have had with some of them, a few asked that certain passages be eliminated from their narratives or that others be made more oblique. I have obliged such requests. Their stories touch other people's lives, which may or may not correspond with the named—or unnamed—individuals' subjective reading of these women's narratives. The women trusted me with some of the most intimate aspects of their lives, and I have no reason to think that they fabricated their experiences and their entire life stories. "Unlike the reassuring Truth of the scientific ideal, the truths of personal narratives are neither open to proof nor self-evident" (Personal Narrative Group 1989, 261).

Another serious problem I had to contend with also emanates from retaining these women's real identity. The difficulty had to do with the degree to which I could communicate some culturally taboo topics they shared with me, such as homosexuality, bisexuality, sexual dissatisfaction, and rape. These topics are known in the literature on Pakistan, of course. "Between you and me," sometimes they would say, or during a lunch break when the tape recorder was off, some revealing comments were made. A few of them specifically asked me not to mention such topics in the text, at least not in great detail, despite my attempts to encourage them to talk more about them. Some did not make a secret of these subjects as far as their own lives were concerned, but sometimes they made reference to other people's sexual preferences, which might be problematic and potentially offensive. In such situations, I have taken refuge in the long-standing tradition in anthropology of masking the identity of the person in question, leaving out the references to particular individuals, making the variations on sexuality oblique, or omitting the issue entirely.

All of the women featured in this book are educated, with professional jobs, although Rahila Tiwana was campaigning for political office on a Pakistan People's Party ticket at the time of her interview, and Nilofar Ahmed maintained an unpaid position. All have a positive, almost visionary sense of themselves and of their activities. All speak fluent English, except for Rahila, who speaks well enough to make herself understood. My conversations with her involved much greater segments in Urdu, and we switched back and forth between English and Urdu. A glossary for Urdu terms is provided at the end of the book. All our conversations were taped in the course of several days or weeks.

Organizing a Life: Chapter Structure

Each chapter centers on the life of one particular woman and is divided into three major segments. I introduce each woman in the first segment and give a quick synopsis of the circumstances surrounding our meeting.

The second segment features the text of each woman's story largely in her own words. I intentionally have retreated to the background and removed the text of my questions, though my voice is not entirely silenced. I agonized over doing so, not only because the reader may miss the questions I asked, but also because the nuanced responses and emotions expressed may get flattened without the give and take of questions and answers. The advantage of retreating, however, was to give the women's narratives maximum space, so their voices can be heard uninterrupted. Not all questions carry the same weight. Some are fillers and primarily for the purposes of prompting and clarifying. Leaving them in the text would have slowed the flow of the narratives. I tried to recapture the gist of some of my questions in the subheads, to redirect them in the first line of the women's responses, or, when absolutely necessary, to reproduce them in the footnotes. The footnotes form a major part of the text and are used extensively to clarify many references made in the narratives. To convey the feelings expressed, I also describe in brackets the speaker's mood, tone of voice, or emotional reactions to some of my questions or to their own contemplations. Nonetheless, given the length of my interviews and the limitations of space, I have had to condense the narratives, eliminate some repetitions, and rearrange passages. I have not smoothed out the emotional or intellectual contradictions or the apparently personal or cultural inconsistencies that may have been expressed.

I conclude each chapter with a third segment that discusses one or two themes from each woman's life story that bring out the uniqueness of that individual's life trajectory while situating it within a cultural context and within current anthropological and feminist frameworks. Because I came to know Kishwar Naheed and Ayesha Siddiqa for a longer period before interviewing them and continuing our friendship, I had a chance to interact with them on many occasions, which I draw upon in their particular chapters.

Many other issues and interpretations can be derived from these women's commentaries and reflections. Their social analysis and interpretations of Pakistani culture and society are often sharp, insightful, and informative, though, as it is in the nature of social sciences, one may disagree with some of their interpretations, as indeed they disagreed with each other regarding issues such as feminism and fundamentalism in Pakistan. The kind of ethnography that emerges from the confluence of the thick description, multivocality, and cross-referenced dialogues and discussions between these women and me is what I call "shared ethnography." In this kind of ethnography, social analyses and interpretations are a prerogative not only of the anthropologists, but also of the indigenous scholars and professionals. The representation of the self and other in ethnographic text, in other words, is the product of the joint effort between the ethnographer and the "natives."

No Shame for the Sun is organized in three parts. Part one, "Against the Grain: Revealing Our Selves," includes chapter 1, which sets the historical, cultural, and theoretical contexts for the six narratives that follow. Part two, "Contesting the Culture of Dominance," involves social and cultural transgressions and includes three chapters focusing on identity, violence, and legitimacy. In chapter 2, Quratul Ain Bakhteari (b. 1948) describes her coming of age and her gradual awareness of the cultural clash and traditional divide between her own sense of her developing feminine identity and individual desire, on the one hand, and her parents' expectations and her society's normative codes, on the other. Chapter 3 revolves around violence against women and the torture and the alleged "rape" of Rahila Tiwana (b. 1964), a young woman political activist in police custody in 1990–91. A young feudal lord, Ayesha Siddiqa (b. 1966), in chapter 4 expresses her ambivalence toward the legitimacy of being a woman with substantial financial power in a rigidly hierarchical male-dominated feudal and urban setting.

Part three, "Face-to-Face with the Text," explores religious and legal transgressions and includes women's narratives focusing on marriage, kinship, and religion. Religion and culture here are not taken as reified and bounded categories, but as two powerful yet fluid frameworks and concepts that can facilitate organization of ideas and discussions. In chapter 5, Kishwar Naheed (b. 1940), a well-known Pakistani poet, speaks of her determination to make a culture of her own by arranging her own marriage and by challenging the traditional male-dominated literary forms of poetry. Sajida Mokarram Shah (b. 1951), in chapter 6, describes movingly the plight of widowed women among the Pathans, while underscoring her determination to raise her own children rather than live with her in-laws, as is culturally mandated. Chapter 7 is about a Sufi mystic woman, Nilofar Ahmed (b. ca. 1940), who is reinterpreting the Qur'an and the received traditions from a feminist perspective. She is working hard to empower Pakistani women by educating them about their religion, which in her view has given Muslim women many rights that historically have been obliterated by male scholars' (mis)interpretations of the Scripture.

Because each chapter ends with concluding remarks, the book's conclusion is short. It briefly revisits some of the major themes that have emerged in the women's life stories.

PART ONE

Against the Grain: Revealing Ourselves

1

Stating the Problems
Theoretical Contemplation

Journey East: Journey of Self-Discovery

FOR MORE THAN TEN YEARS NOW, I have immersed myself in Pakistan society and culture. I found Pakistan culturally, religiously, and politically quite different from Iran, where I was born. I felt strangely at home there, though. After a long colonial domination, Pakistan was partitioned from India in 1947 in one of the most wrenching human tragedies of the twentieth century. Pakistan is a young nation-state superimposed on ancient and ethnically distinct cultures—Punjabi, Pathan, Baluch, and Sindhi. It is a fragmented postcolonial society in search of ideological legitimacy and national identity. Iran was never colonized, at least not directly. It did not suffer crises of identity—until well into the twentieth century—and the Persian language has survived many years of upheavals and foreign invasions. I became fascinated with the syncretism[1] of Pakistani cultures and religions, the multiplicity of ethnicities and languages, and the "exoticism" of their postcolonial cultural practices. I also was touched by the generosity with which many Pakistanis treated me. I was impressed specifically by the indomitable spirit of the Pakistani women I met and befriended.

I first headed for India and Pakistan in 1987, after having lived in the United States since 1968, when I left Iran. Iran and the United States—my country of birth and my adopted home—were at loggerheads diplomatically, and their rhetoric of mutual enmity left me emotionally exhausted. I was disillusioned and discouraged about the political events that unfolded rapidly in Iran after the revolution in 1978–79 and found unbearable the war of attrition

---

1. For a description of religious and cultural syncretism in South Asia, see De Tassy 1995.

between Iran and Iraq (1980–88) and the tragic loss of hundreds of thousands of young lives. Returning to Iran in search of new research objectives did not appeal to me, not then. I had already joined the growing number of indigenous anthropologists, the "holies," who had studied "their own society."[2] But why go to Pakistan? I was neither a Pakistani wanting to study my own society nor a white Anglo-American with the birthright legitimacy to study the "other."[3] Indeed, I was neither the "self" nor the "other."

In retrospect, I was at a point in my life when I needed to go east. My wish came through when a postdoctoral grant from the Social Science Research Council funded my trips to India and Pakistan in 1987–88.[4] Pakistan was then under the military dictatorship of General Mohammad Zia ul-Haq (1977–88), and his Islamization policies seemed to be in full swing. With the experiences of Iran's Islamic Revolution still fresh in my mind, I recoiled from staying too long in another apparently oppressive or—to use the popular catchword—"fundamentalist" society. I limited my stay in Pakistan to a few weeks and instead spent most of my research time in India.

I realized in India and later in Pakistan that what had inspired me to go east was perhaps an obscure sense of identity crisis and existential loneliness that had precipitated like a fog in my mind and heart. Neither fully an American or an Iranian, I was the object of displaced anger in both the United States and Iran and welcomed in neither. I became a scapegoat minority overnight in both places. I was an "I-rainian" in the United States and an American-educated woman—guilty by association with the "Great Satan"—in Iran.[5]

In India, where Muslims form a minority, I gradually began to have a sense

2. Altorki and El-Solh 1988; Haeri 1993a. For a discussion on the term *halfie*—that is, an anthropologist who by the virtue of being bicultural disturbs boundaries of self and other—see Abu-Lughod 1991.

3. It is ironic to note here that some Pakistani women scholars also did not see my endeavor as "legitimate," apparently being used to seeing primarily Western researchers.

4. This project involved archival research on Persian manuscripts in the major libraries in northern India and Pakistan.

5. In their attempt to help me cope with the hostage crisis in Iran (1980–81), some of my classmates from UCLA facetiously disguised my identity by calling me Sheila Rodriguez. In a similar mood, Lisa Suhair Majaj, an Arab American poet-writer reflects, "I knew that Arabs . . . thought me foreign, while 'real' Americans thought me foreign as well. . . . Arab culture simultaneously claimed and excluded me, while the American identity I longed for retreated inexorably from my grasp" (qtd. in Naber 1996, 7).

of our shared marginal experiences and gained some insight into the intellectual vitality of some South Asian Muslims.[6] Traveling across northern India, participating in various cultural events and performances, and having intense dialogues with Indian Muslims, I came to see more syncretic, reflective, tolerant, and worldly "faces" of Islam and Muslims. I spiritually felt a bit revived. I did identify, of course, many of the same "faces" of intolerance and bigotry that I had seen in Iran during the consolidation of power and authority following the revolution of 1979. I happened to be in Pakistan again in 1989, when the Indian government banned Salman Rushdie's book *The Satanic Verses* under the pressure of some Indian Muslims. I witnessed the frenzied demonstrations and protests against Rushdie and had heated debates with some Pakistani intellectuals on censorship, freedom of speech, and the hopelessly all-purpose East and West opposition. Nonetheless, I gained a better sense of perspective. What was and has continued to be significant to me was the energy and vitality of many intelligent and intellectual Muslims, women and men, to question, challenge, resist, accommodate, and engage institutions of state, law, religion, and custom in discourses of democracy, gender equality, human rights, and civil society.[7]

Relative to the thick political and religious oppression in Iran at that time,[8] and despite the presence of the military dictatorship in Pakistan, I found the cities of Karachi and Lahore to be vibrant, pluralistic, and intellectually fascinating, if sadly impoverished. I was surprised to discover how I had integrated much of the prevalent perception about Pakistan—that is, an awareness pri-

---

6. I also met several Indian Hindu scholars and other professionals with whom I had ongoing discussions on the politics and poetics of South Asia, partition, Pakistan, and communalism and with whom I shared an Indo-Persian cultural heritage.

7. In a similar impression, Leila Ahmed writes of her return visit to Cairo: "It was a sense of enormous intellectual vitality and cultural richness of this city and a sense of an almost palpable vibrancy and ferment: this place that was (as it has been for millennia) a meeting place of so many histories, so many ways of thought, so many forms of belief. And this sense of the complexity and mental aliveness of the place was there despite the growing presence of fundamentalism and fundamentalism's deadly intent to curtail freedom of thought" (1999, 301–2).

8. In time, the same sense of self-criticism and questioning gripped Iranian society as well. The sociopolitical criticism that has been leveled against many of the "hardline" leaders since the election of Mohammad Khatami to the presidency in 1997 and the ongoing debates on the relationship between church and state are a testimony to the growing vitality of intellectuals in Iran.

marily of its religious intolerance and military oppression. I met, talked, and interviewed women—women who belonged to the Women's Action Forum (WAF), Applied Socioeconomic Resource (ASR), and the Aurat Foundation; women who were academicians, politicians, activists, artists, poets, actors; women who were members of the Jama'at-i Islami (JI)[9] and housewives—and have remained in close contact with some of them. I found them socially conscious and self-critical, focused on their feminist objectives and critical of the state's human rights and gender policies. Feminism is, of course, an evolving phenomenon and is not monolithic in Pakistan or anywhere else in the world. Women's strategies diverge, and their interests differ depending on their class, ethnicity, profession, education, and lineage. Nonetheless, a majority of women I met and many more about whom I read share clear objectives about improving women's lives and liberty. In subsequent trips to Pakistan, I became more aware of some of the intractable sociocultural problems facing Pakistani women, which the women's narratives in subsequent chapters will disclose.

In Lahore, I was invited to a conference on ethnicity,[10] funded and organized by the foundation of the late Begum Kishwar (Baji) Abid Hussain (d. 1998), whom I had come to know and admire greatly.[11] In a dazzling variety of

9. The first JI woman I was told to meet was an American Jewish convert to Islam who had emigrated to Pakistan in the 1950s and assumed the name Maryam Jamila. She became an ardent follower of Maulana Abul'ala Maududi (d. 1979), the founder of JI (1941), married one of his devotees, and settled in Lahore. She is reclusive to the point of being disoriented when she leaves her home. When she does go out, she is completely covered in a *burqa*. She became somewhat of a cult figure for American male researchers who went to Pakistan in the 1980s and early 1990s; she would receive them from behind a curtain to discuss Islamic issues. I met her several times and found her to be a nice and gentle woman, more interested in Sufism than in orthodox Islam, though she was hesitant to talk much about it. She has written prolifically about Islam and society, but she is not active on the political scene in Pakistan. Neither the other JI women I met nor the more modern professional women found her life and religious ideas relevant to their cause.

10. The conference was called "Establishing Ethnic and Sectarian Peace in Pakistan" and was held on December 26, 1987.

11. Baji was born into the prominent Maratib Ali family in Punjab. She was involved in several social and charitable activities and frequently hosted American and European intellectuals, scholars, and diplomats. Her husband and brothers occupied many positions of power and influence in the new state of Pakistan, and her only daughter, Begum Abida Hussain, was the Pakistani ambassador to the United States during Nawaz Sharif's first term as prime minister (1990–93).

languages (English, Urdu, Punjabi, and Sindhi, among others), Pakistani male and female participants discussed the expectations and disappointments of various ethnic groups, stressing almost uniformly the adverse effects of policies adopted by General Zia's military regime on ethnic relations.[12] Their heated arguments on ethnicity, on local and federal nationalism, on the Sindhis' threat to secede, and on the military regime's divide-and-rule politics sounded reflexive and relatively uncensored to my ear. Learning of the ethnic and linguistic diversity in Pakistan added nuance to my earlier assumption of Pakistani ethnic and linguistic mosaic. I was also unprepared for the depth and range of emotions expressed in discussions and reminiscences about the partition. As an Iranian living in the United States, I had at times a sense of being an exile and could appreciate the intermittent longing for a "return" home. Many Pakistanis, of course, have no desire to go home, for home is simply not there. But a degree of nostalgia was there, mixed with memories of loss and tragedy and with the anxious restlessness of "what ifs." The partition resonated strongly and seemed to be on many people's minds, at least those I met.

The Pakistani English-language press likewise seemed to exercise a healthy amount of freedom, which again was a pleasant surprise to me. I remembered that, with the exception of a few short periods, the press in Iran was hardly free under the Pahlavi shahs (1925–79) or under the Islamic Republic.[13] I met people—ordinary people and intellectuals—who showed generosity of spirit and introduced me to feasts of Pakistani cuisine that forever changed my palate and cooking habits, which I now call Perso-Pak cuisine. In no time, I was adopted by the Pakistanis, and I fell in love with the country and the people. I now think of Pakistanis as my *rishteh dars*, my kinfolk. And, indeed, I think of them as my *rishteh dars* in more than one way: historically, culturally, religiously, and politically. I realize that this confession makes me vulnerable to accusations of subjectivity and personal bias. But I take heart in the changing ethnographic attitude that challenges the "central assumptions of mainstream

12. Mazari (1983), likewise, locates the increase in ethnic violence in Zia's Islamization policies. For specifics on ethnicity and the tension among different ethnic groups, see Jalal 1995, 108–9, and I. Malik 1997, 110.

13. Exceptions are to be made for short periods during the Constitutional Revolution of 1906–11 and Mohammad Mosadeq's prime ministership 1951–53 and immediately after the revolution of 1979. After the election of President Mohammad Khatami in 1997, the press momentarily enjoyed a greater degree of freedom, only to be closed down en masse in 1999, when the regime felt the heat of its criticism.

social science" regarding "objectivity" of the "detached observer" and "the effort to create a formal vocabulary of analysis purged of all subjective reference . . . and the claim to moral neutrality" (Clifford Geertz, qtd. in Rosaldo 1993, 37).[14]

Lahore always held a particularly special place for me as an Iranian. I grew up with stories of its imperial majesty and magnificent monuments. My parents had taught me some Persian poetry of Pakistan's celebrated national poet-philosopher, Iqbal-i Lahuri (as Iranians know him),[15] and I had memorized and recited some on various occasions in my elementary school. Even as a child, I loved to repeat—rather loudly and dramatically, the way my mother had taught me—the refrain *az khab-i giran khiz*, where Iqbal admonishes the South Asian Muslims and their leaders to wake up from their deep sleep of backwardness. I did not realize then the depth of the poetry's meaning. But becoming familiar with the way some Pakistani leaders had mismanaged the affairs of the state, I felt like repeating it just as loudly again.

In the streets of Pakistan's major cities, I breathed a sigh of relief to see unveiled and veiled women side by side. This commingling—just like Iran when I was growing up—signaled a degree of personal and individual freedom. The bright and lively colors of their apparel and their veils contrasted sharply with the black and drab-color veils worn by Iranian women. Unlike Iranian women, Pakistani women are not mandated by the state to veil. The former are required to wear black veil or dark-colored overcoats and scarves, the so-called Islamic veiling,[16] whereas Pakistani women wear the modest yet beautifully color-coordinated two-piece suit, locally known as *shalwar-kamiz*, which is almost always accompanied by a long, rectangular, thin scarf known as the *dupata*. I wondered why Iranian leaders of the Islamic Republic did not emulate Pakistan, another Muslim society, as a role model for fashioning a standard

14. See also Behar 1996, 28–29.

15. Sir Mohammad Iqbal (1873–1938) was born in Sialkot, Punjab, and lived the greater part of his life in Lahore. His subject matter included "patriotic, philosophic, humanistic or Islamic themes" (Kanda 1990, 216–17). For an excellent discussion of Iqbal's views on individual, community, and nationalism among South Asian Muslims, see Jalal 2001, 165–86. See also chapter 5, fn. 61, in this volume.

16. In the dramatic victory of the "reformists" in the parliamentary election of February 2000 in Iran, a newly elected male representative from Tehran was asked whether now Iranian women would have a choice regarding their *hijab*, veiling. He said no, but that Iranian woman would have a choice regarding the color of their veil.

dress for Iranian women. Why did they feel obliged to force Iranian women to wear the rather unattractive, dark-colored, and formless Islamic veiling that is closer to nineteenth-century Catholic nuns' habits?[17] In Pakistan, I found an example of women's attire that combined modesty with beauty, while allowing for individual taste and financial resources to improvise upon it.

Before moving into the women's narratives, I think it important to set the stage with a discussion of the emerging contestation over the visions of social order for the new state of Pakistan that frames the broader outlines of the arguments presented in the women's stories. I then discuss the reasons for the invisibility of professional Muslim women, attributing it, among other reasons mentioned earlier, primarily to a growing fascination with "difference"—as the hallmark of identity—and to a preponderance of subaltern studies. Last, I address the issues of citizenship and honor specific to Pakistan before ending the chapter with a brief reflection on my overall approach.

Fundamentalism, Secularism, Feminism

As radicalized religious revivalism became a powerful political force in the late 1970s and in the 1980s all over the globe, discourse on fundamentalism and its impact gained urgent currency in academia.[18] Funding for cross-cultural stud-

17. In time, of course, Iranian women asserted their taste and individuality to refashion the Islamic veiling into a more personalized and appealing overcoat, though they still are restricted to dark colors. As for the reference to Catholic habits, it is interesting to note comments made by Maulana Maududi, the founder of the Jama'at-i Islami Party. Arguing that during wars, women's veiling may be relaxed somewhat to allow them to help with feeding and nursing the wounded soldiers, he then writes "[women] have been allowed by *Shari'ah* to wear the same sort of dress, with a little modification, as is worn by the Christian nuns now-a-days" (1987, 209).

18. Fundamentalism has been the subject of intense scholarly debates and discussions, and any definition of it is necessarily controversial. I use the term loosely, but with both irony and facticity. As a contemporary phenomenon, fundamentalism has as many different origins as it has national manifestations. The term *fundamentalism*, however, evidently was first coined by some denominations of North American Protestants who attempted a more literal reading of the Scripture. Feeling sidelined by the influx of minorities and the loss of political power at the turn of the twentieth century, they set out to write the fundamentals of Christianity. In relation to other Christians and denominations, they came to be known as fundamentalists. See Ammerman 1991.

ies of fundamentalism grew phenomenally.[19] Everywhere one turned, one would hear about a conference on fundamentalism. Although other fundamentalisms were at times included, the prominent position in the academic discourse, in media representation, and in popular imagination was given to Islamic fundamentalism. Discourse on fundamentalism, reminiscent of its predecessor Orientalism, had become hegemonic; fundamentalism in general and Islamic fundamentalism in particular were construed as the "other." Topics such as "Islamic terrorism," "Islamic bombs," "the Islamic threat," and—as the language of academia gradually became more tolerant—"Islamic feminism" crowded endless panel discussions. The publication of a stream of books on Islamic fundamentalism, pro and con, became overwhelming. It seemed as if, at least for a while, nothing about the religion or the people could be said that did not have *Islam* or *Muslim* as a prefix or suffix. Nor was the ubiquitous "veiled Muslim woman" left out of any textual or visual representation.[20] Fetishized in both the United State and Muslim societies, the Muslim woman's veil became the dominant—hegemonic—image and thus concealed a more nuanced knowledge of the "other."[21]

For me, fundamentalism had a different urgency. I personally wanted to make sense of the implications of the politicized Islam that was unfolding in Iran and of the upheavals that shook Iranian society to the core, forever changing the configurations of its political institutions, religious legitimacy, and gender hierarchies—and by implication, its gender dynamics. I was also interested in exploring academically the confluence of religion, law, and gender dynamics.

I returned to Pakistan in 1991 to conduct research on a project I called "Contested Identities: Women, State, and Fundamentalism." I was interested in the interplay between fundamentalism and secularism, which I construed, more or less, to be structural opposites.[22] The effects of modernity and nation-

19. Pioneering among them are the multivolume work *The Fundamentalism Project*, edited by Martin Marty and Scott Appleby (1991–95), as well as works by Lawrence (1989) and Riesebrodt (1993). For a comparative review of global fundamentalism, see Stump 2000.

20. A quick glance at the cover jackets of books published regarding women in the Muslim world reveals the general fascination and obsession with veiling. A corollary to the obsession with veil and veiling is the visual representation of violence on the cover jackets of books written about Islam and fundamentalism.

21. For a comparative study of the veil in Iran and in the United States, see Shirazi 2001.

22. Filali-Ansary argues that secularism in Europe is viewed as a process, but in the case of Muslim societies the question becomes: "Is Islam compatible with secularism?" Secularism in

hood that gained momentum in the late nineteenth century intimately touched and forever transformed traditional gender relations and the status quo in much of the world, including Muslim societies. By choice or by forces beyond their control, women moved into the public domain and into the workforce. Such far-reaching changes disoriented both men and women, but they disturbed men in particular, who as custodians of the social and moral order often perceive the effect of women's professional autonomy as *fitnah*, chaos.[23] Frustrated or unable to put things back into the idealized—imagined—order again, men saw their power, privilege, and control over their women and children slipping uncontrollably out of their hands. In Pakistan, religious parties wholeheartedly supported General Zia's Islamization policy and embraced his efforts to push professional women behind their veils and the walls of their homes (chador and *char diwari*).

Faced with strong adversaries, professional Pakistani women mobilized themselves into consciously feminist and political organizations such as the WAF, which was established in 1981 and is the most prominent. Like their counterparts in other Muslim societies, the women realized that in their society, given the rapidly changing religious and political alliances, knowledge of the sacred text *is* power. I attended several WAF meetings and observed Pakistani professional women and human rights activists debate the ongoing issues in their society. They challenged legal inequalities and social injustices and demanded accountability from their political leaders, particularly with regard to violence against women.

I became deeply involved in the intellectual and social life in Lahore, contacted various nongovernmental organizations (NGOs) and traveled widely within the society. I participated in many political activities, attended artistic performances,[24] and marched in a few demonstrations on the Mall Road, a major thoroughfare in Lahore, with other women demanding justice for acts

---

this sense is understood "as an alternative to religion, not as an alternative way of ordering society and of conceiving the world" (1999, 6).

23. *Fitnah* is an Arabic term meaning "both a burning and a trial, or temptation, and by extension a seduction or a charming—an enchantment" (J. Williams 1995, 26–28). Many verses in the Qur'an warn Muslims regarding *fitnah*, and one states that it "is worse than killing" (2:191, 217). In one hadith, women are said to be "the greatest *fitnah*" for men.

24. Of particular interest is the socially conscious "alternative theater" group Ajoka, which takes a political and feminist approach and focuses on dramatizing cultural conflicts. A husband and wife team jointly write and direct it.

of violence against women.[25] I visited the JI headquarters, Mansura Complex, in Lahore and interviewed several of its high-ranking men and women leaders. In Karachi, I met with Begum Sufi, a leading member of Tahrik-i Islami, and had a lively discussion with her and some of her supporters.

I focused intensely on learning Urdu, although as the well-known scholar Malik Ram told me in India, "One does not go to Lahore to learn good Urdu. You should go to Locknow or Delhi!"[26] Lahore is the center of Punjab, and the majority speaks Punjabi, though Urdu is the language of instruction. For them, Urdu is a second or third language, and many speak it with a Punjabi accent. For much of the professional class, however, English is their first language, though not their mother tongue, courtesy of a long period of British colonialism.[27] There are several daily English newspapers, and many more weekly and monthly magazines. Although learning Urdu in the midst of so many competing languages was frustrating, communicating easily in English was important in several ways. Unlike their Iranian counterparts, for many of

25. See chapter 3, Rahila Tiwana.

26. Malik Ram Baveja was a diplomat and a scholar of Islamic studies. Among his many books is *Women in Islam* (1981).

27. To determine the percentage of Urdu- and English-speaking populations in Pakistan is tricky because although neither language is indigenous to Pakistan, both occupy positions of importance. According to the information attaché at the Pakistan embassy in Washington, D.C. (May 2002), Urdu is the national language and the language of instruction. Extrapolating on that, he suggested that if the literacy rate is 35 percent in Pakistan, one can assume that at least 35 percent of the population has a good to functional knowledge of Urdu. English, he said, is the official language, and all governmental transactions and communications are done in English. Approximately 2 million people (out of a total population of approximately 150 million) work in the federal and provincial governments and should have a minimum English proficiency to be able to perform their duty. This does not include the educated middle class or upper middle class, for whom English is their first language. It is worth noting, however, that in 1979 the government of Pakistan established the Muqtadira Qaumi Zaban (National Language Authority) "in furtherance of the objectives in Article 251 enunciated (1) of the Constitution of Pakistan, 1973, to formulate and present recommendations to the Government for the formal adoption of Urdu, the national language, as the official language, and to develop linkages for cooperation and collaboration with various academic, research, and educational institutions" (www.pak.gov.pk/public/govt/ministry_population_welfare.htm). According to the Web site www.polisci.com/world/nation/PK.htm, the breakdown of the percentage of the languages spoken in Pakistan is: Punjabi, 48 percent; Sindhi, 12 percent; Saraiki, 10 percent; Pashtu, 8 percent; Urdu, 8 percent; Balochi, 3 percent; Hindko, 2 percent; Brahui, 1 percent; English, less than 1 percent; and Burushaski, less than 1 percent.

whom speaking English is a struggle, Pakistani academics and professionals have direct access to and engage in various international discourses on feminism, politics, and religion. Their fluency in English, colored though it is with local concepts and idioms,[28] has been ethnographically an asset in minimizing the linguistic and cultural problems of translating that have beset anthropology (Asad 1986).

Soon it became apparent to me that in Pakistan secularism and fundamentalism are not structural opposites, though among certain social strata religious opposition to social change is fierce. Nor are they monolithic entities. Their "boundaries" are more permeable in real life, and institutional alliances and individual solidarity are shifting constantly. Nor do Pakistani feminists speak with one voice. Several national as well as ethnically organized feminist organizations are active in Pakistan and involved with politics of community and of the nation.[29] The phenomena of feminism, fundamentalism, and secularism in Pakistan, as in other societies, are animated processes, are situated historically, and have evolved in response to the global currents of modernity, industrialization, and colonialism (D. Ahmed 1994; Said Khan 1992, 1995; Saigol 1995). What is also true in the case of Pakistan, given the circumstances surrounding its creation, is that it has a particular sense of calling and destiny about itself and its mission on earth.

Culture, Religion, and Women in Pakistan

The contradictions of being the granddaughter of an ayatollah and yet not veiled had never occurred to me until I was confronted with it in 1988 by Dr. Christian Troll, a scholar of Islam and a Jesuit priest living in India at the time.

28. For an interesting representation, see Yule and Burnell's *Hobson-Jobson* (1989). Originally published in 1886, "*Hobson-Jobson* . . . remains the indispensable lexicon for the innumerable words which entered into the language of the British expatriates during the Raj. These words came from the Indian languages of the provinces, and from Arabic, Persian, Turkish, Portuguese, Burmese and a host of other tongues, all subjected to the peculiar phonetic distortion that was the privilege of the sahibs. The word 'Hobson-Jobson' perhaps illustrates this phonetic journey best, derived originally as it was from 'Ya Hassan! Ya Hosain!' " (from the cover jacket of the book).

29. For example, the Sindhiyani Tehrik (Sindhi Women's Movement) was founded in response to the wider political movements in Sindh Province and is rooted in rural Sindh (Mumtaz 1989).

"How is it possible?" he asked. "How come your grandfather did not ask you to veil?" Indeed! "Why hadn't he?" I wondered. What was specific to him or to Iran at that time in history that made it seem perfectly natural—or so it seemed to me—for him to let his daughters and granddaughters go unveiled? "Perhaps," I told Dr. Troll, "it was partly because he was an enlightened ayatollah, well read and well traveled. But also because"—I tried to come up with a more sociological answer—"in the decades of 1950s and 1960s, Iran, like most other Muslim societies, was undergoing the process of modernization and Westernization." The "force of modernity," to borrow from Bruce Lawrence's book *Defenders of God* (1989), was such, I thought in retrospect, that even ayatollahs were impacted by it. Perhaps they, too, thought the march of "progress," the increasing secularization of legal and political systems, and the direction of social transformation were unavoidable and inevitable.

The shock I might have given my Jesuit friend for being incongruously Muslim and unveiled was similar to the ones I felt when observing religious practices and rituals in Pakistan that were different from my expectations and from what I had learned and seen in Iran. Hearing the electrifying devotional music, the *qawwali*, for the first time in the Shrine of Data Ganj Bakhsh [30] on the edge of the old city of Lahore, I was transfixed with fear. Who dared play music in this holy place? I had never heard music played in the vicinity of a mosque or a shrine in Iran! At least not among the Shi'ites who constitute the majority of Iranians. But here they were, facing the shrine and seated on a narrow bench, four or five men playing tabla and harmonium while singing—now together, now solo—the devotional poems with a most heartfelt passion. Nor had I ever seen pilgrims dedicating stringed red roses or jasmine to the shrines in Iran.

Most strikingly different from its Iranian counterpart is a Pakistani wedding. Weddings are good examples of the articulation of religious injunctions, local traditions, and political regulations in the Muslim world. In a Pakistani wedding or *shadi*, the Muslim marriage contract or *nikah* is the least elaborate of the rituals. The Family Law Ordinance, passed in 1961 amid much political

---

30. Ali ibn Uthman Data Ganj Bakhsh Al-Hujwiri, a Chishti mystic and author of *Kashf al-mahjub* (Unveiling of the hidden), was from Ghazna and went to live in Lahore later in his life, where he died in 1071. His mausoleum is a popular religious shrine located on the outskirts of Lahore and at the edge of the old city (Schimmel 1986, 88).

tension and dissent from the religious establishment, legally tried to shift the agency from the family to the individual by granting Pakistani Muslim women a range of rights, including restrictions on polygyny, divorce, and mainte-nance (Esposito 1982). Yet few women are aware of their rights or are allowed, paradoxically, by their families to take advantage of them.

The most elaborate part of the wedding is by far the marriage ceremony, lasting a minimum of three days. It starts with *mehndi*, the tradition of coloring women's hands and feet with henna; moves on to the *nikah*; and ends with *wal-ima*, the final feast, which usually takes place on the final night, marking the consummation of marriage. Brides wear an exquisite red costume, sit still, looking positively demure. Even the most vivacious Pakistani woman, I have seen, follows the tradition and sits almost motionless throughout her wed-ding. Similar to the Hindu marriage exchanges and cultural practices, the bride's family is obliged to pay a dowry, *jahiz*, to the groom and his family.[31] Although not part of Islamic law, dowry payment "is a firmly established cus-tom" in Pakistan (Esposito 1982, 87). The wedding ceremonies and rituals I saw in Lahore and Karachi were almost entirely South Asian[32] and com-pletely different from the middle-class weddings I had observed and partici-pated in Iran.

The *nikah*, the Muslim marriage contract, of course legitimizes marriage in Iran as well. There, however, brides wear white, actively participate in the marriage ceremony, and are under no obligation to take material goods to their husband's household, though they may and often do so. Similar to the Family Law Ordinance in Pakistan, the Iranian Family Protection Law of 1967 and 1975 brought about changes in the legal status of women but was aban-doned after the Islamic Revolution of 1979. Under pressure from Iranian women, however, many of the same legal changes gradually were incorpo-rated into the Islamic marriage contract and are presently active in Iran. They

31. Legal texts use the term *dowry* or *dower* to refer to *mahr*, bride-price, the legally binding money and gifts given to the wife by the husband (Balchin 1994; Fayzee 1974, 132; Mannan 1995). Popular usage has followed the text. *Dower* or *dowry* is also used to refer to gifts trans-ferred from bride to groom in South Asia. For a classic treatment of differences between *dowry*, *bride-wealth*, and *bride-price*, see Goody and Tambiah 1973.

32. For a similar observation among the Indian Muslims of the late 1950s, see Vreede-de Stuers 1968, 17–27.

are now known as *shurut-i zimn-i 'aqd,* conditions set at the time of marriage contract (Haeri 1993a; Kar 1999). In both societies, however, many restrictions still prevail.

More fundamental and often misunderstood in the assumption of all religion and no culture in the Muslim world is that although Islam grants women a degree of agency, local traditions in various Arab and Muslim[33] societies have prevented them, in the very name of Islam, from exercising it. Religious scholars from different schools of Islamic law[34] have disputed the parameter and the extent of a woman's legal agency and the degree to which her consent is necessary to draw a marriage contract. Nonetheless, Islam grants a legally mature woman—legal age varies slightly from one Islamic school to another—the right to choose her own marriage partner and maintains her consent as fundamental to the *validity* of the marriage contract (Balchin 1996, 45; Engineer 1987; Haeri 1993a; Hussain 1987). In Pakistan, the dominant Hanafi School of Islamic law and the Family Law Ordinance of 1961 recognize the right of an adult woman, sixteen years and older, to contract her own marriage independently from her father or guardian's wish (Balchin 1996, 13; Hussain 1987, 455–56).

South Asian Muslims have followed strictly the local cultural tradition of arranged marriages and parental control, however. Arranged marriages are, of course, nothing new to Muslim societies or, for that matter, to non-Muslim societies. What is noteworthy in Pakistan and in much of South Asia is the degree to which parental rights to arrange marriages and a daughter's obligation to obey are legitimated in the name of religion and sanctified culturally. The parental sense of sacred entitlement, however, has less to do with religion and more to do with a coalition of ancient feudal and tribal practices and with the culturally held hegemonic values of purity and chastity that converge in the deeply charged phenomenon of honor, *izzat.* Given the cultural assumption that purity and family honor are intimately tied in with women's sexuality and conduct, the increase in violence against women who assert their individuality

33. A distinction between Arab and Muslim must be noted here. Although most Arabs are Muslims (there are Christian and Jewish Arabs), the majority of Muslims are not Arabs. Arabs live primarily in the Middle East and North Africa.

34. The four officially recognized Sunni Islamic schools of law include Shafi'i, Maliki, Hanafi, and Hanbali. Shi'ism forms a separate branch of Islamic law.

by choosing their own marriage partners becomes less surprising, though no less shocking.[35]

In all these cases, the same religion, Islam, articulates with cultural practices and local structures of power to manifest itself in widely different rituals and ceremonies. Anthropologically speaking, as Geertz has argued, religion is "a cultural system." This is to say, although religious beliefs render the mundane world of social relationships and psychological events graspable, they also provide a template for people to conduct their daily secular lives. In his view, all religions articulate with specific cultural practices and traditions to create moods and motivations for culturally meaningful symbolic action (1973, 124–25).

Religion presently does appear omnipresent in Pakistan and in Iran, given the designation of Islam as the basis for the creation of Pakistan and for the Islamic Republic of Iran since the Revolution of 1979. Many actions and intentions, in particular the public ones, are cloaked formally in the garb of Islam.[36] But if Islam in Pakistan manifests itself differently than it does in Iran and is observed still differently within different communities of each society and among various ethnic groups, that difference falls in the realm of changing cultures, involving the vagaries of other local traditions and structures of power that must be accounted for (see also Jalal 1995, 239).

Culture[37]—and not just religion—I submit, must be incorporated seriously into social analysis in the Muslim world if we are to understand both the articulations of cultural specificities in the Muslim world and the universal principles of Islam. In Pakistan, many religious beliefs and rituals are filtered through the local practices as evolved in the social organizations of lineage system, *bradri*, and feudalism. Deeply integrated in these multilayered social structures are the values regarding property, *zamin*; gold, wealth, *zar*; and (control of)

35. See the noted journalist Beena Sarwar's many articles in the Pakistan daily *International News*. The cold-blooded murder of Samia Imran in 1999, allegedly by a hired gunman on behest of her parents, is a case in point.

36. For an excellent discussion of "religion as difference" and "religion as faith" in South Asia, see Jalal 2001, 574–78.

37. Many anthropologists have become increasingly skeptical about the argument that "culture" explains the difference (Kuper 1999). Shweder (2000, 7–9) warns against tendencies to disown "culture" totally, and Abu-Lughod (1991) cautions against an essentialized notion of culture and argues that anthropologists must write "against culture." See also Rosaldo 1993.

women, *zan* (Barth 1970; Haeri 1995b)—the three most sought-after commodities in Pakistan. Embedded in these particular sociopolitical formations
of patrilineal affiliations, land ownership, and patriarchal control of women
and in the warp and weft of the fabric of Pakistan's social life are the ancient
cultural beliefs of gender hierarchy, female purity, and male honor, *izzat*.

That Islam requires women to veil is understood by Muslims to be a universal Islamic principle, contested though this injunction is even on religious
grounds. But the ways veiling and the segregation of the sexes are experienced
and practiced individually and actually in the Muslim world presently are
mandated by political considerations and mediated by cultural traditions and,
in that sense, are culture specific. As a part of his Islamization program, for in-
stance, General Zia ordered Pakistani female television newscasters to veil
while broadcasting. They had to wear an attractive, thin head scarf that barely
covered their heads and elegantly draped over their shoulders. The present
Iranian authorities would be scandalized to allow anything like that to flash on
the television screen because it is un-Islamic in their view. The veil Iranian female television newscasters are prescribed to wear is a subdued overcoat and
head scarf that not only cover their entire bodies, but their heads, part of their
foreheads, and their chins as well. In both cases, the prevailing political power
elite enforced, in the name of religion, the ways they perceived veiling ought
to be practiced. In both cases, women were deprived of making a choice and
were obliged to obey the authorities or face disciplinary action. In both cases,
a coalition of forces, not merely religion, was brought to bear upon the state
decision.

The difference is that General Zia required "spot veiling" with an eye to manipulating both the fundamentalists, whom he relied on to legitimate his military coup of 1977,[38] and the more modernist groups who clamored for
meaningful social changes. The Islamic Republic of Iran, however, in a radical
reaction to the Westernization policies of the previous kings and in its desire

38. Begum Nusrat Bhutto, wife of the deposed prime minister, challenged the legitimacy of
General Zia's military coup on constitutional grounds. Unlike the previous military takeovers
by General Ayub Khan (1956) and General Yahya Khan (1962), in which the Constitution of
Pakistan was abrogated, in 1977 the Supreme Court recognized General Zia's martial rule "only
as an extra-constitutional step required under the peculiar circumstances of the country at that
point in time and subject to certain specified limits including only limited license to amend the
constitution" (Sardar Ali and Arif 1994, 6).

to establish an Islamic moral order, required that all women, Iranian or foreign, wear a veil on all occasions when appearing in public.

An Alternative Vision of Order

Early in the morning of December 12, 1991, I received a phone call from Baji,[39] who in her disarmingly delicate yet assertive way said, "Come walk with us." For a few weeks prior to that, public discussions had been hovering around the violence and the gang rape of a few women supporters of the Pakistan People's Party (PPP). What precipitated the demonstrations, simultaneously staged in major cities, was the alleged gang rape of Veena Hayat, the daughter of a distinguished retired Pakistani leader and a former friend of Pakistan's founder, Mohammad Ali Jinnah. Veena Hayat, a close friend of Benazir Bhutto and her husband, accused Irfanullah Marwat, the son-in-law of the then-president Ghulan Ishaq Khan, and his men of having committed the crime (Haeri 1995b; see also the 1991 issues of the Pakistan periodicals *Herald* and *Newsline*). As we marched down the Mall Road, many male lawyers, lawmakers, and judges also joined the march before we eventually congregated in front of the governor's house. Several women lawyers and representatives of women's organizations, including Veena's younger sister, accused the state of antipathy toward women and inactivity in redressing the rising violence against them. They demanded an end to violence against women and an immediate apprehension and punishment of the perpetrators. Several Pakistani feminists groups and NGOs arranged numerous smaller gatherings and consciousness-raising events, including several hunger strikes in which Benazir Bhutto and some PPP members, who at that time were in the opposition, also participated.

Understanding the significance of women and men taking public stands against rape and violence, crimes that have long been kept secret because of the shame involved and so are perpetrated against women with impunity, requires a knowledge of the history of the birth of Pakistan and of the shifting visions of an alternative sociomoral order. I am not suggesting that these issues were the only problems Pakistan faced, but rather I am focusing attention on how the shift in conceptualizing a different order of society awakened women to the possibilities of realizing their talents and potentials and of demanding their rights. In this book, Quratal Ain Bakhteari describes refugees' indefatiga-

39. See fn. 11, this chapter.

ble struggle to rebuild their lives in the newly created Muslim nation of Pakistan. Kishwar Naheed talks of the euphoria of freedom after the creation of Pakistan, and Nilofar Ahmed expresses similar sentiments in one of her articles, as she did to me: "The independence of Pakistan, in 1947 brought along with it the independence of some women. . . . Once in Pakistan the women threw off their veil and set about the task of educating themselves, or at least their daughters" (1992, 29).

Birth of a Nation: Pakistan's Origin Myth

The idea of a separate nation for Indian Muslims broke the Muslims' mental siege and liberated them to imagine different horizons, to think of "alternative visions of power" (Said 1991, 151) and to wish for a different "order of things" (Foucault 1973). It animated Muslims toward a demand for social agency and sovereignty (Geertz 1994). Although no one could have imagined the extent of the tragedy and the horror of human suffering set in motion in the aftermath of the partition of 1947, the idea of a nation-state presented Muslims, including women, with multiple opportunities, challenges, and paradoxes.[40]

From the beginning, the very idea of the partition was contested, not just by Hindu nationalists who opposed the dismemberment of "mother India" and the existence of a separate nation for Muslims, but also by many Muslims who viewed as problematic the concept of two nations for India and Pakistan.[41] The Indian Muslims disputed vehemently among themselves as to what par-

40. The moment of the creation of Pakistan also can be conceptualized in terms of Sahlins's theoretical "structures of conjuncture." This is to say, there are "moments in history in which different systems of thought and practice . . . come into engagement with one another and potentially set in motion radical kinds of conceptual and practical unraveling" (qtd. in Ortner 1996, 5).

41. In a more recent reading of the narrative of partition, Ayesha Jalal attributes a degree of complicity to the Indian political leaders: "Just as Jinnah feared that the Congress would exploit the particularism of his provincial followers in the Muslim provinces unless he got grouping, the Congress High Command for its part feared that sharing power at the center with the [Muslim] League would enable the League constantly to dangle a bait before its own Congress following. It was quite conceivable that Congress, a medley of political opinions, might split up along ideological lines soon after a British withdrawal. This, together with the possibility of a re-alignment of parties along political rather than specifically communal lines, suggests why the Congress High Command was so averse to sharing power at the center with rival High Command" (1985, 245–246). See also Jalal 2001, 180–83.

ticular political form a "Muslim nation" ought to take. At the same time, it provided the "modernist" and "traditionalist" Muslims with the prospect of having a real opportunity with an alternative vision of power or of "realizing a long cherished dream of religious and social transformation on a society wide scale" (Hefner 1998, 6). In this context, the acclaimed scholar Eqbal Ahmed (d. 1999) told me, "The whole idea of creating Pakistan for Muslims where Islam is adopted by modernist Muslims as the raison d'être of the creation of a new nation-state is a contradiction in terms" (personal communication, Lahore, March 16, 1990). The idea of a separate Muslim state, however, he said, was the crowning triumph of the "modernists," who, following Sir Sayyid Ahmad Khan (1817–98), had become involved in their society's politics and pursued modern education.[42] The most vociferous objection came from Muslim religious leaders, who were highly fragmented among themselves (Alavi 1987). As the traditional custodians of the sacred knowledge, they perceived their role and legitimacy as being eclipsed by founder Jinnah, who in their view was a British-trained lawyer and an advocate of a secular Pakistan.

Once Pakistan became a concrete reality and the initial euphoria wore off, it did not take long for various groups with incompatible interests to lay claims to exclusionist visions of order while trying to legitimate their particular vision of power and order in the name of Islam. Although Islam, as the basis for the reality of Pakistan, loosened the religious hierarchy's monopoly of sacred legitimacy, it gradually and ironically became synonymous with a "legitimacy" in which diverse groups vied to interpret it subjectively and to appropriate it for their own particular objectives. Religion, as a "primordial" institution, argues Geertz, is at the core of people's sense of self and identity and of necessity is in conflict with "civic ties" (1994, 29). The reason for this conflict is that the two major motivations of a modern state are a desire to be recognized as responsible agents and a demand for progress, effective political order, and

42. Alavi also identifies Sir Sayyid as "the father of Islamic modernism" (1987, 33). For Indian Muslims, Sir Sayyid Ahmad Khan (1817–98) is a towering figure, whose teachings and philosophies revived the Muslim community in India. He "grasped the challenge of modernization which British rule had brought to India . . . [and] led the Muslims to enter the stream of modernization through four avenues of reform: political, educational, religious, and social" (H. Malik 1980, 21). Sir Sayyid "organized societies for the translation of English works into Urdu and for the teaching of civics to the Indian public. In 1875 he established the Muslim Anglo-Oriental College at Aligarh, which later became Aligarh Muslim University" (Harris and Levey 1975, 38).

greater social justice. The idea of citizenship, which has become "the most broadly negotiable claim to personal significance" (Geertz 1994, 30), is what makes the two motives intimately related.

I will not rehash here the long and contentious debates over the "correct" reading of the narratives of partition and the creation of Pakistan.[43] My interest lies with the implication that designating Islam as the unifying element for the creation of Pakistan had for women and for women's own vision of a new order. It must be noted, however, that South Asian Muslim women, similar to men, neither shared the same dream regarding the establishment of Pakistan nor spoke with a unified voice once the nation-state of Pakistan was created, as is apparent in the following chapters.

Mohammad Ali Jinnah, Pakistan's founder and leader, provided the conceptual framework for change. In an address at Aligarh Muslim University in 1944, he said, "it is a crime against humanity that our women are shut up within the four walls of the houses as prisoners. There is no sanction anywhere for the deplorable conditions in which our women have to live. You should take your women along with you as comrades in every sphere of life" (qtd. in I. Malik 1997, 143). In opposite ways, two major events specifically brought into sharper focus women's vision of social transformation and a feminist alternative. One is the development of the Constitution of 1973, drafted by Zulfikar Bhutto (1969–77), and the other is the passage of the Hudood Ordinance (*hudood* means "punishments") of 1979 under General Zia's military regime.

One of the major accomplishments of Bhutto's government was the drafting of the 1973 Constitution, which granted greater opportunities to women. It maintained that "there shall be no discrimination on the basis of sex alone" and that "steps shall be taken to ensure full participation of women in all spheres of national life" (Said Khan 1988, 5). Early in 1976, the senior Bhutto set up the Pakistan Women's Rights Committee to "consider and formulate proposals for law reforms, with a view to improve the social, legal, and economic conditions of the women of Pakistan and to provide for speedier legal remedies for obtaining relief in matters like maintenance, [and] custody of children" (Said Khan 1988, 5; see also Weiss 1994). The committee recommended that women be provided with education, employment in all occupations, and the right to participate in sports, culture, and the media. Female

43. For an excellent overview, see Gilmartin 1998.

literacy reached its peak in the mid-1970s, and "women were just beginning to participate in larger numbers in both general elections and labor politics" (Weiss 1987, 97). The Bhutto years marked a period of definite progress for women (Mumtaz and Shaheed 1987, 130; Weiss 1995).

In making these changes, however, Bhutto was "to overrule most, if not all, the premises on which he had started building a new popular order in Pakistan" (Jalal 1991b, 317). And so the tide turned against him, bringing down on him the wrath of the radicalized religious parties who saw the economic and social transformations that Bhutto had accelerated, particularly those for women, as contrary to their interest and ideal. But that was not all. Dissatisfied supporters also abandoned him in droves. Such changes or simply the perception of the social changes to come threatened or damaged the dominance, prestige, and continuity of the traditional values of honor, female purity, and gender hierarchy. They dislocated masculine sensibility (Cornwall and Lindesfarne 1994) and provoked cries of "Islam is in danger" from the radicalized religious parties.

Zulfikar Bhutto's ambitious programs were brought to a halt by General Zia, whose military coup d'etat deposed Bhutto in 1977. In spite of an international plea for his pardon, Bhutto was hanged in 1979.[44] General Zia subsequently instituted Islamization policies and undid much of what Bhutto had accomplished or promised to do. Supported by the JI and by other religious organizations, General Zia shelved plans for the political and economic empowerment of women and so dashed women's hopes for a supportive and democratic regime. Worse yet, the military state supported religious organizations' call for women to be sent back to "chador and *char diwari*," the veil and the four walls of their homes.

Most detrimental to women's—and civil society's—aspirations and health was the resurrection of articles of Islamic criminal code that led to the passage of the Hudood Ordinance in 1979. This law includes punishment for theft,

---

44. The timing of General Zia's military coup and the launching of his Islamization programs are very significant in view of regional events. They coincide with the former Soviet Union's invasion of Afghanistan and the Iranian Islamic Revolution, which resulted in massive U.S. aid to Pakistan (Jalal 1995, 108). Part of the aid was to help the Islamic insurgents in Afghanistan who were fighting the Soviet Union and part of it was intended to take the initiative away from the growing power of fundamentalism and the spillover of the effect of the Iranian Revolution.

drunkenness, adultery, rape, and the bearing of false witness. The crucial article in the law establishes the treatment of rape as adultery, zina (Zia 1994, 23–37).[45] "Zina," writes noted human rights lawyer Asma Jahangir, "includes all forms of extramarital sex" (1992, 52B), which became punishable with imprisonment and whipping after the promulgation of the Hudood Ordinance. Under the Hudood Ordinance, it is virtually impossible for women to press charges against rapists because they are required to produce four male eye witnesses of the rape. Otherwise, they can be accused of adultery, which Islamic law punishes by death. Therefore, Pakistani women theoretically are caught in a legal double-bind: assuming that they can overcome cultural inhibitions and feelings of shame and dishonor, they are likely to be accused of adultery if they file a court complaint against a rapist (Jahangir and Jilani 1992). Women thus are strongly discouraged from seeking help, rendering "sexual justice" practically ineffective in Pakistan, denying women "legal protection" (Iqbal 1988, 9).

Since the passage of the Hudood Ordinance in 1979, the number of women in police custody has increased dramatically (Jahangir and Jilani 1992). Despite the rape, torture, and abuses that women face in police custody, many are reluctant to speak up or to file charges against the responsible officers for fear of police reprisals. Women's predicament in such situations—given their fear-inspired reluctance to pursue justice—is complex and multifaceted. Their misgivings are owing in part to the shame of dishonor they and their families feel, in part to the intimidation by the agents of law and order, and in part to the equation of rape with adultery under the Hudood Ordinance.[46]

Although the discourse of the Hudood Ordinance has become dominant in Pakistan, the degree of its implementation and impact is contested. Its application has varied according to class, ethnicity, education, professional background, and, above all, personal connections. Equally conditional has been the politics of implementation pursued by General Zia's regime itself. General Zia, being a shrewd politician, appropriated Islam to placate the fundamentalists or even to undermine the threat of Islamic resurgence, but at the same time

45. Rubya Mehdi (1997) argues that one of the consequences of the Hudood Ordinance was to reduce the emphasis placed on the crime of rape.

46. Men are also convicted for adultery and fornication, but where charges of rape are brought against them, at the High Court level "they are often converted into the lesser charges of adultery and fornication as a prelude to conviction," according to the Human Rights Watch report Double Jeopardy: Police Abuse of Women in Pakistan (1992, 65–66).

he was careful not to alienate the elite, the military, or his huge bureaucracy, according to Eqbal Ahmed (personal communication, March 1990, Lahore). Supported by a massive aid program from the United States (much of it to fight the former Soviet Union's presence in Afghanistan), General Zia cautiously mediated between fundamentalists and opponents of his Islamization programs (Richter 1987, 137) and did little to counter the charges that his Islamization program was antifemale (Kennedy 1987, 1990, 76).

Women's Vision of a Just Society

The passage of the Hudood Ordinance and the unprecedented Islamic punishment of a hundred lashes given to a woman (Haroon 1995, 182) galvanized Pakistani middle-class and upper-middle-class women (Bari 1995, 135–36; Fernandes 1995, 88–89; Kamal 1995). Faced with an increasing brutalization of social sensibility and a strong adversary bent on restricting women's rights and movements, some women came together in 1981 to form the Women's Action Forum, a self-consciously feminist organization.[47] The WAF is an urban-based umbrella organization and has come to represent one of Pakistan's most influential—and contested—political and feminist organizations. It has been vigilant in the past two decades and has continued to play a vital role in keeping women's issues alive in the public consciousness and in the state's agenda.

In their informative book *Women of Pakistan: Two Steps Forward, One Step Back?* (1987), Khavar Mumtaz and Fareeda Shaheed bring out the sophistication with which Pakistani professional women debated issues and policies of importance to them and to their society when they began to organize.[48] "We did not debate issues related just to women and Islam," said Nighat Said Khan,

47. It must be noted, however, that the WAF was not the first women's political party formed in Pakistan. In fact, it consciously was called a "forum" to distinguish it as a coalition rather than as an organization, as one of WAF's founders, Nighat Said Khan, explained at a talk given at Harvard University, September 22, 2000. Several political and charitable women's organizations already functioned in Pakistan when the WAF came on the scene, though the WAF is the most politically active and vocal. See Fernandes 1995, 92.

48. Mumtaz and Shaheed wrote their book soon after the creation of the WAF. Much has changed since then, and although the WAF has maintained its central position among Pakistani feminists and activists, it now has many other affiliates, which are just as active and vocal in their demands for women's rights. For a more recent review, see Said Khan, Saigol, and Zia 1995.

"but also issues of universality and specificity, democracy and dictatorship, lib-eralism and survival, women's rights and human rights within a patriarchal sys-tem."[49] The speed with which the WAF grew in number, popularity, and power caught even its founders by surprise. Its primary objective was to func-tion as a pressure group, to "raise consciousness and to promote and protect the rights of women in Pakistan" (Mumtaz and Shaheed 1987, 125; see also Weiss 1987). In two WAF founders' assessment, "it cannot be denied that [WAF] has accomplished more in terms of raising consciousness in its short history than can be claimed by any organization or group to date" (qtd. in Mumtaz and Shaheed 1987, 125).

Because the WAF was established by upper-middle-class women, it is per-ceived popularly as "elitist" and continues to maintain a politically contested status in Pakistani society (Fernandes 1995, 91). Whereas Fernandes perceives it as an "inward looking and class-based" organization (1995, 91–92), others argue that it is not monolithic or undifferentiated in terms of its political agenda and activities. According to one of its founders, Nighat Said Khan, the Lahore chapter has been most varied, active, and vocal. The WAF was also in-volved, with other political and activist groups, in forming the Women Work-ers' Center in 1989 to mobilize women industrial workers and to increase awareness among them (Parveen and Ali 1995, 123). Iftikhar Malik (1997, 141) also challenges the charge of "elitism" against the women's movement in Pakistan and contends that even though the activist women were mainly from urban centers, they attempted to make people aware of the plight of women in general. The WAF viewed General Zia's regime as being repressive of women "not simply because it is a martial law regime, but because, in addition to being politically and economically reactionary, it has been characterized by socially retrogressive programs dressed in Islamic colors" (Mumtaz and Shaheed 1987, 130).

The WAF decided early on that it had no option but to work within the framework of Islam: "it seemed pointless to oppose the supposed word of God with the mere words of women" (Mumtaz and Shaheed 1987, 131; see also Weiss 1995, 347). This position, however, has been contested hotly within the rank and file of the WAF and challenged by both right- and left-wing or-ganizations. Hina Jilani, a well-known lawyer and one of WAF's founders, opines, "Early in our struggle, in 1981, we . . . were getting into controversies

49. Talk given at Harvard University, September 22, 2000.

over what Islam said and what it didn't say, but then we realized that as women, this source of lawmaking didn't suit us. So Women's Action Forum was the first-ever political or non-political organization that said in its manifesto, we are secular."[50] Nonetheless, WAF members are aware that "in Pakistan, Islam has become so intertwined with national culture that people often fail to distinguish between what is Islamic and what is merely social custom" (Mumtaz and Shaheed 1987, 131).

Faced with the hostile rhetoric of various Islamic parties and the passage of the Hudood Ordinance, the WAF negotiated its options and created its own publicity and rhetoric. As part of its effort to convey its message to people, it—and later on some of its affiliates—held public meetings, arranged poetry readings, and sponsored performances of humorous and sarcastic skits on the theme of women's desire and cultural oppression. They arranged public seminars, debates, and workshops and became prolific in writing resolutions and proficient in holding press conferences (Shaheed 1984). Commenting on WAF's vision of a new sociomoral order, Mumtaz and Shaheed write, "what was new was that for the first time, [such programs] were being implemented by women in their struggle for their own rights; what was commendable was that many were used in defiance of martial law regulations and orders" (1987, 136; see also I. Malik 1997, 139–67, and Weiss 1995). Asma Jahangir likewise observes, "The women's movement put Pakistan on the map of the world as a country where women were aware and struggling for their rights" (qtd. in I. Malik 1997, 161; see Jalal 1991b, 78–79, for counterargument).

Defiant and organized, other woman's associations also have come of age in Pakistan.[51] The gang rape of Veena Hayat in November 1991 shattered the

50. Interview given to Amnesty International, November 2000.

51. Many middle-class and upper-middle-class professional women, while maintaining their WAF affiliations and alliances, also have channeled their energy into creating several well-staffed and fully functioning NGOs that address the educational, legal, religious, cultural, and psychological problems of women. Some of these organizations include branches of Shirkat Gah in Islamabad (established in 1975) and Lahore (1976), which was "set up by a few professional women and concentrated on establishing a hostel for professional women and writing books/research on women" (Fernandes 1995, 89). They are very useful resource centers. The Aurat Foundation (established in 1976–77) provides legal and medical assistance to working women (for details, see *Dossier* 7–8 [1989–90], 59). ASR is another successful women's organization that in addition to consciously addressing and promoting women's issues is also a publishing company devoted to publishing books by Pakistani and non Pakistani feminists. ASR

belief that only poor and peasant women get raped and that women of the elite are safe. Women Against Rape (WAR) established its Lahore chapter, and as stated in its by-laws, its objectives are "to help the rape victims morally, legally, psychologically, and medically, punishing the culprits, improving the laws relating to rape and creating a rape free society . . . and breaking the silence on sexual violence and rape." Thanks to the dedication of WAR activists, the work of other women's organizations, and all the publicity campaigns surrounding rape cases in Pakistan, the issue has gained greater social and political currency and significance (Yusuf 1992b, 49). In 1991–92, one such publicity campaign prompted Prime Minister Nawaz Sharif to visit rape victims, to promise swift justice, and to provide a small amount of money to the victims and their families. This is not to say that Nawaz Sharif had a change of heart overnight, but that women's organized demand for justice compelled him to respond favorably.

Women's movements in Pakistan represent the most crucial contest between state and civil society (I. Malik 1997, 141). The political reality of Pakistan, where the military regime had been all powerful, suddenly changed, and a new generation of Pakistani professional women "became spokespersons for the largest underprivileged section in the Pakistani population. They stood against human rights violations and raised their voices against legal, social and physical discrimination on the basis of gender" (I. Malik 1997, 146; see also Weiss 1987, 98).

Urban Professional Women: The Invisible Other

A paradox I confronted in Pakistan began to make sense when years later I read an article by Eleanor Dumato, who expressed frustration over the available literature on Muslim women that confirmed the very stereotypes she was trying to undo.[52] "How come," she asks, "much of [the existing] literature deals

---

established the Institute for Women's Studies in Lahore in 1994 (Said Khan, Saigol, and Zia 1995; Shah 1994b, 82–83). For a guide to various organizations and references on Pakistani women, see Shaheed 1992.

52. In response to an exam Dumato gave to her students in which they were asked to "explain how the Middle Eastern Muslim social system can work for women's benefit," Dumato received the following answer, which she thinks is typical: "Muslim women are controlled by men. They have to do whatever men tell them because the Koran says that men are superior to

with problems and personal turmoil which describes no one I know?" (1996, 11). I share Dumato's sense of cognitive dissonance. The women I have met in Pakistan and the women seen through my students' or the popular imagination's eyes are quite different.[53] The point is not that the image of oppressed and victimized Muslim women is totally wrong. Some women *are* abused and victimized. The problem is that this dominant image conceals other images and faces of Muslim women.

My exasperation leads me to pose yet another curious paradox. One of the anthropologist's perennial problems is that of accessibility, particularly to Muslim women, who are often perceived to be or actually are secluded. As citizens of a newly created nation-state, however, Pakistani professional women are both accessible and visible, and yet they have gone unseen and unacknowledged.

The apparent invisibility of professional Muslim women in the ethnographic literature and academic discourse and the theoretical silence on their role in the changing configurations of power and knowledge in their societies are puzzling. This category of women has become reflexive of the changing sociopolitical situation and cultural transformations domestically and internationally in the past few decades. These women are mustering intellectual, political, and economic resources to claim their rights in their societies. They are, in Geertz's words, "authoring themselves," in the sense of demanding that attention be paid them (1986, 373). Attention, ironically, is what they have not received, at least not from Western anthropologists in the mounting research done on women or, paradoxically, from Muslim feminists who live and work in the United States. This inattention is all the more conspicuous when

---

women. They have to have a vaginal examination by a mid-wife to prove that they are a virgin before they can be married. They can be divorced at any time by their husband, who can take away their children, and he can take four wives in her house. Women reproduce the system because they don't know any other. If they try to lead a different kind of life they can be killed or their family can throw them out" (1996, 11).

53. Muslims themselves may not be necessarily free from biases or aware of accomplishments of other Muslims in their societies. As a Muslim woman from Morocco, Leila Abouzeid was surprised by what she observed at the Universities of Homs and Haleb in Syria: "In Homs I met an impressive women's group, consisting of university professors in different disciplines. I was amazed by the dynamics and diversity of the group, which included traditionally educated women and Cambridge graduates, veiled, religious women and feminists in the Western sense of the word, all acting and interacting in complete harmony and acceptance of the other's opinion" (1996, 13).

we consider that middle-class urban professional women from all over the Muslim world (with the exception maybe of Saudi Arabia and Afghanistan under the Taliban) have moved into the public domain.

The general invisibility of professional women in the academic literature ironically contrasts with their visibility in their home countries, where their social activities are often contested and the extent of their public presence resented. Sometimes they are perceived as collaborating with the colonialists; other times they are dismissed as Westernized and thus inauthentic, elitist, and, worse yet, un-Islamic.[54] The resistance to the public presence of professional women in the Muslim world, however, ebbs and flows depending on the kind of regime in power at any given point in time—theocratic, autocratic, military, or democratic.

In academia, the feminist awareness that swept the globe in the late 1960s and early 1970s initially operated within the two frameworks of Orientalism and cultural anthropology, which determined the requirements for both ethnographic research and funding. "The all-too-powerful Orientalist discourse" of the Islamic world came to be "the most bounded and authoritative field" (Gilsenan 1990, 229). In time, feminists began to challenge many of the assumptions in the anthropological approaches to the study of gender in the Middle East and elsewhere. Feminist anthropologists have produced excellent work about the Muslim world to challenge some of the prevailing assumptions and stereotypes and to humanize the unitary image of Muslim women and of the Islamic monolith. However, they, too, for the most part seem to have searched for their "distinctive other" among the peasants and tribal women or among the urban poor.[55]

It is a wonder then that feminist anthropologists, non-Muslim and Muslim alike, have not "studied up" (Nader 1974)[56] by looking at the life and experi-

---

54. It is interesting to note how the perception of professional Muslim women's "(in)authenticity" is reflected outside Muslim societies. A British-based publisher rejected the first proposal for this manuscript, despite the reviewers' unanimous support for publication, primarily because the series editor felt that the middle-class and upper-middle-class women it features were "unrepresentative" of Muslim female population and hence "inauthentic."

55. Several exceptions are to be noted. Some have focused on one or two elite women (Shaarawi 1986; Nelson 1996). Sizoo (1997) brings together a collection of personal memoirs and life histories by a group of professional women including those from the Muslim world. Esfandiari (1997) has written on upper-class women's attitude toward the Islamic Republic of Iran.

56. Such a tendency is not unique to anthropology. Messner observes, "Sociologists have perhaps most often studied 'down'—studying the poor, the blue- or pink-collar workers, the

ences of like-minded middle-class educated women. I argue that, in addition to the broader reasons stated earlier, this oversight has occurred primarily because of the fascination with difference, the generally antielitist strain in anthropology, and presently the preponderance of subaltern studies that for the most part have framed and guided research in the Muslim world and perhaps beyond.

Fascination with Difference

Responding to a growing criticism from women from other cultures, colors, and classes, feminist anthropologists abandoned their earlier assumptions of "women being women everywhere" (Moore 1988)[57] and became sensitive to cultural differences and variables of class, race, and ethnicity. They became increasingly sophisticated in their methodological approaches to issues of "representation of the other," "voice[s] of the natives," "position" and "location" of the self, and the embedded power inequality between the anthropologist "subject/self" and the native "object/other." Redirecting their gaze and refocusing their attention on the difference, feminists celebrated it with relish. Fascination with the difference seemed to liberate feminist anthropologists, who in their identification with the "other"—that is, in relation to the male "self"— tried to give voice to that voiceless "other." But by studying women or the downtrodden or both in communities so different from their own, they reified, perhaps unwittingly, the boundaries between anthropologist/self and native/other more concretely. Such ethnographic encounters in turn confirmed the self's difference and position of dominance. Difference became synonymous with identity. Whether the focus of study was peasant, rural, or tribal women or the urban poor, the *difference* from the feminist anthropologist was glaring enough to make the *object* of study easily identifiable, bounded, and so analyzed.

The fascination with difference as the hallmark of group identity has con-

---

'nuts, sluts and perverts,' the incarcerated. The idea of 'studying up' rarely occurs to sociologists" (2001, 401).

57. See H. Moore 1988 for a description of the difference between anthropology of women (based on sameness and biological denomination) and feminist anthropology (based on cultural, racial, and ethnic differences).

cealed the similarities between self and other.[58] If the West is assumed to be so different from the rest—particularly from the Muslim East—or if anthropology is a "discipline built on the historically constructed divide between the West and the non-West" (Abu-Lughod 1991, 139), then how can Muslim Pakistani professional women be similar to Western professional women? Who is a Muslim woman if she is not veiled? How is a Muslim woman to be identified and thus safely differentiated from the Western self? Who *is* she? Where does she belong if not behind purdah? The conflation of the self and the other also challenges the dominant—though presently contested—epistemology of binary oppositions in Western thought (Morris 1995, 5), leading to methodological dilemmas of definition: how to define this all too familiar other and to distinguish it from the self. The blurring of the boundaries between self and other by this all too similar other is discombobulating.

My point is not to draw a one-to-one correspondence between professional Muslim women and their Western counterparts or to insist on likeness based on their common physiological denominator, but to point out that an exceptionalist view of Muslim women—and by extension of gender relations as well as of political relations—militates against grasping Muslim women's lives as familiar and their struggles as akin to those of women in other countries. My stress on similarity is to highlight, in Rolf Trouillot's words, that "the Other, here and elsewhere, is indeed a product—symbolic and material—of the same process that created the West" (1991, 40; see also Kandiyoti 1991, 4).

The attempt by middle-class, professional Pakistani women—heirs to the postcolonial legacy, citizens of a nation-state—to create a niche in the public domain approximates that of their Western counterparts. They speak English fluently—for most of them, it is their first language—and are educated in prestigious English-speaking colleges. They pursue a wide range of careers, which their families may or may not contest, contribute to the economic welfare of the family, and exert power and influence in the family and society. Stated differently, they are "a complex product of local traditions and values, coupled with ideas of science, rationality and thought derived from their Western edu-

58. In an analogous situation, Brown (1998) argues that "resistance" and its use in anthropology have become trendy to the point that cooperation and harmony are no longer given any attention.

cation" (Saigol 1995, 25). On a more trivial level, they also drive their own cars—though some also have drivers.[59]

One may also wonder why Muslim women anthropologists, the "natives" and the "halfies" who by virtue of being in the profession blur the boundary of self and other, have not studied the life experiences of like-minded women. One can advance the same broader theoretical and financial constraints, namely the prevailing dominant discourses and the funding agencies, that have restricted non-Muslim anthropologists from studying up. But Muslim anthropologists have an added constraint. As natives, they have to show their "difference" from the community they study so that they will not be accused of not being "objective" from the beginning. Morsy articulates the problem succinctly: "I defensively explained that I had never lived in an Egyptian village before and that my social background is very different from that of peasants. I now recognize this defensive posture as an illustration of how anthropological academic socialization promotes ideological conformity and internalization of the Cartesian separation between observer and observed" (1988, 75).

It could be that, as Soraya Altorki notes, women from the same background of the native anthropologist demand the anthropologist's greater conformity with their culturally ascribed role and status (1988, 53–55). Or, of more serious consequence to research, in her view, is that the researcher potentially may pose a threat of exposure and judgment (57). It could also be that, as the Pakistani feminist activist Nighat Said Khan suggests, having inherited the British colonial baggage, most " 'westernized,' middle class, urban feminists find it very difficult to talk about themselves, except intellectually" (1995, 118). I concur with her observations but only partially. I did have the opportunity to meet a few Westernized intellectual women who were reluctant to talk. But I also have had intimate conversations with many professional middle-class and upper-middle-class women, including those whose narratives are included in this book.

Soraya Altorki is among the very few native anthropologists who has gone against the ethnographic grain to study up, while acknowledging the dominant constraints. Her reasons for researching among "the elite families" in Saudi Arabia—of whom incidentally she is one—are that such studies are

---

59. One significant difference between Pakistani professional women and their American counterparts is that the former have the luxury of having several servants, helpers, and nannies.

"rare in anthropology," and that "[t]he history of anthropological fieldwork has been a study of commoners, the poor, and the marginal. Anthropologists, whether working in their own society or in another, have traditionally studied people whose status is below their own" (1988, 51–52).[60]

The overall effect of such theoretical and canonical constraints and individual neglect has been to mask the active roles urban professional women have played in mobilizing and politicizing—if not always reforming—ideas of gender hierarchy, political relations, citizenship, and human rights in their societies.

Citizens of Pakistan, Honor of Their Men

After having lived in Pakistan for some time, I abandoned assumptions regarding the binariness of fundamentalism and secularism. However, I also came to realize the complexity and dynamics of the cultural and political tension between them. These issues are politically important both nationally and internationally—people situate their lives and activities in relation to them, and they refer to them often. Their sense of self, identity, and ethnicity are closely bound up in these conceptual frameworks and social structures. Against this background, women's identities, in particular those of professional women, are more contested than ever before because the autonomy and independence associated with their public activities disturb the traditional boundaries of public and private domains and hence of primordial values (Geertz 1994, 30; see also D. Ahmed 1994) associated with female immobility and chastity. At the heart of the contestation lies the dilemma of citizenship and honor. Perceived as individuals, as citizens of the nation-state of Pakistan, women are accorded or denied certain rights, depending on the political orientation of the ruling regime. As members of certain ethnicities, lineages, and classes, women culturally are perceived in relational terms and as the embodiment of purity and honor. As the tension has grown sharper between Pakistan's national identity and various ethnic groups' claims to greater autonomy and identity, the state has exerted greater ideological pressure to forge a national identity, and it often does so in the name of Islam. Jalal argues that forging unity on the

60. Referring to C. Mohanty, Margery Wolf (1990, 12) similarly writes that anthropologists are vulnerable to charges of superiority over those they study because they typically study the rural, the poor, and the uneducated.

basis of "Islamic ideology" in fact paradoxically has militated against national integration (1991b, 288). One of the concessions the state has made consistently is to allow, directly or indirectly, different ethnic groups to restrict women's rights and options in the name of "respect" for culture and tradition.[61]

National identity for professional women implies a series of added conflicts and tensions that ensnare them in further contestation of their aspirations. They are caught in national, cultural, and ethnic double-binds: between national opportunities for appearing in public and pursuing a profession, on the one hand, and the ethnic and cultural ideal of women's seclusion and immobility, on the other; between opportunities to be socially active in the public domain and the cultural meanings and symbolism of honor perceived to be located in the female body. These conflicts are emblematic of larger sociocultural clashes between the expectations raised and opportunities provided or strategically withheld by the state and the ancient and well-entrenched customary codes of honor sharpened by the emergence of feminism and fundamentalism. And honor, *izzat*, is the heart of the matter.

A Matter of Honor

Izzat is a complex primordial concept with multiple connotations and overlapping meanings, including respect, esteem, dignity, and reputation. "The spirit that motivates people to protect their *izzat*, in turn, is called *gairat*" (Murphy 1996, 106). *Izzat* is also a dynamic sociocultural construct, constantly adjusting and responding to the changes happening in the state and society. As a South Asian society, Pakistan carries the legacy of Islam through the cultural idioms of caste and class, gender hierarchy, and female purity.[62] Both men and women have, of course, dignity and honor and are expected to show their *ghairat* appropriately. But the main components of their honor are effected differently, both domestically and publicly. Honor is male centered in Pakistan

61. The reaction of Pakistan's Senate to the cold-blooded murder of Samia Imran is a telling example. The Senate refused to condemn the killing (allegedly arranged by her parents, who perceived as dishonorable her desire to divorce her abusive husband), arguing that it was a matter of "honor" and so a long-standing tradition and hence beyond the jurisdiction of the state. See also Chhachhi 1991.

62. For a discussion as to why honor and purity of lineage are vested in the sexual behavior of women and how the development of female purity and honor is connected to the development of the state, see Ortner 1996.

and is acted out in public. Men are expected to be brave, generous, authoritarian, independent, fecund, and protective of their women. A man's "honor demands that he should fully monopolize his wife; this is a virtue in men; it epitomizes masculine dominance and autonomy" (Barth 1981, 87).

A woman's honor, in contrast, is perceived culturally to be an inherent condition of her being, namely her purity and chastity. Both men and women are expected to be honorable and obedient to their elders, leaders, culture, and God, but women bear an added obligation. Honor, symbolized in the female body and reduced to women's sexual purity, is perceived as a "natural" foundation for social and moral order. Women's loss of honor—whether by force or choice—bears directly on the honor of those primary male kin who, as the presumed custodians of women's chastity, are expected to take public action to maintain their good name. In Pakistan, political scores oftentimes are settled and a political rival is dishonored through the rape of his womenfolk (K. Ahmed 1992; Haeri 1995b). Hence, the threat of women's mobility and autonomy.[63]

"Honor," argues Stewart, "is a notoriously paradoxical topic, and one of its most famous puzzles is the effect that women's behavior can have on men's honor" (1994, 107). In Pakistani society, the concept of honor is tied intimately in with a sense of men's "natural" right to possess and control women. Objectifying honor in the body of a woman, *zan*, men culturally are believed to possess honor, just as they possess gold, *zar*, and land, *zamin*—as I mentioned earlier, the three most sought-after commodities in Pakistan and presumably at the root of all conflicts. It follows logically that women cannot possess honor in the same way as men. Men *have* honor. Women *represent* honor; they symbolize honor; they are honor. Objectified into manipulable possessions, women conceptually lose a sense of individuality and autonomous identity in the eye of the community. Educated Pakistani women, however, systematically have challenged such traditional and male-centered cultural perceptions of women's individuality and sense of honor, while trying to generate greater honor parity.

In the name of honor, some men perpetrate crimes and violence against women. They do so with impunity, knowing full well that in the eyes of many of their compatriots they are heroes and will be rewarded according to the same honor code. If they ever receive punishment, it is usually light and is

63. See Mandelbaum's discussion on the symbolism of reproduction, in which "men provide the seed, the woman the field," hence the necessity to keep women constrained so that the seed grows in a pure field (1988, 72–73).

done in the name of religion with the state staying at a distance. According to Islamic criminal justice, killing is a punishable offence and a crime against society in a modern nation-state. Reinterpreting the Qur'an within the context of a modern nation-state, Nilofar Ahmed, a religious Sufi woman whose life story is recounted in chapter 7, argues that the punishment for the perpetrators of the crime of violence against women can be as severe as execution. Presently in Pakistan, however, although crime and violence against women are on the increase, the punishment, if there is one, is not commensurable with the crime.[64]

Although the state's ambivalence to punish crimes of honor may stem from its hesitation to upset the feudal, tribal, and religious status quo, men's motivation to commit the crime is often rooted in the honor code itself. "Honor," argues Montaique, "is a matter of self-help," and "[he] who appeals to the laws to get satisfaction from an offense to his honor, dishonors himself" (qtd. in Stewart 1994, 80). Men take it upon themselves in Pakistan to punish "disobedient"—read autonomous—women, and the state often looks the other way. Whereas the state is presumed to protect the rights of its citizens, women who seek justice usually are frustrated in their attempts, and those who try to help them often come under attack. The problem is compounded by the fact that those in power continue to be drawn mainly from traditional, feudal, and tribal backgrounds (Hussain 1990, 191; I. Malik 1997, 92).

Feudalism, Patrilineage, and Purity of Women

One frequently hears of or reads about feudalism and feudal attitudes in Pakistan, and the public attributes much of the country's social and political ills to feudalism and to its concomitant practices and worldview. A review of the historical and cultural differences between feudalism in Pakistan and in Europe is

---

64. It should be noted here that professional Pakistani women' sustained political agitation both inside and outside of Pakistan and their attempt to bring the issue of violence against women to public attention may have borne some fruit. In April 2000, General Parvez Musharraf, the military leader who overthrew the elected prime minister Nawaz Sharif in October 1999, convened a national conference in Islamabad to address specifically the issues of "honor killing," violence against women, women's and minorities' human rights, and the so-called blasphemy law. Prior to that date, Riffat Hassan, a Pakistani professor of religion sent an open letter (*Pakistan Today*, February 24, 2000) to General Musharraf, urging him to devise means to protect women's lives against violence and honor killing in Pakistan.

beyond the scope of this section.[65] Suffice it to say that *feudal* in the Pakistani context means a relatively small group of politically active and powerful landowners. It also means "a moral category," in the sense that Pakistanis often talk of the "feudal attitude"—"a combination of arrogance and entitlement."[66] In describing the character and form of feudalism in Pakistan, Iftikhar Malik writes that whereas in the South Asian colonies "feudalism itself has undergone a dramatic transformation, the feudal dynasties . . . have continuously redefined their role so as to guarantee their self-preservation" (1997, 81–82).

Within this context, the juxtaposition of powerful women such as Benazir Bhutto and the many powerless women who live in abject poverty appears paradoxical. Such extreme oppositions may be explained against the background of Pakistani feudal and patrilineal, *bradri*, systems. *Bradri* (or *baradari*), according to Mann, means "brotherhood" and is an "internalized sense of solidarity extended to its members, but denied to those outside its limits. It is imbued with a sense of honor *(izzat)*" (1992, 44). *Bradri* membership among Muslims is ascriptive and "functions similarly to a caste among the Hindus" (Mann 1992, 44). These restrictive and superimposing social structures that snare landless and poor women and men into lifelong servitude and compounded poverty paradoxically also can be enabling to some women of feudal lineage. Perhaps the specificity of feudalism in Pakistan and much of South Asia lies in its multiple capacity for extreme brutality and oppression of many women and for concentration of tremendous wealth, power, and authority in the hands of a few. Power and authority are drawn from land ownership, and women, by inheriting land, are placed in a position to exercise feats of national greatness and authority. The enabling mechanism, however, is *not* the ownership of land alone. It is also the strong and special relationship between a lineage patriarch and his daughter. His support recognizes her as an autonomous individual and bestows power and prestige on the daughter and legitimates her presence and activities in the public domain.

Anthropological literature is rich in documenting, describing, and analyz-

---

65. Whether feudalism in Pakistan is similar to its namesake in Europe has been debated in the literature on Pakistan. For a brief review of feudalism in South Asia and in Europe, see Murphy, who argues that feudalism in South Asia is not necessarily the same as the one in Europe (1996, 101–10). For a view on the history and the changing nature of feudalism in Pakistan, see Gardezi 1983.

66. Richard Murphy, personal communication, 1995.

ing variations of father-son relationships in patriarchal and patrilineal societies. The oft-repeated emphasis on the significance of father-son relationships for the continuity of social structure has had the effect of reifying the
relationship. Although the father-son relationship may be indeed the ideal
model, it may not—and often is not—the normative one. The problem with
superimposing the ideal model onto the normative one and assuming a perfect
fit between the two is that it tends to mask the dynamics of other existing relationships that actually may be operating, competing, or countering the ideal
model. Consequently, little information is available on the intricacies of the
relationship between a patriarch and his daughter, whom he may indeed favor
over his sons, who are in a structural position to dislodge the patriarch from
his position of authority. By bestowing land, power, and prestige onto their
daughters, powerful and prominent male leaders in fact groom their daughters—sometimes at the expense of their sons—to assume political leadership.
The riddle of the preponderance, relatively speaking, of South Asian women
prime ministers is solved once viewed within this particular father-daughter
political alliance.[67] Even while in jail, the senior Bhutto continued instructing
his daughter Benazir—not his sons—to carry his political philosophy and
leadership mantle (Bhutto 1989, 145–46; for another politically influential
father-daughter relationship in Pakistan, see Shahnawaz 1971).

Also partly solved is the nature of the conflict and the simmering animosity
between Benazir Bhutto and her brother, Mir Murtaza. He returned to Pakistan from exile during his sister's second term in office (1993–96) and immediately demanded that the leadership of the PPP be turned over to him. Begum
Nusrat Bhutto, Benazir's mother and the PPP cochairwoman at the time, supported her son, much to Benazir's consternation. The pain and frustration Benazir consequently felt is achingly articulated in her interview with Etienne
Duval in a documentary on her life in politics, *Benazir Bhutto: Walking the
Tightrope* (1995). Mir Murtaza apparently assumed, in line with the ideal patrilineal patterns of feudal filial relations in South Asia, that his sex gave him the
birthright legitimacy to political leadership. He was mysteriously murdered in

67. Citing Carol Mukhopadhyay, Erin Moore offers a different explanation, but one that
sees religion as the prime factor. According to Moore, Mukhopadhyay argues that "because in
Hinduism both gods and humans turn to powerful women for assistance, protection, and leadership, Hinduism legitimates—and the populace accepts—female exercise of power and leadership in domestic and extradomestic domains" (1998, 32).

Karachi in 1996, however, and many allege that Benazir's husband, Asif Zardari (jailed since the ouster of Benazir in 1996), masterminded the killing.

Benazir Bhutto's political leadership symbolizes tensions between religion and culture as well as between citizenship and honor. Her leadership of a Muslim state created much uproar in Pakistan and in other Muslim states because it effectively turned traditional gender relations and political hierarchies upside down. Yet religion was no barrier to her being elected prime minister twice. Prime minister, citizen of Pakistan, and professional woman par excellence, she negotiated political alliances with her foes, while maintaining her honor by agreeing to a marriage arranged by her kin. She covered her hair and avoided shaking hands with local or international male dignitaries.[68] Overriding religious objections, the strong ethos of masculine superiority and dominance, and the embedded code of purity and honor, the Pakistani feudal system makes it politically possible for women to assume leadership, but not without serious cultural and emotional tensions.

Female Honor, Gendered Space

Feminism has brought a paradigm shift in the perception and the symbolism of honor and of gender roles and relations in Pakistan. Active in public, professional women defy the central tenet of traditional beliefs that requires women's seclusion, invisibility, immobility, and subservience to men.[69] By action and words, these women challenge, sometimes not without ambivalence and often at a risk, the perception of women as the embodiment of purity and the repository of their husbands' or their lineage's honor. Exorcizing honor from their bodies, they embody their individuality. So doing, Pakistani educated and professional women locate honor in their action and in their moral

68. The reason for the prohibition of cross-gender handshakes, according to Bouhdiba, is that adult males or females have already known the pleasure that touch may arise in them. Therefore, touching each other's hands is permitted only between two children or "two old people sheltered from temptation" (1985, 38).

69. In a study of inner-city women in Lahore, Anita Weiss argues that two-thirds of the women who had to withdraw from school in her sample of one hundred did so because of the perception that their activities outside of the home were a threat to their *izzat* (1992, 34).

courage to pursue personal and civic objectives, as men have done all along. They draw legitimacy both from a feminist interpretation of the Qur'an and from the charter of a modern nation-state. They challenge the historically received religious practices and beliefs regarding women and instead uphold the original Islamic fundamental respect for equality and individual dignity.

Cognizant of the potent symbolism of the female body and sometimes emotionally conflicted because of it, Pakistani feminists lay claim to honor *not* as something accorded them as females related to and dependent on male kin, but as something basic to their humanity, as a sense of self. Professional women demand to be treated as citizens of a modern Islamic state, with equal rights, privileges, respect, and indeed honor: honor based on their personal worth and on their professional participation in society, not on the "symbolic capital" of female chastity and purity—that is, honor "as having certain worth . . . as a right to respect" (Stewart 1994, 21).

Female honor in Pakistan, I argue, ought to be viewed as a multifaceted expression of female agency in public and of inner strength to pursue objectives in the face of unjust demands and oppression—attributes that have always been associated with men. Public domain has been historically an exclusive arena for male activities, creativity, and performance. Consequently, resistance to gendering this space has been fierce in Pakistan and elsewhere. Writing on the anthropology of cities, Low points out that cities are arenas where women "are still not full citizens, in the sense that they have never been granted full and free access to the streets" (1996, 390). Women's agency in the public domain and the gender competition over utilization of public space have provoked violent reactions in Pakistan and have confronted the state with inherent contradictions. Are women to be treated as citizens of a nation-state or as symbols of male honor and lineage purity and thus as objects to be controlled or disposed of capriciously? A state's role theoretically is to protect its citizens' rights, but the state in Pakistan is often unwilling or unable to do so because it continues to be dominated by tribal leaders, pressure groups, and feudal lords.

It is against this highly complex and conflictual background of crosscutting, constantly shifting, and superimposing political, ethnic, and ideological rivalries, alliances, and values that middle-class professional Pakistani women situate their lives, talk about their journeys of self-discovery, attempt to gain self-respect, and effect social change.

Liminal Ethnographer

"If seeing," as Joan Scott argues, "is the origin of knowing" (1994, 366), then in the case of Muslim women her observation is obviously inadequate, if not inaccurate. What has been seen in the Muslim world is, paradoxically, not the visible, unveiled professional woman but the veiled Muslim woman, the sight of whom does not begin to add much to one's knowledge of women in the Muslim world. Perhaps the desire to reveal the forbidden and to make it seen and presumably known has been a strong motivating factor in focusing attention on the veiled women of the Muslim world. The veil has been perceived as synonymous with the Muslim woman and thus has become the hegemonic image of "Muslim women"—reductionist in any case. In tandem, many anthropologists' wish to make the voices of the downtrodden and the subaltern heard has rendered those voices gradually hegemonic in academia. Hegemonies are powerful, but they are not eternal or total (Ortner 1996, 172), and so the image of the veil or the voices of the subaltern should be viewed as providing only part of a complex whole (Ortner 1996, 18). Therefore, if professional Muslim women have remained invisible and unheard outside their own countries, despite their relative influential status, and if they have been represented only sporadically in the existing ethnographic literature, it follows that our knowledge of the Muslim world and of Muslim women is fundamentally flawed.

This book attempts to fill in some of the gap by bringing to light the lives of professional women who have been un(under)represented in the West. It offers stories of women who have gone against the cultural grain and social expectations and have—willingly or unwillingly—jeopardized their family's honor and prestige in doing so. They did not challenge the law or culture just for the sake of doing so. They did it because they knew that what was facing them ran deeply against their sense of self-respect and dignity. Their resistance against oppressive cultural expectations and religious obligations, accidentally or intentionally, created a new awareness of themselves and of their society. It was precisely by taking action that they laid claim to self-respect and individual dignity—indeed, to honor. Having the courage of their convictions, they claimed their honor in and of itself, not on the basis of their gender or their relation to a particular man from a particular patrilineage, but as a measure of their moral courage and personal struggle.

By making the lives of professional Muslim women visible, I, too, have gone against the cultural grain and the ideal of the primacy of community over individual in Muslim societies. I have focused on the lives of individuals in a society where individuality and individualism are perceived with ambivalence or more often as subservient to the centrality of the community and communal values. I also have attempted to historicize the lives of particular individual women in a context where historically little significance is assigned to an individual's life experiences (Zonis 1991), least of all to women's.

Together, the six women whose life stories are told in the next six chapters take us into their worlds, which are as intricate as they are compelling. Sharing with us their intimate feelings and experiences of success and failure, they take us along their journey of self-discovery, awareness, and action. Their narratives simultaneously concentrate attention on the uniqueness of individuals and bring into focus overlapping cultural denominations and patterns. Their life stories provide an ethnographic tapestry of Pakistani culture and society, wherein the diversity of women's actions and experiences refocus attention on the complex and nuanced ways in which middle-class, educated Pakistani women perceive themselves, their families, and their society and on the ways in which they craft their identities and negotiate with various structures of power.

My journey east became a journey of self-discovery as my life intersected with the lives of these and many other Pakistani women. Anthropology, by nature, is a journey, and ethnography often becomes a journey of self-discovery, as indeed it was for me. Approaching ethnography as a process of self-discovery opens up vistas of enlightenment about the other instead of fixing the other in the straightjacket of preconceived theories. "There is more in a human life," Hillman states, "than our theories of it allow" (1996, 3). I sought collaboration, mutual contemplation, and interpretation from women themselves and consequently did not wish to squeeze their lives by dispersing their stories into aspects of my social analysis. What we have created in the process is a shared ethnography of Pakistan.

A traveler is transient, moving through both personal and historical time while passing from place to place. She evaluates the distances traversed, the wonders observed, the enlightenment received, and the new experiences gained in a particular time and space. Having gone east in search of clarity and meaning, and having been given the gift of many Pakistani women and men's friendship, I see my role as a feminist anthropologist not so much as a "translator" of culture. Pakistani professional women do that quite eloquently. Nor do

I see my role as a "border ethnographer" (Dossa 1999, 159) or as a "native" or "halfie" anthropologist in Pakistan. I see my role rather as a liminal ethnographer—and anthropologists often are liminal—who crosses different geographical, cultural, and linguistic boundaries, traditions, and histories and is positioned as neither a self nor the other, as neither an outsider nor a native, yet in her liminality has the potential to bridge them both.

PART TWO

Contesting the Culture of Dominance

2

Identity
Contested Visions of Womanhood and Society

Meeting Quratul Ain Bakhteari

QURAT, as Quratul Ain Bakhteari is commonly known, answered my telephone call personally and was most cordial and receptive when I indicated my interest to interview her for my project. In less than thirty minutes, I was at her house. It was a hot summer day in June 1998. We barricaded ourselves in an air-conditioned room, drank lots of cold water and lemonade, and instantly bonded. I visited her at her house for two or three consecutive days, and we talked, had lunch, and talked some more. Lunch was prepared for us every day by her servants while we were deeply involved in our conversations and interview. No one else joined us for lunch, and the two of us talked about her work, my work, our mutual interests in research, Iran, and Pakistan. She invited me to join her at the education workshops and seminars she organizes in Quetta, the capital of the province of Baluchistan, where she is currently director of primary education. Much to my regret, I had to decline because I was on my way to Iran the same day she was flying to Quetta. Qurat is a proud mother of three sons and is a young grandmother.

Qurat was highly articulate in English and did not need much encouragement from me. As soon as she understood the objectives of my research, she began telling me the story of her life systematically, chronologically, and eloquently. It is the story of a woman caught in the dilemmas of being a wife, a mother, and a professional in Pakistan, a woman in search of identity and self-empowerment in uncertain and transitional situations. Let us hear from her.

Quratul Ain Bakhteari

The Frontier Spirit: Seeds of Social Activism

I will be fifty come December 25, 1998. I was born soon after the creation of Pakistan, and my birthday falls on the same day as that of Pakistan's leader and founder, Mohammad Ali Jinnah.

My mother's family is from Agra, India, very near the famous Taj Mahal. Her childhood was spent playing in the lawns of that magnificent monument. She happened to be the youngest of five children until my grandfather married for a second time and had more children after her. My maternal grandfather, Agha Ahmad Hussain, was a very creative architect, and most of the buildings you see in Pakistan today and many in India were designed and constructed by him.[1] He designed the Motta Palace, the Fatima Jinnah residence in Clifton, Karachi. He was one of its designers *and* contractors.[2] He worked for the British and was very Westernized in his orientation. But after the partition, when my mother's family migrated to Pakistan, they faced very hard times. He died before my mother married my father.

My father is from Sunipal, somewhere farther away in Indian Punjab. My parents met at Aligarh Muslim University, where they were both studying, and married soon after they landed in Pakistan in 1948. They were in love and married against everybody's wishes. He was twenty-two and had no job, nothing in Pakistan. She was eighteen or nineteen, also with no skills or money. They lived with my maternal grandmother and her brothers and sisters in one big building that was left by the Hindus when they fled to India. It was very crowded. My mother was a very independent-minded, temperamental, and spirited woman. She wanted to have her own space at all cost and did not like living with many people. This might be because she lived in an extended family in India, and, as the youngest child with younger stepsiblings,

1. Responding to my further inquiries, Qurat sent an e-mail message to me (April 15, 2000) in which she wrote, "My maternal grandfather was born in India but had his construction work in Karachi, Peshawar, and Lahore before partition. Therefore, my mother's family had a home in Karachi as well." It is not clear, however, that her mother actually lived in this house after partition.

2. Words in italics are used to capture the inflections and stress Qurat put on certain terms, situations, emotions, and events.

she suffered a lot. Her father's careless attitude toward her mother generated insecurities in her.

My maternal grandmother was also a very hardheaded woman. When her husband married his second wife, she left him and took care of her five children. She had nothing to do with him anymore and made the best of it by building rooms on her land in Agra and renting them out to provide for her family. Not that my grandfather wouldn't pay for them. He would. But she just refused it, while, in the meantime, he focused only on himself, enjoyed his wealth, and was always surrounded by women. My mother grew up in that kind of environment.

My earliest memories of my parents are that my mother was constantly pushing and pulling things the way she believed things ought to be. She dreamed to make her life the way she lived it—or remembered it—in Agra: huge house, big car, lots of servants. Meanwhile, my father just followed her. He was a very quiet, peaceful, and loving man. He still is. He was very much into his own world, his children, and his solitude, but he let my mother do whatever she believed in, never interfering in her activities. Once or twice he tried to caution her, but she told him to mind his own business and keep quiet.

Knowing now how she struggled as a child, I came to understand the way she related to us. Her attitude was that she knew what was best for her children, that she was determined to have her own home even if it meant a one-room house in a remote settlement area for the refugees—somewhere near the airport. Her family tried to make her see the difficulties that such a move entailed, that it was too far, that her children were too small, that it was crazy, but to no avail. No water as yet was available in that refugee settlement, nor was there electricity or anything else. But she insisted that it would be hers. These are the kinds of arguments I constantly overheard as a child.

Memoirs of Hope: A Child's View of Partition

Finally, we moved to that one-room house. I was only five years old, but I remember, being the eldest child, I was part of my parents' daily struggle. My mother and I would get some mud and a bucket of water and put one brick over another to make boundary walls. This settlement was created hastily by the government to assist the refugees who were pouring in from India. These were people hit by the circumstances, poor but educated people with some civilized backgrounds. It was a community neighborhood, full of understanding, civilized behavior, and loving, affectionate people who were living in an extremely harsh environment and struggling for a better life in Pakistan.

My childhood was strongly influenced by the values promoted in this struggle: partnership and love for others. It has left *very* powerful images in me. I remember my mother working from dusk to dawn. My father, though working hard, would stop after two o'clock to spend time with us, to give us love and care. Half of the time he did not know where our next meal was going to come from, but my parents never showed that worried look on their faces, that "there is no food in the house, what will happen tomorrow?" That insecure feeling we never had. Reflecting back, I wonder how they could make ends meet on my father's earning of 280 rupees per month and my mother's 80 rupees.[3] Yet she had a part-time servant in the house.

My mother was very particular about the way we dressed and the way the house looked, in spite of having no furniture. The floors had to shine. The windows and the doors and the walls had to be absolutely clean. Our boundary wall, although made out of mud, and our floors, which were made of packed garbage, always looked neat and clean. It was just a room, just four walls, two windows, one door—that's it. The government provided nothing else, nothing. People built everything, brick by brick. Everybody was busy working on their houses, children and all. The sights, the hustle and bustle, and the daily movements of people working—it was so electrifying. That is how my childhood was.

My mother walked five miles every day to her school because she could not afford the bus fare. I remember she had just two saris, both blue. She refused to let me wear the traditional Pakistani dress, the *shalwar-kamiz*.[4] Instead, I had to wear skirts and blouses, which she made herself, although in summers she would make me pants. She used to cut my hair the same way as the British girls. She had a totally British orientation. I *never* wore any kind of veil or anything traditional until I was twelve or thirteen years old. Imagine living in that type

3. The relation of rupee's monetary value to the dollar has fluctuated dramatically since the creation of the state of Pakistan. In 1967, the exchange rate was approximately 4 or 5 rupees to a dollar, 13 to 1 in 1987, 24 to 1 in 1993, and 56 to 1 in 1998. By early January 2002, the rate was 67 to 69 rupees to a dollar. In April, the rupee gained slightly, and presently it stands at 59 to 60 to a dollar.

4. The traditional Pakistani two-piece suit, the tunic and pants, to which a scarf (*dupata*) is added.

of refugee settlement and bringing up your children in that Westernized manner! She was struggling hard to keep alive the Western images of *her* past life.

I was not brought up as a vulnerable girl because the entire neighborhood
was caring for each other's children. I was never made to feel that I was a girl,
that I was a good girl, because the struggle was carried at such a higher level
that gender was lost in it. The way women were traditionally treated could not
be done in the refugee camps because there was no luxury of time to treat
women as women. We had hardly anything, but I had a very happy childhood,
full of wonderful memories.

I really did not have much parental supervision and was on the street all the
time. I was a child of four or five years barely and not in school yet. I was
mostly with boys roaming around—other girls wouldn't venture out as much.
Our servant would cry his head off, worrying that I might get lost any day.
There was an air force base near where we lived, and I loved to go there and
watch for hours the planes landing and taking off. I knew my mother would
come home from school at one o'clock. Somehow I would try to reach home
by that time, and if I couldn't, I would get a good beating.

Then my mother would leave again. She had to go to the teachers' training
herself, which her school required. She was trying to complete her education
that was left unfinished in Aligarh University because of the partition. Again
in the evenings I was out, exploring, playing, cycling, doing all sorts of things
that usually happen in the streets. I guess I was a very popular child. I was also
a well-protected child in a *big* neighborhood, where everyone knew whose
daughter I was. When I was hungry, I would walk into anybody's house and be
taken care of. Then I would go out again, playing. Whenever something was
happening, a wedding or a feast, someone would call me in and give me sweets
or make me something here and there. So my days would pass that way. It was
such a wonderful time.

That was the education I got, which is carrying me still today—the freedom, the chance to do my own explorations. If my parents had not been poor
and struggling, I could not have done all that. Had they had a little bit of
money, I would have been locked up inside the house and not allowed to do
anything. But there was no way they could do that. Who would then be fetch-
ing water? I used to go and get water. Who would get the milk from the
milkman's house? Who would buy groceries from the hawkers and the bazaar?
There was no electricity. I had to go out, holding a lantern in one hand and
carrying a pot or something in the other. So there was no way they could treat

me like a girl and keep me locked up in the house, particularly because I was the eldest child, no way!

Like Mother, Like Daughter

I remember the settlement houses had no latrines; there was no sewer system. Fifteen or twenty houses were attached to one latrine, and everybody had to use these public toilets. There was no maintenance for these latrines, and they were manually cleaned. One of the latrines was right in front of our house, so naturally until the sweeper would come and take away the filth, it was all there. My mother—the way she was—fought tooth and nail to demolish those public latrines. From the very first day, the first thing she did was to make our own private latrine. We never used that public one. Every day on her way to work, she would go to the Works Department and ask them to come and destroy it or to shift it away from in front of our house. Mother was so unhappy about this public toilet that she taught me to throw stones at anybody who would use it [laughing]. Finally, one day I saw my mother very happy. Bulldozers were there, tearing down the latrine. That's how single-minded she was.

Perhaps the reason I became so *fascinated* by this structure and involved in designing and constructing latrines has something to do with these struggles.

One time as I was coming home from school with my mother and as we were walking toward our house, we saw a big crowd around one of the rooms in the quarter. We could hear a woman's wailing through the crowd. My mother pushed aside the men who were holding a vigil around the woman and went in. She saw a woman with three small children sitting outside the locked door of her room. Her children were holding on to her and crying. She was crying and sitting on top of her small *buqchah*, bundle of clothes. She was a youngish woman, around thirty. Many *men* were crowding around her. Not a single woman was there. My mother went up to her and asked what the matter was. She said that a man threw her out of her house and locked her out. He had taken over the room in his name because she was a widow.[5] My mother got so furious—the way she was—and started shouting at the men who were standing around and watching this woman cry. The words she used even today I remember: "You useless men, you are just having a nice time looking at a woman crying." With those words, she picked up a big stone, crashed

5. Because she did not have a man to support and protect herself and her children from such cruelty.

through the door, and she said, "If anybody can hold me back, let him try!" She broke down the door and put that woman's belongings back in there with her own hands. I was scared to death, the way my mother was acting. She then put the woman and children in the room and stood in front of the door. "Do what you want to me. I am going to see to it," she said. Nobody dared to move. The man who had taken over the room came over and started an argument with my mother. "You come one step closer," said my mother, "and you will see what I will do!" In the meantime, the Works Department officer came to see what was happening, and my mother related the whole story. She gave them a big lecture and said, "This is *not* the reason we made Pakistan! Is this the reason we came to this country?" Suddenly other men chimed in and started agreeing with her.

These two incidents had a *strong* mark on me. There is a whole lot I don't remember, but I do remember that whenever there were issues concerning anybody, she was right in front of it. My mother was an activist in the Pakistan movement. There were, all the time, women in and out of our house and meetings going on.

Going to School: British Education

Now all of sudden I started hearing the arguments over where I should go to school. *Right* next to our house there was a government school where children had to sit on the floor. "No way. My children are not going to *this* school," said my mother. "Children should *not* be sitting on the floor. Besides, no English is taught there." But, then, no English or missionary school was nearby. The closest was at least ten miles away from our house, and there was no transportation system, and I was only five or six years old! How was I supposed to go there every day? This was a highly reputed Christian missionary school, and only people who could pay the monthly fifteen rupees tuition could go. "*That* is the school my children are going to," mother said. My father asked, "But where are we going to get this money every month, plus the costs of transportation, the uniform, and everything else?" In the government school, things were provided.

"That is my problem," said mother.

What my mother did was to work harder. She started giving private lessons after one o'clock, when her schoolwork was over. So I was registered in that missionary school. Soon after my brother came of age, he was enrolled in it. Imagine—every evening our uniforms, which she made herself, were starched and ironed neat and clean. We were the best-dressed children in the school. There was only one public bus that used to go near the school, and I was just six years old. If I missed that bus, I had to walk.

Everybody told my mother that she was crazy, that this child was going to be kidnapped, or *something* would happen to her. And every evening my parents gave me a lecture. "Do not go with strangers. Do not trust anybody who tells you, 'Your mother has had an accident, and you should come with me immediately.' *Never*, never do that." They pounded that into my head. My mother had our address and a number strung around my neck. She was doing things in those days that *no* other women did. I think whatever I am today is because of that period, that struggle.

I was a healthy, clean, and well-dressed child. Very quickly the bus drivers and conductors and everybody took a liking to me, and they started taking extra care of me. If they saw me running to catch the bus, they would hold the bus a little longer. They would also hold the bus if they didn't see me at the bus stop. There were *many* children around, but I used to get special attention. It was a lovely childhood. There was a feeling of care and love all the time. I don't know what has happened now. People are like that no more. But then all of us were the same class of people, same background. There were no *rich* people around.

I started Saint Agnes Missionary School. It was a *very* good school, and the Christian nuns were very particular and strict, but also very caring and principled. I don't see them that way anymore. It was a coeducational school, and boys and girls got equal attention, until I was, say, eleven years old. That is when I started getting signals that I was different. I was much taller and healthier than other girls my age, and so I was not seen as eleven years old. That is when things started changing around me, inexplicably. I was a good bicycle rider, but gradually my bicycle was taken away, and I was not allowed to use it.

Gendering Qurat

My mother was changing very fast. My father was changing very fast. The people on the street changed. The same people who used to love and care for me changed. Things were tightening around me, none of which I could understand.[6] Resentment started mounting between my parents and me and

---

6. Now that Qurat was coming of age, her parents, in particular her mother, tried to enforce the traditional rules of conduct generally expected of women in Pakistan.

grew stronger day by day, hour by hour. I could not understand it. Soon I started lying to my parents about my whereabouts because I did not change my pattern of wandering off. Then they had to go out searching for me.

The settlement itself was developed slowly, and things were improving. My parents' position improved a little financially, and the school started to operate a pick-up bus for the students, so my parents got the bus for us. Now three of us were in school. I refused to take that bus because it was too boring—being picked up from my home, dropped off at the school, picked up from the school again, and dropped back at home. I was missing all the bus rides, the walks, and all the fun of wandering. Often the school bus would reach home without me, and I would arrive home at five instead of, say, at two. That was because I had no money or had eaten it away and had to walk home. While walking home, I liked exploring new routes. Sometimes I would get stuck somewhere because I got busy picking berries or because we ended up playing too long. My mother got scared to death that something would happen to me, so every evening if I did not get a good beating, I would get shouted at—lots of howling and screaming.

My parents, already under heavy pressure from financial constraints and daily struggle, started losing their cool with me. Mother started using words and language that humiliated me. She used abusive words and called me *kambakht*, wretched one who would bring *beizzati*, dishonor, to the family. She started making me feel like a girl. I was confused as to how dishonor was going to come. My brother and sisters kept away from me so that they would not get the same spanking and blame from my mother. I was all alone. The tension and conflict got so bad that sometimes I would go to school without eating breakfast. But Mother was very particular. She would finish teaching her first three classes at ten, and during her recess she would walk three miles to my school to bring me something to eat. Then she would walk all the way back to be at her class on time. I don't know how she could manage it because she did not have any money.

But what happened to me in this process was that as a teenager, instead of developing a healthy relationship with my parents, I became alienated. Slowly I realized that my parents did not appreciate their surroundings, where we lived and where I was brought up. Mother constantly berated her environment. She insisted that it was not up to our standards, that we did not belong to these people here, that the only reason we lived there was because we could not afford anything better, but now we had to move away. What she was doing constantly was to pound a class structure in my head. She kept saying, "Look, we are different. Live here, but don't mix here."

But she *never* knew my experiences as a child growing up in that refugee settlement. It was beautiful. She did not know how I learned my own lessons. She had no time to reflect and to appreciate because she was so busy all the time providing for us. She never gave us time to reflect together and to appreciate. When she was out all day and there was no food in the house and I was stuck somewhere, she did not know that not even for a day did our neighbors let me go hungry. She did not know those things. Nor did she want to know them. I got confused as to how come she said such things about people who cared for me. I could not rationalize what she was saying—that I should not get involved with a boy of this class or that, that I should not look at them as equals because this was not *her* dream for her children's future.

I see it now, but the way she did it then alienated me completely. It created an environment of mistrust between my parents and me. They started seeing me as a threat to their honor because I was with boys all the time. The conflict continued, and tension mounted till I was in the ninth grade, around fifteen or sixteen. This was the peak of my activities. I wanted to party all the time and to go out with my school friends. My parents caught me doing things which I was not honest about. There was a total breakdown of trust. I remember it very distinctly. This was a time when I was *really* into playing cricket and bicycling, going away for a whole day on bicycles with boys. This was a time when I *did* get really infatuated with a boy who was older than I. That was my first infatuation as a teenager. Rumors flew around and reached my parents. They were *very* harsh with me, *very* harsh. They locked me up and started escorting me back and forth to school, and somehow they arranged a good beating for that poor boy. I felt so very sorry for him.

He would hang around my school or around my class or somewhere, in spite of everything. He was not in my school but was from the same area. We grew up together. Mother kept on saying, "You cannot do this until you get married; you cannot do that until you get married."[7] So the boy's parents sent in a marriage proposal. My parents got wild about it: "How dare they?! It is no match!" They scolded me severely.

---

7. Seeing that young man here and there. That was considered a taboo as far as her parents were concerned.

In the meantime, my parents were counting the days for me to finish my tenth grade—you know, so that I could be sent off, married off.[8] I did not know their plan. Once, as I was arguing with them, I said, "Well, if you say everything depends on marriage, then all right, get me married off to whomever you want!" I just wanted to get married because the home environment had become very unhealthy, *very* unbearable for me. I wanted to get out of that house at all costs. It was a very lonely time for me.[9]

I could not confide in any of my siblings. All four of them kept their distance from me and my activities. I had a totally different life experience, and none of them was ever part of it. Never! Mother threatened them with dire consequences if they ever did anything similar. Given that she was a very high-tempered woman who believed she was always in the right, all my siblings kept away.

Drama of Arranged Marriage and Extended Family Life

Within a week's time there was a marriage proposal, and I was asked to see this person. I thought "fine." Mother told me, "Look, he's a doctor. He has a small car; he can take you places." He was a dentist, and the thought of freedom and going to many places was exciting. I agreed to the wedding. I was excited about all the opportunities that were about to open up to me. Suddenly my parents were so nice and respectful of me, and the environment in the house changed drastically. I became the focus of the house once again. I was consulted about everything, the dresses I would like to wear and the way I wanted things to be. It was a total shift of mind, and I was at an age when I liked to dress up.

Our marriage was arranged. They were a Shi'a family, like us. During

8. Ortner argues that agentic women are "punished" through marriage to make them "passive and humble" (1996, 9).

9. In a similar vein, Durre Sameen Ahmed, a professor of psychology and communication at the National College of Arts in Lahore, Pakistan, describes how her mother, despite being educated in and having a "genuine respect for the West," was "growing alarm[ed] at the way I was 'turning out' as a teenager. There was constant struggle between us as she tried to domesticate and feminize me, wanting me to dress 'properly' and not be so boyish" (1997, 43–44). Her parents arranged her marriage when she was seventeen, and she agreed to it because "My mother and I had reached a high level of confrontation regarding my femininity, and I saw an opportunity to escape" (44).

Muharram,[10] all Shi'a families come together and go all over Karachi to visit one another. People come to know of prospective boys or girls. Someone is always looking; someone always knows someone with marriageable children. Someone knew my parents. But for the 200-square-yard house where my in-laws lived, physically there was nothing *very* elaborate or very rich or different from my house. The only difference was that they had electricity because it was in the settled area, although our area was catching up. But what *was* different was the extent and the nature of rules and regulations in that household, which I was brought up to condemn.

I was married to my present husband the year I completed my tenth grade in 1966. We had the *nikah* [signed the marriage contract] that year. Ten months later we had the reception, and I was formally taken into my husband's extended household.

The In-Laws

My husband's family, like my parents, had an Indian background and had emigrated to Pakistan after the partition. They were from Lucknow [India], and all six of them [four brothers and two sisters] were *highly* educated. They were a very principled family. They used to own six or seven villages in India and had a *huge* number of mango farms. They had seen the very lavish times of nawabs [nabob, a rich person, a ruler of a territory, or a governor of a district or town under the British Raj], a life of luxury and educated conversation that I had never experienced. My background was totally different from my husband's. His family emphasized education. All of them had gone through universities, all of them had read the classic Persian and Urdu poetry and had memorized poems by heart. They could quote poetic verses in every sentence they used. My orientation was not that. I went to a convent for my education,[11] and my orientation was English, English, and English all the time. My parents used to be so proud whenever I said a word or composed a sentence in English. But at my in-laws, I remember, if I used too much English in my conversations, my father-in-law would get angry and say, "But we are Pakistanis. Speak Urdu. Nobody speaks English in this house!"

My husband's parents lost everything when they arrived in Pakistan in

---

10. The Shi'a annual ritual of mourning commemorating the martyrdom of the third imam, Hussain, the grandson of the Prophet Muhammad.

11. On the education of middle-class and upper-middle-class Pakistanis, see Saigol 1995.

1948. My husband was six or seven years old and had a terrible time coping with the poverty they landed in. They were virtually on the streets. He studied under the street lamppost—all six children did. My mother-in-law pawned little by little whatever jewelry or clothes she had brought from India and put the money into her children's education. Her clothes had embroidery of pure silver, so she could sell one of her dresses for a lot of money. She was a *very rich* woman in India, an only child who had inherited all her father's lands and villages. She never knew what was going on in the kitchen, how to serve and how to look after the house. They had many servants.

Back in India, my father-in-law used to be a big landowner, and as a child he was brainwashed to think that because he was a nawab, he did not need to work for anybody else. Although he had a law degree, he had never practiced. At that time, Pakistan needed judges and magistrates, and he was offered jobs, but he refused to serve. Instead he decided to go after small businesses in which he had no experience at all. He had never managed his own land even in India—you know, the way these big landowners are. Naturally he was not a successful businessman, but he could make ends meet. My father-in-law was a very domineering man who needed to control everything. In this family, I saw my mother-in-law being given a daily allowance for food and other household expenses. I never heard money being talked about in my family. I never saw my father giving money to my mother; it was the other way around! It was always my mother who gave and my father who received. My mother would even give him money for bus fare.

As for their [the in-laws'] children, when they passed the tenth grade, they would give tutorials or look for other jobs in order to pay for their own education and to make ends meet. This is how collectively they made it in Pakistan. But the girls used to be tightly veiled. Each wore a *burqa* even in the university. My mother-in-law never stepped out of the house, and if she did, she would be covered by a *burqa*. My mother hated the *burqa* and never wore one, *never*. I was reared not to acknowledge it. At the time of my marriage, my parents made it very clear that I was not to be pressured to wear a *burqa*, and my in-laws did not object.

Identity Awareness

Let me tell you something very interesting about my character. During the *walima*, the marriage feast, as you know, the guests give the bride some money. I collected quite a bit of money, and my parents and my in-laws never took it away from me. My husband asked his father to help me open a bank account. He took me to the bank next door and introduced me as his daughter-in-law. Remember, this was the third day of my marriage and my first time ever being in a bank. And I was only seventeen years old. The bank manager filled out a form and put it in front of me. He had already written my name as "Mrs. So-and-So." There was no Quratul Ain, and I was supposed to sign that![12] Look how my childhood socialization was expressed in what I did! I had no background in women's rights and women's issues. It surprised me at that time. It surprises me even more now.

I looked at that form and told my father-in-law, "This is not my name!" This is *exactly* the sentence I used. I remember it so vividly. They were all so shocked. "This is not my name," I said. I scratched it out and wrote "Quratul Ain Bakhteari." My father-in-law looked at me and said, "All right, do you want it that way?" "Yeah," I said, "this *is* my name." No fuss was made about it, and the bank manager changed the form. This incident had a strong impact on me, and when I reflect on it, I am *happy* about it. I have made it a point, since that third day of my marriage, to be always known as Quratul Ain Bakhteari and not as Mrs. So-and-so. I had no idea about this Mrs. concept. I had *no* orientation at all on women's issues. It is very strange. There were never any discussions in my family as to which name we should use or the implications of doing so. I had just done my matric [finished tenth grade], and that's all, not even a college education. I do not know from where this impulse had come to me. Maybe it was a sense of identity about myself, which I think was always there. So the thought of imminently losing the Bakhteari identity and being cut off from everything in just two days did not sit well with me [laughing]. No way was I going to change my identity completely in just two days!

Dutiful Daughter-in-Law: Trying to Fit In

So I landed in a totally different set up. Here I was seen as the daughter-in-law of a family with many rules and regulations and placed on a very high pedestal: *our* daughter-in-law. This was not an affluent household, but it was a very intellectually rich household. There were strong debates all the time be-

12. It is worth noting that many professional Iranian women generally keep their own maiden name after marriage. There is no cultural pressure to adopt their husband's name, though some do so willingly. El Guindi (1999, 164) makes the same observation in the case of married Egyptian women.

tween the brothers, sisters, and their father. Everybody talked about partition and questioned their father as to why they had immigrated. They spoke to him accusingly: "There was no problem in Lucknow. Nobody forced you to get out. Why did you come to Pakistan?"

Still it is like that, as if Pakistan was made yesterday.

This was the environment in that household: *questioning*, lots of questioning. They were into reading and reflecting, things *my* family never did. We never had any reflections, readings, and intellectual discussions because my parents never had *time*. I mean, it was a family that was just trying to survive. At the same time, the traditionalism of my in-laws was the same I used to see around me in my own settlement. Except for *my* house, the rest were traditional. Women did not work outside the way my mother did. Our friends' homes, too, were similar to my in-laws, with the same kind of relationships my mother used to condemn at home. I registered that difference unconsciously. I was trained to condemn it, to challenge it because of my parents' relationship. I was educated in a convent where boys and girls were taught together. I used to dress differently and wore saris with sleeveless blouses. I used to wear trousers with short tops, things that not many traditional young women did.

So already I was a different kind of woman in their set-up, and because of my socialization I did not receive the proper traditional training that is normally given to a girl. My mother just left me too open. At the same time, she was very *tough* on me so that I would not do anything disgraceful. She did not train me to be a good daughter-in-law because she *hated* this daughter-in-law business, she *hated* the mother-in-law business, and she *hated* all forms of domination. I never saw my mother living with a mother-in-law or in a joint family situation, so I had no way of knowing how to take these strict rules at my in-laws'.

Thanks to their educated background, my in-laws were very understanding and civil. They did understand me to a certain extent, but at the same time they were confused by my behavior and my way of life, which, in their view, was too outgoing, too free. I did not make a social distinction between men and women and would talk to both in the same way. If someone knocked on the door, I would just go and open it and stand out there, talking to whoever was behind the door. But other women [in the family] would first open the door a bit and ask who was there. If there was a woman's voice, then they would open the door and talk, but if it was a man's voice, then a man would be sent out to greet the caller. I was not trained to do that.

If I wanted to buy something from the hawker who was passing by, I would instantly jump from my bed and go out to make the purchase myself. I would talk to him, choose and pick, standing out on the street in front of my in-laws' house. This behavior shocked my father-in-law completely. Then I would get a lecture! Because my husband was never around [he was away in his dental clinic], my father-in-law would severely reprimand me and would give me a lecture, which I could not understand. I would start to cry, more like a child, sobbing and making a lot of noise. It was not a very sophisticated cry, with tears quietly rolling down! And it was never in my room. I used to cry out, "I want to go back to my parents. I want to go back home." Then they would get panicky [laughing]. But they also had a sense that I was unable to articulate something, that I was being honest with my feelings. My in-laws almost respected that and treated me as a naïve child who does not know any better. Being much older and more mature, my husband could not relate to me in this way either. Although I was given civilized support and understanding, I had a very terrible and lonely time.

Marriage: Parental Punishment

I felt this was *not* the idea of marriage that was given to me. I had *no* freedom. What I had been told was wrong. I found out that my classmates and friends had gone on to college, and they were freer than I was. Once or twice a flock of [my] girlfriends drove up in a car and came to see me in my house. I was unable to relate to them. Here I was married after the tenth grade, while they went on. From my home, they planned to go somewhere exciting and have a good time. They had plans, whereas I was pregnant and living with my in-laws, who were looking at them with disdain.

Ahhh . . . [pause] I still remember when the girls left. I was holding onto the iron railing, you know, after saying good-bye to them, and I stood up there and just looked at them. [Long silence, tears rolling down.] I felt betrayed by my parents. The feeling of betrayal was *so* sharp, so sharp that it evoked two feelings in me [pause, weeping quietly]. One was, "OK. This is what my parents did to me. They finally got rid of me in this way. So, all right. Now it's my own life. No more dependency on my parents." I felt emotionally totally cut off from them. Second, I instantly felt strong emotions toward my unborn child [long silence].

I did not feel close to my husband. He was twenty-eight or twenty-nine years old, and I was only seventeen. He was settling down in his practice and clinic and had little to do, emotionally or otherwise, with the woman brought into his life. I was too overwhelming for him and for his family, too. I could not relate to him—being the kind of woman I was. On the face of it, everybody thought that I was happy and quite content because I was vibrant, talkative, extroverted, and sociable. The way I was brought up, I was a people person, and it never mattered to me who came from which background. I had no ambition at all. But because I had no intellectual background, I could not appreciate that these were special people. I just took everybody in the same sweep.

My husband would leave home at eight in the morning and would not get back until eleven at night. I felt abandoned and lonely. Three or four months into my marriage I insisted that I wanted to go to college, and I was pregnant. Because education meant a lot to my in-laws, nobody resisted. They said, "Yes, yes. Fine, go ahead." But, then, how to bring this off? I was on one side of the city, and St. Joseph's College was in the city center. I had to change three buses to reach the college. I would get home tired, exhausted, and pregnant. Three days later I quit. I could not make it, but for a time I felt so good being in the college.

Wife, Mother

My son was born in 1968. It was lovely. He was a beautiful child, and I turned *all* my attention to him, *completely*, single-mindedly. Very consciously I started reading books about how to feed a child, what to do each month as he grows up, and all those things. Systematically I organized my life around my child. My in-laws' tradition was to keep a wet nurse to look after a child. In their Indian Lucknowi tradition, the daughters-in-law were not expected to rear children themselves. The servants did all that work: clothes were washed by a washerwoman, and the cleaning was done by a cleaning woman, and I was there only to look after my son. Again I said, "Maybe *now* I can go back to college," and in less than three months after my delivery, I was admitted to the college. I had to commute by those buses again, although my husband had a car. But, you know, when nursing time came, my breasts would get hard, and milk would start dripping from them. There was such a strong pull in me. I thought, "What am I doing here sitting in this classroom? *Why* am I here?" Three days into college I left again. It was just too hard for me not to be with my child when it came time to nurse, but I still wanted to continue my education. My husband suggested I do it as a private student. You register as a student, but you do not attend classes, only to take your exams. And that's what I did.

By now, my husband had started earning a lot of money, and his practice was picking up. Every day he would come home with fifteen hundred or two thousand rupees and would just hand me all that money, without even folding them or counting them—just like that. He would pull the money out of his pocket and put it right in front of me—every day! But I was still lonely and did not have intense communications with my husband. Nobody knew the person inside me, the way I withdrew within myself. Meanwhile, I learned that my husband was suffering from deep depression. Before we married, people had attributed somebody's death to the tooth he had extracted earlier on. That had a strong impact on my husband, leaving him very insecure and fearful in his practice. I was too *young* to understand his position, though he did at times try to relate his problems to me. I just did not know how to handle all that.

My in-laws, watching their son suffer that way, felt that I might be the cause of all his troubles: the pressures I was putting on him, my needs and demands, you know, for schooling, going out in the evenings, and the like. I *was* very active, planning to do all sorts of things. I was very different from my in-laws. I was not a passive woman, whereas that household was very passive. Besides, I was one of the two girls who had married into the family from outside. Tension [sigh] was building up in me and in the family. My problem was that I had no one to talk to. I had no one to relate to at my level. I was just giving, giving, giving. I felt I was being nice and understanding to everybody. But I was not getting the same in return except for a civilized acceptance and behavior toward me [subdued, pause].

As for my parents, I had already put them aside. They suddenly had no role in my life. During all this time, I never stayed at their place. Once a week or in the evening I would go with my husband for a visit. They did not know anything about what was happening in my life and what my husband was facing. I *never* confided in them *anything*. Even when my son was born, they were told after the delivery. I wanted my mother-in-law to be there, but not my parents!

It was quite a lonely journey. My son was my only consolation. Slowly he began looking up to me, recognizing me whenever I walked into the room, smiling at me. I would talk to him for hours in that room because there was no other one to talk to, nor was there any household responsibility for me. I had all the time in the world to be with my son. And it was OK. I was preparing for my private exams at the same time, and financially I was having quite a respectable and comfortable life.

But then my husband's depression became more severe by the day. He used to cry quietly. I would talk to him, but he would not respond. He cried before he left for the clinic in the morning and returned tense and worked up. He could not eat and soon developed an eating disorder. He had this very lonely attitude, as if I did not exist. Initially, he was very happy with the child, but even that he did not enjoy anymore.

The problem was, I found out, that as a child my husband was beaten severely by my father-in-law, almost daily. His depression reached a point where he had to go to a psychiatrist. I had never heard the word *psychiatrist* before in my life! I had such a healthy life all my childhood and adulthood that I had never seen even a thermometer until I was pregnant and my doctor put that thing into my mouth [laughing]. Here they were talking about a psychiatrist, mental attitude, and highly technical things—very heavy stuff. I just left everything to my elder brother-in-law and parents-in-law because my husband was their son. I just stood aside as a helpless spectator, waiting to see what was happening. They took charge of my husband, all of them. Then they all trouped to the psychiatrist, the father and the sons, all. The psychiatrist automatically wanted to see me and to talk to me. I was also asked to come along. Here I was sitting in the room with a man I had never met, and he was asking me very intimate questions! I did not know how to handle that, and I got very panicky. I felt very lonely and had *no* one to relate to and find out what was happening.

You see, the psychiatrist was a very modern young man. He started visiting our family, observing our interaction, and talking to my father-in-law, brothers-in-law, and my sisters-in-law. He explained to them that my husband needed to be independent and that we should be living separately [from his family]. So the three of us moved into a small two-room apartment close to my in-laws' house. My parents-in-law resented this move, and I learned much later that my husband did not welcome it either, but he never showed his dissatisfaction to me.

For *me*, the move was an opening! It meant freedom. I was involved in setting the apartment up, buying things, and decorating it. My life became interesting again. In the evenings, I would go out and stroll without asking anyone's [i.e., her father-in-law's] permission. It was great. But for ten to twelve months

I did not have the slightest inkling that my husband was going to my in-laws straight from his office before coming home and that he was discussing his situation with them! He never discussed that with *me*. One evening while my husband was out, my brother-in-law came over and said that his brother was very unhappy and that we better move back with the family again! That was— oof—like a blow because I had had no signals before that night!

"But *why*? This is our home," I protested.

"My brother is not happy here!" he said curtly. "Come over tomorrow and select a room—whichever you like best. You people are not staying here. If he continues living here, he might commit suicide."

Oof! That gave me such a shock: "How come somebody else has to come and tell me that my husband was unhappy here? *Why* was he not happy here? What was I doing wrong to make him unhappy?" Oof! But for his sake and because of the way I was approached, I became a bit concerned. I thought, "He is my husband all right, but he is somebody else's brother, somebody's son, and I am not going to take a risk [with his life]. "OK," I said, "I don't want to take responsibility. We will come over."

Kinship Rivalry: Competing Daughters-in-law

We moved *back*. By now, my in-laws had moved into a bigger house, and I was not the only daughter-in-law in the house. My younger brother-in-law had gotten married, and there was a competitor in the family. My husband and I were in one room, and my brother-in-law and his wife in another. My sister-in-law was older and more mature than I and had a master's in Urdu literature. She was a lot more in control of her life, her husband, the kitchen, and everything else. Because of my husband's situation, I was on a very shaky ground. I became a point of comparison within the family, and my life was made more difficult than when I was the only daughter-in-law in the house. Tension was palpable. They did not condemn me outright but praised her all the time. My husband continued to be his own aloof self, and my depression and my sadness grew more intense.

By this time, I had completed my first year of college, and my son was growing. It was lovely being with him, and I was pregnant again with my second child, who was born in 1970. But this was a very depressing and lonely pregnancy. I used to cry all night, and nobody cared about me. My husband would not look at me, and I did not know how to share my problems. In time, my depression started to overwhelm me, and I became resentful toward my in-laws.

Once, I remember, as I walked into the house, I overheard a conversation about me. My parents-in-law and this new sister-in-law were sitting around the table discussing *me*. They did not know that I had already entered the house and were saying things like, "She gets all the money and has all those resources, but she is misusing them. She goes shopping every day! She has made our son sick, and the poor fellow is suffering. And look at the way she is." It *hit* me hard—oof—it's the *money!* My in-laws must have thought that because my parents were poor, I must have been giving part of his money to them without letting my husband or anybody else know, which I was *not*. I never *did*.

I did not let them know that I had heard them. I thought that if money is what comes between us, why not get rid of it? The next morning I took out all the cash from my *almari*, cupboard, and I went to my father-in-law and handed him the cash. I said, "This is too much of a responsibility for me to handle. Why don't you take over this responsibility?" You see, the way I was reared, money was never discussed. As a child I had never, never established values for money and material things. My parents' attitude was, "Oh, you have lost something today? Don't worry. You will get it again tomorrow." That was their style. What had value for me were *people*, happiness, liveliness around me. That is what I wanted and needed. I also think my husband might have had second thoughts about giving me his money without counting it.

So I gave my father-in-law all my financial assets without even consulting my husband. Instantly he [her father-in-law] became very happy. He said, "Oh my God, you should be more responsible" and other such well-formulated complimentary and traditional words, you know. "Why do you do this? This is a big burden on me," while gently scolding me: "Look at the way you have kept this money." He was stretching the notes, putting them carefully into categories of one rupee, five rupees, ten rupees, and continuing to grumble, "Oh, I'm an old man. How can I take this burden?"

I could see how pleased he was. It dawned on me that here was a dental surgeon's father, and the son, instead of giving *him* his earnings, was giving it to a wife who had just joined him. After that I would go to my father-in-law nightly and just empty the bag of money in front of him, never counting it. Once he said to me, "You bring this money and put it in front of me like garbage papers. *Beti*, dear daughter, this is not the way to handle money. Don't ever give money to anybody without counting." I remember my reply very distinctly. I said "Abba, what you are saying is right. But what I want is a relationship where you give money without counting. Money is not important." I said, "If I give you money and count it back and forth [not trusting him], then in which relationship will I give money without counting?" He just laughed and looked at me. It was as if a new relationship began between us. Being a principled man, though, my father-in-law slowly saved enough money to enable us to buy a piece of land. It was quite close to a piece of land the family had bought earlier.

[Sigh] My husband was just on his own, the same way.

Unremitting Nostalgia

My father-in-law had bought this land in Karachi when he was forced out of rural Sindh, where he had been given seventeen or eighteen acres of land five or six years after the country's creation. He was given that land in exchange for the land they [the family] had left behind in India. It was a rural, barren land, but he was very enthusiastic and wanted to re-create the mango orchards he had once grown in India. But one night local Sindhis attacked the orchard and cut down all his trees—all those young trees he had worked so hard to grow. The attackers also sent him several threatening messages: "You are *muhajirs* [refugees from India]. This is not your land. Just get out of our lands, or your life is in danger." This happened in 1966, two years before my marriage, and it was another setback for the family. He was disillusioned. His children were disillusioned and questioned his wisdom in coming to Pakistan: "Why did we leave our home in India? This land does not belong to us; we do not belong here. We cannot own any property." They felt very insecure, and my father-in-law was put under strong pressure to sell that land and to buy a plot in urban Karachi.

When the construction of my father-in-law's house was completed, we all shifted to his new house. The unmarried brother and sister were still with the family. I had a room there, and my sister-in-law had another. The competition between my sister-in-law and me became stronger by the day. I felt incompetent when compared to her. She now had a son, born around the same time as my second son. With the birth of my son, I had more responsibilities. My loneliness, too, grew more intense because instead of sympathetic sharing there was intense competition in the house. It was not that my in-laws liked her more. They were very intelligent and understood my innocence completely. They placed me quite well. They also understood her completely. But she was older and more experienced than I. She created situations where I would be seen as the troublemaker or as the cause of my husband's depression.

She made it look as if I was incompetent to run my own house, and that's why my husband and I had to come back to the family.

Having two small children, dealing with her relentless competitiveness, and not fitting well into the expected feminine role—the way family women were—left me totally frustrated and isolated. But, being young, I was still eager to go out and play, eager to learn, eager to do things. You know, the "taming" was not done completely. I wanted to get out of that space. I started spending more time at my husband's clinic. I learned how to make dentures and tried to assist him in his clinic's daily management. But, then, because I was young and a bit good-looking—this is what people used to say—I was told it was not proper to be seen by so many patients, that I should not go there, that it was not right! I had gone to his office to give him support because I was also a bit more mature and understanding now. Apparently giving in to the pressure, he, too, thought it was not a good idea. So again I was back home, stuck.

One evening when I was trying to put my children to bed, about nine or ten o'clock, and the house was very quite, I heard my brother-in-law and his wife walking in. They had just seen Elizabeth Taylor's *The Taming of the Shrew*. As they were coming in through the corridor, laughing and joking, my sister-in-law said, rather loudly, "Tayyab *bhai* should see *The Taming of the Shrew!*" She was talking very *loudly*. Suddenly somebody said that I was in, and then there was silence. After a week or so, I also went to see this movie. Then I realized how they were placing me. They could not see the honesty and love between the couple but only the "taming," and *that* was the message they were trying to send to my husband.

Raising Children, Finding Self

My first son was showing signs of intelligence, and I wanted to find a school or nursery for a two-and-half-year-old child. Purely by chance I found a Montessori school. I sat in some of their classes, and I *loved* it. I decided, "My child is coming here." But I confronted huge opposition and accusations from the family: "He is only two and a half. How come you want to send him to school? You want to throw him away in that school because you want to have free time." But I insisted and prevailed. I realized that my husband's passivity had created a space for me to make my own decisions regarding my children.

Every day I took my son to school and spent one or two hours with him there. The opposition slowly died down, and the family began to see things he was learning and sharing. Now they saw the benefits of his early education and agreed that "yes, it was a good thing." This was a new *thing* that I did. The Montessori techniques had such a *strong* effect on me that I would spend hours in the school with the teachers, trying to learn the techniques. By 1970, I had also finished my first year toward my baccalaureate degree.

My second son was very different from the first one. He wanted to cling to me all the time, but my first one was a curious little boy. So in the daytime I was busy with my first child's contradictions and confrontations and at night with my second son's restlessness. I would be up all night, while my husband would be sound sleep. By morning, I would be irritable, angry, and grumbling. *And* I had to put up with all the other household matters and with my sister-in-law's competitiveness, which though unsettling was never uncivilized. My father-in-law was an early riser and would be already in the lounge having his tea and breakfast before the rest of the family. Apparently, he heard my grumblings from our room.

One day I walked out of the room to get something for my son. I was angry, and my face was not pleasant. My father-in-law looked at me and said, "You are a very problematic woman. You have made my son's life miserable. He cannot sleep at nights, and he cannot have peace in the mornings. I am so *sorry* for him!" This was the first time he ever spoke to me like that [high pitched, shocked]! I went back to my room. My son was only three weeks old. I picked up my bag and asked the boy who was helping me [with chores] to get me a rickshaw. Before anybody could know what I was up to, I climbed into the rickshaw and went off to my parents' house.

I left everybody. This was the first time ever my parents came to know my problems. I had never told them the whole story. I said, "I am tired, excuse me. I have been up all night and had *no* sleep. Nobody helps me." I did not tell them the details, but I slept. I slept the whole day, and I slept the whole night. I slept the second day, and I just rested, and because my mother was teaching, I had a good rest. They didn't ask many questions, but they observed me.

None of my in-laws approached me for three days. Their attitude was, "She went on her own account. She should come back on her own account." On the third day, I started feeling the agony of missing my children. Suddenly I had nothing to do. My parents kept observing me. The way my mother was, she went over to my husband's clinic. *That* evening my husband came over,

and we talked. With my parents' mediation, there was something like reconciliation, and we went back. I did not make a big deal about it because I
wanted to go back home. I missed my children terribly, and not seeing them
for three days made me realize that I could never live without them, no matter
what happened.

Those three days were very decisive. My in-laws were angry with my husband for coming after me, but they never said anything in front of me. It was
late when we returned, and I went straight to my room. The next morning it
was as if nothing had happened, no confrontation of any kind. My life went on.

Building a New House, a New Life

In addition to my children's education and upbringing, my third project was to
construct my house on the land I had bought [with the money her father-in-
law saved for her]. I was the architect and the designer of my own house. I was
saving all my money and had nothing to do with what was going on in the
clinic, in the house, or anywhere else. My husband gave me all the freedom to
do it. He was not that involved but was there. His clinic was doing very well,
and now our income had grown to around six thousand rupees per day. I was
pregnant with my third son when we shifted to our new house. It was almost
ready. I was very happy, building my garden and doing things. Once again it
was just like my childhood days, making a wall here and a wall there. Although
I was not getting any attention from my husband emotionally, I did not mind
it. I had a nice life. I was happy. I was much freer than others in the family and
had my own space, whereas my sister-in-law was still in that one room.

Loss of East Pakistan

Then the civil war broke out between East and West Pakistan. All my life, as
you must have noticed in our conversations, I had thought, "All right, my parents betrayed me, and I landed in this marriage, but fine. I continued with my
education. I am not that bad off. I have not lost my identity totally. Life is still
OK." While having my house constructed, I was dealing with the system and
with different authorities. I got excellent responses everywhere, no obstacles.
I believed in the system.

Now in 1971 I was thoroughly confident that the news media was accurate.
I believed it. *Never* for a minute was I insecure. I did not read newspapers before
that. I did not have any world political background because my focus had
been the children, my own self, and my home. But at my in-laws' I was uncon-

sciously taking in the political discussions, though never participating. Intellectually I was not equipped like them.

Then came that fateful day, December 12, 1971.[13] Up until that time the media was telling us that we [West Pakistan] were winning, that we had shot down 111 Indian planes, that we had captured this territory and had done that heroic deed. All very reaffirming and positive news. On that night on Pakistan National Television, General Yahya Khan [1969–71] addressed the nation and declared the fall of Dhaka! Pakistan lost.

LOST! The Pakistan army had surrendered [pause]. I had never had a *clue* as to what West Pakistan had *done* to East Pakistan to reach *that* level of animosity. I just stood there and stared at the television. I still remember it very distinctly [sigh, pause]. The room was dark because of the blackouts of the war. Yahya Khan tried to be reassuring: "This is a temporary withdrawal of our troops. We will get Dhaka back!" Then there was the national anthem. The Pakistan flag was on the TV, and I just sat there like a stone, one son in my lap, and one son in my arm, and one in my belly! What happened?[14]

As I reflect, I think the reason I felt it so strongly was my childhood struggle, my enthusiasm to be part of the refugees' life and their struggle to build their homes, those high hopes and visions. I mean, I felt that my whole being, my whole orientation, was very much rooted in Pakistan, rooted in the people—the way I was brought up. It *hit* me *very strongly.* For the second time, I was a betrayed person [sigh, silence]. This time, by the system.

That night I could not sleep. The memories of the stories I had heard in my childhood came rushing in: stories of miseries, of the terrible things that happened to refugees during partition. My mind kept going to the East Pakistani refugees.[15] "Right at that minute," I thought, "what was happening in East Pakistan? What were the refugees going through? What were their sufferings and separations?" Such losses I could not fathom because I had not experienced any so deep. I had only heard about them. I had not experienced the division of families. I did not know the way refugees suffered. I just knew one life. I was born into a refugee family, but I never saw any comparisons.

The next morning I looked at my children, I looked at my house, and that home suddenly became meaningless to me. Today I can articulate this. At that

---

13. Gardezi and Rashid (1983, xiv) record December 16 as the day Dhaka fell.

14. On the public's shock from the fall of Dhaka, see Jalal 1991b, 313.

15. East Pakistan was renamed Bangladesh after the civil war of 1971.

time, it was all confusion and depression. It was strange. My husband and my husband's family just looked at each other in *total distress*, disbelief. They had believed in Pakistan, and my father-in-law had participated in the Pakistan movement. Now they felt so extremely insecure. Once again my father-in-law had a setback and became the target of his children's anger and insecurity. "*Why* did you come? *What* did you see in this country?" Then everyone—my parents, my in-laws, and others—rushed to the American embassy, British embassy, or German embassy to get emigrations [visas] out of Pakistan. *Out of Pakistan?!* They had no longer any trust in Pakistan. My husband, along with his eldest brother, applied to the American embassy and was given an immigration visa in 1972 or 1973.

Communal Visions

I wanted to get back to the people, to the refugees. I started making a point of meeting the refugees who were coming back from Bangladesh for repatriation, and that is where my time slowly and gradually started going. I came across a family whose four children were killed right in front of their eyes. One son survived only because he had spent two days hiding under the other bodies. Nobody bothered with them, thinking that they were dead. After two days, he pulled himself out from under those bodies, and his mother found out that he was still alive. Her husband was killed, and she was thrown out of one house after another, with no money or resources. She had still eight other children: five daughters and three sons. I found out about them, and somehow I wanted to be a part of their struggle. I asked my husband if I could bring the whole family to live with us. He agreed. I had designed and built a charming kitchen garden with a nice plot next to it. I ripped it off completely and made a small house within our compound. I got them over to our place, and in the neighborhood we announced that they were our tenants. They all lived with us and shared the entire house, our refrigerator, our kitchen, everything.

My husband got their eldest son into his clinic and started teaching him to make dentures, scaling, and all that. Slowly life started to come on track for them. Their children resumed their education, and they stayed with us for many years. During that time, two of their daughters married, and one son finished his chartered accountancy and got a very good job. Then he rented a house where they could all live, and they all shifted to their own house.

Through this family, I was getting information about what was happening in East Pakistan. I also started going to the refugee camps frequently and became even more disillusioned by my house, my luxuries, and my way of life. I was obsessed with the thoughts of similar things happening to my children. Supposing somebody got into *my* house and took my children away? Supposing on the school bus something happened to my son, and he died? This woman had lost four children! Look at her. I could not bear it. I felt *so intensely* scared and insecure that the only way I could really keep myself from going mad was slowly to disassociate and detach myself from my children and family. I had already detached myself from money and material things by handing them over to my father-in-law. Now I was trying to detach myself from my children and from the home I had built. I thought I needed to understand more about life. My journey so far was a very lonely one, and all the learning was done through action and reaction.

I wanted to be a better and more effective mother,[16] so I registered for Montessori training myself. I was *very* happy doing it. For the first time, I was involved with books and experimentation and really enjoyed learning a technique. I had done just barely four out of nine months of training when my husband put a stop to it. He wanted me to be home when he came home in the afternoons for his lunch. This time conflicted with my training, which was from one to six o'clock in the evening. We argued, but eventually I left my training half done. In the meantime, I learned to drive. I picked up my husband, dropped him off, picked up my children, dropped them at school, picked up my mother-in-law, took care of all their chores or whatever, and dropped her home because I was the only woman driver in the family.

Still, after doing all that work, I would go to the closest refugee camp and spend some time there. I began to hear stories from the refugees, *horrible* stories, *horrible* stories. Not only stories of what happened during the civil war, but also stories of what our own army personnel did to our own people in the camps.[17] That left me much more depressed and insecure. All that trust was gone, completely. My parents were already cut off from me emotionally, and the system I no longer believed in. Before, I used to admire an army officer in a uniform and would trust any police officer, but now I questioned *every* power

16. I am assuming that what she means here is to be less emotionally but more intellectually involved in the lives of her children.

17. For a narrative account of the horrors perpetrated by all sides in the war of 1971, see Firdousi 1996.

structure on the street, on the road, around me, in the offices. For *everything* I had a question mark.

The reason was again selfish. It was *not* that I had suddenly become a very aware person. Basically, the motive behind all that questioning was the concern for my own children. If the army could just walk into the houses in East Pakistan, they could do the same thing here as well. The more I went on meeting the refugees from East Pakistan, the more uncomfortable I became. What the army did to our own people—the rapes and the very miserable way they treated people, their own people, in the camps—was all so very sad. That kind of insecurity got into me with tremendous intensity, though I could not articulate it at the time.

My husband never knew what was happening to me and why I was not as expressive or communicative with him.

Desire to Know

Around 1973 or 1974, I decided I should work on my master's degree. I went to Karachi University. I met a friend of my husband, a professor of political science. He talked to me for two hours. He said, "Either you do your education as a regular student, or you don't do it at all. If you really want to have that degree, it should not be just a piece of paper. There should be some substance to it. Take your time. Let your youngest child go to school and whenever you have time to become a full-fledged student in the department and involved in the learning environment, then you should join and do your master's degree."

When I returned home, I was quite clear. I started learning informally and focusing on my family. For the next three or four years [from 1974 to 1977], I became more aware of myself, the type of woman I was. I felt good being with people, sharing their problems and solving them along with them. I also came to another awareness—that I am not a conceptualizer or a theoretician, one who just sits and, you know, ponders and thinks by herself in a room, one who can read lots of books and just be satisfied with them.

I enjoyed being with my children. In the evenings, I would take my children bicycling, to gyms, and I myself joined the badminton team. I was always a good badminton player, and so my children and I would play at the badminton-coaching center. I was playing so well that in a match of the Karachi finals, I ended up as the second runner-up. But when the time came for me to go and take my trophy—which was a *big* event—my husband said, "No, you can't go." He said many people were going to be there, and it was not proper for me to take this trophy in front of everyone. That made me *very* angry. I could not understand his objection. We had an argument, and he said, "If you go, then do not come back to this house." I tried to have my in-laws mediate, but they all said, "Well, if that's the way your husband wants it, then what is so big a deal about a trophy? Forget it. Think about the children, your home, and all these things." So I just let it go, and the next day I quietly went there and picked it up at the office.

By now my parents and my husband had gotten their immigration papers to America. My husband kept going to the United States every year to maintain his residency. He could not decide whether he wanted to live in the States or to remain in Pakistan. He could not practice in the States unless he passed his board exam and received a license. In Pakistan, on the other hand, he was doing very well. It was a tough option, and we were in limbo for some years.

Finally, in 1977, my youngest son was admitted to preprimary school. Now all my three sons were in school. The first day after putting him in school, I went straight to Karachi University and met the same professor.

"I've come now." I said, "I've done my job; my children are all in school, and they don't get out until three o'clock. There is enough time."

He smiled and said, "Are you sure you really want to do it?"

"Yes," I said.

He said, "What are you interested in?"

"Well," I said, "I have taken political science courses before but have had no practical training. Now I realize that after spending time with refugees, I am more interested in people. I am more of a community-oriented person. Do you think that the university has courses like that that I can specialize in?"

He said, "Yes, there is social work."

I asked, "Is social work a discipline?"

"Yes," he said. "There is a master's degree in social work."

I was *so* excited. He immediately took me to the department, and I got admitted. In the department, people were quite surprised because half of them knew my husband, and they thought, "Why on earth does a woman in her position want to join this department and come here to the university?" They knew I was married into such a well-known family, with status, money, name, and fame, and that my husband was popular and famous. I came back that evening and went over to my husband's clinic and said, "I got admitted to the social work department!"

He looked up at me and said, "Oh, so you are now a regular student?"

"Yes!"

From then on, every morning, after dropping off my children at their schools, I would drive to the university. I loved every minute of it. My studies were progressing well, and I was just a totally different person—*so happy* with myself and everything. I was no longer bothered if my husband did not talk to me or that there was no communication between us. I did not care about that. As soon as we were in the bedroom, I would be at my desk, and he would busy himself with his books or papers or whatever. If he wanted to go out, I would say, "You all go. I need to finish this assignment, or I need to complete this book." That started really bothering him.

Reliving Childhood Memoirs: Second-Wave Refugees

The majority of the students in the social work department were from East Pakistan, living in refugee settlement communities that were established by Pakistani authorities. They were very bright students, articulate and politically *highly* charged. I, on the other hand, was without any orientation and had little political background and understanding. I was totally swept off by them, completely. There were times when I completely forgot that I was a wife and a mother. I became politically aware of the situation and got into it with enthusiasm. I spent most of my time with these young men, going up to the refugee settlements and their homes. There were a few women in the department, but they mainly stayed put, while I was drawn away. I was the only woman who went to the refugee camps *and* was in the company of four or five young men. They were younger than I or were my age, and I felt comfortable with them. I was married and had children, and so I thought there could be no scandal or gossip. I visited their families and tried to understand what really had happened during the civil war. They had such moving stories to tell about themselves and the movement. Sometimes I would lose track of time and stay away from home till ten at night. I was in a world of my own.

I had a maid, and the East Pakistani family who lived with us took care of my children and the house. My children would come back at three, and then they had tutors for various lessons, but I was not there to pick them up and drop them off. I was not there to pick my husband up and drop him off either. I was totally preoccupied. I justified this to myself that I had done my duties, and now it was time for me. I wanted to spend these two years on myself intensively.

Things went from bad to worse.

Marriage: Emotional Blackmail

In 1977, my husband decided that it was time for us to emigrate to the United States. I thought, "All right, I can finish my social work studies in America." So we all migrated, only to return to Pakistan after three months. My husband feared that he was not able to make it in America and was in danger of losing his practice in Pakistan as well, so we came back, all of us. As soon as we arrived, I went to the university and immediately got back into the department. It was the second semester, but I caught up very quickly and was doing very well. I never felt study pressures because it was just coming to me automatically. Over these two years, I had my real growth and development. They were beautiful years, although the suffering continued. By 1978, my husband was really *very* angry with me. He said that I was never at home, neglected him, and was not a good mother.

"If you are not going to be at home doing your duties," he said, "why should you be here at all? If you continue in this way, you will have to leave this house."

I was dumbfounded. I said, "But this *is* my home."

"No, it is not." He said. "This is *my* house."

It was, of course, *his* money, but *I* had done all the saving, designing, decorating, and fixing. It was *our* money. I was emotionally involved in it, had invested time and energy in it.

He said, "No, the house belongs to me. The children are mine. Everything is mine, and nothing is yours."

I questioned him three times. I remember, I said, "Are you sure nothing is mine?"

"Yes," he said. "You can ask any lawyer, anywhere. Nothing is yours"—although the house was in my name.

"Another betrayal," I thought [pause]. I reflected about home, family, children, and all that I had worked for, created, lived for. I had thought that this was the securest place, that I could afford to take risks in this context, to seek personal growth. But all that proved wrong. I was being forced out. This was a *very* emotional, very emotional moment in my life. We had lots of fights, and one evening when I came back from the university, he had thrown out all my belongings. Everything! My children were all there. They saw it all. It was very painful [long pause]. His family was standing outside. They tried to intervene and prevent him from doing that. It was a big scene in the neighborhood. Everyone was out, watching. I left that same evening. I took only my books and enough things for my university studies, and I went to my parents' place. By then, they were living in the Center City [a district in Karachi]. They were very surprised to see me then.

I just said, "Here I am."

For the first time since I had been married off, I sat down with them and explained the whole story of the twelve years of my marriage. I explained to them that every time I tried to do something, I was forced to leave it in the middle. I had to leave the Montessori school in the middle of my training. I had to leave my badminton half finished and was prevented from claiming my trophy. I told them that going to the university was something I enjoyed and that it was not fair to be prevented from continuing. They thought for a moment and then said, "Yes, yes. You stay here, no problem." They supported me for three days. After the third day, they started making me feel insecure. "Think about your children," they said. "Somebody will take over them. Then they will never recognize you. When you grow old, who will look after you?" On the third or fourth day, my husband came over to take me back. We had a long counseling session with my parents, but his parents kept away. He agreed not to abuse me again and to allow me to continue my studies.

"Now you must go with him," my parents said. "Give him a chance."

So I did. But now I was physically drifting away from him. I did not like his physical closeness to me, and I could not hide it. I could not, you know, camouflage it. That infuriated him. And to put more fuel on the fire, I continued doing *very well* at the university.

I had a female classmate who apparently felt very competitive toward me, but I had no idea about it. She belonged to a political party and had strong political affiliations. Her gang started calling my house and making up stories about me to my husband—that I was seen going around with young men. I *was* seen all over the city, you know, raising donations and collecting funds for my assignments in the communities. Her intention, however, was to push my husband to put pressure on me to quit the university so that she could have a free ride, without any competition. Her frequent telephone calls undercut my husband's self-respect and his respect for me. I kept on telling him of her intentions, but he would not believe me.

"How can there be a competition to *that* extent?" he would ask. "You *must* be doing something wrong. I have seen you myself with men."

"But have you seen me in restaurants, at seaside, or in some relaxing places?"

I protested. "Or did you see me in places where I am supposed to be in order to carry on my work?"

He said, "Whatever it is, you are in the company of men."

I said, "Well, I have to do this."

He said, "All right, you do it, but you be nice to me."

I said, "But I feel very, *very* hurt, and it is going to take time to be nice to you again. My children saw all that humiliation, the neighbors saw it, everybody saw it. It is not easy for me to get over it. Give me time."

But he was not ready to do so. Basically, the problem was that I was not sharing his bed. As he saw it, my rejection implied that I was seeing other men. That is how he explained it to me. Again, after a month or two and a few arguments, he threw me out. Once again I had to leave for my parents' place. This time I thought, "I am not going back." But in two or three days he came back with his elder brother to plead his case, and they took me home again. Such episodes were repeated a dozen times [long silence]. Yeah . . . a dozen times, coming back home, fighting, and being thrown out, on and on. And each time I would go back because of my children. I missed them terribly. For four long years, this drama continued, until 1982.

I tried to make him understand that I was not a log, that if he humiliated me publicly I could not share his bed, but he could not see things my way. From 1978 to 1982, when I finally left him, we had no physical contact, no intimacy, even though technically we were living under the same roof. He did try to force himself on me. Many times he got very angry and became physically violent, but he could not succeed. Because physically he was weaker than I—he is a very thin and meek man, and I am a strong person—he could not do that much damage. But by holding a stick or something in his hand he was threatening enough, and nobody knew about it. It was terrible.

Everybody found out about us, yeah. Sometimes the neighbors would get into our house and try to reconcile us. Then unsolicited counseling would come from everyone. People would stop me in the street or would call me to tell me to "take" my husband. I mean, everybody! It was awful. I felt very vulnerable. My children were vulnerable. I felt so sorry and sad for these small children who had to bear all that. They were scared to death and suffered a lot. Sometimes they would try to mediate, but most of the time they would just hide themselves in a room or a corner.

In retaliation, he slowly took everything away from me. I could not use the car. The driver was taken away from me, and my cook and maid were sent off back home. He must have thought that if the household work were loaded up, it would discourage me. There were also times when my parents were conniving with him to put pressure on me to stay home and forget about my education and activities in the refugee settlements.

Civic Responsibilities, Civil Society

I had two assignments [from the university] in a camp for refugees from East Pakistan while rehabilitation work was going on. One was to assist the community to build a school and the other to construct houses. This was a self-help program. I created a community committee, who then constructed a girls' school with five rooms, all by themselves. I raised money from the print office and the shopkeepers. This was the first time in the history of the department that a student was actually able to achieve the objectives of a development project, and the department was very proud of it. The press in Karachi covered my rehabilitation work in the refugee camps—*so much* coverage! I will show you some of the newspaper photos and articles.

Fortunately, UNICEF took note of it and offered to collaborate with the social work department. Suddenly I was in the main social development field, and I was about to graduate. This was around 1979, and my master's thesis was on the squatter settlements. This was the time in my life when my husband had taken everything away from me and was not giving me any money, and I was in and out of my parents' house. I was just broke, completely. UNICEF wanted to get volunteer students for their sanitation project, for building latrines in squatter settlements outside Karachi. I enrolled myself in it and received a salary of twenty-four rupees per day. I devoted myself to that work and got intensively involved in the community. In 1980, the result of the master's thesis competition was announced. I had won the first position in the entire university!

By the time I actually received my degree in 1980, I had already constructed sixty latrines for UNICEF—in one year's time! This was a project rejected by everybody for unfeasibility. The objection was that pit latrines could not be constructed inside houses of fewer than two hundred square yards. A Dutch consultant had paid some two hundred thousand dollars to UNICEF for the construction of three hundred latrines. The objective was to demonstrate a sanitary condition that people could maintain and improve themselves. This project was lying in the pipeline for two or three years. The Karachi Ministry Corporation had insisted that people would not let them build it [the latrines], that the Dutch should give them the money to make sewer systems instead. The Dutch consultant was adamant against a sewer system because there was a shortage of water. You cannot have a water-bound system in Karachi where there is no water to flush the pits! The ministry and the Dutch argued back and forth.

Coincidentally, the 1980s was the decade for water and sanitation, and UNICEF decided to pick up this project again. Once again the Dutch moved in and agreed to give them the money only *if* it was spent on sanitation projects with community participation, that it could not be allocated for a sewer system or be given to the contractors or the government. Well, with UNICEF's regular fund, I had already demonstrated the success of pit latrines—that if people are organized, they *can* do it. The Dutch took note of what I had done and were so encouraged by it that they gave the entire money to UNICEF for a similar program. I was appointed as the community organizer, with a salary of three thousand rupees per month! I worked full-time for a whole year, from morning till night. I was really leading a very purposeful life, a very fulfilling life, except that it was also a very painful life because during this period I would be periodically banished to my parents' home, and I could not see my children.

Now my husband was even more resentful because I had done my master's and had a job, though periodically he wanted me to go back home. But now I had become so resentful toward him that I did not want to be in the same space close to him. He had caused me so much pain. I saw my children very rarely. They were humiliated in society, and I was trying hard to protect them. I was surrendering all the time, and finally it had happened. "So," I thought, "I just have to live by myself." I could not put up with him and all the demands and claims he had on me. I could not fulfill them because I was too torn inside. It was just too painful to be a regular wife to him. I could not. And nobody was giving me space, you know, so that I could take care of my wounds.

Other Pastures, Other Homes

My parents finally left to settle in the United States in 1982, and they took my brother and my younger sister with them.[18] But they left the house there

18. In a subsequent question I sent to Qurat via e-mail (April 15, 2000), I asked her why her parents, who came to Pakistan with so much hope, left it for good to settle in the United States.

[in Karachi]. My old servant and his wife continued living there. This time
when my husband threw me out, I went to my parents' house, and I did not go
back to him, not for many years to come. My parents were no longer there to
push me. I was in peace, and I stayed on. For the first time, I was happy with
myself. All my life I had been dependent on others' decisions, and I was just
following what others had planned out for me. Now I felt more confident
about myself. I was *doing* something, and all the pieces in the puzzle were
coming together. It was, of course, *very* painful, very painful. He, too, was
very hurt because in his mind he had provided me with opportunities and
given me liberty to do things I wanted to, but I had rejected him. He was totally confused.

Through it all, the only good thing was the university. I was thriving. Most
of the people in the group I was working with were socialists. They became
my support group, giving me strength and comfort. This infuriated my husband even more. How could strange men be supporting me? What right did
they have? According to him, I should be just left alone, isolated and with no
support. If people supported me, therefore they must have a vested interest.
That was his thinking.

With my parents away in America, nobody ever came to ask me how I was
doing, not my uncles or my aunts or my siblings. They were all apprehensive
to be implicated and fearful that my husband might scold them for not pushing me hard enough to stay home. My sisters were all married, and they had
their own lives. They did not want much to do with me because they felt insecure with their own in-laws. They were afraid that their in-laws might blame
them for what I was doing. There was no support from anywhere except from
the refugee settlement where I was working. They were very supportive and
understanding. I just devoted myself to them completely.

I kept contact with my children through the telephone, the driver, the servants, and secretly visited them in their schools. Sometimes my husband
would bring them over himself; other times the driver would do so without his
knowledge. I treasured the time I spent with them, but even that time was very
painful. They also had a lot of accusation and reservation against me, and most
of our time would pass by me explaining. Then they would go back, and I

She wrote back that her parents felt that they would have a better life in the United States and
that there were more educational opportunities for their two youngest children, who accompanied them.

would just sit back, thinking and crying—all alone. But the next day I would get into my Jeep and go to work.

As the newspapers and the media covered my community work, I had a feeling that my husband, being the kind of intellectual man he was, was trying to understand me. It was very rare for a woman in Pakistan to be working with the community, with the masons and the brick layers, to sit with them to design and construct latrines and toilets and then train them on how to flush them. I was calmer, and we were both worn out. There came a time when my husband, feeling down and very low, would come over to my house for advice and counseling. I would talk with him, and whatever advice I could give, I would do it. You see, he was still suffering from depression. He realized that I was the only person in whom he could really confide. It was also our mutual interest in the children, his clinic, his patients, and the fears he had about life.

Every day he would ask me to go back to him, but every time I would tell him that I just could not do so because I could not fulfill his requirements, that I was still not up to it. Through it all, I learned to have a soft spot for him. You see, my community work taught me to see his point of view. Unlike many Pakistani men, he *had* given me freedom and basically allowed me to do whatever I wanted to do. But, of course, I realized this much later—not until I started working with UNICEF and other women, when I became aware of gender issues. My whole orientation was developmental, so I could see my husband in perspective. I could now understand that he was behaving like an Eastern husband.[19] He was shocked and hurt by the way I had changed. As a husband, he did all the right things—in his mind. As a father, he did all the right things. He worked hard in his clinic from morning till night and would go back home to be with his children and family. He never had a life of his own. Not for a minute did he do anything alone for himself. He was a very dedicated father, and I respected him for all that. But I could not forgive him for what he had done to me personally. All his life he feared that he would not be a "normal" man, so I could see that if he was hurting me, he must have been in extreme pain himself. Spending time with the people in the refugee communities and

19. It is interesting to note the comment an American male editor made on the margin of a copy of this chapter. He wrote, "This distinction is unclear and undeveloped: Western husbands would be just as resentful and threatened by their wives' success and independence."

seeing them in such painful situations taught me to understand pain, to rise above the situation continuously, and to deal with it.

Here, I thought I was being very sympathetic and understanding in my community work but very tough and hard with my husband. This was like having two faces. I thought that sometimes even in the community I was thrown out of some houses. People would say, "We don't want to have a latrine, and you are not going to build it. Don't come to our house. We don't want you." They wanted to keep the old system. So I felt that if I could take it from strangers and not from my husband, then that meant that I am having two standards. That is how I got the strength and stability to continue putting up with him whenever he came around. The other reason for receiving him was because of my children. I wanted to foster that soft corner in him; otherwise, there would have been total blackout; he would have lost hope, and I would not have gotten any love from my children. Basically, he knew that I was a family woman with love for children and family. He *knew* me very well, and I knew him very well, too, his weaknesses and the man he was.

Empower Thyself

But, for all this knowledge, there emerged a clearer knowledge about myself. That was very empowering and improving for me. I did not really camouflage it or hide it. I just made it very clear that what I was doing was very important for me. Perhaps my frankness and straightforwardness and my honesty made him see the kind of woman I was. He began to see the strength of my personality, I guess, and I could see that I had earned a bit of respect from him, an acknowledgment, in spite of everything. That's why I was always invited for my children's birthdays. I used to go back to that house for each son's birthday. I would go as a guest and come back. My children used to ask me to stay, but they also knew that if I stayed, there would be problems, so it was more peaceful this way. They were not lacking in love and care. That refugee family was still there. A maid who had been with us for twenty-seven years was there, and my in-laws' house was very close by. Then my husband stopped working in the evenings and was mostly at home. He was not concentrating well on his clinic, and so he reduced his work time to take care of the children himself.

Early in 1981, John Bitford, a professor from the University of Loughborough in Midland, England, came to Pakistan to see if his recommendations [on sanitation] were being followed. He met with me, and he became *so* fascinated with the latrine work that he invited me to go to the university to be the keynote speaker in an international conference that was to be held in October 1981. UNICEF funded my trip. It was a big event: a woman coming from an Islamic country and working on a sanitation project! My paper was very well received and later published.[20] I got *another* kind of awareness and boost. I became interested in getting a Ph.D. degree. I learned that the University [of Loughborough] offered a Ph.D. program where you could register in the university but carry on your assignments in your own country. *That* was perfect for me. I talked to John, and he said, "I would love to enroll you as my student."

I returned to Karachi, and the arrangement was that I would go to the university once a year and give seminars to the faculty, who would then grade my course work. All my travels were arranged either by the university or by UNICEF because I had no money to do all that. Whatever I earned from UNICEF I invested in my education. A British Muslim woman philanthropist, Mrs. Loreen Ismail, also became *very* inspired by my work and gave me three hundred pounds toward my registration fee. She is still a very loving friend, the only friend who has stood by me.

In 1982, I developed my *own* model of sanitation. With some help from UNICEF, we provided five thousand families with latrines, demonstrated the flushing mechanism and its maintenance. While doing this community work, I came upon an innovative idea, that of home schools.[21] You see, some traditional families do not allow their daughters to continue their education beyond a certain level, nor do they allow them to leave the house and get a job. So my idea was make these families intermediaries in educating children who could not go to regular schools for economic or social reasons. The idea was to get these girls' families to convert their homes into a "school" for two or three hours and for the children to pay them a small fee, which would become their income, earned without uprooting tradition by leaving their house.

Home Schools: An Indigenous Educational Model

I initiated the model for home schools in the settlement communities, and it became so popular. It was not part of the sanitation system but came about from the community. The way it developed is such an interesting anthropological

20. "People's Participation in Slum Upgrading," Water, Engineering, and Development Center Group, presented February 1982.

21. See chapter 5 and Kishwar Naheed's references to these home schools.

case. What happened was that some people were still not flushing the latrines properly. I had to go door to door with the community organizers to teach them how to flush. This was to show them how to save the water that was already scarce.[22] Having to do this was getting on every volunteers' and the masons' nerves. Finally they said, "Baji, every day you go to the same houses, and you say the same thing. Why don't you write down the instructions?"

"All right," I said. "We can write them down." So we sat in somebody's house—I never had any office, I had *nothing* at all except my salary—and we wrote down the instructions for flushing and maintenance, and we went back to the houses to distribute them. We told the women who opened the door that from then on we were not going to be coming around and bothering them. They could, instead, simply follow the instructions.

The women looked up at us and said, "But who's going to read it? We don't know how!"

And I looked at the men. I *knew* the women were not literate, but I just let these guys continue with it, so that they could understand for the first time this handicap of their women.

For almost three years, I could not get the men to work with the women. For three years, I worked only with men. But to start a program for women and with women, *that* was a breakthrough. From then on, men started having meetings on women's education, discussing and planning to do something about it.

Because I was so intensively involved in the community, I knew there must be a model of women's participation to which men would not object. You see, there was already a tradition of teaching at home and offering Qur'an education for young girls. My idea was, Why not build on that and add secular education as well? Through the sanitation committee, we informed people about our training sessions. They went out and found these girls for me, and they

22. Qurat explained, "Either you have a sewer system where each house is connected to it, in which case there should be enough water to push it down to the treatment plant and then to the sea. (That kind of water is not available in Karachi and especially in the poor areas, it will *never* be there.) Or you have the pit latrine system where the human feces are buried underground. It is not connected to the sea, and every household has its own on-site disposal system, on-site treatment plant. The surface could be used by the family for any purposes, as a courtyard or anything. You could dig it right here, under the kitchen floor. . . . That caught on like wildfire. A whole private sector emerged in the community, and people started making their latrines themselves."

were behind it. I mean, it became their project; it became the community's program. The men themselves were motivating their own women to go out and do it. My first teachers' training attracted about ten girls with tenth-grade education. They were the first to become home-school teachers. This meant ten home schools!

I wrote a book on this program.[23] It gives an account of their activities. That's how the idea of HomeSchools came up, and this was a *beautiful* event.[24] HomeSchools is now a trademark term anywhere in Pakistan. Today Home-Schools are all over the country. Most of the programs for women start with HomeSchool projects. It's a movement now, and I have nothing to do with it any longer. Most people do not even know where it came from. UNICEF was promoting it. I never insisted that I put my stamp on it, not even for the sanitation programs, which are all over Pakistan now.

From the HomeSchool program emerged the primary health care program. You see how important the whole process of education was! Each Home-School became a center for primary health education, with a mothers' group—comprising the children who were in the school—at its core. I was invited all over the world to make presentations and give lectures. I still am on the visiting lecture list of the University of Loughborough.

In 1984, UNICEF employed me as regular budget officer with a salary of fifteen thousand rupees per month, plus benefits. I trained and oriented the UNICEF officers of Pakistan. My project became a training ground, attracting many international and national visitors, who came to see the latrines. By 1986, I was already known as an expert on sanitation, and more and more donors sponsored projects for the development of the *kachchi abadi*s, the slum areas. I assisted CIDA [Canadian International Development Agency], UNICEF, of course, and the Netherlands and reintroduced them to ways of working with communities. By this time, I had organized around forty-three community projects, and with the financial support from CIDA I was the

---

23. *Home School for Education* (Bakhteari 1995).

24. In "Gender and Literacy in Pakistan" (www.brown.edu/Departments/Swearer_Center/ Literacy_Resources/women.html), S. Yasir Husain argues, "Bakhteari's project in Baldi town is probably the best example of participatory method which assists the women of the settlement to extend their normal roles and become agents in community literacy and development." See also Bakhteari 1988.

founding member of two national organizations. One was originally called Small Project Office; now it is known as Strengthening Participating Organizations. The other is South Asia Partnership, which brings the Canadian NGOs and South Asian NGOs into a partnership.

Quratul Ain Bakhteari, Ph.D.

In the same year [1986], I left to prepare and to defend my Ph.D. thesis. The pilot phase of the sanitation project was over, and with UNICEF's facilitation it was institutionalized into an NGO called Busta.

When I arrived in England, I had money for only six months of a visit, which was sponsored by the Agha Khan Foundation.[25] I was supposed to do everything in those six months—the library research, the reading, writing, defending, and all. And I did it! I worked eighteen to twenty hours every day and just lived on tea and biscuits. I left Pakistan in July 1986 and my *viva* [oral examination] was scheduled for February 1987. I had two outside examiners, and my dissertation was sent out to four universities before my *viva* could be scheduled. I developed a methodology for the development of and work with communities. My dissertation was later published into a book: *From Sanitation to Development: Case Study of the Baldia Soakpit Project.*

After I received my doctorate, I visited my parents in California. For a long time, I had almost no contact with them, except for occasional phone calls. By this time, my parents had gained an understanding of my work and developed a deeper respect for me. They surrounded me with much-needed care and a peaceful environment.

I returned to Pakistan from England and the United States in 1987 with my Ph.D. in hand. In the meantime, I had saved enough money to buy a piece of land and to construct my *own* small house. I bought a small car, and the same servant who had lived with me for so many years became my driver. For the first time, I had my own home, and *nobody* could tell me to "get out, it is not yours."

As a single professional woman in Pakistan, I was well established, which was highly unusual in those days.

25. Agha Khan is the spiritual leader of the Isma'ili (also known as Agha Khanis in Pakistan) branch of Islam. The Aga Khan Foundation in Pakistan is a country subsidiary of the Aga Khan Foundation, headquartered in Geneva, Switzerland.

Rethinking Marital Relationships

My relationship with my husband, however, remained the same—back and forth. I would call my children once or twice a week, even from England. My eldest son was becoming more appreciative of my activities, even feeling pride that I had successfully defended my dissertation. In the interval, he had traveled to the United States and become aware of other lifestyles. He was developing some kind of Western orientation and was beginning to realize that his mother was a different kind of woman.

After my return from England, my children started visiting me on their own. My husband, too, said that he now understood me more, and I was much calmer by then. I felt at peace with what I was doing and with things around me. My husband was constructing this house [in which this interview took place]. He knew that going back to that neighborhood where I had been badly humiliated would be impossible for me.

"Now I've made a new house for you, a new place for a new beginning. You must come back," he said.

Again I said, "I need time. We have never had a peaceful time together. It was always under threat that you came to get me. Just let me be. I have a home now, and I have made a life of my own. These are major decisions. I have changed a lot. I am not the same person. We have to think about it carefully. But we should start by becoming civil first, by respecting each other's face and space."

But, you see, all this time he had never taken another woman [wife], and there was no scandal about him. He had dedicated his life to our children and worked only half days to be with the children the rest of it. The children did well in school, and he tutored them at nights. Every day he took them to school. Not a day did they ever miss their classes or were not properly dressed, so just looking at my sons, their health and well-being, invoked a lot of softness in me for him. Being a prosperous and well-known man, he was under tremendous pressure to take another wife or do something [divorce Qurat], but he did not. I was no longer in a defensive mood, and we started approaching each other little by little.

Bureaucracy and Community Development

I was quite securely set up in my job and content with myself. In August 1987, UNICEF offered me the position of program officer for the whole province of

Sindh. My salary was hiked to approximately forty thousand rupees per month, and my travel allowances included twelve hundred rupees for every night I spent outside of Karachi, regardless of whether I used it. My benefits were excellent, and I was covered for international travel.

Unfortunately, I soon realized that I was really given a chair and a desk to work on papers. The whole intention was to make me behave like a program officer—*no* more as a community organizer. If I wanted to go out and work at the community level, I would be told, "No, no. UNICEF officers do not work directly with the communities!" I was turned into another bureaucrat working for the government. The problem was compounded by the fact that the government directors and personnel changed frequently, and they were not serious about their jobs. All I was doing was writing a lot of notes for the records: "Such and such thing could not be done for such and such reasons!" Before, I was there *in* the community, getting things *done*. I got sanitation plans going, organized home schools, and developed the health programs. *Here* I was saying that "such and such things could not be done," protecting myself all the time.

In December 1987, I resigned. I thought I was in the wrong place. I was not made for that job. I just resigned, but my resignation was not accepted until March 1988. Once again I was making myself very vulnerable. I did not go to my office at UNICEF. I stayed home. They gave me a one-month sick leave and said, "Think about it." Then they gave me another month of sick leave and said, "Think about it!" Our country representative came to Karachi and talked to me.

"What is the problem?" he asked.

I said, "Your work is OK. I am the wrong person for it." You see, I could also see that they needed work at that level. I said that I was just not happy doing it.

He was concerned and asked, "Why? What is wrong with UNICEF that a person like you is not happy with it?"

I said, "You can hire other people, and they would be very happy with this work, but I cannot accept this position. I am more interested in community development."

Finally they accepted my resignation. Ever since then I have been on my own. I only take work that I *like*, regardless of the pay. If I think it is worthwhile, I take it. That was a decisive point in my life. I traveled across the country, assisting wherever people wanted my help in developing sanitation, constructing latrines, setting up small NGOs, home-school education, primary education, primary health care, and the like.

In the late 1980s, the Dutch wanted to duplicate the Karachi pit latrine system in Quetta.[26] They asked me to assist them, and I jumped at the opportunity. The program was to construct three thousand pit latrines in the city of Quetta. Again I immersed myself in the work. I worked hard but conducted the team training a bit differently, making it a bit more institutionalized from the beginning. The program did *very* well initially, but unfortunately it had to be implemented through [Pakistan] government agencies, and the corruption was so high that finally the Dutch withdrew the funding, and the program came to an end. It was never completed. Interestingly, although the Dutch stopped it halfway, its impact was so great that the masons and the people themselves continued it in a modified form with their own money.

I spent 1989 completely at the policy level in Islamabad. There, I worked as a part of a team to prepare investment plans for water and sanitation for the whole country. I approached the issue from a community perspective and designed a water and sanitation program that included community participation. Today it is being implemented across the country, and the pit latrine system is *all* over. Now the government has made it a rule that the communities have to be involved in building and organizing the sanitation system.

Just as I was wrapping up the sanitation project in Quetta in 1992, the girls' primary education program came up. I was asked to join that project and was given a five-year contract. So far [1998, the time of this interview] I have been in Baluchistan for a total of nine years, four years for the sanitation project and five years for the primary education. I would spend the weekends in Karachi and then go back home to Quetta. By then, my husband and I were reconciled, and he had *no* problem with my being in Quetta. I was very much respected, and all my earnings were spent on my children's higher education in the United States. Two of my sons got married after my husband and I were reconciled.

Girls' Primary Education

When we started the primary education for girls in 1992 in Quetta, only fifty-seven thousand girls were in school, about 17 percent of the school-age girls. We have been able to raise that number to 29 percent in five years. Again it was a community mobilization program. Because of the strict tribal and feudal moral code, Baluchistan was the most backward province in terms of girls' education. Education was a taboo, an emphatic no for girls. But now *every* village wants a girls' school, and there is not much parental resistance to it.

26. Quetta is the capital city of Baluchistan Province.

The way we tried to reach the families and communities was to first learn about the Baluch culture and tradition.[27] We developed a fourteen-step community-supported process for building a partnership with the communities for female education. The first four steps focused on identifying a female teacher in a village. That was the toughest thing to do. Once we identified her, she had to be tested without any biases, and her residence had to be verified to see whether she was actually a resident of the village or the city or whether she was just using the village to get a teaching post and a salary. Steps five through seven involved organizing the community, talking to the parents of *each* girl child in the village, and then organizing them into village education committees. Then the village education committees had to be trained to establish their own schools and to run them for the girls. They had to do that for three or four months without any support from outside. They had to contribute their own funds to establish their commitment to girls' education, that they were not only after a teaching position or getting the money for a building that could be misused as personal property. As soon as communities go through this testing and probationary period, they are put in touch with the government officials, who after grading and testing and looking at the school's operation, will approve it as a government school. Then the government starts paying the salary of the teachers, the material comes in, the building is planned, and jointly the government and the village education committee manage the school. Such a collaborative system had never existed before. In fact, it was never practiced in any part of Pakistan. Now the whole country is following the Baluchistan model, and the World Bank has made it a point that if Pakistan wants any funding for female education promotion, the country must use the Community Support Process of Baluchistan.

I think that eventually the salvation of this society is in this type of community partnership. That is what I have seen through this massive female primary education program in Baluchistan. Despite it being a very conservative tribal and feudal society, there is now a positive shift of attitude toward girls' primary education. But because of the shortage of single female teachers, the percentage of girls in school is still low. Now we are trying to defuse the situation

27. Qurat was cosmopolitan in her upbringing, lived in a large city, and was trained as a social scientist. Her attention to Baluch culture points not only to her personal sensitivity and professional training regarding the "native" culture, but also to cultural and ethnic diversity in Pakistan.

and to recruit male teachers, cautiously. Some communities have already hired male teachers until enough girls are graduated. Then we can shift. Such ideas are coming from the people themselves. If the government were to do that [force the community to accept male teachers], then there would be resistance, but people themselves are now placing male teachers in their girls' schools, and this is a major change of attitude and behavior.

Let me give you an example that I witnessed personally. In 1992, the entire Baluchistan government bureaucracy and the politicians were pressurizing the World Bank to shift the priority of the education project from girls to boys. Their argument was that people do not want girls' education, and so the money will be wasted, the time will be wasted, and there will be no girls in school. But one or two strong women in the bank insisted that if there were no girls' schools, no money would be going to the province. Finally, when the loan was released, and we started working with the community, we realized that there was no such resistance! It was just that there had never been an honest attempt to reach the community and to let them know what education is for girls. Even now there is a continuous push in the government to give more money to boys' school, to take it from the budget for girls' education [high pitched, incredulous]! But we moved so fast that hardly any money was left to be taken away and given to the boys [laughing]. It used to be that in the absence of extracurricular activities from the girls' section, the leftover money would be added to boys' activities, but this time there was a *big* shift.

Community Participation

The girls' primary education program started in 1991, and my component, community participation, was added in 1992 and is still going on.[28] The second phase involves elementary education, which will be added on by the end of 1998. The primary education has been very successful, and now *strong* pressure is coming from the community itself for the establishment of elementary schools. Presently, five NGOs are working across the province, where there were none before. These NGOs have the support of the community, and act like a bridge between the government and the community. They help communities to build up schools, then they withdraw, allowing the community to take over and to negotiate with the government directly. So the forum is pro-

28. Qurat is currently (1998) the technical advisor for beneficiary participation and the director of the Baluchistan Primary Education Development Program.

vided by the NGOs. Every three months I bring all five NGOs together to
train them and keep them updated on new strategies.

Despite all these projects and programs, we still need to develop our human
resources more to work at the community level. I have now worked for twenty
years at the community level, and I can still count on my fingers the number of
professional community workers. That is why I have launched this teaching
and practice course for community development. It is called the Institute for
Development Studies and Practice, for which I have written a concept paper
and gotten some money to test it.

My idea is to bring together [in this institute] a cross-cultural group of community activists from the world's rural areas who have high school education.
Then I have them go through a rigorous training and learning of theoretical
and practical aspects of community work and community development. I
think there is a need to understand the conceptual and theoretical framework
for the community work. Here are many community workers, really laborers,
but no theoretical and conceptual understanding at all. That is why they *never*
rise beyond that. I also want them to practice their learning *in* the community,
the way it happened to me. I was doing my work, I was enrolled in the university, I was reflecting, but I was not taken away from my roots. That is how I
learned. I was working in the community, but I was also involved in learning
and policymaking. We can count just one or two names of individuals who
have got that community base and yet work there.

In Pakistan, there is a stigma against working in the community—absolutely! And to give it a status is why I want to set up this institute and to
conduct a sixteen-week residential training course. I have basically conceptualized it and am the project director, teacher, and everything else in the school
[smiling]. The Asian Foundation has given us twenty lakh[29] rupees for a pilot
project that is presently in progress in Quetta. The grant is not given to me
but to the Society for Advancement of Higher Education, which then gives
it to us.

Our students are community activists who come from all over Baluchistan.
We had 143 applicants, but room for only 27 positions. We try to keep a gender balance. Community development and participatory action research is my
subject. A professor of political science from Baluchistan University teaches
power structures, and another professor from Karachi teaches organization

29. One lakh equals one hundred thousand rupees.

and management theory. The idea is to send students back to the community, where they can be effective community teachers and activists. Initially they take a two-week course work and spend two weeks in the field. Then they come back and take one week of course work and do another two weeks in the field. It goes on like that for sixteen weeks. The last week is devoted to reflections. If this pilot project works effectively, our objective is then to institutionalize it and apply for more funding.[30]

A Role Model

Hmm . . . to a certain extent I see myself as a role model, yes. I learned that basically women are very intelligent and sharp, but most of them get threatened by the inability to deal with the emotional blackmail they face in their daily lives: "Oh, my children, my status, my house," and the like. If they can only learn to deal with that, the rest becomes much easier. There is *no* other way than to deal with it. I think there are increasing stories of women who need to understand themselves and deal with their situation. There is a space for them. But without a process, without backing it up with productivity, the whole effort may lead to more headaches. Just to rebel and do it for the sake of women's rights might not be the whole story. Women get caught in this emotional blackmail because of our marriage structure and lack of legal support. Women have very few legal rights, and most importantly their children belong to the husband.[31]

Painful as it was for me, I never challenged the law. I dealt with it. It is stupid to fight for children because no one can exchange me for another mother, so why should I fight for an established fact? The only terrible thing was that

30. I received the following e-mail message from Qurat: "Institute for Development Studies and Practices concluded its second development course on May 8, 2000. A graceful ceremony held at Rural Development Academy" in Quetta, Pakistan.

31. "Under the [Pakistani] law, the father remains the legal guardian of the minor, regardless of whether he does or does not have actual custody. While rewarding custody the welfare of the child/ren is considered the most important factor, often overriding provisions of Muslim personal law (e.g., custody of children even beyond age limit under traditional Muslim jurisprudence has been granted to mothers; and mothers who remarry have been granted custody). Factors taken into account while deciding welfare include: age and sex of minor; marital status, character and religion of parents; physical and mental wellbeing of minor and minor's preference. For Sunni schools of law, mother has custody until son is 7 years old and daughter reaches puberty" (Balchin 1996, 137). For a quick description of variations on the issue of child custody within different provinces in Pakistan, see Balchin 1996, 136.

they were not near me, but *nobody* can take away my status as a mother. That is something women need to understand. Besides, the Western model is not very conducive to women's self-development either. I find more and more Western women not achieving their career goals because they are stuck with children. Their men leave the children with them, and *they* have the custody most of the time, and they have to cope with the needs of growing children, all the agony of a single parent raising children, and yet have to focus on their work as well. But here when I was told that the children do not [legally] belong to me, that because my youngest child was six years old and already of an age where he would be automatically placed in his father's custody, I thought, "Fine. If that's the case, he can have them! They are growing up, and they will definitely look for their mother, so this is a temporary phase. In the meantime, I am getting quite a good space to work on myself."

As for the sexual, emotional, and psychological relationship between the spouses, that *is* a stress.[32] That has been a limitation in our part of the world. If I had sought physical satisfactions, very soon my whole fight for differences of points of view would have been labeled as "selfish" and "immoral." I would have never been acknowledged for my productivity, for my community work, and for my contribution to the profession. Actually, the whole thing would have gotten confused: "Was it [sexual] freedom she was after, or was it really work [self-empowerment]?" But then, that is the price one has to pay.

Yeah . . . the way marriages are arranged here precludes physical intimacy, definitely.[33] From the beginning, physical intimacy is not there! He is the greatest stranger of all, and then suddenly you are thrown into a room together.[34] In most cases, physical intimacy is *never* established, even until the last day of one's life. But then your attention is taken away by your family and your children. You establish a day-to-day routine for things to be done, and no intimacy is required in that. No expectations are there, from either side.

I believe these cultural barriers to having meaningful physical relations

32. I asked Qurat, "You concentrated on the role of the mother, but what about the wife, the sort of sexual, emotional, and psychological relationship between the spouses?"

33. I asked Qurat, "I was also wondering about the way marriages are arranged in this country. Do you think that because of it, physical intimacy, which is fundamental to marriage, becomes very difficult to establish?"

34. Kakar (1989) argues that the most fundamental and perennial problem among the Indians, Hindus, Muslims, and Christians is sexual.

hamper one's maturity and the development of one's personality, absolutely, for both men and women.[35] This is the problem. I was quite young when I became infatuated, and I could have been involved in that kind of situation, but I had to resist all the time. If I had entered into a relationship for my own self, my children and others would have never forgiven me, and I never would have been able to go back to my family. Always in the back of my mind I knew that one day when everything was sorted out, I would be going back [to her husband]. You see, I had plenty of opportunities. I was still very young, I was living alone, I was traveling all over, and I did come across *very* interesting men. There were some *very* tempting opportunities. It is interesting: because of the kind of woman I am—someone breaking new professional ground as a woman—people from my part of the world find me very interesting [amused]. But that strong pull from my children and from those early years when I single-mindedly dedicated my life to my children was so powerful and so empowering that my other needs became secondary, very secondary. I never focused on my physical needs. All my life, my energy went into creating that space for myself, and maybe the approaches I took were so time-consuming that when the space was there, the opportunity was there, I was no longer interested. But I have a feeling that women in this part of the world have to go through this phase to establish themselves, to get themselves recognized. Maybe once that space is created, then the realization of their physical needs will be acknowledged.

Such issues come up in our Quetta workshops *very* strongly. The only way to deal with that is through sharing and networking. But there are still no breakthroughs, no hard and fast way to deal with them. It is just like getting yourself to feel a bit lighter, that "all that's happening to you is happening to me also." The majority does not have basic education, and there is no infrastructure to fall back upon. That is the whole problem, and our laws and the judiciary system do not support women.

Universal Human Rights

One of the main subjects in our courses is to address the power structures of gender relations and the human rights issue.[36] We are not treating them as sep-

35. I asked Qurat, "Do you think this inability to have meaningful physical relations may hamper one's maturity and personality?"
36. I asked Qurat, "How is one to change *that* kind of power structure?"

arate issues or just as a woman's issue because we have come across many young men who have no say in their own lives either. Many men lead very sad and lonely lives. They are also forced to marry women they do not like, and so they go to prostitutes. A large number of men spend their lives outside on the streets, going home only to sleep. So our courses on power structures start right from the international power structures or relationships down to the kitchen and to the bedroom. And that realization is what the students learn to think about for the first time in their lives.

We do not as yet know what effects, if any, such discussions and workshops will have on the power structures of the judiciary and the state.[37] You see, the community projects are initiated and funded almost totally by international donors. The donors pay the salary of the main leaders, facilitators, and activists. The latter's commitment is therefore mostly to the donors or to the projects rather than to the community. For that matter, many of the programs in the past twenty years are still half-baked. That is why they have had no real impact on the society's power structures—because the amount of money that was pumped in the country through these projects and programs really diffused the vigor of activists and their commitment to the community. It became like a job opportunity, with the objective of shifting positions as fast as possible and following any agency that pays more.

I *did* give up a tremendously prestigious and financially beneficial position [at UNICEF], but not very many people are willing to do that. The reasons for the unwillingness are a lack of basic education and training for self-recognition and of a genuine self-awareness. People seldom stop to think, "What do I want in life? Why do I want to be here?" Most important, the *vision* is not there. Also, when young people look around and see so much decadence and corruption in the larger society, they get disillusioned and fall back on the routines. As I said, there is no institution to nurture the kind of character that is required for community work or a university to teach and demonstrate it. The commitment is there, but it is not nurtured. I have come across young people who have refused positions because they want to work for their own community at the village level. They do not want to leave their villages. There *are* such people, but if only they could have a support system around them to reassure them that this is a respectable position, that maybe they are

---

37. I asked Qurat, "What effect do you think these ideas will have eventually on the judiciary and the state, possibly leading to fundamental changes in your society's power structure?"

not getting much money but that they should be happy with the changes they are creating in their community, then maybe they could be the leaders who will be creating structural changes.

I am very much encouraged by the changes I see. Given its resources, Pakistan cannot afford to pay high salaries. The people who are in demand, who are community based and have professional skills, are paid well by international donors. A time will come when these salaries will go away. The survival of the projects and community work will depend on people who have gone through a local learning process. If we could produce hundreds of those, then we would be on a real course of development. The bottom line is that of community development. The framework is participatory action research, where students learn the logical sequencing of a project. It is the Paulo Freire approach,[38] and a lot of anthropological principles are applied in it: you learn with the community, then you go back to reflect on it, write diaries, and then participate in presenting seminars. It is a very interesting course. I mean, during my week, the first day we focus on the overall process of historical development. The second day we concentrate on community development, which then leads to personal self-awareness. The third day is for learning techniques of social mobilization and participatory action research. Somebody is doing health, someone is doing electricity, someone is doing TV, someone is doing microcredit, and someone is in agriculture. So they have their own programs and projects. Cost cutting is community development, and that comes about with participatory action.

Reconciliation

My husband and I finally made an attempt at reconciliation in 1990. I was traveling everywhere, and he did not object at all. I was living in my own house, and my children came and spent the whole day with me. If I was not there, my husband and children stayed in my house, eating, drinking, and sleeping there. There was no pressure on me. Ahh . . . [pause],[39] my husband would sleep at my house when I was not home, but sometimes he would stay even if I was around but sleep in a different room. Sometimes we would sit together,

---

38. Qurat explained Paulo Freire's approach to education as "community-based education processes that are launched to empower people." See Freire's *Pedagogy of the Oppressed* (1970).

39. I asked Qurat, "Did your husband sleep in your house, too?"

but cautiously, very cautiously. It was not physical yet. I was testing. He was not pushing. Then I started visiting his house occasionally.

It just so happened that when I was in the United States in 1990, visiting my parents, my husband and my youngest son were also there. My son was about to graduate from high school. One day he took his father and me for a walk and a talk. We were sitting around in a park, talking and listening. He said, "What is the problem between you two? I want you together! If you do not make up, you are going to lose me completely in this American society. I will also go on my *own* way."

We talked and talked and talked for the whole day! My husband and I tried to clarify many things, with my son sitting there listening to us as a witness. With his mediation, we agreed to live together. When we came back to Pakistan, we started the process of reconciliation.[40]

Initially I spent three or four nights in my own house or stayed there whenever I wanted to. I could not let go of my house just like that. I had too many memories in that house. My servant and his family were still living with me. It became a family house. Whoever wanted it lived in it. Last year I finally sold it. Instead I bought a small house in front of my parents' house in California. I thought, "When my parents are very old, *maybe* I will end up right in front of them and take care of them."

My mother-in-law became ill and came to live with us in 1991. I took *such* good care of her that she never even left this house to visit her other children. One evening, after I had bathed her and clothed her, she held my hand and looked at me and said, "No one has ever taken care of me as you have done." She just held my hand. It was a nice feeling. I heard her telling my husband that he did the right thing not to listen to them to remarry, that he was wise to wait for me, it was worth it. She died in 1991 at our house. My father-in-law was already with us because his wife was here, but when she died, he actually moved in. He, too, preferred to stay with us. I would make a special trip for him from Quetta on Sundays, and he would wait for me to come to see him. He died a year later.

My husband comes to Quetta to visit me frequently. He would come there

40. In her last e-mail to me (22 August 2002) Qurat wrote, "My family and I have been healing, and we are trying to build the family with new reference points that we developed ourselves. I am very hopeful that this publication will light the way for others, helping them to see alternative ways to empower women."

to be with me, to look at my work, and to read my papers. He is a totally different man now, a changed man. But there are still [sexual, emotional] problems; there are many things I want to talk to him about and share with him, but he does not want to talk about them. He is like, "Just fine. I am happy, you are happy. Let's not talk about it." There are scars on my children, and everyone is working on it. I am working on it.[41] Fortunately my sons' wives are very intelligent girls. My sons chose their own wives. The girls have visited me in Quetta many times and saw my work. They are working with my sons on it [on their difficulties with their parents' marital problems].

Sure they know about me.[42] All of Karachi knows about me [laughter]. If people ask me how I got here, I have to tell them the whole story! It is not easy for a woman to do all that, *not* in Pakistan. I have gone through a lot. If women want to live their own lives, then there are prices to pay. So, yes, I just shared my story with my daughters-in-law before their marriages.

Some Reflections: Betrayal, Defeat, and Self-Empowerment

Qurat's birth, as she said at the beginning of the interview, coincides with the creation of Pakistan and falls on the birthday of Pakistan's founder and leader, Mohammad Ali Jinnah, who is also affectionately known as the father of the nation, *baba-e qaum*. Other than the mystical meaning and personal significance that these associations may have for Qurat, the trajectory of her life in search of identity and self-empowerment, intertwined with the creation of Pakistan, found its wellspring in the refugee settlement located at the outskirts of Karachi in a transitional society. Her exuberant child's eye perspective of her community in the refugee settlement provides a rare window into the life of refugees in an emerging community. Qurat did not hide the refugees' hard life and their daily struggle to survive, but her positive experience of mutual

41. Over our lunch breaks, Qurat and I had a heart-to-heart talk, and she told me that some serious marital problems still existed between them. We talked about psychology, intimacy, and the differences among the sexual habits and traditions of Americans, Iranians, and Pakistanis. I suggested marital and psychological counseling, toward which she seemed to be inclined. I have not included most of her reflections on that topic here because she was not sure she wanted them to be publicized.

42. I asked Qurat, "Did their families know about you?"

aid and civility stand in stark contrast to the mayhem, disorientation, and loss associated with the partition of 1947. Stripped momentarily of their class, ethnicity, lineage privilege, and caste, and in pursuit of a higher ideal, the refugees had come together to Pakistan guided by a powerful vision of national sovereignty and self-realization and by the hope for a better future. Memories of the life they had left behind were, for the most part, the only possession they carried to the new homeland. A "communion of equal individuals" (Turner 1976, 96),[43] the refugee settlement in which Qurat grew up was "civilized" and "caring" and provided her with a sense of basic trust and civic responsibility that became the cornerstone of her identity and personality.

The liminality of the refugee settlements and their status created an environment conducive to "formulating a potentially unlimited series of alternative social arrangements" (Turner 1974, 14) and to the development of behaviors and interpersonal relations at variance with the local traditions or with the refugees' own traditions. Qurat's course of life, in other words, would have been different had her parents had more money and been able to live in a less transient and more traditionally structured setting. They probably would have followed a more traditional and culturally scripted pattern of socialization and upbringing, as indeed they did by the time their other children were born and they were financially more secure. Qurat's sense of self and identity was formed in these fluid years, which later in her life enabled her to draw upon and to reciprocate the nourishment she received from her refugee community. Her gradual awareness of her own desire and needs as well as her sense of commitment to community development, however, seem to have been brought about largely through three "betrayals," which though painful, made her more resilient and persistent to pursue her goals. These betrayals, in her view, were committed by her parents, her husband, and the new state of Pakistan. She distanced herself from her parents and periodically left her husband. Convinced of the soundness of her convictions, she continued with her education, earned a Ph.D., and made a greater commitment to her community, the same community that had given her the best memories of her life.

43. My discussion here rests on Victor Turner's concepts of "liminality" and *communitas*." He defines *liminality* as "betwixt and between" and *communitas* as a "model" for human interrelatedness, which "emerges recognizably in the liminal period." It is a society of "unstructured or rudimentarily structured and relatively undifferentiated *comitatus*, community, or even communion of equal individuals" (1976, 96).

Parental Betrayal: Fearing Dishonor, Getting Rid of a Daughter

Qurat's emerging awareness of her role and identity as an individual and as a woman and of her relationships with her parents challenge some of the existing theoretical and ethnographic assumptions regarding gender relations and gender dynamics in Pakistan. Her gradual awareness of her culture's gender expectations and her own conflicted experiences as a woman simultaneously highlight the fluidity and specificity of gender identity. They also underscore that at a particular moment in the life of a society, a family, and an individual, gender identity, roles, and relations may be different from or improvisations on the norm, which means that the norm itself is subject to historical and situational fluctuations. In other words, normalcy is not a static concept that is formed presumably once and for all. Likewise, gender identity and gender relations do not remain static or unresponsive to social change. Nor can we assume that they always "fit" the cultural ideal.

Far from a general projection of the ever-agentic and domineering masculine image, Qurat's father was loving and caring and preferred to stay home with his children. The mother, on the other hand, was an ambitious authoritarian and a disciplinarian. Within the framework of their marital relations, she was the decision maker, the strategist. Qurat frequently stressed her mother's temperamental personality and her single-minded devotion to bringing up her children in a Western tradition and in accordance with what she remembered to be a prosperous upper-middle-class standard that she enjoyed previously in the undivided India. The irony of it is that Qurat seemed to have inherited her mother's assertive personality, but when she took initiative and behaved like a young "Western girl," her parents, more specifically her mother, "panicked" and fell back on tradition and cultural expectations in order to restrict her activities.[44] The parents' drastic reaction toward their daughter and the mother's abusive and humiliating language burdened Qurat with emotional problems while manifesting the parents' cultural conflicts between their Western aspirations and their traditional expectations.

---

44. In the same vein, an Indian anthropologist, Kamala Ganesh describes: "I wanted to study further. . . . Around this time, my parents were looking seriously for a marriage alliance for me: when they sensed my fear of the expectations attached to a traditional 'arranged' marriage, they flew into a panic and redoubled their efforts to get me married before I became too stubborn" (1997, 28).

Marriage provided the way out for both the parents and the daughter. Arranging Qurat's marriage as quickly as possible would control her and transfer the safeguarding of the family honor to someone else—that is, her husband. For the daughter, getting married implied freedom from her parents' control, an independent adult life, and the beginning of a new identity.

The realization that her parents arranged her marriage to get rid of her was brought about in a crushingly painful reunion she had with some classmates who flocked to see her after her marriage. After thirty years, she still wept as she recalled, vividly, her friends' freedom to continue with their education, while she, pregnant, was restricted to one room at her in-laws. Marriage was not the license to freedom and independence she had been promised it would be. As painful as her experience was, however, it deepened her resolve—however unconsciously in the beginning—to empower herself by seeking knowledge and emotional independence from her parents.

Marital Betrayal: Irreconcilable Expectations

Qurat's moment of feminist awareness, in retrospect, came in the aftermath of her marriage and in the imminent prospect of losing her Bakhteari identity: she insisted on keeping her maiden name. Her independent spirit, her love for life, learning, and experimenting, however, were totally alien to her husband and his family, whom she perceived as civilized, educated but restrictive, and "passive," except for her father-in-law. Her husband, a relatively gentle but insecure and emotionally distant man, could not have been more different than Qurat. Their temperaments and sensibilities were at odds with each other, and their needs and interests diverged at every turn of their lives. He was, however, a "decent man," in her words, tormented though he was about the degree to which he should—or could—allow her autonomy. He was generally supportive of her education and of some of her social activities, but the more she learned about herself and became clearer in her objectives, the more resentful he became.

Supported by law, society, and unequal marital rights, he finally resorted to violence and threw her out of their house, not once but many times. Much to her shock, he claimed she had no rights over the house, any material goods, or even her children. She realized at that moment that, as a woman, she had little recourse to claim either her share in the house or her children, even if she had given birth to them and had invested so much time and energy in them.

State Betrayal: Deceitful Leaders

The state betrayal was just as heartwrenching for Qurat as the others. It came through the crushing defeat of the Pakistani army in 1971 at the hands of the Indian army, their erstwhile enemy, who had come to the rescue of East Pakistan, renamed Bangladesh hence forward. The lies and deceit spun by Pakistani leaders and the atrocities committed by Pakistani soldiers against their Bengali brethren stunned Qurat and disillusioned her regarding her society's values and calling. At the same time, it deepened her resolve and commitment to community development and to the refugees who were pouring in from East Pakistan. She was not about to concede to the state the human dimension that could help the refugees to rebuild their lives, that had sustained herself and her family once in the face of adversity.

Qurat gradually directed the self-awareness she gained through confronting multiple conflicts and serial betrayals toward empowering herself by becoming actively involved in community development and by helping to build civil society. She improved the general hygiene in her city through designing and constructing public latrines. Most significant, she developed an indigenous framework for secular education based on the idea of community involvement and participation. In areas where girl's education was frowned upon, Qurat was able to make some inroads, to gain the locals' trust, and to provide young girls with some means to self-realization and self-empowerment.

3

Violence

Woman's Body, Nation's Honor

Meeting Rahila Tiwana

THE "RAPE" OF RAHILA TIWANA in police custody was one of the more controversial news stories my husband and I learned about when we finally settled in our house in Lahore. By November 1991, several more charges of rape and violence against women, in particular those women affiliated with Benazir Bhutto's Pakistan People's Party (PPP), were alleged in the media.[1] Women's Action Forum (WAF) and Women Against Rape (WAR) arranged several simultaneous demonstrations in the major cities of Pakistan, including one in Lahore. I was hesitant whether to join the demonstration planned for December 12 because I was not sure of the ethics of political participation while one is working in the field. But when a dear friend, seventy-year-old Baji (Begum Kishwar Abid Hussain), called inviting me to "come walk with us," I could no longer hesitate. The feeling of solidarity was contagious, and I marveled at how this respected woman, whose own daughter was at the time a high-ranking representative of Nawaz Sharif's government, actually took a stand against the violence unabashedly perpetrated against women. I accepted the invitation and felt as though I had "found my feet" with my Pakistani hosts in the process.[2]

In tandem with the increase in the level and intensity of violence against women in Pakistan, feminists, activists, and human rights organizations have stepped up their public activities, political agitation, and pressure on the gov-

---

1. See I. Malik 1997, 107–14, and N. Ahmad 1992.
2. The expression "finding one's own feet," is taken from Geertz 1973, 13.

ernment. They are keeping the issue of violence against women burning in the public's consciousness.

Ahmad Rashid, the noted Pakistani journalist, told me about Rahila Tiwana and facilitated my meeting with her psychiatrist, Dr. Haroon Ahmed, and his wife Anis Haroon, who is a founding member of WAF in Karachi. The Haroons also graciously arranged my meeting with Rahila and her brother, Afzal, and shared with me their knowledge of the case. I met Rahila and her brother several times in May 1993 and ended up with more than seven hours of taped interviews with her. Throughout our interview, her brother Afzal was present, and at times the sister and brother collaborated jointly to discuss issues such as Rajput honor, political commitment, and torture. They seemed to have a mutual love and admiration for each other. I have kept his contribution intact in the text because it sheds further light on the state's strategies to break down its political opponents.

Rahila and Afzal invited my husband and me to their house, where we met their mother and two of Rahila's three sisters. At the time of our interview, Rahila was running for a National Assembly seat on the PPP ticket. She and her brother took us to her constituency outside of Karachi, where we spent some time with two dozen women and children. She introduced me to her female constituency as a professor from the United States who had come to interview her. My husband and Afzal stayed outside in the company of her male supporters.

Rahila was a devoted twenty-four-year-old political activist who belonged to People's Student Federation (PSF), the student wing of the PPP, headed by former prime minister Benazir Bhutto. Rahila's life history brings into focus the plight of women in police custody and the abuses of women political prisoners for political propaganda. Rape and violence against women as expendable objects during political conflicts and territorial dispute have a long history and are not peculiar to any one particular society or culture.[3] One may refer to the Serbian atrocities against and gang rape of Bosnian and Croatian women, the mass rape and slaughter of Tutsi women in Rwanda, Indian atrocities in Kashmir, to name only a few, where women's bodies became the battlegrounds for masculine honor and national pride. One can find a certain

---

3. Sexual abuse of women in police custody is not limited to the developing or underdeveloped societies. For a comprehensive report on the issue, see *All Too Familiar: Sexual Abuse of Women in the U.S. State Prisons* (Human Rights Watch 1996).

cultural specificity, however, in the case of Rahila's torture and alleged rape in police custody in Pakistan, despite its global features.

Rahila was arrested, tortured while in police custody, and then hospitalized in a psychiatric ward for more than nine months in the beginning of 1991. Rahila's father was a civil servant, living with his wife, their four daughters, of whom Rahila is the eldest, and one son in a comfortable state-owned house in a colony just outside Karachi. All her family members were devotees of Benazir Bhutto and activists on behalf of the PPP. Rahila repeatedly told me how much she loved Benazir and how worried she was for her leader's life because while in jail she heard her interrogators threatening to kill Benazir.

Before Rahila was arrested, her house was searched, and then she was arrested on the pretext that she had received weapons and ammunition and had passed on secret messages to Indian agents. When she refused to cooperate with the Sindh authorities to fabricate charges of sexual misconduct and national security violations against Benazir Bhutto and her husband, her interrogators turned sadistic.[4] So severely was she beaten and tortured that at some point she lost consciousness and subsequently had to be hospitalized and placed under psychiatric care.

Rahila felt more comfortable speaking Urdu, in which she could be highly articulate, rhetorical, and at times philosophical. We switched back and forth between speaking in Urdu and speaking in English. Although I understood her Urdu relatively easily, I could not reciprocate as fluently, hence our speaking in both English and Urdu. One of the disadvantages of switching from one language and thought process to another might be the presence of some inconsistencies and confusion in this narrative. To capture the nuances of her life story, I frequently have used her idioms and expressions in Urdu. This is her story.

Rahila Tiwana

In Custody

I was held in jail in CIA [Crime Investigation Agency] custody.[5] My father came to visit me and said, "Rahila, you are a Rajput girl.[6] Your neighbor was Bhagat Singh.[7] You have to consider him and honor him. You are in police cus-

4. See also I. Malik 1997, 112–13, and for local coverage see the 1990–91 issues of the *Herald* and *Newsline,* two of Pakistan's most prestigious monthly magazines.

tody, facing all that *mahaul,* environment. You broke all our traditions, our family rule. Now that you are in politics, as a Rajput with our family background,
we expect you to come back to us as a *shahid,* martyr. We will bury you with
pride and *izzat,* honor, in our graveyard. You hold our honor in your hands. But
if you compromise or bend your head in fear, we will be buried alive with
shame. We leave this to you and pray that God will save you from all indigni-
ties and help you achieve your goals in favor of the nation and country. Then
we can wait for you outside with pride, in an honorable way."

I felt my father was crying. The very same night he was taken to jail. I heard
him *chikh,* scream. I heard my brother screaming. I know their voices. I was
very disturbed the whole night. The police were pressuring me to compromise. They wanted me to admit that we were hiding ammunition. Mohammad
Khan [8] kept saying, "Rahila, where is the ammunition?" But I knew what his intentions were. He said that he was going to search my house to find the un-

---

5. "Pakistani CIA has acquired ill repute not only through violations of human rights but also
by becoming an active party in organized crime in the turbulent province of Sindh. During its
hey day under Jam Sadiq Ali and Irfanullah Marwat [coinciding with the time Rahila was in cus-
tody], the CIA practiced victimization, personal vendetta, forgery, car theft, kidnapping, torture of innocent citizens including cases of gang-rape against women and operated as parallel
organization pursuing its own kind of interrogation. The CIA was originally intended to help
the police in its criminal investigation, but political patronage and the exclusive nature of its
leadership helped the agency to run a reign of terror in Sindh until the death of Jam Sadiq Ali in
early 1992" (I. Malik 1997, 112). See also the *Herald* throughout 1991, in particular its special
issue, "Inside the CIA," October.

6. The Rajputs are "a group of clans of the Kshatriya (warrior) caste, who fall just beneath
the Brahman intellectual-priests. . . . [T]heir harsh code of honor and their code of chivalry
have often been compared to those of medieval European knights. The Rajputs would fight
against all odds" (Weaver 2000, 52). "In many ways the Rajput bears such a strong resemblance
to the Highlanders of Scotland," writes Caroe, "with some trifling differences of names and costumes. They had the same reckless daring, the same loyalty to a chief they trusted, the same
love of sport, the same readiness to take offence and quarrel among themselves when they
could find no enemy to give them employment" (1983, 87).

7. Bhagat Singh was a freedom fighter from Amritsar, India. He was arrested trying to blast
the British viceroy's car and was hanged in Lahore in 1929. He became a popular folk hero, and
a ballad about his dying to keep the honor of his country was sung all over the country. He is
probably the only Sikh known as a *shahid,* martyr, and loved as a hero in Pakistan. I am grateful
to Tanvir Khan for providing me with this information.

8. Mohammad Khan and Malik Ehsan were Rahila's two primary interrogators at the CIA
Center.

derground room. You see, my colony is a semi-army colony and is owned by the government. Our house is rented. We could not be hiding anything there. I said, "Look, our war is a war of endurance. We fight a war of ideas. We change minds." But he told me that my kind of thinking was dangerous and threatened me that this night was going to be a very difficult night for me. He was trying to blackmail my father.

My case had become public, and many were demonstrating on my behalf. There was much publicity, and people were horrified by the government's behavior. The government did not expect this, thinking, "Rahila is not famous. She is a woman." This was a very big mistake for the government because the students, liberal parties, women's and human rights organizations, even Sindhi and Baluch women came out on the road to support me. I am so very thankful to my country's women's federations. The government was heavily pressurized, and now the police decided to bargain with my father.

They said, "If you give us five lakhs,[9] we will leave both of your children alone."[10]

My father said, "OK, but first you will have to release me so that I can arrange it for you. I have no big [powerful] man in my family, and all my girls live with me."

"First you give us ten thousand rupees before we let you go," said Mohammad Khan. Then the police took my father and me to our house. My father whispered to me that Mohammad Khan had demanded five lakh rupees. He said, "Rahila, you know the police have demanded five lakhs. What is your decision?"

"If you give in to their demand," I said, "then it means that I have admitted every allegation. I am your child, and I know this is your weak point. You are my father, but I have an obligation to my commitments."

My father said, "Good. I wanted this decision." He then praised me and said that he would fight for me. He went outside with them. Now, that night when we had arrived home, around eight, a student party leader from another party had come to our house to help my mother write a media appeal on our behalf. My father went to his room and brought out ten thousand rupees. The police checked the entire house, looked everywhere, but did not find the secret "underground room." When they did not find what they were looking for, Malik

9. Each lakh equals one hundred thousand rupees.

10. Rahila's younger brother, Afzal, was arrested and jailed at the same time.

Ehsan said, "Arrest Rahila's sister, Amina"—who was only twelve years old—
"and bring her along!" They also wanted to arrest the man who was helping my
mother. My sister was terrified and hid behind my mother. My mother started
crying and pleaded with them not to take her. Malik Ehsan was such a horrible
ghundah man. I think even the earth would not accept him, *zamin bhi us ko qabbul
na karae gi.* He slapped my sister hard and said, "OK, let her be."

They returned us to the CIA Center, and my father gave Mohammad Khan
the envelope with the money. Mohammed Khan kept the envelope in his
drawer and released my father at 11:00 P.M. My father went straight to see my
uncle, Khuda Bukhsh Tiwana, who was then the home minister in Punjab. My
whole tribe stood up together to support me: "How dare they arrest our girl?"
But, you see, only my family is a PPP supporter. The rest of my tribe belongs
to the Pakistan Muslim League [PML].[11] Party loyalty has its place, and tribal
solidarity has its own importance. My tribe thought it was wrong for the government to keep me in jail. They pressurized Nawaz Sharif[12] and Ghulam
Ishaq Khan.[13] That's why the police did not misbehave with me as they do
with other women.[14]

In the morning, they took me to Samiullah Marwat, the deputy inspector
general of the CIA Center in Karachi.[15] They told me this was their last warning. "Here is a blank check," they said, "and a good life or punishment. This is
your choice. You are a green card holder,[16] and we can settle your family in
America and open a bank account for you. But if you do not agree with us, we
will ruin you and your family."

---

11. On the shifting alliances and political rivalries between the PML, the PPP, and the
Muhajir Qaumi Movement (MQM), see I. Malik 1997, 223–56, and Nasr 1994.

12. The arrest and torture of Rahila happened during Prime Minister Nawaz Sharif's first
term in office, 1990–93.

13. Ghulam Ishaq Khan was president of Pakistan from 1988 to 1993. Using the Eighth
Amendment, passed under General Mohammed Zia ul-Haq (1977–88), which gave a president
the right to dismiss the elected prime minister, Ghulam Ishaq Kahn dismissed both Benazir
Bhutto's government in 1990 and Nawaz Sharif's government in 1993.

14. By "misbehaving," she means sexual harassment and rape.

15. Samiullah Marwat was the deputy inspector general of the CIA Center in Karachi in
1991. He was vehemently anti-Bhutto and cooperated closely with Jam Sadiq Ali, the chief
minister of Sindh. See I. Malik 1997, 112.

16. The U.S. permanent residency status.

"No," I said, "this is not possible."

The third night the police made many raids and arrested more people from all over Karachi. They also arrested another woman, Fahima Rima, at 4:30 in the morning. This woman was *ghaddar*, a traitor. Secretly she belonged to the MQM [Muhajir Qaumi Movement],[17] but openly she was with the People's Party. The police took me along to identify my secretary Sabrina's house. I knew that if Sabrina was arrested, she would tell everything because she was not strong. As we were driving around Sabrina's house, I realized that a few boys were sitting around and talking. When our car drove closer to these boys, I said loudly, "Sabrina's house was somewhere around here." Now, everybody knew I had been arrested, so they took Sabrina from her house and hid her someplace else. When the police did not find Sabrina, Malik Ehsan grabbed my hair and hit my head against the dashboard, saying, "You have warned them about us. We wanted to see how sincere you were to your friends. We already knew Sabrina's house." They beat up and arrested her sister's husband and her brother, exactly as they had done with my father and my brother.

Malik Ehsan pulled my hair—this is the place where I was wounded [she pointed to her head]—and returned me to the CIA Center. They were tired that night, so they left us alone. Next morning, on the fourth day, Samiullah Marwat and Malik Ehsan started questioning me again, the same bargaining, back and forth. They wanted me to implicate Manzoor Wassan, our minister for youth. Jam Sadiq Ali [Sindh's chief minister] was bargaining with him. Other ministers had sold out to Jam Sadiq, but Wassan was a very strong and loyal [PPP] man. They wanted me to allege that he was involved in criminal activities with some girls, that these criminals would rob jewelry shops and then the girls would sell the gold in Quetta in order to buy ammunition to use in terrorist activities. "No," I said, "that's not true," because I knew Manzoor Wassan. You see, the government wanted only one allegation against Benazir. If I had agreed to this, then Benazir's character would have been badly damaged in Pakistan. You know, since General Zia's time, it has been alleged that

17. The MQM is a party of Urdu-speaking Indian Muslims who migrated to Pakistan after the partition of 1947. It is essentially a regional organization based primarily in Sindh Province and is "the third largest electoral party in the country," after the PPP and the PML. Its founder is Altaf Hussain. The MQM was split into two factions in 1992. See I. Malik 1997 and Nasr 1994.

Benazir and her brother Mir Murtaza are involved in terrorist activities,[18] so if I had agreed to their demand and agreed that we did have ammunition, people would say, "Oh, the government was right. Benazir is a terrorist."

But the sources of PSF's activities were in college. We were only demonstrating to change our very old educational system. We wanted new technology and computer systems in the college. We wanted free education, at least for the poor classes. We also demanded religious freedom. Islam is our religion, but if you are a Christian and I am a Muslim, this is our own business. Our struggle had to do with pen and paper only. We wanted to change mentality. Benazir wanted to change their mentality through *inqilab*, revolution, but MQM wanted *darr*, terrorism. We [the PSF] had strict orders from Benazir not to use guns. We were told if anyone used weapons, he would be no longer a companion and would be dismissed and black-listed. Benazir's rule was: even if you have only one pistol, you go to jail. She was very strict. She said, "If you die, it brings us honor, but if you kill somebody, it dishonors us." I think this is a very good policy, but we were suffering because of it. So when our [student] president was arrested, we were all very scared because he did have a pistol.

The police confronted Fahima Rima and me. She told them that she was a member of MQM and had done a lot of work for them. It was very difficult for me to deal with this situation. We [the PSF] were not aware of her duplicity. We had had our doubts about her, but now she exposed her true self. First, Mohammad Khan asked her whether she knew me. She said, "No, I don't know her because she is not a good woman." I was shocked by her behavior—on top of trying to deal with my pains and wounds. When we were alone, I told Fahima, "Look, you are also in police custody. The police are not your friends. If you compromise, you lose your personality and our respect, and you won't have any friends. Why do you do this?" But she was very rude and bad-mouthed Benazir and me.

She made a statement against the Peoples' Party and Benazir, and I made

18. Mir Murtaza is closely associated with the Al-Zulfikar Organization (AZO), which was formed in the aftermath of the execution of Zulfikar Ali Bhutto by General Zia ul-Haq in 1979. Mir Murtaza was accused of antigovernment activities during Zia's military regime, and AZO came to be identified—against Mir Murtaza's vehement objections—as a terrorist organization. After hijacking a PIA airline in the early 1980s, Mir Murtaza was forced to live in exile until he returned to Pakistan in 1996 during Benazir Bhutto's second term in office, much to his sister's consternation.

one in favor of the Peoples' Party. I felt the police's mood changed greatly because of the contradictions in our statements. The next morning I saw her in the washroom. I tried to tell her not to give out any names and to pretend that we did not know anything, but she said, "Oh, I hate you." I was shocked. After that we were kept in separate rooms. Then in the evening we met again. Now she admitted that I was the president of PSF, but that she was not like me because I was a criminal like Benazir. I said, "Fahima, I don't know why you are making these allegations. I am not your enemy. You are scared, and that is why you talk like that." Then Mohammad Khan interrupted the meeting, warning me that this would have dangerous consequences for me.

Divine Message

The next day Tayyaba, a Mrs. Subinspector,[19] warned me that they [Malik Ehsan and Mohammad Khan] were going to make an example of me. She gave me a cassette and said, "Listen to this cassette tape." I listened to it. You know, it was the story of Hazrat Bibi Zainab,[20] and how she was tortured by Yazid, the caliph. It was full of *marsiya* song.[21] I love my religion. I believe in my religion. It had such a powerful effect on me. You know, I do not make distinctions between Shi'a and Sunni because I believe in principles. I respect all religions, but I am not crazy about either one of them [Shi'a or Sunni]. But this story affected me strongly. Hazrat Zainab is a symbol for Muslim women. In my view, she made a great contribution on behalf of Muslim women.

I cried a lot. I remembered people telling me that if you go to jail, you bring dishonor to your great family. But when I listened to this cassette, I thought, "Rahila, this is God's example for you. Bibi Zainab was a most respectable lady[22] who made her male captors look small." I prayed to God, "Either include me in the company of the martyrs and make me a *shahid* or give me

19. "Mrs. Subinspector" was Rahila's term of respect for female subinspectors.

20. Zainab was a granddaughter of the Prophet and daughter of the Shi'ites' first imam, Ali, and his wife, Fatima. In the aftermath of the Karbala tragedy and the martyrdom of Imam Hussain in 680 C.E., Zainab was taken to the court of Yazid, the caliph, where she delivered a historic speech against Yazid and his tyrannical regime.

21. *Marsiya* is a poetic genre, an elegy or lamentation for a dead beloved, and is popular in Urdu, Persian, and Arabic literary traditions. Among the South Asian Shi'i Muslims, *marsiya* is the most expressive medium for commemorating the martyrdom of the third imam, Hussain.

22. Throughout the interview, Rahila used the word *lady* instead of *woman*. Given the connotations of *lady* in English, I use *woman* instead, which is closer to her meaning. For an interest-

strength. If I am weakened and give a statement, then I will not believe in you." This was my commitment to my God. Then I felt very relaxed. I don't know where the energy and power came from. I felt very powerful at this time. I don't know why she gave me this tape. Maybe because she is a Shi'a. And she said, "When I saw your face, you reminded me of my daughter."

Punishment: Inscribing the Female Body

When I refused every allegation, Mohammad Khan said, "OK, Rahila, if you do not behave like a human being, we will make you one." I said, "OK, you try your stamina. I'll try mine." He got very mad at me. They tied my hands with a rope behind my back and hung me from the roof like a bag—like this [she lifted her hands over her head and collapsed them together]. I was swinging in the air. Only my toenails touched the floor. Then he beat me, saying, "Rahila Tiwana, where is the ammunition?" Mrs. Subinspector Tayyaba was not present then, but two low-ranking women soldiers were there. My companion was also hung up, with Fahima Rima sitting in front of us. Sabrina's sister was made to sit opposite me because they wanted Sabrina's whereabouts.

The police started beating me. "Now you will tell us where the ammunitions is." I said, "I don't have any. You get me down!" Both my hands felt as if they were being cut off. I felt horrible pain. I was shouting. "Tell us, otherwise we will break your arms and torture you more," Mohammad Khan said.

At that time, Mumtaz [another female subinspector], who was in the *kholi*,[23] the other cell, came in and dropped at my feet and said, "Rahila, for God's sake agree with them. They are *zalim*, very cruel, and will treat you very badly" [she implied sexual abuse also].

That night a powerful cyclone hit Karachi. That got the two women sol-

---

ing discussion of the usage of the term *lady* among anglicized middle-class and upper-class Pakistanis, see Murphy 1996, 111.

23. Rahila described a *kholi* as "a very small, congested, black, and dark room. You cannot straighten your whole body. Usually there are several people in one *kholi*, and you can only sit there. Men have to do everything there, right in the *kholi*, but women go outside somewhere else. The problem is that bathrooms have no locks. Fortunately Mumtaz helped us by guarding the door. But the bathrooms' condition is so bad, so dirty, that they make you vomit when you go there. They are very old. *Ghilaz*, filth, and terrible odor fill the air. Everything is broken there. You know, I am crazy for cleanliness. When I saw that dirty condition, I could not use it. It was so bad that I also dreamed about very dirty places."

diers scared, and they said to Malik Ehsan, "Rahila is innocent. You are hanging an innocent person. Take her down. Take her down. Otherwise you will face God's wrath." Everyone, particularly the women, were pressurizing Malik Ehsan to take me down, but he said, "Who is God, *khuda*, to save Rahila? I am God at this time!" And he kept beating me. My *maas*, flesh, was exposed, and I was bleeding. Malik Ehsan said, "Rahila, if you do not make a move, you will be dead soon. We will throw you away somewhere and put the blame on the [student] federation."

They pulled my hair from here [pointing to her head]. I felt as if my bones were breaking, and I shrieked with pain. I was sobbing, but he said, "This is not all. Give us a yes statement," and he pulled my hair, and it came off with the flesh. I was bleeding. Then he started beating on my nails, like this, with a stick. My fingers were broken, and my nails were showing the flesh. That night he hung me twice until I lost consciousness. Then he left but returned to hang me up again and tortured me for the second time. He left at four o'clock in the morning. Both times I lost consciousness. He was a bad guy. He punched me in my stomach, and I started bleeding from my mouth. The soldiers became very scared. One said to Malik Ehsan, "She is dead. She has turned black. She is dead!" But all the time Mohammad Khan and another person—I don't know who because I was in a very bad state—kept on saying, "We want some allegations against Benazir Bhutto or Nusrat Bhutto or Mir Murtaza or Manzoor Wassan."

They also wanted me to implicate Benazir in Najib's murder.[24] Malik Ehsan said, "You should make a statement and say that Benazir was responsible for Najib's murder because she did not like him. Say that Benazir and Najib had a *ghalat*, illicit, relationship, and therefore Asif Zardari [Benazir's husband] wanted to have him killed. But Benazir found out and had Najib killed." He said, "Make this statement and say that you know about all these happenings." I said, "No, no, no. You can beat me all you want." I don't know how I could say no in this situation.[25] I had a lot of energy. I said, "You stupid *buddha*, old man. Is this your *namaz nishan*, prayer badge? You are a black man, and this is a black behavior." I couldn't say any more because he slapped me hard. My tongue was bruised and bleeding.

24. Najib Ahmed was a president of the PSF and Rahila's comrade. He is described more fully later in the text.

25. I asked her, "How could you keep saying no under such conditions?"

At four o'clock, they pulled me down. It was winter, December [1990], but they made me exercise and used a stick to goad me. My foot was wounded, and they forced me to walk. My flesh was exposed everywhere. They hit me. I fainted. I had to lie down on the floor. I had no bed. My bed was the floor, and I had no blanket or anything. My hands had turned blue. One of the soldiers was a PSF sympathizer. He came to my cell quietly and gave me hot water with salt. He was scared because policemen are not supposed to be involved in political activities, but he looked after me very secretively.

In the morning, they arranged for a doctor to come and see me. Women were crying hard. Fahima Rima also saw my condition and was very scared, but she was very tough. I have never seen a woman like her. She tried to push me to compromise with the government. Then the doctor came in, and when he saw me, he said, "She will die if you do not take care of her immediately. Her stomach is swelling." That day was spent in my treatment. I do not know what kind of treatment. They gave me drips and injections. Several doctors came and went. It was an emergency case. I was vomiting blood.

Now, Afzal was kept in another cell. The police had also tortured him the whole day and the whole night. They whipped his feet with a stick and hanged him—the same way. We were not allowed to meet, and my family could not see me for twenty-one days. One subinspector, who was a friend of my family, told my parents that Afzal and Rahila were being beaten up very badly,[26] so my sister informed the press and also the People's Party. Then several articles appeared in the media about us. She also filed a petition with the court. In the meantime, one of my PSF friends, Zeb, came to see me. She disguised herself as a doctor and saw my conditions. I told her to leave the city because she was also wanted and to tell the other girls to leave. The boy activists were already arrested—maybe two or three hundred of them, and it was the girls' turn. Zeb ran out of the CIA Center and went straight to see my family. She told them, "Rahila is not in good condition. She will be dead if you do not take care of her." Then with my sister she went to Bilawal House[27] to inform Benazir and later on told my companions. It was at that point when they started this movement on my behalf.

For a day or two, I was unconscious. Mrs. Subinspector Tayyaba saw my condition. Now everyone was very scared, including Samiullah Marwat, be-

---

26. Rahila often referred to herself in the third person.
27. Benazir Bhutto's headquarters in Karachi. Bilawal is also the name of her first son.

cause of the publicity and because my sister had filed a case with the High Court. Nusrat Bhutto also got involved because she loves me very much.[28] Benazir was watching [the process]. All my jailers were scared, denying that they had tortured me. Now Malik Ehsan was looking after me, but when I regained consciousness, he started it again. "We will not let your sister alone." They used dirty words about my sister.[29] They said, "This time we will not touch you since your sister has filed a petition on your behalf in the court. But we will torture your brother. You have only one brother. We will kill him."

They did not present me at the High Court until fifteen days later! I don't quite remember the procedures because it was very horrible for me. The day they were to take me to the court, Benazir and Nusrat Bhutto sent several well-known lawyers and party leaders to the court. But the police changed their plan. Instead I was taken to a doctor in the civil hospital for a checkup. The doctors were instructed to fabricate my condition and to give me a clean bill of health. They sided with the police because they were scared. The x-ray report of my hands and feet was declared fair [normal].

When I was presented in the court, Malik Ehsan made a big mistake in identifying the car in which we were arrested. We were arrested in a white Toyota Corolla, but in the court he said we were arrested in a white Civic. I said, "Please note this [discrepancy]. He thinks we are not educated." His inability to be consistent became an issue in the court. The judge said, "You are uneducated. This will be a rope around your neck." This was a big headline in the press. Our fight was very interesting but very painful.

The press was also there, and I told them everything. I told them that Malik Ehsan had threatened to torture my brother if I talked about my torture and spoke the truth, that he threatened not to leave me alive, and that anything could be done to me. I also told the press that Malik Ehsan and Mohammad Khan drank alcohol[30] in front of me and told me they would not leave me alone. But unfortunately the court was not with us [was biased against Benazir

28. She is Benazir Bhutto's mother and until 1995 was the cochairwoman of the PPP. Benazir removed her mother when the latter sided with her son, Mir Murtaza, who laid claim to the leadership of the party.

29. Rahila's sister had a small business. Malik Ehsan started harassing her and eventually forced her to close down her business.

30. Drinking alcoholic beverages is forbidden in Pakistan, at least publicly. Zulfikar Bhutto decreed the prohibition in 1973.

and her party] because one of the judges sneered at me all the time. In my heart, I was crying. I felt very hurt and angry. I thought, "Why is this judge ridiculing me?" I felt so hateful toward the police, the judiciary, everything.

When I was returned to the CIA Center, Malik Ehsan tortured my brother in front of me. They took off Ajay's [Rahila's nickname for her brother] shirt and tied his hands. They were blackmailing me. They were all drunk and beat up my brother.

Afzal: I was beaten up for seven days.[31] They wanted allegations against Benazir Sahiba. They wanted me to sign on a blank paper against her. I refused it. I did not know that they had asked the same thing from Rahila. I only knew a little bit about what was happening to her. I also knew what had happened to the PSF activists when they were arrested during Zia's time, so I guessed what Rahila must be thinking in her cell. I was kept alone in a cell next to hers because they wanted to put pressure on me to sign the blank paper, but I refused. Every time I refused it [emphatic], they hung me, beat me with boots and sticks, and punched me.

Rahila: When I saw them beating and torturing my brother, I went crazy; I felt like a psycho. He is my one and only brother. My mother had prayed hard to have a son. She made a *mannat*, vow, to have a son, and God gave him to us. He is my only brother. Seeing him being tortured, I became really crazy. I told my brother, "Ajay, imagine you are in the field of Karbala.[32] The last cry, *siday-i haq*, the voice of the truth, is coming from Hazrat Ali Asghar.[33] Think you are there. If we die, we will be *shahids*, martyrs." This was my hysterical voice. I don't know why I was saying these things, but I was hysterical. As I was talking with him, he told me that he felt in peace. He was not crying anymore. Then he said, "I hear all of my companions shouting, 'God is great, *allaho akbar.'"

Malik Ehsan got very scared and slapped me hard. He said, "You are a very dangerous, *khatarnak* woman. If you can do this while staying inside, what are

31. In the text, I identify a change in speaker by their names, followed by their comments.

32. *Tom mahsus karu keh tom maidan-i karbala main ho.* Karbala is in present-day Iraq, where Imam Hussain was martyred in 680 C.E. Rahila invoked this scene to ease her brother's pain by associating their fight for a just cause with that of Imam Hussain, who fought against the tyrannical government of Caliph Yazid.

33. Ali Asghar was a suckling son of Imam Hussain who was martyred along with his father and two other brothers at the Battle of Karbala.

you capable of doing outside?" He gave me two more powerful slaps, and as he was leaving, he said, "Next time I will not only beat you, I will give you a horrible punishment."

He punished me by making me stand up—like school children—for five days. My feet were swollen like an elephant. They did not allow me to sit down, but a policewoman came in one night and closed the doors and the shutters to let me rest a little. Generally policewomen were nicer than men. Mrs. Subinspector Mumtaz took care of me like a mother, but if Mohammad Khan had found out that she was nice to us, he would have punished her. I don't know why, but some women were special only to me. They treated me very gently, but not the others. I don't know why they were nice to me only. I am a *pagal* woman, crazy [smiling]. Mumtaz said, "I torture other woman when they are brought to jail, but I don't know why my hands are not free with you." But if Mumtaz doesn't torture [women], then the men would do it, and that is most horrible.

But there were also two nasty women jailers. These kinds of women are selected for this kind of work. Samiullah Marwat or other inspectors hire them personally. The first time Malik Ehsan came for interrogation, two women also came in and started insulting us. We were very timid and scared. These women were thieves and demanded that we give them money. I said to them that we had no money, nothing. One of them said, "Give me your ring." It was in December when I was arrested, and I had no warm clothing except for one sweater I was wearing. She demanded that I give it to her. When I refused, she grabbed my sweater and took it from me. I felt so very cold. I wrapped my chador around me.[34] If the police gave me tablets, toothpaste, or anything like it, these women would steal them.

Honor and Shame

Now all the work on my behalf was happening outside. But [inside] I was told, "Look, Benazir is not here to help you." Fahima Rima was bailed out by MQM after two or three days, while I was still in jail, suffering. Fahima Rima was a black sheep[35] for MQM, while pretending to be with us in PSF. She was sin-

---

34. What most Pakistanis call chador is a large rectangular shawl that they either wrap around themselves or drape over their heads. It is different from the all-enveloping veil that some Iranian women wear.

35. This was her expression, meaning a spy.

cere neither with MQM nor with the PPP. In the meantime, two PSF members were arrested, and under torture they confessed to having committed murder. They also said that Fahima Rima helped them kill MQM supporters, so she was arrested again. This time I told her, "Look, you are suffering in two boats. If you commit yourself to one, you may be saved, but if you are in two boats at the same time, you will get drowned in deep water. So, please, this time make the right decision. Choose one and stick with it." She was very rude and refused to talk with me.

You see, she is a very clever woman. This time she cooperated with the police, and they celebrated her birthday in the CIA Center with lavish cake and sweets, while they behaved very badly with me. They kept me hungry for three days and gave me spit water. They would spit, *thuk*—like this [she made the gesture]—in water and would give it to me. The wounds inside my stomach were swelling and hurting me horribly, but they could not see my wounds. They just wanted to make sure there were no outside marks. After twenty-one days I was allowed to see my mother and my brother. My hands were broken, and my condition was very bad. I was pale and very thin—like this [she held up her index finger].

Afzal: I knew Rahila was beaten because I heard her screams, though when I asked, they [the jailers] denied it. But I recognized her voice. So when I saw her face after twenty-one days, I don't know what were my feelings or what was happening to me. After three or four minutes, I asked her if she was all right.[36] She said, "You can see." There were two or three soldiers with her, and they did not allow us to talk to each other. My mother and Amina, our youngest sister, were also there. When Amina saw us, she started crying badly. Then I learned what allegations the government had made against Rahila and me. I was accused of possession of a Kalishnokov and illegal weapons, interruption of government affairs, and murder. Similar allegations were made against her. My mother told us to be patient and not to worry, that they would get us out. She is a very strong woman. I cannot imagine how she survived under those conditions.

I never contemplated giving in to their demands in order to get out. Actually, the Tiwana family belong to the Rajputs [caste]. In the Tiwana family, if you have given a *wa'da*, commitment, to anybody, you must remain committed. The family honor depends on it.

36. I asked Afzal, "How did you feel when you saw Rahila after so many days?"

Rahila: This is our nature.

Afzal: It is a matter of your life or death. So my commitment to the People's Party and Begum Sahiba [Benazir Bhutto] and Asif Zardari [her husband] must be kept. I take their false blame on me. Why? Because this is our family honor. We prefer to cut our neck than to break our commitment or to kneel down. We never surrender. When you meet our family, you will realize what I mean. That is why we did not accept any allegations [against Benazir]. After the pain of the first punch that Malik Ehsan gave me, I thought, "The pain of one blow is equal to the pain of hundred blows. OK, carry on, beat me."

Rahila: Rajput men never break their promise.

Afzal: No, *never*.

Rahila: You know, our nature is like a dog's tail. If anybody makes a commitment to us, we wag our tail only for that person. You know, in the history of South Asia, Rajputs are known to be very brave people. What matters most for them is their *izzat* and *ana*, self-respect and the family name. All the Rajputs have one quality, star-like quality. They are very sensitive, very brave, and very committed.

Afzal: My father did not try to influence my decision, but when he went to see Malik Khuda Bukhsh Tiwana [the father's cousin], he told my father that if Rahila and I left the People's Party and joined the Muslim League and accepted the allegations against Benazir, he would write a letter on our behalf. The Muslim League actually wanted us because we were activists.

Rahila: The Tiwana tribe thought that we were breaking the tribal rules, all of them. They were very, very angry with us.

Afzal: In December, Benazir Bhutto Sahiba went to the Tiwana tribe and told them, "Why do you blame Rahila? Blame me. Rahila Tiwana is now a member of the Bhutto family. She no longer belongs to the Tiwanas."

Rahila: But then Benazir faced rotten behavior from my tribe because everyone was angry with my parents. They blamed my mother, saying that it was all her fault because she is an outsider [married into the family]. She is an enemy of the Tiwana tribe. My father went to see Benazir and told her that we do not want anything except respect, that at the CIA Center both his children had resisted very bravely. My father is very broad-minded. He said, "My daughters are not bad characters. I believe in them. I am very proud of them." He said to her, "We want to know what you are planning to do." Benazir said, "For the first time, I feel very weak. I am very disheartened for this nation. I lost my father. I lost my brother.[37] Why don't these people understand who is their enemy, who is their friend?"

In the meantime, a few days after my arrest and detention at the CIA Center, a PSF delegation had gone to Islamabad to see Benazir. They told her, "There is this woman student leader who has been tortured horribly. She did not give any statement against you because she loves you very much, because she thinks you are the only person who has come to get rid of our bad laws." They told her, "She really loves you." So when I was transferred to jail [from the CIA Center] Benazir came to see me. She said, "Rahila, you know, you are the source of my power. When I hear about or meet someone like you, then I think, 'Benazir, you are not just one person; you have the great power of many people behind you. Live in Pakistan and stand up for the people.'" This was Benazir's commitment to me.

The court was very quiet. The only decision it made was to warn the police that if they tortured me again, they would be punished. But now my brother was seriously threatened, and I felt I was losing my mind. With the court's decision, Jam Sadiq Ali, the chief minister of Sindh and his chief advisor, Irfanullah Marwat,[38] personally came to jail to see me.[39] At first, Jam Sadiq Ali spoke very softly and lovingly. When I refused to cooperate, he became angry. He threatened me with more torture. Then we were transferred to the Karachi Central Jail [late December 1990]. The jailer's behavior was as bad as the police's. I went to the women's section with a broken hand—like this [she twisted her arm]. They refused to get me a cast. My left hand was still functioning, but my right hand was absolutely useless. I did not have any feeling in it, and my veins were damaged. Both my legs were swollen. My hair was plucked out from here and there. When I entered the jail, I scared the women there. But some of them were also happy that I was so brave.

Afzal was taken to the men's section. But now they put Afzal in a black cell,

37. Benazir Bhutto's younger brother, Shah Nawaz, mysteriously died in France. See her autobiography, *Daughter of the East* (1989), chapter 2, "Death of My Brother," 280–307.

38. Irfanullah Marwat is the son-in-law of Ghulam Ishaq Khan, president at the time these incidents took place. He was alleged to be the perpetrator of several orchestrated rapes against PPP supporters and activists, including the most publicized gang rape of Veena Hayat. See Bakhtiar 1992; I. Malik 1997, 107, 112; and Haeri 1995b.

39. Rahila initially was kept at the CIA Center for a few weeks before she was transferred to the Karachi Central Jail and later on to a psychiatric ward. Some of the dates mentioned here are approximate because sometimes she could not remember the exact dates.

with both his legs in a rod, like a cross. He could not sit or move at all. He was kept in that condition all the time, *and* they kept on beating him. Their motive was to keep my mother under constant pressure, not because they wanted her to persuade him to give allegations against Benazir. This time [in jail], they wanted money, a plot of land, or something like it in exchange for not beating Afzal or for providing him with some facilities. They did not care whether we made allegations or not. It was pure blackmail. Up to now my mother was strong and holding up well for me, but at this point she felt very weak because now my brother was involved. She was crying all the time. I felt terrible. I could not sleep, and I was pacing my cell constantly, thinking about what was happening to my brother. What were they doing to him now? I prayed all the time. But I also thought, "Rahila, you are in jail because of a just cause. Your enemies are mean. If you surrender now, you won't forgive yourself later."

Prisoner of Conscience

When I was taken to jail, I was told to go to the C class. C class is for pure criminals. I protested and said that I was not a criminal. I told the woman officer that we were political prisoners and not *her* prisoners and that her duty was not to order me around or to make other women scared of me. She said, "Those who speak loudly in jail are punished." Prisoners who talk back or question the jailers are taken to the "black room" and live in solitary confinement. They give you terrible food once a day only, and you are not allowed to talk to anyone. Women in jail believe that there are ghosts in these black rooms, and they are terrified. I said, "I do not believe in ghosts." I believe in spirits. I believe in the Kalma, the Word [Qur'an]. I believe that as humans we are very strong because we live to fight injustice. I want to fight all injustice because I am a fighter.

I told the women that if we all united, we could be more powerful and demand better services. They said, "No, no, no, Rahila, we are very scared." The next day the jail superintendent came in for his rounds. The woman officer warned us that if we made any demands of the superintendent, we would be punished.

When he came to the jail, Shehla Butt[40] and I were standing in front of him. My hand was broken, and my condition was not good. I said, rather

---

40. Shehla Butt was one of Rahila's companions.

loudly, "Is this the superintendent?" He was shocked. Nobody had ever dared to call on him.

He said, "Who is calling me? I am the superintendent."

I said, "Why don't you ask us what are our problems here in the jail?"

"OK, what is your problem? What is your name?" he asked.

"My name is Rahila Tiwana. I want to have a bed because I cannot sleep on the floor," I said.

Shehla Butt said, "I need a bed because I am scared of sleeping on the floor. It is full of cockroaches." You see, Shehla was very much scared of the roaches and stayed up all night.

But the superintendent said, "You won't get a bed because you are prisoners."

We said, "Yes, we are prisoners but not *your* prisoners. We are the government's prisoners, and it is your duty to keep us safe."

He said, "OK, OK. What is your class?"

We said, "We are in B class."

He said, "What are you doing in the B class? You are criminals and have to go to the C class!"

We said, "It is not your job to tell us whether we are criminals or not. This decision has to be made in the court!" He decided to fight with us. We said, "This is an Islamic society. Why did you come to the woman's section? You are *namahram*.[41] You should not come here!"

He said, "I know you, Rahila Tiwana. You are a loudmouth and a very bad, *kharab* [morally loose] woman. Now shut your mouth and get lost!" And he left. But the women felt our energy. They were so charged by our exchange.

Then the same woman officer said, "I asked you not to do that, but you did not listen to me. Now I will beat you." She had a stick. As she was about to beat me, I grabbed her stick, but she kicked me. She said, "How dare you stop me?" I kicked her back and said, "How dare you kick me! If you continue, all these women will kick you." The women started moving closer—like this. She said, "This woman is very dangerous." Then she separated me from the others. After three days, my condition became worse. By now, my willpower was also diminished. I was finished.

I was kept in jail and not allowed to meet my mother until a week later. She

41. *Mahram* (lawful) and *namahram* (unlawful, forbidden) are legal and conceptual categories used to determine the extent of gender association and avoidance within and outside of kinship system. See Haeri 1993a, 76–78.

was sobbing, you know, when she saw me in the barracks. I got very angry with her for weeping. I did not want her to cry in front of them. I told her that they would then think I was her weakness and demand more from her. I told her to please stop crying and that, *inshallah* [God willing], we will be victorious. I was talking very loudly. I wanted them all to hear me. My mother said, "She is crazy. I think she has gone mad," and she walked out. I felt horrible, and my condition grew worse. I vomited blood. I became unconscious.

Then the police decided that they should transfer me to the hospital, but then the MQM started protesting against me. They threatened that if I was admitted to the hospital, the MQM would call a general strike. The doctors were MQM's supporters. My own party members also gathered outside the hospital and demanded that I be admitted to the hospital, but I was refused hospitalization, and they returned me to jail.

Now my condition became critical, and it would have been very bad for the police if I had died in jail. I kept vomiting blood and was physically in very bad shape. Then some [Pakistani] human rights organizations pressured the government that it was necessary for me to be transferred to the hospital. Finally, they transferred me to the hospital [January 1991], but I had to be taken to the emergency room. The whole night no doctor came to see me. Only the paramedics were there. The next morning the emergency doctor [the MQM supporter] came to see me. As soon as he found out who I was, he protested, "Who has admitted her? Get her out, get her out!"

When I saw this kind of behavior from people of my own country, I felt terribly heartbroken. Then I don't know what happened. I lost my memory. I lost every feeling. I became absolutely silent. Psychologically I felt numb. I could not remember anything. I could not identify people. I became very quiet, nonemotional. This time when I saw Ajay in jail, I was extremely quiet. I am still quiet.[42] My eyes were open, but I did not talk. It must have been a state of shock. I think it was at this time that Dr. Haroon and his wife Anis Haroon came to see me.[43] He is a great man. *He* admitted me. It was not the police who sent him to me. It was one of my companions, who happened to be a student

42. She implied that she has not recovered fully yet.

43. Dr. S. Haroon Ahmed is a professor of psychiatry at Jinnah Postgraduate Medical Center in Karachi and the president of the Pakistan Association for Mental Health. He has written and edited several books and many essays on conflict, torture, and mental health in Pakistan. See S. Ahmed 1991.

of Dr. Haroon. My friend went to see him and told him about me and told him that he should come and see me for his research.

The police were forced to allow him to come and see me in the jail. They were afraid that I might die in police custody. He arranged for me to be transferred to the psychiatric ward of the hospital. He said that I had a posttraumatic syndrome hysteria [PTSH]. I could not talk for one whole month. This was all because of the way the police had tortured me in jail. The police continued to torture me, but this time indirectly.

Dr. Haroon insisted that my mother should come there to stay with me. He and his wife were very protective of me. But now the police perpetrated another torture. They installed a [closed-circuit?] camera in my room and made two camps outside on the lawn. One camp was for the rangers, and the other was for the police, and they assigned Iqbal, a policeman, to my room. Psychologically this was very bad for me because by then I was terrified of the police. Any mention of the police or the sight of their uniform made me shiver with fear. One day my mother had gone back home to take care of something, and my little sister and one of my friends stayed with me in my room. Iqbal knocked at my door very loudly—you know, knock knock knock. I was terrified. My friend opened the door and said, "What is wrong?" He pushed her away and said, "You *get back.*" Previously he was so nice, behaving very politely, but this night his behavior was very bad. He pushed my friend out and created a big drama. My condition worsened, and the thought of these two young girls left alone outside scared me even more. The next day Iqbal brought more police with him and ordered the hospital management to gather in my room, but by that time I had a relapse, and I was unconscious, in a coma. Both my hands were twisted like this and shaking. The doctors became very worried and protested to the police, but Iqbal slapped one of the nurses and said, "Why don't you release Rahila from the hospital?" He wanted to take me back to jail.

My ordeal was now constantly covered in all the newspapers, so Jam Sadiq Ali threatened Dr. Haroon, "If you do not send Rahila back to jail, I will see you!"[44] Dr. Haroon said, "No, she *is* a genuine patient and is here for a good reason. I am on her side, and I am not your servant to obey your orders. If you want to make this decision [have her removed from the hospital], go to the National Assembly!" Jam Sadiq Ali wanted me to go crazy because he was afraid that if I recovered, I would talk and reveal their secrets. It was also dur-

44. Idiomatic way of threatening someone, meaning "I will punish you."

ing this period that several attacks were made on Dr. Haroon's office. They also attacked his wife, and she had a car accident.

I don't know why, but my doctor said that the person inside me was very frightened. He said, "You put up a brave exterior, but in reality you are scared. This fear has turned you mentally disturbed, *nafsiyati pagal*." At that time, it did not make sense to me. I was totally finished, exhausted. But still they tormented me. I was not allowed to leave my room. I did not want to look at the police because I was scared of them. I was just an ordinary student leader, yet they had enforced such tight security on me. Nobody was allowed to visit me, not even when my family and my younger sister came to see me on Eid.[45] Only the MQM doctors were allowed to visit me. They used to twist the injection needles to hurt me even more. The other doctors were not allowed inside. After that, my hand was numb, and they refused to do any checkups or tests.

Most worrying was my brother's condition in jail. Once my mother came to see me after she had visited Ajay. She was very angry with me. Others were blackmailing her, but she got angry with me. I felt very lonely. I felt rejected. She was supportive of Ajay but not of me. She did not ask me to change my stand, but she said, "One thing you should know: if something happens to my son, I will never forgive you. I will disown, *aaq*, you."[46] I said nothing, only cried and imagined myself as a *shahid*. To top it all, my brother developed jaundice. This was the last straw. These were extremely hard times for my family and me. People would frighten us that this was a very nasty disease and that he was in a dangerous condition. The police continued to behave badly. My mother would take cane juice for my brother, which is good for jaundice, but the police would take it and drink it right in front of her. It was complete blackmail. Again the government officials came to the hospital and said, "Rahila, if you do not change your statements, your brother will die in jail." When I found out that my brother's condition was very serious and that he was denied hospitalization and that the police tormented my mother by drinking the cane juice meant for Ajay, my own condition became even worse. I was very tired and exhausted. I did not know how long I could continue to fight. But still I told them, "No." Then I had my first seizure. My hands and feet were twisted, and I started foaming from the mouth. I thought, "What if my brother

45. A Muslim holy day and holiday.

46. In the context of Pakistani Muslim society, to be threatened by one's parent with being disowned is very serious.

dies. My mother would never forgive me." I felt very weak. The nights were particularly hard. I thought, "Leave it, Rahila. Najib is dead. Haroon is dead. What must Najib's mother be thinking? Why face these people? Go and face God after death. Your cause is great." But when my brother's condition became worse and was almost in his last stage, we [her family] pressured Benazir and Asif Zardari to force the government to transfer him to a hospital. We said that if Afzal Tiwana was not transferred, we would make a case [against Benazir Bhutto]. Then they said, "OK," and he was transferred to a civil hospital.

Afzal: I was sick for three months. No doctor came. Only one who came to check my eyes and gave me capsules, which were prepared inside the jail. That was it. Then Manzoor Wassan came to visit me, and he finally managed to get me transferred to the hospital.

Rahila: I was not allowed to see him, only read about his deteriorating health in the newspapers.[47] Dr. Haroon had arranged for me to get newspapers. He is so great. My father also came to visit me. He was very strong. He would tease me, calling me "a *pagal* woman." My family did not tell me much about my brother's condition in jail, but I was really suffering for Afzal, knowing that he was in jail, badly treated and beaten up. He was there for one whole year.

Then Malik Ehsan was murdered!

Shahla: "What?!"[48]

Afzal: Because he tried to collaborate with Benazir. You see, Jam Sadiq Ali was getting impatient and wanted him to conclude his investigation of us and to get our statement that implicated Benazir in a murder. I don't know why he [Malik Ehsan] agreed to meet Benazir Sahiba. Maybe because he was being unduly pressured by Jam Sadiq Ali. Anyway, he wanted to talk to Benazir Sahiba to tell her what was happening to us and how we were implicated in false cases. But Jam Sadiq Ali found out that Malik Ehsan was about to meet Benazir, and before Malik Ehsan had a chance to see her, he was murdered and his wife was prevented from holding a press conference.

I remember when I was in the civil hospital, my ward was very close to the morgue where the corpses were stored. One evening I could not sleep, and I

47. By then, Rahila had been transferred to the hospital, which was what she called a "subjail."

48. I was stunned by this news. I asked them to explain it in great detail, and the brother and sister took turns describing the events leading to his murder.

saw one dead body brought in with lots of policemen. I knew something must have happened, but I did not know that it was Malik Ehsan who had been murdered. We think because Begum Nusrat Bhutto gave a statement to the newspapers that Malik Ehsan wanted to meet Benazir, Jam Sadiq Ali had Malik Ehsan killed. Soon after, Jam Sadiq Ali himself died of cancer. Some say the type of his cancer was suspicious.

Rahila: You know, doctors were all terrified of him. When he died, it took them a whole day before they actually released the news. Even then it was very secret.

Save the Leader, Save the Nation, Save Me

The conditions in the subjail [hospital] were as bad as those in jail. Dr. Haroon and a Hindu doctor, Dr. Sunder, who is also a great man, looked after me. There was also an MQM doctor, Dr. Rizwan, who knew Najib and me and told me that he respected me. He was good to me and looked after me. He even gave me some flowers because I was not responding to anything. My senses were all numb. I was told that two things might cure me. One was to see Benazir Bhutto because my doctors thought if I could talk with her and cry, that would be good for me. Otherwise, I would be paralyzed. But when Benazir did come to see me, the police made it impossible for her to come to my room. The police surrounded the hospital and did not allow her to come and visit me. Poor woman, she had to go back. She sent her mother, Begum Nusrat Bhutto, but she, too, was forced to go back.

And the other [cure] was to see my brother recovered.

It was not until April [1991] that I began to recognize people: "This is my mother, this is my sister." For four months, I could not remember anybody, could not talk to anybody, and could not cry. Dr. Haroon said that I should try to talk, to show my feelings, to express my anger, even to break things if I wished. I still am quiet. The doctors told my mother to try to make me cry and to talk.

I was listening to a song—*vo kaghiz ki kashti vo barish ka pani* [that paper boat (that we used to float) in that rainwater][49]—when Najib's brother walked in. It

---

49. The text of the song and poem is: *ye dolat bhi lai lo / ye shohrat bhi lai lo / bhlay chean lo mujh se meri javani / magar mujh ko lota do bachpan ki yadain / vo kaghiz ki kashti vo barish ka pani* (take my wealth / take my fame / snatch my·youth from me / but give me my childhood memories back / that paper boat and that rainwater). I thank Ambreen Butt for helping me with the text and the translation of this song.

is a song about childhood. It reminded me of my brother Afzal and the stories our grandmother used to tell us. When I saw Najib's brother and thought of my own suffering brother in jail, I broke down crying. I cried and cried and cried.[50] I don't know why I cried so much at that time [pause, pensive].

My wish was to cry all the time, very loudly—screaming—but I did not want to be seen by anyone. No one has ever seen me crying, not even my mother. If I felt sad, I would go outside to our lawn or to the bathroom to cry. But in the hospital I could not fulfill my wish, so I would listen to a tape [of music] at nights in the dark and then cry. As I cried, I would think about my parents' *bebasi*, helplessness. I felt very bad for them and for the shame I had brought to the family. I am the first woman [in her family] who went to jail. This is very bad for my family because I have four sisters. This gave a bad name to the family.

From the medical point of view, crying was very good for me. My parents' morale was high now because Dr. Haroon talked to them about me. They were there for me. Dr. Haroon said, "Rahila, you talk now," and I began to talk. I talked for two hours nonstop. I was talking all about the jail's conditions. I kept crying and pleading with them to please save Benazir because these people were going to kill her. Malik Ehsan, Samiullah Marwat, and Mohammad Khan, even Irfanullah Marwat and Jam Sadiq Ali—all told me, "If you do not cooperate with us, we will kill Benazir." I love Benazir a lot. She is our leader, and I love her. She is the only person who can get rid of every bad law and custom in my country. I love her too much, and I was very scared for her all the time when I was in jail.

When I was released in September 1991, I was not yet in a normal condition. Dr. Haroon said that I should not be having any new stress burden my mind, that I should relax and not think. Dr. Haroon said that it normally takes three to five years for all those who suffer from posttraumatic syndrome to get well, but he said that I was strong and had will power and would be able to recover in one year. But I did not feel well. In fact, I thought my condition was very bad. Now [May 1993] I feel relaxed, and I have gotten my admission to Sindh Muslim Law College. Classes have started, and I am taking a few

50. I met Dr. Haroon Ahmed and his wife, Anis Haroon, and talked about Rahila's situation. With Rahila's consent, Dr. Haroon showed me the unedited videotape of his conversation with her. I also saw the edited version of the same session, which Dr. Haroon had prepared for a conference on PTSH. Rahila was sobbing the whole time, her hands were twisted, and her face reflected the terror and the unspeakable pain she had endured.

courses at a time. I am taking it easy. I still see Dr. Haroon because I am constantly scared. This is true. Even now, every time I go home, I feel as if the police are coming to get me. My brother, my mother, and little sister also feel very disturbed. If we hear a knock at the door or the telephone ring, we jump. Sometimes when I am talking to you, for example, I feel you are not Shahla, but a policewoman. Sometimes I dream with open eyes, day or night. I am afraid they may catch me again and take me back to the jail or the CIA Center. When I hear of horrible cases or I read of similar cases in the newspaper, I have bad dreams.

Dreams of Survival

I forgot to tell you something. When I was in the CIA Center and being tortured, Subinspector Tayyaba went to visit a holy man, Abbas Sahib, to get me a ta'wiz, protective charm. She told him that Rahila was arrested. He said, "Go and tell her that I am with her and that she should recite the four Quls[51] in the morning. If she recites them ten times, I am with her." Abbas Sahib knows me because every time my mother has a problem, she goes to him for help.

The same night I dreamed of a holy man in green clothes,[52] with a beautiful white beard, a green turban,[53] a long green kurta, and a white dhoti,[54] approaching me with a tasbih, rosary, in his hand. Milk was flowing from his tasbih. He said to me, "You pagal girl! You should not be afraid. You are not an ordinary girl. Why you are sitting like this? Stand up and come with me!" After that, I saw huge dogs, you know, bulldogs, very angry bulldogs, with dyed hair. I saw

51. The four Quls are short suras (chapters) in the Qur'an, all of which begin with the word qul, "say" (Qur'an 109, 112, 113, 114).

52. Green is symbolically significant for Muslims because the first time the archangel Gabriel appeared to the Prophet Muhammad, the hue of his wings turned the sky green (according to a lecture given by Seyyed Hossein Nasr on angels in Islam at Harvard University, April 12, 2000). The color green is particularly meaningful for Pakistanis because it is the color of the Pakistani flag. See also Corbin 1971, 76–80, and his discussion of Najm Kobra's (1145–1226) theory of colors, where the latter argues that "The color green is the sign of the life of the heart" and is one that "outlasts the others," that "the mountain of Qaf . . . wholly takes on the coloration of the Emerald Rock which is its summit" (13).

53. According to popular belief among the Sufis in South Asia, a "pir's spiritual power is connected with the green color of the emerald," which can blind the eyes of the serpents or the enemies of faith (Schimmel 1986, 113, 309).

54. A kurta is a long shirt or a tunic, and a dhoti is a piece of cloth worn round the waist, passing between the legs and fastened at the back.

Malik Ehsan and Samiullah Marwat and all the others. I saw so many dogs, but I kept on passing them by. I was very scared, but I was holding the holy man's hands tightly. We passed an entire pack of dogs. Then he said, "Aamir, take her hand."[55] And he told me, "Rahila, go with him." I said, "No, please, please, I don't want to go with him." But he said, "This is my order. He will get you across safely." He held me with one hand and told me not to be afraid. You know, he said that he could not go beyond that point. Then Aamir said, "Come with me." But I was very scared. We passed more angry dogs. They were watching me. They would have liked to eat me, but they did not touch me. The dogs sat like this—very obedient.

The next day I told Auntie [Subinspector] Tayyaba about my dream. She said, "Rahila, do you know who is Hazrat Zainul Abedin?[56] You must have seen him in your dream. He was often ill. I prayed all night to Hazrat Zainul Abedin because you were also so ill. This is a *mujeza*, a miracle!" Auntie Tayyaba is now an inspector. When Benazir was in the Larkana jail, she was also her guard. She is a Benazir supporter. All Shi'a families support Zulfikar Ali Bhutto and Nusrat Bhutto because they are also Shi'ites. Auntie Tayyaba is Urdu speaking and a Shi'a. But then Fahima Rima is also a Shi'a and Urdu speaking, but she does not support us because she is a *munafiq*, hypocrite.[57]

When I was in the hospital, I would also dream of people with very long faces, especially policemen, who were coming to arrest me and take me away. Big men with long horrible faces, running after me, chasing me, and I was running away. My biggest fear was an attack on my honor—*meri izzat ke upar hath na dalain*. I saw people running after me, and I was running and running. My only reason for running away was that I only wanted security for my *izzat*.[58] I

55. Aamir was a family friend to whom she apparently had made a promise of marriage. At that time, he was living in the United States.

56. Hazrat Zainul Abedin was a son of Imam Hussain from his Persian wife, the daughter of the Iranian Sassanid king, Yazdigird. He is the only son of Imam Hussain who survived the tragedy of Karbala in 680 C.E. because he was ill. Instead, he was taken captive with Zainab and the rest of the women and children and presented at Yazid's court. He is the fourth Shi'i imam.

57. The term *munafiq*, hypocrite, is politically and historically very meaningful for Muslims. There is a chapter in the Qur'an (63) called "Al-Munafiqun."

58. The significance of keeping women's virtue intact is pervasive in South Asia. Nanada writes, "Bahuchara was a pretty, young maiden in a party of travelers passing through the forest in Gujarat. The party was attacked by thieves, and, fearing that they would outrage her modesty, Bahuchara drew her dagger and cut off her breast, offering it to the outlaws in place of her

dreamed that they were approaching me, and I was shouting for help.[59] They attacked me, and I saw my *dupata* being ripped apart.[60] They also attacked Afzal and cut him up into pieces. In my dream, the dogs attacked Benazir's neck. They actually caught me [61] because a policewoman told us horrible stories. She said that she got orders from her superiors to supply them with jailed girls and women. At nights, many of the officers got together and arranged for girls to visit them. She said that "they rape them without rest in a closed room.[62] God knows what they do to them." I felt sick. Then she told us that next time was our turn.[63] We were terrified. She said that the good-looking women prisoners who are poor and have no family support or influential backers are particularly targeted. They are then provided to men with big houses and palaces.

You see, it was her [Tayyaba's] duty to provide those girls. When I heard all this, I made a decision that when I got out of jail and I was fully recovered, I would work with women prisoners. So many women are tortured by the police and at the CIA Center, but they get no help from the government at all. We have a blind government and unhelpful laws. I hate everything. The women have nowhere to go. If they say that the police have raped them, the police accuse them of being *gandi* and *kharab*, bad and corrupt women, and

virtue" (1996, 25). Although subsequently she died, her self-mutilation and sexual purity led to her deification. She is one of the most important goddesses in the Indian subcontinent.

59. Schimmel relates the legend of the *haft afifa*, "the Seven Chaste" women saints from Sindh, who "escaped a group of attacking soldiers and were swallowed by the earth before their virtue could be touched" (1986, 434).

60. In his novel *Shame*, Salman Rushdie satirizes the symbolic value of "the green dupatta of modesty" (1983, 63). The *dupata* is a long rectangular scarf worn by Pakistani women as an indispensable part of their two-piece national attire. The *dupata* is associated popularly with women's modesty and chastity. No respectable Pakistani woman leaves home without it. However, in 1982, rebelling against the military dictatorship of General Zia, some Pakistani women organized a *dupata*-burning session, very much reminiscent of the American feminists' bra-burning episodes.

61. I asked her, "Did they actually catch you in your dream?"

62. Rahila used the word *rape* throughout, never using any indigenous term. There is really not one term in Urdu that can be translated as *rape*. There are several composite words that imply the act, such as *ismat dari karna, zina bil jabr,* and, most poignant of all, one that has to do with the shame of dishonor, *us ki izzat loot gai*"—"she whose honor is plundered."

63. These comments give me the impression that the policewoman might have told them such horror stories to scare them and so to encourage them to cooperate with the police.

then they turn around and bring charges of *zina*, adultery, against them.[64] Besides, Pakistani laws are against women and favor men. I met some of these women [described by Tayyaba], and when I asked them about this [rape], they said when they were tortured, their hands were tied.

No, not like me.[65] *Their* hands were tied in opposite directions. Then their clothes were taken off, and they were raped. It is very horrible. Is this what you call a Muslim society? You know, in the CIA Center and in all the *tahnas*, police stations, a standard police torture is to undress women. When a woman is arrested, if she does not agree to the policemen's demand, she is then undressed and made to wait like that. The police did not dare to treat me similarly because they knew that I belong to a very strong family and a powerful lineage. This was God's help for us, and [Subinspector] Mumtaz also helped me. They also did not touch me because I was unmarried. Fahima Rima and I were both unmarried girls, so I think this was a good thing for both of us. Fahima was not touched at all because she compromised [cooperated] with the police. But I think they do it to married women.[66] You know the cases of Khurshid Begum and Veena Hayat?[67] They both made allegations against the government and the police.

Dishonor: The Shame of Rape

A woman told my mother, "If Rahila makes the [rape] allegations against the government, her case will be very strong." My mother said, "If my daughter did not accept the government's allegations against Benazir, why would she make false accusations against the government? Don't you ever say something like this again because nothing like that happened! She is still clean." I have had so many medical tests and check-ups. So many times I feel very angry be-

64. On *zina* and the impact of Islamization policies, see chapter 1, the section on Pakistan's origin myth.

65. I asked her, "Is this how they tied your hands?"

66. Wendy Doniger argues that people use fantasies of replacement, displacement, and doubling to deal with violence and fear: "it happened to someone else, it wasn't me." Talk given at Boston University, September 8, 1998.

67. Veena Hayat was a close friend of Benazir Bhutto and her husband and is a daughter of a very prominent Pakistani leader. Khurshid Begum is a washerwoman whose husband was a PPP supporter. They both made allegations of rape against Irfanullah Marwat and Jam Sadiq Ali. See Bakhtiar 1992 and Haeri 1995b.

cause this is not politics. Why do people make such wrong allegations? I am telling the truth.[68] That is enough! [emphatic]

Dr. Haroon and Dr. Karim told my mother and me, "You should not lose your temper at any point, and you should not be disappointed. People say these kinds of things. Stay calm." My mother used to cry and say, "Everyone in the family talks about her. She will never get married." For me, this has been a very hard period. I have gone through many *imtihanon*, tests. I am a very shy woman. I don't even talk to my mother about women's problems. Sometimes I feel I am not well because, you know, during my monthly problems I have pain. But I do not show it. I don't even tell it to my doctor. But in this matter [allegations of rape], I am very strong. I say, "No, this is wrong. This is loose talking."

But sometimes, you know, Malik Ehsan's language was very filthy. It felt like a rape. He used dirty language for Benazir and her husband, too. They said that Benazir had relations with other men. They said Najib and I had relations and that I must have had an abortion. They knew Najib was a good friend of mine, but Najib and I were respectful of each other like a brother and sister. I am not used to this type of language. I am a very shy woman, you know. I felt, "Please, *zamin*, earth, open up and hide me inside." His language was very, very bad, so was Mohammad Khan's. They drank bottles [of liquor], and then Malik Ehsan would say, "Rahila, if you do not agree or if you do not cooperate, then half [of the bottle] for you and half for me. Then we enjoy you." Very bad language. When some of my companions and comrades objected, Malik Ehsan got mad and said, "Shut your mouth when I am talking." We had to face this kind of mental torture constantly. You know, every time Malik Ehsan opened the door and entered our cell, we got terrified.

Childhood Upbringing and Kinship

I was born on April 30, 1964, in my grandfather's village in Mirzay Wallah in Jaran Wallah, which is a district of Faisalabad in Punjab. Our background is very historic because we belong to the Tiwana *qabilah*, tribe. The Tiwanas were converts from the Sikhs, and my ancestors converted to Islam, and we are seventh-generation Muslim. By the time of the creation of Pakistan, my grandfather, Khaizer Hayat Tiwana, was the king of our tribe. He used to live

---

68. Whether she was raped was the subject of newspaper and popular speculations.

in Karachi. Hotel Faran used to be a Tiwana house, which belonged to my grandfather. He had a high-ranking position in the police department. One more promotion would have made him a commissioner, I think. He traveled all the time, and his children were growing up not knowing much about their own *qabilah*. My grandfather felt that his children were being spoiled in the city and decided to take them back to his village and to his tribe. He sold the Tiwana House and returned to our village, where we have our Mitha Tiwana [most Tiwanas are from here] in Sargodha. My younger sister is to go to *mitha* Tiwana after her [arranged] marriage to my father's cousin.

My paternal grandfather married seven times but did not have children from all of his marriages. Altogether he had two daughters and four sons. But at this time I have only one step uncle and two aunties. My extended family owned many farms, and because of the *jagirdar*, feudal system, they behaved like feudal lords. My father did not like my grandfather's policies and did not get along with him. By nature, he is respectful of human rights and does not like killing other humans.[69] So he left Punjab and went to Karachi, but used to go home, like an angry kid, to get money and return to Karachi. He joined the People's Party and was one of the most active members of the party.

My mother's father was an Afghan Pathan who migrated to Lucknow, India, and settled there. She was born in Lucknow. He was a police inspector during the British period and died six months before my mother was born. He was killed by some *dacoits*,[70] armed robbers, in a police raid before Pakistan came to being. After that my *nani*, grandmother, who was only seventeen years old, migrated to Pakistan. My mother has no siblings. She is a very fine and a different [kind of] woman. My paternal grandfather gave them shelter in his home and looked after her family. For a long time, my mother did not know that she had a separate father. But she knew one thing, that the girls were to marry within the Tiwana tribe. That is why mother taught us all about the Rajput

69. I am not exactly sure what she is alluding to here. My guess is that her father did not appreciate the harsh treatment of peasants that is common among the land-owning families.

70. The *Hobson-Jobson* dictionary, edited by H. Yule and A. G. Burnell ([1886] 1989) defines a *dacoit* as a robber belonging to an armed gang. The term, being current in Bengal, got into the penal code. By law, to constitute *dacoity* there must be five or more in the gang committing the crime. In 1817, Sir Henry Strachey observed: "The crime of dacoity has, I believe, increased greatly since the British administration of justice" (290).

code of honor and behavior—because she knew we would be marrying into this family and so we should know everything about them.

By the time my mother was thirteen years old—she was very beautiful— my *dada* [paternal grandfather] asked my grandmother to allow him to marry her daughter to his son, my father. He was afraid that otherwise someone else might take her away. My father was nineteen when they got married. That is how my mother got married into my *dada*'s family and got her *tarbiyat*, upbringing, in that household as a Rajput girl. She adopted all the qualities of the Rajput women, even though she is a Pathan by blood. So both our bloodlines are strong. Because my grandfather was a king of our *qabilah*, nobody disagreed with his choice of a non-Tiwana bride. We lived in the village until I was four years old. Then Abbu brought Ammi to Karachi after the death of my grandfather.

When we were in Karachi, my mother constantly told us that we are Rajputs, that we belong to a great family, that we have to look after our characters, and that we should not socialize with bad friends or meet with unsuitable families. I also read some books [on the Rajputs], and when we visited my grandfather's house and village, women were very proud of us precisely because we are Rajputs. Rajput women are very proud of themselves and do not want to talk to anyone [but the family members]. They say they would rather starve and not have many facilities than to marry outside of the family. They want to stay within the family because it has a big name. When we were young, we used to think they were silly to think like that. Later on in life, we realized how much other people look up to our family and respect a Rajput girl. We realized that people respect us. Therefore, to safeguard their respect we could not do anything bad.

When we were kids, many of Mother's in-laws did not treat us well, for a variety of reasons.[71] But now that we are grown up and my sisters are very beautiful, many in our family want us for their boys. But now my mother has decided that if we see a man from a good family, we should marry him and not necessarily marry within the family. She has said no to some of them. People say to my father, "Poor Fazal"—that is his name—"he has four daughters" [laughing]. My mother says, "They are *rahmat*, Allah's blessing. My daughters are very important, every single one of them. Look, all my daughters are

---

71. I asked her, "How did your mother's in-laws treat her as an outsider?"

proper and well behaved. I mean, they know all about housekeeping." I think this is very good change of attitude for us. My mother is a very good mother. She has taught us everything.

When my parents came to Karachi to live, according to our family tradition my mother was to be given two servants as part of her *jahiz*, dowry.[72] But my mother said, "If I keep these servants, my daughters will be spoiled, and they will not learn anything. Who knows what kind of future marriage arrangement they will have?" So she returned them. We used to get mad because none of our cousins did anything, but we had to do all the housework. We used to feel insulted, but our mother was very strict. Now all our male cousins are very impressed by us because we are able to have a conversation in good company. At first, they [the in-laws] spoke badly of Ammi because she put us in coeducational schools. They said it is all her fault and that our father is *beghayrat*, shameless, without honor, because he is letting his daughters go to coeducational institutions. But my parents are very good friends [with each other]. They have discussions before making any decision. Sometimes they might fight, but they always have table talks,[73] and afterward they consult with us. They take our opinion into account. This has created self-confidence in us. Many families gather at table to gossip and talk badly about others, but we always have dinner together, and my father discusses all kinds of issues with us.

I remember my parents were both very active members of the People's Party. They were crazy about Zulfikar Bhutto. A major reason was that Bhutto was very supportive of women's rights. My mother has a big picture of Bhutto in her room in our house. We listened to all his political talks and everything that has to do with Bhutto. Naturally I grew up to be a Bhutto supporter.

Religion and Politics: Learning the Political Ropes

Before entering college, I knew I wanted to work with people, to help people. When I was in the tenth grade, I became interested in the Tablighi Jama'at and their idea of human rights.[74] This is before I became involved with the PPP.

72. Whereas *mahr*, the gift and payment legally owing to a wife from her husband at the time of marriage, is commonly translated as "dower" in Pakistan, the payment and gifts given to the husband from the wife's family is also known as *jahiz*, "dowry" (Esposito 1982, 87).

73. "Table talk" was one of her expressions, by which she meant negotiation or discussion.

74. On Tablighi Jama'at, see M. Ahmad 1991.

You know, I love Qur'an and everything related to it. My father does not say *namaz*, his prayers, or *rozah*, fast, but my mother is very devout. I learned to read the Qur'an when I was in the eighth grade and joined Qur'an classes in our colony. This included reading the Qur'an, interpretation and translation. Some rich senior officers' wives arranged these classes on Saturday evenings. I felt they treated poor people rudely. I asked them why they did so because the Qur'an does not teach this, and God does not like snobs. One of the wives told me to mind my own business. She said that Qur'an and personal life each have their own place. Then one day we finished reading Surat al-Nur (Qur'an 24) in which there are passages warning one against *tuhmat*, false accusations. I heard some women gossiping about other women. The Qur'an clearly says that she who talks behind someone's back and she who listens to it are both partners, and God will not be their partner because Allah Pak would be very angry. When I brought this to their attention, the officer's wife became angry with me, accusing me of loose talking. She showed no respect for me because she thought she was big [important]. I told her, "Auntie, there is no difference between big or small. This is God's order." But Auntie was angry with me.

My father used to laugh at me and told me that I was wasting my time. He said, "Why do you waste your time? This is politics of *begums* and rich ladies. They give *dars* [Islamic education] in the air-conditioned rooms to amuse themselves. They should go to small areas and teach the Kalma there. That is the real *dars*. Like our holy Prophet, they should join ordinary people and do hard work." I said, "OK, I will do this hard work." I started going to low-income areas in the same colony or in nearby smaller villages, where people did not know the Kalma and started teaching them. Then I joined the Tablighi Jama'at and used to go to small areas to teach Qur'an lessons. My father was still laughing at me. His view was: "Rahila is crazy. She believes in mullahs because she is emotional and always takes an extremist stand." Mother just laughed and would not say anything. My parents firmly believe that children learn by their mistakes. Therefore, there is no need to pressure them.

Then one day I saw Aftab, one of my classmates with whom I had done my metric [matriculation or tenth grade] in 1982. When he realized that I had become a religious fanatic, he said, "Rahila, when you work from a small platform, your struggle becomes small. Why don't you join us and empower your voice, *avaz ko taqat var banado*, from a larger platform?" I was in the first year of college and said, "I won't do it. I hate them [the Bhuttos]." He said, "You should not hate before you find out more about them. Besides, what are your reasons for hating them?" I said, "Bhutto is a *kafir*, infidel, because he drinks." He said, "Who doesn't drink? These are stupid reasons." You see, because of my religious lessons, I had come to believe that women who wear the veil are better. These women were against Bhutto and thought that he was a *kafir*, and so was his daughter because of the way she dressed. Besides, she was jailed, and decent girls did not go to jail. I was young and repeated whatever I heard.

When Bhutto Sahib was murdered, my father was demoted and severely punished for being a party member. They were going to throw him out of his job, but there were too many people from my family in the army. Instead, they discontinued my school bus. You see, at that time [1979], I was very interested in the arts. I loved them, and I wanted to be a great artist, like my uncle Sameeh. I got admission on the basis of my talent because otherwise they admit only intermediate students [equivalent to twelfth grade of U.S. high school) at the Arts Council. But I got admitted after my tenth grade because they saw my talent and also because I was related to Sameeh. But then Bhutto was hanged. The managing director of our colony stopped my bus [service] and did not allow me to use it any more. I was then very angry at Bhutto. I felt like I wanted to kill somebody.

Now I realize the reasons why I turned against Bhutto. When the bus service was taken away from me and all other services were taken away from my father, then I questioned what had Bhutto done that was so *bad*, such a big sin that being his supporter was considered such a big offence! This must have been a great *gunah*, sin. I thought we were penalized because my father took Bhutto's side. There was so much security on us. I started hating lots of things. For a year after I was admitted to college, every time I opened an art book, I wept. That year I could not take my exams because I cried a lot for this loss, as if a child had been taken away from her mother. It was very painful. My mother said, "When you are older, you can learn the arts, but now you should finish your education."

I can understand it now. I was a child then and had limited thinking. Besides, I was surrounded by a group of religious people. After that, I started reading, and my *zehn*, mind, got enlightened, *khulta chila*, that what mullahs teach us is not Islam. In fact, Islam is exactly what Bhutto was telling us. Then I started my own research on Qur'an by studying the interpretation of the Qur'an. I studied by myself because my father used to read a lot. My father's room is like a library. He has done his law degree. Abbu used to leave books by my bedside. When I returned from school or college, I would look at them. In the beginning, I did not enjoy them. Then he gave me books on the struggle of the Palestinian people and an English translation of a book about the Russian Revolution. He gave me the novels of Nasim Hijazi, who is a famous writer in Pakistan. My father would not say anything. He would just leave them there, and I would pick them up and read them. This is how my mind totally changed. Father also gave me literature on the behavior of the army and why they hated Bhutto. After that, I started hating the army.

Taking Action, Joining the Student Federation

During 1983, I read and researched about PSF and the People's Party, and with Aftab's encouragement I joined PSF in 1984. Aftab introduced me to his friend Najib, who was the president of a small unit of PSF at that time. Najib and Tariq Aziz Masudi later became my best friends.

Everyone inside PSF respected Tariq Masudi. He was considered to be a very intelligent and sensible person. It was said about him that he could change minds. That's why he was told he could change Rahila's mind, that she was a very bold girl and that if she joined PSF, it would be very good for the organization because they did not have a girls' wing in the PSF. You see, in a planning meeting they had, Dr. Zafar Arif, a high-ranking party man who used to instruct them, had told them that they needed a girl who would be bold and capable of taking a stand. Aftab knew me since high school. He remembered me from a fight that had erupted between members of the ninth and tenth classes. I was in the ninth class. Many of us were consequently blacklisted. When the colonel[75] came [to school], I was the first person who threw a stone at his car. I was standing right in front of his car. The colonel got out and said, "What is it?" I said, "Why have you blacklisted both our classes?" He said, "So that no child will act this way in the future." We said, "This is not a fair decision." You know, in my school I was also a leader. Aftab remembered that.

Father used to be very strict and did not allow us to go out with boys, even though he let us attend a coeducational school. We were also not allowed to walk around the neighborhood or play in the playground. We had to stay home and read books all the time. But my mother is very bold and would tell my father, "You should believe in your daughters. If you trust your daughters, then your daughters will honor your trust and confidence in them. If you do

75. I assume that her high school was in the same army colony where they lived.

not trust them, they will behave like thieves, act sneakily." So gradually our friends could visit us at home, and we kept good company. Around this time, Aftab came to our house to get my father's permission to let me join politics. My father also wanted me to join the party, as he had already been in the Peoples' Party.

The women's wing was not in the People's Party, but in PSF, which was located in the college. My companions said, "We want Rahila to represent us." Then I was made president of a district in late 1984. I did very little studying. Instead, I would go to college, and there, with my friends, we would pass out literature and discuss political issues. I would go to the canteen and start talking very loudly: "Bhutto was a very good man because he provided a good college education for us. But where are your teachers and your friends now? Why do they not get us books or provide sports facilities?" I gathered all of my best friends in the colleges, and we agitated for a better use of the college funds. One of my closest friends was Farhat.

I said to her, "You know, the college receives funds for education, but we never see them used in the college. There are no books in the library, no scientific resources, nothing. We don't have any sports facilities although we pay the fees for it and our parents have to bear all those costs. If we ask Miss [the teacher], she says, 'We don't know.' Where does everything disappear?"

She said, "Rahila, what should we do?"

I said, "Let us take a stand!" Then we made groups of five girls to go and fight with the madam.[76]

In Pakistan, if you want to shift the blame, the easiest way to do it is to spoil that person's reputation. Blame the girl for being *bad kirdar*, a bad character.[77] She will then be in a difficult situation to defend herself and will be intimidated. This is what the college did to us. They said that we did not have good characters. They threatened us that if we did not stop our activities, they would send letters to our fathers. I discussed this in the meetings with my friends Najib and Tariq and told them that I was *khauf zadah*, worried.

When I joined PSF, I did not tell my parents about it. I was scared because my father was very strict and did not like us making friends with boys or joining PSF, where there were all boys and not a single girl. I was the first girl

---

76. Principals and head mistresses are called "madams."

77. "Bad character" in a Pakistani context means "loose morals" and is used to describe a girl who befriends a boy and has sexual relations.

who joined PSF. It was after six months and after I had become very active that I got my father's permission. What happened was that Aftab and Najib came and talked to my parents. They said, "Auntie, Uncle, please, we request that you give permission to Rahila. She is a very shy woman." You see, I am very strict. I don't know why, but this is my nature. My behavior was very strict—even rude—with my cousins because I knew that they were interested in me. If I were to be free with them, they would propose [marriage] or say something. I was not strict or rude with Najib and Aftab, only with my cousins. So my mother said to them, "Her behavior is not good with her cousins, and if you take her to the federation, how would she get along with you? She is like a Hitler.[78] Why do you want to make her president? She is not suitable because she is a very shy and religious woman." My parents did not know yet how involved I was. Then Najib and Aftab said, "Auntie, this is our headache. We promise you that Rahila will trust us. We are responsible for her *izzat* and everything. You should trust us and give her permission." Najib said, "I will pick her up and drop her back if you give her permission." My mother said, "She is the one to decide." And my father said, "We have never stopped our kids. They are responsible for their actions. If she wants, she can go." Then I said, "I want to join PSF." My father said, "If you want to join, then work with *imandari*, honesty, and don't consider it a joke. Otherwise, you will lose your *zindagi*, life. When you start this work, *pahna*—wear it like you wear a dress."

We started our struggle under martial law and organized many student meetings, but all in secret places. We made business placards. Because I am a good artist, I made very good drawings for posting, all in secret. Nobody knew my face, only my name, or that a woman in PSF was doing this work. We had a promotion in the Karachi division of PSF. Najib was made a general secretary, and I became the girls' president. The police were watching us all the time, but we continued our movement at the University of Karachi. Sometimes we met in my house because nobody suspected our house of any activities. In one of these meetings, we decided to boycott our classes. Our objective was to unite students under one platform to get rid of martial law. We wanted democracy. We organized a rally of PSF in March 1987 and invited all the student federations of Pakistan, and all our 150 girls took part in it.

78. "She is a Hitler" was another of Rahila's expressions, by which she meant being tough or strict with some men.

All my companions were arrested. Najib was the first to be arrested. No girls were yet arrested. When I went home, I received a telephone message from one of my companions: "Rahila, the police are making raids, and everyone has been arrested. You should leave your home." I was so worried. I talked with a friend and told her that I would go to her house under some pretext and spend a week there. I told my mother that my friend was getting married, and I needed to spend this time with her to celebrate it. I stayed there for two days when I received Najib's message: "Go back to your house because we have reached an agreement with the government that if they arrest or try to catch our girls, we will make *giriftari*, trouble, for them. We have told them that we have presented ourselves for arrest, that they can arrest us, torture us, but they cannot do this to our girls." Najib was detained for two months. Did you see the "Free Najib" placard in our house yesterday? I made it! All eleven members from the Karachi division were arrested. Only I was outside. My friends asked me to organize a demonstration with the girls inside the university. You saw that picture of ours where we were demonstrating. They were all girls from the university—about fifteen of them.

We did not get our instructions from the PPP, Benazir, or other party leaders.[79] The instructions came only from the students. We were liberals; we made our own decisions. Besides, PSF would not take any instructions from the high command. But now we had to make our policies in coordination with People's Party. Before, we were free, and we did not work under PPP. We had our own policies. We worked under Najib because Najib was very powerful in PSF. He was a student leader and a gift from God for Pakistani students. But after him we did not have a good president. Everyone was a black sheep, a spy. They were not sincere. Najib was a sincere boy. Najib and I had a lovely coordination because I was very sincere, too. We had gathered all the different *qaumoun*, ethnic groups and races, to make our Karachi division. We worked hard and had strong coordination. Whatever decision we took, we took it jointly and firmly. If we had a meeting, a job, a demonstration, or if we were doing a strike, we preplanned everything in detail.

Then something happened that was unprecedented. Usually the students who graduate with a master's degree receive it within the university, but under the martial law in 1987, Ghaus Ali Shah, the governor of Sindh, or-

---

79. I asked her about the nature of the relationship between the PSF and the PPP and about the hierarchy of command and control.

dered that the degrees must be picked up from the governor's house. Obviously he was afraid of entering the university, and also he was very arrogant. This was a big insult to the students. We decided that no student should go there. That is why in September 1987 we took over the university, surrounded it, and told him that he should come to the university to award us our degrees.

We were arrested after that. By then, Najib had been let out of jail, but he was arrested again. The police filed cases against Najib for *dacoity*, armed robbery. They alleged that Najib and all his companions were *dacoits*. But, you know, Najib is *har dil aziz*, loved by everyone. Even ordinary and neutral people wanted him out and demanded his release. He was released after one month but with many cases pending against him. The police alleged that he had ammunition. He *was* a very crazy boy, but he never had ammunition! I was arrested, too, but only for two hours.

This time the police were not that bad. They were cautious because we were all girls from the university. You know, we were arrested after our companions blocked every road but one and burned tires. They maintained their roadblock for nine hours, and after that the police opened it. The government was very scared and under pressure because this was a very big student federation. The police were very angry and tried to talk to us: "You are *achchhi*, good girls. Why are you doing this? Why do you support Bhutto? He was a criminal, and you know that! Bhutto's daughter is also a criminal. She is not a good lady. She has destroyed our *qaum*, nation. She is a *kharab*, bad woman and is spoiling our girls [is a bad role model]." Oh, it was so very sad. Then a policeman said, "You must stop these kinds of activities." But we started singing Bhutto songs, which disturbed the police more because we were not scared.

My parents had no idea that I was arrested for a few hours. We were arrested around three in the afternoon, and I got home around seven. My mother is a good friend, and I told her everything honestly. She said, "Oh, God." I said, "But I am released. I am standing in front of you." My mother calmed down a little bit and said, "OK, but you be careful now."

A New Order: Death of a Military Leader

Then General Zia died on August 17, 1988. His plane exploded over the Ojhri Camp in Punjab. In Karachi, we stood in awe. Just prior to that, our student federation, in a show of unity, had decided to have a big convention to announce the united students' platform. We had arranged a very big convention in the university and were planning to have a big demonstration against General Zia, all planned for August 18. Benazir was to come to the university and join in the celebration. Then at noon we heard that Zia was killed! We were very happy, really very happy. But then Benazir called us and said, "If you have your convention now, it will be very bad for us under the circumstances." We thought, "Oh God, why didn't you have this [Benazir's call?] happen yesterday so that we could have the opportunity to announce the cancellation!" We were all so upset because we lost one lakh of rupees, the money we had worked hard to earn by fund-raising and selling tickets.[80] We had arranged for this convention six months in advance. We were in tears—Najib, Tariq, Amin Mustoyi, and I. We said, "No, *please.*" But she said to be patient and not to worry. Besides, we were rid of Zia ul-Haq! That was great news. We consoled each other that if we had to cancel our convention, it was because of Zia's death. Then further news came out from the Ojhri Camp, and we learned that the bomb was planted in a crate of mangoes that were presented to Zia from the army and that some general was involved. We do not know exactly what happened because the mystery explosion has not been solved yet.

When I was detained and interrogated at the CIA Center, Mohammad Khan said, "Tell me, how did you people kill General Zia?"

I remember my reply vividly. I said, "Oh, you know, Najib was a very naughty boy. He liked to play with his *ghulel,* sling shot. He used a little stone and targeted, *nishana,* the general's plane and the whole thing exploded. Najib was surprised, too!"

"Shut up," he said. "You are making fun of me."

I said, "You are making fun of *me.* This is a very big case, and you question me about it? Shame on you!"

In March 1989, we arranged a big rally, demanding the abolition of the CIA Center, a ban on all arms in the university, and the creation of a new educational curriculum.[81] We invited all the students to unite under this platform to continue our struggle toward these goals. You see, some students did have

---

80. I asked her, "Where did you get so much money?"

81. By then, Pakistan had held its first postmilitary election and Benazir Bhutto had been elected as the prime minister.

weapons.[82] There was no education in the college, but only clashes between different groups, and students dying. We demanded a stop to all clashes, and all [student] federations joined us except for MQM. Because this was in March, our slogans were "First March," "Long March," "Our March." We had a huge rally and went over to the Mausoleum of Quaid-i-Azam. People were very surprised to see so many strong girls attending the rally.

Do you know, when I was in jail, my jailers told me that they were shocked to see me mobilizing so many girls. They said, "You are a dangerous girl. We have special orders to stop you and make you an *ibrat*, example, so that no other girl ever dares to join the student party or lead it."

Our rally was a huge success. We were arrested afterward but were soon released. This boosted our morale. We joined forces for the next election. We planned where and how to cooperate with the PPP, and in the polling station we tried to educate the public, and we arranged our party's duties. We campaigned for the party, and our companions performed many duties for the election and for Benazir Bhutto. Since she had became our prime minister, we had so many crises because now we were the *sarkari*, government. This time we were called *sarkari ghundah*, bullies and bad characters. So we [PSF] decided on a cooling policy toward the People's Party.

In the meantime, because Najib was Urdu speaking,[83] the MQM wanted to claim him as a hero for the new generation. Najib was famous and challenged the MQM for calling themselves *muhajir*. He said, "I am not a *muhajir*, a refugee [from India]. *Muhajir* means suffering.[84] I am a Pakistani. I was born in Islamabad. Why don't you say you are Pakistanis? Pakistan *is* our homeland." This kind of talk made the MQM very scared of Najib. He was a very bold boy, very handsome. When the MQM did not succeed in winning him over, they decided to kill him and started using blackmailing tactics.

I don't know why Benazir bargained with the MQM to make a coalition

82. On various student federations in Pakistan, their rivalries and conflicts, and their resort to violence in the major universities in Pakistan, see I. Malik 1997, 123–25, and Nasr 1994.

83. "Urdu speaking" often means a person whose history goes back to India and who emigrated to Pakistan after partition, hence a *muhajir* or refugee.

84. *Muhajir* literally means a refugee, but in the context of the painful partition of the subcontinent and in the language of the MQM it connotes suffering, deprivation, and discrimination.

government [pensive].[85] She had said she would never do so. The MQM is a terrorist party. Our student federation did not like that and did not agree with her compromise. We hate the MQM because we lost so many of our companions to them. We thought it was not fair, but because our leadership had agreed, we kept quiet.

Comrades, Rivals, Lovers

Najib was caught in a dangerous situation. We all agreed that MQM was out to kill Najib, and my companions and I decided that he should leave PSF and Karachi and go to Islamabad. I was asked to relay the message to him. I told him, "Najib, you have been the PSF president for two years. If you don't mind, leave PSF for one year and then come back. Right now you have many enemies. Please leave this city, leave the country." He was very stubborn, *zidd*, and foolish, *bewuquf*, and did not want to leave his post. He said he was not a *buzdil*, coward. We told him it was cowardice *and* foolishness to stay. Then Tariq told our companions that he would listen only to Rahila, and that forced Najib to quit his job. He said, "What you are doing is not right, but I cannot refuse your request. So I will leave my post as the president of PSF." After that, we asked Najib to leave Karachi also. Najib was very angry with me. His condition was, "If you want me to leave, then you should also come to Islamabad with me." But I was needed here, and there were lots of things that I had to do in Karachi. We had a bad fight. He left for Islamabad, and I stayed back.

You see, I asked Najib to leave PSF because he was perceived to have become the [MQM] black sheep [spy] inside PSF. It was for his own safety. He went away to Canada, where his older brother lives. Before Najib left for Canada, he came specially to tell me that he would never believe anything bad anyone says about me. He said, "You will believe these black sheep, but I will never succumb to that. I request you, Rahila, never to misunderstand me and always have faith and trust in me. I want you to believe me, Rahila. This is my

---

85. If Benazir Bhutto made a coalition government with the MQM for political expediency during her first term as the prime minister, her party reversed the trend in her second term in office. The two parties confronted each other "in the worst show-down" in Karachi's history (I. Malik 1997, 259).

request." I said, "OK, OK, Najib. Why do you think I am a weak woman?" But I really *am* a very weak woman because when Najib left, I believed all the gossip I heard, that he favored one faction against me and that he had said he would not speak to me when he returned. I am very crazy. I don't know why. I thought, "OK, if Najib is talking this way, I don't want to see his face either." I should not have believed them.

When Najib came back, I pointedly ignored him in public gatherings. Najib felt very insulted because all those who told me about him had also told Najib the same things about me. They said, "Rahila says you are a bad character and that you are a terrorist." But Najib did not believe them.

Then Najib celebrated his birthday, which turned out to be his last. We had a pact. He always wanted me to give him a gift that I had made with my own hands. He insisted on that. He said that the time I would spend making something for him, I would be thinking about him. He would also give me something he had made himself for my birthdays. He celebrated his birthday only for me, he said, as a slap on the faces of the black sheep [within their rank and file]. He said, "You must come." I said, "OK." But I had *shaitan*, the devil, inside me. He came to my house personally to invite everyone, including my mother. My mother wanted me to go to his birthday and said, "Rahila, I will be angry with you and will not speak to you if you do not go. You are *zalim*, a cruel girl. You are a Hitler." Sometimes I really am a Hitler.

I did not go to his birthday party. He waited for me until the last minute. As a gift, I sent a picture of him I had taken earlier on in which he was crying, for some reason. He threw that away and cried a lot. He complained to my mother. He complained to our friends. Two days later the MQM fired at his house. I called him on the phone and said that I wanted to see him. He said, "No, I will never see you again. You broke my heart. I have no faith in you anymore. You were my hope. You killed my hope." At that time, I realized he was really in love with me, but he had never told me so.[86] I knew it, but I discouraged it because I thought it was not good for my federation. I did not want to think about marrying him because at that time we had serious crises, and I was of two minds because of my promise to Aamir. Aamir was a school fellow, and I had known him since 1976. He has loved me since we were kids, but now I feel he has changed.

---

86. I asked her, "Do you think he was in love with you?"

Death of a Hero

But Najib's uncle died, and Najib had to come back to Karachi [from Canada?], where everyone who is close to Najib is Urdu speaking. I doubted very much that they were sincere with him. I wanted to tell him to be careful. But Najib and I were having a "cold war" and were not on speaking terms. I was very worried and tried to get in touch with him, but he had left for Larkana to attend Bhutto's death anniversary.[87] On the fifth of April, he attended his uncle's *chehlum*[the forty-day ritual after death], and on the sixth of April, when he was returning home from his uncle's house, he was faced with a roadblock. He tried to take another road but was fired at. Bullet casings were strewn everywhere. They found five hundred on the ground. We still do not know how many bullets struck him, but two very powerful bullets hit the windshield. One penetrated Najib's neck and the other his chest. Our companions in the car were also wounded. Despite being hit, Najib borrowed a bicycle from some passerby and biked to the hospital. There he had himself bandaged and asked the nurse to call the police and also to have him and his companions transferred to the Aga Khan Hospital.[88] Otherwise, he said, MQM people would come there and finish him. In five minutes, Najib was taken to the Aga Khan Hospital, where he gave his statement.

He was still conscious and could talk, according to the doctor. After cleaning Najib's wounds, the doctor told him that he was out of danger but that he should be taken to Liaqat Hospital for a special test, even though the Aga Khan Hospital was the best-equipped in Karachi! I cannot imagine that! Najib asked his brother-in-law to go and bring his mother to the hospital, and so his brother-in-law left. This was a great mistake. Najib *should not* have been left alone, but this we discovered afterward. Najib was conscious and talking when he was taken to Liaqat Hospital, but by the time his brother-in-law returned, Najib was in coma. After that, he was just about finished, *khatam*, gone. We think that whatever happened must have happened in the ambulance because Najib was all alone. There was nobody with him.

His parents happened to be at our house. We did not know what was going

87. Larkana is the Bhuttos' ancestral village, located in Sindh Province, where Zulfikar Bhutto is buried. He was hanged on April 4, 1979, so these dates are very significant for Rahila and her companions.

88. This hospital is funded by and named after the Isma'ili leader and imam, Karim Aga Khan. It is the best hospital in Karachi, if not in all of Pakistan.

on. Around four in the morning, Najib's brother-in-law told Najib's mother. You can imagine people's reaction when the next day they heard that Najib had been shot! The army came out in full force. Najib was a student leader, not an important personality or a powerful politician. Why get the army out? This was the first step toward blackmailing Benazir's government because they knew that Najib was a *har dil aziz*, and that if they killed him, students would come out on the streets. This was a major reason for dismissing Benazir's government later on.[89]

On the morning of April 6, I heard that Najib was shot. The previous night I had a dream about Najib. He came to me at four in the morning. This is the time Najib was being transferred by an ambulance from Aga Khan Hospital to Liaqat Hospital. I saw Najib coming toward me. In my dream, he said, "Rahila, please help me. I am dying." I opened my eyes and thought, "Oh my God. What's wrong?" I started praying and using my *tasbih*, rosary. My younger sister also had a dream three days before Najib was shot. She dreamt that Najib came to our house and told her, "Lubna, could you please try to work out my friendship with Rahila." This was her dream, but her dream was incomplete, and mine seemed to complete it. Lubna had told me this in the morning. My mother had said, "Rahila is a *jallad*, an executioner. Why do you tell her that? I hate her decision [to not go to Najib's birthday]. She has a hard heart." My mother was very harsh. I said, "OK, OK. I won't do it again." My sisters were also very angry with me. But on the morning that I heard the news, I rushed to Najib's hospital. I was feeling very, very guilty, praying, "My God, please give me one more chance, give me another chance." I had a panicky heart and was very sorry for Najib.

I remembered our encounters. We were at a Palestine program ceremony, sitting around a table. I knew Najib liked one spoon of sugar in his tea. I put sugar in the cup of all our companions, but when Najib's time came, I said, "Please, how many sugars?" He said, "Oh, you mix in poison. I will do it myself." So all the time I was pricking him, jab, jab, jab. Now Najib lay unconscious in the hospital.

I did see him in the hospital, but he did not recognize me. Najib's sisters were also there. His sisters loved me. His mother loved me, but sometimes she also hated me very much because she knew my temperament. He was in a

89. Benazir Bhutto's first government was dismissed by then-president Ghulam Ishaq Khan on August 6, 1990.

coma. His eyes were closed. But you know, when Najib expired, I think at twelve on April 11 [1990], I was praying the whole night, using my *tasbih*. I was standing in Najib's room praying for him. Najib's mother came to me and said, "Rahila, you go and rest. This is an order, go."

I went to another room, and I was in a delusional state, with *tasbih* in my hand. I saw Najib standing in front me, crying with bleeding eyes.

He said, "Rahila, please help me. Don't let me go, please."

I said, "Oh, Najib."

I opened my eyes, and I heard a woman wailing. "What's wrong? What's wrong?" I screamed.

Najib's sister said, "Najib is dead. Rahila, Najib is dead."[90]

Then I don't know what happened to me. I was senseless, completely. [Pause]

After Najib was bathed [ritual ablution], a woman came to me and said, "Rahila, you saw his face [in a dream], and that is why you are upset. You saw his face." I was crying. I knew I had seen Najib's face. As I was crying, his cousin came in. She said, "Rahila, is this what you made for Najib?" This was a handkerchief I had made for him. "Yeah," I said. "Look, Rahila," she said, "he kept all your gifts in this packet. Everything has been kept very carefully, lovingly wrapped as if they are *Qarun ka khazana*," the legendary Qarun's treasure. I felt horrible. I felt as if I had tortured him. But then I saw Najib's picture, the weeping pictures. Najib's eyes were red. I felt as if Najib was laughing at me. It was as if he was retaliating. My condition was very bad. This was what our enemy wanted. This was a very great success for our enemy. All our work and my life was burnt.

We tried to tell the members of government who came for investigation that many of our friends had been martyred by the MQM. You know, the MQM burned, *jala dia*, five boys alive and threw their dead bodies in front of us. Everywhere we turned, we found the mutilated bodies of our companions—in cars, in bags, in the streets, everywhere [talking fast, high pitched]. Everybody knows that MQM's torture is very horrible. The army knows it; everybody knows about their horrifying torture cell.[91] Do you know, every time one of our friends was killed, the MQM celebrated with lights and distributed sweets, *mithaei taqsim karna*. This was very bad for us emotionally. We

90. At the time of his death, Najib was twenty-five years old.

91. For more detail, see I. Malik 1997; see also the *Herald*, November 1992, and *Newsline* throughout 1991–92.

were very angry at our government. Why has Benazir compromised [collaborated] with the MQM when they are killing our companions? I don't know why, but this was very strange [pensive].[92]

The murder of Najib was very suspicious, and I was really mad now. I said to Benazir's government, "OK, if Najib was to expire, and you say that you could not do anything about it, then I will wage a guerilla war. I have been attacked and shot at twice. My only brother's car was fired at full blast twice. How can we remain silent? If Najib had to die, then we will not let any happiness in any home. We will drop dead bodies in every home, most prominently in the homes of the ministers and office holders of the People's Party. We will drop them in the homes of the bigwigs of the MQM. But we will not harm ordinary people." We told the government we would burn everything.

Benazir's reaction was to call us. She is a very intelligent lady. She called Najib's mother, who had initially filed a complaint. Then Najib's mother came to see me and said, "I don't want to see another mother suffer the way I did. Rahila, you are like my daughter. All of you are like my sons or daughters. I don't want anyone else to be in the situation of being Najib's mother. If you kill someone, it is as if you have killed my son or daughter. I know Najib's death has been very painful for you, but that is how I will feel if any Pakistani child dies." She said, "Save your generation. Najib gave a great sacrifice. Keep his name alive. If you are dead, the enemy will be happy, and then who is there to enjoy the bad times the enemy will have to suffer? *Zindeh raho*, stay alive to see the bad times of your *doshman*, enemy. And leave it to God."

I said, "It is cowardice to leave it to God. When one cannot do anything herself, one leaves it to God."

Najib's mother handed her *dupata* to me and said, "I know that today my son is not alive to cover my head, but you are my daughter also. I want you to cover my head.[93] I threw the *dupata* on the auntie and started crying. I cried and cried, telling the auntie that we had only one recourse, and she had snatched it away from us.

Najib used to say, "Rahila, keep these pictures with you. They will kill us [young men], but you stay alive to continue our cause. I know you will need

92. On the initial coalition between the PPP and the MQM, and on their subsequent breakup and animosity, see Alam 1989 and I. Malik 1997, 223–44.

93. To cover a woman's head is a sign of respect and protection. It is also a sign of clout that comes with association with men—that is, husband, son, or a patron.

these photos for posters. I want you to pose crying because I want a good picture of you grieving." I remembered everything he said. I was thinking of this
and wanted to do something for him. But what could I do? His family, sisters,
and brothers made a big sacrifice, *azim qurbani*, to compromise with the authorities. Najib had two brothers and three sisters. It was all so cruel and ironic.
One of Najib's sisters, who was only a year older than he and loved him dearly,
used to faint whenever she heard something bad about Najib. Six months after
Najib's *shibadat*, martyrdom, she died of a brain hemorrhage. So, emotionally
and psychologically it was a horrible time.

I felt very guilty about having been so angry with him. My companions
said, "If you had made up with him"—because he only listened to me—"then
you could have stopped him. You could have sent him out of the country.
Why were you angry with him?" All our friends think that if I had not fought
with Najib, he would be alive today. After our fight, he was very disheartened;
he was smoking all the time and fighting with everyone. One day before his
death, I think it was April 5, he arranged a tea party at Zeb's house, a PSF companion. She said, "Rahila, you should come and have tea with us." I said,
"Why?" I knew having a tea party was not Zeb's own idea. My sixth sense was
telling me that Najib must have arranged it. I called one of my friends and
asked him whether Najib was in Karachi or Islamabad. She said, "You don't
know? He is in Karachi." I did not go to Zeb's house. Later Najib telephoned
me and said, "You are a stupid girl. Please, Rahila, this is my request. For the
last time, have a cup of tea with me. Otherwise, you will regret it." He said, "If
you do not come to have a table talk with me, I will be dead." I said, "OK, I
have seen so many people who say, 'if you do not do this or that, we will be
dead.' But I have not seen any dead bodies or coffins!" As he hung up the
phone, he said, "OK, next time when you come to see me, it will be at my
death bed."

Love and Memory

When I was detained at the CIA Center, the police said, "You know, when we
arrested your Najib, we beat him up severely. We did a great job on him."
They were so cruel and said it very proudly. I felt a surge of power and said,
"OK, we will see. I am not dead." They said that Najib and I were "married"
[had illicit sex]. When they said nasty things about him, I refused to listen to
them. I cannot bear to hear anything against him because he was *imandar*, the
most honest friend I had. Besides, I have these guilt feelings about my fight

with him. It was all my fault. They would say, "If your Najib was alive, would he leave you in the CIA Center?"[94] I would reply, "My Najib is very much alive today. He is living in your mind, *zehn*." They would say, "We do not understand you. You are very dangerous." They talked like that because of all the lies that Fahima Rima had told them, that Najib and I had relations—all fabrications and lies. I told them I was involved with Aamir, you know, because I had Aamir's letter in my bag. I had told Fahima Rima about Aamir, but she would not believe me. Anyway, Najib's own life is on the record. He liked me, but I was not sure because I know our ways. I don't know why, but then I was thinking like that. I liked him as a friend. This is my feeling. But he was a crazy man, though he was very careful, very delicate with me, very protective of me. So I do have a soft spot for Najib, but I broke up with him because I was angry with him. I still am. It is my nature. If I am annoyed with someone, I stop talking to them. This is a very bad habit of mine, and that is how I behaved with Najib. He would say, "Rahila, beat me or fight with me, but for God's sake don't ever stop talking to me." I said, "Najib, *asa vaqt na lana*, don't make it come to that point." But then they [the MQM?] made us fight, and it came to that point. We were both misguided.

I have a block in my nature. When I promise something, I cannot break it. So this [not reciprocating Najib's love] was because I had made a promise to Aamir. I made a promise to Aamir because he was going to America and because my mother was pressuring me. She kept scolding me, "Why do you not want to marry? You are blocking your sisters' chances." This was heavy pressure and very bad for me. So I said, "OK." I thought, "I sacrifice for my family." I compromised with Aamir because Aamir was not living in Pakistan. Whenever I felt something special for Najib or he said some nice things to me, I felt responsible to Aamir. Najib knew about my promise to Aamir and was angry. Once he said, "I will kill him" [smiling—an indirect way of expressing his love for her].

Once later Aamir talked to me about Najib—and he was right. He said, "Rahila, no revolution is coming. Why do you waste your time and energy? Look, where is your Najib today? He is buried under tons of *mitti*, dirt. *Nobody* knows him today. People remember him as a criminal." I got very angry at him,

94. Implying here that Najib was really not an honorable man because no "real" man would let his wife (or intended wife) become involved in political activities to the extent of eventually being thrown in jail. It would be against his *izzat*.

and I said, "OK, Najib, eh . . . Aamir, you go. I am not talking with you any-more." The next day he came with his brother-in-law, and he started crying. He said, "Rahila, you have lost one Najib. You would lose another one. You have the habit of falling in love with images, *tasvir*." I got very scared, and then I made up with him again. But I know that we can never get along, we can never be friends [marry].

Aamir never asked me what happened in jail, but I am 100 percent sure that this [alleged rape] must have been in his mind, too. That is why he ignored me. He is a very shy man. He is a very suspicious man. After Najib's death, he returned to Pakistan and came to visit me. Because Najib's picture—a big pic-ture—is in my bedroom, he said, "Oh, you see Najib all the time." I said, "Yes, because I respect him as a brother. Why are you jealous?" Then I said, "Why don't you wear the *shalwar-kamiz*?" [like a Pakistani man] I like my country's na-tional dress. He said, "Oh, you want to make me into another Najib." I said, "No, Najib was a very brave man. You are not made like Najib" [laughing]. But he does remind me of Najib. He is not good for me.

Many times I feel very sad. But I am human. Sometimes I think I should go and live in America. Then I think, "No. I have done so much work, and so much is left after Najib's death." This is my promise: to complete Najib's work. *Inshallah*, one day I will realize Najib's aim. Wherever I go, and any time we have discussions, Najib's name inevitably comes up. I know Najib is asleep. I have a feeling of connection with him. When I was at the CIA Center and being tortured, I thought of Najib. I think he helped me. You know, Najib was my great teacher. He warned me about police behavior: "Rahila, you know, they try to misguide the companions. They tell you that your friend has made a statement to fool you to admit it. Beware of their tactics."

I remember, one day Fahima Rima told me—I don't know whether this was the police scheme or that Fahima was very naïve—that Mumtaz had sug-gested that we escape at night and go home.

I said, "How are we going to do that?"

She said, "Mumtaz will arrange everything."

"How do we get outside?"

"We go to the washroom with Mumtaz. Then she arranges a taxi for us, and we sit in the taxi and run away."

I said, "OK, Fahima, this might sound like good advice, but what time will she do that?"

She said, "At twelve midnight!"

I said, "Look, we belong to good families. I have never left home at night without my brother or someone. If we leave the jail at night, will we be safe? Will we not get into trouble, or the taxi driver might not take us to his home? From here, we can be taken to worse places. How do we know that the police have not planned this scheme? So far they have not been able to prove any allegations against us. But if we were to escape at night and they caught us at some place, it could turn into a horrible situation for us. I will not go, but if you want to go, it is up to you. We are both educated. Besides, we are not criminals. *Inshallah*, we will leave this place with honor." After that, Fahima asked me not to discuss this plan with anyone.

I have also warned my girls at the PSF against the police cunning. I explained my ordeal to them and told them, "If you get arrested, the first thing to do is make up your mind as to what is your stamina. If you feel strong and powerful, then do not surrender. If you feel weak, do not give a statement to the police. Give a statement only in the court because the police beat you, and torture is just terrible. Then you can tell the truth in court. The police are very *makkar*, cunning, and *munafiq*, hypocritical. So if you admit one case, the police start so many cases against you. Then it becomes very difficult to fight it. If you compromise with the police on the first case, they will make life hell for you. And if you don't, they will still do the same thing. So it is better to take the path of strength and never come under their influence at all."

Gendered Violence

There is this hell, this fire inside me, fire as big as an *atish fishan*, volcano. This is what moved me and gave me strength. My civilization and my government have treated me very badly. They took my friends away from me, spoiled my childhood dream of going to the Art Council by taking the bus service away from me. My good friends were killed. My helpless and *baizzat*, honorable, father was tortured [harassed], my mother's feelings were hurt, and I was badly tortured. Once [Irfanullah] Marwat said, "We kill you in the CIA Center." I said, "Fine! If I am dead in the CIA Center, this is your triumph, this is your reward. But if I go outside, I am your death. This is my promise." He said, "You are a crazy woman." I said, "Yes, because you think women are very delicate and weak. I am a student leader, and I am a Muslim woman. I show you who I am, what is my character, and what is my background. Definitely, *zarur*, I will show you!" They were all so scared. They were scared of what I could be able to do, so they tried to be alternatively compromising or strict with me.

When I came out [of the hospital] and moved around, I realized how badly women are treated in my society. They are reflections of my face. My fight is to reveal the police secrets in public. This is good for me emotionally. Once I told Malik Ehsan, "You have arrested me, but I do not feel shy because I am not a criminal. I am not guilty because I know my *zamir*, conscience. I am in pain, but I am not guilty. When I go outside [of jail], I will tell everything. I will talk about my experience." When I heard the judiciary's unfair verdict, I was filled with hatred.[95] I felt the poison inside me. I decided to give it back to them, and it was my wish to stay alive and not die. I was certain I would not die.

When I was sent to America, I gave talks about my ordeal in the CIA custody.[96] I gave a complete report regarding the government's behavior. I told people that in my government some *rij'at pasand*, retrogressive, mullahs do not like to see women educated and progressive. They challenged Benazir because she is the first woman leader in all the Muslim world.[97] Further, I told them that one reason for the existence of torture in my country is that it is a police state. Rich men use the police for their *shahinshahiyyat*, imperial authority to scare ordinary people. If you scare poor people and harass them, they are not able to demand their rights, and you can rule. In Pakistan, the rich classes rule through the police. That is why we are subjugated. Our big problem is the army. The army does not want to stay in the barracks and protect the borders. They enter the government and impose dictatorship. That is why we have martial law in our country so often.

You ask me how I survived? I must say, this was because I met so many good people, loving people, true and devoted ones, who gave me power and energy. I was getting this energy from friends as the moon, *chand*, gets light from the sun, *suraj*. I have friends from all races, religions, and colors. I remember a Christian sweeper[98] who brought me some beans to eat. She had seen my state

95. She refers to the verdict to return her back to jail, despite her having been tortured.

96. Benazir Bhutto and her party sent Rahila to the United States for a few months for further rehabilitation.

97. At that time (1993), however, Tansu Chiller was prime minister in Turkey, as was Khalida Zia in Bangladesh.

98. Most sweepers in Pakistan are Christians, as they are in India. Moore, conducting research in India, writes that when she identified herself as Christian, her informants "gasped," as-

and saw that I had been punished and had to go hungry for three days. She told me, "I am very dirty [being a sweeper]. I am very poor, but this food is clean. You eat it." That gave me power and energy. The police were bad, and so were a lot of other people, but many others were so loving and caring. That gave me energy to fight and to believe in the goodness of humanity. I am not special. I am a normal human being, but that created a soft spot in my heart. I felt very powerful.

Anywhere in the world some people are mean, like my enemies, but my aim is to change them. This time, my first aim is to campaign for elections. This is good for women. I am not disheartened or disappointed. I want to continue our struggle. Election is one part of the struggle. When I go to the [National] Assembly, I will change the laws. Old laws are dead laws. So my wish is to have electoral power. Then I can change the system of Pakistan.

I will not compromise.[99] This is my nature. I know that Benazir had to compromise, but my law is the law of no compromises. I made one resolution when I was in the CIA Center. *Inshallah*, when I make it to the Assembly, I will try to change horse-trading.[100] At this time, horse-trading is the law of land in my country. So my wish, when I am in the Assembly, is to ban horse-trading.[101]

My ordeal took a long time, although I am telling you the whole story in two or three days. Now I feel I am in the last stages [of recovery]. Sometimes I feel as if I am still in the CIA Center, and Malik Ehsan is using bad language. Then I don't understand what is going on with me. Every time I see my parents' faces, I feel very heartbroken. I listen to music. I like Sufi *kalam* music. When I listen to this kind of music, I feel, yes, we are humans and must be ready for sacrifice. I read a book called *Muhsen-i insaniyyat*, the benefactor of

suming she was an untouchable converting to Christianity to escape her caste identity (1998, 17).

99. I asked her, "How are you going to do it? If Benazir was unable to make any significant changes, what makes you think that you will not have to compromise, as Benazir was compelled to do?"

100. "Horse-trading," or crossing the floor and switching one's party and political loyalty, is a perennial political problem in Pakistan. Pakistanis humorously call a party horse-trader a *lotta*, a wobbling water pitcher they use in the toilet.

101. Rahila apparently became dissatisfied with the PPP, and by the mid-1990s she switched her party affiliation and political alliance to the PML, headed at the time by Mian Mohammad Nawaz Sharif. Last I heard from Rahila (May 2002), she was the president of the women's wing of the newly created Sindh Democratic Alliance.

humanity, which is about the life of the Prophet (Peace Be Upon Him). When he would go for missionary work, he would confront very bad behavior and hardship. Then I feel comforted. When I remember how I was insulted, I think about the great women leaders such as Hazrat Bibi Zainab, Hazrat Bibi Sakina, and Hazrat Bibi Ayesha[102] when she was accused of wrong doing.[103] When people say bad things about me, I think about these women, and I feel very comforted. This is my willpower [smiling]. I know one thing: we are our own doctors at all times. When I feel sad, I don't cry. I become very quiet. I rest and I think. I will try to find a solution. This is my nature. For this reason, I do not regret. You know, this time I have compromised because I know that I have returned from death. You know, after Najib's death I was very puzzled, all the time. I was sick, mentally sick. But I now realize the meaning of life. This time I have an aim in my life.[104]

Some Reflections: Strategies for Survival

The etching of political rivalries onto women's bodies for national honor—or to inflict dishonor—is *not* unique to Pakistan, though Rahila's case involves elements of individual and cultural specificities. A global glance at the ways political and ethnic conflicts are expressed across cultures reveals the symbolic significance of violating women's bodies as a means for dishonoring the enemy while underscoring national identity and masculine honor.

The politically motivated violence perpetrated against Rahila while she was in police custody and the terror unleashed on her to force her to do the bidding of the state, I argue, is a variation of feudal rape. The target of humiliation and shame, in other words, is not necessarily a specific woman. It is

102. These women are, respectively, the sister and daughter of the Shi'ites third imam, Hussain, and the Prophet's favorite wife.

103. Ayesha, the Prophet's favorite wife, became embroiled in a controversy of "proper conduct" for a wife of the Prophet and was left vulnerable to wrongful accusations. The Prophet, while sending her back to her father's home, agonized over how to respond to these accusations and how to treat her. He received a revelation, in which Ayesha's innocence was upheld (Qur'an 24:11).

104. Toward the end of our interview, Rahila said, "You know, this is my first complete interview. I don't give many interviews, but this is very, very deep. I am very happy because this is very important."

rather a political rival—an old enemy—on whom revenge is to be taken (K. Ahmed 1992, 36–37; Haeri 1995b).[105] As for the violated woman, she does not seem to exist as an individual.[106] She is culturally perceived to be the property of her husband or her lineage, expendable or jealously guarded. As more and more women become politically active, however, they, rather than their male kin, become the specific targets of violence and humiliation. They bear the multiple burden of being violated physically, shamed culturally, and dishonored publicly. In Pakistan and elsewhere, violence against women, including rape, is often institutionalized and has the tacit and at times explicit approval of the state.[107]

Violence against women theoretically and variously has been conceptualized in terms of controlling female sexuality, in terms of restricting women's autonomy, in terms of humiliating and so keeping them out of sight,[108] and in terms of maintaining male control and dominance. Although these ideas are relevant, there is something more I wish to emphasize in the case of Rahila. Her case involves an act of revenge aimed at humiliating and dishonoring a powerful and potentially threatening rival, but with a gender twist that makes it poignantly meaningful in the cultural context of Pakistan.

Here, the "enemy," the political rival, was none other than Benazir Bhutto! How is that possible, one might ask? She herself is a woman. Precisely the point! Although out of office at the time, Benazir Bhutto was a powerful rival with whom the opposition had to contend. When female members of her party were tortured and raped, not only individual women were dishonored, but Benazir Bhutto herself—the leader of the opposition, a woman of feudal lineage, a notable citizen, and the model of womanhood[109]—was "raped" sym-

---

105. Khalid Ahmed (1992, 36–37) argues that feuds are settled through the rape of an adversary's womenfolk. Yusuf describes the particular form of rape in Pakistan as a form of "feudal vendetta" (1992a, 47).

106. Ward (1996, 261) argues that in gang rape the identity of the woman or women assaulted is irrelevant.

107. For discussions regarding rape in India, see Kakar 1989 and Sunder Rajan 1993, 78.

108. Kakar (1989, 33) argues that one way of making women unagentic is to humiliate them sexually or, worse yet, to subject them to the violence of rape, which sends a double message: stay out of sight and behave or else pay the consequences.

109. "All nationalist discourse," write Breckenridge and van der Veer, "appeal to primordial images—of blood, of kinship, of soil, and of sexuality—in order to imbibe the nation with the force of bodily self-interest" (Breckenridge and van der Veer 1993, 11).

bolically by association.[110] How could a nation, any nation, thereafter choose to have a raped leader? Conversely, how could a leader who is unable to protect herself or her followers protect her country from being invaded by its "enemies," real or imagined?[111]

Doubling: Rahila/Benazir

Pakistani women for centuries have buried in their hearts the rage and anguish of rape. In the interests of family honor and from fear of ostracism, they have been forced to keep quiet or face humiliation and abandonment by their families. Raped women have been forsaken even by their state, as they were in the aftermath of the 1947 partition, when the mass rape of women of all persuasions took place in the ensuing communal riots and animosities.[112] Pakistani families customarily shun raped women or hide the "shame" of those women whose *izzat* has been "looted." The society actively discourages public disclosures of rape and, until very recently, has preferred not to know.

Rahila potentially faced the dilemma of all raped women who put their own honor and that of their families in jeopardy. Determined not to allow that, Rahila categorically rejected being raped, notwithstanding the lingering doubt in the public mind, and so acted "appropriately." Her denial secured her

110. In Kakar's view, rape, "actual or attempted" (as in Indian films), is the worst kind of degradation a woman must bear for her "transgression." He sees it as a "collective sado-masochistic fantasy" (1989, 33–34).

111. Compare the apparently culturally perceived offensive thought of a female leader's violated body in Pakistan, even by association, with the following: "While [Queen] Elizabeth occupied the throne, any threat to the body of an aristocratic female . . . was nothing less than an assault on the nation itself" (Armstrong and Tennenhouse 1989, 13). To minimize their sexuality and to reassure their male followers and opponents of their leadership prowess, one woman (Bhutto) donned a religiously symbolic scarf and refrained from shaking hands with men, and the other (Elizabeth) wore costumes that also signaled distance and inviolability. The latter remained officially virgin. I am grateful to Kaveh Safa for bringing this parallelism to my attention.

112. See Bapsi Sidhwa's novel *Cracking India* (1991), which was converted into the movie *Earth* (1999).

social acceptance—ambivalent though it might have been—and her honorable return to her family and saved her family from the shame of living with a "raped" daughter. She supported her claim to purity on the basis of her family background and lineage, insisting that the police did not dare to touch her, even though they routinely rape women in custody.[113]

Rahila herself ironically seems to have internalized the state's projection of her sexuality and dishonor onto Benazir. She clearly identified her persona with that of Benazir Bhutto and appeared to imagine herself as Benazir's double.[114] She repeatedly denied accusations of sexual misconduct made against Benazir Bhutto and appealed to female religious figures to underscore her own honorable intent and conduct. Rahila perceived herself as not "an ordinary woman," like Benazir Bhutto, and argued that Benazir (and, by implication, she herself) is a "a savior" of the nation and that, above all, she has managed to become a woman leader, something Rahila aspired to in this highly patriarchal society. By adamantly denying any possibility of rape, Rahila protected not only her own honor but also that of her leader/double and thus of her nation as well. Saving her leader, for whom she repeatedly proclaimed love, she refused to substantiate allegations of sexual misconduct against her. In turn, she ensured her own salvation not only psychologically but also politically. Benazir Bhutto publicly acknowledged Rahila's plight by arranging for her to be sent to America for rehabilitation and gave her a party ticket to run for an Assembly seat.

Moreover, Rahila's persistent refusal to implicate Benazir Bhutto in the face of extreme brutality saved her and her leader from being trapped in a cultural and political no-win situation (Doniger 1999, 283). She escaped the possibility of being rejected by her family (and by the nation in Benazir Bhutto's case) as well as of being destroyed by her own and Benazir's enemies. She upheld her *izzat* as a member of the Rajput tribe and as a pure (sexually unspoiled) woman. Her public stands for social justice and her categorical denial of rape, in turn, denied her tormentors and Benazir's "enemies" the satisfaction of having broken or dishonored her. In fact, it did the opposite and allowed her to gain a degree of self-respect. It enabled her to run for a political seat and restored a degree of honor to her family.

113. See Bakhtiar 1992; Human Rights Watch 1992; "Trial by Torture," *Herald* (November 1992).

114. For a fascinating study of doubling and splitting, see Doniger 1999.

Body, Space, Mobility

Rahila's active political participation and agitation for democracy and civil society challenge many an outsider's view of Muslim women, who are imagined to be generally passive and without social visions.[115] They also threaten a radicalized segment of her transitional patriarchal society that has increasingly felt compromised by professional women's autonomy and independence. This "radicalized traditionalist," whom Riesebrodt identifies as fundamentalist (1993, 177), sees women's public appearance and activism as contrary to what they consider the ideal gender relations and as an infringement on the male privileges that, in their view, are sanctioned by divine command.

Rahila had her parents' blessing for her political activism but emotionally seemed not to be sure how to behave in her society or where to locate her conduct in the cultural and political landscape. Her active political involvement potentially put her in a precarious position vis-à-vis the cultural ideal of female vulnerability, chastity, and purity. Her wish to safeguard her *izzat* at all costs simultaneously underscored both her determination not to seem like a woman of easy virtue *and* her ambivalence regarding women's political mobility, honor, and control of her own body. Her close associations with men in her party riddled her claim to propriety with contradictions and hence made it culturally suspect.

Rahila's leadership quality guaranteed her a rapid rise on the party ladder, which boosted her ego but also mired her in party loyalty, political rivalries, and gender dynamics. As president of a branch of her student federation, she competed discretely with Najib Ahmed, a "handsome" popular male student leader whom she described as "loved by everyone" and with whom she developed a "lovely coordination." Her youthful, complicated, and often twisted description of their emotional involvement and political relationship points to a strong undercurrent of mutual affection, if not love and desire, but she chose not to acknowledge it. She apparently perceived a romantic relationship as culturally inappropriate and perhaps as politically disadvantageous. If they had been lovers, not only would she have publicly confirmed all the gossip

---

115. Even in the violent grip of the Taliban, many Afghan women manifested courage by performing educational, medical, and civil services in their society, however discretely and secretively. See Benard 2002.

(though her parents seem to be fond of Najib), but she probably would have had to take a back seat to him politically. Rahila clearly had political ambitions.

Again, she tried to escape the cultural no-win situation in which politically active women may find themselves. Not only did she deny her own emotional attraction to Najib, but she blocked his efforts at expressing his love with her frequent reminders of her marriage promise to Aamir, a suitor who lived conveniently far away in the United States. Rahila used her promise of marriage to Aamir, a childhood friend of the family, as a concession to cultural ideal and as a protective shield to ward off gossip in the party rank and file, accusations of impropriety by the public, as well as pressure by Najib. Claiming that they respected each other as comrades and liked each other as brother and sister, she upheld her purity, acknowledged the cultural control of her body—however uneasily—and thus expected and received respect from her society.

Caught off guard by his tragic death, however, she manifested her love, that tormented cultural commodity,[116] for Najib posthumously and silently by hanging a life-size poster of him in her bedroom, where she could see him all the time away from the public gaze.

Empowered by Religion

Rahila had a mystical sense of her religion and frequently invoked religious imagery to underscore the justice of her political objectives and the propriety of her actions as well as to rationalize the personal consequences of her imprisonment. In dreams and in wakefulness, she identified herself with prominent religious female leaders such as Hazrat Zainab (the Prophet's granddaughter), whose political courage and purity while held in captivity by her enemies became legendary and exemplary. Rahila upheld the leading Muslim women as models par excellence for womanly conduct and moral courage. She conjured up images of martyrdom and invoked the moods and the ambience of the massacre of the Prophet's grandson in Karbala to calm down her brother and to reassure themselves of the justice of their political action. The spiritual power she received from Islam intimidated her male captors

---

116. On love and longing, see chapter 5, Kishwar Naheed's life story.

while providing her with a means to cope with her ordeal psychologically and culturally.

Religion simultaneously granted Rahila yet another strong link with Benazir Bhutto. She intellectually downplayed religious differences between Shi'i and Sunni and claimed not to have much tolerance for the religious schism. But because she, like Benazir, happened to be a Shi'a Muslim, she found another emotionally meaningful way of finding her double in the latter. Her heroic refusal to cooperate with Benazir's enemies not only saved her leader/double—and thus herself—but also redeemed her religiously.

Having spent several intense days with Rahila, I found myself in agreement with others that she was indeed "not an ordinary" woman, as she said of others' perception of her. I was impressed by her ability to distance herself from her horrifying ordeal, to reflect on it, often philosophically, and to speak about it in such great detail. More important, her powerful imagination and her determination helped her to develop her survival skills during both her torture and her recovery, maintaining her sanity and strengthening her ability to enhance her budding political career. Above all, by denying being raped while identifying her plight and her conduct in jail with the experiences of leading religious women, she situated her suffering within appropriate cultural and religious contexts. Triumphant, in a sense, Rahila thus laid claim to her honor unambiguously.

As painful as raped women's experiences have been, they have confronted Pakistani society with a moral tension, leading to greater public awareness of the issue of violence against women. They also have strengthened the resolve of many Pakistani women activists to reclaim their bodies and voices. These women are determined to speak out, realizing that to remain silent for any longer is a "crime," in the words of Kishwar Naheed:

> The desire to see you silent
> Billows up even from the grave.
> But the speech is urgent
> When listening is a crime.
>   (1991c, 31)

4

Legitimacy
In the Boots of a Feudal Lord

Meeting Ayesha Siddiqa

I MET AYESHA in early 1992 a few weeks after she had announced her engagement. The decisive, articulate, and assertive manner in which she expressed her ideas and opinions impressed me immediately. She did not mince words, although she seemed a bit shy and self-conscious. Later, in April, my husband and I joined Ayesha to celebrate her twenty-sixth birthday at her ancestral estate, Khanqah Sharif, seventeen kilometers outside of Bahawalpur in central Pakistan.[1]

The three of us arrived at the small but charming Bahawalpur Airport on a windy, dusty, but pleasant sunny afternoon. The walkway leading to the small terminal was covered on both sides with colorful rose bushes, whose fragrance greeted us enjoyably as we walked toward the terminal. Three men greeted us right outside the gate. One was her driver; another her *munshi,* secretary or bookkeeper; and the third her *maulvi* sahib, who reads the Qur'an at her ancestors' and parents' graveyard weekly.

Ayesha owns a seventy-five-acre mango and citrus orchard, at the entrance to which stands a large, four-room concrete house. Her servants came out to greet us. There was Choti (literally, "the little one"), Bachol, the *maulvi* sahib's beautiful twelve-year-old daughter Asfa, and a whole list of others, young and old. Having rested a while, we took a walk around the orchard, with Ayesha's old *mali,* the gardener, keeping pace behind us. Ayesha, clad in blue jeans and

---

1. Bahawalpur is located in central Pakistan and is one of the major divisions of the Punjab Province.

a loose shirt, kept talking to him, sometimes asking a question, sometimes instructing him, and sometimes giving orders without ever looking back at him.

As we circled the orchard and approached the house, reaching the space
around the triple-decker fountain in front of the house, her staff of several
men, women, and children had already gathered there to greet her. First, the
men one by one—and one quite old—walked toward her and, in the symbolic
tradition of expressing hierarchy and status in South Asia, bent over to touch
her feet. Stretching back to stand up, they then shook her hand quickly, while
exchanging complements with her. Then the women approached, again one
by one, bending over to touch her feet, and she in turn placed her right hand
on their heads, after which they quickly held that hand with both of theirs.
The women were completely hidden under colorful *burqas*, and most of the
men wore *lungis*.[2] Almost all had a request, which Ayesha referred to her manager and accountant, who were standing behind her.

An old man with his wife and their young child requested Ayesha to bless
the imminent marriage of their daughter by giving them a *ta'wiz*, amulet. Later
on, when we were resting in the living room, Choti brought in a piece of bread
for Ayesha to give it her *dam*, breath or life, to bless it. Ayesha held the piece of
bread close to her mouth while whispering a few lines from the Qur'an. When
I asked her half jokingly what exactly she recited from the Qur'an, she said
rather seriously, "Something having to do with animals." This bread was then
given to a nanny goat that was about to deliver. Later that evening Choti burst
into the room laughing, hugging two tiny black-and-white kids.

Ayesha also arranged for a woman to come and sing at her house the following night. She humorously referred to the performance as "chamber
music," adding, "we have still kept some of those nice traditions!" We did not
get a chance to sit in the "chamber" to listen to the singing until some time
after midnight. The singer was accompanied by her husband, who was also
her tabla player, and by another man who played the harmonium.[3] Their five-
year-old son, half asleep at their feet, must have been dragged out of bed to
make it possible for his parents to perform at that late—or early—hour.

The night before her birthday, around midnight, Ayesha took us to the ancestral *mazar*, tomb, where her parents also are buried. We walked in front of a

2. A *lungi* or *dhoti* is a piece of cloth worn around the waist and between the legs.

3. They appeared very deferential toward Ayesha, and that is why they waited patiently
until Ayesha was ready to receive them.

group of male servants. They were followed by female servants and village female singers who accompanied the crowd, playing their tablas and singing.
All around us a large number of children skipped, hopped, and danced, sometimes walking alongside us, sometimes running ahead of us. We walked the
short distance to her ancestral *mazar* and went to the large, covered structure
where the tombs of at least twenty of her male ancestors, including her father,
were kept impeccably. The graves were raised above the ground, and every
single one was draped with a green piece of clothing with Qur'anic verses
printed on them. Some of the graves had a pillow placed where the head was
to be. The grave keeper, who had been following us, stood in attendance,
holding a basket full of rose petals. Ayesha and I whispered our *fatiha*, the
Qur'anic prayers for the dead, and then a thirteen-year-old boy with a
scratchy but warm voice sang a few songs and recited a few poems. We tossed
the flowers over the graves.

We then walked toward the end of the big shrine yard and to her mother's
tomb. Ayesha, in front, walked fast, and the rest of us followed behind. The
women's graves were scattered all over the shrine yard, not protected by a
cover, and were much less elaborate than the men's. They, too, were raised
slightly above the ground, but their mud coat was not hidden by green
drapes.[4] One or two graves, including one that belonged to Ayesha's step-
mother, who died in 1971, had a little structure built over them. As we cleared
the shrine yard and turned toward the northwest, her mother's tomb came to
view, and it was a sight to behold. The tomb was located inside a large glass
and steel structure, the size of a large room. It had a marble floor, and candles
and incense were burning inside. The trembling shadow of the candles on the
wall created a mysterious and mystical mood. Rose petals almost hid the red
piece of cloth stretched over the grave. After our silent prayers and *fatiha*,
Ayesha gave orders to the singers, who had filled the room and had sat quietly
on the marble floor all around the grave. They jumped to their feet to perform.
In appreciation, we put some paper money on the grave, and the head woman
singer immediately claimed it. Shortly after that, we left.

At Ayesha's home, three chairs were placed in the yard for us to sit on. We
faced the crowd of dancing, singing, and tabla-playing women and children.

4. Except for her mother's grave, women's graves ironically were outside and uncovered—
unveiled?—whereas men's graves were inside and covered! I am grateful to Kaveh Safa for
bringing such an astute observation to my attention.

Choti's six-year-old youngest son, Jamal, imitated Michael Jackson's dancing to devotional and folk music, while Choti directed him to shake his head and hands just like Michael Jackson. More singing and dancing followed and continued until 1:30 in the morning, when Ayesha dismissed them.

During the dancing, Ayesha's *munshi* and others approached her chair and held various denominations of rupees over her head and then gave the money to the head singer and coordinator. My husband and I followed suit: after circling some rupees over Ayesha's head, we gave them to the head singer. Holding the rupees over her head not only symbolically blessed the money but also expressed the audiences' appreciation of the singer's art as mediated through Ayesha's presence. What was fascinating now was that the male staff sat politely behind the women—at a respectable short distance, reversing the customary pattern of gender hierarchy and sex segregation—while participating in the ceremony leading to Ayesha's birthday, planned for the following day, April 7.

Early in the morning of April 7, Ayesha was decorated with flower and money garlands.[5] She was led toward a big scale that was already set up in her large back yard. She sat cross-legged on one of the scales, with my husband and me and the rest of her staff watching and giggling as she tried to keep her balance on the wobbling structure. Some of her male servants started placing huge bags of wheat on the other scale, while the *maulvi* sahib held a copy of the Qur'an over her head and recited a few prayers, blessing the wheat. Every year on her birthday she is weighed, and wheat seven times her weight is distributed among her servants and the villagers.

Her beautiful orchard was decorated for celebrating her birthday. *Diyas*, small earthen lamps, were lit and arranged less than a meter apart from each other all around the rose garden and around the small fountain in the middle. After a sumptuous dinner, a group of men, dressed in red and yellow costumes, performed the stick dance, accompanied by two men playing a tabla and a bagpipe while walking all round and in between the dancers. The dancers increased their tempo, dancing faster and faster, jumping high to strike their sticks together. Their exuberance and energy were contagious. As the men left, women dancers moved to the front of the garden and danced and sang be-

5. Money garlands, *noton ka haar,* are very popular gift items in Pakistan. They come in all denominations, and people, depending on their resources, present them at various ceremonies.

fore they were followed by another group of male dancers and singers who performed variations of the torch and bear dances with zest and flare. Ayesha sent them away after midnight, and the party was over by one in the morning.

Ayesha is a charismatic young feudal lord, and in her village she is respected, worshiped, and feared. Within her own feudal family, however, she is a controversial character, and her activities are scrutinized closely by her extended patrilineage. She treats her servants strictly and is not shy about heaping abuse on them. When at the end of her birthday party I asked her why she was screaming at and abusing her driver and said she should not do that, she told me to mind my own business. She said that in her feudal society "the sound of a blow means respect."[6] Ayesha also does not hide her affection for her servants, particularly for their children, of whom there are quite a few. They are, as she told me frequently, "like my family."

Ayesha initially was not willing to be interviewed for my research, but as our friendship developed into mutual respect and affection, and she gained greater knowledge about my project, she agreed to it. She would drop by our house in Lahore frequently, asking me to read poems from the collection of the celebrated Hafiz of Shiraz, the master *ghazal* composer, and to interpret the fortune that the poems "divined."[7] By then, we had established a strong emotional and intellectual rapport. Our conversations were at times intense and argumentative, particularly when we discussed feudalism, fundamentalism, and feminism in Pakistan. In retrospect, listening to the tapes of our conversation, at times I wince to hear myself questioning, quizzing, and probing, but then perhaps my persistent inquisition encouraged her to be more reflective. Our conversation was taped in May 1992. By the time of the interview, Ayesha's engagement had been broken off, and she was feeling restless and bothered. Her mother had died four years earlier, leaving her with mounting emotional conflicts and legal suits regarding property ownership brought

6. Power is something women discover, writes Heilbrun, "once they perceive the great difference between lives possible to men and women and the violence necessary to men to maintain their position of authority." (1988, 16).

7. Shams al-Din Muhammad Hafiz (1326–89) was born in Shiraz, Iran, and is the most celebrated lyricist Persian poet. Next to the Qur'an, his *Divan* collection of poems is the most revered book, one that is kept in almost every household in Iran. Iranians popularly believe that Hafiz has mystical power, and they read his poetry as a way to divine their fortune.

about by her maternal and paternal relatives. In the meantime, she was trying hard to survive as a civil servant,[8] while managing and supervising her estate and her affairs in her village in Khanqah Sharif. But she was also excited about the prospect of going to King's College in England to start her Ph.D. program in the Department of War Studies.[9] Let us hear from her.

Ayesha Siddiqa

Family Drama: Paternal Love, Maternal Discipline

I remember there were times when we were driving three hundred kilometers from Bahawalpur to Lahore, my mother would make me dress up as a boy. Once or twice she said, "I feel so secure going out with you like this. Everybody will think you are a boy, and I am traveling with a man." That insecurity was very much part of her and was transferred to me, but there were times when I would *want* to dress up like a regular girl, wear beautiful things. Sometimes her friends would say, "Jamilla, we think your daughter should be dressed like a girl." But she would look up at me and say, "Do you want to dress like a girl?" And I *did not* have the heart to disappoint her. What I had heard about her life from her or others was that it was a pretty bad one. I did not want to add to her disappointments.

My mother comes from a typical middle-class family. My father comes from a *wedera*, feudal, background. I was raised more in the shadow of my mother than of my father. My mother was my father's second wife, and there was always the fear of his leaving, like there is in a feudal family.[10] Because my father had no sons, he married my mother in the hope of having one. They *had*

8. Ayesha was an assistant director at the Pak Telecomm Corporation accounts office. She was in charge of computerization and of the telecommunications engineering and establishment section, which were the mother feeding sections of the entire cash account. She was grade seventeen, and the maximum is twenty-two.

9. The term *war studies* may sound awkward in American English, but the Department of War Studies, according to Ayesha, is one of the most prestigious departments at King's College, University of London. War studies does not involve combat training, but includes subjects such as defense economics, policymaking, intelligence, military technology, war literature, and the like.

10. See Tehmina Durrani's autobiography *My Feudal Lord* (1997).

a son, but he was killed, actually murdered, by the rest of the [paternal] family members.

I did not know him. He was born three years before I was. The story is that my infant brother was not feeling well—my father was away in Bahawalpur—and they needed a doctor. So a male cousin brought a woman doctor to see my brother. She kept injecting him with a drug [medicine], and by the evening he was dead. The doctor herself died in a mysterious car accident a few months later.

No, I don't think my father was heartbroken [by his death].[11] Evidently he did not care. He was basically a feudal lord, though never rude to my mother. But he made a very cruel comment, my mother told me. He said, "Well, I am glad your son died; otherwise, you would have taken all the property." You see, that is what was fed to him [by the extended family]. That "that is what your wife would have wanted if she had had a son."[12] Only twice did my mother mention her son in my lifetime. Once when I was too naughty, and another time, when I was 21 years old, she said, "I wish I had my son." I think she was a very strong woman but the desire to have a male around her was very much there, very, very much there. She was a woman, again as I said, with middle-class values, one who would worship her husband, like, you know, he was God.

Their marriage was a typically arranged one. The story is that once my maternal grandmother was traveling by train, and in the train she was talking to a woman who happened to be my father's maternal aunt. They were discussing personal things, like they do in Pakistan. So she said something like, "Well, I have daughters, and I am worried about their marriage." My father's aunt got interested. Soon after, a marriage proposal arrived at my mother's house, and the *nikah*, the marriage contract, was performed in 1959. My father did not have a formal education. He was brought up like a prince and had some knowledge of music, Persian language,[13] and that's that. He was artistic, in his own way. His life was spent gardening—growing plants, roses, and things like that.

11. Thinking formulaically about the strong attachment of a feudal lord to his son, I said, "Your father must have been devastated to hear the news of his son's death."

12. His cruelty could be understood, if not appreciated, against the feudal and *bradri*, lineage, systems specific to Pakistan. On filial rivalry, see Barth 1970.

13. Among the Mughal emperors who ruled North India for more than three centuries (1526–1857), the Persian language was the language of the court, the elite, and the literati until

My mother, on the other hand, was very well educated. She was a writer, a *very* good writer.[14] I say that not because she was my mother, but because she *was* a very talented person, quite unusual in a feudal family. There was little intimacy between my parents, and nobody made a conscious effort to come closer. My mother with her middle-class values and my father with his feudal values just did not meet eye to eye. They were very different, and there was no equality between them. They had no communication, and I generally did not notice them talking a lot. The basic conversation would be for my father to ask in the morning, "What are you going to cook today?" The irony of it was that she never cooked for him! The cook did. In that kind of an atmosphere, he would drink, and my mother could not force him to stop it. Sometimes she would tell me, "You know, your father takes this medicine. It is not good for him. Why don't you tell him." Like a simple child, I would go and say "Baba, why do you drink this? Please don't," not knowing what it was. Then he would say, "All right, I won't." [Laughing]

My father had little to do with my upbringing. He never scolded me. He was very loving. I used to sleep in between my parents. When I slept, I would always have my arm around my father. My fear was that he might go away. I was afraid that when I got up in the morning, he would not be there, so I would hold on to him. I do not know how this feeling came about. It seems as if I sort of grew up with it. Maybe because I was so attached to him when I was *very* young. My mother told me that when I was only a few months old, whenever my father left for Bahawalpur I would develop a fever. Until I was in grade three, he used to hide from me to go to the village. The train station was very near our house, and I used to play alone. The train would slowly pass by, and suddenly I would catch his sight [see him], and I would start shouting and screaming. I used to say, *"Baba bhag gaien,* Baba ran away" [laughing]. I would cry and cry and cry. That is how I was attached to him.

I was thirteen when he died. I don't know. Maybe God was being kind to me because if he had not died, there could have been a divorce. Things had come to such a head. My father had other women in his life, local women from

---

the British outlawed it in 1835. Persian was held in great esteem, and until recently many Pakistani schools and colleges offered regular courses in Persian.

14. Ayesha's mother used her maiden name, Jamila Hashmi, professionally. Among her novels are *Atash-i rafteh* (Extinguished fire, or Gone glory) (1941); *Rang bhum* (Spoiling a good time) (1987); and *Chehra be chehra ru be ru* (Face to face) (n.d.).

Bahawalpur [subdued].[15] The women did not come from very good families. He was not dating gorgeous, sophisticated women. They were just ordinary women, like my servant Choti. He was a typical feudal lord minus the temperament. I mean, he would not go around abusing his wife and beating his servants. Besides, he had other people in his life. He did not belong entirely to me. He had another daughter. He had his grandchildren. I was a *part* of his world, not his whole world, like it happens in normal families. So it was this fear, my mother's fear of losing him, that was transferred to me. As I have grown up, I have gotten so used to fearing something all the time. That shadow of fear incarnate is always there with me. Fear of the unknown.

At the same time, he was very supportive of my mother's intellectual activities. I mean, coming from *that* background, he allowed my mother to have a car of her own. She would go around meeting people, especially men writers and literati. Her friends used to come to our house, and my father was *very* friendly with all her special friends, like Dr. Jamil Jalbi.[16] He is still a very good family friend. My father never objected to that. He was unique in that kind of environment and was very liberated, but although he was liberated, he lacked direction.

You know, when my sister and I sit down and compare our notes about our father, *her* father is a different man, and *my* father is a different man. She is thirty years older than me. Her father was twenty-one years old, a young man living in a world where for a man to carry his own child was not something to be done, not on. *My* father was a different man who would pamper me, who would allow me to sleep with him, would take me out, would befriend me. A totally different man. Besides being my father, he was my playmate. My relations with him came more naturally to me. I could discuss cars with him. I could play toys with him. I could listen to English music while he was around—but could not do that when *my* mother was around.

I would hide the fact that I was listening to English music. For one, she would say, "I do not want you to listen to English music. Every ordinary child listens to it, and I want you to be extraordinary." That, I could not be. I am not

15. It apparently is known, even expected, that men from the feudal background take mistresses. Prime Minister Zulfikar Bhutto (1971–77) had several mistresses, one of whom became his permanent companion, much to the dislike of his wife. See Wolpert 1993.

16. Dr. Jalbi mediated a land dispute between Ayesha and her half-sister, with whom she had a very tense love-hate relationship.

made up that way, probably. Second, every song has something to do with love, and that she could not stand. She thought English love songs amounted to corruption. She listened to old Indian songs, and I would get angry. "Why is she fighting with me? Why can't she understand that all these old Indian songs she listens to are also about love?" I never had the courage to go and tell her that.

I remember I was not feeling well, and the homeopathic doctor had said that I could not take any milk products. Being a child, I used to be desperate for ice cream. My father used to take me out, and he would tell my mother, "We are going out for a ride," and secretly would buy me an ice cream—something my mother would *never* do. Well, for the good of me, but it was something that my father did for me, too. It was more a normal kind of relationship. He would buy me toys, and he would spend all day in the toy shop with me. One big event of my life was to buy a special toy. Every year I used to get one expensive toy, three hundred, four hundred, even seven hundred rupees. For *that* I used to really spend some time in the toyshop, buy something worth the time and money. It was always a walky talky or a gun or a motor car or a train set—boy's stuff, tanks and many, many pistols.

From the day I was born, I had this commitment toward my mother. It has been a strange kind of relationship. Less of a friendship, more of fear and commitment. Actually, I think we were not too close to each other. It was circumstances that put us together. Like every mother who knows her child, she knew me very well. I have always been extravagant, but until the day she died I would get money from her—and I was growing up. The last few months before she died were very bad, you know. One day I wanted to buy this "naval forces and military technology" calculator. I was never too fond of buying clothing and jewelry and all that stuff. I had gotten out of the habit! I said, "Amma, why don't you start giving me some pocket money?" You know, it was very strange. She was a writer, she was bringing me up, she was my mother, but still she was *very* innocent of the ways of bringing up a child. The first time I started wearing my undergarment [bra], she did not even know about it. She said, "But I give you everything." I said, "I want to have money of my own. Please give me one hundred rupees." Then I said, "The calculator for naval forces is ninety rupees, military technology is ninety, give me two hundred rupees." I could see the pain in her eyes. Suddenly she realized there was something she was doing that was not right. I *had* no life of my own until she died. Sometimes I think I still do not have a life of my own.

She said, "All right, I'll give you five hundred rupees." Now, *five hundred* rupees sounded great to me. She said, "No advances."

I said, "All right, no advances. That is a deal."

I do not know what she was scared of. She was scared for me. She was afraid
that I would get too friendly with boys, even boys younger than me. She tried
her best to keep me away from the world. Actually, it was an act of saving me
from the cruel world that she had seen. She never thought of dying, but she
did not take good care of her health. She was [de]fending me, you know,
against the world. I was in class eight when she hurried me to take my metric
exams [matriculation, tenth grade]. I took it. Then after I did my metric and it
was time to go to college, she said, "No. There are older girls there, and they
talk silly, and I do not want you to be exposed to all that!" So she said, "Now
you do your 'O' levels." She chose all my subjects. But when in 1979 on the
way back from England my father had a heart attack and died on board the aircraft, she handed me the travel checks, the passports, and everything and said,
"You take care of it; you are in charge." She sat down and cried. That is the relationship I could never understand between her and me—that enigma, our
relationship—to this day. I feared her. I loved my father without any fear, but
I loved my mother with both fear and commitment. Commitment toward her
till today is like a passion.[17]

I don't know fear of what. Fear of everything, of failing her, maybe. I have to
tell you, when you bring up a child with lots of restrictions and focus all your
attention on that child all the time, the child does develop a kinky kind of personality. That is how I ended up, very kinky [laughing]—you would not want
to know how kinky!

My father used to smoke, so I used to smoke sometimes, you know, that was
for fun. But after he died, she discovered it. I lied to her that I did not. It was *not*
because she would beat me up and she would scold me. I simply did not want
to disappoint her [pause]—God, if she had seen me now, she would be thoroughly disappointed and disgusted both [laughing]. You know the lack of
confidence that I face sometimes is one of the things I acquired. Every time I
said something or did something, I would be looking toward her eyes for approval or disapproval. Despite all that—and after all, I was a child—she would

17. Ayesha organizes an annual memorial lecture in her mother's honor, where she invites
local and international scholars and artists to commemorate her mother's work and achievements.

still scold me for going overboard at times. Let me tell you, Shahla, I *did not* really go overboard. It was going overboard by *her* standards. In a way, I am glad she died when she died because I was growing up and I was turning into a wild horse.

My mother's greatest wish was to see me as a writer, and I *did not* want to be one. I do have the capability to write. I was six years old when I started writing. We had gone to Murree,[18] where we stayed at a rest house, my father, my mother, a servant, and myself. I bought some beautiful papers and markers, and I wanted to use them. The first thing I wrote, literally, was something like "the smoke from the fire is stronger than the smell of the roses." My mother got it published! Every birthday I had, when I was a young child, whatever I had written in that year would be published. *But* because of all that pressure, her rules and the kind of people and writers I saw around her, I *did not* want to [become a writer]. So we would argue about that. I was never rude, but I would argue. But she would never take an argument from me. *That* would amount to rudeness in her eye. It was out of the question. Without arguments, you cannot have a relationship. If I was naughty, she would make me realize her displeasure. Then I would go down on my knees, begging, apologizing—"please, please forgive me." It was always me who apologized. I never thought of disobeying her willfully. I did not want to hurt her. It was not her fault. She was really innocent, in a certain way, of relating to me, because she did not know how to bring up a child.

I am not making excuses for her. I am trying to tell you how it all affected me. I always had this craze for airplanes, and when I was sixteen or something, suddenly I wanted to become an aeronautical engineer because women could not become pilots. I thought, "I will become an aeronautical engineer," and I wanted to study physics. When I told her that, she put her foot down and said, "Nothing's doing. You are going to study literature, and that's that." My subject had been chosen for me. I did not stamp my feet. I just accepted it [pause]. I don't know why [pause]. I always accepted all that she said because *that is* how it should have been. It would have been, anyway. She also always chose the fabrics for my clothing.[19] Hmm . . . I do not think she always chose the right kind of fabrics.

18. Murree is a resort hill station north of Islamabad, the capital of Pakistan.

19. Most Pakistanis buy fabric and have clothing made. Although ready-made dresses are becoming popular, the vast majority of people have their clothing made.

I am the kind of person who lives between two extremes. I have the extraordinary capacity to suppress all kinds of emotions, and I can let them go, all of a sudden, the whole of it, either in this end or that end. I think one reason why it is so is because of the way I was brought up. I still remember being hurt. One day I was really angry with my mother. That was one of my arguments in years with her. She said, "Ashur." I said, "Don't call me Ashur"—my father used to call me that—"I don't want you to call me Ashur!" It was Eid Milad al-Nabi,[20] a holy night, and she was praying. She came to me after she had finished her prayers and said, "Do you know what I prayed tonight?" I said, "What?" She said, "That I may die the day you do not need me anymore." That haunts me. What she said was very upsetting. At times now, when she is not there and I am very naughty, I remember how well she knew me. She could see the good in me, the bad in me, and the evil in me, more than I. *That* night she died [in 1988], I was twenty-one years old. Whatever she said to me follows me like a shadow. It haunts me all the time, especially when I am enjoying something, something that I have created myself.

I do feel guilty. Call it that. Everything is spasmodic in my life, I would say. As soon as I begin to enjoy something, I remember halfway, well, should I enjoy it? Would she like it? I am used to putting so many questions to myself. I still have not gotten out of this habit because when I was young and she was there, she expected me to understand and follow every movement of her eyes. She was very demanding, she was. I mean, she did not get you; she was very sensitive, very emotional, a creative person. Still, very thirsty for love herself. Maybe that is why she was so possessive of me. She did not want to share *that* love with anyone else.

So I grew up. One day I was sitting next to her. Suddenly she said, "You know, it is very strange. I am surprised how well you can get along with your father's family"—although today I say it was certainly for my good that I was kept far away from them. Still, when I would get back to them, I would enjoy it. I am not a very difficult person. What are my weaknesses? Happy faces and people laughing. I can, you know, go around like a clown. What my father's family and many other people enjoy about my company is that I make them laugh. I say funny things. I make an effort to make people happy. Whenever I was with my father's family, we would get along quite well. My mother was surprised because she did not. For one thing, she was an outsider married into

20. Celebrations for the Prophet Muhammad's birthday.

the family. Two, she *had* kept herself away from them. Well, it is true they are not worth it. But all human beings are worth something! The point was that she always sat with them, talked with them, and discussed things, but she wanted *me* to avoid them.

Look, Shahla, now that you have started talking to me about her, I think I do not know her. Actually my problem is that I know my mother in a certain way [pause], as I would. Very secret sides of her I do not know. She would socialize with them, she liked being with them, but again I do not know. She kept me away. She was very friendly with my stepmother, with my aunts. They would sit together and talk through the night. But when it came to me, I do not know why she was creating a shell and pushing me into it. I really do not know whether she really liked them or not. I think she did. To her friends she would say that they are a good family. Her friends would say, "Well, you have had all these civil suits and court litigations with them, and you say they are a good family!" They *are* in a way a good family. They are not that bad. I am surviving. They are all *males*, thirteen males, and I am surviving! It is not because I am, you know, something extraordinary or I am very brave. It is because they are not too bad.

I remember two days before she died, she suddenly asked me, "What will happen if I die? Would you want to go back to your [father's] family?" I said, "Well, no." The typical emotional sentimental answer: "No, you are not going to die. If you die, I die, blah, blah." She said, "Tell me honestly, would you go back to them? Don't go back to them." So she did not want me to be like my family. The wild character—my romantic nature is like my father's [long pause]. Now when I am trying to clear up all this mess and to reconcile with my sister—I find it relaxing to stay with her—with whom I have had a constant battle for four years, I keep thinking, "Am I defying my mother?" She told me to do certain things, but I cannot go on any longer doing them the way she wanted me to.

Another thing that I have learned from her circumstances and from her is to doubt everything and everyone. Now, you know my relationship with my sister. You know, I was telling you a couple of days ago that Dr. Jamil Jalbi said that my sister wanted this land, which is [worth] about ten to fifteen hundred thousand rupees, and I gave it [to her]. I am quite conscious about money and all that, in my way. But that day I could not refuse her because it was so nice having this feeling of warmth toward her. For four years I have been pushed, thrown away, thrown out. But still, like a fool, I am willing, every time, to try again, to reconcile.

Wish to Fly

Let me tell you a little about my life, about my father. With him gone, it had to be a shell. I was living in two shells at the same time. One shell was created by my mother—her morals, her values, her standards, and everything that would satisfy her. It was so dry. It was such a hard life. So, in order to survive spiritually, I had to create a shell of my own. In my shell, there was no human being, no relationship. There was no love, just planes and aircrafts. I have this postcard picture of an aircraft and those small badges that I have collected on my Lufthansa flights. You know, right in the middle of the night I used to be sitting and imagining myself as a pilot. I used to be really nuts at that time. Whenever there was an aircraft going past our house, I would *run* out. I still do it [pause, pensive]. Probably I wanted something to take me away, fly me out of this mess. I felt like a caged bird. I wanted to have the ability to do things, to have control, to fly away.

I used to be so jealous [protective] of my property. I had a briefcase in which I used to keep all the badges, all the postcards, picture of planes, and everything. We used to get *Newsweek* or maybe *Time*, and if there were pictures of aircrafts, I would cut them and paste them and make my own collection. My mother never made any comments about that. She was quite happy because this kind of occupation kept me away from people or from wishing to make friends. I would be very happy with those things. I survived because of that love for aircrafts.

You know, when I started my training in the Civil Service Academy in November 1988, all of the sudden I began to feel very miserable. I thought about it. After a couple of months of this, I said, "Damn it. I know why I am miserable." It was because I had suddenly stopped daydreaming. You know, that shell, that protective shell I wear all the time around me, that hides me, that saves me from this nasty world. People can do whatever they want, but I am safe in my world, within which I am in charge. Sometime I am the pilot of an F-16; sometimes I am a nuclear scientist. I dream about it. I am the main character. I do such fabulous things. It keeps me *so happy.*

Making a Face of Her Own

I had two boyfriends, real ones. Now I am totally off romance, and I am into other romances. I cannot tell you why I feel off romance now. Oh God, my mother would have fainted [if she were to hear this]. She had no concept of

me having an independent life of my own. Either I stand right there not entering it, or once I am in it, I go too far into it. Something I do not like myself. I
am a person at the extremes. The moments that are nice have something
wrong with them three minutes later. Like when I drink. There is just this one
moment, one brief second, in which I feel great and I talk giddy—those few
seconds that are at the core of the whole thing. I do it for that. I am trying to
tone down everything about me. I still use the same extreme expressions. I
started toning down on that. Now I try to use *mild* kinds of expressions that say
the same thing because people are people, and they do not accept these ex-
tremities. People can do very vile things themselves, but they are not willing
to forgive the violence of another creature. So I try to avoid that. I am not a
very successful person, I must say, but I try.

There *might* be a tension between what I want and what I think I ought to
be. Once I told you about the two faces of human beings: one that you can see
in the mirror and another of the physical person under the facade. The face inside is *my* face. Right now the shape of it is raw plaster paste. It is no solid face,
has no solid features. I am trying hard, sometimes messing it up, but I have no
knack for art. I better leave alone making a face of my own. So there is no face
really, no solid face. *That* is probably what is creating the conflict. *That* is probably what gives rise to my low self-esteem. You see, for so long I have lived the
life of my parents—never had the chance to live a life of my own. All actions
which I did as a child and which I do now, I end up feeling tense about them. I
feel guilty. So it is actually still their life that I live. I am trying hard to make a
face of my own, have a life of my own. The day I do that, probably, that will be
the end of the low self-esteem. That will be, maybe, a milestone. I have been
jogging for a couple of days, along with Chima. What we do is to set mile-
stones, so I push myself to make it to a designated point and have a break for a
minute and then start running again to the next milestone. Today I was thinking, "Well, God, isn't it like life, from one milestone to the other?"

Conflicted Self, Confused Gender

Going for my Ph.D. degree to Kings College would be a very important milestone.[21] You know, I really do not know what my interest is in. Somebody
asked me this question yesterday, "Why do you want to get a Ph.D. in war

21. Ayesha started at King's College in September 1992 and received her Ph.D. degree in
1996.

studies?" You know, I had no answer. I admit it. But one interesting reason for my interest in war studies is that I think that basically I am a careerist. I should have been made an engineer or something. *Now*, another reason, I think, is because of the intensity, the fire, the blood which is related to war studies [long pause, contemplating]. Or, another reason could be the success factor related with war. I mean if you succeed, if you win a war, that is a great time in any nation or individual's life. Or, it's maybe the destruction bit of it. Everything we do not like, or we do like, burns.

Another thing I think could be is that when I am operating in the world, I keep observing myself: "What am I doing?" I have this habit or nature of trying very hard to appear equal, if not superior, to any man around me. All the time I am competing with them. You see, when I fell in love, it was beautiful. The feeling itself was very beautiful. *But* then I began to hate. You see, my problem is that I love a person, you know that kind of love, until I take a U-turn. Then I am really ruthless. Why do I hate to be in love? Why do I take a U-turn? When you are being loved, when you are a beloved, you suddenly see yourself as a woman. All of the sudden, you have to behave like a girl, being delicate [in high-pitched voice], attracting attention. And suddenly I realize, God, I am trying to be delicate and feminine and all that! God damn it! Then I would take a U-turn.

So one major reason for my interest in war studies is that it is one 100 percent a subject within the male domain. What I enjoyed during my training in the Civil Service Academy and afterward was that during the special training we were taken to Wah [22] and to the ordinance factories. We had fifteen days of military attachment. There were nine girls, and the rest were men. Now what I really *relished* about the total training business for those days was to surprise men—the brigadiers, the colonels, and the majors. I would be sitting there questioning them about military affairs, not like a person who does not know, but with deep interest. I used to be arguing with them. I remember in one of our training sessions there were twenty-four boys, and I was the only girl. After the lecture by the colonel in charge, we had a question-and-answer session. All the men sat quietly. I was the only person who was questioning them about purely military affairs, talking in purely military terminology, quoting from the military technology and naval courses. They would get flabbergasted. They would be going around asking, "How does that girl know all

---

22. A small town between Islamabad and Peshawar.

that?" [laughter]. *That* was a great feeling! None of those twenty-four boys knew a thing! So my interest in war studies is, number one—you see what my mother pumped into my head—that I had to be extraordinary. Probably I am very ordinary, more ordinary than any person could be, and maybe I won't have the capability of being extraordinary, but her desire for me to be extraordinary stuck in my mind. Not many civilians, let alone girls, *dare* to enter this field. Number two, it is that it is a male domain, and I manage to make them uneasy because men *are* uneasy [hearty laughter].

In Murree, I was telling you, Chima and I used to go to play this video game. There was one game of shooting. A few men were standing around and looking at me, quite flabbergasted to see a girl aiming so well. Then we went to Patriata [a resort area between Islamabad and Murree]. Suddenly there was this man, you know, with the balloons and air gun. I thought I would try it. First I shot all the balloons in the small doors. Then the small buttons, I started aiming at those. I must have struck terror in the hearts of those poor men [laughing]. The Pathan said, "Well, madam, what good aim." Finally I said, "Wait a minute. Don't do these buttons. Put a pin." So he put a pin on the board and said, "Take aim." Imagine a small needle and you have to aim and break it with two shots. I managed it with three. I had never taken any shooting lessons, except that when I was a child, I had played with an air gun. Whenever I get a gun, I shoot. The very fact that there were men standing around, feeling amazed—you know, a girl doing that! Now I have gone into a different field. I want to be extraordinary in *my* way. One way, I think unconsciously, I can do it is to go into a field where even men do not dare go, to take *their* place and tell them I deserve it.

My mother knew of my passion for war studies. I remember the night she died. She used to work in her library. There was a master bedroom, and there was my room. She came to my room and sat on my bed. I don't know why, but that day I read her a poem. We remembered my father, and I read her a poem about death by [Rabindranath] Tagore. She cried. I suddenly felt sorry. I felt guilty. I said, "Why are you crying? I have never made you cry." She said, "No, I am crying because the lovely things that you could do, you can do, and you should do." She said, "In particular, I mean studying abroad. You cannot do it because of me. You are suffering because of me." She cried that day. She died that very day. She had an infarction. So I think that the point with being extraordinary is that I am not satisfied; I do not want to do things except to excel.

You know what I *hate* doing? Mother never liked me cooking. She never taught me how to sew. She hated it. *She wanted me to be a man, her son.* So now I do not want to be delicate, to do delicate things, like being an artist, have a boutique, or something designing. When I set my heart and mind to it, I would probably excel. *But* what I *hate* is the fact that some people would say, "Well, that is a girl's job. That is what women are supposed to do, what they are created to do." I am going into war studies with two objectives. One is to pursue the subject with a very creative mind, and two is the satisfaction I will draw from hearing people say [in a masculine voice], "Well, she excelled in a man's world" [laughing].

You know, one day I went to the British consul. There was this army chap who was going to England to study a military subject at the government expense. He was so surprised—[broad smile] this is what gives me satisfaction—and said, "Are you going for war studies?" "*Yes,*" I said. And I said it, you know, pretty confidently, thoroughly enjoying myself [smiling]. I like it because of the very satisfaction I get from shocking people, *men* in particular. It is constantly a woman-against-man kind of a thing.

But, you know, so far I have been criticizing what my mother did to me, but there are things which she really gave me. I *am* a weak person and cowardly in certain respects. Sometimes when I get this extraordinary *strength*, it is because of what she told me. When I used to do mathematics, the way I am, I would go for the simplest questions first. Mother would say, "No, go for the most difficult questions first." She would make me work hard and do difficult things. I never had the concept of an easy life. When I get upset these days, it is normally because there is not a thing which can tire me. She formulated my personality in that way, according to my genes, my nature. But one moment of ecstasy is worth, at times, everything. When I talk about drinking and intoxication—I think *intoxication* is the wrong word; we all get intoxicated when we drink. The hangover is quite a while. But I am not after intoxication. It is actually the ecstasy I feel, just for a few moments. So when you are working *hard* and whipping yourself, ecstasy is when you succeed. When you are going through it, striving to achieve your goal, and you get it, it is momentary ecstasy. It is so beautiful. Maybe something like what you would feel when you have sex or something. Ha. Ha. So I have to keep running and running and running.

What I think of ecstasy, today, is a bit different. Like I was assigned ten men who came to my section for training, out of a total of eighty-five. The rest went to other sections. Now I began training them, giving *them* a hard time and giving *myself* a hard time. I worked hard preparing tests for them, very technical things. When they got into it, they enjoyed it because they were gaining much more than anyone else out of those eighty-five men. The funny bit is that out of those ten men, two of them were from my office. So when the training of the men from my office finished, I had to give them a certificate. One of them who did not perform well came to me. I said, "I am sorry, but I cannot given you a certificate. You did not qualify, and I think you have to put in at least another ten days of training." You know what he said? He said, "Madam, I have come because I don't want to go to another division because there you do not learn anything. At least I am learning something here. Please write to the administration section. I do not want to go to other divisions." And *that* was a good moment.

I like my lifestyle. Why? Because it makes me *different*, different from other girls and even different from many men. I draw a sheer satisfaction from it— operating in a man's world, maybe like a man, *better* than a man. I was reading in *Time* magazine a statement about this woman, I don't remember the name, saying to myself, "She is a man I would like to meet" [laughing]. It would be an insult to women, you are very right [laughing heartily]. But speaking in my context, mentally, you see, I am not like a young girl, but like a young boy. I like playing games which boys would. Now *there* is a paradox because I am twenty-six—I was born on April 7, 1966. Mentally I would be like a boy of fifteen or sixteen, with the physical age of a twenty-six-year-old woman. Now the paradox is that I *enjoy* doing what I am doing. *But* in my part of the world, it would mean moving toward rejection by people. I mean, I am not willing for a second to change myself into a smart, slick girl, behaving like one, pretending, or actually putting forth this idea before others that, well, girls are vulnerable. I say other people are vulnerable. That is what the girls do around here, and they get rewarded. My contention is, all right, I am very lazy. I would rather shout for my servant to get me a glass of water, *but* the minute a few men are around, I would like to do everything myself just to show them that it is not only they who can do it; I can do it, too! I think a major reason for my interest in war studies is that I am in a state of conflict all the time, sometimes with my parents, sometimes with the male members of the society around me. *It is a world of conflict I live in all the time.* And in between, in order to survive, I have this dream world of a shell. The shell never leaves me.

I was talking about a paradox. Now, what *happens* is that in the social market you are no longer a valuable commodity. Because of the way you are, people are scared. They are annoyed by what you are, by what you are portraying yourself as. Honestly, I can tell you one thing. I am *far, far, far* less harmless than many cute-looking, well-behaving women and girls that I see. My only fault in life is that I am very blunt with my likes and with my dislikes. If I like a person, I tell them that. I try to do something to contribute to that person's happiness. Most of the time people begin to take me for granted. When I dislike the person, I do not hide that fact either. You see, I never use the word *hate* because *hate*, which we use so recklessly—we are really reckless with our use of words—is a very strong feeling, at times stronger than love. There is very little difference between the two. So my dislike, I am telling you, is graded. So I am trying my best to establish myself in a man's world. I am *very* happy the way I drive, pretty crazily.[23] *But*, you know, when a boy is sitting in my car complimenting me, well, I enjoy that compliment. They say, "Women don't drive well"—here they really don't—"but you drive differently." I like that! I mean, I am not used to compliments. They really confuse me.

Yesterday I went to see this friend at my office headquarters. He had seen me after a year and a half, and he said, "Oh, you look pretty." These kinds of comments, you know, I really do not know how to react to. They make me pretty uneasy. I am not used to compliments. I have a general opinion about myself, that people do not like my face, *and* they end up disliking what I try to be. I mean, it makes men uneasy. Well, they are excited for a while, but then they say, "Oh God, she is a dangerous commodity." And women, they do not like you because you do not like them [pause], especially after my mother's death. I cannot help being what I am. I am constantly fighting men. I fight them because I do not want them to feel that I have chickened out. Now I am trying to come to terms with my sister and to sort out my problems. I am beginning to think that there is more to life. It is not worth fighting [with her sister]. Try to get out of it. Find other frontiers for yourself, frontiers worthy of you. So I am trying to mend my relations with people around me. One thing my mother could not teach me was how to have relationships with people.

Family Feud: Land and Lineage

I became aware of the conflict between my sister and my father when I was six or seven years old. Before, I was too young and too busy with games and such.

---

23. My husband and I had a taste of her "crazy" driving in the deserts of Bahawalpur, going toward the Drawar Fort, when she asked her driver to let her drive.

I felt good seeing my sister when she came for visits, and she may have felt the same. She was involved in a five-year litigation with her own father over land. Her husband started it. During the five years of conflict and litigation, her husband forbade her to see her father. I remember—I will never forget that night—she came out to see us without her husband's knowledge. She cried, and my mother cried, and father had tears in his eyes. Although my mother was a stepmother, they hugged each other, and they cried that evening.

Well, my father died, and again the litigation started. For twelve years we have been fighting each other in the court. The conflict between her and me is a conflict that should have been sorted out by our father. With the conflict not there—I think, I hope—it would be more peaceful. I could then sit down and dedicate my life to the work that lies ahead.

The bone of contention is the mango orchard at Khanqah Sharif. It started when my father gifted it to my mother. My sister's husband then started this whole litigation. He said that it could not be done. For five years they fought with each other in the court. Then Father died, and twenty days after his death the court litigation started again. They challenged my mother's right to the orchard. In fact, one of my father's sisters charged that my father had divorced my mother, but she had the audacity to want me to marry her second son! I refused. After my mother's death, my sister and I saw each other for a year, and then we stopped visiting altogether. Then her younger daughter was getting married. I was in Karachi. I got a call from my servant, Choti. She said, "Najma Bibi has called, and she is inviting you to her daughter's marriage. What are your plans?" I said, "Nothing's doing. I will go." And I went. She was so happy to see me. We kissed each other, and we hugged and we cried. This was last year [1991].

After that, we started seeing each other. She invited me to go and see her in Murree, and I was happy to do so. I used to go to Europe without telling her. She would get very upset. Then one day my sister called and said, "I am tired. I am old"—she is not that old. "I do not know how long I will live. Let us resolve this." She talked with me and said, "I can give you my share [of the orchard]. But I want *our* problems to be solved. I can give you my guarantee, but I cannot guarantee on behalf of my children. I do not want you and my children to fight, and I do not want your children and my children to fight." [Long pause] We are now trying to talk to each other. So for six months she kept coming to Lahore, and we went to see the mediator, and we talked it out. It is taking some time.

You see, we have been fighting each other since November 1979. It has gone on and on. Initially, when we would see each other, nobody was abusive, nobody was too angry, and nobody even mentioned that we had a court case. In the meantime, the case kept dragging on in the court, but nobody was inclined to resolve it; nobody was willing to mediate it. Now we have the inclination and a mediator to sort things out. The point of our dispute is that she claims that she has a share in the orchard, and I say that it was gifted to my mother.[24] It would take another twenty years to fight it, maybe more than that, and lots of money. So we said, "All right, let us negotiate outside of the court." The mediator suggested that I forgo my share in the Bahawalpur property and that my sister forego her share in the orchard, and we accepted it because our relationship is important. You see, this change has been brought about by my sister. If she had been willing to fight, I would have fought her to my death because my contention was, "I am not going to resolve it just because you think I am weak. I will resolve it when you treat me as your equal." She used to perceive herself as superior to me. Now she has come to me, asking me for *bakhshish*, a gift.

Shahla, every minute of a life can be a new discovery of life itself, of what you can do, of what others can do to hurt you, to love you, of love itself.[25]

A few months ago when my sister was coming to Lahore, and I told you that I did not really wish to see her, it was because there were so many gaps between us, not just the age gap, but so many other gaps. I was less sure of her. She was coming for reconciliation, and I was getting worked up because when you stay away from people, you have a tendency to get attached to things rather than to people. That time I was more attached to money. Let me tell you, at that time even if she had fallen on her knees before me and asked me

---

24. According to Hanifi law, a Muslim, male or female, may make a gift of his property during his lifetime, and there is no limit on that, but he cannot do so after his death by will. In the latter case, he can bequeath only one-third of his property by will (Fayzee 1974, 217; Mannan 1995, 207–8). In the same vein, Maulana Thanvi writes, "If someone gave anything to anyone and he accepted it or did not say anything and the thing was left in his hand, then it becomes his property and no longer remains of the giver. This is called 'hiba' (gift) in religious code" (1981, 355). Ayesha's claim that her father had gifted the mango orchard to her mother before his death means that her sister or any other heir legally could not stake a claim to it.

25. I said to her, "I remember once when I saw you, you said that you were supposed to pick your sister up at the airport. I think it was after you had broken up your engagement with Hassan. You said, 'I don't like her.' What changed?"

ten times for a *bakhshish*, I would have said no. Now that I have had a chance to stay with her and heal, I feel yes, she is my family. I stopped thinking of medieval benefits, and I started thinking more humanely, more like a normal human being because in these three or four months my relationship with her has also developed. When she came then, she was my opponent; she was coming for the resolution of a conflict. Now she is my sister. It was so moving when she said,. "*Bakhshish*," and I said, "All right, take it." I will go to Bahawalpur, and I will be God again. She had tears in her eyes. She said, "It's not just the money factor that has made me happy. You have forgone your share of the property. I can now raise my head before my husband and say, 'Well, we have resolved our conflict. Now I can boast proudly that, yes, she has given me this.' " You see, if I have my ego, she also has her ego. I thought of that. If I have to look straight with my head up and strut about proudly, she also has to do that.

What may happen next and how our relationship may develop, [pause] I have left it to God [pensive]. I am relaxed now. You see, I am reminded of a story I was told when I was young. A young girl was told to go to a certain river and throw her net to catch a fish, inside whose belly she would find a precious ruby. She threw her net and caught a fish. Inside the fish she found that ruby. But no sooner had she gotten it that it slipped and fell into the water. She was despondent. For three days, she prayed, "God, I really want that ruby." The fourth day she threw her net again and caught a fish. Inside the fish she found a ruby. This time she could have it. The moral of the story is that it is not just your efforts that are important, but also God's will. A lot of things have to be left to him. I mean, at best what you can do is try.

In Saraiki, there is beautiful saying.[26] It is an allegory of life: *Poches pe karu, allah rang lesi*—"You draw the sketch, God colors it in." I feel very peaceful now. I feel that I have an anchor now, I have a family. You know, it is beautiful. Now when I think of going to Bahawalpur, I also desire to take the time off and go to Murree and stay with my sister. One day we were strolling and I saw a hat that I wanted to buy. My wallet was in her purse, and when I asked to have it, she said, "Let me get it for you." I said, "No, I have money." She said, "Let me have the pleasure of being the elder sister." You know, when I take people out normally, I pay for them myself. This time she was paying for it. It was so nice,

---

26. Saraiki is one of the major languages in Pakistan and spoken primarily in central Pakistan and in the Bahawalpur Province. Ayesha is fluent in Saraiki.

like having a family all over again. Now those same fifteen lakh rupees [gifted to her sister] probably does not matter that much, considering what I can get.

The out of court settlement involves my forgoing a twenty-five-acre share of land in Bahawalpur in exchange for her foregoing her twenty-two acres in the orchard [which is seventy-five acres total]. But my [legal] dispute with my maternal aunt is continuing.[27] Right now I no longer see my *khala*, my aunt. It is because she does not understand my lifestyle. She wants me to be totally dependent on her, which is not possible. I could be dependent on her if she helped me with all spheres of my life, including litigation and everything else. That she does not do. Twenty days after my mother died, and after eight years of not seeing each other, my aunt, who lives next door, automatically acquired the role of my guardian. I did not realize how totally I was dependent on my mother's guidance. So being a dependent person mentally and having that kind of attitude, I became dependent on her initially. I see her because she is my mother's sister, but lately I have sort of started going blank everywhere.

Marriage Feudal Style

I think that the person I am in love with has to be very considerate, has to understand me, because till now my relationship with the men I fell in love with began with either this feeling of "Well, she is a good victim. Have her. Enjoy her wealth" or *this* feeling *plus* pity. I am reminded of a novel by a Swedish author, *Beware of Pity*, in which he says that those relationships that are based on pity are not long lasting. It is not that *they* were to be blamed entirely. I ought to be blamed for who I am. Because I *was* looking for sympathy, which ended up in infatuation or love or whatever word you would like to use. I was fishing for a different thing. I keep looking for shoulders and leaning on shoulders to cry on, which I should not. I had no image of male love for me, other than that of my father. I really do not know how it would be. But I know for one—and I

27. The maternal aunt claimed an inheritance right to Ayesha's mother's property. Ayesha contended that her mother was a Shi'a and therefore no one but her has a right to her mother's inheritance. According to the Shi'a law of inheritance, in the absence of sons a surviving daughter precludes all others from the paternal and maternal sides. The Sunni law, however, maintains that if there is only one daughter, she takes one-half of the estate, but two-thirds if there is more than one daughter. The rest goes to the agnatic heirs (Fayzee 1974, 464–65; Balchin 1994, 273–74). For a quick review of inheritance law and its application in different provinces in Pakistan, see Balchin 1996, 148–49.

assure you it is not a prejudice or bias for myself—that I am not too *bad* a human being from inside. Somebody has to give me a chance. God has given me all sorts of opportunities to survive, but I also need this one opportunity. This would be not only from God, but also from the person involved with me. He has to relax as far as I am concerned.

There was no love involved with Hassan [not his real name], not even a factor of liking.[28] You see, the way our society is, as far as the subcontinent is concerned, everywhere you turn, you hear, "Well, all alone! God, that's blasphemous!" I was tired, and four years of running [since her mother's death] can be very, very tiring without anyone around you. When you are running, you need a reassuring look, a glance. Like, I was jogging today, and what I enjoyed was panting, slowing down, and Chima [her friend] saying, "Come on, buck up, a little more, you can do it." I like that. So that is the kind of thing you want in your life, too. People just turn around, friends who would not move a finger to do anything for you, and they say, "Why don't you get married?" I usually tell them, "Well, the kind of dumb person I am, nobody is interested in marrying me."[29] I mean, the kind of person I am, why would they come to me? You know, people have such double standards. These girls are so delicate, et cetera, et cetera. They can be so conniving and cunning. They really get things out of men, make life so miserable. If I marry a man, I would like to be his companion. I want equality—equality in the sense that if I am tired, he should buck me up and help me. If he is tired, I should do the same.

It was not even based on understanding—my engagement with Hassan. To begin with, it was very stupid of me. I am basically an idealist. I want to find all the solace, success, *everything* inside that individual, inside the house. I was comfortable with the idea [of marriage] *because*, number one, I used to have a relaxed relationship with his family, and I thought, well, adjusting would not be very difficult. They are the very unconventional kind of family, very modern, more modern than I could imagine initially. But I was being very foolish.

28. By the time of this interview, Ayesha's engagement had been broken, and the marriage arrangements were off.

29. Ayesha actually was being facetious here. In fact, she had several suitors and marriage proposals, suggested to her by her maternal aunt and her sister, notwithstanding various conflicts between them. She rejected them all on different grounds, mostly for being after her money or being intellectually inferior to her. She nearly married a man handpicked by her sister but broke off the relationship at the last minute, much to her sister's consternation.

Second, adjustment with him was not a problem at all because he was not
interested in me. His family wanted it. They told me later that they had been
after him for a year, telling him, provoking him to get to this idea of marrying
me. Otherwise, there was no way he could have gotten married. Nobody
would marry *him* in Bahawalpur or in the adjacent areas. To begin with, he suf-
fers from schizophrenia. Some people think he is gay. Well, he is pretty ef-
feminate. Plus, he was forty-three years old and not just a bit but very cold
emotionally. When I thought of marriage and settling down, I had his family
in mind, not him, not a *bit*. In fact, after our engagement got arranged, I would
ring up from Lahore, and I would be talking to his family all the time, instead
of to him, unless he happened to be around.

"Do you want to talk to Hassan?"

"All right, if he is there."

It was that sort of thing. I desperately wanted a *home*. I have a house. I
wanted a home. And that is what is so beautiful about my present relationship
with my sister. When I go there, I have a feeling that I am in a home instead of
a house. So I thought I would be having a home, would have people besides
my parents' brothers and sisters who would be interested in me, who would
take care of me. Not in the literal sense, taking care of your bread and butter
and all that, but that if you cried and if you laughed, they would be interested.
Like a child, I wanted attention and I wanted love. So, really, I had no relationship with Hassan. He was not capable of giving any love or feeling intense
emotions. I am a very intense person, and he is very, very cold.

There is no comparison between him and my father.[30] No way! He was so
much unlike my father. My father was a man who was capable of falling in
love, of making love. Hassan was incapable of anything, particularly of making it [laughter]. Father was a very tender person. He also was tender with my
mother, but he shouted at her, though never in public, anyway.

What happened was that there was a marriage proposal by a friend of
Hassan's nephew, who was a year younger than me, a captain in the army.
Now, I did not like to live where his family lived. I would not want to go there.
When he proposed, I asked him, "What if I say no to living where you live?"
He said, "Well, we are to suggest it"—and that meant suggesting that his
mother should move in with us. I would not want that either. So I told Hassan's

---

30. Because Hassan was also from a feudal background, I asked Ayesha, "How do you compare him to your father?"

sister, "I am saying no to your nephew." She said, "No, no. Hang on, hang on. Come down to Bahawalpur." I went to Bahawalpur, and I was asking her what was people's reaction generally to his proposal. I finally asked—just like that— what was Hassan's reaction? She said, "Well, he was jealous and said that he wanted to propose to you." So I said—jokingly—"Why didn't he?" He did.

Then his family was really after me. I thought, "What the hell?" They are a good family, and they would not be greedy and to hell with the man. So that is why I accepted. Nobody told me then what was wrong with him, which I *later* discovered, and that was very traumatic. They never told me that he was not normal. I expected him to behave like a normal man, but he was not, so it blew up. I am glad it did. Besides, they are too modern for me. I have some principles and values [long pause].

You see, the conflict within me is the conflict between the woman that I am or the man that I am and the men that are around me. With Hassan, I had no relationship. I was trying hard, but you know one thing? I was trying hard, when he was around, to become the woman, the wife. I was trying to mold myself for that future role. But fortunately because he was not man enough—I had realized this—it was writ large that I would still have to be the man around, earning my own bread and butter—in fact, earning and working for him also. The conflict, Shahla, was how to face the people around me. I come from a rural background. It is a different world altogether. It is purely a man's world. When a woman marries, her man should be the type who can take charge of things and of her. Hassan was not that kind of a man. The conflict that emerged then was that I also had to fill in the blanks for him. I had to push him. You know, when I would go to Bahawalpur, I used to tell him, "Please don't work, but be there. Come with me to my village. When my *munshi* comes, you just sit there please and chat with him." I knew that he was worthless as a man. I knew I would end up doing most of the things myself, but I was doing it [getting married] to earn a home for myself.

After the breakup, I was devastated [she lit a cigarette, took a long drag, and paused]. The reason I was devastated was *because,* number one, by the time it ended, I had settled down with the idea of marriage. As I said, I come from a rural background. It was very difficult facing the [village] people. Although the entire world knew that he was not normal, when an engagement breaks in our society, the woman is to be blamed: "Well, something must be wrong with *her!*" That and, plus, for so long I had resisted getting married and rejected my suitors. That is a stigma in itself in this society—a woman who acts like a man and does not want to get married. Facing people's reactions, that was devastating. Also, I now think the reason the whole thing blew up could be probably because his sister also did not want [the marriage]. Much later she told me that their relatives had warned them against his marriage with me: "Don't marry this girl, or she will take all the property!" Well, of course, I already have my own property, but, you see, that is what they had on their mind. That is probably what she also had on her mind. Right now she is the only able successor of that family's property. Hassan is not married. *Now* there is no chance of him getting married, so it is she who will inherit after he dies, whatever his property is. In the feudal setup, these things, these long-term plans, do matter; they do take place.

Feudal Lord, Civil Servant

Uh . . . [sigh] well, that is another frontier I have been fighting.[31] You see, my mother believed in genes. We used to have a Founder's Day. On Founder's Day, every child from every grade had to stand and get a prize. My mother used to attend. After the Founder's Day intermission, my mother would say, "You know, that kid got the first position." I would say, "You know mother, that kid, *that* particular kid, is brighter than me, and I have a low opinion of myself." She would say, "Why are you looking down? Why don't you look up?" I used to be bothered about it. So when I was doing my BA, what really made me work to pass my exam was a comment she had made earlier. She had said, "In your family, nobody has ever done a BA, and you will not do yours. I am sure. You have taken after your father's family." That hurt me so much! I said, "I must do my BA," and I worked hard. I made it.

I really worked for it because *she* wanted it—my civil service exam. Well, the result of the civil service final exam was declared in March [1989] after she had died. After that, there were times when I was really leery, but it is good that I did it. She wanted me to go into the civil services, and I was against it. Out of college, everyone has ideas. I did not want to face life. One day she sat me down and said, "Listen, child, when you do not have a father, you do not have a brother, you are not married, you do not have an uncle, then you have to stand on your own two feet. You have two alternatives, either you write so well that you make your name in a short time, and everywhere you go people

31. I asked her, "What made you decide to go into the civil services?"

recognize you and welcome you. Or else you have to go into the civil services." The second option was much easier.

But there is so much corruption in the civil services, and the fact that you
are a girl [can be a problem]. There are very few exceptional cases of women
who are willing to work as officers and *not* present themselves as women in a
male society. Now my conflict in my office is that my director wants to give
me certain facilities [advantages] *because* I am a girl, but I refuse to take them. I
say, "No way. I am an officer. I have competed, and I should be treated as one.
If you want to be harsh with me, go ahead [banging the table]. If you want to
be lenient with me, go ahead [bang]. But it should be equal treatment." Another reason for the differences of treatment is that of rampant corruption, as
I said. The boss is involved in it. If you do not join their club and do what they
want, you have to stay out. There are lots of things you have to do in the bureaucracy. You have to laugh to please your bosses; you have to be sorry to
please them; you have to cry to please them. A boss is like a husband, without
any of the advantages of having one [laughing]! It is worse than having two
husbands! So I try to act in my office in a very *awami*, commoner, style.

They know some things about my background, that I am a rich girl and that
I do not give a damn about anyone, but my relation to the junior class is cordial. They are not allowed to make any phone calls from any place in the office, so they come to my office and say, "Madam, can I make a phone call?"
And I say, "All right." "Madam, it is a long distance." I say, "Oh, all right, go
ahead." Of course, I do not pay for it; the government does! But, you see, if I
can make a call, why can't they? Now I am training a few grade-eleven clerks
for grade thirteen. They have to take an exam. My office is air-conditioned. I
make them sit there and lecture them, and every day I treat them to a cup of
tea and biscuits from my own pocket. Nobody has ever done that in that office. I told them from day one, "Listen, nobody in this office is superior, nobody is subordinate. We are all here to learn." Then I gave them a test and
asked them to evaluate the trainer. This was something that had never been
done before. No officer has ever stood up and said, "I do not know." So my relationship with my subordinates is much better than my relationship with my
superiors because seniors behave in a certain way. Bureaucracy is bureaucracy.
It is very difficult. You have to behave in a different way; you have to be very
pleasing to your boss and please him all the time. What is expected normally
is that you just go and chat with him and say pleasing things to him. I do not
do that—the kind of artless person I am, I don't know.

There are five hundred men, and I am the only woman working in my office. It does not bother me that there are no women. My only problem is that I should have someone to talk to. I am friendly with a few clerks. They are very kind. These days I am so busy training these men. I chat with them, joke with them, sometimes joke at my own expense. Now the atmosphere is more relaxed. Whether my relationship to my boss or superiors has changed since I have been hired, I cannot tell. You see, I am a very complex person, keep switching. But I think I have some understanding now.

Coming from a feudal background has its problems in your mental development, and that is because you are so used to exercising authority. It is very different when you are taking orders from someone. At times, it is very difficult for me, and I feel as bad as a child would who has to go to school in the morning. "Oh, the director said this, the director said that." But I am slowly getting used to it. I say, "All right." At worst, what is he going to do? Shout at me? They are not going to throw me out. "You want to shout at me, go ahead." It is not that I do not carry out his orders. I do. But if I go wrong somewhere, I am not scared. I used to be scared. I say, "All right, the worst is that he will shout at me. Fine! I will take that." That is something that is very difficult for a feudal to adjust to.

Uh . . . well, my servants may take my screaming as very similar kind of thing, but they take it because I also carry them along with me like a family. The problem in my office is that my work is too technical. When I took charge, it was really learning on your own. Nobody told me what my duties were. The work was not charted out for me, anyway. Sometimes there are errors. You screw up. My boss does not shout, but he gets angry, and I have been forced, slowly, gradually, to change myself. You know, yesterday there were a few clerks in my office. They are really good human beings and come to my help when I am in trouble. So one of them said, "Madam, I think you should start learning how to play chess [laughter]. That will teach you a lot about government services and how they operate."

Being in the government, being in the bureaucracy rather, *is* like playing chess. You cannot go around displeasing people because, you see, they are all too related. The way you are working, people come to you with their problems and expect you to sort them out. If you start fighting with people, on principles even, soon you will be isolated. There are ways to fight. Two years back I was a person who would fight about everything and anything, make everything into an issue and everything a deep principle. Now I have begun to sort out things. If you are in the government service with a lot of idealism, you can expire in no time. You are expected to deliver some goods, and you should do that. You should do your duty and try to be just with people. That is an art that I could *never* have learned in my feudal background and environment, which I could learn only as a government servant.

My civil work can come in handy in the feudal setup, yeah. It comes in very handy in life, because, you see, once you are away from your land—it is a small domain—you are nobody. You have to learn how to operate. I mean, in your feudal setup your ego—my God—gets inflated. You are handicapped in a feudal environment. You are used to insulting people, not to taking insults. What I am saying is that I have gained a lot out of my civil service experiences, namely how to operate with people like your equals. You cannot order them all the time; you have to obey them at times. This [change in attitude], too, came about gradually. You see, I would not go around trying to please anyone. Me? Pleasing anyone? No way! Now I have learned that it is not just *me*. Last year there was this clerk who had to take a course. He asked me to talk to the director of my department. Now, very recently I had an argument with my director, and I said, "No way am I going to his office. Until he calls me in and says what the issue is, I would not ask for any favor." But for two days there was this conflict going within me, conflict between my ego and that poor man's interest. I finally thought, "My ego is not *that* big that I should sacrifice this poor man's interest." So I made up with my director. Fine! Do not join this club, I thought, but at least by standing at the edge of the door of this club you can benefit so many others.

Women, Work, and Feminism

I think it is very important for women—talking about the feminist movement—who live in the big cities, this elite class whose daughters go to good institutions, to strive toward sending their girls to work [for the government]. You know, a very old saying in this country is: "we are not educating a girl to make her work." But I say, why not? The atmosphere has to be changed. Attitudes should be changed. More girls should come to work. For all the people living in the posh areas, rich people, for them college is considered to be a marriage market, especially Kinnaird College.[32] I say, mothers should be con-

32. Kinnaird College is located in Lahore and is one of the oldest and most prestigious English colleges for girls in Pakistan. See Maskiell 1984.

vinced that their girls should be made to work [emphatic]. More girls should do civil service—because we need more women to do the work. There was this [marriage] proposal for me.

He said, "Can't you leave your job?"

I said, "No way!"

"Why is it such an ego problem?" he asked

"No, it is not an ego problem." I said. "Every day I go to work for five hours, at least. Those five hours are mine. I present what is the best in me and what is the worst in me. It is all me."

Now, when I joined my office, my director threw me this challenge: "You take the computerization." For fifteen days, I worked day and night trying to understand how to do systems analysis and designs, and I mastered—sorry, I still won't use the word—learned how to do it. Today, I feel so happy. Whenever there is a team that comes from the headquarter, or anywhere, to talk about computers and computerization, I am called immediately. I feel happy. That is *my* achievement, a projection of *my* ability. That is very important. Like there were two sides of my mother: she was Jamila Hashmi, and she was Begum Sardar Owaisi. In Khanqah Sharif and Bahawalpur, she never introduced herself as Jamila Hashmi, always as Begum Sardar Owaisi. Once I asked her [about it]. She said, "Listen, this is your father's domain, and here I am Begum Sardar Owaisi. When I go to my domain, then I am Jamila Hashmi." So even for women who marry I think it should be a matter of satisfaction to have their own domain. You know, it is very satisfying to have your own domain. Every day you have to face bitterness, you have to face excitement.

I do not want to be part of the feminist movement, the WAF [Women's Action Forum]. The reason, Shahla, is that most of the women who take part in it, except for a few, are very confused about the whole thing, about the feminist movement, about feminism itself, and, more than that, about the status of women in Pakistan. They talk of freedom and of liberation, but when they are mothers themselves, they behave differently. OK, in my view feminism in Pakistan is the struggle to thwart the male part of society, to say, "Listen, we are as much human beings as you are. What we want is to be treated equally, not as some creatures who are dependent on you, who want nothing but your love and your sympathy and your appreciation as you would appreciate a fellow male." Women fight against injustice. Fine! The idea is not misplaced. The way they are doing it is misplaced.

To begin with, if you want to have a successful feminist movement, you will

have to amend—restructure, rather—the entire society itself. The majority of
the women involved belong to the upper class. They are in the movement not
just because they believe in it, but because they need to do something with
their time and to feel important—people like Kishwar Naheed.[33] I have seen
that woman from childhood, and I know that she is *not* a feminist. Male chauvinism in this part of the subcontinent is directly related to female chauvinism.
In fact, it is the female chauvinism that gives birth to male chauvinism. If you
want the feminist movement to succeed, you do not have to change the men
only. You have to change the women and the family structures.

My great desire for war studies—to do it practically, not fight a war but be
a part and parcel of it—is because of my peculiar background. My strong desire to establish myself in a male-dominated society is not because I am in conflict with a male-dominated society alone. It is also the conflict with my
mother [banging the table]. In a war, everything is so very fluid. You destroy a
thing, and you construct a thing [bang]. You destruct what is there [bang], and
you construct a new thing out of it [bang]. In the subconscious, it would be
there, I am sure. The family structure is very important. In Pakistan, it is the social structure that is the problem. You start with all these marriage ceremonies,
all these mothers who at times pretend to be so liberal. When it comes to their
daughters-in-law, their family, their sons, they are darn conservative.

There are two sets of women here—three sets, rather. One set lives in the
villages, in the rural areas. They are working along with the men, are taking all
the pressures of life along with the male members, and are earning side by
side. They do not brag about feminism and the movement and equality and all
that. When they want to have lovers, they have them.[34] Their basic problems
are not equality and justice. It is poverty. It is financial injustice.

The other two sets of women come from the city. One includes the *begumaat*
[sing. *begum*] and Mrs. So-and-so—those who live in posh homes. Either they
totally appreciate what their men do, or they may try to spend some of their
time usefully—as they say, engage in some activities. These are older women.
The second set includes women who work in the government or elsewhere.

33. Kishwar Naheed, chapter 5, was a close friend of Ayesha's mother; Ayesha addressed her
as *maasi*, mother's sister. At the time of this interview, Ayesha and Kishwar seemed to have developed some personality conflicts.

34. Several times during the interview Ayesha asserted that many women in her village have
lovers, and so long as it is not flaunted, nobody cares.

They can be divided into those who believe in the cause—and they are very few—and those who consider themselves a part and parcel of the government and the establishment. You see, what is horrible about bureaucracy is that those who are in it have no face. Their faces are mutilated. I know the daughter of an ex-chief minister of Sindh who is the assistant commissioner here in Lahore. She was in the foreign service and reappeared in the civil service exam, and she was reallocated to district management. One day we were talking, and she said, "Do you know, women and jobs do not go together!" I said, "What are you doing here?" See, they would rather be under the shadow of a protective male. This concept of male protection is, again, deeply set in our society.

I have not been directly involved in the feminist movement, but I think the kinds of problems we have—of feminism, of male chauvinism—have to be sorted out practically. Otherwise, you get into a solution like the creation of this country. Muslim League was basically a leader's party with four hundred members.[35] Muslim League is a concocted party. It never existed. Not just because they have split into various factions, but because they never existed from day one! You see, Muslim League was never a populist movement.[36] It has never been. The first thing we should have done after the creation of this country was to disband Muslim League. Now what they do is that every now and then they wake up and say, "Well, Muslim League created Pakistan, and anyone who is against Muslim League is anti-Pakistan, blah, blah, blah." They start blaming people, framing people, and that's that. Muslim League has never made it to the throne without the help of people in charge of politics and of the government. It is not the movement, it is not the party; it is the powerful people. Well, you know the story about these elections; otherwise, Muslim League could not have survived. In the end, when they had to create this country, the *quaid* had to go around making those pacts with feudal lords.[37]

35. The Pakistan Muslim League (PML) was first established in undivided India in 1906 and later on became associated prominently with Pakistan's leader and founder Mohammad Ali Jinnah. The PML continued to function in Pakistan after partition, though it has splintered into several factions.

36. Akmal Hussain similarly argues that the PML as well as the Pakistan People's Party "were taken over by landlords whose political interests lay in constraining the process of political development within the confines specified by the military bureaucratic oligarchs" (1990, 190).

37. By which she means that the entrenched feudal system frustrated the development of political institutions in the emerging nation-state, which in turn militated against a gradual de-

That is why we are not surviving today and are yet to emerge as a nation after forty-five years. I do not believe in such kinds of solutions. I know that the WAF and the feminists are struggling against the repressive laws [emphatic] that the government has lately been trying to impose—the Shariat bill,[38] the Hudood Ordinance, and all that. Good. Fine! But I think this problem will never be sorted out because, you see, the Jama'at-i Islami, the fanatic mullahs, the people who think conservatively, they are the sons of the soil. You have to do something with them, bring revolutionary kinds of change in *their* thinking.

Sons of Soil, Fundamentalism, and Feminism

I read a few books on the Iranian Revolution, and I came across some very interesting facts, that those who were initially involved were directly or indirectly connected with the university. You see, the middle class—and middle class is the most confused and most complex—form the majority of those people who go to the university, where they begin forming ideas. Now I have come across this feudal family, where both the paternal and maternal grandmothers were British. The boys went to England, and when they came back, they were so dejected that they grew beards and joined the Tablighi Jama'at.[39] You see, they have to be [dejected]. Like when you are going on a ship, or when there is an air pocket, you feel dizzy. Whatever the changes to be brought about should not have that effect. I am totally for this idea that you have to have change, but you have to do it practically.

In my village, the tradition among the big [important] families is that when a child is born, the mother does not feed him or her. A wet nurse is kept. The woman who fed me had a son, who is like my brother. Fifteen days ago when I was in Khanqah Sharif, he came to see me. He always comes to me for help. He is divorced and has one daughter.

---

velopment of democracy and political institutions in Pakistan (Hussain 1990; Jalal 1991b; I. Malik 1997).

38. With his Islamization policies in full swing in 1986, General Zia ul-Haq proposed the Shariat bill, which had profound implications for women and minorities. Despite strong protest by WAF and other Pakistani organizations and individuals, Prime Minister Nawaz Sharif was finally able to pass it through the Parliament in 1991, but in a more diluted form (Weiss 1994, 436, 442).

39. See M. Ahmad 1991.

He said, "Well, my in-laws are threatening to take away my daughter."

I said, "Why are they doing this?"

He said, "Because I married my brother"—the *watta-satta*, exchange marriages we have—"and in exchange she [his daughter] will have to be married to the brother of my brother's wife.[40] My in-laws threaten to take away my daughter because they do not approve of this thing. Please help me. Write a note to the police that they should help me."

I said, "Siraja, you have a right on me; you are my milk brother.[41] But in this case I will not help you. I am not willing to help a man who trades his own daughter. Sorry."

Watta-satta is a parental exchange and is one of the more popular variations of marriage traditions in Bahawalpur and in the rural areas. If you have all sons, and you are not fortunate enough to have many daughters, then you really are done for. When you want to marry your son, you have to pay lots of money [as bride-price]. If you do not have the money, you have had it, or your son will not get married! Unless he has a love affair, and they elope! It means a give and take. I mean, a brother and sister are exchanged with another brother and sister.[42] So there is no exchange of bride price. None whatsoever. Age is not a barrier either. Sure, it is un-Islamic, but practiced anyway. It is very dangerous because it may happen that a couple cannot get along, and the wife refuses to live with her husband and goes back to her parents. The other girl [in the exchange], who might be living happily, will have to be sent back, forcibly. Sometimes the kids are kept; sometimes they are sent back.

40. His brother is married to a woman whose brother is promised to be married to the speaker's daughter. In other words, A marries B's sister in exchange for the marriage of B to A's brother's daughter (A. Ahmed 1989)—hence, the expression "I married my brother." This kind of marriage is known as *watta-satta* and still takes place in the rural areas in Pakistan. Akbar S. Ahmed describes a variation of this form of marriage among the Pathans, *badal*, as "straightforward brother-sister exchanges" (1989, 41). But some forms are more complicated, such as the one Ayesha describes here.

41. According to Islamic law, if nursed by the same woman, children under the age of two are considered "milk siblings." They legally are prohibited from marrying each other if of opposite sexes (Thanvi 1981, 330).

42. Although the ideal pattern of this form of marriage is the exchange of a brother and sister with another brother and sister, it does not necessarily have to be between two siblings, as the case of Siraja indicates (see fn. 40, this chapter). *Watta-satta* marriage is similar to the *shighar* type of marriage that existed in pre-Islamic Arabia and is prohibited explicitly in the Qur'an (Haeri 1993a, 221, fn. 20).

So, you see, we need to have movements on parallel lines, not just against the government and its rules and regulations, but also to transform the society and its customs. That's maybe what the feminists want [emphatic]. But *that* is what they are not effectively doing! Once I was engaged in a conflict and was very perturbed. Somebody suggested, "Why don't you beat those people on their own ground? Use the weapon they use." Our problem is—the problem with these ladies also—fine, the Hudood Ordinance and Shariat bill. That is the kinky side of the mullah's religion. This is not Islam. I say, use the religion as a weapon. The fanaticism that is here is because nobody knows what the Holy Book says!

I remember one day I had some guests in Khanqah Sharif. I told my servant, Choti, to make a few dishes, make chicken. Later I saw her running around quite wild. I said, "What are you doing running around?"

"I am looking for some man," she said, "who can *zibah*, slaughter, the chicken."

"Why look for a man? Do it yourself," I said.

She was shocked! She looked at me and said, "Me? Will you take *haram* [forbidden] meat if I do it?"

"Dear Choti," I said, "the Qur'an does not say that! There is no place in which it is written that a woman cannot do it [43]—if she is in the right state" [that is, not menstruating]. I said, "Damn it! If it's *haram* or *halal* [permitted], I am going to eat it, and I will be responsible, whether it is *gunah* or *savab*, sinful or proper. You do it."

So, you see, religion can be used as a weapon.

It is not a matter of awareness only! I say use the Book as a weapon against those fanatic mullahs. I am not saying that feminists do not have such objectives. I said this should be stressed. Certainly there should be a movement, but I was not talking about ideology. I was talking more about practical matters. Certainly I am all for a women's movement, and I would not say that they are entirely wrong. What I say is that there should be correction and amendments to their entire plans. They should be more organized. They should have more ordinary people involved. They really have to sit down and think about it. Right now they are going at a very slow pace. They have to move fast. Right now the situation of women, especially in cities, is not good. You see, I do not

43. According to Maulana Thanvi, "The slaughter of an animal is in order by a Muslim whether by a man or woman, clean or unclean" (1981, 340).

see many problems in the rural areas. There are more problems in the cities, where once a woman is married, she has no life of her own but for the life she has acquired through her husband and his family, middle class, upper class, and whatever. Upper-class women do not do anything. Their maids do the shopping, and that is about it. I have seen Kinnaird girls participating in the WAF meetings, in the demonstrations even, but in the end what they do in their life is almost the same as their mothers. You see, it should not be just games.

Fine! You really cannot compare the life of rural and urban women.[44] If a wife is beaten up, she is beaten up everywhere, in town or village. In the village, at least she can have a lover. Another factor is that when a woman in a village picks cotton, her husband does not have *any* right to the money she earns. She picks cotton and is given her share, the money, directly. She can have clothing made, buy jewelry, anything. It is *her* money. But in town, men take that money, what the wives earn.

What I think is that the feminists should take the women's movement and turn it into a more populist movement. Do not restrict it to a few elitist kinds of meetings. Some solid planning has to be done. Funds have to be raised. That is very important. You cannot have a movement without proper funds. You have to have written materials. You have to have lectures. You have to have teams going to places. They all have to be done.[45] Well, we have never received a single team from the WAF or any other feminist organization in my area. Right, there are thousands of villages in Pakistan, but why don't they organize?

You see, in our country, you cannot change the social structure until you have literacy. Despite many difficulties, the urge is very much there. I am not able to help those people because I have my interests here. This is where self-ishness comes in. I enjoy the city life. I want to work as a civil servant, to develop contacts, and to survive. People who have the ability and the resources never put themselves to the task of doing it. What I should be doing, if I want to serve my people and my nation, is quit my job, spend less time in Lahore, where I am miserable, and go to Khanqah Sharif. I know it would be painful and hard, but sit there and start a school. If I am there and if I have a school, I

44. I asked Ayesha, "Can you really compare the life of women in rural areas with that of urban women?"

45. I said to her, "But this is what WAF and other feminist organizations such as Applied Socioeconomic Resource are doing."

will manage. People will come, people will study. But my commitment is also not there [banging the table with the enunciation of every word]. So, like me, people do not have that commitment. You see, poverty and fanaticism are related. I am reminded of a very beautiful statement made by a professor of social studies in Holland. He says, "Are we poor because we are too many or too many because we are too poor?" In the rural areas or in Khanqah Sharif, Jama'at-i Islami as such does not exist. For the poor people, the Jama'at-i Islami, People's Party, Muslim League, and any political party are all very much alike politically. But the situation is different in the cities.

Religion and Politics in Rural Areas

A Sindhi writer, Nurul Huda, told me a profound story. She said there was this boy who had committed a few political murders and was hiding. "One day," she said, "he came to me. We discussed his problems and the political situation." She said, "I told him, you are sitting here full of vigor, agitation, and intensity. Do you know that you are like those twigs that the politicians put into the fire to warm their hands?" She said that suddenly the young man grew so silent, as if all energy was drained out of him. That is what the status of Jama'at or of any other party is. At the grassroots level, they do not exist. A poor man today is as lowly and alone as he was forty years back when this country was created. The Jama'at has a strong hold in the educational institutions in the cities. They provide guns there. But in the rural areas the poor are so poor that they cannot be bothered by religion. The mullah tells them, well, this is right and this is wrong. They do the wrongs knowing that they are wrongs, but they have to do it. There is a lot of loose life in Khanqah Sharif. People take drugs; people may take lovers, may have illicit relations, and nobody is bothered, not even the mullah because a mullah is also financially poor. He has to go from one hamlet to another begging for his meals. Either he goes himself, or he sends his agent, who is a boy learning Qur'an in his *maktab*, to collect the *roti* [bread] every evening. The mullah is poor. The people are poor. At least in my part of the country, the Jama'at does not exist for the poor men.

One day I was talking to this man who tills the land for me—very poor. I lectured him for half an hour on how good it would be if Benazir Bhutto came to power. After a while, when I was thoroughly satisfied with my performance, I said, "How do you feel if Benazir Bhutto comes to power?" He sighed and he said, "Well, it does not matter for me because the fertilizer would be sold at the same price, maybe more expensively, the water rates would go up, or they would be the same. The price of the seeds, the cottonseed that I sell, would not go up, maybe it falls. So it does not really matter." It goes the same for women, too. There *was* no excitement about Benazir Bhutto among the village women either.

You see, Shahla, what you have to realize is that a man or a woman at the helm of the affairs does *not touch* the life of the downtrodden people of this country. When Benazir Bhutto comes to Bahawalpur, which she does often, she sits there amidst such uproar. The party men are fighting amongst themselves: "This man is in business and has so much money. That person is in that business and has that much money. I want a seat. I want a party ticket. I want this. I want that!" She is so much engulfed in it. Nobody reaches out for the common man. It is very funny when you go to these meetings and talks. Bahawalpur is the largest division of Punjab, and I can safely speak of that part of the country.

At the grassroots level, there is no party organization. Take any party—be it Jama'at-i Islami, People's Party, National People's Party, any party. Nobody reaches out for the people. It is part of the top that matters to all the parties and all the leaders. And naturally it is the men of the area, the elite, who matter. That is because we have very much a tribal system as far as regional politics is concerned. You see, what the common man is concerned about is who is the person that can deliver him the goods. When there are elections, members of parliament go and say, "Please give me your votes." Then the people say, "All right, kindly construct that school, construct that road, get us electricity." Those are what matters. I am speaking from experience. Because of my position in Khanqah Sharif, the People's Party always comes to me for help, and I always help them. Once somebody from the Saraiki Quami Movement, rang me up at eleven at night and said, "We want a candidate. Would you be one for us?" I said, "Firstly, I am working for the government, and, as per rules, right now I cannot. It would take some time for me to resign and do that. Secondly," I told the gentleman, "there is a decent time to call a lady, and *this* is not the time, please!" [Laughing]. He never called again.

Secularism or fundamentalism also do not exist or matter in the rural areas. As I said, and I *insist* on what I am saying or what I have said, when you are poor, your bread is your god. Your survival is all that matters. It is a day-to-day survival. I give two hundred rupees per month to a woman who does some work for me. Her husband is a drug addict. Her two very young sons also work. She would be earning, altogether, say one thousand to fifteen hundred rupees a month. While she is raising seven kids with fifteen hundred rupees, feeding them, buying their clothing, and providing for her husband's addiction, what time does she have, tell me, to sit down and think whether the mullah is right or this Benazir Bhutto, who is very modern and liberal? Or to even begin to think what is liberalism and what is fundamentalism and fanaticism? She does not have the time for it. So it is for men. I mean, they are working very, very hard. It is a matter of *survival*. They are very good-hearted people.

Women and Religion: Female Pir

Take my example. I sit there as a *pir*.[46] They accept me. Try to understand that. Men with long beards, old men, fall on my feet crying, asking me to pray for them. Now, why is that? Why do they do it? I am a woman, a young woman. If Jama'at-i Islami's influence or fundamentalism was that rampant in the rural areas, they would say, well, she is a woman. You see, I was reading a newspaper ten days back. The Sindh commissioner's daughter has an important position in Lahore. Her clerk refused to work for her, saying that it is against Islam [for men to work for women]. This can *only* happen in a city, where people have a little more time to think, even about religions—good or bad, the mullah's religion or real Islam. Religion, I say, is the problem of the middle-class people, of the city people, not of the poor people of the rural areas who do not have time to think about religion.

Anywhere in the world where life is fast, where there is too much success, where there is too much failure, people need to find an anchor. Every human being needs an anchor, something solid to which to cling. When those poor people come to me, it is because they need me, not just financially, but spiritually or mentally, I would say. They are illiterate. They cannot go beyond a certain point. They have their limitations as far as their thinking is concerned. When they are hurt—in emotional, spiritual, or mental pain or even in physical pain—they go to a *pir*. Now, it does not bother them that I am a woman. I belong to a spiritual family. They think I can deliver them the goods:[47] deliver them from their bondage of poverty, deliver them from their physical pains

46. Literally meaning an old man, *pir* refers to a spiritual guide or a holy man. In South Asia, *pirs* and sheikhs have a special place and are very popular. They also often have been the subject of criticism by the orthodoxy and the modernists.

47. See I. Malik 1997, 89, on the length that rural and tribal Pakistanis will go to please their *pir*, who, as it often happens, may also be the local feudal lord. See also Jalal (1990, 288), who ar-

when they come to me. I can deliver them from the persecution that awaits them, according to what the mullah says. A mullah is a mullah everywhere. He tells them, you are a sinner: you do this, you sin; you do that, you sin. Sometimes when they have time to think, they actually begin to think they are sinners. So when they go to the world hereafter, they need to be helped, and they need to be delivered from the misery that awaits us. So I am the person they can go to for help to break out of that. They may even think that I have *barakat*, divine blessing. So it does not *matter* for them whether I am a man or a woman. They think I can deliver, and they come to me, and I have never heard any discontent against me, *never*.

Conflict Resolution: Women, Land, and Violence

In Khanqah Sharif, I have a piece of land that was claimed by another *zamindar*, landowner. This family claimed that their girl was raped by another landowner's son. Medical examination [to determine rape], chemical examination, it was all paid for by the latter, but nothing was proved. The dispute continued. Finally I went there. So far I was supporting the boy's family. I went to the girl's home. I talked to the girl, and I could see that she was acting. After I talked to her, I called her father and said, "Listen, give me these documents that you say you have. Although you have been molesting my people, my servants, taking my land, I give you a guarantee that whatever you do with me would be a different affair. Your daughter is my daughter. Don't worry. I want to satisfy myself that you are right. Although I have supported the other party so far, I am with you. You have been wronged. This is not on." Now the police was messing things up without helping either family. Finally, both parties went to the police and said, "Whatever Bibi"—they call me Bibi—"decides for us we accept."

You see, it was a local drama, a rivalry between two men. The poor child was a victim of that, even if she had to put up this act. I said to them that whatever the issues, rivalry or whatever, you ought to sort them out here. You see, *they* all knew it was playacting, the girl was pressured to pretend. Actually, the whole conflict was over a piece of land that her family wanted. I said, "Rather

gues that *pirs* or *sajjadah nishin*s are often feudal lords who control religion and do not allow political parties to mobilize the rural areas.

than fighting amongst you, let us sit down and call the *patwari*, accountant,[48] so that he can present you with the clarifications [of land ownership]." The girl's "rape" was a nonissue. The issue had been created. So when I pinpointed what exactly was the problem, they forgot about the other issues, and the case was settled before reaching the court.

In another case, once this man came to me and said, "My daughter was married to another family through a *watta-satta* marriage, but now their daughter is refusing to marry our son. She has run away, eloped with this particular man, but we consider her our daughter-in-law. Please help us with the police to retrieve her."

I asked him, "Listen, has the marriage actually been done?"

"No."

"Then if she does not want to marry your son, why are you making it into a problem? I cannot force a decision on a person against her will. I cannot help you."

But, you see, our main problem, Shahla, is that in a male-dominated world, where all our mediators and arbitrators and judges are men—men who have feudal mentality—their decisions are made according to *their* aspirations, according to the way *they* have been brought up, according to *their* environment. What we basically need, people need, more than money is education, education introduced on a revolutionary platform. What we need more than feminist movements today are NGOs [nongovernmental organizations] and organizations who are willing to put themselves into implementing the development of literacy. Right now, the villagers do not know what their rights are, what the laws are, what the rules are. They cannot read. They cannot fight the wrongs that are done unto them. And they do wrongs unto others.

You see, injustice has two sides to it. Number one, injustice is done because the other person is unjust, is an aggressor. Number two, injustice has been done to you because you were not capable to protect yourself. The problem of these people here is of the latter, illiteracy. When they are taken to a police station, they do not know what is their right, what is being done to them.

---

48. Ayesha described a *patwari* as "the man who has the records of land." According to the *Urdu-English Dictionary*, he is "a village registrar or accountant; a keeper of the records and accounts of lands, a land steward."

How can they save themselves? You see, literacy can bring about higher consciousness, and I can see it. All those young boys who have done their matriculation from Khanqah Sharif are less impressed by the feudal of the area than those people who are illiterate. For illiterate people, there is no way out. In the cities and urban centers, it is a different story. Fine. They may not be able to get justice either, but at least they can fight for their rights. There *has to* be a beginning somewhere!

They definitely need guidance. The fact that I have not brought them education is because I am not sitting there. I do not think that the feudal can continue to prevent literacy from reaching these villages[49] because I do not think that the feudal have total monopoly over their bread and butter. In my area in Bahawalpur division, there has been lots of industrialization. In ten kilometers from Khanqah, there are about four factories—a big sugar mill, two textile factories, and other industries. In fact, there is an agricultural labor shortage for the farms. And people have their small farms themselves, a few acres from where they earn their bread and butter. Why they need the feudal is because every place has to have a system. There is injustice that is done for which they need justice, and they have to go somewhere to some authority. The [male] feudal wrangles that position from the people who deserve it and places it on himself to give justice, which he cannot.

You see, my mother started a system of scholarships in my father's name. For any boy who would top the metric [matriculation] exam in Khanqah Sharif, she would issue a scholarship that would take him through his entire education till his BA. I sometimes call them, and I talk to them. I say, "Listen, you are the future if not of this country, at least of this area."

One reason I am today struggling to settle my affairs with my sister is because my plan is, after I am back [from England], to teach in the International Defense College at least for a year. Then I would want to quit the job, go back to Khanqah Sharif, and settle down at home, start a school, and work with commitment. Why I want to is because the status of the mango orchard is doubtful—because it is a disputed property. Once my matters are settled with my sister and a few other relatives, the orchard will be entirely mine, *inshallah.* That place can then be turned into a central planning [area].

49. On feudal lords' opposition to education, in particular that of women, see I. Malik 1997, 83 and 285 n. 12.

Feudalism in Flux?

My family, like many feudal families, is losing much of its power and prestige. They used to be very big landowners, but they are going down very fast. There are other people with more land. My family still has the power in their hands. You see, in a feudal setup, your personal authority and power are derived primarily from your family, although you may gain personal power if you also have extraordinary qualifications, such as a high degree in education or a high-ranking position in the bureaucracy or military, and a good reputation. My family is fast selling their land, and what scares me most these days is the vacuum that would be created once these people dive down or leave [the country]. There would be no one capable enough to take their place. There would be upstarts, but they would be really reckless. Feudalism is not just a position. It is also an attitude. You could be an upstart and nouveau riche but have a very feudal approach to life. Let me tell you, it is very fanciful, very fascinating. You are sitting there like a lord, like a king. There would be people around singing your praises and telling you how good you are, how beautiful you are. Nothing you do can be wrong. It can go to your head, and people are fascinated by it. So I think what is needed is a lot of commitment from people who can think, not short-term but long-term planning. What is painful about the feudal system is that it mentally stops people from questioning authority, even in their own minds. Our governments—whether it is that of Benazir Bhutto, Nawaz Sharif, or any other—*cannot* deliver to the people what they deserve. If we have to have education, it will have to be done by NGOs.

That it has not happened is not because our system is centrally controlled. It is because the richer we grow, the more selfish we become. I have bank balance [account] in Lahore, in Khanqah Sharif, and I now struggle to have bank balance in England and in the United States. That is my entire aim in life because, again, the social system is such that there are lots of uncertainties, and people want to leave behind lots of rupees for their children. Nobody wants to sacrifice anything for anyone—starting from our intellectuals down to the businessmen.

In the Boots of a Feudal Lord

It is very tiring, switching hats, moving from being a civil servant in Lahore to a feudal lord in Khanqah Sharif. Here [in Lahore] I am a civil servant who goes to her office, who is scared that her director might say something nasty or be angry for something she has not done right. I live in a big city. I have to pay the bills and go to places and learn to live with people as equals. Suddenly within one hour and ten minutes—that is the flight time to Bahawalpur—I am the person in charge, not only of my land, but of people. See, a *murid*, devotee, comes to you, he presents what is inside and what is outside. You are a God sitting there. This is my problem. You have the power to help them or to shun them.

Once, with a few friends, we were discussing what is the concept of hell. A lawyer from Bahawalpur said, "Hell is the state of utter hopelessness." So when I am there and I am a *pir*, I am a person who is trying hard to save those people from the hell that is hopelessness. Women come to you and say, "Please, we want an amulet." "What for?" I say. "I have a stone in my kidney." Now, for a city dweller, for a woman from the feminist movement [sarcastic tone], the very logical thing to do would be to say, "Listen, this does not help. Go to a doctor. This is illiteracy; you are being an idiot; you are being stupid believing in false values, blah, blah, blah." But knowing those people and their state, it would be like pushing them into hell if I refuse. They are so poor, they cannot go to the doctors. The doctor would charge them at least fifty to one hundred rupees, plus prescribing a whole list of tests—ultrasound, blood tests, urine tests—and would give them a big list of medicines. Or I can send them to a quack who would give them small bottles of medicine prepared by himself, water mixed with some concoction or something. They will have to keep going to him and paying five to ten rupees here and there, which is again too much for them. I cannot. You see, there are two ways. Either I can send them to a doctor myself—but there are financial restraints with me, too—or try to help them as much as I can. Again there are limitations. If I tell them, "Buzz off, I am not helping you," they will die before dying physically. Let me tell you, Shahla, I think dying mentally and spiritually—physically you die once—is like dying every day. It is very painful. So why should I take away that hope they are clinging to? All right, I give them an amulet, and they dream. They think and hope that because of this amulet they will be all right, that they will get healthy. So why shouldn't I do it? I do not take any money from them, which all the *pirs* do. And I normally do not accept any gifts, which is often given in the form of animals, *desi ghee* [local clarified butter], eggs, and home-made bread. These gifts, though, sometimes I take.

In my house, the family tradition is when you are sitting there [being present in the village], food is prepared every day. Any one who comes to your house, you give them food to eat. Besides, every weekend when I am there, people come, asking for money, medicine, a daughter's dowry, or construction of their house, or whatever. I keep giving whatever I can. You see, my grandfather was a *pir*, a holy man, in his own way, although he married twice, for reasons I do not agree with. He used to give out a lot. *Urs*, or the anniversary of the death of a *pir*,[50] or *pir's* day, is basically a day when all the devotees gather. The tradition is for them to give gifts to the *pir*, not the other way. Food, of course, is given out. The rest of my family members take from the *murids* [money or other gifts]. The *murids* contribute even to the *langar*, food distributed to the poor, at the time of *urs*. When my father was alive, a team of men would distribute the food, with him sitting there surrounded by his *murids*. Now, what I remember is that these men would be standing there with sticks, and anybody who tried to be naughty they would hit. I have sort of changed the tradition. For *urs*, I do not take anything from anyone. I have my servants cook food. One day I went and I said to the men with the sticks, "Forget it. I will do it myself." I told them, "Listen, damn it. It is food. I am not asking you for work. This food that they are eating is what is fated for them. It is what was given to them. Besides, what you give them is not a lot." I stood there, and they took till two o'clock in the morning. What I have started doing is after the *khatam*, prayer recitations, I say, "Please sit where you are in a very disciplined way." We have these earthenware utensils, which the servants put the rice in and put each dish before two people. I announce, standing there, "No person will be turned away until they have had their fill." My *munshi* kept telling me there was not enough food. I said, "Fine, cook more!"

Yeah . . . unfortunately, I will have to skip the *urs* next year. That is a sacrifice I will have to make for myself. I cannot have other people do it while I am away. I am dying to go to Kings College and do my study there, but I would hate to stay anywhere but in the Khanqah. Today that is the way I think. You see, being with the common people is one of the loveliest things we have in the village. They are crude. They are mean, very mean. They are so mean that you can *see* it. They are very down to earth, the way they love, they way they hate. Actually, they do not hate. It is just jealousies and competition. The first competition took place between the two sons of Adam, Cain and Abel. So it is

---

50. In its Sufi rendition, *urs* means "a wedding, when the longing soul will finally unite with its beloved" (Schimmel 1997, 154).

the same kind of competition [laughing]. I love being with these people. You learn so much about life.

I was reading Eric Fromme, and what he was saying was, "It is not when you are happy or too content that you learn things. It is when you are under stress, facing pain while living your life, which teaches you things." The misery that you see around you teaches you a lot. It shows you another angle of your own life. All right, these people are miserable, but they also are happy where they are, I have learned. I am not saying that everyone gets to learn that. It depends upon your human development, your mental development, how much time and effort you spend in developing yourself, caring for your environment. I mean, there are males around me who are feudal, who are *pirs*, who are living amongst those very poor, downtrodden people, but who are reckless and ruthless and brutal, and who do not learn a thing. They just cherish the fact that they are riding around in big Pejaro cars.[51] They have a couple of bodyguards with them. They can spend money and throw away money and believe in things that really do not matter. But, again, it is all like an intellectual exercise we do not indulge in.

I cannot stand more than ten days in Lahore because life is so made up, so artificial, in the city. People smile and laugh because other people want them to. They dress up because people want them to. They behave in a certain way; they enjoy in a certain way; and everything is done for other people. In this country, people have grown toward the worst, not toward the better. Many are so "feminish." They talk about love affairs or intrigues. They do not talk about healthy love, but unhealthy love. They discuss other people's affairs, and women gossip. I have sat with elderly women, and I have been in a girls' college; I know what girls talk about. They do not talk about love, but about love affairs of other people, not their own. See, my problem is when I sit down with girls, I can listen to clothes and to makeup and to movies, Indian movies, and to song and to the feminist movement, but I do not want to be part of them. I do not want to talk too long about them.

In a rural life, women fall in love, they make love, they are lovers; the silly things they do or the good things they do are purely for themselves. Even if it is for their survival, it is for *them*. There is no pretense. There is them and then

51. Pejaros are sport utility vehicles and are very popular among the affluent classes in Pakistan.

the world, their desire and the world. You are so close to nature when you are with them, their surprises, the shock in their eyes. You know I smoke and sometimes drink, but when I go to my village, I dare not. I go to the toilet and smoke, which I do not do in Lahore, or I sit in a secluded room and smoke. Except for a few of my servants, nobody knows I smoke. It is not because they will just stop coming to me or stop respecting me. It is because I do not want to shock them. Whatever their beliefs are, I do not want to break them. Then again, my aunt, my father's sister, thirty-five plus, is having a rip-roaring affair with her own driver. She is very much married, and he [the husband] knows about that, too. It is a public fact. No outrage. She is accepted. She is not an outcast. You see, her husband does not object to it, at least not openly, because she has more property than he does.[52] If he forces her out, she would probably run away with everything she owns. And it won't do to accuse her of zina either.[53] That takes place in Punjab, but not in my father's county. People are very docile. They go to her. She also gives ta'wiz to some people who may perceive her as a pir. Nobody rejects her.

Rural people, Shahla, do not have so many inhibitions—also because they are too tired. Our problem is that when we start thinking about rural people, village people, we talk about them in our own terms. We, the city people, go around in big cars on concrete roads, we go shopping and to movies, we watch MTV and Star TV, or watch VCR, enjoy modern art, theater, or other such thrillers. But think in terms of the village people in their context. Their cinema, their VCR, their Star TV, their concrete roads, their dreams, fantasies— everything is there. Their excitement, their sorrow, their pain, their anger, their hunger, their food—everything comes through that very soil. Gossiping is part of their survival. Their feelings are very basic: jealousy and love. There is not much hatred, I would say. They would not go out killing. We do not go out of our way to hurt somebody. The jealousies are there. It is very, very close to nature. When these women fight, they abuse each other like hell, abusing each other's daughters to begin with. But in a couple of days they are sitting in the same place, eating together and merrymaking, and their marriages are all there, all those harsh words forgotten.

52. Husband and wife do not automatically form a communal right to each other's property after marriage.

53. I said, "But she can be accused of zina, adultery," which is punishable under the Hudood Ordinance.

Some Reflections: Female, Feudal, Family Drama

Contemplating what has come to be known as the prototype of the family drama, Sophocles portrays in his play *Oedipus* a paradox that has survived for twenty-five centuries. Family, though a sacred institution that protects individuals and sustains them in a web of meaningful relationships, is also a source of conflict and tension in the physical world. Ayesha, often bewildered by her family intrigues, revisits her own family drama and articulates honestly and movingly the agonies of her love-hate relationship with her extended family, of coming to terms with her conflicted identity, and of her parents' relationship with her. She tries to make sense of the ambiguities of her parents' relationships with her, while expressing ambivalence toward her own gender role and status in feudal and civil societies. Her major crisis and conflicts, as she expresses them, are the result of the accident of her birth. She was born a female in a feudal family who yearned for a son.[54] Yet when a son was born, jealousy of his eventual power and authority seems to have caused his untimely

---

54. On January 13, 2000, Ayesha sent me the following e-mail message from Bonn, Germany, where she had a research grant. "Here is more food for your thought and your book. I would appreciate if you actually use this material. Let me tell you what surviving in a feudal system does to a female or even a male. It deprives you and ravishes you of your sensuality and sexuality. Now that I have grown away from the times when I kind of had a weird pleasure in winning battles against my rivals and enjoyed every victory in court, I feel, at times, less strong even to admit that I have been through those times. The biggest victim was my sensuality, my appreciation of the other sex. In those times, the other sex had only one color, and that was of an opponent or an enemy. My mother, for whom the greatest issue was to survive and help me survive, tried to shut all doors that would ever lead me to realize who I was—not a male child but a female child. There are times when I look back and think about the times when I was so proud of acting like a boy. Those were the days that deprived me of the ability to feel sensuous like a female would. The ability to think of a man not as a rival but as a creature who can invoke certain ticklish feelings inside you and stir romantic feelings. There are times when I have this great urge to fall in love, to let myself go. I know I love Omar [her husband] and all that, but it is more a matter of routine than anything else. Maybe one does not have to go through the experience of a roller-coaster ride and definitely not at this time in my life, but the craving is there. I am sure it must be fun. But I never came even close to this pleasure because I was trying to survive. I fell in love once, or so I claim, and even that experience got shrouded and mixed with trying to cater to your basic biological needs and looking at the affair from the perspective of finding one who would help you survive. Let me tell you straight and simple, I wouldn't curse even my worst enemies with being born female in a feudal system."

death—or murder, as Ayesha believes it was. Ayesha survived perhaps because she was born a female. Yet her survival in a feudal setting with its medieval intrigues and attitude, paraphrasing her words, involved real struggle and several paradoxes that challenge both cultural expectations and theoretical speculations. Stories of her life reveal multiple inversions of culturally expected relationships and ambiguities of legitimacy that complicated her personal and emotional maturation, while allowing her to assume control and to exercise authority. Did her mother love her because of who she was, or did her mother mask her desire for a male child by bringing up Ayesha as the "man" she wanted her to be, not as the girl child Ayesha.

Ayesha's special bonds with her father and his unconditional love for her compounded the ambiguities and confusion of her gender identity. She "feared" her mother but loved her father "without any fear." Is the fact that he was apparently not devastated by the death of his son a tacit indication of his fear of dislocation by filial rivalry and of his desire to have a daughter instead? Did he love Ayesha for her own sake? The question of "who Ayesha was" was a profoundly existential issue not only for Ayesha, but also for the people who tended to reject her, finding her "neither fish nor fowl."[55]

In the next three sections, I discuss the theme of ambiguous legitimacy in three areas of Ayesha's life: her relations with her father, with her mother, and with herself as a woman with solid financial resources and potential political power.

Paradox of Patrilineay: Father, the Love Object

In chapter 1, I briefly argued that the cultural mechanism that enables some women of feudal background to assume political power and authority in South Asia is the strong and loving relationship between father and daughter, combined with the ownership of land. Sometimes the strength of the filial love is expressed in the absence of sons, other times regardless of the existence of sons or even at the expense of sons. This situation I call the paradox of patrilineay. In patrilineal and feudal societies, male children are strongly desired, and South Asia provides a notorious example (Bumiller 1990). Descent is

55. For a fascinating discussion of the abomination of uncertainty and "in-between" creatures, see Douglas 1966.

traced through the male line, and power, prestige, and privilege automatically pass on to male descendants. Yet the father-son axis potentially and sometimes actually is the nexus of tension and rivalry, where the two may in fact fear or resent or even eliminate each other. South Asian history provides ample examples of fatal rivalries between the imperial fathers and coveting sons. This is not unique to South Asia, however. From Sophocles' tragedies to Japanese filmmaker Akira Kurosawa's visual representation of Shakespeare's *King Lear* in *Ran* to Iranian poet Ferdowsi's poetic epic *Rostam and Sohrab*, deadly filial rivalries abound. Dwarfed by the preponderance of literature on father-son relationships, however, the father-daughter kinship bond and its specific individual idiosyncracies and cultural patterns curiously have gone unnoticed by anthropologists.

Born in a feudal setup and by and large without a brother as a rival, Ayesha was groomed to breathe life into the spirit of her dead brother. She was brought up as a boy and treated as one by her parents. In light of the previous discussion, the father's sense of relief regarding, or at least his apparent indifference toward, his son's death may not come as a surprise, for this death also deprived his second wife of economic power and a lineage anchor, which she desperately seemed to desire. Instead, Ayesha was dressed like a boy, taught horseback riding, polo, and other activities generally associated with that of boys in her culture. While she was brought up to fill the shoes of a son, the son was conveniently dead. Ayesha filled the place of a potentially contentious son and an emotionally distant wife. The father integrated Ayesha into his life, took her on his visits to their villages, and had her sit next to him in public hearings, where, as a *pir*, he dispensed local justice or blessed villagers, their children, and their animals, a tradition Ayesha inherited.[56]

The love between Ayesha and her father throws a paradoxical shadow on the "traditional" pattern of family relations and the father's role in patrilineal and patriarchal family system in Pakistan. Ayesha's characterization of him as "a very tender person" and of their relation as "more natural" inverts the image of a father as an agent of discipline and punishment, as a distant figure in the

---

56. It is worth noting here that as a young man Ayesha's father apparently did not have the same loving relationship with his elder daughter from his first wife. By the time Ayesha came on the scene, he already had been married twice, neither of which marriage was emotionally satisfying to him, though he was a more experienced father.

daughter's life, and as a stern feudal lord. It was indeed her father's unconditional love that fostered and supported her sense of masculine power and entitlement and ultimately legitimated her authority.

Maternal Ambivalence: Mother, the Superego

Ayesha's relationship with her mother, although more complicated, also involves multiple cultural and psychological inversions. To begin with, Ayesha
"feared" her mother; her relationship with her mother "did not come naturally"
to her, as it did with her father. A beloved son unquestionably would have an-
chored the mother's status within her husband's feudal family, but he died, so
the subsequently born Ayesha was dressed as a boy and actively encouraged to
pursue her interest in masculine games, activities, and behavior. From photo-
graphs of her in childhood and early adolescence, it is difficult to recognize
the female child beneath. Yet the mother, having to contend with the realities
of her daughter's female sex, also anxiously kept Ayesha close to herself and
did not allow her the freedom of movement and expressions that come with
being a boy. Treating her at times as an extension of herself, she gave Ayesha
mixed messages that frustrated both the daughter's emotional maturity and an
integration of the appropriate gender role, as expected in her culture.[57] The
mother, on the other hand, also facilitated her daughter's going to college,
and, being herself a professional writer and a literary person, she strongly encouraged Ayesha to pursue a professional career. In other words, she helped to
create that space for Ayesha that women of her own generation had to fight to
obtain. In short, it was the mother, not the father, who acted as the disciplinarian and the superego in her daughter's life.

The mother's feelings of insecurity concerning her own position as an outsider married into a feudal family—who for the most part viewed her with
hostility and her belief that only a son could give her prestige and legitimacy
within the family—were communicated to Ayesha throughout her life.
Whether it was her husband's death that gave her the chance or her own desire
to avenge herself for her affines refusal to accept her, Ayesha's mother did her
best to keep her daughter away from her paternal kin. By obliging her daughter, at her deathbed, not to "go back" to the father's family, she in fact may have
frustrated her daughter's means of gaining self-confidence and mooring.

---

57. Parts of my argument here are inspired by Chodorow 1989.

Ayesha did go back to her paternal kin because her social identity and prestige came from her association with them, a well-respected feudal family in Bahawalpur. Feeling guilty for having disobeyed her mother, however, she paid her tribute by building an elaborate mausoleum for her and arranging for the annual memorial lectures in her mother's honor in Lahore. Her relationship with her paternal kin, nonetheless, continued to be legally and emotionally conflictual. She was left with a profound sense of ambivalence and anxiety regarding her own identity and authority.

Ayesha's passion for war studies and for pursuing a fully masculine profession may be seen as a symptom of her wish for parental approval. She knowingly or unknowingly always had a conflict with her mother, which she tried to suppress for as long as her mother was alive—not the type of conflict that would burst into the open, but the kind that inhibited her own individual sense of growth, spontaneity, and separate identity. In wars, certain issues are resolved one way or another, as she explains. As a young child, she did not have the courage to argue with her mother, to try to establish her point of view. She was unsure of the justice and fairness of her own point of view. She thought whatever her mother said was probably right. Her mother had, after all, her "good at heart," as Ayesha rationalizes it, though she still "remember[s] being hurt." When it came to her mother, Ayesha apparently had not cultivated her combative side. Instead, she turned it inward and seems to have displaced it partially with a passion for aircrafts and airplanes—instruments that could fly and take her away. On a manifest level, Ayesha's determination to get a Ph.D. in war studies may have been motivated by her desire to achieve something significant on her own and thus to establish her independence from her mother. On a deeper level, however, it also may have been motivated by a need to win, yet again, her mother's approval because it is a manly profession. A degree in war studies was also a way to fulfill an unspoken promise to her father, that she would make herself worthy of being entrusted with his feudal "mantle," something she may have thought he would have wanted his son to achieve.

Ambivalence of Authority

In Pakistan, as in many other patriarchal societies, authority and power are associated with men, in their actual and symbolic forms. Power and authority are believed to be intrinsically masculine, desirable in men and desired by men. They also are inscribed in the age and gender hierarchies in Pakistan. Vacillating between being physiologically a female and yet desiring to perform masculine tasks—or being like a man or competing with one—Ayesha was confused and confusing to herself and to others. She wielded power and exercised it often with authority and flare. However, not only was the legitimacy of her masculine position shaky, but her status also was not firmly grounded because she was twenty-six years old and not yet married. Such merging of masculinity and femininity was as confusing to her as it was to her male employees and female workers. The former, often older than she, did not know whether to relate to her as their *izzat* or reluctantly to ignore expressions of her autonomy or to carry out her orders begrudgingly. The latter, likewise, did not seem to know exactly how to treat her: as a naïve unmarried girl who needs protection, even manipulation, or as a powerful sahib to be obeyed.

Ayesha was expected to behave like a man, and she appeared to do so quite competently for the most part, but she was denied, however discretely, the privileges that often go with the power possessed by men. Although her male servants' livelihood depended on her, they resisted her authority and subverted it whenever they could. The constant battle to keep them under tight control and her doubts about their loyalty left her emotionally discontented, insecure, and unsteady. Maintaining her authority and power became a matter of sinking or swimming. Ayesha was determined to act authoritatively and did not hesitate to show her power by verbally or even physically punishing her servants, male or female. She enjoyed the authority that came with her financial holdings and said she detested behaving like a delicate female, yet she seemed to feel ambivalent about her power and the "fit," as it were, of the "feudal boots" she was expected to wear. She frequently expressed her wish to have a close male relative—that is, a brother or, more appropriately then, a husband—to support her, to manage her estate and her staff, and to validate her authority in the eyes of the public.

Because Ayesha was a young unmarried woman with economic power but no parental supervision, her extended relatives perceived her to be potentially in a position to risk family honor. Her maternal and paternal kin minutely observed her conduct, and her defiant rejections of their marriage proposals and their attempts to arrange her marriage lent credence to their anxieties. She was not against marriage per se. In fact, she did want to get married, very earnestly indeed. She was well aware of the enhanced social prestige that accompanies marriage in Pakistan and, consequently, of the strengthening of

her authority and power over her estate, her property, and her staff. She, however, resisted the lead of her extended family, whom she generally viewed as
having had adversarial relations with her mother and with her after her
mother's death. Were she to have acceded to her paternal family's marriage
proposals, it seems to me, it would have been an ultimate betrayal of her
mother's wish that Ayesha stay away from her father's family. The man she was
interested in marrying would have to be, as she specified, more emotionally
and intellectually compatible with her.[58]

Thanks also to her mother's encouragement to take the civil service exam,
Ayesha became a professional woman with a serious job and responsibilities.
She was determined to stand on her own two feet and to establish her independence and individuality. Toward furthering that goal, she soon left Pakistan against the wishes of her extended family and went to England to
complete a graduate program in war studies.[59]

58. In 1995 and through an arranged match, Ayesha married a Pakistani man who was not
from a feudal background, but who met the requirements given here.

59. Ayesha received her doctorate from the Department of War Studies, King's College,
London, in 1996. Her dissertation title is "Defense Management and Procurement and Produc-
tion Decision-Making in Pakistan."

PART THREE

Face-to-Face with the Text

5

Marriage
Making a Culture of Her Own

Meeting Kishwar Naheed

A BBC CORRESPONDENT once asked one of Pakistan's most controversial contemporary female poets, Kishwar Naheed, to name a poem that best described her. "If one poem could represent me," she replied rather swiftly, "I'd stop writing!"[1] In an interview by me, however, she was less rhetorical and more reflective, if no less defiant. Fully aware of her contested public persona, she recited her poem "The Grass Is Like Me," which challenges and dismisses her culture's assumptions about women's actions, intentions, and motivations. With a playful smile, she said, "Many say this is a sexy poem."[2]

> The grass is like me.
>> It learns to love life
>> Only after feet have crushed it.
>> By becoming wet
>> Does it mean to show
>> Modesty's warmth, or
>> Passion's heat?
> The grass is like me.
>> As it lifts its head,
>> The mower
> Promising to turn it to velvet,

---

1. Kishwar was being interviewed at Lahore's Pearl Continental Hotel (May 10, 1992) and asked me to join her there.

2. From her collection, *Galyan, dhoop, darwazey* (Lanes, sunshine, and doors, 1971). See also *The Scream of an Illegitimate Voice: Selection of Poems of Kishwar Naheed* (Naheed 1991c, 34).

Levels its lifting top.
You really labor
To put women down,
But the desire to grow
Dies neither in the earth
Nor in women.
Hear me,
The old idea to make a track was good.
Those who shy [away] from the heat of courage
Will still be trampled
To make tracks for authority.
But they are straw,
Not grass.
The grass is like me.

I first saw Kishwar Naheed reciting her poems on Pakistan Television when I had just arrived in Pakistan in November 1987. It was not until 1990, when I returned to Pakistan for a short visit, that my Pakistani hosts invited me to go along to visit Kishwar. She had just undergone a hysterectomy and was recuperating in her elder brother's house. Despite being in pain, she was in good humor and received me with much grace and interest and was particularly intrigued by my Iranian nationality. Our interactions and friendship became regular and intense and have continued since. In our subsequent meetings, we read poems by the foremost Iranian feminist poet, Forugh Farrokhzad, whom Kishwar admired, saying that she thought of herself as the "Forugh Farrokhzad of Pakistan." Kishwar is one of the most prolific contemporary poets and writers in Pakistan. She regularly contributes a column to the *Frontier Post*, one of the daily English-language newspapers, in addition to writing articles for various journals and participating in numerous literary and artistic functions. She is also a controversial woman, and her views, literary works, and personality evoke a whole range of positive, negative, and ambivalent reactions from the public. She is aware of her eccentricity and frequently stresses her difference from other women in her society.

Because of political rivalries between the Pakistan People's Party (PPP), which Kishwar supports, and the Pakistan Muslim League (PML, headed by Nawaz Sharif), Kishwar intermittently has been promoted, demoted, or removed altogether from her job as a civil servant. At the time of our interview

(1992–93), she was in one of the periods of forced "retirement" imposed on her by Nawaz Sharif's government (1990–93). She was actively involved, however, in supervising several projects for poor women through the Yukki Gate nongovernmental organization (NGO), located in the old city of La-hore. Kishwar has become an institution in Pakistan. Although earlier I had decided not to interview famous Pakistani women for my project, I changed my mind in her case. She does not mince her words, as we shall now hear.

Kishwar Naheed

Choosing a Husband, Losing Honor

I was married to a family from Punjab, but they are originally Kashmiri, and we are *sayyids*. In South Asia, *sayyids* think that they are supreme and cannot think of allowing their daughters to marry non-*sayyids*. The cultural barriers were very high between the two families. I was the only educated woman in their family, you see. My mother-in-law was scared of me, thinking that be-cause I speak English, I must not know how to cook and how to run a house. Soon they realized that I knew everything, starting from cooking to typing to partying. Then the whole family descended on us from Karachi—they were not refugees from India. I had to run a joint family of twenty people at home. It was such a stupid affair. I was working hard and making money, and they were enjoying it. One can live up to expectations but not to exploitation.[3] I was spending my whole earnings. My father-in-law was not working. My younger brother-in-law was not working. My sister-in-law—she was married and had three or four children—would come to our house every day and spend the whole day there. They just sat around and had fun!

My husband Yousef was a class fellow. Both of us were doing our master's at Punjab University [late 1950s]. Mine was in economics. Yousef was writing poetry, too. I used to go to the intercollege *mushaeras*,[4] poetry contests, where I felt apprehensive without a companion. I had no contact with men before, so when he started going with me, I felt safe, that I was not alone in the company of men. There was no [love] affair between us, but my elder brother, who was

3. I asked her, "Do you think they expected it?"
4. The *mushaera* is a form of poetry recitation and contest and is very popular in the subcon-tinent.

studying in the statistics department, saw me going to debates or *mushaeras* with him. Being from the same *sayyid* traditional *maulvi* family, he informed [on me] at home. My parents and brothers got together and called me in. They said, "Is it true?"

Now, I had read Marx and Lenin, and I was a very revolutionary person. So according to my theory, I said, "Yes."

They said, "What do you want to do about it?"

"Nothing. He is my class fellow. He goes to *mushaeras* with me."

"What do you mean?" they asked. "What are you up to?"

"Up to nothing yet!" I replied. "But when we finish our classes, we get a job and earn money. Then we will be able to make a house"—it was all theory in my mind—"and then we will get married." My parents were furious.

They said, "Young lady, the world doesn't operate like that. Who has given you permission [to see him]?"

I said, "I do not think I need permission."

"Now listen," they said, "we have sent someone to fetch him. If you thought that you wanted to get married, then do it right now! Or from tomorrow you will not be going to the university. We will marry you off within a week. The fun is over."

Yousef was summoned. He had never been to our house; there was no occasion. My parents did not really care to find out who he was. My brother had already told them all they cared to know: he was studying economics, his family lived in Karachi, and he lived in Lahore, his income, that he was a Kashmiri, not a *sayyid* and not from Uttar Pradesh [the Indian province from which Kishwar's family migrated to Pakistan].

Yousef came. He was confronted with the situation. He said to me, "I am not ready to get married."

"Look," I said, "they gave me an ultimatum. Now, under these conditions I cannot go to the university. I cannot let myself marry anybody else. So I ask you, just agree to the *nikah*, marriage contract, for the moment, and if you do not want it, then we go out of this house, and you can divorce me. Please help me."

I do not know how I got this courage to say such things at the age of nineteen, but because I knew there was a ditch on the other side, I thought I must be ready, I must. He was two years older than me. I persuaded him, and he agreed to have the *nikah*. Half a kilo of *laddu* [sweetmeats] was made, and my *bhabi*, sister-in-law, graciously brought me one of her *ghararas* to wear. I said,

"No, I get married in whatever dress I am wearing." We sat down, and our *nikah* was held that day, in 1960. My brothers, my mother and father, the whole family was there, but my mother did not say a word.

Yousef was living in a room, and I went along with him. I was so stupid. I did not know just what happened. After intercourse, I was hurt. I was bleeding. I thought I had my period. I said to him, "I have my period." He was so stupid. He said, "Go have a pad." He was not a virgin but did not know anything either.

He said, "It always happens the next day!"

"It does not."

"It always happens," he repeated.

Afterward he slept, and I sat on the stairs, thinking, "What will happen tomorrow?" How could I go to the university and work? I could never imagine my life to be as such!

You know, it took me ten years to write about the experiences of the first night of my marriage! It is called "Arusi," wedding:

> The night of my wedding
> Lonely,
> Felt like one hundred nights
> Weeping,
> I thought
> How is it going to be?[5]

The next day when I went home to pick up my clothing, my brother said, "You cannot have them. You do not belong to the family. You have nothing here. Everything was closed to you on that day." My parents refused to see me until after my first son was born, but after that night I never again stayed at my parents' house.

It was a sort of punishment they wanted to give me. They just wanted to throw me out, and that was their legal way, letting me have my choice. The family felt dishonored because I did not behave according to their expecta-

5. "Shadi ki pahli raat / main ne tanha, sainkaron ratian gozarain / jag kar ye sochte / kes tarah hogi bhala." From *Benaam musafat* (Nameless distance, Naheed 1991a, 95–97). This poem begins with a different verse, but because Kishwar was reciting it by heart, she improvised on the first verse.

tions. I know that for months people would go to my mother to pay condolences for the way I got married [pensive].

My husband's family behaved the same way. One night one of Yousef's cousins came to our house. He was very fond of me because I was already becoming known in the university. He came to tell us that my sister-in-law was coming to throw us out, so we all went to a movie. It was December. She came and took everything we had, even the *lihaf* and the *dal*, the quilt and the lentils. That night we slept in our jackets.

After eight days, I got a job, and we rented a place. I was the assistant editor of *Development*, a monthly magazine at the local government [Punjab]. When the editor came to know that I was in trouble and needed a job, he asked me to go to his office. He said, "Go over to that desk and sit down. You have a job!" Yousef got a job after three months. I would get up at 5:00 in the morning, take care of the household chores, and leave for my university at 7:00. From the university, I would go to my office around 11:30, leaving the office at 5:00 P.M. to return home to make dinner and take care of more household chores. Still I had to listen to all that nonsense [from her in-laws]. That was the lifestyle I started.

For a whole one and half years, no family member came to see me, but, you see, I had very good friends and elders, like Faiz Sahib[6] and his teacher, Sufi Tabassum.[7] He was very well known in Iran also. These elders appreciated my poetry, and they gave me their blessings. They shared our every moment.

---

6. Faiz Ahmad Faiz (1911–84) is "recognized as one of the foremost Urdu poets of the Indo-Pak subcontinent. . . . Faiz is one of the few poets of our age who have been prominent in public affairs. . . . He had a varied career as teacher, army officer, journalist, trade union leader, broadcaster and script writer" (Kiernan 1971, 7). He distinguished himself as the editor in chief of the *Pakistan Times*, which developed into "the largest chain of newspapers in Pakistan" (Kiernan 1971, 7). He had a strong sense of "commitment to the socialist ideology" and was a dedicated poet. "An admirer of Karl Marx and a poet of the people, Faiz was honoured by Soviet Russia with the prestigious Lenin Award for Peace" (Kanda, 1990, 306–7). For some of his political activities, Faiz Sahib was jailed for four years, starting in 1951 (Kanda 1990). He was one of Kishwar's supporters and role models, and his political ideas had a strong impact on her.

7. Sufi Ghulam Mustafa Tabassum was "A poet par excellence" who "wrote with equal ease and facility in Persian, Urdu and Punjabi. . . . [H]is headquarter in the Government College became the headquarters of Lahore elite in intellect. Here one saw not only budding poets, who came to have their verse corrected, but eminent men of all vocations—authors, publishers, printers, jurists, lawyers. Sufi Sahib had a profound knowledge of the Qur'an and the Sunnah, he was widely read in exegesis and it was a treat to hear him explain so lucidly complex problems of jurisprudence" (A. Iqbal 1986, 168, 173).

They were so nice and kind that I never felt I was without my elders or relatives. Also, I was so much engrossed in my own problems. I had to finish my
master's. I had to attend my office. I had to do my household chores. And because I was earning so little, I would also participate in *mushaera* contests.

I remember the first time I got five hundred rupees from a *mushaera* contest!
Ahh . . . it was such a great feeling! We bought a cupboard. We had nothing,
no boxes to keep our clothing or anything. That was our first purchase in our
house. The whole night I looked at that cupboard and thought how beautiful it looked, how nice it was having it there. That was the way we built
everything.

Marital Drama

Yousef never let me forget that it was because of *my* insistence that we got married, and so he thought, "You suffer." He did what he wanted to. He was a carefree person, particularly when he left for his job in the United States. A man
who had never mixed freely with women got free reign. American women
would call him at his place and had free relationships with him. For him, it was
a big opportunity. He enjoyed it and utilized it to the maximum. After three
months, he suddenly left me. I used to cry. I would have fights with him. My
mother-in-law chided me, "This is the profession of men"—to go out. "There
is nothing new in it. He will come back to the house. Why are you crying?
Why are you making scenes? He is a beautiful man. He is a smart man, and
women like him." It was just terrible. He kept reminding me that it was my
choice we got married. His choice was to be open to American women, and he
behaved in the same way throughout his life. He did not care much for our relationship. He turned vengeful.

But at the same time he would make allegations if I were to go out for any
meetings. I never went to dinner parties in my official capacity because he
would never come with me. If I got an invitation for him, he would say, "I am not
going. Why should I go as a Mr. Kishwar Naheed?" And he would not let me go
by myself if I wanted to. He would sit in the study, making a big face, frowning,
and talking nonsense the whole night, keeping me awake, and having a quarrel.

You see, it is always like this with men. Earlier, when I had my show on television, he would say, "You want publicity." But when I arranged for him to
come on the television, he would stay the whole night. I said, "Why are you
staying there the whole night?" He said, "You do not know how much time is

required!"[8] I thought, "Has he forgotten that I got *him* introduced there?" [Incredulous]. He was full of contradictions, and it [the situation] was full of agony for me. He would send my sons to my office to see who was sitting there. If it happened to be an official meeting, whoever happened to be sitting next to me would come under his scrutiny. "Why is that man sitting there?" he would say. It was very bad like that, a very bad relationship. I had to continue with it. Early on I had decided many things with myself. He tried to stop me from writing in my own name. He said, "Do not write such poetry; it is shameful. You are washing your dirty linen in public." So I could only have a dialogue with myself. I had nobody to talk to. I thought, "If I stop writing poetry and if I stop going to my office, he is not going to stop going to women, stop drinking, and stop going out, so what will happen to me? I'll die further down. I'll not be able to have any sort of expression. I'll be a mad woman. So if he is going to continue like this, I should at least continue with my achievements of being a writer, and a professional."

I never knew what he was earning because I was earning myself and spending it all. He would give me money [for the house], but only what he wanted to. He never gave me the full amount, as is the tradition.[9] I never asked him for more money. This was the system of our married life. Also, because we lived in a joint family system, my sister-in-law and mother-in-law would constantly make insinuating comments about how it was useless to be educated, how I was the ugliest person in their family. I never fought with them, and I never allowed them to fight with me because I wanted to keep my self-respect, at least. So I never let them, never dared them. But they were up to it every time. After my husband's death, I had a choice to live with them. What helped me make my decision was a bunch of letters I found in Yousef's returned luggage—letters sent to him by his family members, me, his girlfriends, and others. His family had continuously implied that since I was living by myself, I must be enjoying my life [having illicit relations]. That is because I did not allow them to

8. Yousef became a TV celebrity, while Kishwar "dropped out of her final year at Economics and went to work to support him through his final year. Their marriage remained unconventional but the relationship appears to be somewhat ambivalent, a far cry from the fairy-tale ending the youthful poets in love might have expected it to be. A strong streak of cynicism runs through the personal poetry of both poets in later years" (R. Ahmad 1990, xii).

9. By "tradition," Kishwar means both a local and an Islamic one. Muslim men are obliged legally to support and maintain their wives financially, regardless of whether or not the women have their own independent source of income.

interfere in my life. They had every chance to come to my place. Our friends, including men, would come to see me as they had done when Yousef was around. In their view, this was bad. Whoever was my friend was a bad person.

So I decided, "Why the hell should I accept to live with them? I will be earning, and they will be eating at my table." After a fortnight I said, "He has died. Anything that is damage to you is damage to me. Suffer it yourself. I have to go to my office." After forty days,[10] I started going to my office just to get rid of them. You know, I put my in-laws' luggage—*every one* of them—in my car, and I told them, "Where should I take you?" Nobody was prepared to leave, including my son. He was married. He, too, did not want to go, not out of love, but that I should keep on earning, and they should keep on enjoying. That was their attitude, and that was all they wanted to do. They tried in so many ways to come back, hoping that maybe after a fortnight or a month they could have an entry in the house. Every time I told them, "I have no relations with you."

Twice I tried to get a divorce, and twice he refused to divorce me. He wanted to show the whole world that he could control me. He never wanted to let me have the freedom [emphatic]. He said it!

"I will never divorce you. I will not let you get a divorce. I'll take away the children."

"OK," I said.

Then he said, "No. I'll not let you take rest."

He continued [with the relationship] just to show that I could not get divorced, that he was in charge. Just chauvinistic! It was a very, very bad time. I had to put up with [the relationship] for two reasons. Now listen, Shahla! It was nothing emotional, but two basic logical reasons.[11] One was that people would say, "*You* wanted to get married. Now you are a defeated and failed person." Second, in our society the labeling of a man is very significant. It is as if you keep a dog at the gate. Just keep the husband at the gate and stop people from making up stories about you.

Children

Because my children were brought up in a joint family system, much of their relation with me was mediated through the family. My husband and his family influenced my sons against me, and I was not able to do much about it. You

---

10. The ritual of mourning commemorating the fortieth day after death.
11. I asked her, "Why did you stay in this relationship?"

see, this is a very strange psyche. I do not know how it is in Iran. Because I have an aptitude to change the social structure, I decided that I would remain a dedicated daughter-in-law—that whatever they do or feel, I should be part of it. Here, when daughters-in-law go to live with their in-laws, they never really mix with the family. They do not become part of the family. They are not granted the status of the in-houser [kin]. But I stayed with them. I did it willingly for the joint family. I cooked for them. I got them married. And I did everything as an elder member of the house. But I never realized that they were not feeling the same way. A basic drawback with me is that I am a very sincere person. I had never thought that the other side was not sincere. When my sons [sixteen and thirteen years old at the time] started talking back to me in a tone of voice that was unfamiliar to me, I began to realize it.[12] I was amazed to hear them say, "What have you done for us? You go to your office every day. You are busy with your poetry. We have been brought up by our *phuphi*, father's sister." Then I realized that the language that is spoken when I was not there was something else. My in-laws' relentless character assassination of me as a working woman had gone on to the point that it was getting back to me.[13] I felt really bad. The life I had spent! The torture I had taken for everything just for the sake of my children. I wanted to give them respectability in society, to have the father's image. I had given them everything, and after all that, this! They made my sons resent me and spy on me, and I did not realize it. It was a very, very heartbreaking situation.

Now that my children live far away in different cultures, they are having a better appreciation of their mother. Earlier they did not. One lives in America, and the other in Spain. Now they are busy with their own lives and with their own families. I am living my own life. They also know that I am busy with my own activities. They say, "Mother is not going to stay with us for a day more than it is necessary!" [Laughing]. Once a translation of one of my articles was reprinted in a Spanish newspaper. My son's Spanish girlfriend saw it and asked him, "Isn't she your mother?" He said, "Yes." She said, "I have been living with

12. In her poem "Déjà vu," Kishwar writes, "I once told my mother / I hate you. / I was proud of my courage / Until today. / Today, my son told me: / I hate you. / My childhood / Flows in my veins / As mercury" (Naheed 1991c, 41).

13. On the "shame" of "women who earn their keep," see the short story "Disdain" by Khadija Mastoor (1994).

you and never knew how important you are!" Now, she is telling everybody that Mizu's mother is a famous writer [smiling].

When we lived in the joint family, I became very upset with Mizu's decision to get married early.[14] He did not even appear for his graduation. It was done on the instigation of my father-in-law, who wanted to retaliate against my marriage to his son. He encouraged my son to get married. Children do not realize. You know, I suffered because of my sincerity, because I invested all my confidence in them, as with my own family. I let things happen on the assumption that they are going to safeguard my interests, but they did the reverse.

My Mother, My Self

My family started making overtures to see me because I was making money. I had a job. I had a child. I had my own house, and it was fully furnished. I was a respectable citizen [ironic smile]. I was OK, and Yousef was OK. So they must have thought, "Let's accept her." But they started coming back just in a token way, not very enthusiastically or in a broad-shoulder way. I did not care whether they wanted to see me again. Never! The scar in me was very deep, *very* bad. I am a very mean person. For that I have not been able to really reconcile with my mother. I do not have a longing to be with her, the way mothers and daughters do. I do not want to. I never felt any love from her, *never.* There are also other reasons. My younger brother, like me, married against my mother's wish. My mother showed the same sort of anger and distance she had shown toward me. She had so much jewelry and other valuables. She gave them to my other five siblings but did not give anything to my brother or me, even after our reconciliation. When my father died [1976], he left a very small amount of money. My two elder brothers said, "We give our portions of inheritance to Kishwar and Akhtar because they did not get anything during their marriage." I refused to accept it because my mother had never thought of it. She did me injustice, and I am not prepared to take any *kharaj*, tribute. I have made sure that nothing from my mother's house is in my life.

You see, it is very bad to be outstanding among your siblings because they relate to you through your public persona. Now I am related to everyone who is not even related to me [laughter]. Now everybody claims me. I find it very

14. He did marry early and had two children but was later divorced.

strange. It must be among the families from Uttar Pradesh. Brothers and sisters have a reserved relationship, unlike the Punjabi families. I don't know how it is in Iran. Punjabis are very close. They talk to each other, they care for each other, and they look after each other's welfare. Our family is very reserved. We talk to each other, but not with each other. They cannot talk with me. I mean, none of my sisters has ever asked me or advised me or thought of finding out how I spend my life or how I feel living alone or whether I should get remarried. That hurts, *hai na?*[15] They just assume, in their own way, that I am a very carefree person, that I am enjoying the best of life, because I never cry before anyone, because I never look as if I have something to worry about or that I miss anything in life. I am very composed. They still think that because I meet men, I must be having relations with them. Otherwise, why meet them? It is just a logical thing in their view.

I was not angry at life because of the way our families treated me. I had accepted life. Life for me is in the toil. Otherwise, there is no life. I never wished to be a *begum.*[16] I never wished to be a person with jewelry or with cosmetics or with things like that. I wanted to be myself. I wanted to like myself just as I am. You see, what made me different from my sisters is our choice of marriage partners. My two older sisters were married to *sayyid*s. These guys are very, very innocent to the point of being stupid. They are very calm and quiet, and I never liked either one of them. So when I was in high school, I decided that I would not get married to a person chosen by my parents because they would give me to another stupid person. That was my reason. But all was premature on my part. That made me hasten my decision to get married to Yousef because they had opened the gate. If my parents had not confronted me with the dilemma of either marrying Yousef or staying home, I might have waited and not gotten married. But they forced me, and I made my decision.

I now realize that I go for hard decisions in my life, and I stick to them. *And they have saved me!* I decided to stay in the job that in the end saved me. If I had not, Yousef would have never left me a penny in his bank or otherwise. He spent all his money on his own, on his girlfriends, or on liquor. Not a single

---

15. An Urdu expression—"isn't it" or "doesn't it"—frequently used in conversation, whether the conversation is in Urdu or in English. Perhaps its American equivalent is "right?"

16. *Begum* literally means "lady," but in the Pakistani usage it may be a derogatory reference to wealthier women, who are lackadaisical, have many servants, and do not do much except for their occasional charitable activities.

penny was in his bank account, despite the fact that he was working in Saudi Arabia [at the time of his death]. I would have had to go out begging if I had not stuck to my job. My own toil and my status have given me respectability in the entire country and abroad because of my writings.[17] He was never sure if he wanted us to build a house. This house [in Lahore], I built it by myself. [Zulfikar] Bhutto Sahib allotted this plot to me as a writer in 1970. You know, at that time he also offered me the membership of the National Assembly. I refused it. I said, "I do not want to be a politician. I am a writer. Whatever I can do to change the world, I'll do it through my poetry." Bhutto was very angry and said so.

Death of a Husband

Yousef died of a heart attack [1984]. He was barely forty-five years old. Shahla, what a strange thing! He was going to Saudi Arabia. I knew he was running off, and I knew this was the end of our relationship because I would never go to him, and he would never ask me [to go to him]. I had my senior post here, and I knew he was interested in somebody else, a Pakistani Christian woman who had gone to America, but he continued his relation with her. But I knew he never had the courage to get married to any other woman. I knew he would be continuing with other relationships and with her and that he would spend all his money, whatever he earned, on her [pause]. That is why there was no bank account.

When I heard the news, I felt pain and relief both.[18] I felt relieved.[19] The

17. Kishwar is one of the most prolific writers and poets in Pakistan. Her poetry is translated into several languages, including Persian.

18. I asked Kishwar, "How did you feel when you heard the news of Yousef's death?"

19. I told Kishwar a short story I had read by Alifa Rifaat, an Egyptian writer, called "Distant View of a Minaret" (1987). It is the story of a complex asymmetrical sexual relation between an Egyptian woman and her husband. After sexual intercourse that leaves her unfulfilled as always, he falls asleep. When the woman returns to bring him a cup of coffee after performing her ablutions, she finds him dead. "She returned to the living room and poured out the coffee for herself. She was surprised at how calm she was" (4). Kishwar said, "Every Pakistani man falls sleep after making love, and they feel angry if women complain. Pakistani men care only for their own satisfaction. They never care whether you are ready. They never care to make preparation. They do not believe it. They only care for their own needs."

torture and agony were over [whispering].[20] It was March 9, and I had gone to the annual Industrial Exhibition with a few journalists. I came back at 10:30 P.M., and at 11:30 I got a telephone call. The person on the other end kept asking again and again, "Where is your son? Is somebody else in the house?"

I said, "Is there something about Yousef?"

"Yes," he said.

"*Main-i ne kaha?* Is he dead?"

"Yes," he said.

"How long ago?" I asked.

"Two hours ago," he said [long pause].

I rang up my eldest brother. I did not tell my son because he was not old enough. I did not tell my in-laws either. The messenger had told me that it would take at least eight days for the coffin to be returned to Pakistan. There was nothing they could do that night. My brother came over and suggested to stay with me or to have his maidservant come over. I said, "No. I'd rather stay alone." The whole night I sat up, and the whole night I thought of the life that this man had left me. No memories as such! The way I should remember him, the way I should miss him. What an unlucky man! I thought this man enjoyed the best of life and early on refused to accept any responsibilities. Every moment of his life he spent as he wished, not caring much for others. Even then, I thought, I was going to make all the preparations [for his funeral], but I did not know [the complexity of her own emotion]. I had never seen women cry that much! I must have been crying out my agonies in public [incredulous]! I did not stop crying for the whole forty days. It must have been my old torture because it was so bad.

People from all over Pakistan came daily to see me and to express condolences. It was so painful. All along my sister-in-law, sitting in one corner, kept on saying, "She made him die. She made him die." Not to my face, but others told me. I think it is that Eastern tradition. Indians do that, too. Through

20. In a poem called "The crackling sound of sadness," Kishwar expresses her conflicting emotions: "Death is a doorway in life leading to the land of exiles. / Death is the light which is drawn from our eyes / To be sown in the earth. / Death is a lamp which glows in the rain / And draws life from hurricanes. / Death is the sound of footsteps / Which can be seen but not heard. / Death is a heading / Which appears on every page of a book / With a different name. . . . Death is that moment of awareness / in which even grief, buried in oblivion, / Appears as abodes of happiness. / For forgetting, even a moment feels like a burden. / For remembering, even a lifetime is not enough" (Naheed 1991c, 120).

words and gestures, women taunt you. They want to hurt you, to humiliate you, by hook or crook. This is in our sadomasochistic psychology.

But, you know, there are very different stages of experience. After his death, on the third day,[21] and after he was buried, I wrote a poem about the stifling coffin. I wrote many more poems thereafter, invoking his memories, but the first one I wrote was a homage to him. It is not a *marsiya*,[22] elegy, in that way:

> From the tree on which sparrows were wed,
>> He chose the timber for his last journey.
>> The same silver shade
>> Under which lovers are joined,
>> He chose for his last robe.
>> With the same blind belief
>> Which turns trust to worship,
>> He closed his eyes
>> In a new surrender.
>> The urge to keep love secret
>> Needs sealed lips.
>> He gave poise to the burdensome quiet.
>> Like grass hidden under water,
>> I watched him
>> With waves gathering on my face.
>> He was an ocean,
>> Yet he appeared confined.
>> I, a small stream,
>> Spilled over the banks.
>> Till the wedding of the age of sparrows,
>> He will still live in the soul of that tree
>> And I shall search for him
>> On the island of my ignorance.
>> But, till the wedding of the next to next,
>> And even later generations of sparrows,
>> He will still live in the soul of that tree.[23]

21. Muslims are required to bury the dead as soon as possible, within three days at most. At the end of the third day, they perform the ritual of *khatam* (literally the "end") for the deceased.

22. See chapter 3, fn. 21, on *marsiya*.

23. Naheed 1991c, 117. Kishwar did not have the text of her poem, so she improvised it during our interview. "He is gone," Kishwar said, "in a box whose wood was made from a tree, in

[Long pause] I did love him in a sense, yes, but then there was also hate or tension—you could say.[24] You see, I come from a very traditional family. In spite of all my revolution, from within I was the daughter of my mother. I was never prepared for marriage until I got married. I could not have taken that revolutionary step to jump from one man to another. Besides, working in an office made me realize that men in general react the same way. If I were to change one man for another, I would not be gaining much, except that I'd be comparing them [to Yousef] all the time, and they'd be adding to my injuries by remarking about the first husband. So it is better to forget the messiness in your life, accept it, and get involved in other activities so that you do not think about it.[25]

Humm . . . he *was* in my mind all the time! But, no, I was not trying to forget him all the time.[26] I wanted to forget what is culturally expected, accept what is there, and go on to doing other things. I had a sword hanging over my head. The whole family was watching me, waiting to see when my marriage was going to break apart, so I acted as a martyr to prove that I was a most dutiful wife until my husband died. Even now nobody knows what happened to me, how my life was. They think I had the best life. They still think so.

Swimming Against the Currents

Before my husband's death, I was living alone for one year. One night my elder brother came to me and said, "Why don't you come to my house? It is big. You

---

which birds used to get married. So nothing to be sorry about! He is with those birds, who are always getting married. He is listening to their voices in happiness and music." The poem in its totality is reprinted here to underline Kishwar's sense of longing and her complex love-hate feelings for her husband.

24. I said to Kishwar, "You seem to be having a lot of ambivalence toward your husband. On the one hand, there is love," and she finished my sentence, "and you could say hate or tension." I continued, "Yeah, because the way he treated you. You really loved him at some level."

25. In her poem "Non-communication," Kishwar writes, "In the tumult of my days and nights, / you announce your existence / Like a comb passing through hair. / But rage and love, / Like my half-ripe hair, / Knit a web inside me. / Like scattered patches of clouds on the sky, / The moth-eaten leaf of life / Does not even have the value of scrap. / You thunder like a cloud, / And I pour like rain. / Like two deaf singers, / We are trying to sing to each other" (Naheed 1991c, 142).

26. Following up on my previous question, I asked, "You were trying to forget him all the time, but he was in your mind all the time?"

can take the guestroom and stay there, and I'll not ask who came and who went."[27] See the twist of the sentence?[28] I said, "*Bhai jan,* you have been tolerating me all throughout. I am different from other women. If I do not spend two or three hours a day in my library, I am nobody. This is my lifestyle. I cannot write anywhere except in my study. I am made up like this. I cannot live in families. I cannot talk about children. I cannot gossip. You have heard so many stories about me, and you have tolerated me. Whenever you wanted to own me, you owned me. I never asked why. Whenever you wanted to disown me, you disowned me. I never grumbled. It was your sweet choice whether to own me or to disown me. Please, leave me be like this." So I said, "*Bhai jan,* you are also living all by yourself!" He is not married. "I am not going to ask you to come to my place. You are a human being living alone. Nobody is making up stories about you. I have activities more than a man. Why should *anybody* object to my living alone? And if somebody does, please tell them you have no relations with me. I'll not mind it."

After my husband's death, I made several decisions and many restrictions. Earlier, anybody could drop by without an appointment, as it is among friends. Then the whole family was there. Yousef was there. If I was busy in my study, they would sit with Yousef and have a drink with him. After his death, they wanted to continue the same tradition. People would come with their half bottles to have a drink before their meal, as it is usual in Pakistan. You do not drink with your meal. I thought they might have the same expectation of me as they did of my husband. Then they'll go out and make up stories: "Oh, she is all alone. She calls us to her house and wants to spend time with us." "Better make a decision early," I thought—like I did with my in-laws. I had to make a new culture, ethics, and style in my life. So I told people, "I am alone, but I am not lonely. Do not come without an appointment. I'll not welcome you." It *happened* many a time that someone would come for a visit. "I am sorry," I would say, "I have to meet a deadline. I cannot see you at the moment. I am writing." And, really, I *was* writing. Even to my family and people who had been coming to my house for thirty years I said the same thing.

Still they made up stories: "God knows *what* she is doing if she is not prepared to see anybody without an appointment!" But I had decided: "*I'll make a culture of my own.*" Then I told my servant, "Listen, when I expect somebody, I'll

27. She repeated her brother's sentence in Urdu: *"keh kon ata hai kon jata hai, mai nahi puchunga."*
28. She implied that he suspected she had improper relationships.

tell you, but if anybody happens to drop by and say *'begum sahiba hain,'* say she is not here." *Ye baat hai.*[29] It requires great self-discipline because without that you could not succeed. But that took only a year or so, and after that my friends were also disciplined [laughing].

That first year of strict disciplining made my life easier. But, you see, there are times when *I do want* to be with someone. You cannot read all the time. You cannot write all the time. Sometimes I touch my telephone to see if it is working! I *can* get tired of reading. When I do, I go out and just drive along the canal, but I *never* peep into somebody's house without an appointment, and I *never* let anybody come without an appointment. Many have asked me, "Why don't you keep paying guests? You won't be alone." I said, "I am *not* lonely." I have had enough of the joint family business, of crowded houses. I do not want any crowding. Social life in Pakistan is an ongoing process.[30] So many of our writers, artists, and politicians do not do a thing. You become used to socializing, and there is very little of your mind in your books.

Love, Marriage, and Desire

I *have* fallen in love—one could say. It was not so much in terms of being very intimate, but I have felt soft on occasions. Although, you see, I had not had many chances because often *I* was the beloved. Many of our elder poets and others fell madly in love with me. Stopping them, making a barrier between us while not spoiling the relationship, understanding their message while pretending I did not—most of my energy went for self-defense [laughter]. So I had very little opportunity to be in the company of many people. When I reached forty or forty-five, there came the younger generation! And *that* was another trouble. The younger men would fall in love with me and sought my

29. *Ye baat hai*—"That is the thing" or "that's the point"—is a popular Urdu expression, and Kishwar frequently used it as a way of concluding many of her arguments and opinions. Its American equivalent would be something such as "that's it." To minimize repetition, I have eliminated some uses of this expression.

30. My husband's and my social life in Pakistan quickly became overwhelming. Not only would old and newly acquired friends invite us to their homes regularly, but our own house became a refuge, a hangout, for some friends who knew that as Americans we had a good supply of wine and beer, commodities that one cannot easily obtain in the legally "dry" Pakistan. As much as we enjoyed these gatherings, we eventually had to limit our socializing in order to be able to get some of our work done.

company. If you are mature and have grown up sons, you tend to treat them like your sons. Then they would fall in love with you! Once or twice I was tempted but could not get my conscience free.

There was one occasion, however, at an international conference in Moscow. I met a man who had a doctorate in *Ramayan, Bhagvad-gita*.[31] He became my interpreter on the first day when he heard my speech. He said, "I heard your speech and am very impressed. May I be your interpreter?" I said "OK, if your official duties do not restrict you." You see, being a government official and working in mixed groups, you tend to behave like men. Men do not fascinate me. I do not have the fascination of the touch of a man because we all shake hands, we talk, we joke, we travel together, we have joint company and joint meetings.[32] For love, you need fascination. That is a big, big, *big* need. That is a minus point for me. This man was very much impressed by Indian culture. He behaved like a typical Indian—not expressing, not telling, but being there all the time, like a shadow [laughing]. The last day of the conference he said—and it made me really *feel* for him—"I am not going to see you off at the airport. I cannot bear to see you off. Someday I will meet you somewhere in Bangkok or Singapore or anywhere, and when we talk again, we'd remember that . . . ahh . . . some twenty years earlier we had met and stayed together." It is moments like this that I feel *sweet* and soft. He died ten, fifteen years ago.

When love is not in your life, you write about it.[33] When you do not have it, you desire it. When I was younger, I just wanted to fall in love [laughing] but could not do it. I was busy. Naturally, I want to be loved. You want to be loved. I have been so loved by people from all sections of society that I do not have any complaint about it. But your personal love—the child in you wants to be

31. Hindu religious texts, including "the Sanskrit *Epics*, the *Mahabharata* and *Ramayana*, the *Puranas*, the 'books of Sacred Law,' and the collections of hymns and poems . . . [o]riginally secular histories and cosmologies, . . .became sacred by virtue of receiving religious interpolations. The most famous of these is the *Bhagavad-gita*" (Inden 1990, 109).

32. In the context of Pakistani culture, what Kishwar is referring to here is the religious and cultural disapproval of men and women shaking each other's hands. The extent of this prohibition may become clear when understood against the background of an official directive banning men from shaking hands with Benazir Bhutto. Even visiting foreign dignitaries were informed to observe this protocol.

33. I asked her, "Our marriages are seldom love marriages, yet our poetry is filled with love and this longing for love. Why is that?"

captured by somebody, to become awed by somebody. If I fell in love, I would not mind getting married again. I like it. No moral or physical thing is dividing me. Physically you feel for it. When I have my migraines, I know it is the tension of my body that is reflected in my headache. I cannot help it. I cannot have a lifelong migraine [laughing]. People ask me, "Why don't you get married?" I say, "If I find the right person, I will. But if I don't, I won't." Some married men want to come and spend a few moments of their life with me. They expect me to cook for them and to make my house and myself available. But if at times I want to have *their* company, they would say, "I am busy." What is this? To be a second fiddle, just to be a keeper of somebody? Why? Why should I?

Childhood and Growing Up

I was born in 1940 in the city of Bulandshahr in North India, thirty miles away from Delhi. The majority of the population was Muslim. The families did not send their daughters to school. They followed Sir Sayyid's philosophy.[34] He realized that under the Britishers' domination,[35] Muslims had badly fallen behind in education and progress. He said, "Educate your boys, and teach your girls the Qur'an." All my uncles and my brothers graduated from Aligarh Muslim University, which at that time was the only university in the whole of India that was perceived as the *best* and most *elegant* university. People from Punjab and even Calcutta used to go to Aligarh. That was *the* prestige symbol. But *none* of the girls were allowed to go there.[36] Here is where my feeling of retaliation started.

My maternal grandfather was adamant against girls' education. It was my mother who dared to oppose him and decided to have her girls educated. My grandfather said, "Then I will not allow you to come to my house." She said,

34. For a discussion of Sir Sayyid Ahmad Khan's views on Muslim education, see Hafeez Malik 1980, 125–72. See also note 42 in chap. 1.

35. "Britisher" is a popular Pakistani expression.

36. Sir Sayyid's objection to girls' education is underscored also in the following statement: "We wish our women to be educated. But if education means letting them loose to mix with whom they please; if it means that as they increase in learning, they shall deteriorate in morals; if it means the loss of our honour and the invasion of the privacy of our homes-we prefer our honour to the education of our women, even though we may be called Obstinate, prejudiced, and wrong-headed." I am grateful to Ayesha Jalal for providing me with the text of this quote, before her book *Self and Sovereignty* (2001) was published.

"I'll not come!" And she did not go, as far as I remember. My mother facilitated her daughters' study, a chance she herself never had. My father, too, was not well educated but was a highly paid person. He was a *patwari*, the village comptroller. At that time, it was quite enough to study up to the primary school. He knew Persian language and literature and Urdu poetry. He believed that what you earn depends on your luck and not on your education. He, too, was unwilling to have us educated, but my mother had made her decision against her father and her husband both.

Yeah . . . I have inherited my mother's will [laughing]. My father said, "I am not going to increase the monthly expenditure." She said, "You can give me the same amount. I'll cut down the food, but I'll not cut down their education." And she did that! But, you see, the revolution of that age had its limitations. She did not want her daughters to continue beyond high school. After my two senior sisters finished their high school, she made them stay home to wait for a *sayyid* family to come their way because they could not get married to any other man.

Coming of Age, Coming to Pakistan

We left India in 1949, two years after the partition. On the night of the independence [August 14], my father was arrested and kept in jail for two years. He was the [Pakistan] Muslim League's district secretary.[37] I remember going to jail with my brother to see him. At the time of his release, there was a ban on mobilization of refugees. The path between Pakistan and India had taken up such a big mobilization of people that it could not be tolerated any more by either of the countries.[38] Neither India nor Pakistan could accommodate the refugees. Both countries sealed their borders and decided that those Hindus that had remained in Pakistan should stay there, and the Muslims who wished to go to Pakistan had to have an immediate relative employed by the government of Pakistan. My paternal auntie's son was in the excise department. He declared my father and my mother as his parents and my sisters and brothers as his sisters and brothers. We came to Pakistan in September 1949, when my father was out of jail, but he could not come with us because there was a ban

37. See chapter 4, fn. 35, on the PML.

38. For a piercing satire on the unwillingness of India and Pakistan to claim their "intellectually challenged" members left on the border of the two societies, see the short story "Toba tek singh" by Saadat Hasan Manto (2000, 9–16).

on his travel. He concealed himself somewhere and came in some disguise after quite many months. It was a very bad experience.

In Pakistan, refugees were given evacuated property allotted to them in exchange for the property they had left behind. But my father said, "I have mobilized and come to Pakistan not for a reward. I'll not take any property." And he did not, so we had to stay in my aunt's house for three years. He could not buy a house because his money from his estate was not transferred until three years later. He then was financially able to handle things, and then we rented a house of our own.

If I were to trace my awareness of the world, it goes back to three events. It begins with my mother's activities on behalf of the Muslim League in India. What women did was to put aside one bulk of *atta*, flour. You see, people used *atta* to make *paratha*, fried bread, for breakfast, for lunch, and for dinner. So with every meal they put away some *atta*, which amounted to a substantial quantity. Then it was the children's duty to collect that *atta*, take it to the shop, and sell it. Whatever money was collected would be given to the Muslim League office. That was the way funds were collected for the Muslim League. It was the women's own wisdom to find ways to fight for their freedom, and all of them were housewives.

Also, when my dad had a meeting, my brothers and me—I was in between, one was older and one was younger—would be playing outside. We would be running around and reciting this verse at the top of our voices: *"lay ke rahain gay Pakistan, ban ke rahe ga Pakistan"*—Pakistan will be established; it is inevitable [laughing]. You see, I used to play boys' games. I never played with dolls. I never played girls' games. *Ye baat hai.*

Then came the riots—the Hindus killing Muslims in those areas. I remember a girl, the only one from our city who went to Aligarh University, was abducted. She was a law student, and we looked at her as if she was a film actress. She was our heroine, our role model. We never thought in our *lives* we would go to the university. After quite some time, she rescued herself and ran off. It took her a long time to get back to Bulandshahr. I remember everybody went to see her. I do not remember if I saw her face; I know I only saw her feet. They were all bloodied.[39] I still have terrifying images of feet in my mind. I know of

39. For a discussion of "male inhumanity towards women"—be they Muslims, Hindus, or Sikhs—"to assert dominance over men of other communities" during the partition of 1947, see Jalal 2001, 553.

many cases where the entire families were killed. My cousin who facilitated my family to come to Pakistan—his whole family was killed, including his in-laws. He was left alive only because they believed he was dead. After a few days, he crawled out and rescued himself.

To come to Pakistan we had made train reservations [pause]. A few friends of father—they were Hindus—learned that the Hindus were abducting or killing girls and snatching everything else. Because our father was not coming along with us, they advised my mother not to go by train, but to sell the entire luggage and go by plane. So my first journey out of India was in a Dakota plane, coming from Delhi to Lahore. I sat on one of my brothers' lap. I remember everybody was very happy to come to a free country because we had struggled for it, and my father was jailed for two years. But now the whole structure has changed. You see, it was a freer society then. Women were coming out. Before [in India], women were carried in *palki*, a covered "chair" carried on the shoulders of two men. In Pakistan, they could just go out and feel freer. Although one should not say it was a free society, it was, in a way, almost a freer society then. Nobody knew who was who. One would try to seize a house, another to get hold of properties and factories. Many did anything to make a fortune. That was the very bad thing about it. Yet, at the same time, there was this sense of euphoria, that something exciting was created. *Ye baat hai*, that's the thing.

So given the significance of Aligarh and the Pakistan movement, my awareness of the world included the role my mother played in the Muslim League, working for children's education and organizing women's meetings. Next is the partition and the way women were being abducted and brutally raped or murdered. But then, ahh . . . the freshness of being in Pakistan, everybody feeling better, going out, doing something—life was looking so much better.

Birth of a Nation, Vision of a New Order

From the very beginning, Pakistan started on the wrong foot. The father of the nation [Mohammad Ali Jinnah] died [1948], and the men who took the helm of the affairs were not politically astute. They wanted to make the best of their luck. If you place much food before a hungry person, he would like to eat it all. He might get ill, but his appetite will not be satisfied. The same goes with our leaders and people. They were flabbergasted with the idea of being free. They never thought of having a plan of action. That system of temporariness continued and penetrated all sections of society.

Also, because of Kashmir, we have pampered the army like anything, and the army has taken over the country. Many nations are called martial nations, but we became the martial law nation: an autocratic social structure with a crazy character of a nation. Just as people were the slaves of the Britishers during the British time, in Pakistan time they became slaves to their political and military masters. They bow before every power structure for their own petty interests. But you have to make decisions as to whether you are only after your personal interest or you are interested in a broader good. People are trapped in their personal interests, and that trap is tempting. Once you are entrapped, then another trap is ready for you, and the vicious circle continues.

In this part of the world, when uniculture is taking shape, the ethnic political structures are simultaneously growing. So at this time Pakistan is also facing the same type of ethnic problems faced in other parts of the world. Yesterday there was a *hertal*, strike, in Baluchistan. A call for strike was sent out in Sindh as well. But we shouldn't worry about such things if the nation is strong enough to bear it. It is easy to break a person, but it is difficult to break a nation, if one *is* a nation. Our first priority is therefore to be a nation.

On the one hand, socialism is gone, but, on the other, the world does not offer any system that while doing away with socialism can provide the basic necessities for the poor. If people say socialism has failed, in the same way democracy has also failed because it has not made people flourish. I think though ideologies do not fail, the administrative structures do. The point is that thinking and planning for a broader community, for the world community, have to be oriented toward [providing for] people. But who is going to do that? The West has made governments in the name of emancipation, while still women have not achieved equality with men. The East thinks of women as a commodity. As long as feudalism continues in the subcontinent, the definition of property includes women as well. Realize the point of articulation. The point of articulation lies in that we should aim for an equitable system where men and women work and are rewarded according to their qualifications and capacities, and not [according to] gender specificities that deprive women. We can achieve that only if we reinterpret every system of learning, including religion, anthropology, psychology, economics, and others. Up until now, the interpretation of all the educational systems, learning and teaching and religion, has been done by men only, and for only 50 percent of the population. We need a reinterpretation of society *and* culture *and* ethics.

In Pakistan, in the 1970s elections, 82 percent of people who turned up in the Assemblies were educated. For the 1988 elections, it was 60 percent. And in the present Assembly, it's only 38 percent. Most of our representatives are illiterate.[40] The system works on the basis of *bradri*, tribal or feudal, loyalties. You do not need education and qualifications. You rely on your tribal affiliations and alliances [to get votes], not on democratic institutions. If a democracy is to exist [in Pakistan?], it has to reinterpret itself.

Self-Awareness and Desire to Know

I started school in Lahore. Because we lived in a joint family [with her paternal aunt's family], my mother became very vigilant. She would slap us if we talked to any of our [male] cousins. You see, earlier in India, I had been taught the Qur'an and read the *tafsirs* [interpretations of the Qur'an]. I learned the *tahajjud*, midnight prayers, and the *namaz*, daily prayers. So [in Lahore] I had no choice except to take refuge in books. One of my elder brother's friends, who was very fond of literature, gave me novels. I read books that were required to pass subjects such as Persian and Urdu literature. By the time I did my matrics [matriculation exams, finished tenth grade], I had read almost all of Dostoyevsky, Tolstoy, and anything else I could get my hands on. I did not play much with my sisters or my cousins, all of whom got married here in Lahore.

I fought to go to college. I fought for everything, you see. I wanted to be educated more. My mother said, "None of your sisters has ever gone to college. You cannot go!" I said, "I want to." She was adamant. Then I went on a hunger strike for eight days. Finally my brother asked me to please stop it, and he assured me in writing that they would allow me to go to college. When I was younger and wanted things, my mother used to beat me. I would say, "You can beat me, but I'll not stop." Father had no say. He used to say whatever they [mother and older brother] said.

I got my admission to college [University of Punjab, Lahore] in the eco-

40. Members of the Assembly must be literate, though what Kishwar means by literacy is not a minimum requirement for reading and writing.

nomics department in 1959. In college, I would go to intercollege debates, poetry recitations, and *mushaeras*. One of my professors who saw my performance
said, "Why don't you write about the college events, and we can give you a
stipend for it." I was so *happy*. I came home and said to my parents, "Do not
worry about my education. I'll earn [money] for my education. I have been offered a job at the college." *And* there was a hue and cry all over the house [pro-
longing each word as she pronounced them]. My mother started crying. My
brother said, "We will stop you."

Such crying came so many times, you see. The first time it happened was
when I had passed my matric exam, and there was a contract from Radio Pakistan for me to appear on the children's program. We used to have *bait bazi*—
you might be having that in Iran, too—poetry contests.[41] We would be having
a *bait bazi* contest with me on one side and the whole school on the other! I had
memorized many poems, and my parents were very happy about it. A very famous radio artist was living near our house. She was known as the "Golden
Voice of Radio." Once she came as a judge to our school's poetry contest. She
said that I had a very nice voice, spoke well, and had a good repertoire of poetry. She thought I should go to the radio. She got my address and sent a contract. Oh, it was an occasion of death. It was *so* bad! My God! My mother cried
and cried and said, "She is a *sayyid's* daughter. The voice of a *sayyid's* daughter
is not heard even in the *mardana khana*, men's quarters. Now she wants to have
her voice heard all over the city. How *besharam*, shameless, she is!" So I could
not go to radio at that time.

You see, the drawbacks and the conflicts that I had to face made me
stronger. Something did not let me behave in the conventional traditional
way, like others. When I was barely five years old, my mother asked me to
grind *masalla*, spices. I could not pick up the *patthar*, the stone with which we
grind *masalla*. It was too heavy, and I got scratches in my hand. I started crying

---

41. I told Kishwar that what Pakistanis call *bait bazi*, is called *mushaera* in Iran. It is a very popular game, and I used to play it frequently with my parents, my siblings, and classmates at school
or at other social gatherings. It can be played between two individuals, an individual and a
group, or two groups. The game begins with one party reciting a verse of a poem. The oppos-
ing party must reciprocate with another poem that begins with the last letter of the first poem.
It continues back and forth until one of the parties can no longer respond appropriately, poetically speaking, and thus loses the game.

and ran out on the street, saying, "She is not my real mother. She is my step-mother to ask me to do this!" [Laughter].

[Pause, reflecting] I am tracing back my sense of retaliation and my memory of going against the tradition. You know, I am a very self-analytic person. I remember that I was just seven years old in 1947 when I was made aware of being a girl. This is when I was first forced to wear a *burqa*. I remember I could not walk, I could not see in front of me, and I kept falling down. I protested, but everybody said, "No, no you are from a *sayyid* family" [and thus must wear it]. Yeah . . . this was despite the fact that my parents were so politically aware. You see, like your ayatollah family, mine was very religious. But when we were coming to Pakistan in 1949, we were told not to go by train because still after two years all trains were being looted, and girls were abducted. There was one small Dakota plane that could take thirty-eight passengers that was traveling between Delhi and Lahore. For children up to twelve years old the ticket was half price, and I was only nine years old.[42] If I were to travel with my *burqa*, then I could not use the half-price ticket [would be considered an adult]. So I came to Pakistan unveiled [smiling]. For the sake of honor, they put on the *burqa*, and for the sake of money they took off my *burqa*. So the awareness was gradually setting up in me, you see.

I was in *burqa* until I went to the university. In the university, I used to go to intercollegiate debates. Because I was going with boys and on the team, I used to take off my *burqa* and keep it in the ladies room and get my prize. Then I would put on my *burqa* to go home. I concealed my prizes either in the dustbin or in a jar so that my mother would not see it. Otherwise, she would make a huge hue and cry.

I remember in 1952 a young Pakistani poetess called Zehra Nigaah returned to Karachi from London to perform at a *mushaera* contest.[43] She was only sixteen years old, but she sang such marvelous *tarannum*.[44] Oh . . . it was spellbinding! She still is. Oh, if you could only hear her—if she comes to Lahore, next time I'll invite you. None of the great poets present, including Faiz,

42. Upon reaching nine lunar years, Muslims girls traditionally are expected to veil and to cover their hair.

43. See R. Ahmad 1990, xv-vi, 65–78; Imam 1991, 179–80.

44. *Tarannum* is a kind of singing and modulated recitation of Urdu poetry, popular in South Asia.

could match her. People wanted her to continue. Later I heard all these men saying, "How could she write them [these poems]? A man must have written them for her. She is not a poet."[45] I was very young and not a poet at that time, but I felt very humiliated. It might be that those men's attitude toward Zehra Nigaah and their damnation and humiliation of her made me the rebellious person I am. It might be that their denials and accusations triggered my brain to write poetry differently.

In a Different Voice: Poetry of Retaliation

I was still not writing poetry when I went to college. I had my poetry call, but not like this. While I was in college, one of my Urdu teachers asked me to enter into intercollege poetry contests. I said, "I don't know how to write." "Try it," she insisted. I hesitated, and finally I said, "OK, I'll try." I used to study at nights. Otherwise, my brothers, my sisters, and my mother would see the books I was reading. If I was reading novels, they would snatch them and throw them away: "Did you buy such books? You should be only reading schoolbooks!" Everybody wanted to keep me away from books. For Urdu books, they generally did not raise objections. Only for English books—"Oh ho, what tongue is she speaking?" But even for some Urdu books. There was a case against Manto, and his book *Thanda gosht* [Cold meat].[46] I said to my brother, "I have read this book. I don't find anything objectionable in it. Why is the case going on against him?" He slapped me in the face and said, "How dare you read such a thing?" And, you know, he had not even read it [ironic laugh]. So I made up my plan of studies. I used to sleep at seven or eight at nights and get up at two in the morning to read my literature books. I either

45. Zehra Nigaah is not the only woman whose literary creativity was either denied by the male literary establishment or assumed to be the work of a male ghost writer. Ismat Chughtai (1911–91), one of the foremost literary figures in South Asia, initially was believed to be her brother's pen name. Parvin I'tisami (1907–41), the renowned Iranian poet of the turn of the century, initially also was believed to be a pen name for a man. Some never let go of their doubt and argued, even as late as 1977, that her poems were too good to have been written by a young woman who also happened to be shy and unglamourous (Garakani 1977).

46. Saadat Hasan Manto (1912–55) is considered one of the greatest contemporary Urdu short story writers, and his themes explore the many horrors of the Indian partition of 1947. His depression regarding the aftermath of the partition drove him to drink himself to death by the age of forty-three. See Manto 2000.

borrowed them from the library or from a friend of one of my brothers, who knew I liked literature.

All these things made up my rebellious personality. When I began writing poetry, I did not show them to anyone at home. For a whole year, I continued going to *mushaera*s and won the second prize in one of them. My older sister, who was studying with me, informed on me at home. One day, after a few months, my father locked me in a room and said, "You wanted to have some life and activity around you. You have had it. Now from whomever you have borrowed these *ghazals*, poems, return them." I tried to make my father believe that I was writing them myself. He never believed me. He said, "Don't talk. I heard you. Now stop it."

I became used to keeping my writings concealed. When I was married, my husband criticized me but in a rather more vivid way. He would say, "Why did you write this line? Why did you write that image? What would people say about me? What would people think about you?" He began to see my books in the same way as other people were seeing them, so I started concealing my poetry from him as well.

Luckily, by the time I went to the university and started reading my poetry, I attracted the attention of our senior poets and writers. As you know, the earlier tradition of our great poets was that they would begin by becoming a pupil to a great poet master. You had to rehearse to become a good poet. I started my apprenticeship by sitting in their presence and listening to their poetry, their talks and discussions, and absorbing them in my head. In Sufi Tabassum's house, there would be five or six people coming together. He was the most senior person, and he was living next to our house! I used to say that I was going to buy a book or to go to the library and secretly would go to his house and sit down. For hours, they would have discussions on Hafiz, Sa'di, Rumi, and Iqbal's poetry.[47] I would just sit there, listening and absorbing. It was fascinating to learn the great length they went to in their debates, criticism, and evaluations to understand literature and poetry. *That* was my basic training in literature.

When I started writing *ghazals*, they were purely romantic and in the classic

47. Shams al-Din Muhammad Hafiz (d. 1389), Muslihuddin Sa'di (d. 1291), Maulana Jalaluddin Rumi (d. 1273) are three brilliant jewels of Persian lyrical poetry, mysticism, ethics, and philosophy. See Arberry 1967. Sir Muhammad Iqbal (1873–1938) is one of the great Indo-Pak poet-philosophers, who composed poetry in both Urdu and Persian. See chapter 1, fn. 15.

mode.[48] I was trained in the classic tradition, and I used the same vocabulary. My tone and diction were completely classical. I changed my tone when I started writing *nazm*, free verse.[49] Even now, when I write *ghazal*, it is classical. When I talk about change in my tone, I think of it as a kind of death. I burnt all the *ghazal*s I wrote in college. It was from the university period, from 1960 onward, that I kept my poetry. My earlier poetry was only a rehearsal. I do not count it as my own original thinking. You see, one thing I like about myself is that I am a good critic of my own work. When I read out something, sometimes I think I don't want to reproduce it. I trash it out, "This is not good. That sounds right."

The themes I wrote about were a mixture of old and new at the same time. I think I was bidding farewell to my youth. I will recite one of the couplets, and you will realize how it is: "daikh kar, jis shakhs ko hunsna buhhut / sar ko us ke samne dhakna buhhut.[50]

You see, in our culture when you are in love, you want to hide a little, to cover your face from the beloved, to conceal [revealing and concealing at the same time]. So I was bidding farewell to my tradition, my youth, and it was reflected like this. Again, of the same period, another couplet:

kochh youn hi zard zard si Naheed aaj thi[51]
   kochh orhni ka rang bhi khulta houa na tha.

---

48. "The *ghazal* has been rightly described as the pride of Urdu poetry. Though not an indigenous verse form, it has been thoroughly assimilated into the Indian cultural stream and has, over the years, proved its worth as a fit instrument of artistic expression, fully responsive to the complexities of human experience. . . . As it is, nearly three-fourths of Urdu poetry is in the form of the *ghazal*. To get an idea of the popularity of the *ghazal*, we should attend a *mushaira*, a public session of poetry recitation, where the best of living poets, drawn at times from the entire subcontinent, regal their audience with their select compositions, mostly *ghazal*s" (Kanda 1990, 1).

49. "In a broader sense [*nazm*] is used to describe all 'kinds' of poetry, as distinguished from prose. However, in its literary sense, a *nazm* is a well organized, logically evolving poem (unlike *ghazal*), where each individual verse sub-verses the need of the central, controlling thought or theme. Though the *nazm* is traditionally written in rhymed verse, there are many examples of *nazm*s in unrhymed verse, or even in free verse" (Kanda 1990, 330).

50. Kishwar did not translate this poem but gave a general sense of it. A literal translation would be something such as "To see this person and to laugh." Naheed 1991b, 57.

51. In the tradition of classical Persian and Urdu poetry, the poet sings off by mentioning his or her name or pen name in the last verse.

(The color of her *dupata* reflected her [Kishwar Naheed's] paleness today.)[52]

Again, this is bidding farewell to my youth. This one is with new diction but the same thought:

> dil mai hai mulaqat ki khahish ki dabi aag
>> mehndi laghai haton ko chhupa kar kahan rakhun.
> (In her heart the burning desire to meet her lover / but where to hide her
> hennaed hand).[53]

You see, I never had *mehndi*[54] because of the way I married. It is like passing through a phase, when I analyzed it later. Another wave comes in:

> ghar ke andar katti hai tiregi
>> ghar si bahar rah ke bhi, durna buhhut
> (Fear of staying outside / inside the house darkness devours).[55]

This expresses my feelings about men. You see how things are coming up?

> main teri khuy-i talawwun ke kuhle sahra main hoon
>> wo kahan tak apni surat ko badalta jae ga.
> (I know your fickle habits. How long are you going to change your face with
> the loved ones?)[56]

This is a poem from 1962, and again about male character and his fickleness. Here is another from 1965:

> chhupa ke rakh dia phir agahi ke shishe ko
>> iss aineh main to chehreh bigarte jate they.
> (Hiding the mirror of awareness, because it distorts faces reflected in it.)[57]

---

52. Naheed 1991b, 86.

53. Naheed 1991b, 111.

54. Part of the marriage ceremony in which the bride and her close female friends and women from the groom's family decorate their hands and feet with henna.

55. Naheed 1991b, 58.

56. Naheed 1991b, 71. In reciting this couplet by heart, Kishwar combined parts of some verses from pages 70 and 71.

I was articulating the changing faces of people. Passing through that "deathlike" phase, my poetry became more multi-imaged, physical, passionate, and philosophical. You see, I had many things going on in my life. I was having a child. I was a young woman working at an office, where men looked at me greedily—like this [she bulged her eyes while smiling]. I would go to recite poetry in the Halqah-i Arbab-i Zoq,[58] the literary circle in Lahore, and male poets would stare at me—like this. They felt very jealous of Yousef. I could judge it. You know, here we have a bad habit. We could judge what people are up to from the very first sight. That even helps us to decide how to behave toward them [laughing].

Yousef was well aware of the competition and was very jealous of it. You should see his books.[59] It is all about it. I had no woman friend to talk to, and a male friend was not possible, so all these events and issues were reflected in my poetry. I could not talk about them to anybody. I could not talk to my husband. I had no friends. I had no family to talk to, to get support. They had *no idea* of the magnitude of the problem I was going through. The only communication I had was through my poetry, which sustained me. I was reflecting all such feelings in my poetry. In one poem from 1970, I wrote:

> din main to daftaron ke mashaghil buhhut se hain
> > raton ko dil ka chor na soae na sonay de.
> (Your time is occupied during the day [with office work]. But the desire
> > in your heart does not let you sleep at nights.)[60]

---

57. Naheed 1991b, 94.

58. Halqah-i Arbab-i Zoq is one of the most well-established and respectable literary circles in Pakistan, which takes place in an old teahouse in old Lahore. It meets regularly, although it is now under the threat of being brought to an end because the owner of the teahouse wants to sell his property.

59. Kishwar's husband, Yousef Kamran, unlike Kishwar, published only one book during his lifetime: *Akaile safar ka akaila musafer* (Lonely traveler of a lonely journey, 1981). It is dedicated to Kishwar. His second book was published posthumously: *Safar tamam hova* (The journey is over, 1984). This book has two introductory essays by Munno Bhai and Kishwar Naheed. The title of Kishwar's essay is "Oh God, Let the News of Yousef's Death Not Be True."

60. This is Kishwar's own rendition of "Khab main khab ka darr" (Fear of dream in a dream). Bakht has translated these lines: "There is plenty in the office / To keep you busy during the day. / But at night / Your own conscience / Will not let you sleep in peace" (Naheed 1991c, 23).

So fresh themes were coming up in my poetry. I remember I met a Bengali senior poet in 1969 just before the first collection of my poems came out. His name was Dr. Andaleeb Shadani, and he was the dean of Bangladesh University, Department of Humanities, at that time.

He said, "Do you know a senior lady called Kishwar Naheed?"

I smiled and said, "I am the one."

"No. It is impossible."

"Why?" I asked.

A few people who were there laughed and said, "Why do you not believe her?"

He said, "It is just that the language she uses is not a joke; it sounds like that of a senior person."

Contemporary Poetry in Pakistan

The aptitude for poetry, in a way, is a God-given gift. You do not need education, and you do not need a university degree. The knowledge of your surrounding and cultural wisdom carries you through. But this is no longer possible because of the economic changes in Pakistan. Now it is the law of maximization and diminishing of the importance of literature. When the colonial system invaded our society, it started giving *khairat*, alms, and *jagir*, properties, to people to bring them into their [the colonial administration's] association and to encourage spying [to pacify the public]. Scholars were thrown to jail, and spies were given positions in the colonial administration. So the benefits went to the *jagir*s, the feudal [lords]. The cultural system changed at that time. People tried to grab lands rather than knowledge. Since the 1970s, the society's norms have changed yet again, from grabbing land to grabbing petrodollars. Ten years from now it might turn into yet something else.

This kind of psyche prevails in all circles, from the literary to bureaucracy to religious. Before, we had the *alim*s, the scholars, the poets, such as Ghalib and Iqbal.[61] Now we suffer because of the shallow knowledge of the *maulvi*s,

61. Asadullah Khan Ghalib (1797–1869) "is primarily a poet of love—love that is real, passionate and jealous. He has given us subtle insights into the mind of the lover torn by conflicting forces of desire and frustration, love and jealousy, anguish and ecstasy, submission and self respect. He is a master of the condensed style, and a specialist of the poetry of suggestion. . . . His creative imagination enabled him to transmute his suffering into song, and his indomitable

the clergy. There is a difference between a poet and a versifier. We do have poets, but more versifiers. The age through which we are living now does not allow one to make this distinction. Many poets or creative people are not distinguished in their own lifetime.

The subcontinent has a long literary history. The poets used to be *mosahib*, companions, of the king, or they were his *wazifa khar*, salaried [personnel]. In the subcontinent, it was always conceded that you could expect no responsibilities from a poet. A poet could not be trustworthy and could not be expected to sit down for two hours and work [do office work]! But with our age group, including Faiz Sahib and Rashid,[62] we started the tradition of taking up a profession. But still that dismissive kind of attitude toward poets has remained. People say, "Oh, *ye to shaer hain? shaer to kia kareh? vo shaer hain*" [sarcastic].[63] But this forced me to work twice as hard. You do not want to hear that because she is a woman, she cannot work equal to men. Or because she is a poet, she cannot be responsible [to pursue a career]. Two swords were all the time hanging over my head, and I had no choice except to prove. A woman's life passes through every stage, proving something. Men bear no such stigma, no such burden. They do not need to prove themselves.

I was the talk of the town. For five years, people discussed my poems, arguing, how can a woman write *ghazals*? Writing *ghazal* in Urdu means expressing love and desire for a woman. I was writing as a woman would feel when she falls in love. So the first debatable issue about me in the entire literary circle was, "Can a woman be given the right to express her love the way she wants to?

---

will strengthened his commitment to life" (Kanda 1990, 116–17). Sir Muhammad Iqbal (1873–1938) "is the inheritor of the tradition of Ghalib. . . . His poetry, like that of Ghalib, is a blend of deep thoughts and intense feelings, which he expressed in a forceful, Persianized style. . . . Though Iqbal is an indisputable master of the *ghazal*, a bulk of his poetry is in the form of *nazm*—a poem with a single, ventral theme" (Kanda 1990, 216).

62. N. M. Rashid (1910–1975) is among the most significant Urdu poets of the twentieth century, known to be one of the pioneers of the "modern poetry" literary movement and of free verse, *azad nazm*. Rashid's core contribution to Urdu poetry is his ability to "metamorphose the disposition of Urdu *nazm* by converting it into a vehicle through which the personal angst and ecstasies of the poet could be expressed." His contribution to Urdu poetry is immense because it brought about radical changes in form, diction, technique, and overall complexion of Urdu poetry, as well as removing it from the dominant shadow of Persian poetry (www.shayaranamusic.com/adab/NMRashid.htm).

63. "Is she a poet? What can a poet do? She is a poet" [disdainful tone].

How can *she* talk about men?" It was so senseless. And that created hue and cry from everybody. Many wrote that "the tradition does not allow her to behave like this".[64] Only a few agreed with me; the rest did not like my expressions.

I believe in the experience of equity, and I write about it. Where are the books? [She searched for her books on the table.] You see, in my first book of free verse, *Benaam musafat*, I wrote, *"mere harif bannu, to main tum ko chahun bhi"*: "if you become my worthy rival, then I can love you. Then we can fight [compete] with each other [as equals]."[65] Or, in this one, called "Agahi," awareness.[66] When I was a young girl, I saw my mother having one child in her belly and another in her bosom. I decided, "I'll not be like my mother. She has a bowed down back. I don't want my backbone to bow down because I know that just as nobody looked after her, nobody will look after me." I wrote it when I was twenty-six. Or, in another poem, "Zaval-i istishal," decline, I wrote, "I have the hands, which are not decorative hands. The veins in my hands are bulging, my fingers have gone crude, not because I am cleaning the dishes and doing everything with my hands. These are the hands, not of a rich woman, nor of a beggar, but of a self-made woman."[67] You see the hint? "Don't take this as the destruction of my body! This is the destruction of society that is shaping in my veins." You see, the person who is under attack always retaliates, so you can call this poetry of retaliation.

My earlier themes were less politically aware and more about human relationships. Thereafter they became all mixed up because human relationships also grow and develop in a politically free society. In a repressed society or in a revisionist or fundamentalist society, human relationships also suffer, more than anything else. When you cannot take your anger out on society, you take revenge on whomever you feel upset about at the moment. But, you see, as I said earlier, for a woman, her fights never end.

Munir Niazi loves himself [laughter].[68] He is a good poet, but he is a complete narcissist, like most of our male poets. Women poets such as Fahmida

---

64. See Mehdi 1984, 211.

65. Naheed 1991a, 33.

66. "Awareness," in Naheed 1991c, 16–17.

67. See Naheed 1991a, 49. Also given in Naheed 1991c, 21.

68. I asked her, "Last week I read an interview by a Pakistani poet called Munir Niazi. What do you think of him? He seems to think that there are no other poets in Pakistan except for himself!"

Riaz[69] and Parvin Shakir[70] and others are coming along, writing about their emotions and feelings. It is interesting to note how Zehra Nigaah's poetry has completely changed from the ones she wrote in 1952. You see, the effect of our [feminist] writing is obvious in everyone's work. She is now writing about "chador and *char diwari*," the veil and the home,[71] adultery and women jailed under the Hudood Ordinance. Everybody now writes about man-woman relationships. Earlier the same people would say, "How can women's poetry be about man-woman relationships?" Their objection was both to the style and content of modern poetry. Ten, fourteen years ago, when I started writing modern poetry, everyone said, "Is this poetry?" Now everyone does it.

In the Mirror of the Other

I had a miscarriage, my first pregnancy, so I wrote a poem to the unborn child, which shocked the established literati. Such subject matters perturbed them. This was a different style. This was a different tone. They said, "How can this be a *ghazal?*" They were all so used to the classical tradition of *ghazal* writing that they were not prepared to accept any change, *especially* by a woman [flabbergasted].

For five years, the writers and the critics reacted to my poetry by ridiculing my work, *complete* ridiculing, discussing me, and particularly mentioning this couplet: "kochh orhni ka rang bhi khulta houa na tha" (she looked pale, like the pale color of her *dupata*). Again and again they kept saying, "How can this be poetry?" Even once Faiz Sahib said, "How can this be poetry? Poetry cannot be like this!" [using free verse and regarding profane subjects].

69. Fahmida Riaz is a contemporary of Kishwar and like her is a well-known feminist poet. Under General Zia's military regime (1977–88), she was "editor and publisher of a magazine, *Awaaz* (Voice). A total of fourteen court cases of sedition were filed against the magazine, one of which (under section 114A) carried a death penalty. She escaped to India whilst out on a bail with her husband and two children where she lived for seven years" (R. Ahmad 1990, xiii).

70. Parvin Shakir was born in 1952 in Karachi. She has published numerous books of poetry, and for her achievements she was given the Pride of Performance Award, which is the highest award given by the Pakistan government (see www.urdupoetry.com/profile/parveen.html). She died in a car accident in 1994.

71. The phrase "chador and *char diwari*" (literally, the veil and the four walls of the house) became popular with the coming to power of General Zia's military regime. The contention was that women ought to stay home and be covered.

Many of our Urdu writers, including Intizar Hussain,[72] and all this crowd, have been calling me a *na-aurat*, not-woman, because they feel threatened by an unconventional woman. Deep down they appreciate only a traditional woman—even Intizar Hussain. It does hurt, *hai na?* My contemporaries were jealous of my literary recognition.[73] Because my books generated discussions, I frequently appeared on the television, and I spoke like a man—or like a human being, rather. They would say, "Why is she there, talking with no inhibitions, meeting people, shaking hands with men, embracing them, talking about sex, menopause, and marital experiences as if friends are talking?" They could not openly and honestly admit that "she" is talking about sex because that is what has created them or [what is] arousing them, and [that] it is an academic discussion. I did that to educate them to behave like a human being. But they did not, not fully [laughter]. They were just scared how I might react, so they kept quiet but gossiped furiously about me, referring to the first line of a poem I wrote:

> Umr main us se bari thi, lekin
>> pahle toot ke bikhri main
>> sahil sahil lehrain theen
>> darya darya utri main.
>
> (Although I was older than he, I was the first to break down and scatter;
>> that is, even though the sea is older / bigger than the river, it breaks /
>> scatters into pieces [rivers/revolute] when hitting the shore.)

They kept saying, "Oh, who is this younger one with whom she is in love now?"[74] It has been the same with every single poem! When my poem "The Grass Is Like Me" was published, many said, "Oh, it is a sex poem."[75]

---

72. Intizar Hussain was born in 1929 in Meerut, India, and presently lives in Lahore, Pakistan. He is a master of modern Urdu fiction and one of its most significant practitioners (http://www.yugantar.com/fall98/intizar.html).

73. Kishwar "held a powerful position above her peers as the director of a prestigious monthly for several years, which meant that many of her male colleagues have had to put up with her cultivated stroppiness however much they have resented it" (R. Ahmad 1990, xi).

74. Apparently the "gossipers" took her poem literally, whereas Kishwar was using the relationship between sea and river as a metaphor for expressing her own emotions and experiences. See her collection *Malamaton kay dar mian* (In the midst of humiliation, 1976).

75. See fn. 2, this chapter.

I do not feel conflicted by such reactions, but they do.[76] It is a continuous process, you see. Here I completely agree with Simone [de Beauvoir]. She said, "I thought by the time I am forty years old the scandals, gossips, and conflictual attitude would stop. Now I am sixty-eight"—when she wrote *The Dutiful Daughter*—"and realize that so long as a woman is alive there is no scantiness of scandals about her, and people will never resolve their ambivalence about her being." So they have *never* resolved their ambivalence toward me! You have to keep your own discipline and determination; then things may subside. Otherwise, there is no end to it, if you listen to people.

It does not bother me that people think like that! *I know* that they are thinking like this! If I had not known it and if I had been living in a fool's paradise, then I would have thought that they are good people, that they think well of me. They are not progressive. They are not realistic. They are traditionalists. They think that women are meant to lure men. They cannot think of women any other way. I do not expect many good things from them. But then, of course, there are many others, like Masood Ashar and Anwar Sajjad Sayyid, who think highly of me, saying that "she has the courage to live honestly where many men do not."

There was an article in a newspaper, reprinted in India, including a photograph of Fahmida Riaz and me. Somebody wrote that women like us are prostitutes of literature, that they talk about men-women relationships and wash their dirty linen in public, and that they prostitute their work and themselves. I do not remember the name of the person who wrote the article. I do not keep such things with me, and I do not reply to them because what I have learned from psychology again and again is that if you want to move around in this world, and if you are to maintain your sanity, you must ignore them. Otherwise, you will be constantly busy replying, and you will never get time for your own creative thinking. That has really helped me.

You see, one should be prepared for such things because if everything you write is acceptable to people, then there must be something wrong [laughing]! Still in our Oriental subcontinent culture, femininity means willy-nilly women who are ever so polite, who never disagree with men, who just happen to be in love all the time and alluring to men.[77] That is the definition of Oriental

76. I asked her, "So, how do you resolve such conflicts? Did you see it as a conflict?"

77. Compare her characterization with that of Fahmida Riaz: "A woman in traditional Urdu poetry is a concept, not a person . . . an ideal with rosy cheeks, shiny black eyes concealed shyly under long, dark eyelashes and a shapely swaying body" (qtd. in R. Ahmad 1990, xiii).

Woman. If you do not fall in that category, if you do not agree with it, then you are a *na-aurat*, you see. One of our poets, Munir Niazi, in a much-quoted line from an interview he gave in 1969, has said, *"Main to apni bivi ko Kishwar Naheed si purda karvata hoon"* [I will veil/hide my wife from Kishwar Naheed! If she starts behaving like her, what will happen next?] Many others have written articles like this.

You see, the feminist movement in America started in the late 1960s, while we were already involved in this process. You know, when Erica Jong's book of poetry came out in 1972, a few of our writers said, "Oh, Kishwar Naheed writes like Erica Jong." I said, "But my book was already printed when she started writing! So you could say she has taken from me!" But it is really not a matter of who is taking from whom because women's awareness is so alike, so similar that when you talk to women from Siberia or South Africa or Yemen or anywhere else, their attitude and reactions to male domination are exactly the same.

Certain things, as I said, I resolved early on, as I did in my relationship with my husband. I resolved that it was not going to improve, so I better do something else. I resolved that I would not get remarried because I did not want somebody interfering in my life. I resolved that when I live alone, many things are going to happen. People gossip about me because no other woman had, in those days, lived alone like I did. You see, if you resolve with yourself that such things are going to happen, then things become easy. If you are not clear in your head and nasty things happen, then you feel damaged, and you get nervous breakdown.[78] I did not get nervous breakdown because I *knew* it. It is not that I do not feel lonely, it is not that I do not feel shattered, it is not that I do not feel hollow inside, but that I do not get the repeated breaking of my conscience, as I was experiencing it when I lived in the joint family system, with my husband and my in-laws: nobody agreeing with me, and all expecting service from me, not caring a bit what was happening to me. Now I live within my walls and my doors and my bed that do not react contrary to my desire. That is a great, *great* consolation for a person who, for eleven years, lived with seventeen persons who did not understand a *bit* of a line of poetry and for whom I

78. Sara Shagufta is a case in point. She was a contemporary feminist poet who was "deeply pained by the cruel indifference of a chauvinistic poet husband who was himself surrounded by 'critics/friends' ready to deride her work." She challenged their double standards and unfair dominance. Their marginalization of her work and her husband's indifference, according to Rukhsana Ahmad, drove her to commit suicide in 1984 (1990, iii).

had been cooking and washing and doing everything. *And* I did not get any attention, any commendation, or any appreciation from my husband [pause— pensive and subdued]. Many things one resolves after experiencing many odds. You see, you accept some ill after going through some bad times. I have seen very, very odd times.

Violence of a Different Order: Sexual Harassment

Under General Yahya Khan [1969–71], the administrator of Punjab, was a man called Jalil Niazi. He proclaimed publicly that he wanted me. He had seen me somewhere in a meeting. He jailed Yousef and his father and complained to one of my bosses, "Many times I have indirectly communicated to her that I want to be with her, and she has refused me. So I put them in jail, and now she will come [to me]!"[79]

The charge against Yousef and his father had to do with the house they lived in. It belonged to some army colonel. He had complained to the provincial government that when he went to collect rent, they [Yousef and his father] insulted the military regime by saying, "Martial law is a stupid thing." They were then sentenced to a one-year jail term.

Then I went to see him [Jalil Niazi]. He said, "Oh, now you have come!"

I said, "Come, tell me where do I have to meet you?" [Pause]

He gave me the address [whispering voice].

I said, "What time do I have to come?"

"Five o'clock."

"Promise that when I come to you," I said, "the next day my husband and my father in-law will be out."

"I promise you," he said.

I went to my brother's house and said to him—I was not driving at the time—"Give me your car and driver."

He said, "Where are you going?"

"Just let me go for an hour," I said. "I have to go alone."

I took the car and first went to the cantonment to see the chief minister of Punjab, Tikka Khan, who was the sub-martial law administrator. I was so stupid. I did not even know his residence, and I was roaming about in the canton-

---

79. For a more recent and comprehensive report on sexual harassment of professional women, see Zaidi 1994.

ment. Finally I found his house and sent the chit with my name. My heart was pounding, and I was reciting Qur'an and prayers. The *chokidar*, gatekeeper, came out and opened the door and asked the driver to bring the car in. I went to the porch, and somebody opened the door. I did not realize that he was Tikka. You can see how stupid I was! He led me inside the house, where he was entertaining some guests. When they saw me, they said, "Oh, it is Kishwar Naheed! How lucky to meet her!" At that time, I appeared on the television regularly—every third day was my program.[80] After ten minutes or so, I realized that the old man who greeted me at the porch was Tikka Khan himself!

I said, "Sir, I want to talk to you."

"Oh, OK," he said.

I was served tea, samosa, kabab, and everything. I was getting panicky because it was about half past four, a quarter to five. Finally he led me to his study. He told me he knew about my husband's imprisonment because it was discussed in the press every day.

I said, "Sir, there is something I'd like to discuss with you."

"What is it?" he asked.

I said, "I have promised General Niazi that I would go to him at five o'clock at such and such place. I have come to tell you that if such a thing happens under your leadership, and you do not say anything, then I am resigning."

"And if you are wrong?" he asked.

"You can put me in jail," I said.

"I'll come with you, then, in your car," he said.

"OK," I said.

He said to his guests, "I'll be back in ten minutes," and we left together. God was with me! That man was pacing in the corridor of his house, where I was to meet him. General Tikka Khan said to me, "Lie down. He shouldn't see you." When Tikka saw him, he asked the driver to turn back, and we came home. He said, "Now you can go, and tomorrow your husband and father-in-law will be released."

Tikka gave Niazi hell! I heard that it was very bad. But the next morning at ten o'clock General Niazi gave me a ring. He said, "You have to come and sign some papers, and they'll be out before two." When I went there, he said, "If you had come and told me like this, I would not have touched you. I admire

80. Kishwar was a moderator for a literary program and conducted talk shows on social issues.

you and I love you, and that is why I asked you. Why, did you think I am going to rape you or sleep with you?" I did not say a word because I was feeling so humiliated. I signed the papers, and my husband was out of jail by six o'clock. And by seven o'clock the same evening, he was away from that house, my husband [pensive].

Well, yeah, I did put myself in a compromising situation,[81] but that is because, I think, it was my first experience in such matters. You see, Yousef was shown on the television with handcuffs, and I felt bad. They were in jail for one month [long pause]. Also because, after all, as I told you, I am the daughter of my mother. I think I *was* in love [pause]. When he died, I cried for almost six months.[82] And I thought, "He was the one who tortured me, and he won. *He* left me. *He* went on. And I am crying for him!" Even now, when I am sick, I miss him terribly. Whenever I was sick—he was a great actor in that way—he would not go to his office. He would sit at my bedside, looking after me on that day like anything, pressing my clothing, and caring for me. So all these things, and then seeing him hand-cuffed.

When General Niazi was off [fired from his job], he threatened that he would abduct me because I had humiliated him. But when he was transferred to East Pakistan [Bangladesh since 1971], I really thanked God. I went to have *nafel*, religious offerings, that I was rid of this man.

I have gone through every type of experience. One of our ministers tried to touch my hand when I went to his office. I said, "What is this nonsense you are doing?" The next day he dismissed me from my job. Bhutto Sahib interceded and put me back at the job.

But when he [Bhutto] saw me, he said, "What nonsense! If a boss feels inclined toward a subordinate, she should feel elevated that she is so important. You are an Eastern woman, and that is why you felt humiliated when he tried to touch your hand!"

I said, "I do not feel elevated, and I did not want him [to touch me]. The person that I want, I can do it with, but not with anyone."

81. I asked her, "Why did you want to put yourself in such a compromising situation?"

82. In a preface to her husband's posthumously published book of poetry, *Safar tamam hova* (Kamran 1984, 13), mentioned in fn. 59, Kishwar writes movingly of the grief of losing her husband. Confessing that she was in the stage of denial, she ended her elegy by borrowing a line from Shakespeare's *Richard II*: "You may my glories and my state depose / But not my grieves, Still am I king of those."

The Bhuttos

Yousef and I were involved with Bhutto Sahib from the time he created his party [1969–70]. From then until 1977, when he was removed by the military coup, I was in charge of the National Center, though holding various positions. Bhutto was the person who knew to whom one should go, where to go, whom to contact, and what to do. His memory was so swift, so exact. In 1969—might have been 1968—before the party [the PPP] was created, some of us met with him, including Hussain Naqi, Yousef, and a few others. We were sitting in Bhutto's room in Pearl Continental—Intercontinental then. A chit was sent in, written by Kausar Niazi.[83] I laughed and said, "Oh, you are now meeting with the intelligence people, with police people."

He [Bhutto] said, "Listen, Kishwar Naheed! Everybody has his own importance."

I did not see him again until 1972, when he invited me to his office. I said, "Sir, may I come in?"

He said, *"Han, tu us din Kausar Niazi ne tumhara fikra son liya tha"* [That day Kausar Niazi overheard your comments].

After three years, he remembered our dialogue! I had forgotten it [amazed]. He was *so* smart.

Once I went to see him. My boss was very temperamental and behaving in a very bad manner. I said to Bhutto Sahib, "Why are you keeping him? He is such and such kind of person."

He said, "Look"—you see the feudal in him—"what is your minister paying him? Only four thousand rupees! My dog eats up to five thousand rupees every month!"

I said, "But your dog doesn't bite anyone, and this man is biting us" [laughter].

I have not been very close to Benazir in the same way because she was out [of the country] after 1977. She did not know much about what happened to us. When she returned to Pakistan in 1986, she then started learning of the situation, and people gathered around her. I do not believe in hanging around leaders. If somebody has the courage to talk about pressing issues or has something to discuss, it is fine. Otherwise, I would never go to anyone just to say, "Hello, I am so and so." But just last year [under Nawaz Sharif's government], when we had the country's Opposition Leaders' Conference, we hosted a din-

83. Zulfikar Bhutto appointed Maulana Kausar Niazi a federal minister.

ner. She said to me, very nicely, "Why don't you and me have a Muslim women's conference?" I said, "OK. Since Sattar Niazi[84] has recommended that you talk about it, now let us have it." I sent her the names of the scholars of various Muslim countries that she could invite. But we have not had it yet. I think she has forgotten about it. She might be busy with other things.

Women and Islam

There *are* feminist Islamists, such as Dr. Riffat Hassan in our country.[85] She is a feminist, but at the same time she talks of Allah, Musalman, and *rasul*, the Prophet, and in that sense she comes closer to the fundamentalist. She is not a fundamentalist, but in the last analysis she takes the same course, to a certain extent. Fatima Mernissi [a Moroccan sociologist] is not a feminist Islamist, but at places she also says, "Oh, God says this thing, the Qur'an says that thing, and the Prophet says this." But a historian and sociologist who never talks about these things is Dr. Nawal El-Sadaawi [an Egyptian physician and writer]. She does not talk much of religion. She talks about the history and religion and all this, but in an anthropological vein.

What happened in Pakistan, frankly, is that the progressives[86] disdained the *maulvi*s, the clergy. The literate class was primarily progressive, but many were fashionably progressive. The upper and upper-middle classes were not progressive, but they were Westernized. The progressives were anti*maulvi* and relegated every religious category and activity, starting from *azan* to the *durood* and *khatam* and *fatiha* to the *maulvi*s. They excluded themselves. Very few people really knew about religion. I give you an example.

As a girl growing up in a *maulvi sayyid* family, I had been educated to read Qur'an and understand Islam with *tafsir*. But my husband and many others had not read Qur'an. In the subcontinent, even those who learn Qur'an through

84. Maulana Abdus Sattar Niazi was the minister for religious affairs under Nawaz Sharif's government.

85. Dr. Riffat Hassan is a professor of religious studies at the University of Louisville in Kentucky. Some of her publications include "Made from the Adam's Rib: The Woman's Creation Question" (1985) and "On Human Rights and the Qur'an Perspective" (1982).

86. In the context of Pakistan history, by "progressive" Kishwar means both a left-wing individual and the political movement that came to be known as the Progressive Movement in prepartition India and later in Pakistan. On the Progressive Movement in Pakistan, see www.iisg.nl/archives/html/.

*maulvi*s do not really learn proper Islam. As long as you do not read the Qur'an meaningfully, you do not understand it. Until General Zia's time [1977–88], nothing was at the altar. Being or not being a Muslim was not tested [in a punitive manner]. Nobody's understanding of Islam was challenged. General Zia's Islamization held a hammer to everybody's head, particularly to women's and after he promulgated the *zina* and Hudood Ordinance in 1979 and later the Law of Evidence in 1984.

Then women became the object of national obsession. I remember very vividly in 1977 or 1978, when I was in the Ministry of Information, for a full four hours the discussion in the ministry circled around whether [Pakistani] women should wear sari. If they did, whether they should wear a half-sleeve blouse or full-sleeve! Sleeveless blouses were out of question. The meeting ended with a recommendation that women should wear full-sleeve blouses! Then it would be OK [to wear a sari]. Then in 1978 a circular was sent around mandating that all female employees were to wear chador.[87] All of us working women took the stand and threatened that we were not going to wear it in the offices, and we *did not!* But in the educational institutions, women and girls started wearing chador. Zia was apparently so scared that he did not repeat his order again. Many of us in those days and in retaliation to these orders mostly wore saris.

Now, the Westernized and the upper-middle-class women who had not learned the Qur'an as a part of their education, who had gone to the English-speaking convent schools,[88] who wanted to get married to a bureaucrat—their freedom was at stake in the name of Qur'an, so they started reading the Qur'an and talking about it because challenges were coming at them relentlessly. Now the ball was in their court because the *maulvi*s knew these women did not have the knowledge. At that time, Riffat [Hassan] had gone abroad. She was writing on the subject, and she was taken as the only [educated, secular] person here who knows the Qur'an. Of course, all the Jama'at-i Islami [JI] women know Qur'an, *hai na?* Many women came to me, and I was given prominence only because I knew Qur'an already and could speak good Urdu. So I started

87. A Pakistani chador is different from the Iranian one. The Iranian chador is a long and all-enveloping garment, whereas the Pakistani one is a large, rectangular, thin shawl draped over one's head and shoulders.

88. Many of the children of the upper middle class and upper class go to English-speaking schools and colleges, and for them English is their first language if not their mother tongue.

writing for them, writing posters, writing replies for all these upper-middle-class WAF [Women's Action Forum] women. The religious education of upper-class women had started!

Local Feminism: The Women's Action Forum

I was part of the WAF, but I did not sign the contract because, you know, as a civil servant I am very cautious about government service. I helped write and organize various activities, but I do not do the work where I could be caught. So I did not sign the founder membership list. I also have not joined any other parties for the same reasons. When the WAF was founded in 1981, we had our first public meeting in the YMCA hall. I gathered about 700 to 750 women from all circles, and I told these upper-class WAF women to please charge registration—one rupee per woman. I also asked them to make these women members. This would allow WAF to expand. But they got scared. They said, "No. This is not a trade union. This is our association." This was the Women's Action Forum's first mistake, and they have continued doing it ever since.[89] WAF is the preoccupation of the very few. It is not the activity of the common women. For that, you only find a few selected ones on the road; the same faces you saw on the very first day you see on the last, too. Any real movement comes from the people. It does not come from the top. And when you make it a top-down system, it never really works.

I am not saying that WAF has not had any effect in society. The press is now motivated to cover WAF's activities, but the press also sensationalizes the news: "A girl was raped, and oh . . . the WAF retaliated against the maulvis." Then the next day they print—because the press wants juicy stories—other people's reactions to such encounters. So they bring lust into it.

That the WAF has kept the issues alive is correct, but only among themselves. They have not penetrated among the people. It would work only if they include the common people. Then they would be more effective. WAF does not include people from the public because it takes a lot of labor. It makes them go to the people. Sitting in a foundation's office or in somebody's house and continue smoking your cigarettes and deciding about issues are not con-

---

89. Fernandes levels the same criticism at the WAF: "The inability to develop a platform or movement to represent the masses is a sore point with WAF, an ideological handicap" (1995, 91).

ducive to mass movements. But because WAF's activities are now being covered in the press, especially the English press,[90] it has come to the attention of the Western press as well. When the Western reporters come to Pakistan, they talk to WAF and write about their activities and personalities.

WAF has not achieved much except that they claim themselves to be a pressure group. A pressure group is to create hue and cry and mobilize public opinion. WAF has no definite goals. It issues statements, sends messages or resolutions or suggestions to the ruling parties and to the ruling juntas in the Senate and the Parliament. Early April [1993] there is going to be a United Nations meeting regarding equal rights of men and women—human rights— in Manila. Pakistan is not a signatory to it because Zia ul-Haq said it is against Islam. At the moment, WAF is campaigning to convince the members of the [Pakistan] National Assembly and the Senate to pressure the government to sign it, but I reminded them that many members in the Senate and the Parliament had promised us right up to the night before the Shariat bill[91] was to be decided that they would rather resign than sign on them. The bill came into the House, and it passed within half an hour! Nobody came to know about it until after the third reading.

90. "English press" implies the few English dailies for the elite and the educated. The masses read Urdu newspapers. The distinction is made popularly to imply class distinctions within Pakistani society.

91. The Shariat bill of 1991, passed in the last days of Benazir Bhutto's first government, affirms the supremacy of Islamic law, as laid down in the Holy Qur'an and upheld by the Prophet's tradition, Sunna, as the supreme law of Pakistan. Its preamble states the document's intent and identifies five major principles: (1) sovereignty belongs solely to God, but authority is to be exercised by the people through their chosen representatives "within the limits defined by Him as a sacred trust"; (2) Islam is declared the state religion, and all Muslims must live according to the Holy Qur'an and Sunna; (3) the protection of life and justice are guaranteed in "accordance with the moral values of an Islamic state"; (4) obscenity, gambling, prostitution, "and other moral vices" are proscribed; and (5) future laws are to be enacted in "consonance with the injunctions of the Holy Qur'an and Sunna through a recognized mode." The enabling legislation subsequent to the preamble excludes the personal-status laws of non-Muslim citizens from the effects of the law. See Haeri 1993b, 213 n. 122; Jalal 1995, 111–12; "Text of the Shariat Bill" 1991a and 1991b. The act states that all statute law is to be interpreted in light of the Shari'a and that all Muslim citizens of Pakistan shall observe the Shari'a and act accordingly. Section 20 of the act states that "[n]otwithstanding anything contained in this Act, the rights of women as guaranteed by the Constitution shall not be affected."

International Feminism

I have not been seriously involved with international feminism, though I have been in touch with some Arab feminists, such as Fatima Mernissi and Nawal El-Saadawi. I should be translating Saadawi's books. I have not had much contact with American feminists, although I have read some of the works of American and European feminists. I thought Betty Friedan's first book was very good and useful, but not the second one. Same with Germaine Greer. By the way, where is Gloria [Steinem] gone?

I think the objectives of the American and Pakistani feminists are more different than similar.[92] We have to fight on the ground of our existence and basic human rights. They have to fight for higher levels of recognition. We in Pakistan are respected and accepted through our relationship with our men, whereas American women are dealing with the problems such as whether to have an abortion. We have the fundamental problems of whether we should be educated, to be allowed to participate in the political process, to become a senator or a minister, or to appear veiled or unveiled on the television. We have the basic problem of being accepted as a person! Their problems are different. We do not have much in common, except in one thing: in the nature of our marital relationships and the consequences of our marital afflictions.

Many things we inherited from the Britishers are much more progressive than those of the Americans, but much of the media is not covering it. The Western media talks much about our oppression, but they do not talk much about our freedom and privileges. So many do not know about us. The Western women are beginning to realize the disparity among the women even in their own country.

The very first thing that a Pakistani feminist can say to a European or an American feminist is this: international cooperation and coordination. As I told an international conference, if five thousand women get together and sit in front of the White House for forty-eight hours and demand equal wages, the Parliament and the Senate would pass the law.[93] But that needs political thinking. The American nation as a whole is not politically aware, the way

92. See also Naheed's article "Aurat ki azadi, maghrib va mashrig, qurbatain or faslaih" (Women's liberation, west and east, close or distant [similar or different]) (1988, 13–30).

93. In his last State of the Union Address, January 2000, President Bill Clinton underlined the necessary justice of equal pay for equal work.

that the women of the third world countries are. I do not blame them because the whole cycle of the economic system is such that it puts people in a very tense situation. They have to get up at five in the morning and fall into bed at eight in the evening. They have nothing to think about; they do not know much about literature, about politics. They only know how to earn their bread and how to make ends meet, and for that they do not have much knowledge. The third world women are more politicized, aware, and enlightened.

Because we have had the experience of fighting against colonialism, we, the women of the subcontinent or the third world, have a higher political consciousness. If we communicate with American and European women, they understand why political consciousness is needed in order to get your rights, and for that you need political foresight. Black Americans have been trying to get their rights. If they [white feminists] learn from them [black feminists], they can get together and get their rights. But American women are not conscious of their rights. They talk about other things than their rights.

We can learn three things from American feminists. First is labor and consistency. We talk of working, but the amount of work an American woman does is hundred times more. Second is to be nonemotional in our work and arguments. This is lacking in our structure. Third is the approach to problems. Even in our revolution, our approach is romantic, whereas their approach is very methodic. My own idea is that these three basic things are needed not only for [Pakistani] women but also for men generally and politically.

When I was undergoing my hysterectomy, my friends, male and female, gave me hundreds of books to read. Their advice scared me, "Do not go for a hysterectomy. You will grow a mustache." And all those books around me, giving one advice or another. Then I had the operation, and everything went well, no side effects, no complications. So I said to them, "These books are all written to scare women, not to help them." Half of the literature written around the world—starting from anthropology, psychology, matrimony—is to scare women. It is amazing to think why society is so scared of women to the point of creating so many barriers around her that she should feel everything is horrible and she shouldn't come out [into the public arena]. Well, I think the fear is rooted in the male psyche, and that is because they come out of women's womb [laughing], and so they think women are inherently powerful.

Fundamentalism: Real and Imagined

Fundamentalism is not a phenomenon peculiar to Pakistan. It is all over the Muslim world, in Egypt, in Libya, and, more recently, in Iraq and Somalia. In any society where illiteracy is high, the only thing that can be effectively manipulated is religion. It is part of your culture. You are born into it. It is embedded in your psyche. So, in spite of being secular, all of us, in the garb of culture, continue to be religious. This is not necessarily bad as long as religion is taken to be part of culture, but when religion is manipulated as a means to divert the country away from progress, away from being a just society, and to deny people education, then it becomes a problem. And it is not only the Muslims who do it.

Representing Islam

I have noticed in Pakistan that the moment fundamentalism became an issue, much of the Western media started pouring into Pakistan and conducting interviews. There was an American woman—what was her name?—who translated *Bihisht-i zewar* [Heavenly ornaments], a religious text written for women, a book that was given to women along with a copy of the Qur'an to take to their husband's home.[94] She came to Pakistan and stayed here at the State Exchequer for two years. She had the best of life in Pakistan.

She came to me and said, "I am translating this book. What do you think?"

I said, "I hate the book because it is against women."

"How do you call it against women?" she asked.

"It might be looking fascinating to you," I said, "like *Alice in Wonderland*, but it is very problematic for us."[95]

---

94. Maulana Ashraf Ali Thanvi (1863–1943). This book is also translated from Urdu into English by M. M. Khan Saroha (Thanvi 1981). See also the short story by Zahida Hina regarding the male abuse of the reciprocal rights and obligations of genders in "The Earth Is Ablaze and the Heavens Are Burning" (Hina 1994, 109–33).

95. In her novel *Blasphemy* (1998), Tehmina Durrani also describes the gulf between indigenous educated women and visiting scholars and journalists. She narrates the encounter between a white female journalist and the highly secluded wife of a violent and evil *pir*. The journalist naïvely praises the *pir* and seems totally unaware of the plight of women under his abusive control, nor is she willing to find out. The journalist "swooned" over the *pir's* devotion, whereupon the abused wife reflects, "I thought that she had passed a judgment and drawn a conclusion without realizing that there is always a cruel method behind undying devotion. Could she not see the terror in our eyes? . . . I couldn't help glaring at her when she exclaimed, 'so much tran-

She then complained to the ministry and told them that I was not working according to the needs of the government [incredulous, high pitched]. She could do that because she had very close connections in the ministry. I do not remember the details of it, but she was a guest of the government, and I was directed by the government of Pakistan to talk to her. She wanted to talk to me as an intellectual, and when I talked to her like one, she grinned, she misbehaved, and she said, "What do you want? Why do you want to fool women of Pakistan?"

I said to her, "What do you think? We have grown out of this nonsense. Why are *you* translating it? Why are *you* trying to fool other people in the name of Islam?"

They think what they do is Islam. They want to damage Islam [high pitched]. I have noticed that so many journalists who come here to write about fundamentalism sensationalize it in their own media. Then they have other people talk against it. Then they print *that* [agitated]. They create a lobby for it and create a lobby against it. Then they sit back to watch the *tamasha*, the show—what a joke!

Islamization in Pakistan

Islamization was brought about by Zia ul-Haq because of two reasons. One, Zia, who was brought to power and prominence by Bhutto, primarily implemented the laws that were made by Bhutto. It was *Bhutto* who banned alcohol and under the instigation of Kausar Niazi, the minister of religious affairs, declared the Qadianis non-Muslim.[96] The second important reason for Zia to try to push for Islamization was that all our aid was coming from the Americans via the Saudis. The Saudis wanted a replica of their own monarchy here. Our political plight went from bad to worse in 1979 when the Soviet Union attacked Afghanistan, and they came right up to our border. The Americans and the Soviet Union threw money, weapons, and forces on Pakistan. The Jama'at-i Islami was strengthened like anything. So much money and arms and other resources were given to them that it became almost the ruling party. Now, after the eviction of the Soviet Union from Afghanistan and its dismem-

---

quility in the midst of poverty can only mean one thing. He provides the people with something divine.' Fool, I thought" (151–52).

96. Mirza Ghulam Ahmed (mid-nineteenth century), the founder of the Ahmediyas or Qadianis, as they are commonly known, claimed to be a latter-day prophet (Richter 1987, 134).

berment, the challenge to the United States' interest has subsided, so the Americans no longer need the Jama'at-i Islami or Pakistan. The USAID people are leaving Pakistan. Now the Americans have started talking about liberalization policies. Now the prime minister [Nawaz Sharif] himself goes to the family of a girl who was raped or talks about changing the Eighth Amendment.[97] Now his regime disavows any relations to fundamentalists[98] and claims to be progressive! So the reasons for religious resurgence in Pakistan are different from those in Kashmir or in Serbia or in Palestine.

You see, after China's liberation and the establishment of communism in 1949, and after the Korean War and the Soviet Union's treaty with India, America paid full attention to Pakistan. During that time, a consistent effort was made to keep all the Asian countries away from the Soviet Union sphere of influence. Pakistan was not allowed to move politically closer to the Soviet Union. All the scholarships offered by the Soviet Union used to be wasted. If one visited embassy personnel or met a Soviet citizen, one would be attacked and notes would be taken and reported to the Intelligence Bureau. Nobody ever questioned all the people from the Foreign Office who were sent to the American universities for leadership courses. But once when a Soviet ambassador hosted a reception in honor of Pakistani writers and intellectuals, everybody was put to task by the government: "Why did you go to the reception?" Likewise with India. Even now, if you want to go to India, you have to get intelligence clearance; otherwise, you cannot be given a visa. It was all a very senseless effort.

Well, the Americans were scared of socialism at that time.[99] That they already had the [Pakistan] government in their pocket is not the point. They had to divide and convert the people. There was no choice; otherwise, they could have made it a liberal state. They knew that at that time the newly independent states were all moving toward revolution and socialism. Pakistan could have also

97. The Eighth Amendment was constituted by General Zia ul-Haq. It gave the president the right to dismiss an elected prime minister and to dissolve the Parliament. Benazir Bhutto was dismissed twice, and Nawaz Sharif was dismissed once under this law. The amendment was modified in part under Nawaz Sharif's second term in office, when his party was in the majority. Benazir Bhutto's party supported him on this issue.

98. In his first term in office (1990–93), Nawaz Sharif made a coalition government with the JI.

99. I asked her, "Why do you think Americans would be willing to fund Pakistani fundamentalists?"

gone that way—the way India did. Such a big area of the subcontinent, starting from Asaam up to Baluchistan would have gone out of the American's hands, and they wanted to maintain some of their stations in the area. And they had it.

They made Jama'at-i Islami play a major role in the national politics and started funding it from 1953. They encouraged the Jama'at's influence in all spheres and institutions of the country. They started calling *us*, [those] who did not agree with the Jama'at, antinationalists. You see, the Jama'atis are not patriotic people; they make people defensive. Well, if the fundamentalists also say that they are more authentic, I do not question it,[100] but I just resent their hypocrisy. Qazi Husain Ahmad [the present leader of JI] was to have an operation three months ago, and he went to London. Why? The cardiology section of the Services Hospital [in Lahore] is one of the best in the area. Maulana Maududi [the founder of the JI in Pakistan, d. 1989] also went to America for his treatment.

Gradually all our institutions fell under the spell of Jama'at-i Islami. Most of the posts in the army were in the hands of Jama'at-i Islami. The JI was given one task—namely, to disrupt growth and development. That is it. I was scared. Many people like me were scared as to what the hell they would do, now that they have all that opportunity. Since they did not have any training or administrative leadership, we came through it. We then realized that the Americans, or whoever their masters were, were scared of giving the Jama'at basic administrative training.

The Jama'at is politicized in opportunism. You see, the Jama'at-i Islami has been trained in this country to sabotage, not to change. You know that, and I also know by whom [laughing].[101] The Americans are training the Jama'at-i Islami through Saudi Arabia. I am not saying that the Americans orchestrated the whole religious resurgence. They are not doing it now. Now they are even afraid of resurgence of Islamic fundamentalism. But in the beginning they were. I think it *was* intentional because fundamentalism is not inherent to the Pakistani society.[102] You see, in 1977, when the military moved against Bhutto—and I have very, very vivid images of the situation. With only

100. I said, "But the Jama'at also claims that they are patriotic and you are not."

101. I asked her, "How do you know that?"

102. In the same vein, Said Khan writes, "Islamic fundamentalism . . . was created and encouraged by global capitalism, by the United States, for its own political and economic purposes" (1992, ii).

twenty-three boys, the Jama'at-i Islami managed to create trouble around Data Sahib,[103] several mosques, and crowded locations. The crowd has no sense. They go wherever the emotions go. There were the same faces, same motorcycles, and same goings-on all around. The crowd was directed and controlled because the Americans feared Bhutto might be moving closer to the Soviet Union.

The government could also mobilize huge crowds, and Zia created the biggest circle of people or constituency in the name of *zakat.*[104] When Zia ul-Haq came to power, Jama'at-i Islami fully supported him till his death in 1988. They had seven ministers in Zia's cabinet, including the Information Ministry. I, as a person, was scared of them because of the terror that I saw them unleash, the way they controlled the anti-Bhutto demonstrations, and the speed with which they took over the universities. I knew it would be a fascist government, and it would be terrible.

I was in the Ministry of Information and know personally that the moment the JI minister and his associates took over the ministry, they indulged in talking—for months—just talking about what to do and how to manage things, never actually doing anything. *Then* I was convinced that they were trained by the Americans just to disrupt the system, not to take charge of it. That is a very, very important thing that I have learned through personal experiences and through observing the JI in operation. You see, there are two kinds of psyches: a defeated psyche, which aims to disrupt and is a terrorist psyche, and an active psyche, which is a psyche that can give results. They [the Americans] do not want anything better in our countries than to have the fundamentalist forces well entrenched.

Now the Jama'at has lost its attraction to the Americans because of the changes in the region. For that matter, the Jama'at-i Islami of Pakistan that

103. See chapter 1, fn. 30, on Ali ibn Uthma Data Ganj Bakhsh Al-Hujwiri.

104. Pakistan's *zakat* system was an essential part of Zia ul-Haq's Islamization program, which he referred to as "an essential pillar of Islam's social welfare system" (Clark 1987, 79). *Zakat* is a "tax of two and half percent paid annually on total worth assets" and is one of the "thirteen sources of revenue" that apply to contemporary Pakistan (Weiss 1987, 3). It "is to be used for helping the destitute and for creating a safety net to catch those that a modern economic system fails to reach" (Burki 1987, 57). "If the zakat system can separate itself from national politics, rampant rhetoric, and Islamic fantasy, and concentrate on doing well the things that this system can do, it could be a very positive, if modest force, doing a lot of goods for many people who need help" (Clark 1987, 79).

used to praise America now talks against America, as if they are the most socialists of the parties! They are alienated, and their front has been brought
down; otherwise, the Punjab police would not have dared to enter the privacy
of Punjab University if they had thought that the Jama'at still had their alliances and their stronghold.[105] When they are weak, the police attack. The
police never attack the strong.

Sovereignty: Individual, National

My file in the Ministry of Information is a very historic file. I had a chance to
see it. When the Jama'at-i Islami minister took over, many had already told
him about me, that "she is against Islam"—on their own presumption—and
that "she is advocating socialism." They recommended that I should be
thrown out because I did not side with them. The minister was given the
names of thirty-two people in the ministry who were known to be progressives and so should be thrown out. The general who was at the helm of the affair at that time said, "If I throw them all out, who is going to work? The rest of
them aren't alive [laughing]. How can I make the dead work?" So he did not.
The minister wrote on my file, "Can this ministry not run without Kishwar Naheed?" [laughter].

But it was not just them that I did not side with. Once Appa Nisar Fatima [106]
[a female member of parliament and a onetime member of JI] said to me, "Tum
buhhut zahin ho. Hamare sath ao, to phir pata challeh ga": "You are very smart. Come
to our side, and we can work together." But I refused. Women like Appa Nisar
Fatima got so much "Women and Development" funds. So, you see, in the
name of Islam an associate of government gets such resources. At that time, no
woman was prepared to go along with Zia ul-Haq and the martial law administrator. JI collaborated with Zia, and because she was in the JI, she got money.

Where minds are not encouraged to grow, then there is every possibility for
explosion and exploitation. I went to Iran in 1973, and I visited many parts of

---

105. "Despite the Jama'at's electoral defeat, its power and influence in today's Pakistan
should not be underestimated, for it is derived from the group's symbiotic relationship with the
ruling regime [General Zia's]. It tends to function as a pressure group rather than a political
party and uses its influence with government agencies to achieve its objectives. The Jama'at has
acquired a firm grip over the universities and wields a powerful influence over the government-
owned and controlled broadcast media" (Alavi 1987, 36).

106. See the introduction, fn. 17, on Appa Nisar Fatima.

the country. I thought Iranians were more liberal and freer than anywhere else I had seen in the region. We in Pakistan used to say that there was *too* much liberalism in Iran, too much. Any liberalization, if it is not accompanied with education and development, either turns into a situation like in Iran [revolution] or the Philippines and Thailand [promiscuity]. When you turn the whole society into consumers, the minds do not grow. The material culture grows, the income level grows, but the mind does not.

In the developing world, we are not sovereign. We are still ruled by others' ideologies. It is perpetually taken for granted by the bosses of these countries that people have no opinions, that they should be controlled, and that they should be kept desperate in order for the leaders to handle the situation. The moment a leader starts becoming independent, he is either thrown out or is punished, like [Zulfikar] Bhutto. What Bhutto was trying to do was very small in magnitude. I do not agree with many of his policies, but his "crime" was that in the 1974 Islamic Summit he said that if the Islamic countries use oil as a weapon, they would be more effective than the hydrogen bomb. So the structure of conquering the countries has changed. Earlier it used to be with warriors and through battlefields. Now it is through having the vote on commercial and economic needs. You just put sanctions on any country and get the country nose down to obey your orders. This is economic slavery that has taken the place of political slavery, which is more dangerous.

Fundamentalism

You see, one is born in a certain family within a certain culture. Human beings are brought up not to depend on themselves or to have self-confidence, but to believe in something that is beyond their imagination and their limitations. The reason is that the human mind could not understand the workings of the cosmos and the mysteries of the universe, so to safeguard themselves every religion created a God. Because society was controlled by the male species, so God was given all the qualities of a man. All of us [Pakistanis] who claim to be liberal have religion deep down in our heart and psyche. Sometimes we polish it; we control it and do not declare it, but when we are distressed or when we feel despair, we talk to God. Fundamentalists call it *namaz*. People with a more secular knowledge call it a self-dialogue and a moment of refuge. Hindus call it yoga. These are all different shades of talking to yourself and of holding somebody other than yourself responsible for things and events.

Fundamentalism is not peculiar to Muslims only. It is everywhere, among the Christians, the Jews, or the Hindus. The point is that the leaders and the politicians have not been able to deliver any meaningful vision. Being completely disillusioned by the politicians and by the present economic system, people realize that the poor have become poorer and the rich have got richer, and the distresses and the problems of the people have not been solved. Being a liberal and a nonbeliever has not gotten them the better life they expected, so they think if they go back to religion, they might get their identity and spiritual freedom, comfort, and what is promised out of religious experience.

Oh ho . . . [laughing heartily] How has fundamentalism affected me? You see, before this religious resurgence, I was a subject of controversy. In 1972, when I was appointed director of the National Center, there was a great hue and cry. Well, not just that, but astonishment that a lady was appointed the director and that she would be controlling the affairs and calling the shots. From the very beginning, I was wearing sleeveless blouses. Nobody ever used to wear long-sleeved blouses with a sari. So in the next six months that I was the director, every day in every newspaper, whether English or local, but particularly in the locals—and there were many of them—there would be at least one article about my clothing, the way my bare arms were showing and my sari was hanging around my body! Nobody ever talked and wrote about what I was doing, how I was managing and conducting the functions of the center, and how I was organizing the council. I got so fed up that I called my tailor and said, "Go and take it off. If this is the only problem of this country, I dislike it. Take all these blouses and put sleeves on them!"

Now, at the same time, in 1972, Bhutto Sahib for the first time had created the Ministry of Religious Affairs and Auqaf.[107] To make it more ridiculous, Bhutto merged the Ministry of Information and Ministry of Religious Affairs into one because he wanted to appoint Maulana Kausar Niazi as the minister. Now, Kausar Niazi, coming from a religious family and being a *maulvi* himself and a Jama'at-i Islami stalwart, instituted the Juma'a *khutba*, Friday sermons. What he did was to prepare a *khutba* to give to all the *maulvi*s of big mosques to deliver it at the same time all over the city. He also ordered the National Centers to hold Islamic programs and Arabic lessons.

I am telling you the way religion started getting injected into our culture and society and into the bureaucracy and the offices. He [Niazi] instituted

107. *Auqaf* is plural for *waqf*, meaning a property that has been gifted for religious purposes.

programs on *basirat,* attributes of God and the Prophet, to be aired on the television because the ideology of the newly formed Religious Ministry was to be propagated. He made us have programs, for example, on *hajj,* pilgrimage, policy or on the role of the ulama in Pakistan movement and in the democratic government!

When I was told to conduct such programs, I rang up some of the ulama, like Maulana Abdul Qadir Azad of Badshahi Mosque [in Lahore]—he has been there since 1972—and invited him to come and give a talk! They told me to go away and "Keep quiet," amazed that a woman had dared to talk to them on the phone. I said, "This is Bhutto Sahib's and Kausar Niazi's order. If you do not come, I'll report it." The service required that they should come, and they came. I intentionally wore a sari on that day. I noticed that when I was talking to them, they would be looking like this [she turned her face away], so I would go to the other side, then they would look the other way [she turned her face the other way, laughing]. They did not want to look at me. "Doesn't matter," I thought. I introduced them. I sat down on the stage. I talked to them, all of them, and I initiated the discussion. The next day I got a phone call from Maulana Azad. I expected them to show me some resentment and object to my wearing a sari. Just think!

He said, "Oh, I am so happy that we all came. You are such a learned person. You talk so well, and you know so much about religion, and you facilitated the discussion so nicely." Then he said, "But one thing I want to talk to you about."

"Of course," I said, "You are like my brother, and why shouldn't you be talking to me [ironic smile]. And, of course, frankness is always the spice of Islam!"

"You see," he said, "you were very proper, your language was very good, your tone was correct, but your dress was not" [laughter]!

I said, "Has Islam given any special design of dress for woman?"

"You see," he said, "we have our own style of dress. We have the *shalwar-kamiz* and the *dupata,* but you wore a sari."

I said, "Azad Sahib, in the case of my dress, I have never even listened to my husband; it is my choice. So I am sorry. I should have told you from the beginning."

"OK," he said. "This is your choice, but I wanted to sincerely advise you not to do it."

After that incident, nobody tried to force me to change my dress. They could not because, you see, early in my life I had decided I was going to be myself.

But their retaliation came later.

After 1977 [the commencement of Zia's Islamization polices], I was transferred almost ten times from one place to another—just because they said that
I was spreading anti-Islamic themes and churning out anti-Islamic publications. It was primarily the Jama'at-i Islami and people like Appa Nisar Fatima
and others who demanded that my books be banned. And they did ban my
translation of Simone de Beauvoir's *The Second Sex* and withheld my promotion.
You see, I have not been given promotions for the last eighteen years, since
Zia ul-Haq overthrew Bhutto's government. Three cases were instituted
against me. One was that I had translated and published *The Second Sex* without
government permission. Second, that I had violated the copyrights permission,[108] and third, that what I had published [*The Second Sex*] was vulgar and
pornographic. My friend, the policeman whom you met the other day, was
posted at Attock. He came all the way to Lahore to get me freed on bail and to
transfer the case to his department because I was to be arrested that day by five
o'clock. The case was dismissed three years later.

My elder son was at college during Zia ul-Haq's regime. I had constant
telephone threats: "Behave! Otherwise we are going to snatch up your sons." It
was such a constant worry. One of their team leaders had apparently talked to
my elder son, trying to induct him into the Jama'at. When I was at the university [until 1969] the Jama'at-i Islami had no strong hold. He was told, "Do not
tell your mother. We will give you a motorcycle and five hundred rupees a
month"—in 1977 or '78, five hundred was good money—"and you become a
rafiq," which was the Jama'at's term for a supporter. When he refused to join,
then all those telephone threats came. I put him in an FC [For Christian] College because I knew that at that time the FC College was not a target area of
the Jama'at-i Islami, but it turned thereafter in 1982. So I sent my sons abroad
just because of such threats. I was so worried about their safety that I used to
drop them at the college and pick them up.

Fundamentalism is not only connected with the Zia ul-Haq in that way. I
remember I was given an independent posting in 1967, but then I was told
not go to the office because the staff had protested in writing that they did not
want that shameless woman to be given an officer position, that they were
not going to tolerate me. You see, there was no other woman beside me.

---

108. Pakistan does not honor copyright law. My book *Law of Desire: Temporary Marriage in Shi'i
Iran* was reprinted and translated into Urdu as *Muhabbat ka qanun* (Lahore: Qaumi Digest, March
1993) without my knowledge and permission.

The secretary called me and said, "Such a letter has come, and they are requesting that you be posted somewhere else."

I said, "Let me try it. I could change them, and if I do not get hold of them, you have every right to transfer me."

He said, "There shouldn't be any law-and-order situation."

"Do not worry. Let me try."

I found out that the person who had instigated all that was a Jama'at-i Islami man. He had called a meeting of all the long beards and talked to them about culture and Islam. I went to his office and said, "May I come in? Would you offer me a cup of tea? I want to talk to you!" No man at that time—now the situation has changed—was that blunt to say get out of my office. He offered me tea, and we chatted. I said, "Just introduce me to everyone because you are the senior person. You just go in the front, and I'll follow you." Then he walked out, and everybody was amazed to see him actually introducing me. There was no problem then. He kept his reservations, though, and he kept on writing anonymous letters against me all the time, but he could not say anything at that time. The gist of the letters was that as a woman I was not behaving Islamically, that I met men in a shameless manner, and that I did not observe veiling—all these fundamentalists' concerns. But he would not say it in my face.

You see, religious women like Appa Nisar Fatima wanted to talk to me a few times when the Women's Commission was going on. She said, "If you come to our side, you'll get promotions and a lot of admiration. With the kind of crowd you are hanging out, you cannot get it." I said, "Thank you, I am not a political person." But in the secular crowd, especially among those dominated by men poets and writers, I got recognition because of the fact that I never behaved like a woman. I tried to break norms and taboos every day. I told you about the literary circle in Lahore. That is the place where writers and poets get together. Women did not used to go there. I was not going there every day either, but once a week or once every two or three weeks I would go there and sit and participate in the ongoing discussions. This was more or less accepted, with a little sensationalism, of course. When women participated, some writers would say, "Oh, I sat next to so and so because she wore a low cut dress."

I used to tell them, "What about you? What if we were to talk about you in the same way?"

"Oh no," they would say, "You always turn a joke into reality."

I said, "But do you like it if somebody looks at you as a sex object?" You see, women, too, have not been meeting men in the same capacity as equals, as a trained species.

The Dilemma of Professional Women

The moment a woman assumes a high position in the government, you see, people automatically start calling you, thinking that you are available. That is a very difficult milieu to operate in, because they [men] think that all professional women behave in the same way. And if they don't, then all kinds of rumors go around. For women of integrity, it is a very, very difficult life. But it is not only religious people who do this labeling. Labeling comes from the liberals as well. If you do not behave as a subordinate to the group, then you are not a good woman—because you defy them, you question them, and you talk about all these issues, and they do not like it. This is a kind of violence. They are different from the religious guys in that the liberals are hypocrites. They may talk about equality and write on progressive issues, but in their personal life they behave differently. I have seen the majority of the progressives in this country—they have *never* contributed to women's causes. They have never genuinely supported it. In their own personal life, they never practice what they preach and have no intention or plan of doing so. On March 8, when I was speaking on Madiha Gauhar's play,[109] I addressed the progressives and said that they have not supported our movement in any way. They have not contributed anything, not in their writings or other things. So as long as men and women keep on running on two parallel lines, we are never going to meet—*ye baat hai*, that is the thing. Men have been traveling on a line where they do not feel that women exist. For example, in the Soviet Union they claimed to have created a classless society, but when I went there in 1975, I said to them, "You do not even have a classless Communist Party! Women's

109. Madiha Gauhar and her husband, Shaheed Nadeem, direct Ajoka, an alternative theater group, in Lahore. Ajoka is a political and feminist theater group "with a conscience." It focuses on "cultural conflicts," addressing issues of violence against women, women's rights, class structure, and the rise of Islamic fundamentalism. They "question previous and current state policies that have curtailed the rights of women and secular individuals" (Afzal Khan 1997, 41–42). What is most significant about Ajoka is the group's conscious effort at performing in the "streets" and in various poor quarters in the major cities in Pakistan.

section is separate from men's section. How can you have a classless society when you do not have a genderless party?" Faiz Sahib was very angry with me. He said, "You keep on talking about your issues everywhere you go." I said, "Why shouldn't I?"

When I was writing my book *Aurat: Khab or khak ke dar mian*, [Women: between dream and dust, 1988][110] I asked everyone about the role women played in the Russian and Chinese Revolutions. My big [famous] friends, starting from Faiz Sahib, knew nothing about it. They said that they had never thought about it! See, in spite of WAF movement, in spite of the lawyers' movement against the laws passed by Zia ul-Haq [i.e., the Hudood Ordinance], and all that, there has never been consistent support from men for women's causes.

For the last twenty years, many people have been hired but without proper training. They get scared of me, as they do of women who are articulate and independent. We do not get our promotions and posting. Even for some men it is like this. They [government officials] were very scared of Fraz because he was unconventional, and such people are never treated well. Even my sons used to say, "Amma, what are you talking about? In this house, even dogs keep away [subdued]." So you can well imagine how you are being accepted in society. You see, this *was* very intimidating. But some of these incidents would hurt them, too. Their intimidation was basically derived from the same philosophy that also motivated my family, my in-laws, and others.

But the economic needs are forcing people to break their shallow barriers. I think many things have changed automatically, but many problems remain. Yesterday I was talking to one of my assistants when I got a telephone call. Every day on the average I get calls from at least two battered wives who want me to help them. They just want to talk to me about their abusive husbands. These are not women just from the inner city, but from very modern offices like IBM or the like. The story is familiar. The husband does not quite know what to do with a working wife who goes to the office and meets male colleagues. As soon as she gets home, after traveling for more than an hour on the bus, her husband makes a scene in the presence of the children, and he abuses her loudly. She has nowhere to go. She would like to talk things out and to have a discussion. These are such common problems all around, and I was

110. This prose book includes seventeen long and short articles on women and various institutions in Pakistan.

amazed to find that so much is going on in this society. This is a cultural pattern, and it really doesn't matter which class. Child abuse is even more horrible—child abuse in both forms, sexual and physical.

Prognosis for Change

You see, our society is not a uniform society. Unlike Western societies where the process of development has been smoother and on a much grander scale, so far in our society our development has been done in a very fringe way. Twenty percent of our population is going toward the twenty-first century, and 80 percent of the population is still living in the fourteenth century. Those who work either in the civil services or in poetry or literature, somehow they belong to that 80 percent. Their faces reflect the English and the Western image, but their background is rooted in their body. The dichotomy of the two systems that are in them does not let them behave as civilized people. So all the time they are acting, and when you meet them closely, they are exposed, "Ahh . . . the Emperor has no clothes" [laughing]. It goes for both men and women. You see, having money in your pocket, sitting in a car or a plane, and feeling rich do not mean that your brain will feel the same velocity.

NGOs: Strengthening the Civil Society

You see, I never wanted to be a teacher. I hated it because I found all my teachers to be very dull. They read notes from 1938 reprinted in the Urdu bazaar and assigned all those boring books that they wanted us to read. I never felt attracted to my teachers. So, as I decided about my marriage, I decided never to be a teacher. I joined the government service, knowing that a teacher has more than six months holidays, while government servants have no holidays and are employed for twenty-four hours a day! You see, there are certain people who do not want to swim according to currents of the river. They want to swim according to their own will.

Well, I have not been thrown out yet, but I have been told by the Nawaz Sharif's government "to stay home and get your salary!" I do not have the posting. That's it! I am still a government servant. This means that because I have no posting, I do not go to office nine to five every day. I have not asked them for a posting thereafter! Why should I ask? I am doing my volunteer work. That is more important to me.

Sometime in 1984 a woman who was working at the Lahore Development

Authority came to see me at the National Center and said, "Why don't you take charge of this organization and do something with it?" So I did and started working. This was an old NGO. It was a club! Women would come together to have tea. They did nothing, no practical training or anything. When I joined, I had a survey done of the kinds of training women received there. I discovered that most of the women were piece workers and were exploited by their employers. I talked to the UNICEF. They said, "Why don't you write a proposal?" I suggested that I would train them to become self-employed. Then the UNICEF gave me funding for the training, and I brought in professional people to train women. One of my associates was a medical doctor who promised to provide me with medical supplies, nurses, and two doctors. I do not draw any salary and am the only volunteer person there. Now we have five projects going on at different locations in the city, but unfortunately all these women are now being exploited by the ready-made market. I am encouraging every woman to bring her crafts to a fair we are organizing in Faisal Town. We are going to have the inauguration on the twenty-first [February 1993].

Another agency I launched is called Hawwa [Eve] Association. Its objectives are documentation, feasibility, and planning—that is to say, documenting women's work and writing manuals for self-employment for women. So far I have written four books on various projects, reports, and feasibility. These books include craft guides and are targeted for women and all the NGO agencies and others who are working with women. These books are also available in the bookstores.

I am also involved in a project to bring out a quarterly called "Crafts *kahani*," crafts stories. In 1993, my book on the portrayal of women and craft, particularly those that have become independent through their crafts, will be published. The last part of the year will be about crafts done by Punjabi women. Many things like that are happening. I have written articles, discussing that it is useless to rely on the government and to think that the government can do everything. It is more productive to train women and allow them to take care of their own needs. Come March, I am going to start a HomeSchool[111] for girls and women because in the inner city of Lahore 73 percent are not allowed to go to regular school. So teaching girls in their own environment while they are learning a craft can be very productive. As I go along and learn

111. See chapter 2, Qurat's life history, where she describes HomeSchools; see also Weiss 1992.

of the existing handicaps [for women], I assimilate them and think of ways to deal with them.

We give women small loans. Sometimes we may give them bigger loans, up to twenty-five thousand rupees [approximately one thousand dollars in 1991–92]. I guarantee them. I go to the bank with them, and the bank charges them 10 percent. I started giving women loans in 1989, but the first Women's Bank was instituted in Pakistan last year [1989–90], and they are charging 18 percent interest. I have had several meetings with the chairwoman of the first Woman's Bank, and I told her that poor women could not afford that. She had meetings with the board, and they decided that, yes, poor women cannot be expected to pay such high interest. And you know, poor people are very reliable. We have not had any fallouts, any defaulters.

It is very interesting the way our organization is perceived in the community. We have a community health program that sees to the needs of the community. There are some forty welfare agencies in the northern part of Lahore. They are going to have a meeting tomorrow morning at 10:30, and I am going to attend their meeting. They said, "We want your organization to be associated with ours because you are our *pir behen*, spiritual sister." Early on [it] was difficult [to reach women in the community], but now it is changing. Tomorrow I will be going to this meeting, and at 12:00 I will go to Shadara and the next day to another association. Things are taking off. Now people accept you and people want you, and they want themselves to be associated.

We have never received any threatening notes or been harassed by any men or groups. Not at all. Earlier it was that some men did not allow girls to attend. Not any more, not now.[112] You see, some fundamentalists wrote a few articles in the *Nawa-i Waqt* [an Urdu daily] against us. The same people who used to write the same old stuff against "Kishwar Naheed." I never paid them any attention. They wrote against us because I never invited them to any of my functions, so they felt humiliated, and they continued writing against me personally—not the organization. That "she is unpatriotic, she is an agent of the Soviet Union, an agent of Hindustan," and all that nonsense. When Faiz Sahib was alive [d. 1984], we used to laugh and say, "We were nobody until somebody wrote against us!" So now I believe we were nobody. But by writing against us, the *Nawa-i Waqt* gave us a big personality, and by talking about us,

112. Compare with Qurat's similar comments, in chapter 2, on the gradual favorable reaction to girls' education in Quetta, Baluchistan.

people now want to meet us. If they hadn't written against us, we would not have been anything [laughing]. They still write against me whenever they get a chance, both personal and political. But because now I am not in the service, and they know that whatever I am doing is voluntary, they have kept quiet.

Other Landscapes, Other Experiences

My international travels have taught me a lot, but what has given me courage are my travels within this country and within the province of Punjab specifically. This was facilitated because I was in the local government. My job required that I spend some nights out in the field to observe the implementation of development projects. I was the woman development officer. I could travel alone and/or with my male coworkers. This was after 1967, and by then I was already married. When I transferred to the Information Ministry, I traveled abroad and had a chance to visit every corner of Bengal [then East Pakistan] both as part of my job and as an invited guest in *mushaeras* to recite my poetry. The literary attention I received gave me much strength and saved me from frustration. It reassured me that in other corners of the world my poetry was appreciated. Whenever I meet people, especially women, I find out that many share my concerns, think like me, and want to get rid of the slavery imbedded in much of our relationships [with men]. That gives me reassurance and courage to continue.

I find Bengali women more aware of their rights than Punjabi women because they are more educated and much more politically oriented. They are also more honest because they have less religious inhibition. Men and women work together much more comfortably there than here in Pakistan. Politically they are more alive for the same reason—educated or uneducated. Punjabi women are not made to be politically alive because of their cultural environment. They are either a feudal [lord's] or a peasant's wife. As a peasant's wife, she is not aware of her situation and is not given any identity. You know, in rural Punjab women who are working with their husbands in the field are not counted as working persons. The bonded laborers and the kiln workers—the whole family works, but the wages are registered in the name of the husband. So as long as you do not grant her the consciousness of her being, how can she be conscious of the injustices of the social structure?

Sindh is a different matter. Many are *haaris*, landless peasants, working for the feudal lords. The feudal is God. If they do not please him, he won't let them eat bread! You see, when they go over to Ayesha's house[113]— you might have seen it—people do not turn their back [to the feudal lord] when they leave; they go like this [she walked backward].[114] Here a human being is not that different from an animal before the feudal lord, and they do not think. But still, Sindhi women are politically more aware than the Punjabi women. When the retaliation comes, it comes with force. They have nothing to lose except the chains of their slavery.

"Story of a Bad Woman"

Everybody is asking me when am I going to write my autobiography [amused]. My publisher has been asking me, too. The government of Italy has offered me a grant for the second half of 1993 to go there and to write my autobiography.[115] The only reason I may want to write my autobiography is that I think women of my generation have seen many happenings in their society and the world. We have seen the rise of science, of psychology, of economics from Malthus to Karl Marx, and of the space development. Besides, we have seen the fall of the Soviet Union. We, the women like you and me who have visited the third world, have seen countries emerging from colonial domination to independence and falling in the ditch of fundamentalism. We happened to be the generation who has seen the changes of these cycles and has gone through the experience. If we do not write of things we have observed and the pressures that have been forced upon this fragile body, we will not do justice to the next generation. We have to record history. If Pushkin had not written, we would not have known what types of mothers were at the time in Russia. If Dostoyevsky had not written, we would not have known about the psychology of his characters. It doesn't matter that they were fictions. You see, Ibsen's *Doll's House* gives you an idea of what it was like to be an upper-middle-class woman in Sweden. Natasha of *War and Peace* gives you an idea of how women had to behave in Russia. So we need our reflections to be published. And it is not necessary that you be Anaïs Nin [laughter].

113. See Ayesha's life history in chapter 4.

114. Ayesha's estate is located in Punjab and not in Sindh, but her family is feudal.

115. Kishwar went to Bellagio in northern Italy (1993–94), where she wrote her autobiography, *Buri 'aurat ki kutha* (The story of a bad woman). It was published in 1995 (reprinted in 1997) by Sang-e Meel Publications, Lahore.

I have thought about writing about some of the same themes we have been talking about.[116] What I might have left out [in our interview] may emerge as I start writing.[117] When you start writing, the windows to your memories begin to open—you cannot close them. One of the major themes would be the tension between being a professional mother and wife. Throughout history, women have given life to children and are therefore expected to leave everything for the sake of their children. If you don't, you are made to feel guilty for not being a good mother *and* [for being] an unfaithful wife if you meet male colleagues. And why shouldn't you meet other men? Why should loyalty and purity be expected only of women? Why not from men? You are made to prove your purity and loyalty every day at the altar of pain. A man is not expected to prove his faithfulness to his wife. Why has equality never existed on this earth? Why is everything interpreted for the benefit of men, particularly in religion? What about women?

Why? *Because* men are perceived as *majazi khuda,*[118] false gods [high pitched, agitated]! Still, we teach our women to bow before them. When we were having our empowerment session in the old city [of Lahore], we showed a film made by the Pakistan Women's Lawyer Association. It is about a legal condition in the *nikah namah,* marriage certificate. Signing this clause gives women a right to sue for divorce.[119] One hundred percent of the girls and women who saw this film were unaware of this clause, and they were *all* married. A majority of the families do not allow their daughters to check that clause because they think it is *manhus,* unlucky, to talk of divorce at the time of marriage.[120] So the subjugated subconscious of being a woman continues. There is a need for

116. In her autobiography, she touches on some of the issues she discussed with me, though not as extensively.

117. I asked her, "What are some other points you would like to add that I might have not included?"

118. That women ought to be obedient to their husband, "to seek their husbands' pleasure and to follow the wish of their husband" is underlined in the book *Heavenly Ornaments* (Thanvi 1981, 461–64), whose translation Kishwar objected to.

119. The Iranian Family Law of 1967 made similar changes to personal law but was thrown out by the Islamic Republic in 1979. However, under the persistent pressure by Iranian women activists, the Islamic regime reinstated most of the original conditions formulated in the marriage contract of 1967 and 1975. All Iranian marriage certificates presently have "legal conditions" printed out in them, which are read to the bride and groom at the time of marriage.

120. See Nilofar Ahmed's similar comments in chapter 7.

this subjugation: keep women at home to serve men as a cook at times, as a maid at times, and as a bedmate at times. No need for compatibility. What you and me need, what we desire, is compatibility between two people.

Some Reflections: Defiance, Desire, Dishonor

Kishwar Naheed's reflections on her society and culture are astute and insightful, and her social commentary needs no further elaboration and commentary on my part. What I would like to comment on is her own life experiences, which seem to have evolved as a continuous contestation of ideas, ideals, and identities between a woman's desire to exercise her own agency and a patriarchal society that implicitly or explicitly punished her for being assertive. She resisted the culturally normative and proper role for women and attributes her resistance to her "aptitude to change the social structure" and her determination to "make a culture of my own." Three interrelated themes stand out in her narrative: defiance, dishonor, and desire.

Defiance: Questioning Traditions

In her poem "Decline," written when she was twenty-six years old, Kishwar rejects traditionally expected female servitude and challenges the gender and political power structures in her society, while anticipating change and transformation.

> These are my hands,
>   Their swollen veins
>   Are forerunners of autumn.
>   These veins were once
>   Liquid fire,
>   Rather like a fish out of water.
>   These hands were never lifted to plead.
>   These hands never disgraced themselves
>   By begging.
>   These hands were both the savior and the murderer
>   Of their own desires.
>   The anguish of labour
>   Pressed every knot flat

In the fingers of these hands.
Every nail looks like a jagged shore,
A mirror of ugliness.
This is the beginning
Of the picture of my better days.

Naheed 1991c, 21.

Defiance is the theme that emerges with most force from Kishwar's re-counting of her life experiences; she seems to take a mischievous delight in it. The flip side of defiance and autonomy in Pakistan, however, is notoriety and dishonor. But what is defiance? How are we to understand it within a particu-lar historical and cultural context? What are the social consequences and emo-tional costs of defiance? "Defiance," writes Wagner-Martin, "on a woman's part in the 19th century need not have been the murder of a parent, a lover, or a minister; it might well have been her decision not to marry or not to become a part of her community" (1994, 9). A century later and in another locality, Kishwar Naheed's defiance meant just that! She challenged her parents' cultur-ally perceived sacred authority to arrange her marriage to a "proper" *sayyid* and instead married a young college classmate. Her disobedience and defiance not only provoked her parents' wrath, but also gained her lifelong notoriety.

Kishwar scandalized the male literati by appropriating *ghazal*, a lyrical po-etic style identified primarily with the expressions of male love in Urdu litera-ture (B. Mehdi 1984; R. Ahmad 1990). The defiant tone, the unconventional themes, and her distinct voice startled them. They cried foul. How could a woman be allowed to defy the "Tradition" and to reveal "shamelessly" what ought to be concealed?[121] But this was not the first time the legitimacy of Kishwar's voice was questioned. Much earlier her mother had vehemently ob-jected to her speaking at a children's program for Radio Pakistan. Kishwar gave in then, but once she reached maturity, her voice was never again stifled. Though the echo of her voice in the *mardana khana* realized her mother's fore-boding of the "shame" that awaited her, it evoked a much more complex re-sponse from the male literati, one mixed with envy and contempt.

The male literati punished her for being assertive by labeling her a *na-aurat*, not woman: an epithet that both denied her the privileges of her sex and re-

---

121. Likewise, writing "confessional poetry and being frank" in the Western tradition has been considered a male prerogative (Heilbrun 1989, 63–64).

jected her membership to the male club. Years later, in her midfifties, she felt secure enough to write a frank and confessional autobiography, *khud nivisht*, satirizing her ascribed public identity by titling it, *Buri 'aurat ki katha* (The story of a bad woman; originally published in 1995, reprinted in 1997). By publishing her autobiography, Kishwar committed, yet again, multiple transgressions and subversions. She expressed herself in a literary genre that is rare in Pakistan, particularly by women, whose voices were not to be heard in the *mardana khana* of the public. Worse yet, she showed little modesty or shied away from the public gaze. In a culture still trying to shake loose its traditional preoccupation with covering and concealing women's bodies, muting their voices, and restricting their mobility, Kishwar's unabashed visibility shocked the sensibility of a majority of the public.

Her iconoclastic and unconventional poetic narratives became increasingly intertwined with social activism and feminist awareness. Prodding women to empower themselves, she deconstructed the traditional and sacred gender roles and gender hierarchy. A quick glance at the titles of her poems reveals the extent of her cultural transgressions and her departure from the traditionally desired image of womanhood: "We Sinful Women," "Farewell to the Uterus," "Punish Me," "Who Am I," "Censorship," "Decline," "We Have Flown Away All Birds of Desire."

Contrary to many outsiders' stereotypes and insiders' expectations, however, Kishwar was not vanquished. She thrived professionally in a conservative and patriarchal society, challenging and changing the form and content of a well-established male literary tradition. Her voice gathered strength, echoing in various corners in her society and abroad. She was celebrated abroad as an outspoken feminist poet, which in turn elicited, albeit begrudgingly in some circles, a greater recognition and acceptance of her creativity at home. Despite some individuals and institutions' best attempts, she was not browbeaten to submission. Rather, her focused attention and determined personality led to raising social awareness in her society and to creating a "smoother" groove for women who followed in her footsteps.

Desire: Literal and Literary

Whether it was a yearning for love—that apparently scarce cultural commodity yet ever so pervasive poetically—or her college friendship with Yousef that ignited her lyrical creativity, Kishwar's rapid poetic popularity and her desire to express her deepest thoughts, feelings, and emotions generated multiple obstacles for her.

Disbelieving his daughter's poetic talent and her rising popularity in college, Kishwar's father accused her of "copying" other people's work and then getting prizes for them. He demanded that she should "stop it." Her husband, though fascinated by her because of her creativity and difference from other women, feared the content of her poems and accused her of "washing [her] dirty linen in public." He demanded that she stop writing on personal topics.

In the end, Kishwar's greatest rebellion—breaking the chains of custom and marrying her beloved—turned out to be her greatest punishment. A patriarchal punishment both in its specific and general senses of the term: Yousef neglected her—and neglect seems to be the harshest punishment for Kishwar—and her parents disowned her. Resentful of being pressured into marrying Kishwar, Yousef withheld his affection from her but lavished his attention and money on other women. Until his sudden death in 1984, he never again allowed Kishwar to persuade him to act according to her wishes, not even when she asked for a divorce—divorced though they were for all practical purposes. All along, however, Kishwar loved Yousef desperately, although she felt anguished about the relationship. She serenaded Yousef in many of her poems and after his death paid him homage frequently, reflecting her deep emotional ambivalence toward her husband, their torturous relationship, and her unfulfilled desire. When I visited Kishwar in Pakistan in January 1998, she held the prestigious position of director of the Arts Council, and a framed photo of Yousef and herself in a loving embrace was on her office mantelpiece.

The most complicated hurdle, however, was placed in her way by the male literary establishment. They questioned the style and content of her poems and debated whether what she wrote was indeed poetry. "Can women adapt," Mary Jacobus asked, "traditionally male-dominated modes of writing to the articulation of female oppression and desire?" (qtd. in Heilbrun 1988, 42). Echoed Kishwar in Pakistan, "The first debatable issue about me in the whole literary circle was, Can a woman be given the right to express her love the way she wants to?" Appropriating the traditionally revered literary style of *ghazal*, she reformed it with her own experiences of oppression and desire. "I was writing as a woman would feel when she falls in love. . . . And *that* created hue and cry from everybody. Many wrote that 'the tradition does not allow her to behave like this.'" The Tradition could not have allowed it because, in the words of Baqer Mehdi, "Women were the object of *ghazal* themselves, the beloved. They could not be the creator of *ghazal*, the lover" (1984, 211). Consider the passion and tension in Kishwar's poem "And then, a long drawn silence":

> By the canal, on the autumn-tainted road
>> You and I looked like ambassadors of spring.
>> Playing children saw us.
>> Perhaps, our smiles were innocent like them.
>> Burning in the shade of impatience,
>> We felt the quiver of all the canal's waves
>> Taking form in our own bodies.
>> And the roots of our well being
>> Appeared to grow in the womb of those trees
>> Which had bared their branches
>> To show the mirror of union
>> To our arms.
>> Sinking feet in the wet earth,
>> Felt as if we were walking in dreams.
>> We were reminded of the first day of our thirst.
>>> Naheed 1991c, 143.

Kishwar was criticized for infusing the "profane" aspect of her daily experiences with the more "sacred" topics of [male] love and transcendence. They said, "How can it be poetry? It was so senseless." Not so senseless, apparently, to her male colleagues, for "Women's access to discourse involves submission to phallocentricity, to the masculine and the symbolic: refusal, on the other hand, risks reinscribing the feminine as a yet more marginal madness or non-sense" (Jacobus, qtd. in Heilbrun 1988, 41; see also R. Ahmad 1990, i). Kishwar's refusal to submit to the patriarchal poetic tradition and her insistence on expressing her own voice left her vulnerable to accusations of double violation. More attempts consequently were made to marginalize her as a woman and to dismiss her as a poet. It meant a violent negation of her persona as a woman. She was in the "no man's land," literarily speaking, and hence was perceived as a freak, a *na-aurat:* neither man nor woman. But Kishwar was not to be intimidated into silence or submission. "The drawbacks and the conflicts that I had to face made me stronger," and "their protest triggered my brain to write poetry differently." In short, their criticism made her the kind of person she was, to paraphrase her statement.

Dishonor: Breaking the Chain of Custom

Family honor in South Asia, writes Mandelbaum, "is inevitably tested when the marriage of a daughter is arranged" (1988, 23). The dishonor Kishwar brought on her family apparently was felt so strongly in the community that for months afterward people paid condolences to her mother instead of con-gratulations. Kishwar is perhaps among the luckier women who defy their parents' "sacred" authority to choose their own marriage partner. Many Pak-istani women in a similar situation have found themselves caught in legal suits brought against them by their own parents—primarily their father or broth-ers. They are separated violently from their (self-selected) husbands, jailed, abducted, ostracized, abandoned, and in some cases even murdered.[122] Many parents apparently see it as their inalienable right to choose their child's spouse. Their sense of entitlement is reinforced by deeply held cultural values of *izzat*, honor, that permeate every aspect of belief and behavior in Pakistan (Mandelbaum 1988, 20).

In chapter 1, I mentioned that the Hanafi School of Islamic law and the Family Law Ordinance of 1961 clearly recognize—at least on paper—the right of adult women (presently, sixteen years and older) to decide their own marriages. Most Pakistani women, however, either are not aware of the law or are prevented from taking advantage of it by their parents, who vehemently contest the law on cultural grounds and, according to some beliefs, on reli-gious grounds.

In 1997, Saima, a young woman of twenty-one, infuriated her father, a highly religious and conservative man, by marrying her younger brother's tutor against her father's wishes. The father in turn brought one suit of forni-cation against his daughter and another of abduction against her lawfully mar-ried husband, who was promptly jailed. The father's argument was that because his daughter did not have his permission to marry, her marriage was therefore illegal and tantamount to fornication. The young couple's ordeal gained international recognition and prompted local feminists, lawyers, and

---

122. On April 6, 1999, Samira Imran, a young Pathan woman of twenty-nine, was murdered in cold blood in her lawyer's office in Lahore by an assassin her parents allegedly hired. Her "crime" was to ask for a divorce from her abusive husband, who happened to be her maternal cousin, and her desire to then marry a man of her own choosing. For a fictional account, see *The Bride* by Bapsi Sidhwa (1983).

NGOs to rally around her case. The court eventually found in her favor, but the couple had to flee the country to escape the father's wrath.

In another case, Farzana, an eighteen-year-old girl, took refuge in a women's shelter to prevent her family from forcing her to marry against her will. She came from a prominent Pathan family and wanted to complete her college education before marriage. She also did not like the man chosen for her. "Her refusal to the marriage was seen as a slight to [the family's] honor as they would be seen as having lost control of their daughter" (Balchin 1996, 15).

Indeed, honor, with its presumed primordial moral value that integrates individuals with a group (Gilmore 1987, 3), is the driving force in all these cases, including Kishwar's. A woman who defies her father to choose the man of her life publicizes her desire and openly demonstrates her willfulness. Worse yet, she dishonors her father publicly by negating or challenging his manhood and moral standing within the community. Her action places the two men in what Gilmore calls "masculine rivalries" (Gilmore 1987, 10), which then poses a threat to the integrity and identity of the father. Inflicting shame and outrage on another man by defiling a woman through rape—or, by extension, through an unapproved marriage—is like forcing entry into "the father's house" and hence perpetrating a symbolic violation of the father's manhood and honor (Herzfeld 1985, cited in Gilmore 1987, 11). Indeed, some Pakistani fathers—and brothers—seem to feel such a symbolically loaded and dishonorable intrusion so strongly that they can see no other option but to retaliate violently.

In Kishwar's case and in contradistinction to Gilmore's explanation, it was not so much her father who was outraged at his daughter's unauthorized relationship with her future husband, but rather her *mother* who felt shamed and dishonored. It was her mother, though assisted by Kishwar's elder brother, who was the driving force behind the daughter's ostracism. What is noteworthy therefore is the role some women can and do play in upholding family honor by becoming agents of patriarchal punishment to enforce cultural traditions. Throughout Kishwar's years of growing up, it was consistently her mother who played the role of the family watchdog. She repeatedly intimidated Kishwar to stifle her desire, tried to shame her into submission by underscoring the necessity of upholding the family honor because they were *sayyid*s. Kishwar's father, contrary to the dominant image of men in Pakistan—and, by implication, in the Muslim world—had little input, in her view, and often followed his wife's ideas and decisions.

Kishwar's determination to live alone in Lahore in the early 1980s and to continue her career was no small matter. Her bold action provoked more gossip about her private activities and threatened to compromise her honor even more. Her poetry and creative activities, although a cause celebre, continued to be contested and at times negatively perceived. By no means, however, has Kishwar been universally condemned in Pakistan or in the subcontinent. She has many admirers, both of her person and her poetry. Her high-profile professional success and her social activities in various NGOs have given her greater acceptance and legitimacy in Pakistan. And here is what may appear to an outsider as a paradox in Muslim societies: the ability of some professional women not only to write and publish but also to flourish and succeed in a highly patriarchal and conservative society such as Pakistan. Whereas Kishwar's willfulness and individuality evidently brought dishonor to her family and dissatisfaction to her husband, her economic success and professional prestige validated her public activities and muffled the criticism.[123] Honor, we may note, is "a symbolic summary of past achievements and a main element in present power. Power, properly deployed, enhances *izzat*" (Mandelbaum 1988, 22).

"Now everyone claims me," said Kishwar laughingly.

---

123. Zarina Bhatty makes a similar argument in "Women in Uttar Pradesh: Social Mobility and Directions of Change" (1975, 25–36).

6

Kinship
The Crime of Being a Widow

Meeting Sajida Mokarram Shah

I ARRIVED IN PESHAWAR AIRPORT on a cool sunny March day in 1992 and was greeted warmly by Professor Farzand Durrani, the chairman of the archeology department at Peshawar University. At the university, he introduced me to Professor Shaheen Sardar Ali, who taught law and women's studies.[1] This provided a wonderful opportunity for me not only to get to know her, a most engaging and knowledgeable person, but also to get to know of other people through her. She graciously invited me to give a semiprivate lecture for her female students in her office, which was an occasion to cherish. Around eight or ten young women, some of whom wore a white head scarf, huddled in Shaheen's office. Once the veiled women were assured of my position on veiling, that it should be a matter of individual choice, they warmed up, and we had a lively discussion on women's legal and human rights under Islam in Iran and Pakistan. I interviewed some of the other people Shaheen introduced me to before I was led finally to meet Sajida Mokarram Shah during the last hours of my departure from Peshawar. I met with her briefly, during which time she told me stories of her life, and we decided on a date for me to return to Peshawar, where I would stay at her house and interview her more extensively.

I returned to Peshawar a few weeks later in April and stayed at her house for four days. We talked in the evenings and went around to her office at the Agency Coordinating Body for Afghan Relief (ACBAR), where she worked as

---

1. Shaheen Sardar Ali is a lawyer and at that time was a professor at University of Peshawar. Among her publications, see *Blind Justice for All?* (Sardar Ali and Arif 1994).

a program officer during the days. Aware of her high-ranking position, she clearly enjoyed being in charge and acted with authority. She was critical of the management of some of the international agencies operating in Peshawar at the time, accusing them of nepotism and greed. I met some of the expatriate researchers and scholars and spent some time with a male American Fulbright scholar who was particularly annoyed with Sajida's authoritarian style of running ACBAR.

Her spacious, attractive, walled-in house is in an exclusive area in Peshawar. As we walked to the TV room, Sajida pointed to a bed in the corner of the room and said, "I sleep there. Ever since my husband died, I have not been able to sleep in our bed in the bedroom. I can't face it. Initially I had my children around me in this room until I gradually sent them to their own rooms, but I continue to sleep in this room." Zainab, her eldest daughter, who was fifteen, joined us, and after dinner we watched an old Urdu feature film, *Ulad* (Children), on Pakistan Television. At around 11:15, when the movie was over, Zainab said goodnight, and Sajida and I started talking. We did not stop until 2:30 in the morning. That night Sajida was most engaging and emotional and talked candidly about herself, her parents, and her husband. My small tape recorder malfunctioned, and I had to write down everything by hand for this particular interview. I had the machine fixed the following day and taped the rest of our conversations.

Sajida's stories revolve around a complex situation in which law and religion clash with cultural practices. It involves the tradition of levirate or "widow inheritance" among the Pathans of the North-West Frontier Province in Pakistan. When her husband died in a tragic car accident, Sajida was expected to leave her own house and live with her four children under the protection and supervision of her husband's brother. She rebuked her in-laws, who were anxious to have financial control over her children, and challenged her own father, who demanded, more persistently than even her in-laws, that Sajida move into her brother-in-law's house. With the prospects of dishonor looming large, Sajida was ostracized, for the most part, by her extended kin and most pointedly by her own father. She repeatedly stressed her bitterness against him, his stinginess, his punitive attitude toward his wife and children, and his act of practically disowning her. They seldom met afterward, and, in her view, he never cared much for her or her children. Sajida never recovered from her father's insensitive and, in her eyes, calculated treatment of her. She thought he seriously was worried that she and her children might become an economic burden on him. She was fortunate to have inherited from her husband a car and the house they lived in. She kept the house, sold the car, and decided to live.

Sajida Mokarram Shah

The Widow Who Chose to Live

What I was saying the other day was that, as females, we are suffering twice. First there is religion and all that taboo it puts on us. Then there are the customs of this city, this society. Everything is for the benefit of men. I find it very frustrating because I, as a female, am able to do *better* than most men. But even so I am considered a female, and men think it is *their* right to dictate to every female, that they must regularly order me according to their whims! Not one of them stops to think that I am accomplishing twice what they are doing. I am working as well as looking after the house and my children, and that is just expected. That makes me so angry [raising her voice]. And the minute I stop or complain or even so much as talk to a colleague—God forbid!—I am branded a bad woman. These things make me *so* angry. Why is it that women are never given their recognition?

You see, the minute I became a widow, everybody tried to give me advice, men and women. Everybody had an opinion in the beginning [high pitched]. They thought they had a right to give me advice [sarcastic tone] and expected me to follow that [advice] because as soon as I became a widow, my IQ dropped immediately. I was not able to think for myself. The irony of it was that it was in this very society that when my husband was alive, people would ask *me* for advice. They would call on me, and they would get me involved in all kinds of internal household matters because they felt *I* always gave them sane, rational advice. But the minute he died, our telephone did not stop ringing. It was people—men and women alike—giving me advice, how I must behave, what I must do towards my in-laws, what I must do for my children. It was *never* ending, until I got this job. Then people realized that I was not listening to anybody, and I was just chalking out my own future.

For this society, whether male or female, I am a bad woman. I am a nonperson, rather, because not only did I commit the crime of becoming a widow, I compounded that crime by wanting to bring up my own children independently instead of going and begging people. *That* would have been fine by the society.

A widow is despised. If the children don't grow up as model children, then she is blamed. If she has an opinion, that is ignored because it is not worth listening to. She is despised *because* she is a widow. She is not good enough for the society or to be given the same attention. She is low caste and merely tolerated. Most of the time, most forget she is even there. The moment the husband dies, the widow goes out of existence [high pitched].[2]

But, you see, I know that very few widowed women have been able to stand on their own feet. In Peshawar, with all the people I know, it must be less than half a dozen. Then, again, I don't know all the widows who survive in this city because I am exposed to just a certain class of females, the rich and the semi-educated. Most of them have been left with a lot of money. The difference between them and me is that I was left with no money, and maybe that is what made me stronger. From day one, I had to start thinking of what's going to happen to me and my children.

My advice to women in my position is to stand on their own feet, definitely! I feel there is *nobody* in this society who is going to turn around and help them, and one day they find themselves out on the street if they don't do something about their own life. But if they want to bring up sane, normal children, then they have to take care of their own lives. They have to develop that courage to drown their own weaknesses and to stand up and say, "Well, OK!" You see, it has taken a lot out of me, and it will take a lot out of them but for this one single satisfaction that the children grow up in a normal household, that they are not beholden to the society. Because of this I have lost a lot, but at the same time I feel secure that I am bringing up four normal children who will not be a burden to the society, who will not be misfits, and who will not have any complexes. For a mother, *that* is the biggest achievement.

Death of a Husband

It was a hot summer day in 1983. I was happy to have Mokarram back home again. He had just returned from England where he had gone for further train-

2. Compare: "For a Hindu woman, widowhood is considered a punishment for the crime committed by her in her previous life. Hence, she is looked down upon as a sinner" (Patil, qtd. in Lopata 1996, 22).

ing in endoscopy. We were waiting for this day for a year now, and our children were all excited about spending time with their father.

A week before Mokarram's return, my uncle [father's brother] had died, and my father-in-law felt obliged to go to his village in the north and pay his respects. He wanted Mokarram to go with him on this trip, and I did not want him to leave, not then. I tried my best to dissuade my father-in-law from going then or taking Mokarram along, but to no avail. Mokarram also was unwilling to refuse his father but was exhausted enough to suggest they postpone their trip for a day or so. His father agreed, but that evening he had a change of heart and decided that they should leave immediately after their *sahari* [predawn meal for the beginning of fasting]. He said that they could go quickly, pay their respects, say their *fatiha* [prayer for the dead], and return in the morning. Mokarram agreed.

I was irritated and refused Mokarram's offer to accompany them on this trip. I wanted to spend some time with him but did not want to share that moment on the road with his father. I am not angry with my father-in-law because that is how it is in this part of the world. In fact, he was a very considerate man and was particularly fond of me. I was his favorite daughter-in-law. He liked me a lot and deferred to me. My other two sisters-in-law always commented on that.

They left. By eleven o'clock, I started feeling worried, you know, the type of anxiety one gets in uncertain situations. I prepared lunch and finished cooking quickly. Mokarram hated for me to be in the kitchen when he was home. I waited for him. Then I got a telephone call from the wife of Mokarram's boss. She said, "How is Mokarram?" I knew immediately that something must have happened to him. I said, "Why don't you tell me?" She said "No, no. I just asked." Two minutes later her husband called and said that he was coming over. He came here and picked me up and took me to the hospital.

For some inexplicable reason, my father-in-law had instructed his driver to stay behind in Peshawar in case I might need him. Instead, he had Mokarram drive him to their destination outside of Peshawar. On their way back, a speeding bus that was trying to pass another bus had a head-on collision with Mokarram's car. Mokarram was badly injured, but his father was spared. He managed to get his son to the hospital in Peshawar and had the on-call doctor call his son's boss, the same man who brought me to the hospital.

My father-in-law seemed fine by the time I got to the hospital, though he was being watched and was under the doctor's care. A few beds further, Mokarram was lying unconscious. His father was more anxious about his son, who was his favorite, and implored the attending doctor to "please look after Mokarram. I am fine." Strangely, as soon as the doctor walked away and went toward Mokarram's bed, my father-in-law had a massive heart attack and died instantly. Mokarram died six days later. He never regained his consciousness.

[Silence. Tears welled up in her eyes.] Mokarram was lying unconscious for six days, and for six days I did not leave his bedside [tears rolling down, long pause]. All our friends gathered there. The whole hospital was focused on him. The nurses took every occasion to look after him and to work for him. The nurses and his patients turned the hospital into a shrine, praying for his recovery all the time. [Weeping—long pause—looking around for her cigarette.] I never smoke in front of my children, but in such situations I need to smoke. A policeman said, "This was the biggest funeral in Peshawar that I ever remember."[3] Suddenly he was gone.[4]

My father-in-law was a self-made man. He was from a poor background but managed to study law and pull himself up. By the end of his life, he was a very wealthy, well-respected lawyer and popularly known as Pir Sahib. He did not trust the banking system in Pakistan and did not deposit his money in the bank, but kept it in a black suitcase. When he died and before Mokarram breathed his last, Mokarram's two brothers managed to hide that suitcase [subdued]. They deprived my children and me of their rightful share of inheritance. Up to this day [1992], they have not given them a penny.

This was not the first time or the only time a woman was deprived of her husband's share of inheritance in our family. A few years back my father had perpetrated the same act on his own brother's wife. He is loaded with money but has not given his sister-in-law and her two daughters their share. They had joint property, but my father and his sister divided the property and did not give anything to their sister-in-law.

My father tried to force me to live with my in-laws. Half the community

3. Sajida became very emotional recalling the events of the six days her husband lay in a coma in the hospital. She paused frequently because crying would not allow her to talk much. We both cried. She sobbed. The grief she was reliving I could observe only from a distance. I almost never smoke, but I shared a cigarette with her.

4. At the time of his death, Sajida was thirty-two years old, and they had two sons and two daughters: Motayyib, nine; Zainab, six; Zara, two; and Masood, nine months.

tried to force me, mostly out of goodwill, to live with them, but *he* just wanted to get rid of me [agitated]. Then he went around telling people he was giving me four thousand rupees! That man did not pay for his wife's funeral [tears rolling down]! When the proposal came from my brother-in-law, [asking me] to live with him, my father sent a message wanting to know how much money I needed. I had no savings because all our money had gone to England with Mokarram for his training, but I did not want to accept money from him. I did not want my children to be subjected to the same treatment [long pause]. When I said no, he was so happy because his money was saved. He just went away.

I do not *think* he did not want to support me [raising her voice]![5] I *know* so! I have no illusion. I have been a widow for nine years. My husband was lying in his deathbed in the hospital, and my father sent a cousin to ask me to apologize [for taking care of her two younger sisters against her father's wish] and then he would support me! I was furious. My husband was difficult to live with, but he was a wonderful man. My father is a smooth talker but an awful man. My biggest resentment against him is that he did not let me mourn my loss properly.[6] I was basically forced to look for a job immediately after my husband's forty days of mourning were over.

Mokarram was the eldest brother and had one older sister and two younger brothers. My brother-in-law might have been willing to let my children have their share if only I had complied with his wishes. He is after Mokarram and his mother's favorite and a hypocrite, despite his claim to being a devoted Muslim. He is a Tablighi,[7] educated and articulate, but he is a hypocrite and is dishonest. I detest him. Appearance is all that matters to him. In front of people, he says he would treat me and my children like his own. He would say that he could not bring back their father for them, but that he would do exactly as their father would do. But he wanted to take my children out of their school—which is a very good school—wanted me to sell my car and to move

5. I asked her, "Do you think he did not want to support you?"

6. Ten years had passed since her husband's death, but Sajida still felt very angry toward her father. She wept when she recalled how he pressured her to accept the offer to live with her brother-in-law and how he simply abandoned her when she refused to do so. She resented him strongly, frequently choking with emotion while recalling his insincerity in the face of her predicament.

7. See M. Ahmad 1991 on the Tablighi Jama'at.

into one room in *his* house and to share that with his wife and children. What he really wanted was to have a free servant. I never liked him and was not about to put my fate and that of my children at his disposal. If my father-in-law was alive, I would not have hesitated to move in with them and allow him to take care of me and my children, but the situation had changed dramatically. With my mother-in-law also dead [seven months before this accident], I had no desire to live with my brother-in-law.

Despite all that, I was careful not to alienate my children from their paternal relatives. But when my eldest son, Motayyib, once witnessed how his uncle screamed at me, from then on he never went there. My in-laws don't want to see me either because in their view I am a *behaya*, a shameless woman.

Many people, along the way, have been good to me, but I think this is the most vicious society anybody could have. It is hypocritical and full of double standards. When a woman's husband dies, her fate is decided by her in-laws. She is forced to marry her brother-in-law or a husband's cousin or a nephew, and nobody asks *her* consent. Because she is our *sharm*, honor [angry, sarcastic], she is the property of her in-laws and must be kept in purdah. But when one of our distant relatives lost her rich husband and she fell in love with her cousin-in-law, the whole society turned against her. Why? Because *she* wanted it. Even her own family cut off their relations with her. Normally they would have jumped to control her and to arrange her remarriage. This is the norm of this society. But because she decided it herself, everybody turned against her. When I became a widow, she, too, said nasty things about me, but then when she learned that I had defended her marriage, she came to apologize. If I have the opportunity to raise my voice against hypocrisy, I would do it.

Arranged Marriage and Love

My husband was studying medicine in England when his parents decided that he should get married. They asked him to return to Peshawar, and they got him engaged to the sister of a well-known politician. But, for some reason, the Tablighi brother did not like this woman and, while Mokarram was back in England, managed to convince his mother to break off the engagement. They returned the gifts, and nobody bothered to ask the girl how she felt. She was very young. Mokarram must have been twenty-six then. For him, it did not matter, and he did not involve himself. Neither Mokarram nor the other woman had much input in the whole affair.

After that, his father was looking for another suitable wife for him. He sent some people to my father. My father did not know much about Pir Sahib's family background, though he knew who he was. By then, Pir Sahib was a well-established, prominent lawyer, so my father requested some time to think, but Mokarram's father wanted a quick response. Then my father started asking around, and some people told him that if they had a daughter, they would be happy to give her to him with much interest. So my father told Pir Sahib that he would let me marry his son only if he [her father] took a liking to him [Mokarram], and Pir Sahib agreed.

I was not consulted. Nobody tells you anything. In March of 1973, once again, Pir Sahib summoned his son from England to Peshawar. On March 17, my father met him, and by the end of the evening the two of them were certain they liked each other. A week later, on March 28, we were engaged, and on March 30 the marriage ceremony, *nikah*, was performed. I was not even present at any of these events, not even at my own *nikah*,[8] the legal marriage ceremony. And two weeks later, on April 19, we were married [i.e., had the public celebration]. We never set eyes on each other until the day of our marriage. I was scared of him and did not look at him for a good three days [laughter]! It was not until the papers were signed and the marriage contract legalized on April 19 that I was taken to his house, and then we saw each other. The whole affair took a little over a month. It happened so fast. I was twenty-two years old.[9]

I felt terrible![10] Marriage is terrible. How can you go to bed with someone whom you have just met? The husband wants you, and you go to bed. Women are passive. I felt OK, but I always felt very self-conscious and still feel that a person's body is such a private thing to allow a man to get into it. We were more friends than husband and wife. The thing I miss the most is the friendly companionship. From the moment we met, we liked each other, and I don't want my children to get the impression that our marriage was less than ideal.[11]

8. According to Islamic law, both men and women can give the power of attorney to a third person to represent them during the *nikah* ceremony (Fayzee 1974, 91).

9. Sajida was born in 1951.

10. I asked her, "How did you feel?"

11. Just as Sajida was expressing her feelings about intimacy and sexual relations, she paused and then abruptly changed the subject. It seemed to me that she felt conflicted about talking about sexuality and physical intimacy. I tried to persuade her to feel free and to continue, but she reiterated that she did not want her children to think of their parents' marriage as something less than ideal.

Two weeks after we were married, Mokarram went back to England, and I joined him by June 1, 1973. This was my first journey alone, and I was exhausted, but he was there for me in the airport. He said, "Whatever time we have here in England, consider it your honeymoon. You should enjoy it," and I took advantage of it. Every time he might lose his temper, I would say, "Look, you are forgetting your promise." There are no words to describe him. He had a temper, but he was so caring. He was a good son to his parents, a good husband, and a very dedicated doctor. He would work long hours and would stay in the hospital when no other doctor would be working. He loved his job, and soon I realized that I could not compete with his interest in his job, but he was also very devoted to me. Rather than nagging him about his total involvement in his profession, I decided to get involved in my own areas of interest. He was a decent man but would never support me if I were to get involved in some professional activities the way Shaheen's husband is.[12] Whatever I have achieved, I have done it on my own and am proud of it.

You see, despite all these things, I am grateful to God that I have never felt jealous of other people. I am never in competition with others. I could be very bitter, seeing all these doctors and Mokarram dead. But so long as I have enough to run my house and keep my children happy, I am grateful.

Pathology of Patriarchy

[Long pause, hesitation] I would feel uncomfortable with expressing emotions—maybe because my parents had such a terrible relationship. My father did not like any of his children [five girls, of whom Sajida was the eldest, and one boy, who was the youngest], and he *hated* my mother, though she adored him. They were cousins, and their marriage was arranged, but from day one he knew that she was just his wife. My mother was a typical Pathan woman—obedient. Suddenly he started thinking he was above her. He was educated, she wasn't, and because of his own deep sense of insecurity, he behaved like a bully. He was psychotic.

My father suffered from a profound sense of insecurity within his own family. As one of seven siblings—he was the one before the last—in a rather traditional family, he was made to feel very competitive with his older brothers. Because my grandparents were dead, my father's older brother became in

12. See fn. 1 in this chapter.

charge of his younger siblings. He treated the three younger boys very harshly. Worst of all, they teased my father mercilessly for being of darker complexion compared to his other siblings. They called him *tore*, "darky." [13] My father had three sisters. The eldest died before we came on the scene. His second sister is dead, and one is surviving. *This* woman is very manipulative and tried to control her brothers.

What do you mean by feeling *distant* from my father [raising her voice]? We avoided him like the plague because he would beat the first person in his way. I mean it wasn't as if he would ask for us! He would come home and start shouting and abusing the first person in his way. I don't remember *ever* having a rational conversation with him. He did not think we should go to college, but because he was competing with his brothers, he did not prevent us, though he wouldn't pay a rupee for us. Our asking for even one rupee would get him to hit the roof. Going to college wasn't easy for us. He was so competitive with his brothers that he wouldn't even see our achievements. Even though my sister was doing so well in college and my uncle's son was failing his studies, my father would say, "I don't understand why his children are doing so well!" [Incredulous.]

Professionally he was not as successful as his brothers, and his military career took off rather late in his life. He made it only as high as colonel. So, to cover his own insecurity, he abused my mother and would get violent if we argued with him. He would beat us up to no end and with whatever came in handy. He felt we were his property. That man needed psychiatric treatment and should not have been let loose on his family. He did a lot of damage, and there is so much resentment among us because of that. I don't know how he is with his new family [he remarried in 1991]. His new wife is much younger than him, though she had not been married before and is rather homely. He has another daughter now. I am not interested in what goes on with him, anyway. He could not decide to be modern or traditional. Sometimes he would get up at four o'clock in the morning to do his morning prayers; other times he would insist in participating in every function of the [military] club.

My mother died in 1989 at the age of fifty-seven. She had a massive brain hemorrhage, but that had nothing to do with my father, though he was very abusive toward her. I cannot understand how she could have wasted forty

---

13. Generally speaking, Pakistanis privilege lighter skin colors, and many families indulge children with lighter skin.

years of her life with a man who broke her totally, physically and mentally. That is in fact my biggest resentment against society. She could never bring herself to ask for a divorce because from early on we are taught *sharm*, humility, honor. We, the Pathan women, never dare to ask for a divorce because its stigma is so great.[14] Can you imagine someone to be married at the age of sixteen or seventeen and to go through a life like that? There was not a day she did not get abused, verbally or physically.[15] We children could not understand their relationship and did not give her an opportunity to speak with us. She took it as part of life. She was utterly lonely. My mother's brothers are a useless lot. If a wife's brother stands by her, then her husband would hesitate to mistreat her.

My father had a lot of affairs, and my mother knew about it. We did not know about his outside activities, and my mother discovered it by chance. He had his own room at the entrance of the house.[16] Once when she was out, she came in through the back door and discovered him. There were times when she found it very difficult to take his abusive behavior. She would then come here and stay with me but would resent it if we said anything bad about him. Soon she would miss him, and she would go back.

The contrast between my father and my husband is tremendous. Although my husband was at times bad-tempered, he came from a normal family. His father loved him, and his mother doted on him. He never abused his wife or children. There are no words to describe him. He was bad-tempered but was also very caring. He thought I was the most beautiful thing walking on earth. As a doctor, there were always nurses around him, but he never had any rela-

14. Based on specific verses in the Qur'an (2:228–32, 236–37, 241; 65:1–7; 4:35), Islamic law allows for divorce and dissolution of marriage. Among the Pathans, however, divorce is synonymous with dishonor and so is highly contemptible, as shown in the example given in chapter 5, fn. 124.

15. Against this harsh background, it is interesting to note that according to Akbar S. Ahmed, " 'Pakhtu' . . . means modesty, shame or integrity; strange for those supposedly warrior people to draw their cultural tones from distinctly feminine trait: modesty. *Torgul* (black flower) and *spingul* (white flower) are Pathan masculine names" (1977, 112).

16. "The wife acts out the ritual of subordination to her husband by never asking him any questions and by allowing him his freedom. . . . Men with guesthouses or guestrooms may occasionally have parties with prostitutes or promiscuous girls of the village. Such entertainments are regarded by the wives as the prerogatives of their husbands" (Lindholm 1982, 20). See also the short story by Zahida Hina, "The Earth Is Ablaze and the Heavens Are Burning" (1994).

tions with them. It is strange. In my father's house, there was no love, and I got used to it. Then I became the focus of another man's love for ten years, and I got used to it [whispering]. And suddenly it was gone.

My father was not a feudal [lord] because in our area we did not have big landholdings, only small-time landlords. He was not so rich when we lived in South Wazirestan, and he would not give any money to my mother. But when he came to Khyber and became a commandant of the whole area, he made his fortune. He is about seventy years old now [1992] and lives in a village in the North-West Frontier Province. After retiring from Khyber in 1975, he entered politics in Peshawar. But suddenly one day in 1980, he decided he did not want to have his family live in Peshawar anymore. The younger girls were in college, and my brother was in high school. My sisters did everything to change his mind, but he said, "No, my sister has a better idea." He put the girls in a hostel and turned my brother out of the house and told him to get lost. My mother could not do *anything*.

Yes, the son he expected so much, his only son! That is what I am saying. This was a young boy of fifteen. He loaded my father's stuff in the truck—my father was too big [important] to do it himself. But because my brother was very tired, he decided to stay in Peshawar overnight. The next day when my brother got to the village, my father turned him out because he had disobeyed his order by not immediately following him to the village. My brother had to come back to Peshawar to live with my sister. My brother-in-law is very easy-going, but not my husband—he was not very talkative. My brother and my husband never developed rapport, and he could not feel comfortable with my husband.

My younger sisters had to leave the hostel because the university closed down after three months, and they had to go and live with my father in the village. But my father made their life so miserable that they left and came to live with us. That man is a real bad psychotic case. He beat one of my sisters so savagely once, all because she saw a snake and had one of our servants kill it. He beat her up, for what right had she to kill the snake?! None of my sisters got any financial help from him. We have been taking care of my two younger sisters since 1980. My husband would always leave money for them on the mantle piece, with a note saying "for the girls." It would be there so that I would not have to lose my pride [asking him for money]. My husband and my brother-in-law paid for my sisters' and brother's education, and they all completed their education.

My father for all these years would not let my brother go and see him. My brother tried because he thinks it is his religious duty, but that man just would not let him in. My mother would come to visit us, but she had no say in the matter. If she opened her mouth, he would yell at her to get out and get lost, and for her to open her mouth would be a crime.

Kinship Drama: Dancing to the In-Laws' Tune

My husband was the first of three brothers and had an elder sister. He was a decent man but bad-tempered. He was very different from other members of his family. He loved me, but his family would put lots of pressure on him to control "his wife" because they realized that I was different. Sometimes to goad him into action, they would chastise me in front of him, and this would sometimes get to him, and then we would have a fight. Our sons never grow out from being their mother's sons. He was such a fine person but sometimes needed to show his mother that he wasn't being manipulated by me. That is why I sent my son away to Italy. If they become that much attached to their mothers, then they cannot have good relations with their wives.

Our first son, Motayyib, was thoroughly spoiled by his paternal grandfather. He would get my son just about anything he ever wanted. But my son suddenly grew into a mature young man. He wants to continue his father's profession and to become a doctor [beaming with pride and pleasure]. My father-in-law would do anything for my son. When he was born, my in-laws celebrated lavishly and distributed gifts and sweets to everyone generously, but they did not want to do that for my girls. Poor girls! It seems as if they descend upon us of their own choice! So I decided to celebrate just the same for my daughters. In our culture, little girls always have to defer to boys, young or old. If a little girl wants to have a cookie, she is scolded to wait for her brother. That is why my sisters and I are such strong women because we did not have an older brother. All men are terrible in my family [laughing]. Too often families don't take care of their daughters, thinking that they are for other families.[17] They think that their sons will take care of them when they are old, but most often it is the girl who takes care of her parents.

My husband, like me, had very clear-cut ideas about how things should or

---

17. The belief that girls are raised "for other families" is very widespread in South Asia and is not exclusive to the Pathans. Because marriages are arranged and are usually patrilocal, young women leave their own families to live with their in-laws, hence the expression.

should not be. Naturally, because he was the husband, he expected that in those areas I should give in [amused]. Well, I had lots of problems with that, and we had lots of arguments. I would give in, in the end. Even so, I would find it difficult to reconcile to something with which I did not agree, but which I had to force myself to do because he expected it. He never interfered in the household affairs. Our arguments were mostly regarding our relationships with his family, enforcing certain restrictions on me because that is what his father would have liked or that was what his sister expected because he was living in *this* society. He was very conscious of the society around him, and he expected me to live within the framework of the society and family, but I always felt [laughing] that the society was never worth my living within its framework. But he expected that of me, and I found it very difficult to do that [laughter].

He was his mother's child, as I told you. Sometimes we had *big* arguments, but then he also was a reasonable person. When he did listen to his mother, he would immediately come home and somehow pick an argument with me. But then he would stop, and I would be the one who would be really screaming and battering [laughter]. I would start screaming. Then he would go back and sort of think about the two, and if he realized that it was not my fault, he would come and apologize. He would always come back with a present. You see, that was the greatness in him. I mean, a hundred times I knew it was my fault, and I never said sorry to him, but he would [prolonged laughter].

He had only one sister. She was older than my husband, and his mother felt that we should all be dancing attendance on her and her children. I could not do that. I mean, like it was not as if I did not want to, but it is just not in me to dance attendance on anybody! I believe that people are friends, or people are relatives, and you just get together and you talk and things like that. But getting up every time somebody enters the room and seeing somebody off to the door every time that person is walking—that kind of thing I just cannot do. Then there are things like hospitality etiquette [exaggerating the vowels].[18] If guests came to my mother-in-law's house, I would greet them, I would serve them. But if this visitor was not for me, and it was for my mother-in-law, then

---

18. Pathans are famous for their *melmastia*, hospitality, which forms one of the four major codes of honor or Pakhtunwali among them. The other three include *jerga*, the assembly of the elders; *nanawatee*, peacemaking; and *badal*, revenge (A. Ahmed 1976, 1980; Caroe 1983; Lindholm 1982; Moorhouse 1984).

I would just go back to my room and read a book. She did not like that. She expected me to be there the whole time.

We lived with my in-laws for four and a half years after we came back from England, so it was really very petty things, but they were still there. I mean, like for me they were petty, but for them they mattered a lot. I mean, I don't blame them because in the sort of society we live, generally people accept the demands of the society. Hospitality is a major part of that. If a guest comes, even if it is not your guest, you just sit there very attentively because it is expected. You see, this is part of the custom in this society. I did not really agree with her, but, again, it is expected that you dance attendance to the husband's sister, the whole family. This is customarily expected. I thought, "Fine." I mean, I told my husband, "I am not against you doing whatever you want for your sister. If you want to see her ten times a day, please do!" I mean he can go and spend the whole day or night with the sister for all I care, but you cannot expect that from the wife [high pitched]. But *that* is expected of the wife. Then if I did not do things she [her sister-in-law] expected, she would go and complain to him. It would bother him, but you see that is because he loved me so much. He really cared so much, and he did not want anybody saying anything negative about me. That is what used to make him angry. He felt that with a little effort from me, nobody would say anything negative about me. It was not as if he was more for them or cared more about them and less about me. That was not so. But it was just that he could not abide anybody saying anything negative about me. For me, it was not a big deal. If they wanted to say negative things, let them [laughing]. That was the difference.

Religion, Custom, Women

Women's position has *always* been bad in this society [raising her voice]! And I cannot say that it is getting better or worse with this so-called Islamic revivalism. This is the way it has always been since my childhood, and I do not see any changes happening in the near future. I can talk myself blue in the face, but it will be still the same. It is not going to change in our generation. Perhaps one could talk about a "fundamentalist momentum," if one were to take the perspective of the country as a whole. But its impact as yet has not been felt in Peshawar because what you are feeling right now or see to be happening has always been there. I mean, OK, take the Hudood Ordinance[19] or the clause for stoning a woman to death for adultery. Women have *always* been stoned to death in this society.[20] If a girl elopes or has an affair with some-body—whether she slept with him or not is beside the point—she will be hunted down and killed. The punishment has always been there.

She will be killed just the same, even if she was raped. Her father or broth-ers would be the first ones to kill her. Her body will be found somewhere. They do not want to bear the stigma. It is immaterial whether she did it vol-untarily or was forced. The shame of it is there. I remember when I was very small, twelve or thirteen years old, there was this young girl who was never al-lowed to leave the house, so she could *not* have had an affair with anybody. All she did was apparently smile at a young boy who used to pass by her house. They must have liked each other's looks [laughter]. There was no question of an affair. The two were found and not just killed but cut off [dismembered] [pause]. Where there is even some vague feeling that a woman's modesty is compromised—whether it is rape, elopement, or whatever—her body will be found somewhere.[21]

I am telling you, this society makes me *sick* with its hypocritical standards [raising her voice]. *And* these [standards] are *not* what religion has done to us. They are what *this* society has done to us [long pause]. A lot of people do not even understand religion or what it says. I mean, it is just convenient to say that this is Islam. Nobody knows whether it is Islam or not because they are not conversant with Islam, but it is an easy thing to hide behind religion to get their own way. It is not really the impact of [General Zia ul-Haq's] Islamiza-tion. But because people are more educated in big cities such as Lahore, Islam-abad, and Karachi, their *reaction* is stronger.

Women's Action Forum *is* a failure.[22] OK. I won't say these women should not keep talking. They should because a point *might* come when we may have

19. See chapter 1 on Zia's Islamization program.

20. I suppose by "this society" she means Peshawar and not Pakistani society in general.

21. "No woman in the world," writes Moorhouse, "can be more jealously possessed by their menfolk than the women of the Pathans, and it is both rare and dangerous for a male outside her family so much as to look upon a Pathan woman's face. The most innocent exchange of this kind could mean death for them both, and a simple touch of hands most certainly would" (1984, 185).

22. I asked her, "What do you think of the Women's Action Forum?"

some sane, rational people sitting at the top who will listen to all this. In Peshawar, most women do not even dare to raise their voices in their own house because, according to their husbands, they should not even be having an opinion. What do they understand about world affairs?

Community of Women

Most women, married or unmarried, young and old, feel insecure in their relation to a widow [laughter]. I am a female. Our indoctrination is such that even females don't understand what I am doing. I don't think my life inspires any change. Not at all. I have left a lot of my friends because of that, mostly those whose husbands were my husband's friends. It was not as if these people were my friends—it was not. My husband and their husbands were friends. Then I noticed the slight strain if I visited, so I said, "Fine." I mean, I don't want to be the cause of anybody's distress. I backed off because frankly I did not have the time and energy to waste on people who felt that way. I would much rather waste my time and energy on more constructive things, so I just backed off. I felt there was no point. It wrecked relationships, but even if there were the slightest tension, I would back off. It is understandable, I think, because in a society like this there is so much frustration amongst men. And men—despite this closed society that they have made, where they will not allow their wives and their daughters to move around freely, to think freely, to act freely—get really fascinated by a woman like me! [Amused.]

With my relatives, it was this other thing. Knowing that I did not get along with my father, they felt that if they were too friendly with me, then they might lose his friendship. You see, he is a well-respected man in society. People run around him because he has wealth and status. What can a widow give them? It is a matter of prestige to be seen in the society of people like that.

I have got about a half-dozen friends whom I meet about once every two months. We sit together and have a good chat, and we are all comfortable with each other. I am also close with my cousins. I have got to like my father's brother's daughters and feel *very* close. We can rely on each other. I can depend on them and their husbands to be helpful whenever I need it. It has never been a question there.

I do not think the bond between women is greater in our male-dominated

society, no, not at all.[23] There is so much insecurity amongst women themselves that they will never even think about giving each other support.[24] Basically the environment makes us such that we are concerned only with our own
petty problems. We never think on a larger scale. So, at least in the near future,
it is never going to be that. The concept of a support base for females amongst
themselves and for themselves is just not there. It does not happen here,[25] the
community of women. I do not know about other places. I have never studied
society that way to know, but I know that at least it *does not* happen here because the concept is not there. If you were to turn to a female for help or advice, she would be at a loss as what to say. I am not talking about small things
like a few friends helping with one's party or a wedding. That is a different sort
of thing. What I am talking about is when you are in a real problem. They
would be completely at sea, even if they wanted to help. I do not know about
other women, but as I told you, I look at myself. I have never been able to talk
about things to anybody, not even to my sisters.

I have got this strange attitude. I always feel that everybody has enough
problems of their own, and I am doing nobody any favor by burdening them
with my problems when I know most people do not have any answer to them.
So what is the *point* of just talking about it and giving somebody else even half
an hour of tension and worry? My easiest way to release tension, if something
really drastic happens and I am very unhappy about it, is to come home and
close the door, read a book or magazine. I would just pile up a whole lot of
things, and I would read and sleep, read and sleep, and that may go on for a
good two days. Then I get into my car, and I just go for a drive and *that is* that.
By that time, I have come to terms with it. I find that a better way than burdening people with problems.

But, you see, I have never been that intimate or close to people because I
have always felt it is none of my business to ask people probing questions or to

23. For a different and fascinating account of the community of Punjabi women, see Suleri
1989.

24. See Tehmina Durrani's novel *Blasphemy* (1998), where she dramatizes the terror unleashed by an evil patriarch who controls all the economic and emotional resources and how it
therefore prevents women from forming alliances.

25. Sunder Rajan (1993), an Indian scholar, makes a similar point in her interpretation of the
short story "Prison."

ask about their life. I think that it is something very private, and you really have to be very close to a person before you do that. For that matter, I have never unburdened myself, and that is why I have never tried to interfere in other people's lives. I have tried to help people, but I never ask them questions. If I see somebody who requires my help, I will just go and help. But I have never asked anybody for help. I would feel very uncomfortable if I became too dependent because the only person I was very close to was my husband.[26] I have so far not felt the need that badly enough to become too close to anybody else.

No Replicas, No Replacement

No, no. It is not because I am afraid I might replace my husband with someone else; as I told you, I like people with clear-cut direction. I have always had very clear-cut ideas. So the question doesn't arise because for me the minute he died, I assumed his role and my own. I always knew that my children came first. Even if I unburdened myself to somebody, it would never be somebody to replace *him*. He had such a special place that nobody could take it. I was thinking that *that* situation has never occurred. I have never found any person with whom I felt I could unburden myself or that I could get too close to. It has never happened. If it happened, I would just let it happen.

Well, maybe unconsciously I might have not let it happen. I mean, there are times when I make comparisons, but then, mind you, as I told you, he was a difficult person, so I knew his weaknesses also. I mean, the thing is that I have never tried to replace him with another person—not because of myself, but because of my children. Although a few times when my children were naughty, I threatened them that I would get married and leave them. But I feel that no man is going to give my children the same love, the same affection that their own father would have given them. Maybe mentally that person wouldn't even accept them because they are another man's children. I have never felt that urge bad enough that I must confide in somebody. That is my pride. I *do not* want the entire world to come and know about my problems. I do not confide in my siblings either. We sort of talk on the surface, but we never have gone too deep into things because it is the same with all five of

---

26. For a depiction of an extreme fear of dependence and the will to be self-reliant, see the short story "The Hand Pump" by Khadija Mastoor (1981). From a Sufi point of view, one is to be dependent on none other than God (Smith 2001, 25).

us—that pride. We don't want people asking probing questions. We don't want to confide in people to that extent.

In Search of a Job

My husband died on June 28, 1983. I was trying to come to terms with what was going around me and getting things sorted out. But after the forty days was over, I started the job search, and by September I had a job. I had to look for a job because my father was pushing me to live with my in-laws [agitated]. He wanted to get rid of me. I did not have any money [sigh], but I had a car, and I had to manage to get money from somewhere. The car was the easiest thing to dispose of. That allowed me to keep some money in the bank so that I could keep the house running. I own this house. At that time, there must have been no less than seventy international NGOs [nongovernmental organizations] in Peshawar. I probably could not have worked in a local office, and my family and in-laws would have made greater objection if I, a Pathan woman, were to work for local offices. I must have walked to each and every office. I was footsore from going around to agencies. I was just lucky to find a position at the UNHCR [United Nations High Commissioner for Refugees]. In fact, it was a very lucky break for me, and I am *very* grateful to God for it because it was one of those things that just happened. You cannot plan it. It happened because I went to UNHCR. They called me for an interview with twenty other females. They selected me and another girl for the finals. Our qualifications sort of balanced out. She knew Persian, but then she was too young. But my English was better, and my age was just right as far as they were concerned. We were both called for a second interview.

Now, the governor of this province also had a candidate, a very strong candidate. He just called the head of the office and said, "I am sending this woman, and you give her the job." The head of the suboffice that interviewed me was scheduled to have lunch with the governor. The commissioner of the Afghan refugees was also going along to the same lunch. They were fated to travel together. On the way, the commissioner asked the subhead what happened with the interviews. The fellow said, "Well, my colleagues have interviewed them, and the best person will be chosen," because he did not want to commit himself to him. The commissioner said, "What about Mrs. M. Shah?" The fellow said, "I just told you, my colleagues interviewed them, and they will give the report." But this name sort of stuck in the commissioner's mind—

Mrs. M. Shah. He did not know who this Mrs. M. Shah was. When they arrived at that governor's house, the first thing he [the governor] asked was, "What about that job? I sent you a lady for it. Give it to her." Now the commissioner did not want to commit himself to the governor because the governor would then keep sending people, and the commissioner would be forced to employ them. So it just popped out, and he said, "I think my colleagues have selected Mrs. M. Shah" [laughter]. And the other man quickly added, "Sir, do you remember Dr. M. Shah's widow?" Then the governor said, "Oh, fine. Fine. Better than my candidate. You give it to her. She deserves it."

That is how I got my job! Then you start believing in fate, in luck. Can you imagine? I was footsore for going around to all these agencies. Then I got this job just like that! It does not just happen. God has been extremely kind to me. Touch wood. I am really very grateful for all he has done because I have always managed to be at the right place at the right time where jobs are concerned, because the minute I start feeling economic pressure, something comes along to alleviate that.

I worked for UNHCR for about four and half years, and from there I went to the United States Information Service [USIS], where I worked as the cultural affaire's officer for two and half years. Then I moved to ACBAR as the head administrator, and I have been there for almost two years. Maybe because it is such a diverse community, my status as a widow did not affect my relationships at UNHCR at all. All those expatriates have been exposed to so many cultures and peoples. In fact, everybody took great care of me because they felt that I was somebody who must be given special attention. I mean, I used to have my moments of real tension and depression, and there were times when I would scream at my boss. I just could not help myself, but he would smile and never shot back or tried to show me my place. UNHCR was a unique experience, I think. My first loyalty, as I keep telling everybody, is always to UNHCR, no matter where I go. They were so good to me. If I ever get an opportunity, I would love to go back there.

The USIS position came along at an ideal moment because I needed the money at that time. The children were growing up, Motayyib changed schools, and I was paying much more for his new school. He was a teenager and more expensive, and so I needed extra cash. Initially there was tension in the USIS. It was because I was given the senior-most position above people who had already been there for many years, and they were all men. They were all Pakistanis, and they could not understand why this woman who has come out of the blue is being given the senior-most post while they were being ig-nored. Some were older than me, some were the same age—different ages. But that [attitude] must have lasted a maximum of two months. To this day, they are all very close friends. Sometimes I feel as if I am still running the American Center [laughter]. There were a few women, but they were secretaries and re-ceptionists. I was the only one with authority.

At ACBAR, however, the resentments *are* there because there are two or three Afghans who feel that as a woman I should not be there to begin with, particularly since I am a woman of this area. You see, they can accept expatri-ate women because they think that is what they do. But *me*? A woman? A Pathan woman? I should not be there in the first place, and if I needed to be there, then their concept of a woman is that she should always be below them. I should have been either a secretary, a receptionist, or a library assistant, but as head of the administration, I am the one who develops policies and pushes them down their throats whether they like it or not, so that is the cause of re-sentment. But it is me as a woman they resent and not as a widow. My relation with my women coworkers is much better.

Education and Empowerment

I did my matriculation at Presentation Convent in Peshawar, and I received my BA from Government College for Women in Multan in 1969. Then there was a gap because I was interested in doing my MA in political science. That was not available in Multan, and my parents would not send me to hostel, so I had to wait till my father was posted out to a place where I could do it. We came to Peshawar, and I got admission in political science, but by that time Mokarram had come along [laughter], and so I got married. That was the end of my education then. There was no time. Then I became a widow, and I thought, "I have got to do something. I do not have *any* qualifications for any-thing." I thought, "With my BA I will not be able to get a job good enough that I can bring up four children [her youngest child, Masood, was talking with her, distracting her momentarily], and I have got to do my MA." You see, I started doing it immediately. I got admission as a private student in the politi-cal science department while I was doing my job. I would come home, and be-cause the children were so small, I had to give all my attention to them and their studies. Two were in school, and these two [pointing to Zara, eleven, and Masood, nine, now playing in the room], were very small. So at nights, after I put them to bed, I would do my studies. I had this regular arrangement of studying between twelve and two or twelve and three o'clock in the morning. These two years went along fine, and I got through. There was only one paper left for me to clear.

I missed my final paper because one of my children was not well. Frankly, I did not prepare for it, and I felt I just could not leave my sick child. But by that time I had gotten used to the university atmosphere and going to school. I thought, if I have this opportunity, why not go into a profession? I thought that maybe a profession in the long run would help me more. I knew a little bit about law. My father-in-law was a lawyer, and he would discuss things with me at times. I thought, "Let me try to see if I can get admission in the Law College." I was lucky and managed to get admission.

Admission to the Law School has become pretty strict over the past few years. In my case, it was doubly difficult because I was doing a job, and so I had a problem of attendance. And I was past the age for normal admissions. There was an age limitation. I had to get clearances from the Ministry of Education to be able to get admission. There were multiple problems, but somehow I stuck it out, and here I am [laughing]. I started law school in 1986 and finished it in 1989. Well, it used to be a two-year term, but now they have made it into a three-year term, but there was a long gap. The university was closed because of unrest, and another reason was that there were massive irregularities in the examination hall, and because of that the university administration canceled the exam. So we had to sit for a second time to take the exam. That is why it took longer than usual.

Legal Apprenticeship

I am not concentrating on any specific area. It is general law—constitution, civil law, and criminal law—*all* kinds of law, generally. We also learn all about Muhammadan law and Muhammadan jurisprudence. After that you become an apprentice to learn practical law. That is where you can decide for yourself what specialization you are more interested in. Then you can concentrate on that one. I mean, it depends on one's own aptitude and interest. For me, the interest is just legal aid wherever it is needed; I will just do that. But at the moment I am not even thinking of practicing because I feel that unless I have a real knowledge of law, it would be unfair.

As part of my legal apprenticeship, I go to the chambers as often as I can.

My boss, Nasserul Mulk, is a very accomplished lawyer. He is a barrister-at-law from England, and he gets all kinds of cases. He is very popular. I am not keeping away from studying, though. Every time a case comes up, you pick up one book, and you read it for a particular law; then it refers to another one, and so on. Right now, I feel, "OK, I can go and fight a case." I have that kind of confidence, but I do not think I want to do it yet. Unless I myself am confident enough that I have really understood law, and at this moment I don't feel I have understood it as such, I would rather work as an apprentice. I go to his chamber and prepare cases there. In the preparation of a case, lots of things are needed. He gets very diverse cases: criminal, civil, and banking. I am not interested in the banking laws *at all*, so I have never even looked at a file—even if he has asked me. There are times when he asks me to read a particular file. I say, "Nasser Sahib, I can't do it. It just doesn't register, even when I am reading. So why make me do it?" But he is a *fantastic* teacher. He is a good guy. He has got the patience of a saint. I mean, his patience would put a saint to shame [laughter].

He will put a file in front of us, and he will say, "OK, that is the file. Read it." First, you have to understand what is being said, under what section of law a person is being tried. Then you have to find out about that section, you see, because there are so many sections of law that are very difficult for us novices to remember. You have to keep going back to the books. Then we have to find precedents. If we are on the defendant's side, then we have to find precedence for the defense. If you are the prosecution, then you have to find precedence for the prosecution. That is how you learn: when you constantly find precedence, then you find a judgment; then you try to find a loophole in the judgment that you can use in your own case because no two cases are similar. Some are different, but you have to find justification, and that is how you learn. If we find precedence and feel that it might be even slightly compromising to our case, we just forget about it. So a case of conflict with the Shari'a does not arise for us. You see, it is for the judges to interpret the law. Most probably, what we have set aside the contending lawyer will bring up. You just hope that the sitting judge has a broader concept of law and will decide the case on its merit rather than stick to this particular point.

The prosecution does not try to inject Islamic law into cases—at least not in all the cases that have been tried in front of me. That has not happened, ex-

cept if a case was specifically under the Hudood Ordinance. I think that basically they are also a bit worried of applying something that may have reper-
cussions later on. Right now the Islamic laws are all being constantly
interpreted and reinterpreted, and I do not think the lawyers want to get
mixed up in that. For the time being, law is the Anglo-Saxon laws that we have
inherited from the British. There have been modifications and amendments to
it, but basically it is still those books.

You see, we have got a big problem with our judiciary. Our judiciary is not
independent of the executive, and our judges are all political appointees. *And*
we have all these special courts. So far there is no clear distinction about the
lines of duties and responsibilities of these authorities. It has created even
more confusion than there was before. We now have got three parallel judicial
systems: there are the regular courts; there are the federal Shari'a courts;[27] and
then there is the Special Court.[28] So we have now got three systems running
every which way, and they have created a whole lot of confusion, especially
with the special court, which has gotten special privileges and special protec-
tions. They seem to have started feeling as if they are somehow a little above
the regular courts, although they are *not.* They are a normal court, with normal
judges. But even when you are talking to them generally, you get this feeling
that they think they have more authority and that they have more freedom to

27. "The Federal Shariat Court (F.S.C.) and the Shariat Appellate Bench of the Supreme
Court were incorporated into the constitution [of 1973] and to the detriment of other constitutional bodies, given enormous power in the domain of legislation. The F.S.C., by the very nature of its functions is unique. Its creation was motivated, ostensibly by the urgent desire to
determine whether or not a law was in conformity with injunctions of Islam" (Sardar Ali and Arif
1994, 10).

28. The incorporation of parallel judicial systems into the Pakistani Constitution began in
the aftermath of the military coup of 1977 by General Zia ul-Haq and against the specific order
of the Supreme Court, which "cautioned the Martial Law Administration against establishing
parallel judicial forums" (Sardar Ali and Arif 1994, 7). Sardar Ali and Arif argue that through the
"dubious use of his limited powers" General Zia amended the Constitution and changed "the
rules in the middle of the game" (1994, 6). "The constitution as it stands today, includes three
distinct judicial systems, i.e., the Federal Shariat Court and the Shariat Appellate bench of the
Supreme Court, the criminal law forums established under Article 212B of the constitution, and
a newly inserted Article 2-A. The interpretation of this article (2-A), may cause all the constitutional courts to exercise jurisdiction parallel to and at times overlapping each other and perhaps
even to the legislature" (6).

do certain things. So the prospects for changes in the human rights in Pakistan *are* a dream.

Human Rights

I want, at some point, to be able to sit on committees that are drafting laws on human rights. I have seen so much misery around me—so much poverty, violence, and abuse. There is such a *big* gap between the haves and the have-nots. The have-nots, male or female—I have never made a distinction between men and women where human rights are concerned—and the poor just get the wrong end of the stick every day, and that really bothers me. I'll tell you about a case.

There was a man, a very poor man—it was lucky for him, I guess, that I was in the chamber at the time when he came to see Nasser Sahib. He had almost no shoes on because they were all torn and they were tied with strings in places. He had those *chappa*les, which at some places were tied with strings. He was an old man. His son had been murdered in front of him in the field. He was the eyewitness. He had the machete, the murder weapon, but the other side, who committed the murder, had more clout. They had money. They had status. He just felt so miserable and powerless because the fellow who had committed the murder was acquitted in the lower court—they said there was noncorroborated evidence. And they tried to prove mala fide intent. But this man knew that because his case was off for hearing before somebody who was known to the council for the accused, he would never get justice. He did not have the money to approach anybody. Because he was from Swat, somehow somebody had directed him to Nasser Sahib [also from Swat]. Nasser Sahib does a lot of pro bono [work], but he was frustrated and did not know what to do because the case was off for hearing the next morning. He did not know what the case was all about. This man had just come with an application, asking if the case could be shifted from this one court to the other.

I happened to be there. I said, "Well, give it to me, and I will give it a try," because, you see, it wasn't to go before the court, but before the district administration. Smaller cases don't come to the courts as such. It was before one of the district officials. So I said, "Let me give it a try." I said, "I know one of the fellows in this department, and if I can catch him, maybe he will be able to change the venue." I went there, and I had to sit till 10:30 at night just to get the signature of this fellow to change the venue. That made me *very* upset. You know, I was always aware of it, but it just brought out the difference between the classes that we have developed in this society. That is why, for me, human rights mean rights for all—male, female, children, everybody.

Human Rights Record in Pakistan

Maybe the human rights organizations here started out well and with all the good intentions. Even now they have all the good intentions, but they sort of developed into an elitist group, which sits amongst itself. They exchange information with each other, and they are not very open to outside people. They do not reach out really to other people. They do not want to draw people. They do not want to find out what kind of potential there is in the society with whom they can work. Now, every three or six month there is a seminar, and the group comes together. People read about it in the papers, and their names seem to be kept alive, but the actual work? I am sure they are doing a lot of work, but the actual work they are doing is not coming out [publicized] so that it can motivate other people so that they can do similar work. You see, there might be a lot of people who have good ideas, who have good intentions, but they do not have that kind of courage, and they need a leadership who can show them the way, and *that* is not happening. The Human Rights Commission is just not doing that.[29] So, at the moment, I doubt that they would have much influence on the law or any *significant* influence on any aspect of social life in Pakistan as far as human rights are concerned. If they just stick to this narrow outlook of things, reading papers [in seminars] is not good enough. You see, even when you have a seminar and workshop, and there are certain recommendations, they have to walk to the corridors of influence and *push* those recommendations down people's throats—those sitting in positions of authority. Those people must be made to realize that these things need to be done. They have to be pushed into that situation, if those recommendations are to be followed up. See, they have to force people—those in power—to take action; otherwise, they are not going to. I mean people in high places, those with a house on two *kanals* [approximately one thousand square yards of

---

29. The Human Rights Commission of Pakistan (HRCP) was established in 1986. It is an independent, voluntary, nonpolitical, not-for-profit, and nongovernmental organization. Its headquarters are located in Lahore. "Nationally, the HRCP has provided a highly informed and independent voice in the struggle for human rights and democratic development in Pakistan" (www.hrcp.cjb.net/).

land] and with three cars, sitting in position of power—they are not bothered about what happens outside their houses.

Another problem is that the human rights groups have never sat down and taken the trouble to really understand Islamic law. So when somebody comes along and says this is in conflict with Islamic law and reads off a few *suras* and *ayaat* and gives out his interpretation, then they think this is Islamic law. You see, this is a long debate. They do not know the answers, and this is what they have to do. They have to understand Islamic law. They have to understand the historical background in which Islamic law came into being. There are a lot of positive things in Islamic law that need to be stressed, but because we do not know what they are and we are very vague about them, we cannot fight the so-called torchbearers of Islamization.

Religion and Culture: Fanaticism and Feudalism

In a feudal society such as this one, you are also up against custom. All these people who are for human rights have servants. I am telling you, we are talking a lot about Islamic law, but if that Islamic law were ever to come into conflict with what is customary *here*, people would forget about Islamic law and stick to their customary law [high pitched].

Look what is happening in the Afghan refugee camps here in Peshawar. It is becoming more and more difficult for women and some male refugees to benefit from or to collaborate with the international NGOs.[30] This is insecurity. It is not religious insecurity. It is cultural insecurity. You see, families are broken up in different camps. They are afraid of being ostracized by their friends if they were to go back to the same society. They are afraid because they have this certain framework in which they live. Kabul is a different place. Kabul is a very modern city where the girls roam around in jeans and T-shirts,[31] but the rural areas are all very conservative. This change [in the refugee camps] is threatening that way of life. It is *not* threatening Islam. It is threatening that way of life, and they are afraid that when they go back, they will not be able to fit into the cultural framework that they once had. They still have this naïve thinking that after thirteen years they are going to be able to have that same

30. Sajida's comments resonate strongly in view of the Taliban takeover of Afghanistan in 1996 and their strict policy regarding women's education, health, and movement.

31. This was before the Taliban took over and imposed a puritanical code on the public, in particular banning unveiled women from the public domain.

framework, which is not going to be possible anyway. But, according to them, they are trying to preserve that way of life so that when they go back, they won't be ostracized.

That is the point I was trying to make about human rights organizations—that they are up against the custom, against breaking this feudal custom and the custom of political nepotism, and not so much against the religion as such.

Civic Sensibility

It is very difficult for me to say why this sense of civic duty is rare in Pakistan. You know, basically this consciousness is never developed in us because from childhood you see servants doing your job for you. OK. You grow up in a certain atmosphere, and it *makes* you selfish. You do not think beyond yourself. It is something that has to be inculcated. I have a sense of it because we were always told from childhood that a servant is a human being, that you have to always be polite to them. The servant is there with you all the time. That was the basis of caring for people. If you start caring for that servant, then automatically you develop the instinct toward other people. If you feel sorry for the servant, then you start feeling sorry for others also, eventually. Also, we saw my mother suffer, and we always wondered whether there was something we could do for her to help her.

The servant is only for your benefit. It is that selfishness that comes with it. Outside of your gate, you do not feel that that is part of you or part of your environment. Cleaning the street is the government's job. And the government doesn't help, you see, because the government says we are a poor country. But the examples they put before us are *not* those of governments of a poor country. How come [raising her voice] the bureaucrats have their cars changed every other year? How come the president and the prime minister go on those ridiculous trips abroad for no purpose at all? They go for pleasure trips at the state expense. People see that and think that if the government can do all these things, then they must be having enough money to deal with cleaning the city. It is a very narrow outlook. You see, I am walking through this dirty street. It is affecting me. It is not affecting Nawaz Sharif [the prime minister] or Ghulam Ishaq Khan [the president], but people don't think that they [themselves] also have some responsibility. They feel it is up to the government to do *everything*. If the bureaucrats can do all these other things, why can't they clean up the mess?!

Save the Children

Well, personally, I was always doing things and helping with all sorts of things—I mean, if somebody came along who wanted to go to the hospital, needed money, or things like that. But then I decided, along with a friend of mine, that we should do something for poor children. Because for our children—you can hear them in the yard [her two younger children were playing in her yard]—this is the playground they have. So I told her, "Look, we are lucky enough to have houses and facilities. If there is a park concert, we can take our children there. But what happens to children who don't have any kind of access to extracurricular activities?" We talked with the patron of Pakistan Children's Academy in Quetta and asked her if she would permit us to open a branch of the academy in the North-West Frontier Province. She said, "Fine, go ahead." But she said, "You have to do all the work yourself, and you have to raise the funds and whatever administrative or logistic support is needed." We said, "Fine." So first we went around convincing ladies that this was a very good thing and they must get involved in it. After that, wherever we could find a spot, where people were willing to rent a room or to allow us to use their big lawn or yard, we would just use that for painting or drawing competitions for children. We would arrange interschool competitions, or we would just let the children run wild. We had children from the inner city who had never even seen the open skies properly. We just got them out and got them together.

We would go to various schools—it is difficult to pick the children up from neighborhoods—and we would ask the principals if they were interested in making their schools a part of this whole system. If they agreed, then we would have them. We started holding functions where we could invite female government officials because that was how we had to raise the funds. Now we are in a position where we can donate school uniforms and books to needy children in schools. We go around, the four of us. You see, it was tough starting it, but now it is a big group. Now I am not even actively involved because it is on its own feet.

Donating Blood

Another thing with which I have always been very deeply involved is the blood donor system. I discovered at the age of fifteen that my blood type, A negative, is very rare in this part of the world. I discovered it because there was a woman in the Lady Reading Hospital desperately needing blood type A negative. We got an urgent call in our college to donate blood. I went, and mine matched. Since that time I have never looked back. I am a voluntary donor on the International Committee of the Red Cross list for Afghan refugees. I am also a voluntary donor for the Khyber Hospital—and for anybody else who might need it [laughter]. When I was in the Law College, I organized the college into blood donor groups, and each group would know when it would be their turn to go and donate blood.

I am still on the blood bank's list of donors. I mean it is a standard joke in my house. Sometimes they announce it on TV that bed number such and such in ward number such and such needs a blood transfusion. If I happen to be in front of a TV, I automatically pick up my chador, and I go to the hospital. If I am not there, my children start shouting, "Ammi, the call has come for you" [laughing]. There have been times when within one week I have donated blood twice. Yeah, I am assuming it is OK for me.

Previously I also thought that one should not donate blood more than once in three months. But what happened was that somebody was sick in Khyber Hospital, and they needed blood. It was 12:30 at night, and they had to operate immediately to remove faulty kidneys. I was called to give blood because my husband was working there [at the hospital]. In fact, my husband called me up and said, "This guy is to be operated on. You come and give blood." I said, "Fine," and went there. A week later, again it was evening, and it was pouring cats and dogs, and this doctor called me up—a relative of mine, a gynecologist.

He said, "Sajida, I want you to come in and donate blood because we have got this newborn infant. The only other A negative that we are aware of lives in an inaccessible mountainous place. The car couldn't go. Nobody could reach that guy."

I told him, "Shafiq Sahib, I am willing to donate blood. It is your patient. You are the doctor. You tell me, it is only a week since I last donated blood. Is it all right?"

He said, "Well, Sajida, let me put it this way; it is a matter of life and death for this child. How would you feel?"

"Fine," I said. The child survived. After that, I have never thought about it twice.

I remember once I was off on sick leave. My boss called me up and said, "Sajida, if you can manage to come to the office for half an hour, I would be grateful because this high-powered delegation is visiting, and you know how to handle these things. Please give me a half-hour of your time." I went there, and this Red Cross man came along. They all have our cards—the ones who are voluntary blood donors. This man came with a card and went straight to my boss's office, and my boss told him, "Look, she is running a high fever; I cannot ask her. Besides, she is doing me a big favor by coming to the office for half an hour to sort out this visit." So the man came to me and said that this Afghan refugee needed blood.

I said, "OK, fine. How bad is the patient? Can it wait till tomorrow?"

He said, "Well, the man is already on the operating table. He is that bad. If he doesn't get an amputation, he is going to die."

I said, "Well, OK, let's go. If you have a couple of aspirins in your office to spare, I would be grateful," and we went there.

The doctor said, "Sajida, I know we have got you under very difficult circumstances because you are not feeling well and everything, but come with me. I must show you what you have done it all for." Shahla, that was *very* satisfying because that fellow was a multiple amputee. I mean, it is like one of those things that I have never felt upset about.

I mean, some things you have to sort of balance out. Me or a person's life—because it might be that somebody's life depends on my blood. OK, I would feel weak for some time, but I am a normal healthy person. It affects me, sure, but it is nothing that cannot be improved by taking care. Thank God I can afford to take good food, lie down, and relax. So it is something that I have tried to balance out. I have always felt that human life is too precious to be ignored. This is such a small consideration.

Medical Scholarship

When my husband died, I decided that I would try to pay the educational expenses of one doctor, and I have kept that up ever since. When one person finishes, then I pick up somebody else's tuition fees from the time they actually enter the medical school. This time it is a girl. Like I told you, for me, it is never a question of male or female; it is just human beings. The first one was a boy. The second one is a girl, and she will be a full-fledged doctor this year, going in for her internship. To choose a particular medical student I have always approached another doctor. My philosophy is that I never let them know that I am paying for their education. They know that somebody's helping them, but that is all. I don't want the gratitude. It is something I feel strongly about. Education is one thing about which I feel *very* strongly. There is nothing I can do about the system because you are talking to brick walls. This is my small contribution to the society. That's all.

I select them on the basis of need and talent both. I have made it clear to the doctor who helps me that it is pointless for me to pay for somebody who is needy but who does not have the talent. What is the point of burdening the society with another below-the-average doctor? It is not going to help a thing. Like this present girl—she is always amongst the top ten bracket in her class. Every year when the exams are over, I always find out what her results are.

Helping the Needy

And then there are three children whom I have picked up [sponsored]. This is a recent development, about a year. Three kids whose father died. The mother is not highly educated. There *is* enough money that they can make ends meet, but I felt that the mother, because she is not that well educated and her family is not that well off to support her, needs to be supported. I thought that a time might come when she might say, "Well, their education is too much of a burden, and let's forget about it." So I thought the best way to help her was to pick up their education fee. She is a distant relative. She knows I am helping her; she does—I mean, because I have to pay to the mother. But again I have taken a promise from her that the children must never find out. I have told her that her children or anybody else must never find out that I am paying for their education. I told her, in fact very clearly, that if I find out that somebody comes to me and says, "You are giving money for these children," I will stop it. No more! So it is a clear-cut understanding. She has a brother and a mother, and, at least so far, they do not know about it. She does not have to give them accounts. You see, her husband left her with enough income. They are not going to find out unless she specifically tells them.

Prison Work

I have only recently started to help women prisoners. It took me a while to come to terms with the idea of visiting a jail, so I must not talk about it [the project] because it is at its very early stages. I don't know what shape it [her help] will take, how it will develop, but first of all I want to be able to help the children in jail—in whatever way I can. That would be my priority. There was the case of a woman, with another lawyer, that kept pending and pending and pending, and no decision was being made on it, and the deferring process went on. That got me put off, and I just felt like visiting this woman in jail because I had heard so much about her case—that it kept going back and forth, that the case was being postponed, that the council was not present, and the like. So I just decided to go and visit the jail to see what was happening. There was another woman with me who had already gone to a jail a couple of times before because she has been a lawyer for a longer period. I would want to identify if there are any medical problems, if there is any possibility women prisoners can be educated.

Waiting for a Savior: Prospects for Change

You know what? I have developed, in my mind, a hero who is a mix of Hazrat Umar [the second caliph, 634–44], and Mustafa Kemal Atatürk [1881–1938] of Turkey. A blend of the two is our only salvation. He would not last very long, mind you. Somebody is going to do him in [laughing]. They did, of course, then, too! Hazrat Umar was assassinated [in 644]. Yes, you are right. One is totally religious and the other secular, but both of them, in their own ways, loved the community they lived in, and they strove to relieve their communities of some of the problems that were brought about by custom and by tradition. First of all, Hazrat Umar was basically a clever administrator who manipulated situations to his own advantage, but he was a very fair person. He set his own example. Like if he came up with a new law, he would impose it first on himself and then on others. There was the case of a Jew who had a complaint against him. Everybody said, "Oh, a Jew? No big deal." I mean, how can he complain against the caliph? But Hazrat Umar brought in a *qazi*, judge, and he stood with the Jew before the judge and asked him to hear them both out and pass judgment. You see? That sort of thing was his only weapon. Then he was strong enough—in a way, he was a dictator—that if he felt somebody was giving him unnecessary arguments or unwanted criticism, "Out! OK fellow, you are not needed." That is the sort of leadership we require in this society because that was generally for the uplift of the people. I mean, look at it. If you really think about it, that is when Islam spread.

Well, Mustafa Kemal is secular, right? I mean, OK, Islam says government and religion are synonymous; they both have to be. But *he* was able to separate them. *He* did not turn Turkey into a non-Muslim country, but he just managed to separate the two. He said, "OK, government ought to be a separate thing, and religion is a separate thing." In the time that Islam came, those two could work together because they were a small community, easily manageable, but in today's world both [religion and state] cannot be the same. Mustafa Kemal managed to separate the two. The man had the courage of his convictions.

You see, I always like strong people. I have no time for people who are weak. Atatürk was a very strong man. He stood by his convictions and managed to get his message through to the people. Somewhere I read this very interesting story. I don't know if it is true because I don't know much about his life. It is just a small bit of information you pick up here and there. The story was that he laid down the law that in mosques nobody was to utter anything political, that they are just to teach people about religion, about goodness, about God, about that kind of thing. He said that if he ever heard a *maulvi* commenting on political matters, that mosque would be razed to the ground, and a new mosque would be created in its place, but that mosque and that mullah are finished [laughter]. It was a very drastic command. But, you see, at least he knew how to get a clear-cut message through to the people.

General Zia [1977–88] was not like that! The difference between General Zia and Atatürk was that Zia never gave us any clear-cut message. That man was ambivalent. He did not know whether he was a religious leader or a military dictator! This is my biggest gripe against him, against *all three* military dictators that we have had. You *come* as a military dictator, then behave like a military dictator. You *are* dictators [raising her voice]. Just dictate the law! You say, this is this, and that is how you behave or else. These people came as dictators, and then they tried to portray an image so that people should fall in love with them, and they managed neither [Laughter]. Not *one* of our politicians is honest with people in this country. Well, this Jama'at-i Islami leader may say *he* is honest. Given a chance, he would be a dictator, too. I mean, he does not know his own mind. He has resigned three times from the cabinet, and he is back in it again! So how can a person like that take this country to its salvation [agitated laughter].

"Witless" Leader

Benazir Bhutto lost a beautiful opportunity. She lost it herself. She is *entirely* to blame. First of all, she came with the wrong motives. She came so that she could vindicate her father. You cannot run a country like that! What happened to her father happened. She—if she were a real politician—must have realized that in a lot of ways her father brought it on himself. To hang him was a very drastic action. It was very wrong. It should not have happened; that sort of precedence should have never been set in this country. But still, that man was no angel! You see, with Benazir one gets even angrier because she was educated. She had the support inside. She had the sympathy abroad. She had a superpower like the United States supporting her. She could capitalize on all these resources. What does she do? This witless woman! Nawaz Sharif has won the election [of 1990]; whether by fair means or foul means, he has won the elections! You have to work with him, and she goes to Lahore, and she makes that nonsensical statement about us against them, he has said this and that.

In a society that is male dominated anyway, a woman has to be ten times more hard working and ten times more careful in what she offers, in what she says. You go on a confrontation course with the army?[32] You go on a confrontation course with the president? OK, you know that the president was not in favor of giving you the government—and I think she should not have accepted the government—but she was young and grabbed the power, anyway. You are aware of that. Now you have to prove yourself. Whatever the reason, he [the president] was pushed into giving you the authority [the prime ministership]; you should realize that *that man* has equal power with you. So you have to bring that man to a working relationship with you [highly agitated].

The opposition did, mind you, try to provoke her, but that is what I am saying! Those guys behaved very badly toward her. They did. OK? I am not denying that. But if she were a clever politician, once she came to power, she should have realized that it meant that those guys, despite their likes or dislikes, *gave* her the power. She had to manipulate them, to bring them to a working relationship with her. You see, Ghulam Ishaq [Khan, president 1989–93] is not a fool. He would never have gone in confrontation against her because he wanted the world to think that Pakistan has got a fantastic president in the person of Ghulam Ishaq. He wanted to portray that image of complete neutrality, see, so he *never* would have come openly into conflict with her

32. "The army's confidence in the civilian government of Benazir Bhutto seemed to remain high. . . . However, differences between Benazir and the army intensified over ethnic tension in Sindh. . . . But where Benazir favored a more restricted role for the army in Sindh . . . the army saw an opportunity to reassert its influence beyond restoration of order." Further, her policy with regard to Afghanistan and India alienated the army. "Such discords indicated that Benazir was bent on reasserting civilian authority by overriding the army. Had she succeeded, her policies could have carried far-reaching implications for the premiership and the future of Pakistan" (Monshipouri 1995, 97).

once he accepted her as the prime minister. But she made all the wrong moves after she became the prime minister, and that is something!

Nawaz Sharif was very much against her, too, but she was the one who made the first speech openly. It was an open invitation to confrontation, and the *stupid* people and advisors around her—and she had this massive load of them—not one of them advised her on that. They all kept saying, "Because the Peoples' Party has popular support, we are going to hold our own against all others. We can go it alone." But they did not have a clear majority. How could they go it alone? The ANP offered their support to her also.[33] She managed to alienate them within three months of coming into power. It was her arrogance. It was her complete and total arrogance.

I don't think she has learned her lessons. No! None of the politicians would in this country. For every politician, it is "make hay while the sun shines," and they are not even thinking about the country. They are not even bothered about its intractable problems. They do not even know what our problems are! You see, they do not come for the purpose of doing something good for this country. They just come with one sole aim: to do away with their enemy or political rivals and to make as much money [as they can]. These are the only two considerations.

Female Heroes?

I am not one of those people who think of people as men and women.[34] I just think of them as human beings. I *could* have thought of Indira Gandhi or Golda Meir [instead of Umar and Atatürk]. Again, both of them have that streak of dictatorship, and I love those women. Anything I could find about Golda Meir I would read. This was from my childhood because she was in power when I was pretty young. I have *always* loved that woman because no matter what she was, she was very clearheaded. She knew in which direction she should take Israel. OK, Israel was in conflict with the Islamic world, it was. But she had her priorities right, and she worked toward those. I was reading one story where she had a cabinet meeting in her house at seven o'clock in the morning. That

33. The Awami National Party, founded in 1986, is a regional party headed by Khan Wali Khan and composed primarily of ethnic Pathans.

34. I said, "It is interesting that you, who are such a strong woman, such a capable woman, someone who has done things that men perhaps would not have been able to do, choose two men as your heroes."

woman, who by that time was past sixty, got up to prepare breakfast for these gentlemen. She is the prime minister of Israel [incredulous]! She could have had her own servants. You see, I like people like that. But she realized that the money that Israel had was to be used for other purposes than her own luxury.

This is what I loved about Indira Gandhi. I visited the place where she used to live. It was a small house, British built, typical cantonment house. You can see hordes of them [in Pakistan]. But our senior officers do not want to live in those houses, which are relegated to officers of major or colonel rank. They want bigger, newer houses. Indira Gandhi lived in a house like that. She walked from her house to the office and from her office to her house.

It beats me why Pakistan does not produce leaders like that.[35] I have tried to think about it from every angle, and it just beats me. The only answer I can come up with is that we have never been blessed with the kind of leadership that we can use as our role models. You see, people do need role models. We have just been unfortunate in that. We have no role models. I don't know why. It is something that I can never answer. I don't have any answer.

What would I do if I were the prime minister [laughing]? I will never be the prime minister because I don't have the money. Well, yaah . . . I do have the conviction, but here you do not become prime minister on convictions. I do not know of *any* public representative who is really a public representative. He is only his own representative, whether it is male or female. They are representatives only of themselves and their families.

Retrospectively Speaking

I'll tell you one thing. Despite what I've said about the society of Peshawar, for me people have been very helpful, wherever I have gone to anybody, and usually I don't go for my own needs. It is people needing help. But any person I have called, anybody I have requested for help, they have given it. So despite the fact that it is a very hypocritical society, it has got many double standards, it is very vicious, it is nasty, it is terrible, even so, personally I won't change it for any other society. There are things I would like to change *in* the society, but individually the people I have come across, the people I have associated with, they have always been lovely people. I wouldn't have managed without this knowledge that these people are there to help and support.

---

35. I asked her, "Why do you think Pakistan has not produced such leaders, women or men?"

Some Reflections: Improvisations on the Theme of Sati

Sajida's journey from being a protected and beloved housewife to a "despised" widow began the process of her social and individual awakening and of her becoming the agent of her own destiny. Her determination to live and in the process creatively to seek "strategies for survival" (Sunder Rajan 1993, 77) and to balance her family life with her professional activities amplifies multiple areas of conflict and tension between individual desire, religion, and cultural practices. It is specifically the story of a widow who chose to live, who refused to commit symbolic sati[36] and rejected the cultural expectation of "self-immolation" at the funeral pyre of her husband. Whereas the discourse of sati, the Hindu tradition of widow burning, has become rather prominent in post-colonial studies, the story of the life that awaits widows who choose to live has been as neglected among scholars as it has been despised among the public, excluding some films and literary work.[37] Here and there passing references are made as to the existence of the practice of levirate in Pakistan and among the Pathans but without much elaboration or ethnographic detail regarding the life the widows actually live (A. Ahmed 1989, 41–42; Lindholm 1982, 128).

The religious and cultural revival of sati in the 1980s in North India caught many by surprise. The Mughal court strongly discouraged it, and Emperor Humayun (d. 1556) is credited to be "the first Mughal ruler to make attempts at preventing widow burning" before the British finally outlawed sati in 1829 (Das 1986; Narasimhan 1990, 109). Roop Kanwar's dramatic self-immolation in 1987 was glorified culturally—much to the horror of some feminists—and her burning was sanctified religiously with the immediate erection of a shrine on the spot where she burned to ashes. Her enigmatic self-sacrifice catapulted the issue of sati to a hotly contested public discourse, prompting the state, activists, feminists, and politicians to revisit issues of its legitimacy, intentional-

36. "Sati has now come to mean widow burning, but the original sense in which it was used was different; it meant a virtuous or a pious woman. The word sati is derived from *sat* meaning truth, and a sati was a woman who was 'true to her ideals' " (Narasimhan 1990, 11). *Suttee* is the act of immolation, and *sati* is the woman who burns herself (Lopata 1996, 23). I follow the generally accepted practice by referring to both the act and the woman as *sati*.

37. Helena Znaniecka Lopata has done extensive work on widowhood in India and cross-culturally (see Lopata 1996), but not in Pakistan.

ity, religious symbolism, and cultural meanings (Narasimhan 1990; Sunder Rajan 1993).

I do not intend to involve myself with the debates regarding whether sati is suicide or murder, or whether the widow is the agent of her action or is compelled culturally. Rather, I want to draw parallels between the two traditions of sati and levirate and to argue that both involve a set of highly institutionalized, superimposing religious and cultural rituals and beliefs used to control women in order to maintain the purity and honor of the patrilineage. Sati is, of course, more drastic, leading to the physical destruction of a woman. With her body burned and purified by fire, she is then rewarded with deification as a goddess, *devi*. Levirate does not lead to the bodily annihilation of the woman and could be argued to be potentially protective of some older widows and of women who choose to stay within the family. Lopata, however, dismisses that argument as a myth and suggests that despite the "idealization of traditional cultures," in fact "all indications point to serious impingement on personal safety, happiness, and all sorts of rights by members of a dependent individual's own family, in the past and present" (1996, 21).

Women, as outsiders, occupy a paradoxical position within their husband's patrilineage because "the patriline's purity of descent is made vulnerable by the affinal women who must bear its next generation" (Bennett 1983, 125). A widow's activities, particularly if she is young and has children, pose a serious threat to the lineage honor. The surest way of keeping the purity and honor of the patriline intact is to have the widow "voluntarily" burn herself, which literally and symbolically purifies the patriline, or to have her submit to the will of the lineage and live under the supervision of the dead husband's brother(s). Among the Pathans, Lindholm writes, "A widow without sons is obliged to marry her husband's brother or one of his *tabur* (cousins). She is not allowed to marry outside her husband's lineage." If she has a son, "[s]he is then prohibited from ever remarrying" (1982, 128). Either way, the threat of dishonor and financial devolution is averted, and purity of patriline is maintained.

In short, both sati and levirate are institutionalized means of preventing or controlling the remarriage of widows. Although remarriage is forbidden by religion for "Brahmin widows and strongly discouraged among all higher castes" (Gujral 1987, 51), there is no Islamic prohibition against widows' remarriage. In fact, Prophet Muhammad himself set the example. Except for his wife, Ayesha, who was a virgin, the rest of the Prophet's wives were either widows or divorced women. Underscoring, however, the tension between religion and culture, Lokhandwala writes, "the Pathans as much resented the introduction of remarriage of widows amongst them by Shah Ismai'l Shahid and Syed Ahmed Brelvi as it was resented in other parts of India" (1987, 5). The similarity of the negative attitudes toward the widows and of the prohibitions against their remarriage among Hindus and Muslims clearly underlines the shared cultural tradition in South Asia, despite the religious differences.

What is significant is that both sati and levirate are fundamentally religious institutions, with this difference: one has its roots in Hindu religion, whereas the other traces its origin to biblical and Israelite tradition.[38] Sati also remains primarily exclusive to the higher castes among the Hindus, whereas variations of levirate spread wide and far as well as up and down the classes. Both sati and levirate are strongly associated with patrilineal social organizations and patrilocal marriage residence patterns. But whereas sati remains exclusively a religious tradition and restricted to India, levirate has taken on local colorings and cultural meanings.

The Pathans, as part of the South Asian culture area as well as a strictly patrilineal and patrilocal ethnic group, incorporated the tradition of levirate and have practiced it since time immemorial. Although Islam explicitly condemns levirate and widow inheritance (Qur'an 2:234, 240; 4:19), the Pathans practice it nonetheless, believing it to be Islamic. Whether Sajida was aware of this tension between religion and custom and knowingly refused to follow the levirate tradition is not quite clear. What is clear is that she was able to thwart the custom of levirate because she was of some means and educated and was determined to support herself and her children. More important, it is clear that Islam is not, textually speaking, simply the repressive instrument it is so often made out to be. Religious discourse, Islam, is hegemonic neither in Pakistan nor among the Pathans; nor is it monolithic. As I argued previously, reli-

---

38. "In biblical times a widow who had no male offspring was obliged to marry her late husband's brother (and the brother was obliged to marry her) 'to build his (late) brother's house.' If the brother refused to marry her, the widow could not marry someone else unless a levirate ceremony was performed. The widow had to remove her brother-in-law's shoe and spit in his direction to degrade him. The ceremony had to be performed in the presence of 'the elders.' At present, the Jewish religious practice does not approve of polygyny, thus the widow's marriage to her brother-in-law is not enforced. However, remarriage of a widow (who has no male child) is possible only after the above mentioned ceremony of levirate has been duly performed" (Katz and Ben-Dor 1987, 243).

gion is a cultural system, and, in this sense, religion and culture have evolved historically and manifested themselves as mutually constitutive.

Sajida was aware that her in-laws perceived her action as dishonorable and considered her as *behaya*, shameless. Even her own father cut off association with her, though he did so perhaps for financial reasons, as Sajida believed, and not so much for moral reasons. Sajida, however, conjured up her inner strength and rescued not only her own life but also that of her children. She then went on to pursue a profession and assumed civic duties and charitable activities. Had she been a man who exhibited similar authoritarian characteristics, admired so much by the Pathan in their leaders, she would have been celebrated as a hero, accorded honor and respect. Sajida was born a woman.

Postscript: I returned to Pakistan in late November 1992, having spent that summer in the United States. I called Sajida, hoping to go to Peshawar to visit her. No answer. I tried again. No answer. After several unsuccessful attempts, I called a mutual friend.

"Where is Sajida?" I asked.

Pause. "Didn't you hear?" she responded ominously.

"What did I not hear? What happened?" I asked anxiously.

Pause. "Uh . . . the plane crash. Didn't you hear it?"

"Oh God. No!" I screamed.

I remembered reading about the crash of a Pakistan airline upon landing in Katmandu, Nepal, but at the time I had no reason to think that Sajida was on *that* plane.

7

Religion
Reinterpreting the Text, Reinventing the Self

Meeting Nilofar Ahmed

IN THIS CHAPTER, we meet a Sufi feminist, who discusses her approach
to Scripture, social values, and women's human rights.[1] Nilofar Ahmed elabo-
rates on how religion for women can be empowering rather than restrictive.
Not willing to relinquish the spiritual world to men, yet not being satisfied
with the direction spiritualism has taken historically or in the "Islamic revivalist" movements, Nilofar and many women like her from the Muslim world are
reclaiming religion. Indeed, they are demanding a return to the principles of
equality and social justice they claim the Scripture envisions for all humanity.

I had read about Nilofar Ahmed before I went to Pakistan and called her as
soon as I arrived in Karachi in June 1998.[2] We met at the elegant Sindh Club,
a beautiful colonial building, from which Indians were long excluded under
the colonial domination. It was a hot breezy day, and we sat beside the pool
under a shady tree, drank ice tea, and talked. Nilofar is a delicate-looking
woman in her mid- to late fifties. She is reserved, soft-spoken, and gentle.

She asked me questions about my project, and before we actually taped our
conversations, we talked about social issues in Pakistan. She started by talking
about feudalism in Pakistan and how it has prevented genuine progress and
change, whereas feudalism in India had been broken up. In her view, Liaquat

---

1. *Sufism* is the generally accepted term for Islamic mysticism (Schimmel 1986, 3). The literature on Sufism, mysticism, and Muslim mystics throughout the centuries is inexhaustible. In
this chapter, the references made to mystic personalities are not intended to be exhaustive but
are drawn from a limited number of sources.

2. See Goodwin 1994, 74–75.

Ali Khan, the first Pakistani prime minister after the partition, was assassinated in 1951 because he wanted to reform feudalism. "Even behind [General] Zia were the feudal generals who helped him to stage the coup against Zulfikar Ali Bhutto. The feudals are heartless people, like Bhutto's own family. They are preoccupied with honor, and honor here means that they should have the final word. It is all a power game. Honor is a matter of power."

I asked her if the recent detonation of the nuclear bomb in Pakistan in May 1998, following the detonation in India, was therefore also a matter of honor. "It is not a matter of honor," she replied. "It is a matter of national security. For Hindus, religion is intertwined with their land. If land is alienated, they consider it a matter of high treason. So partition of the motherland has been very difficult for India. East and West Pakistan were considered the two arms of India, and they think they must take them back. They have never accepted the division."

Then we moved on to talking about religion and fundamentalism. Nilofar perceived many (Pakistani) religious leaders as opportunists and hypocrites. "Several male scholars gave *fatwa*s [religious decrees] that a woman is not allowed to become head of a state in Islam. Then later on, when Benazir Bhutto organized a conference, they all came running in and wanted to be sitting with her [accepting her headship]," she stated. "In my view, a woman can be the head of the state. There is nothing in the Qur'an and hadith that says otherwise. In fact, there was a *fatwa* issued from Deoband[3] that a woman can be the head of the state if she does not take decisions unilaterally and has a team of advisors to assist her. But isn't this true for men as well? Isn't this the Sunna of the Prophet himself?"

I asked her whether she thought Benazir Bhutto's ouster twice (1990, 1996) as an elected prime minister had anything to do with the fact that she was a woman. "Benazir Bhutto," she said, "was corrupt to the core, and her removal had nothing to do with her being a woman. When people ask me why a woman prime minister did nothing for the women of the country, I say because she is a feudal lord first and a woman second. No one is as corrupt as Benazir Bhutto and her husband."

---

3. Deoband is ninety miles north of Delhi and is known for its religious, cultural, historical, and educational importance. Its significance was enhanced with the foundation of the world-famous religious and educational institution known as Darul-Uloom (House of Knowledge). The Deobandi branch of Islam is most popular in South Asia. See Nasr 1994.

Assured of my interest in Islam and feminism and aware of the approach I was taking, Nilofar Ahmed agreed to be interviewed and taped on the condition that I would send the text of the chapter to her before publication. She chose her words with care and precision and often paused to reflect before giving a response. I did send her a draft of this chapter, and she made some minor editorial changes. She was particular about the use of bracketed terms describing emotions—*laughing, pensive,* and so on—and wanted most of them removed. Where she made a change in the text, I refer to it in a footnote. Let us hear from Nilofar Ahmed.

Nilofar Ahmed

Daughters of Islam

As I told you, ten of us got together and discussed the fact that now in Pakistan women are free, almost, to get any kind of education they want. We felt that women were not opting for religious education, and also we felt that they did not realize that their whole life was controlled by religion, that everything had to be sanctioned by Islam. If you were going to go out of your house, you had to prove that this is what Islam has allowed you to do and so on and so forth. We also felt that a lot of the *ilm* or knowledge that has been handed down to us is based primarily on tradition and is a matter of interpretation. We realized that male scholars passed down all these interpretations, and we did not find any female scholars in this line. We were suspicious that there was a lot of masculine interpretation involved in what we were told to do or not to do. Even the most sincere male scholar with the best of intentions could not look at the law from a woman's point of view.

This is the main reason women have to look at the original texts and to reinterpret them for themselves. This is why some Muslim feminists have come forward the world over in order to examine some burning issues and try to find solutions for them. Well, a Muslim feminist is a person,[4] male or female, who is interested in giving women the rights that have been given to them by Allah and His Prophet and that have been taken away by men. You know,

4. I asked her, "Who is a Muslim feminist?"

Marmaduke Pickthall[5] called the Prophet "the greatest feminist the world has ever known." So we got together and set up the Daughters of Islam [DOI] as a nonpolitical, nonsectarian, nonprofit organization.[6] Our basic aim is to promote knowledge, especially among women and children, and to carry out several projects. By knowledge, we do not mean just religious knowledge. We mean all kinds of knowledge, starting from literacy going up to research in Islamic studies, especially about some of the controversial topics, like veiling or divorce and the way it is practiced in South Asia.

I am presently the secretary general of DOI, and I am one of the ten founder members of the organization. [The] Women's Islamic Center and Library is one of the main projects of Daughters of Islam. We do have regular meetings and have at least one monthly meeting for the executive committee. We also organize lectures and other programs. We do have membership. We invite people to become members. Somebody might introduce another person, and we meet them for some time to see if they are what we expect them to be, and if they like us as well, then we invite them to join us. It works both ways. But nobody can just walk in and become a member. It is by invitation.

Of the original ten members, one is dead, and another is terminally ill, but our founder, Ozma Zafar, is going strong, *mashallah*.[7] But every time you try to ask her to participate in activities, she says, "Oh, I have retired. I have just left it all to you. But she is our guiding light. Except for our founder, who is childless, the rest have children, but she has stepchildren, and some of them are really nice to her. She must be in her late sixties now. She is a feminist in the true sense of the word. She is not ready to give in or compromise where women's

5. Marmuduke Pickthall was a British convert and is best known as a translator of the Qur'an "who produced the nearest thing to an 'authorized' English version of [the] sacred book. . . . But he once enjoyed widespread acclaim as a novelist" (Kritzeck 1970, 109). See Pickthall 1977.

6. It is interesting to note that as far back as 1908 some Muslim women in South Asia were active in forming associations. They established the Anjuman-i Khawatin-i Islam (Society for Muslim Women) in Lahore and engaged in reform movements even in the face of verbal abuse hurled at them by the traditionalists. In 1915, the first ever "Muslim ladies" conference took place, attended by wives and relatives of leading Muslim professionals. In 1917, the Anjuman passed a resolution against polygyny, which "caused a minor furor in Lahore" (I. Malik 1997, 142–43).

7. I expressed an interest in meeting the DOI's founder and interviewing her, but she declined, citing ill health at that moment.

issues are involved. She is the one who wants to go out to the street and demonstrate, but other people try to restrain her. You see the reason is that if she starts protesting and doing these things, then we fall in the same category as some other organizations that are purely feminist. We want to keep our image as a religious organization, which we are.

Justice for Women, Justice for All

Our religious feeling is that there should be justice for all, especially the downtrodden, including the women. Well, there are ways to attain justice in a very unjust society such as ours.[8] For example, you might have to go to court; you might help people who are in the court to fight their cases; or you might publish articles to raise awareness, which we have done. I brought you a copy of this paper that I presented at a conference.[9] Some parts of this were published in *Dawn*[10] as an article in two parts. This article gives a lot of quotations from the Qur'an, briefly, and discusses a lot of the issues that the Muslim feminists have been concerned about.[11] People really appreciated it because most do not have these quotations at their fingertips, but at the same time there were some religious women who wrote against me, against feminism, and against all the arguments. This was one of those extremist groups.

Their objection was more like an emotional outburst. They said that the feminists are products of the West, et cetera, et cetera. They did not realize that all the thinking and the arguments were given within an Islamic framework, you know. It wasn't an outsider's view. There was really no chance to get engaged in a dialogue with these extremist women. In the newspaper, there is a limited time and space for which you can discuss certain topics, so for two or three weeks after my article was published, the discussion continued. Some of our members also replied to them, but you can't carry it on endlessly. Of course, there were a lot of very positive responses, too, you know. Some of the men responded so well, which is very satisfying.

8. I asked her, "How is justice attained in a restrictive and unjust society?"

9. N. Ahmed 1992.

10. *Dawn* is one of the most popular and prestigious English daily newspapers in Pakistan.

11. Her booklet (N. Ahmed 1992) includes an introduction; four short segments, consisting of "The Central Teaching of Islam," "The Liberative [sic] Aspects for Women," "The Oppressive Aspects of Religion," and "The Ongoing Women's and People's Movements"; and notes.

Dialogue and Disagreement

Women who are working against us are prominent members of these religious parties. When there are functions and some extremist religious groups are participating, they try to dominate and force us to take a second seat [emphatic]. You see, it is very difficult to get along and to see eye to eye on everything with every organization. So we might have something in common with one organization and something else in common with another organization. If we do, then we cooperate with them. You see, a lot of these religious organizations are not even happy with the name of our organization because it is in English, and they say, "Oh, what kind of women are they supposed to be here?"—you know. They think if you are religious, then you ought to have everything in Urdu or in Arabic and maybe Persian. This is how closed-minded some of these people are.

Maybe they [men from other religious parties] think this is a purely women's organization [pause], I don't know.[12] We haven't thought about this, but maybe this is the point.[13] In several of our functions, we have invited men to participate. We have even invited some male scholars as speakers. But, you see, they think if the name is in English, then a lot of our work will be in English. This means we are all educated in English, and therefore we are a different kind of women. Ironically, we speak mostly in Urdu and not in English at our gatherings. It depends, though. You see, even the Pakistani government conducts all the official work in English. So we ought to have officers to work in English. In our library, we have about 50 percent of our books in English and 50 percent in Urdu. Our library is very small, but it is something different [from the existing ones].

I have been doing some research on divorce and veiling and have written on blasphemy and honor killings, which are some of the very controversial topics in Pakistan. And as a group we have had some successful projects.

12. I asked her, "Do you think they oppose your organization because there are no men at the helm, as there 'should be,' and that they think this is a purely women's organization?"

13. Compare her statement regarding DOI's independence in Pakistan with Dawn Chatty's observation regarding Oman: "In the Middle East, more so than in other parts of the world, there exists a resistance and a hesitancy on the part of the governments to allow women to come together in formal groups. And although a narrow range of women's associations, unions, and cooperatives does exist, these are most often created and tightly organized by men for women" (2000, 241).

Divorce

I don't know how divorce is done in Iran, but in Pakistan a man can just stand up and say "talaq, talaq, talaq." Khalas! That is it.[14] Although legally he has to go to the court and a verbal talaq is not accepted, in actual practice people still think that if he says it thrice, then that is the end of it. Even if they do go to court after that, it is simply to register what they have already done. Most of the schools of Islamic law in Pakistan still say that if you say talaq thrice at one go, that is the end of it! You see, the Qur'an is the touchstone, and you should check everything with the Qur'an. If you cannot find an answer, then you go to the hadith. And if the answer is not clear in the hadith, then you use your own intelligence or go to a scholar for a fatwa. In the case of talaq, the formula is most clearly spelled out in the Qur'an. It is all there, and still there is so much deviation. I have started writing on talaq, but I haven't finished it yet. It is an extremely complex topic.

The reason men have not paid any attention to it is [that] most Muslim men—and not just men—do not read the translation of the Qur'an [in Urdu or in English]. They read it in Arabic, and of course they don't understand Arabic. Very few people sit down to read the translations. The tradition of triple divorce is traced to Hazrat Umar, during whose time people took talaq very lightly. He made a ruling that if a man just says "talaq, talaq, talaq," his wife will become forbidden to him.[15] She had to go, and he could not take her back. You see, his fatwa was that if you say it thrice all at once, the talaq would be

14. "[T]he triple talaq pronounced in one sitting with or without witnesses . . . is by far the most common form of talaq among Hanafi Muslims" (Balchin 1996, 92). However, "Under Muslim Family Laws Ordinance (1961), husband may unilaterally exercise right of talaq, but talaq must be written and notification provided to Union Council and wife. Talaq is only effective after 90 days (or delivery in case wife is pregnant, whichever is later); during this time, Arbitration Council must be constituted for purposes of reconciliation. Talaq-i-bidat [thrice divorce] has no legal validity" (Balchin 1996, 91). The Shi'as historically have disputed the legal validity of the thrice-told talaq and do not recognize it as valid. For a discussion of the variations of divorce in Islamic law, see Sheikh 1989.

15. "It is further recorded that Hazrat Umar made three pronouncements at one sitting, an irrevocable talaq as the punitive measure to punish those who had made a vain sport of the injunctions of the Holy Qur'an and Sunnah. Hazrat Umar, in spite of accepting such a talaq as final[,] used to punish the persons who resorted to it. . . . Hazrat Umar repented later on as the change introduced by him was not strictly in accordance with the Holy Qur'an and Sunnah, and it made divorce easy for those who wanted to indulge in it" (Women's Rights 2000, 29).

final, irrevocable.[16] Take that one ruling that was meant for a special time and purpose, and apply it to this day and age, especially when the Qur'an has the whole formula spelled out—I don't think it is right.

The Qur'an's formula is that when the man pronounces the *talaq*, he and his wife have to continue to stay in the same house.[17] He also has to make sure that she is cleared of her menstrual cycle. Then he has to wait a whole month while also continuing to support her. He can then say the *talaq* again after a month has elapsed, given that all the above conditions are met. During these two months, he can always take her back. But if he does it [pronounces the *talaq*] the third time, after another month of waiting, then the divorce becomes irrevocable.

I think the wisdom behind this [process] is to give a chance for tempers to cool down because it is so easy for a man to get mad and say "*talaq, talaq, talaq.*" So if he has to live for a month with the same woman in the same house, it becomes clear to him whether he wants this woman or not, whether he wants to live with her, and I suppose it becomes clear to the woman as well. You see, in this kind of *talaq*, which is initiated by the man—there are different kinds of *talaq*, and I am sure you know all that—the woman cannot take initiative, but she can decide whether she wants to come back to him or not.

But, of course, there are other kinds of *talaq*s, which a woman can initiate. Let me tell you about this very interesting point. In the Hanafi School of Law, women are allowed to have a right to initiate the *talaq*, which, as far as I know, is not recognized by the other three Sunni schools of thought.[18] Technically this is a little different from *khula*,[19] where a woman initiates a divorce, but for

16. Reconciliation between husband and wife is possible only if the woman marries another man, divorces him, and then remarries the first husband. This procedure is known legally as *tahlil* or as *halala* in local Pakistani usage (Qur'an 2:230).

17. Qur'an 2:228–32, 236–37, 241; 65:1–7; 4:35.

18. The Shi'a School of Law has provisions similar to that of the Hanafi School of Law.

19. "According to Muslim jurisprudence and the law of Pakistan, a woman may ask the court to dissolve her marriage when, from her point of view, she can no longer live with her husband 'within the limits prescribed by Allah'—in other words when an irretrievable breakdown of the marriage has occurred" (Balchin 1996, 97). "Courts granting *khula* usually rule that woman has to give up her dower as *zar-i-khula*; where wife fails to pay this amount, husband has to file separate suit for recovery of *zar-i-khula*" (Balchin 1996, 91). The logic here is that whereas *talaq* is a unilateral right of the husband, *khula* is a form of agreement, a contract, to which the husband must agree, and for that matter the wife needs to compensate him in order to secure her divorce. See also Fayzee 1974, 163; Mannan 1995, 466.

which she has to go to court. But the Hanafi school of thought allows a woman at the time of her marriage, *nikah*, to ask to have the right to initiate the *talaq*. *And* the strange thing is that it is actually written right there in your *nikah namah!*[20] But 99.99 percent of the Pakistanis don't know this, and the *qazi*, judge, who comes to perform the marriage ceremony just crosses it out!

Why? That is because he does not want the woman to have this right! If somebody brings up this clause [at the time of marriage], everyone says, "How can you talk about *talaq* at this happy time? It is like a bad omen." This is emotional blackmail. If something were to be accepted from the very beginning, then it wouldn't be considered a bad omen. One of my aunts is a bit of a feminist, and when one of her nieces was getting married, she said, "We want to keep this condition in the marriage contract." But other people criticized her, and because it wasn't her own daughter, she could not push it further. Also the *qazi* said, "Listen, I have already canceled it!"[21] You know, so often women get the *nikah namah* in their hands, and they can read it, but somehow to talk about this condition—*talaq* at the time of marriage—is taboo. But I have met a few young women who have taken advantage of this right. You see, the idea is not to encourage divorce, which, even though permitted, is disliked by God, but simply to benefit from Allah's mercy, grace, and wisdom, which is hidden behind this permission.

At our organization, we do occasionally talk about it [taking the right to divorce at the time of marriage]. You see, in Pakistan the marriage ceremonies and conditions are set mostly by the parents. Even if the girl is educated, she does not really interfere in terms of deciding on the kinds of conditions, except to say "yes" or "no" for the selection of the boy.

20. "Standard [Pakistani] *nikahnama* carries provisions for delegated divorce and restrictions on husband's right of divorce (columns 18 and 19). Column 17 of *nikahnama* specifically provides for insertions of any special conditions to the marriage (e.g. restrictions on husband's right of polygamy); column 20 allows for any other documented stipulations for dower, maintenance (wife's pocket money) etc." (Balchin 1996, 57).

21. In Iran, various "conditions" also are stipulated in the marriage certificate. The change was brought about under the Family Protection Law of 1967, which was further amended in favor of women in 1975. Although the Islamic Republic of Iran initially made the Family Protection Law illegal, gradually the courts admitted the "conditions" to be exerted in the marriage contract. The marriage registrar or the mullah who performs the ceremony presently is obliged to read every single condition out loud and to allow the bride and groom a chance to decide whether they want to sign their agreement to the conditions. They can sign their agreement to some or to all or to none.

We get very different reactions from women when we talk to them about such feminist interpretations of divorce, depending on their way of thinking and their backgrounds. You would be surprised to know how many young Pakistani educated women think conservatively! Sometimes they are what in the West they call "fundamentalists." Some of them might not be veiled but still follow the tradition blindly.[22] What I am trying to say is that not 100 percent will buy what we are saying. For example, I have spoken about veiling, and I did a bit of study on the topic. You would be surprised how many young women, quite well educated and very intelligent, said that they did not want to believe that there was no face veil prescribed in the Qur'an. Even though they themselves did not wear a face veil, they insisted that this is what is prescribed.

Veiling

I'll tell you something secret. I have done some serious research on veiling. The reasons why I have not published it is that what I have found is so liberal that if I were to publish it, I am sure I would not be able to live even for a day. Of course, I do believe I will live for as long as I am destined to live. My life is already ordained for me, but what I mean is that no one will be able to accept what the truth is. I wouldn't be saying things of my own. I'll be just quoting from sources, and yet people will not like it. This is the reason I have not published my research.

Nowhere in the Qur'an does it say that women have to veil so obsessively, as they presently do it in Iran,[23] Afghanistan, Saudi Arabia, or parts of Pakistan. You see, the word *hijab* is not used for a woman's garment in the Qur'an [33:59]. I always wonder, how do Iranian women keep their thick black veil on while moving around and doing their work?[24] The way they do it makes them look as if they are helpless. How can they do it in the heat?

Don't they see the contradictions, that they wear Western garments under

22. In the same vein, see also Jalal 1991a.

23. Some women, in particular women of the religious elite and parliamentarians, wear a scarf underneath a thick, black, all-enveloping chador. The Iranian chador is open in the front, and the two sides of the black veil constantly must be held in place and over one's face with one hand.

24. It is worth noting here that a few women who were elected to the sixth Iranian Parliament (2000) publicly expressed their intention to wear the "Islamic veil"—a loose, long overcoat and a large scarf—rather than the traditional all-enveloping black chador that up until then women parliamentarians wore. Several male members of parliament and one or two

their veil? The Persian veil is open in the front, isn't it? What happens if your veil flies open?[25] This presents a problem when you wear something so different underneath from what you wear on the top, doesn't it? Somebody told me that they attended a corporate conference in Islamabad where some young Iranian women also attended. They came in their chador to Islamabad, and they attended the conference in their miniskirts! When they returned to Iran, they put on their chador again! I find it confusing. Something contradictory is going on in a person's mind. Similarly, Saudi women throw off their veils the moment their plane leaves Saudi air space. The two main concerns about Muslim women's clothing are modesty and practical comfort, which I find in Pakistani dress.

Of course, you must have noticed that the majority of educated young Pakistani women do not cover their heads, but I know of one very intelligent, highly educated young woman who wants to cover her face, too, but her husband does not allow it [laughter]. So this is some food for thought for the Western world. The Western world thinks that Muslim women are forced to wear a veil, but it is not necessarily so. Some people might be forced, but a lot of people do it by choice. For example, this Pakistani scarf [pointing to her *dupata*] that I have on, according to some *maulvi*s might not be good enough [as a veil] but according to most Pakistanis, it is acceptable. There was a time I did not cover my head, and I had short hair. I sort of started feeling the need to wear my scarf because of some internal feelings I was going through. In the beginning, I would wear it just when I went to the Juma bazaar because it is so crowded. Then I started wearing it to other shopping centers, and after quite a long time I started to wear it even when I was going out with my husband. Initially, he wasn't too happy about it, but then he got used to it. The point I am trying to make here is that women are not always forced to wear *hijab* or a veil. They may do it willingly. Then again, I never forced my daughters to do it, even when I became convinced that this is what I wanted to do. I have left the choice to them.

---

women strongly objected to this decision and warned the new female members of dire consequences, but the "reformers" succeeded.

25. There are humorous stories about women's loose veils blowing open, exposing them, or about women themselves manipulating the veil judiciously to attract attention. A sizable majority of women in the big cities have adopted the Islamic veiling, which includes a long, loose overcoat and scarf.

Haji Camps

One of DOI's regular programs is the Haji Camp for the pilgrims to Mecca. You see, many cities do not have direct flights, and so the pilgrims come to Karachi to take care of the formalities. They are here for two to three days, and in that time we try to catch them in order to teach them something about the *hajj* rituals. A majority of them are illiterate. They are going to *hajj*, but they don't have a *clue* about anything. When I said we are concerned about knowledge, that applies here as well. We take up anything that we feel contributes to the spread of knowledge.

There are rooming houses at the Karachi Haji Camps where the pilgrims stay. We go to these places and announce our program. We also put up notices, but many of them cannot read. We don't organize such meetings for men, but sometimes they can sit outside [the room] and listen to what we are saying. We distribute a booklet on the *hajj*. Sometimes women say, "My husband can read, but I can't," so this way men can also benefit from having the booklet. We feel the instructions written by scholars are too complicated, so we simplify everything to essential rituals and teach them the easiest and most basic way of doing it. We feel that once the pilgrims master that simplified way of performing the pilgrimage, then if they want to do another *umra*,[26] they can follow more detailed instructions. This is the first time that a little book has been written by women for women, in which more emphasis is given to women, in the sense of discussing women's problems such as menstruation, et cetera. You see, most of the instruction books on *namaz*, daily prayers, and *hajj* give the whole prescription from a male point of view, the way men ought to do it. After you have tried to remember the instructions and all that, then they say, "*But* women should not do this; they should do that!" So women's concern and instruction came as an appendage, not as part of the main body of the text. I used to be annoyed. In this booklet, we have done just the opposite. The main instruction is written for women, and we say, "But men can do this or should do that."[27]

Oh, the program is very popular with women. We have found that during the past ten years since we started distributing our booklet, every year the new

26. *Umra* means making the pilgrimage to Mecca anytime other than during the annual *hajj*, which takes place in Zilhijjah, the last month of the Arabic lunar calendar.

27. *Hajj Made Easy: A Manual Explaining the Rituals of Hajj.*

batch that comes along is better informed. Sometimes we ask them where they heard about our booklet and us, and they say from people who had returned from the *hajj*. Even though we have this function only in Karachi, you know, we are getting known around. We had a camp once in Islamabad, but we don't have it anymore.

Violence Against Women

As an organization, we do not take any formal political stand on issues, such as rape and violence against women, the nuclear bomb, Benazir Bhutto's leadership, or the like. The fact that we have not done that so far is because some of us think we should go out in processions [demonstrations], and others think that we should not. So we stay on the safer side, and we don't go out on the street and protest. *But* the kind of work and research we do deals with some of these concerns more thoroughly.

For example, there was the case of a girl in Lahore who had married against her father's wishes.[28] He had taken the case to court and argued that since the father was a Shafi'i,[29] he had the right to decide to whom his daughter should or should not be married and that she had no right to marry according to her own choice. And since he had not given her permission, she had committed *zina*, which stands for both adultery and fornication.[30] Her lawyer was a well-known Pakistani woman.[31]

Through our organization, somebody approached me and asked, "Do you know what is the Hanafi School's position on women's right to marriage?" We gave them some books and references regarding *fiqh*, or jurisprudence. It is stated in the Hanafi texts that a woman can appoint her own agent to arrange

28. See the section titled "Dishonor: Breaking the Chain of Custom" in chapter 5 for a fuller description of a case in which a father brought a suit of fornication against his daughter for marrying against his wishes.

29. In rereading this chapter, Nilofar added that the father had become a Shafi'i "over night." Shafi'i is one of the four schools of Sunni Islamic law. The other three are the Hanafi, the Hanbali, and the Maliki. Shi'i Islam constitutes another school of law, though it shares aspects with the others. According to the Shafi'i (and Maliki) tradition, "a woman is denied the right to enter into a marriage at will and must be given away through a contract arranged by her guardian— or *wali*" (Balchin 1994, 7). For a fuller discussion, see Lokhandwala 1987, 48–51.

30. Punishable under the Hudood Ordinance, discussed in chapter 1.

31. The lawyer was Asma Jahangir, an internationally known human rights lawyer and the chairperson of the Human Rights Commission of Pakistan.

her marriage [unlike in Shafi'i texts]. It does not have to be her own father. So, theoretically, I think she could be her own agent. In the end, the girl won the case. You see, even though the father claimed to be a Shafi'i, a judge could use Hanafi ruling to make a decision.[32] We felt happy to be of help in this case. We think these issues are worth fighting for so that women can get back the rights given to them by their religion.

How effective or influential DOI has been is difficult to assess, but cases such as this one help in changing the whole future of women's decision making. If a woman is allowed to choose her own husband, then she will be considered to be an individual, so we are trying to establish that a woman should be treated as an individual. I also think we have been more successful with urban educated women. Rural women are just too far out for us to reach, but the benefits will filter down to them in time.

One hears a lot about violence against women, not just rape in [police] custody but also within the household, but we have not worked on these topics yet. I myself have wondered why not much is written [in the religious texts] on rape, but I wonder whether at the time [of the advent of Islam] the concept did exist.[33] Actually, I have been trying to find commentaries on rape in the hadith and *fiqh* and other texts. So far I have not found anything. I do have my own interpretation as to what the punishment should be, but the [religious] sources do not spell it out. In Sura al-Maida [Qur'an 5], there is something about the punishment for people who are disrupting the peace in the city, like a highway robber, or people who force themselves onto others and exploit them. The word for such people is *muharib*, warring, and the punishments for them are very severe. You would be surprised to hear that the Qur'an[34] has the punishment of crucifixion for highway robberies, *dacoity*, and things like that. This is my own interpretation. I think the punishment for rape should be

32. "The court may, by applying the Hanafi law under the doctrine of *Talfiq* [mixing], ameliorate the condition of women governed by Shafi'i law" (Lokhandwala 1987, 51).

33. Rubya Mehdi also argues that "the phenomenon of rape might not have been common in the early period of Muslim history." But, without defining it specifically, she states: "whether or not this was the case, the traditional Islamic concept of rape is not applicable in Pakistan today" (1997, 99).

34. "The punishment of those who wage war against God and His Apostle, and strive with might and main for mischief through the land is: execution, or crucifixion (*yosallabu*), or the cutting off of hands and feet from opposite sides, or exile from the land: that is their disgrace in this world, and heavy punishment is theirs in the Hereafter" (Qur'an 5:33).

based on this *ayat*, which prescribes either crucifixion or cutting of hands and feet of the opposite sides [of body] or even the death penalty. You see, the punishment for *zina*, fornication and adultery, is clearly spelled out in the Qur'an. Adultery is something in which you have the consent of the other, and yet it is condemned. So what about something where you have this double crime of forcing yourself on somebody? It is like being a *dacoit* you know, forcefully taking away something which is not legally yours [long pause].

For the moment and in the absence of other interpretations, this is what I would say because I could not find anything else in the texts. It *could* be that women were considered a man's property, but, you see, rape is committed against someone who is not your property, against whom you are not allowed to do this!

Sharing Public Space: Claiming Mosques

Traditionally, women in Pakistan have not been allowed to go to mosques even though there is no legal restriction [amazed].[35] I have heard people argue, "Yes, you know, when you say that at the time of the Prophet women used to go to every mosque, and even in Saudi Arabia now women go to all the mosques,[36] those were different times, and times are bad these days."[37] My argument is, if we allow women to come to mosques, it will encourage men to

35. Whether Muslim women can go to mosques has been debated hotly among Muslims. Maulana Maududi, the foremost religious scholar in Pakistan, offers several hadith, on the basis of which he concludes that women have been banned from offering their prayers at mosques, but he also cites Prophet Muhammad for having given women permission to go to mosques, which Maududi opines should be under the banner of darkness. Maududi's subjective reading of Prophet Muhammad's action becomes clear in the following passage. It concerns the second caliph, Umar, who would keep quiet whenever his wife, Atikah, would ask his permission to go to the mosque. Maududi argues that Umar was aware of the Prophet's conditional permission for women to visit mosques, and, by remaining silent, Umar "would neither stop her nor permit her in clear word." But being "a lady of her will," he adds, she would go to mosques anyway (1987, 202–5).

36. In Iran, too, women go to mosques, though after the revolution of 1979 their section has been curtained off from the men's section.

37. This argument apparently was made by Abu Hamid Imam Muhammad Ghazali (d. 1111), who, according to Valerie Hoffman, "endorsed forbidding women from going to mosques," while "recognizing that the Prophet ordered men not to forbid women to pray at the mosques." Imam Ghazali's rationale was that "morals had deteriorated since the time of the

behave, to respect women, and to give them their space, you know. What I am trying to say is that if the times are bad, you can make them good. "Times are bad" means that men do not behave properly, so you can make them behave properly by letting women come into the mosque. The longer you keep women hidden, the more you allow men in fact to misbehave. Men should be made to respect women as individuals.

So it would be helpful if the government makes some kind of allowance or announcement [pause]. This [awareness of and ability to go to mosques] is one thing we are interested in starting, like the Haji Camp that I told you about. I remember some seven or eight years ago there was a case of a German woman convert who went to a mosque in Peshawar—and you know how conservative they are in Peshawar—and the imam of the mosque tried to throw her out. She fought back. This was a big case. I don't know exactly what came of it. So, even though there is no legal restriction, since we don't have the tradition, women are scared or feel intimidated.[38]

You see, it always happens.[39] When a new power or party takes over, it tries to persecute the last power. When the British took power away from the Muslims in India [eighteenth and nineteenth centuries], they always tried to do something to weaken the Muslims. Naturally men became very protective of their women. I don't know if you have read about the kind of purdah and the kind of restrictions that women had before partition, the Muslim women?

There is an interesting story about one of my mother's great uncles. She remembered it happening, you know; she was a grown woman then. There were two brothers. The younger brother took his family by train somewhere, and the women were all fully covered. This time, though, he decided that he would not make the servants hold up the sheets for the women of the family to

Prophet, and it was no longer appropriate for any but the old women to leave their homes" (1995, 229).

38. Schimmel writes of the tradition in which "numerous women" were in the Prophet's close proximity. "It was also understood . . . that they [women] should participate in the prayer service in the mosque, for one hadith says: 'Do not prevent the handmaidens of God from entering the places in which He is worshiped.' Even the second caliph, Omar Ibn al-Khattab (ruled 643–644), had to adopt this tradition, albeit not very happily" (1997, 31).

39. I asked her, "How did the tradition of women not being allowed to go to mosques come about in Pakistan?"

walk in between [compartments?] because the women were totally covered in their *burqa* anyway. The elder brother came to know about this and was so furious with his younger brother for dishonoring the whole family that he *never* spoke to him again as long as he lived! Can you imagine the amount of restrictions? When all this happened, naturally women could not go to mosques. This is where the tradition developed, that the women should stay home to say their prayers. In Karachi, there are a few mosques where they have space for women, especially during the Ramadan and the *tarawi* prayers, but it is not like I could just walk into any mosque at any prayer time and say my prayers. I have been inside a mosque in countries like Saudi Arabia, Malaysia, Thailand, Turkey, and America. I felt so spiritually elevated. And no matter which country it was, the men present always seemed to display great respect for the women in the mosque. I feel that it is my religious right which is being denied for some obscure reason.

[Laughing] No, we have not thought of going to a mosque and claiming a space for ourselves![40] [Pause] You see, if we were to go as an organization, then we would have to have the consensus of the members. As I already said, our members are not in agreement at this point, like on street protests and that kind of behavior, so the next best thing to do is to try to get some of the authorities on your side [pause]. On this particular point, we have not approached them yet, but we are going to have a meeting soon in which we plan to focus on that [pause].

We are in touch with the Ministry for Women's Development,[41] sort of [pause], but for things like this I think the minister for religious affairs would be more effective. If the Ministry for Women's Development announces these things, then people won't take it too well, you know. They would say it is a feminist demand, but if the Ministry for Religious Affairs announces something like this, it would be easily acceptable.

40. I asked her whether they thought of just going to a mosque and claiming a corner for themselves. She found that question very amusing. Elizabeth Fernea, in her film documentary *A Veiled Revolution: Women and Religion in Egypt*, follows a group of women going to mosque to meet in a study group. This film was directed by Marilyn Gaunt and produced by Elizabeth Fernea (First Run/Icarus Films, 1982, twenty-six minutes).

41. "The Ministry of Women['s] Development was established in January, 1979, as a special organ of the Federal Government to uphold the status and enhance the socio-economic role of women" (Ministry of Information and Broadcasting 1991, 264).

Nature Versus Culture?

I find the issue of *fitrat*, nature, a very difficult one.[42] Sometimes, even among very conservative people, you find the woman of the house to be very dominant and domineering and her husband submissive, which means that this is how they were made. Nobody taught them to be like that. In fact, what is taught is just the opposite in our culture, so it is very difficult to make laws about these things. But when a final decision has to be made, I think the safest thing to do is to go back to the Qur'an and the hadith, [pause] for our limits. For day-to-day interaction between husband and wife, mother and son, brother and sister, I think we just have to leave nature alone. What I am trying to say is that a sister might be more domineering, she might be wiser, she might be more intelligent, and she might be able to handle the family business better. *But* you cannot use this argument to give them both [her and her brother] equal share of the inheritance because the Qur'an is quite clear on that [two shares for boys, one for girls]. This is where you have to draw the line. This is to prevent society from falling into a state of anarchy and confusion because some higher power or wisdom has to guide us. But I don't feel that in everyday interactions you have to worry about nature and women having to be submissive or a husband being necessarily the head of the family.

42. Nilofar and I discussed the issue of nature, *fitrat* at some length. Because her responses are directed to several questions I put to her, I provide a shortened version of my question in this footnote. I told her that one of the arguments often used to assign gender roles in Muslim societies is that of the nature, *fitrat*, of woman and man. The assumption is that it is in the nature of women to yield, to want to be protected and governed, whereas it is in the nature of men to be politically dominant and sexually more needy. I told Nilofar of my meeting with another Pakistani scholar, Khawar Chishti, at a conference at Harvard University (May 1998), who addressed the issue of nature. In her presentation, Chishti argued that Islam was "misinterpreted" by the Muslim elite, "misunderstood" by Muslims, and "misrepresented" by outsiders. Arguing that a paradigm shift was needed, she then suggested that we ought to go back to the nature model, the *fitrat* model. She ultimately did not propose a perspective fundamentally different from the classic Shi'i and Sunni view. What she did not address, I told Nilofar, was the question of who is to decide whose nature is what. How is one to understand the changing nature of gender roles and relations? How do we account for individual and cultural variations? How do we understand social change historically? What is this nature business? How are we to understand the physiological differences between men and women without essentializing their social roles and status to their mere physiology?

What I am saying is that there *are* differences of temperament, and this is something you cannot tamper [with] by law. *But* when you come to these final decisions about inheritance, et cetera, you cannot say I am wiser than my brother, and therefore I should get an equal share. Qur'an is quite clear on that, and you don't challenge the Qur'an.

Sure, Qur'an can be read from a feminist perspective, and that is what we are trying to do, but there are some things that are absolutely clear, in which there is no confusion, no ambiguity. There are certain verses, the *muhkamat*, in the Qur'an whose interpretation cannot be challenged, such as the ones about inheritance [pause]. These precepts are quite clear, final, and irrevocable. But there are some verses that are ambiguous, the *mutashabihat*, like on veiling. This is why every culture and every age have interpreted the style and concept of veiling differently.

Within Our Limits

I do not think such an approach leaves women vulnerable to having their nature being interpreted for them all the time. You see, whether women can or should leave their home without their husband's permission is, again, something that can be interpreted. Where does the Qur'an say that women should not leave the house?[43] It is not there in the Qur'an, and prohibiting women cannot be justified on the basis of their nature and being "provocative." Again, this is a matter of interpretation. What I am trying to say is that when you come to issues that are ambiguous in the Qur'an, then you can challenge their interpretation. For example, the matter of veiling can be challenged. Maududi says cover your face, and I have challenged his teaching on the subject. The Qur'an does not say that! And Maulana Maududi —Have you read his work?—in his book called *Purdah*[44] devotes at least 60 pages of a 180-page book to talking about the West.

He is more interested in challenging the West—and that is what most of the conservative scholars are doing in Pakistan—rather than trying to understand what is happening in their own backyards. In his book *Purdah*, Maududi contradicts himself. He says, "Even though the face veil has not been prescribed in the Qur'an, it is Islamic in spirit." In another place in the same book,

43. Maududi argues that women are not to leave home, based on "Divine laws for the movements of women" (1987, 200), without citing any Qur'anic commandments.

44. See fn. 43.

he says [pause]—this is not an exact quotation, but the sense of it—"Women should cover their faces until the day when we have the courage to *pull out* the eyes of those men who stare at women's face [raising her voice]. And when we have the courage to do that, then the women can come out without a facial veil." I find it quite ridiculous! I mean, he is trying to justify what is in his own mind [pause]. There is a hadith attributed to the Prophet in which he reportedly told Asma bint-i Abu Bakr that when a woman grows up, she can leave her face uncovered. Even when he refers to this hadith, Maududi concludes that women are to cover their faces!

He does seem to be attributing that [facial veil] to nature because he neither has the courage nor do men have the education to avert their gazes, as they have been instructed to do [Qur'an 24:31]. But he is not really blaming the women. He is blaming the men for not having the courage to pull out the eyes of those men who are bad, and for that women have to suffer. They do not educate men. Is this supposed to be the character of a Muslim man, so uncouth and undisciplined that he cannot tolerate to see a woman without a face veil?

In many respects, I found the Iranian scholar Ayatollah Murtiza Mutahhari's book quite good, but he also says that women have this uncontrollable urge to display themselves! How does he know? I wanted to write to him, but then I learned that he is dead.[45] The response that came to my mind was: Who is the one who wants to stare at women? Why can't men control their gaze? Another thing he mentioned was that women are allowed to uncover their faces, but that we should not tell them that because if we do, then they'll take a step further, and not only will they expose their face, but blah, blah![46] This he was quoting from another scholar as if it was a secret that all scholars had among themselves.

See, this is the problem that we are trying to challenge, this nonsensical cause-and-effect relationship, you know. That is why we have set up the Daughters of Islam and the library. Even the best minds and the most sincere

45. See Mutahhari 1974. Mutahhari was assassinated at the beginning of the Iranian Revolution of 1979.

46. Maududi also admits that during war times the Prophet allowed the purdah restriction to be relaxed: "In order that they may carry out these duties efficiently [helping the wounded], restrictions of purdah have been considerably relaxed. In fact, they have been allowed by *Shari'ah* to wear the same sort of dress, with little modification, as is worn by the Christian nuns now-a-days" (1987, 209–10).

male scholars cannot really look at the problem from the woman's point of view. It is so easy for them to say that all women should cover their faces. Now, ask the women who have to cover their faces what they have to go through, what their problems are. So this is the time when women have to go back to the original text, the Qur'an and the hadith, try to honestly understand and reinterpret these texts and injunctions for themselves.

Well, we accept whatever feels right to us![47] If it doesn't seem right, or if we refer to the text and realize that the concept that has been given to us is not in the text, then we don't accept it. Like I don't accept the injunction about veiling that the scholars give because I feel the Qur'an does not say that, but when I find that there is something clearly stated by the Qur'an, as a Muslim I accept it because it makes sense to me, as I said earlier about inheritance. Because I don't have to support myself and I don't have to support my family, even if I get half the inheritance, that is plenty, but my brother has to support all the females in the family legally or traditionally. So if he gets double of what I get, then I think maybe I am getting a little more than my share.

Your observation about some men in South Asia sitting around smoking their *hookahs* and doing nothing is also true for Pakistan.[48] But men are not supposed to sit around and smoke *hookahs*! They are supposed to be out there in the field, helping their wives [laughing]! I also understand the growing problem of economic necessity and the demand for a dual family income. [Pause] As a Muslim, however, it is very difficult, you know, to challenge something that is so clearly stated in the Qur'an. But, you see, we cannot just look at one *ayat* in isolation. We have to look at all the others that go with it. Take the

47. I asked her, "If this is the case, why should you accept some injunctions and not others?"

48. I asked her, "But given what has happened in the world presently and the increasing need for dual career families, both men and women have to work to make ends meet. In Iran for the most part, the middle-class women in particular have to work. In the rural areas, women work more than men. So what is the justification [for men's receiving twice the inheritance than women]? I have been traveling in northern South Asia, and I was amazed to see so many men sitting around smoking their *hookahs* while women were working in the fields." Later, in the course of writing this book, I came across the following observation by Indira Gandhi: "I remember my astonishment on my first visit to Manipur, at seeing women not only worked in the fields and wove their textiles but dealt also with the marketing of their produce and occupied themselves with other important civic duties. What do the men do, I asked? They sit and smoke!" (qtd. in Visram 1992, 14).

word *qawwamun*, for example. First of all, the meaning of the word is a matter of interpretation.[49] In Pakistan, you find scholars who say *qawwamun* means "rulers," that the man is the ruler of the woman.[50] But there are other scholars who say that it means "supporter," "protector," and "somebody who gives security."[51] In the Qur'an [4:34], the next sentence reads, "Because they [men] spend of their wealth." There are some women who say, "Since we are our own breadwinners, we do not come under this injunction" [pause]. So Muslim feminists say the interpretation of this verse can be challenged. Maybe not really challenged in isolation, but looked at from a wider perspective to see what other conditions and regulations there are in the Qur'an that go with that particular *ayat*. I don't think I can recommend rethinking the *muhkamat*, those verses which are unambiguous, simply because of the changes in the modern times,[52] but if there is something that can support your reinterpretation from within the Qur'an itself [pause], well, maybe. What I am trying to say is that [pause] you cannot reinterpret the *muhkamat* according to your own wishful thinking but only from what is already there in the Qur'an [pause].

Because the secular feminists are not religiously inclined, their interpretation might be a little different from the reinterpretation of somebody who has faith. I have been to a few conferences and seminars with such people, and you can see the different stands and conclusions that they derive. I would be care-

---

49. Qur'anic verse 4:34 has created one of the most contentious debates among Muslims, in particular among feminists of all persuasions. See Stowasser 1996, 32–33.

50. "Nowhere does the Qur'an state," argues Badawi, "that one gender is superior to the other. Some mistakenly translate 'qiwamah' or responsibility for the family as superiority. The Qur'an makes it clear that the sole basis for superiority of any person over another is piety and righteousness not gender, color, or nationality: 'O mankind! We created you from a single (pair) of a male and a female and made you into nations and tribes that you may know each other. Verily the most honored of you in the sight of Allah is (one who is) the most righteous of you. And Allah has full knowledge and is well acquainted (with all things)' (Qur'an 49:13)" (1995, 6).

51. In her perceptive article "Women and Citizenship in the Quran" (1995), Barbara Stowasser cogently argues that this Qur'anic verse is unambiguous regarding the essential differences in the roles of male and female in the family and that it was revealed to strengthen the patriarchal structure of family. But she challenges its extension by Muslim scholastic interpretation to areas beyond the family to the point of its becoming "a fundamental legal principle of male social and political preeminence in the Islamic *umma*" (33).

52. I asked her, "So, are you saying that it is possible to rethink some of these issues even though they may be part of the *muhkamat* verses?"

ful about touching the Qur'an. But if somebody does not have that stand or does not feel that limitation for themselves, then there is no limit to what they can suggest.

I usually do not get into arguments with secular feminists. Actually our objectives are the same. We are not really at loggerheads with each other. We want to liberate women from this very oppressive hold that the male scholars have on women. I personally get along better with secular feminists than with the fundamentalists or the orthodox women. I find them more humane and concerned about issues. I admire their efforts to work against rape and violence against women. Fundamentalist women tend to blame women themselves, and that to me is less humane.

There is no tension between our organization and the fundamentalist women, at least nothing openly, but we do have more differences of views with some of the politicized religious women. They are extremely militant. I believe people take those approaches to their faith that suits their personality.

Childhood and Upbringing

I was born in Moradabad in Uttar Pradesh, India, which is famous for its craftsmanship in copper, brass, and the like. I was the second child in my family and was about to start school when we left India after partition and migrated to Pakistan. My older brother had started going to school, and I remember I used to wait for him to come back from school like it was something special. My mother was not allowed to attend school in her time. My maternal grandfather was quite a well-educated person, but he felt that he could not send his daughter to a non-Muslim school, not just to a British but not even to a Hindu school. He felt our value system was different. He did send his sons to school, of course. I don't know. Maybe there was also a Muslim school for boys, but even if there had not been one, he would have [sent them to a British school]; I am sure he would have. My mother very much resented the fact that she was not allowed to go to school and that her education was not important to her family. When she was only about five years old, she used to tell us, she would climb onto the window in the morning just to watch this other girl, one of her distant relatives, going to school. My mother thought that the fact that a young girl could go to a public school was exciting, even though this girl used to be totally clad in her *burqa*. My mother was tutored at home by relatives.

She was even taught to read the *Gulistan* and *Bustan*[53] in Persian, along with some household math and English. I guess, if you don't have something, you don't realize what you are missing, but she did realize that she had missed out on education. My mother was very intelligent and creative, and a person like her realizes that she could do a lot more if she had the opportunity. She also suffered more than the women of her generation because she never really could accept all the restrictions they put on women in the name of religion in those days. My father was educated. Now both my parents have passed away.

My family migrated to Pakistan a few months after the partition. At the time of migration, I had one older brother and a younger sister and brother, and my youngest brother was born in Pakistan. Luckily we managed to get onto a military train, and the only thing we could take with us was the family jewelry. I vaguely remember the train journey to Pakistan and somehow remember that every now and then the train would stop and send or receive signals as to whether to proceed. It was a very difficult journey. We had little or nothing to eat. We would get water from the steam engine to make tea. The toilet facility was very bad. I remember a pregnant woman who started her labor pains during the journey and had to be taken out and carried away on a bull cart. Mother often wondered whatever happened to that woman and her child. My parents did not feel nostalgic for India. They did not want to go back. Most people who migrated to Pakistan never talked about the loss. They seemed to be fired by the idea of the separate homeland for Muslims. I once said to one of my brothers-in-law that his family must have migrated because Muslims were being slaughtered all over the place in Delhi. He said that wasn't true. His father was in the government service, and they were secure in their home when they opted to come to Pakistan. The hope of a new life was much greater. When I reflect on it, though, I think I can never imagine taking my children's hands and just walking out of my house, my country.

Education

In Pakistan there was never talk of my not going to school. Never! In fact, when we came to Pakistan a few months after the partition, it was my turn to start school, and my mother was upset that I might miss a year. She was very

---

53. *Gulistan* (Garden of roses) and *Bustan* (Garden of fruits) are the two literary masterpieces by the thirteenth-century mystic Persian poet Sheikh Muslihuddin Sa'di (d. 1291) of Shiraz.

concerned about that. Here you had all this rioting, and people were being killed all around you, people were worried about their belongings and how they were going to survive, but my mother was worried about getting me to school! My father, though not very supportive of education for women of his wife's generation, was very supportive of mine. In fact, I remember he would sit me in front of his bicycle and take me to school in the early days.

I went to a convent school. Ironically, Pakistanis admire nuns because of their moral values. Even in the North-West Frontier Province, families send their girls to convent schools.[54] Muslims did not have a well-established tradition of female education in South Asia. The nuns did not force us to study their religion, nor did they teach Islamiat. In fact, they resisted doing so. They said, "If we have to teach another religion, we will close down the school." The government did not care or think about it then. All religious teaching was done at home. I did miss out on some fundamental education that children learn earlier on nowadays in Pakistan. Now even Cambridge University cannot give O-level exams in Pakistan without Islamiat and Pakistan studies.[55]

On the whole, I got along well with the nuns. The nuns still looked down upon us because of the British Raj tradition. We had a principal who once in a while would make derogatory remarks about Islam and Pakistan. So some of my friends got together, and we decided that if she did that again, we would confront her. But somebody informed her, and so the principal came to our class and admonished us, though she did not apologize for her behavior. I stood up to her. She did not punish us but threatened us. Interestingly, however, after that incident the principal gradually changed her attitude.

We were the first batch admitted for a three-year course in BA. This was during Ayub Khan's regime [1958–69]. But if the exams were difficult, students would riot.[56] They did riot frequently also because the time required to get a BA was changed from a two-year term to three years. They demanded that we should be allowed to go to the university for an MA directly after two

54. See also Sajida's life story, chapter 6. For a study on the Pakistani educational system, the attitude of the upper middle class, and the relationship between the state and education, see Saigol 1995 and Zafar 1991.

55. See Saigol (1995, 62) for a discussion of Islamization of secular knowledge in Pakistan and of the relationship between Pakistani private schools and the universities of Cambridge and London.

56. In some of the major universities of Pakistan, students still riot and protest if they perceive the exams to be difficult.

years. Finally the government gave in, and we all graduated overnight. We came to be known as the "overnight graduates." My BA was in history, psychology, and English. I feel embarrassed to say that I have a degree in psychology because I never had any practical training. My master's degree is in English literature. After I finished my MA, I received a Fulbright fellowship, and I went to the University of Alabama, where I stayed from 1966 to early 1968. I completed another MA in English literature because I was very much interested in short stories and in the American southern writers. When I returned to Pakistan, I wrote a serial for the *Illustrated Weekly of Pakistan* called "No Serenade for Nina." I also wrote for *Dawn* of the Herald Group.

Love and Marriage

I married in 1969 after I returned from the United States. I did not want to stay on in the United States. My marriage was arranged, though I had met my husband earlier, and he had visited my family several times before we actually got married. A friend introduced me to Saleem, my husband, at a dinner party. He had just come back to Pakistan from America, where he had gotten a master's degree in architecture. His family wanted to arrange his marriage, and they kept on arranging for him to meet some girls, but nothing happened. Then my family received a message from his sister that they were coming to visit. We all pretended that it was just a visit. When they came, it just so happened that some of our relatives were there with a marriage proposal. When they saw Saleem's family, they immediately knew it [their intention], and they got upset, but my mother never wanted me to marry a relative, anyway.

I did not really know him, but I had no problem with the idea. I have no objection to or resentment of arranged marriages. Having gone to America had not changed my attitude toward marriage customs in Pakistan. Every girl would be happy with a [marriage] proposal. By then, I had done everything I wanted to at the time, and I was ready to settle down. From the time his proposal arrived to the time we got married took only a few months. First he came with his sister. Then the men came with the proposal. When my family accepted the proposal and after a respectable passage of time, the men negotiated the *mahr*, the dower.[57] Finally, the women came separately to negotiate the marriage arrangements. After that, Saleem and I went out a few times,

57. Nilofar preferred the term *dower* as opposed to *bride-price* as a translation for *mahr*.

along with my brothers, and met in the presence of my family to get to know each other. He said that he wanted an educated and self-confident wife, someone who could "go to bank alone" [laughing]! Meanwhile, my family conducted inquiries regarding his family, his job, and his lifestyle and habits.

We did not go on a honeymoon immediately after the wedding. It is considered rude because all your relatives and family come for the wedding. The advertising agency I was working for did not let me work part-time, so I quit. But after my first daughter was born, I went back to work. Since we were living in a joint family, I did not have any responsibilities, and there was a woman looking after my daughter. My mother-in-law never objected to my working, but after a while I started feeling guilty for neglecting my child. Last year, when I went to America [in 1997] to visit my daughter, I stayed for the whole year, and we spent our time together and made up for the lost time. I have three daughters. The eldest is presently in Texas and has done her master's in architecture. The second one is in Turkey doing her BA in graphic design, and the third one is studying in Karachi.

Poetry and Mysticism

When I was studying in America, poetry was pouring forth from me, good poetry. Everything was coming together to give me inspiration. But when I returned to Pakistan, the flow seems to have stopped. Now I write mostly prose and not poetry. I published my poetry in a literary journal in the United States. I wrote a poem while I was still in America called "Flying to Istanbul" in which I tried to reflect the sense of doubt I was experiencing. It is about the whirling dervishes. At that time, I knew little about [Maulana Jalaluddin] Rumi,[58] but these things pervaded the atmosphere and existed subliminally. In Pakistan, early in the morning over the radio you hear the recitation of the Qur'an—it is

58. Maulana Jalaluddin Rumi was born in Balkh (present-day Afghanistan) in 1207 (d. 1273). His family gradually settled in Qonia (present-day Turkey), where he received his early education in Persian from his father. Rumi assumed the rank of sheikh, forming "a fraternity of the disciples whom his ardent personality attracted in ever-increasing numbers" (Arberry 1967, 215). The most significant and influential episode in the poet's life is his encounter with the mystic Shams al-Din of Tabriz. "The meeting took place in 1244 when Shams al-Din, a wandering dervish of some sixty years, arrived in Qonia. Jalal'l-Din found in the stranger that perfect image of the Divine Beloved which he had long been seeking" (Nicholson 1950, qtd. in Arberry 1967, 215). See also Schimmel 1986, 309–28.

beautiful. When I was growing up, you would also hear Rumi's *mathnavi*[59] recited after the Qur'an in Persian in a very special way. When I was studying
Yeats, I realized that my poem on the dervishes echoed his esoteric philosophy. Looking back now, I realize that I must have had some streak of mysticism and Sufism in me. Well, at that time I was going through a period of
doubt. My doubt had to do with the existence of God, but I did not talk about
it in Pakistan. There is, of course, the tradition of doubt in Islam.

Imam Ghazali's doubt was never about God, but about theology, theories of
religion, and certitude.[60] There is an interesting story about him. Being a great
doctor of law, he was posted in Baghdad as the director of one of the great universities of the time and was sought after by the nobles and princes. Baghdad
was a cosmopolitan city with people of innumerable religions, sects, and
schools of thought being at loggerheads with each other. One day as he was
strolling in his fancy robe, which was a mark of his high office, he spotted a
man in tattered clothes and quite unaware of his surroundings. Reportedly,
Ghazali felt contemptuous of the man. That night he dreamed of the Prophet,
who reprimanded him for looking down at a man who seemed to be totally
immersed in the love and remembrance of Allah and the Prophet. Now, Ghazali was already going through a period of questioning and doubt. He had
started wondering about the value of knowledge and scholarship. When he
woke up, he was a changed person. He disguised himself and quietly disappeared. No one knew of his whereabouts.

One day, in the Ummayyad Mosque [of the Ummayyad dynasty, 661–750]
in Damascus, a group of scholars were hard at work trying to solve a certain
problem of jurisprudence. They had been at it for quite a while and seemed to
be getting nowhere. Then the sweeper of the mosque, who had been working

59. *Mathnavi* is a poetic genre popularized by Ferdowsi (d. 1022), Nizami (d. 1209), Sa'di (d.
1292), and Maulana Rumi (d. 1273), in which every two verses of poetry rhyme with each
other. Rumi is immortalized in his internationally celebrated *Mathnavi ma'navi*. For an English
translation of Rumi's *Mathnavi*, see Nicholson's multivolume translations (Rumi 1925–40).

60. Abu Hamid Imam Muhammad Ghazali was born in Tus (northwestern Iran) in 1058.
After finishing his theological studies, he was appointed as a professor at the Nizamyiya *madrasa*
(university) in Baghdad, which was one of the most important centers of learning in the Muslim
world. Despite a successful career, Ghazali had a breakdown in 1095 and left his teaching position to seek a spiritual life. After a long journey though Syria, Jerusalem, and Egypt, Ghazali returned to his hometown and family to teach once again in Tus. He died in 1111. See Schimmel
1986, 91–92.

at the mosque for some time and who happened to pass by, just blurted out the answer! They all looked up in surprise. But, of course, the sweeper was no other than the great Imam Ghazali, who had disappeared so long ago. The story is that he had found his true self as well as his peace and solace in Sufism and in conducting a humble way of life. He was a great *faqih*, learned in Islamic law, but then his resolution came from Sufism. Sufism gives you a retiring attitude. It is the path of love that helps to develop in you an attitude of tolerance. You don't fight or argue with people. You travel toward God and your closure comes from God.

Doubting Self, Finding Faith

I was not a practicing Muslim and was not religious when I went to America. I went through a period of doubting. After I got married, my father-in-law, who was very religious, complained to my father that I was not doing my daily prayers. He told my father, "This is what happens when young people go to America" [laughing]. My parents had all the religious knowledge and values, but they were not orthodox or strict followers. For example, if in the month of Ramadan I woke up in the morning and I said, "I am not fasting today" [because of menstruation or other reasons],[61] they would never react negatively. Many women pretend they are fasting when they are not.

It is strange the way a sense of religiosity came to me. A friend of my husband had some problems and needed someone to help him. He finally found a Sufi master who helped him with his difficulties. I don't know why, but I wanted to meet this person. When I saw him, I felt that there was an amazing magnetism in his personality. His full name was Abu Zia Hazrat Khwaja Mohammad Ghyasuddin Shah Qasim Jehangiri, and he was of the Chishti Sufi order.[62] People called him Hazrat Sahib.[63] I kept visiting him and taking oth-

61. Muslim women are not required to perform their religious duties such as daily prayers or fasting during the period of their menstruation, but they are expected to make up for them later.

62. The Chishti Sufi order was founded by Mu'inuddin Chishti, who was born in Sistan (eastern Iran). He traveled to India in 1193 and settled in Ajmer, in Rajistan. "The Chishti order spread rapidly, and conversions in India during that period were due mainly to the untiring activity of the Chishti saints, whose simple and unsophisticated preaching and practice of love of God and one's neighbor impressed many Hindus, particularly those from the lower castes, and even members of the scheduled castes" (Schimmel 1986, 345–46). Mu'inuddin Chishti died in 1236. See also Currie 1989.

63. Honorific, meaning "His Presence" or "His Eminence."

ers to see him, and he would smile and say, *"Sare jahan keh dard hamare jigar main hain*—the sorrow of the world is in my [your] heart." But, you see, I think a sheikh and a disciple are destined to meet. You just know when you meet him and when the time comes. When I first met him, I did not know that I would be his disciple. No such tradition exists in my family. The only time we ever talked about *pirs* was about the fraudulent ones [smiling]. Initially I was extremely cautious in my dealings with him. I did not think at that time that I had a particular problem of my own, but I was having strange dreams.

I told Hazrat Sahib about my dreams, and from them he was able to discover my problems. He could see beyond the person. My dreams kept changing and started telling me that I should become a disciple. I fought with the idea for a long time and could not accept it because I was not brought up in the tradition. In this long spiritual tussle, I fell very ill, physically and emotionally ill. I asked him what it took to become a disciple and what difference did it make. He gave me an example. He said, "Suppose you are sitting in a room, and you hear a child crying. You listen. If it is someone else's child, then you let the child's parents take care of him, but if it is your own child, you go running to him."

Becoming a Disciple

It would be very difficult for people to believe this, but my final decision was not made by me. It was made by a much higher authority. I just had to give in to that decision. It came through my dreams [long pause].[64] You see, the problem is that you are not allowed to relate your dreams and experiences to other people, so they don't really understand what's going on and start judging you in a negative way. All this time, you know, I was gradually becoming more and more inclined toward religion. At this time, when Hazrat Sahib interpreted my dreams, he said that they meant that I should become a disciple. I said, "Just tell me the name of some books on Sufism. I want to read them first and see what it is all about."

He would never give me a name [of a book by a Sufi master] because, you see, he wanted me to experience it and know it firsthand before I got into the theory. And theory came to me later rather than earlier. I know of some people who know a lot of theory about Sufism, but they have no inner experience of

---

64. Throughout the narration of her relations with Hazrat Sahib, Nilofar was very pensive and reflective. She paused frequently and spoke softly and haltingly.

it.[65] Now when I read the theory, it is so much easier for me to follow what they are saying. It is not easy to read some of these Sufi texts, you know, and I am not saying I can understand every one of them. I have not reached that stage yet. But what happens is that as you keep progressing, you understand a little more, a little better. For example, my uncle gave me Ibn-i Arabi's (d. 1240) *Fusus al hikam.*[66] Every year I would open it religiously and try to read it. It's an old book, and I would just close it and put it away for another year or two. But this time last year [1997], first I read the commentators' interpretation on Sufism, and then quite recently I got a copy of the original, and I am trying to read it now. I mean the original text translated into English. I cannot say that I understand everything, but I can understand much more than I ever did before. I feel that I am progressing and that the more you progress, the more you understand.

It is very strange the way I got back to my prayers. You know, my husband never said his prayers at home.[67] I remember, when my daughter was very young, her teacher told her that when you fast—she was not fasting at that age, but they were teaching her this—you have to say your prayers. If you do your prayers while you are fasting, that is a *rozah.* But if you are fasting and not praying, that is *faqah,* starvation [laughing]. So one day my husband, who would be fasting but not praying, came home, and this little girl went to him and said, "Abba, do you have *rozah* today or do you have *faqah*? [Laughter.] But while he was not praying regularly, he would always go for the Juma, Friday, prayer. One day, it is very strange, when he came back from his Juma prayer, he found me sitting on the prayer mat and saying my prayers. It was probably the first time that he had seen me praying, which was several years after we

65. "Sufism is based on para-normal experience in its authentic form. . . . Sufism as experience can only be understood by a parallel experience and even conceptual schemata of the great Sufis were not meant as philosophies subject to disputations but as signals marking the 'station' and 'state' of the Sufi path" (Troll 1986, 254).

66. *Fusus al hikam* (Bezels of divine wisdom) is one of Muhyiuddin Muhammad Ibn-i Arabi's (d. 1240) mystical masterpieces. He is also known as *"shaikh al-akbar,"* the greatest master, whose writings "constitute the apex of mystical theories, and the orthodox has never ceased attacking him" (Schimmel 1986, 263).

67. In Pakistan, as in some other parts of the Muslim world, men are encouraged to perform their daily prayers at mosques, as opposed to women, who are encouraged to stay in seclusion. See Maududi 1987, 203–4.

had gotten married. Then later, after I finished my prayers and got up, I asked him, "What did you pray for today?" He said, "I prayed that you would start doing your prayer!" So maybe while he was praying there that I should start doing my prayers, here I was doing just that [laughing]. Very strange. It must have been around late 1970s.

Sometimes my husband would come to my sheikh with me, in which case he would naturally hear our conversations and his interpretations of my dreams. But, you see, the tradition is that you don't discuss your dreams with anyone. Instead, you go to a special person to interpret your dreams, and after you have done that, you might relate it to someone else. My husband is a person who hardly ever dreams, so we never really talked about my dreams. But if he happened to be there while I was discussing them with Hazrat Sahib, he got to know about them. What I am really grateful for, though, is that my husband never tried to stop me, even though he did not understand what was going on. He respected Hazrat Sahib a lot, but he was very far from spirituality. I think of him, though, as a kind of Sufi in his own way. He has much tolerance and qana'at, contentment, which are attributes of the Sufis.

You know, a lot of these orthodox people say that even Rasulallah [the Prophet] had no ilm-i ghaib, knowledge of the beyond and the unknown, but how can that be when my sheikh said so many things which came through. One day, I was sitting in his presence and talking to him—he used to call me bitya, [dear] little daughter. As I said earlier, because I wasn't brought up in the Sufi tradition, I had a very bold way of talking to him, which normally disciples do not have. He was very tolerant. He would just laugh, and sometimes I would say, "Oh, you won't tell me this because it is a trade secret?" [Laughter.] I would tease him. He would just laugh, and sometimes he would introduce me to other people as his "favorite child," you know. In Urdu, we say ladli, a child you spoil through extreme love. Sometimes as I was talking to him, I would get this feeling of being above time and space. I remember thinking, "This could be any time and any place."

The general meetings, like the urs [a pir's anniversary] and monthly programs, I didn't always manage to attend, particularly the monthly programs. Even though my husband did not try to stop me, his not being a disciple was a handicap, a disadvantage, because I could not drag him all the time. Also because of the sex segregation, when there would be qawwali, devotional songs—see, the Chishtis are fond of music [68]—women sat in segregated areas. In the beginning, when I started going to the *qawwali*, I protested to him [the sheikh].

I said, "How come you don't make any arrangements for the women? We have to peep out from the windows and doors. I don't like this arrangement."

"OK. Now that you have scolded me," he said, "I will make some arrangement" [laughter]. He said, "You scolded me." [Amazed.]

I mean, these were things that were very unusual. That is not how you talk to your *pir*. Now I feel it wasn't right of me to say those things, but I did not know any better. He had a lot of women disciples. But, you see, what happened was that women were just sitting inside the house and chattering away, you know, making a noise. The music that came though the speakers was just drowned in this chattering. While the *qawwali* was going on and people were in the state of *haal*, spiritual ecstasy, you could not get to experience it at all because you had to keep hanging out of the window or peeping through the door to block out the inside noise. So he ordered to have a lace curtain in the *shamiyana* [pavilion] and to dim the light in the women's section, while keeping the bright light in the men's section of the *shamiyana*, so that the men could not see the women.

Once my sheikh said to me, "You know, *bitya*, nobody knows me." He had hundreds, I don't know how many, maybe thousands of disciples, but he wasn't a public figure. "But," he said, "everyone is going to know you." At that time, I didn't pay any attention to what he was saying, and I wasn't after any kind of fame, you know. I am not saying everybody knows me, but you have come from such a distance to interview me, and you had heard about me. People invite me to attend seminars or conduct programs in spiritual retreats in New York and Texas and from some other far away places like Kuala Lumpur [Malaysia] and Colombo [Sri Lanka]. So, in a way, his prediction has come true. [69]

68. Schimmel identifies the poet Amir Khosrau (1254–1325) as "the founder of the Indo-Muslim musical tradition" of the Chishti music. The Chishtis allowed "the *sama'*, the spiritual concert and dance. . . . They have contributed a great deal to the development of the Indo-Muslim musical tradition, of which Amir Khosrau—lovingly styled 'the parrot of India' . . . — was the first great representative" (1986, 350).

69. I told Nilofar that some six years earlier, when I first started my research, I was interested in meeting a woman with strong religious convictions, one who does not merely mouth the orthodoxy's masculine interpretation. I then met Appa Nisar Fatima, who unfortunately died as a

Death of a Child

I had a son, and I lost him when he was seven months old. He was my last child, my only son. It was a big tragedy [long pause, speaking softly], and we were not planning to have anymore children after that. That was a big tragedy. He became ill, but it didn't look serious to me, you know, like a cough. I named him Abbas because I had a dream about having a baby son before he was born, in which someone said Hazrat Abbas has sent you a son.[70] That is why I called him Abbas [silence]. I also had very strange dreams about his death, later on.

From my dreams, it seemed as if someone wished him ill [long pause]. Not wishing ill on the child, but on the mother who is made to suffer. I have *no* idea who that might be. There are so many people who might be jealous of you. You don't know what is in their hearts. Of course, the main fact is that God willed it, you know. This is the explanation for a cause. His death [whispering] drew me closer to God, yes.[71] That is what convinced me that you are with God, even if you are suffering. His death was a little less than a year after I had started seeing the sheikh.

At the time of my son's death, I was not a disciple. I could not see the sheikh right away because it meant that I had to go to certain areas [long pause]. There was lots of trouble in Karachi and in other cities those days—must have been the late 1970s. His reaction was similar to that of most Muslims. He tried to console me by saying that when an innocent child dies, on the day of judgment that child stays outside the gates of heaven—you see, any innocent person is supposed to go to heaven—and says to God, "I am not going to enter until my parents do" [faint smile]. I don't know how far that is true. So that was, you know, supposed to be a kind of consolation [very long pause]. But that is not something you can console a mother with [whispering] because she is not thinking about herself [pause]—of going to heaven. Then, of course, it is the experience of adjusting to change. How do you get used to *this* kind of change? What inner resources do you have for this kind of grief? Suffering from which there is no respite. One doesn't go through a quick metamorphosis.

---

result of cancer when I was barely halfway through my research. I had to wait some six years later to read about Nilofar and to make another trip to Karachi to interview her.

70. Hazrat Abbas, a half-brother to the Shi'ites third imam Hussain, was also martyred in the battle of Karbala, Iraq, in 680. Hazrat Abbas was also an uncle of the Prophet.

71. I asked her, "Do you think the death of such a beloved child and the idea of death moved you closer toward religion and spirituality?"

Affliction and the Divine Love

By change, I do not mean intellectual change, but more of an emotional change, a spiritual change. Without knowing it, I was leaning toward some kind of spirituality. Do you know the Sufi theory of affliction? The belief is that affliction brings you closer to God. There is an anecdote about Abu Hanifa, one of the four Sunni jurists [founder of the Hanafi School of Islamic law]. He is said to have had some strong pain, you know, in one of his limbs. At times when his pain was excruciating, he would recite a prayer, and he would blow it at his leg, and the pain would go away. Now sometimes the pain would come back, and he would do the same thing, and again the pain would go away. Then he heard a whisper, either in a dream or in a vision: "Abu Hanifa, every time we try to get closer to you, you drive us away." This is believed to be a message from God. The moral of the story is that affliction brings you closer to God and makes you stronger. In another hadith attributed to the Prophet, it is said that a man goes to the Prophet and says, "The love for Allah and His Prophet is growing intensely in my heart." And the Prophet is related to have said, "You should now be prepared for poverty and hunger, *faqr* and *faqah*." It is a strange thing to say, but that's how it is—somehow [pause].

Spiritual Awakening

It was gradual, my spiritual awakening. Every time you go through a new experience, you have a new realization and a new perspective. You might have had the same experience before, but you did not look at it in the same way, and now in your spiritual life, you might look at the same thing in a different manner. When I go through a difficult experience, I say to my friends and sometimes to my children that if this same thing had happened to me so many years back, I wouldn't have reacted positively, but now I have a different kind of reaction. I take things more like being destined for me, predestined. I am able to accept [long pause] suffering and accept those things which I really don't want to do, but I know I have to do.

I would like to go back to my Hazrat Sahib, my *pir,* again because he is the fountainhead of my spirituality. It was maybe in 1979 or 1978, when I went through a phase where I became extremely claustrophobic, and I could not think of stepping into a plane. I just did not go anywhere! I saw a dream, and when I related it to Hazrat Sahib, he said that I will travel a lot and will be in one city one day and in another the next day. He also said that my husband will be working somewhere outside of Pakistan and supporting me. I said, "My goodness, what are you talking about? I am not even going to step into a plane!" This was after my son's death, and I could not even sit in an air-conditioned room unless I was sitting next to a window, where I could see the space beyond. I was so claustrophobic. I mean, it was something quite illogical, but that was something I guess I had to go through.

I got out of it very gradually. My husband helped, in a way. I know that a lot of Pakistani men would have said, "What is this nonsense?" But my husband was quite understanding, even though he couldn't understand what was going on and had some reservations.

What I actually wanted to mention was the spiritual foresight or insight that my Hazrat Sahib had to my dream. He said that I would be traveling to so many places, when at that time so long ago I could not even imagine doing things like this, but this is what I am doing today.[72] He also predicted my husband's future profession. At that time, there was no question of his going anywhere. There was no talk about it. Today that is what he is doing [working outside of Pakistan].

Another thing he said to me—this is much later now, must be about eight years ago—"You don't pay enough attention to Urdu." I told you that I went to a convent school, and there my school certificate specified English as my mother tongue [laughing]! Because that is how they had been doing it in the British schools. They didn't say that the medium of instruction was English, but that it was our "mother tongue." I studied Urdu as a foreign language [laughter]! So, given that my mother tongue was actually Urdu, and we studied Urdu at home—we had an Urdu tutor—and my parents spoke good Urdu, my Urdu should have been much better. It wasn't a very learned Urdu. It was a lot better than that of a lot of people in my school and in my class. Still it could have been much better. Hazrat Sahib knew the standard of my Urdu, and yet he said, "I think you should start teaching the Qur'an in Urdu." I was quite taken aback, and I just didn't know what to say. Later, I thought, "How could he say this to me? I don't have enough Urdu comprehension to study the *tafsirs*

72. Nilofar has been invited to several international conferences and asked to conduct Sufi retreats in the United States and Asia.

[interpretations of the Qur'an] in Urdu!" I can speak it fluently in a conversation, but teaching the Qur'an fluently in Urdu, discussing the *tafsir* is something I had never thought about! I just didn't want to think about it then.

Soon after Hazrat Sahib's statement, a friend of mine who used to live opposite my house in those days came over, and she said, "Nilofar, why don't you start teaching the Qur'an at my house?" Just out of the blue! We had never discussed it. I just looked at her, amazed. Then I realized that this was something I was supposed to do, that I had no choice here. So what I did was to get a tutor with whom I studied the *tafsir* once a week for about two months. Then I felt comfortable enough to go on with the *tafsir* personally and began studying it regularly. I started teaching a Qur'an class in 1989. I also understand Arabic to a certain extent because I had been attending some Arabic classes, enough to be able to distinguish Arabic quotations from the Qur'an and the hadith. I can get a sense of the language now, even though it is not enough. Isn't it strange that there is such a big difference between the hadith, words spoken by the Prophet, and the Qur'an, words spoken through the Prophet?

When I started my Qur'an classes, Hazrat Sahib was still alive. He passed away in January 1990. I started teaching informally. In Pakistan—I am sure they have it in other countries as well—women get together, and they find somebody who knows a little more than they do, and then they study the Qur'an together. I continued to teach the Qur'an for about six or seven years.

A strange thing happened—I am telling you a lot of things that I normally do not *like* to talk about, but I don't mind telling you about it. At that time, I was living in a very large house, and then I moved to this small apartment. This apartment was a little out of the way. Somehow most people who used to attend my classes and seemed to like them a lot just sort of disappeared. Every one of them had one reason or another, you know [pause]. I said to Allah, "I didn't do this for myself, and I wasn't getting any worldly gain out of it. I was doing it because Hazrat Sahib asked me to do it. So why has everyone disappeared?" I was quite upset at times. I kept on trying to establish the class in other places. I thought, maybe my place was not right, you know. I tried somebody else's house, but somehow the class never got established again. Then suddenly it got arranged for me to go abroad. When I was really upset, my second daughter would say to me, "Ammi, there might be some good in it for you. Maybe we don't know what it is, but maybe Allah has some other plans for you." Her words didn't really console me much at that time. But, you know, she was very right because Allah had these other plans for me, that I was going to travel and do my work there [in the United States].

A Sufi Order of Her Own

I went to the States to visit my daughter because she could not come to Pakistan then and was very homesick.[73] I had no plans for traveling at the time, but I didn't want to disappoint her either. So I said, "OK. Let me see. I'll talk to your father, and I'll see what I can do about it." Then I talked to my husband, and he said, "Yes, why don't you go?" But then the question was what to do with my youngest daughter, you know, where should I leave her [in Karachi]? Then somehow everything just worked out, and I went. Initially I went for six months. Then my daughter said, "I am going to graduate in December, so why don't you stay on?" So I stayed in America for a whole year, and some very, very interesting and amazing things happened while I was in the States.

I had written to my eldest daughter, "OK, if you want me to come, you have to find some work for me to do," besides the research that I was doing on veiling. I said, "Besides using the UT library—it is really amazing—I would like to do some speaking." She got in touch with some people from the local churches, and when I went there, she arranged for me to give several talks and lectures. After several talks, my daughter suggested, "Ammi, don't talk about all these facts and figures, talk about spirituality." Quite frankly, you know, I didn't know how to go and speak about spirituality, just out of the blue! I also had dreams, and all these other things had happened. Then I realized that I was meant to start working under my own Sufi order.

Yes! My own Sufi order. That is what my dreams told me. I even called up the present sheikh from America, my *khalifa* [caliph], who is my sheikh's younger brother. I call him Mobin Chacha.[74] I called him from the States, and

73. Nilofar's first daughter was studying at the University of Texas at Austin at that time (1997).

74. His full name is Mohammad Mobin Nasir Jehangiri. In addressing him as *chacha*, uncle (father's younger brother), Nilofar touches on multiple cultural and mystical nodes. In addition to expressing respect for Hazrat Sahib's younger brother, she acknowledges the mystical and kinship hierarchy between the two sheikhs and establishes her closeness and "kinship" relations to both brothers and her spiritual leaders.

I told him about my dreams. I mean, it sounds crazy to talk of dreams all the time [laughter], but I can't help it if I get all these special dreams so often. He said, "Yes, this is what you are supposed to be doing."[75] Just after he had given me the permission, we got disconnected. Then he moved from that house, and nobody knew where he had moved to, you know. I couldn't get in touch with him for a long, long time. He still doesn't have a telephone [smiles]. You see, I was used to asking my Hazrat Sahib's permission for doing everything and asking for his advice and guidance, but except for the permission to start teaching under the order, I got nothing else from Mobin Chacha at that time. I was a little upset, you know. I thought, "What's all this? I am supposed to start a Sufi order here [in the United States], and I don't get any instructions as how to go about it!" I mean, no one ever told me I was supposed to do this.

I have been a disciple of a Qadiri Chishti Sufi order[76] for the past twenty years. But, you see, we don't have a name for every little branch of a Sufi order in Pakistan. For example, in Pakistan you would say, "I know of a good sheikh. I'll take you to him." And people never ask, "What is the name of his particular branch of that order?" But in America you have to have some identification, a name, so we called it the Jehangiri Sufi order. We even brought out a little newsletter, a report from each program, and we called it the *Jehangiri Link.* You know, I had always been told that, according to the tradition, a woman could never become a *khalifa,* a leader of an order,[77] so it was *much* more than just a surprise to me that I was meant to do all this. At times, I would say, "What is all this? You know, a woman cannot become a *khalifa* but she has to do the work!" At the time, I had all these feminist questions coming to my mind. If you go to any conservative Sufi order in Pakistan, they always have men and women sit separately, and a woman will never be asked to address the gathering, with all the men and the *khalifa* present. That is how I had been attending my own programs in Pakistan, from behind the curtain. But in the United States I was out in the open, and I was addressing mixed gatherings and speaking with men,

75. Among the Chishtis, according to Schimmel, "the sphere of influence of a *khalifa* was designed by the master, who determined the areas where the *baraka* of this or that disciple should become active" (1986, 346).

76. Abdul Qadir Gilani (1088–1165) was an ascetic preacher from the Caspian Sea area and is buried in Baghdad. His followers are mainly from the Indo-Pakistan subcontinent, where his order was introduced in the late fourteenth century (Schimmel 1986, 247).

77. In a subsequent reading of this chapter, Nilofar explained that becoming a *khalifa* means being "a deputy of the sheikh and hence for all practical purposes a leader."

and *this* was something that was approved from somewhere. So sometimes I laugh and I say, "Yes, Allah had to choose a feminist to do all this work," and Allah is saying, "OK, you feminist [laughing], you think you are equal to men. Let's see how you will handle all this!"

So my daughter and I started a Sufi program [pause]. For six months, I was talking about Sufism. We would advertise everywhere, like putting flyers around the university. We also called up certain people that we knew [to invite them]. The bookstore in Austin was very nice. They had a community room where we held our meetings and public gatherings. I talked about topics such as the most beautiful names of God,[78] the development of the soul,[79] and free will and predestination. My favorite topic was the development of the soul because I feel this is the main aim and object of Sufism. For every program, we had a theme. We would start with a recitation of the Qur'an, selecting verses pertinent to our theme of the day. My daughter has learned how to do the *tilawat*, Qur'anic recitation, and has a beautiful voice. So then everything would be tied up with that theme. After the recitation of the Qur'an, we would have the main talk, then maybe recite a *qasida* or *naat*, an ode. My daughter and I would sing the *qasida* together in Arabic or Urdu. My favorite was the *qasida burda*, which is in praise of the Prophet's mantle. This *qasida* was written some time in the eleventh or twelfth century by an Egyptian sheikh called Sharfud-din Busiri. The story is that he was very ill. He had a dream in which the Prophet dictates this *qasida* to him. This is actually quite popular in Pakistan, and you can see it on TV on special occasions and hear it recited from mosques. After Busiri wrote this ode, the Prophet covered him with his mantle as if protecting him. In Urdu, we say *"rahmat ka saya"* [shadow or protection of mercy], and the sheikh was subsequently cured. It is a very long *qasida*, and we used only parts of it.

The words are beautiful, and there is so much strength and power in it, so much music in the rhythm. Sometimes, you know, after we sang it, some Americans, who had never heard these words before and didn't know what

---

78. In the Qur'an, God says, "The Most Beautiful Names Belong to Allah: So call on him by them" (7:180). A significant branch of Islamic cosmology is based on the divine names of God. Nilofar also published her talks in the Sufi newsletter *Jehangiri Link,* which she and her daughter published in Austin, Texas. See "The Ninety-Nine Beautiful Names of God," *Jehangiri Link,* no. 6 (1997).

79. "Three Stages in the Development of the Soul," *Jehangiri Link,* no. 5 (1997).

they meant, would come to us and say that it was something really powerful, that they loved it. I would also present a profile of a prophet or a Sufi sheikh. For one of these profiles, I selected Jesus and called it "Jesus in the Eyes of the Sufis." Some people appreciated this program particularly. One American woman came up to me and said, "Why didn't anyone tell me this before about Jesus?" Then we would have some time for questions and answers. I enjoyed that quite a bit. You are really exposing yourself if you say, "OK, ask me any question you want." But somehow I felt protected. I felt like I wasn't doing this work alone, that I had some help, and I was normally ready to answer any questions. I was never challenged by the participants [pause].

Islam, Muslim, and Feminism

Only in one of the earlier meetings held in a church, a lady who had lived in Saudi Arabia challenged me. She was quite bitter. She was a white American Christian and said that she was treated very poorly. She said, "My son was bringing home some groceries, and he was arrested because it was Ramadan. He was not caught eating or anything but was arrested just because he had bought the groceries." That [his arrest] is not even Islamic. Here [in Pakistan] I have to buy my groceries during the day [during Ramadan]! It is so senseless. I told them that they should distinguish between Islamic and Muslim. Islamic is how it should be, and Muslim is how it has turned out to be. The way people are practicing their religion is not really the way it is supposed to be. I said that Saudi Arabia is a police state, and they are not always doing what they are supposed to be doing. They have some very big problems. Their population is small, but they constantly have millions of pilgrims and others pouring in, so they want to maintain their identity and their culture and their value system. But how do they do it? By protecting their own. And protecting of course becomes obsessive to the point of constant controlling of the public.

Did you get a chance to look at that book I gave you yesterday?[80] I got a chance to present that in a large gathering in the same bookstore [in Austin], you know; they had a book-launching series, and they accepted my piece as a book, even though it is a booklet. They said, "We do not get many things on this topic." Some people told me that they had never seen such a large crowd

---

80. She had given me a copy of one of her publications, a booklet on Islamic feminism (N. Ahmed 1992), which I did read. See fn. 10, this chapter.

in there. I don't know about the size of the crowd, but I did feel that the crowd was very excited. It was a very lively gathering.

I also met several feminist groups. Those were some of the most enlightening meetings I had. These were feminist theologians, ministers, and the like. They had a group, and they invited me to give a talk. Since they were ministers, they were already quite well read, but still it is not easy to get the right perspective, even if you are well read. I think they really enjoyed my presentation, at least this is what they told me. It was interesting for them to hear from another woman from another tradition. I keep telling people [in Pakistan] that Westerners in many ways are very tolerant and generous. They invite you to their churches and let you speak about other faiths.

After doing our Sufi program for six months, my daughter and I decided to stop for Ramadan because we thought it would be very difficult to conduct it during the fasting month. Then somebody said, "Oh, no. You have to carry on, and let's continue for another few weeks." They went to talk to the management of the bookstore, and the management said, "We are closing down this room!" Up to *exactly* the time we wanted to have the program, that room was available! It is very strange.

You see, I was working mostly in Austin at that time. Then some people who were visiting from New York and other cities attended a program, held at a beautiful ranch, in which I was invited to give a talk about Prophet Muhammad and Ramadan, and they said, "Why don't you come to our city?" Now they have arranged for me to go back to the States. The people I will meet this time are also interested in Sufism, but their Sufism is different from mine. The program coordinator who telephoned me from New York while I was in Austin wanted to know more about me. What I told her was that I was born a Muslim but that I was not a practicing Muslim until I discovered my religion through Sufism. I actually went back to my religion, or I discovered it for myself through Sufism, after having sort of rejected it. She found that quite interesting [pause].

Unappreciated in Her Own Land

I don't have to continue the work here in Pakistan because the order is already here. Those who want to learn from me are back in the States. I had all these wonderful ideas in the United States but could not do much with them when I returned to Pakistan. It is a very different life. You can say it is like a watertight compartment. I did talk about my experiences to the members of Daughters of Islam. Many of them were very pleased. Our president at the time, Zaibun Nisa Naqvi, was very appreciative. She and I have a good understanding. But there are some others who were very critical because they did not approve of mixed groups—even though they attend mixed gatherings all the time. When I told them how the audience participated in the program by singing along with us and occasionally accompanying us with guitars, they got very angry because they said music is *haram*, forbidden. I do not believe that music is *haram*.[81] The irony of it is that the same people who believe that music is *haram* have the TV and the radio and VCRs on all the time. Even the news is not given without music!

In the Qur'an, it does not say that music is forbidden. In fact, the Prophet encouraged girls to sing, especially on happy occasions. They used to play the *daff*, tambourine. *Daff* was the drum of that time. In a Sufi program I attended in the United States—they were like Sufis but did not follow any one particular religion—they used words and music from just about any religion. They sang the phrase *la ilaha illallah*, there is no god but God, and we all sang it together. They brought the tone down to a whisper, and in that background my daughter recited the Qur'an. It was just *beautiful;* it was amazing! Later, you know, one of the women came up to me and said, "Today I heard what I have been waiting for all my life." She didn't know what it meant, you know. Quite frankly, I think that was one of the most beautiful things I had ever heard. I *know* the meaning of the Qur'an is the most important thing—that is what my work is all about—but there are other beauties and other spiritual effects and healing in it as well.

It is very sad that I could not transfer that spirituality, that beautiful feeling of wholeness, connection, and exhilaration, to my friends here. You see, people in those groups [in the United States] were spiritual—all of them—so it really did not matter what your language or your faith was. But here [in Pak-

---

81. See Ghazali's *Ihya' 'ulum al-din* on *"sama"*—the Sufi practice of listening to music for the purpose of generating religious emotion" (cited by Chehabi 2000, 151 n. 3). Chehabi also cites D. B. Macdonald, "Emotional Religion in Islam as Affected by Music and Singing," *Journal of the Royal Asiatic Society* (1901): 195–252 and 705–8, (1902): 1–28. *Sama'* literally means "hearing" and was a major cause of differences among Islamic schools of law. "There were complicated problems as to whether "listening to music" and "dancing movements" are genuine utterances of mystical states or illegitimate attempts to gain by one's own effort a state that can only be granted by God; the views of the authorities are clearly divided" (Schimmel 1986, 179).

istan] many people hold onto only the form, the rites and the rituals, rather than the spirit. Basically, I have a feeling that spirituality is something you are born with; it's a gift from God.

If I were to give the same lectures here and maintain the same programs and format, I think some would definitely come and enjoy it thoroughly, but many of the people who I think are very religious, not spiritual, will not come.[82] Or if they did come, they would be very critical. I have a very close friend who was very critical of my programs in the United States. She and I attend the Qur'an classes together. She once told me she had several dreams about how she had lost her way and how "From nowhere Nilofar appears. She holds my hand, and she brings me to my destination." It is very strange. I also had some similar dreams about her, which tells me that her nature is spiritual, but her up-bringing is very strict, very literalist. I did try to tell her that her dreams were telling her something, but I think that in her case her mind is stronger than her spirit or her feelings. She just keeps fighting it. She is *more* critical than a lot of people who are not spiritual at all. It is something that you cannot force on someone. I feel very sad for her. She is not aware of her loss.

People who are spiritually inclined feel very happy about such activities. But, you see, somehow because the whole society is Islamic, we don't have sep-arate spiritual groups as such. If you are in a Sufi order, then that is a spiritual group, but if you are studying the Qur'an, that is a mixed group—mostly [pause]. At the moment, the Wahhabi thinking is very strong and is sort of catching on [in Pakistan].[83] I also have the feeling that the more naïve a person, you know, the more Wahhabi thinking appeals to that person [long pause].

You see, these days I know of people who have not been bought by the ma-terialism of Saudi Arabia but are convinced that if the Saudis are doing some-thing, then it must be right—because Mecca and Medina and the Prophet's Mosque are located there. But whether the Saudis promote certain ways of thinking in Pakistan, I don't know.[84] I guess the sense of anti-Sufism has always

82. I asked her, "Do you think if you were to give the same lectures here in Pakistan, people would come?"

83. Wahhabis are the followers of Ibn-i Abd al-Wahhab (1703 [1704]–92), who "demanded a return to the pure Islam of its earlier days. They denounced all the later accretions of saint-worship and Sufism as well as the whole structure of Islamic orthodoxy which had been built up over the centuries" (Mansfield 1985, 134). The Wahhabi or "Unitarian" religious movement started in Arabia and is associated with Saudi Arabia's ruling dynasty (Eickelman 1989, 83).

84. I asked her, "Do you think the Saudis actively promote Wahhabism in Pakistan?"

been there, not just in Saudi Arabia or in Iran, but I mean everywhere. It is a kind of mindset.

You see, Sufism is like a gift, or you could say spirituality is a divine gift. If a person doesn't have that gift, he cannot experience it. And if he cannot experience something, he does not understand it. The problem is that those who have all these beautiful experiences are not allowed to divulge them. It is an unwritten rule not to expose such secrets, so the other people do not really know or understand what you're experiencing. I was reading a certain pamphlet by a certain scholar whom I used to admire. The whole purpose of this pamphlet was to write against Sufism and to degrade it. You know, he took up several points and compared them. See, many people don't even understand that Sufism is the essence of Islam; it is the spiritual or the mystical aspect of Islam.[85] What this scholar—he's supposed to be an important scholar, and I have attended some of his lectures—did in this particular pamphlet was to keep repeating that Islam says this, but Sufism contradicts it. I mean, he took it point by point to discredit Sufism. He tried to, anyway. My reaction was, "If you don't know anything about it, or don't understand it, just don't waste your energy and my time!"

Also, Maududi, in his commentary on the Qur'an, *Tafheem ul Qur'an* [Understanding Qur'an],[86] mistranslates a lot of words just to speak against Sufism. For example, rather than using the word *khanqah*, monastery, where a Sufi *pir* or *murshid* conducts his teaching, Maududi uses the word *botkadah*,[87] temple, which has all kinds of polytheistic connotations.

Enemy of Sufis: British Colonialism or Orthodoxy

These days in Pakistan it is not fashionable to belong to a Sufi order, even though the Sufi tradition used to be very strong in South Asia.[88] Someone told me how the British tried to weaken Muslim institutions so that they [Muslims]

---

85. On the gradual development of the orthodoxy's hostilities toward Sufism and mysticism, see Hoffman 1995; Schimmel 1986, 1997; Troll 1986.

86. For an English translation, see Maududi 1977.

87. *Khanqah* has all kinds of Sufic and poetic connotations conceptually, whereas *botkadah*, literally meaning the place where idols are kept, is associated with temples and idol worship. For a discussion of the meaning and role of *khanqah* in the Sufi worldview and poetry, see Schimmel 1986, 231–35.

88. On the degree of influence and spread of Sufism in South Asia, see Schimmel 1986, 344–402.

would never be able to fight back. One of the most important institutions was that of *khanqah*, you know, where the devotees of a Sufi order regularly met to learn from the sheikh and where strong relationships between the sheikh, the *pir*, and the *murid* [devotee] were formed. So the British set up fake *pirs* who would give a bad name to the whole institution.[89] I have seen and heard about the big quack *pirs* [smiling]. I guess this is the result of what we see today in Pakistan, that the educated people are not attracted to the [mystical religious] system, and if some people are, then they will not talk about it to others. This is the way I am. I do not normally talk about it to my friends, who do not understand these things.

Yes, of course, the orthodoxy has always been a constant threat—not a threat, but an enemy of Sufism.[90] The reason why I don't consider them a threat is that Sufism has always been there and will always be there. No one can do anything to destroy or do away with it. They [the orthodoxy] have also kept people away, even those who are inclined toward [pause] it. So these are some of the reasons why people today do not like to talk openly about Sufism, even if they are members of a Sufi order. They would discuss it only with those who are already in some group or have similar experiences and beliefs. Many of my close friends have no idea about my spiritual life. In fact, women in one of the Qur'an classes that I used to go to were so antispiritual that, you know, there were times when I just could not take that class anymore. Once I even mentioned it to my sheikh. He said, "It is a Qur'an class; keep going to it." I was very touched and continued going. As he predicted, some of them have now softened their stance.

Rethinking the Text

In the beginning, the loss of my son was a very deep kind of suffering. I don't think I was consciously thinking about women's issues then, but it is possible

89. Tehmina Durrani's latest novel, *Blasphemy* (1998), is about one such imposter *pir* family. She attributes the *pirs* ungodly power to the British colonizers (85–88), who used the local bullies as religious personalities to control possible willful natives. See also I. Malik 1997, 89.

90. "Orthodoxy in Islam," writes Syed Vahiduddin, "cannot be understood in the same way as in Christianity because the Muslim creed has never been officially formulated by any Council or Synod. . . . What is called orthodoxy is a very complex phenomenon in Islam and sometimes even among the ultra orthodox there are strong mystic accents" (qtd. in Troll 1986, 263, 265). I have followed the common usage of the term in this chapter, however.

that that suffering made me realize, you know, that there are other people suffering as well, for other reasons. I think I told you that to begin with I wasn't
very religiously inclined, and therefore I did not have much knowledge. So I
started to read the Qur'an. I have read it cover to cover several times and with
particular interest in women's issues and rights. I am not saying that I focused
my reading on the Qur'an just to discover women's rights, but while I was
reading the Qur'an, I had my eyes opened. Some things I read were almost like
a revelation.

Another significant thing is that many people kept inviting me to join one
kind of organization or another, but somehow I never really felt inclined. It
was the first time that I really wanted to join an organization. The visionary
founder of Daughters of Islam invited me to join. She has been a very active
social worker all her life. She was into so many things, and every time she
would try to get me involved in some of her activities, but I never really
wanted to join. This time I did not refuse.

Why? Because I had already started moving in this direction [long pause]. It
is not always that one can see so far ahead or predict or plan. It is just that
when you are confronted with a situation, you contemplate it, approve of it,
and then take the next step [long pause]. By then, I had also gotten to know
Hazrat Sahib and was becoming increasingly involved in religion and spirituality [long pause]. Once I was talking to him, I don't remember exactly what
had happened, but I said to him that I almost died. He said, "No, no, no, you
are not going to die. You have to do a lot of work with Daughters of Islam."
The DOI was already established, but we didn't have a place, and it wasn't
very active. We would meet at somebody's house, or we might have some kind
of a meeting or lecture or something. But it wasn't that active. At that time, he
told me that I had a lot of work to do with DOI! He had met the founder at one
time [her voice is almost inaudible]. She was not a disciple, but she respected
him. Some of the women in DOI are also spiritually inclined, but establishing
DOI had no connection with it.

Officially we registered as an NGO [nongovernmental organization] with
the government of Sindh [Karachi is its capital] and used one of our founder's
residence as our official address. Then, in two or three years we were able to
set up the Women's Islamic Center and Library through a government grant.
Our work has been quite satisfactory in terms of setting up the center and the
library. Whatever work we have been doing, the government keeps track of,
and so far they have found it satisfactory.

We apply to the government for specific projects. For example, they gave us a grant to start and run the Islamic Center and Library for three years. We established the library in 1988,and our grant was good until 1991; from then on, we have been on our own. I wanted you to see the library.⁹¹ Actually, it is very small and situated in a congested locality, but considering that it is a specialized library for women, it is doing all right. In the beginning, we had a rented space that was larger, but it was difficult for us to collect so much funds to be able to pay the rent every month, and we wanted a place of our own, which we have now.

Raising Consciousness, Effecting Change

In terms of detecting changes in the attitude of women and men—I think men need more changes in their attitude than women—I am very optimistic about the role that Daughters of Islam has played so far. Once a journalist from Holland asked me, "Why do you feel so optimistic, whereas everyone else I have met has been unsure?" I said, "Because no matter what you do, people, women, girls have started getting more and more educated." Once that process starts, you cannot stop it. With education comes awareness of intolerance and rejection of ideas based on ignorance. Once women have started getting educated and they have stepped out of the house, you cannot turn the clock back.

The orthodoxy, commonly known as the fundamentalists, I think, are not necessarily against education. Nor do they object to women working outside. You would be surprised to know that the women of the religious parties are out of the house all the time! They work toward getting the political campaign ready, and they have some other projects and social work [pause]. But, then, another thing I would like to mention, I am sure you already know this, is that in Saudi Arabia women are highly educated. They may not be appearing in public or in mixed gatherings, but, you see, they are there; they have all the education and knowledge [pause]. There was a visitor from Saudi Arabia, a wife of an important senior executive. She said she had a Ph.D., her daughter-in-law had a Ph.D., and her daughters all had top degrees. But she said that at the college for girls no males are allowed to step inside the premises, not even male professors. A gatekeeper works outside while his wife would be working from inside the premises. If you want to give any messages, you have to give

91. I was pressed for time and unfortunately could not coordinate with Nilofar to visit the DOI's library.

them to him. He then talks to his wife, and she then conveys the message. Also, the bus driver who takes the girls home or brings them to school is accompanied by his wife, who sits next to him in the bus [women are not allowed to drive].

I was very upset, and I said to myself, "Is this supposed to be the character of a Muslim man who cannot protect a Muslim girl who might be the same age as his daughter? What are we teaching our young men and boys?"

Our men, I think, need education of a different sort. Our [religious] scholars here are supposed to be very well educated, but they have all these regressive ideas. They talk about human nature. What is this human nature? We are not wild animals that our "nature" cannot be tamed and civilized! Human nature—I always like to go back to this story again and again. It is the story of this little Indian girl who was kidnapped as an infant by some wolves and brought up as one of their own. When they discovered her, she was about twelve or thirteen years old, and she was walking on all fours, she was howling like a wolf, she was eating raw meat, and she was scared of human beings, but she was quite comfortable with the wolves. This is a real story, you know. This means that it is the upbringing that makes the human being a human being. It is not something inborn [long pause].

In Pakistan, a religious scholar who is considered to be a women's advocate once said that women are raped because they go out of the house dressed up in a provocative fashion![92] So I said, "What about all those women in the villages who dress modestly and keep their head covered and still get regularly raped? What about all those minor girls who are raped every day in this country?"[93] Of course, they don't have an answer for that! What I am trying to say is that they do not want to take responsibility or blame the perpetrator for his actions. To me, it's like shedding responsibility, responsibility for the right kind of upbringing and responsibility for suffering the consequences of your actions.

---

92. Compare that belief with an opinion given by an Italian judge, who sometime in 1998 opined that the claim of rape by women who wear blue jeans is invalid because blue jeans are presumably too cumbersome to undress easily! The learned judge opined that the sexual act must have been therefore consensual.

93. See Durrani's 1998 novel *Blasphemy*; various reports by Women Against Rape; the annual issue on rape in the *Herald*, January 1992; and Human Rights Watch 1992. See also many of the publications by the Human Rights Commission of Pakistan.

I always wanted to write an article and call it "The Safari Park Culture." I never did write it, but I had the title before I had the article [laughter]. You know, Safari is the park in which the wild animals are loose, and the civilized people are enclosed. I think Pakistani culture is turning out to be somewhat like that. The harmful people are let loose, while the harmless are controlled.

Women: The Noblest of God's Creatures

Let me answer your second question first—namely, why all over the Muslim world many women are deprived of their basic rights. As I said earlier, people want to shed their responsibility; they want to feel superior. It is like a power game, power politics. For a male, the most immediate way of feeling superior is to have a woman whom he thinks is inferior to him. You see, for men it is already difficult enough to go out into the world and find something to make them feel superior. But it is easy to find a woman. They have to find some kind of sanction for their actions and what better justification than the text. Historically men have interpreted the text. Look at the hadith. You never find a [male] religious scholar who would emphasize how the Prophet esteemed his wives and helped them. The fact that Muslim societies are backward is because they keep 50 percent of their population—women—deliberately backward. That society will never be able to develop fully where half the population is not allowed to develop. I am not saying that Muslims should throw out their values and have their women work for eight hours a day outside the house, but that women should have a choice. Maybe this is what men are afraid of, that if they allow women to come out, all these values will be lost.

As for my vision for Muslim women, I think that Muslim women should come out and think and study for themselves—think of themselves as ashraful makhluqat, the noblest of God's creatures [in the chain of evolution]. Are they or are they not? Are only men ashraful makhluqat and women there to serve them?[94] Men think so. I think women *will* come forward through scholarly work and dissemination of knowledge. By working outside of the house, they will be able to maintain their dignity and to prove to men that they are also

94. In a critical review of the role of women in human evolution in which all activities and developments are attributed to "Man the Hunter," Ehrenberg asks rather sarcastically, "And what of 'woman' meanwhile? Was she sitting at home, twiddling her thumbs, waiting for 'man' to feed her and increase his brain capacity and abilities until he became 'Homo sapiens sapiens'?" (1997, 15–20).

ashraful makhluqat. How can women maintain values so long as they are kept from developing into a complete human being? Men and women can be educated to maintain Islamic values and taught to have the right moral values and not to bring in lust and sex into everything. Islam has been given a bad name in the world—that it envisions no rights for women. I think Islam is *the* religion in which the text talks about the rights of women! It is the interpretation and tradition that have kept women behind men and so the societies backward.

Often people ask me, "How can you be a Muslim and a feminist?" I say that I am a Muslim feminist, and I believe that the rights given to women by God and Prophet Muhammad should be given back to them. This is what women can and should demand within the limits of Islam. As I said earlier, Marmaduke Pickthall called the Prophet Muhammad "The greatest feminist the world has ever known." I believe this sums up a Muslim feminist's vision. I would like to see that women everywhere in the world are given their human rights and treated as the noblest creatures of God. I am convinced of what I have set out to do. There is no turning back.

Some Reflections: Path of Fate and Faith

As a Sufi woman, Nilofar Ahmed is heir to a rich legacy of mysticism and Sufi tradition in South Asia.[95] She shares the historical precedence with her spiritual sisters, such as Bibi Jamal Khatun (d. 1639)[96] and her disciple the Mughal princess Jihanara (d. 1681),[97] as well as Sassi and Sohni, folk heroines from Sindh and Punjab.[98] Her religious calling and eventual turn to Sufism came about gradually and haltingly, but in retrospect almost inevitably. The threshold was reached, and the "streak of mysticism and Sufism" that was dormant in her life early on was energized specifically in response to two events: her jour-

95. My reflections in this segment are based largely on two excellent books by Annemarie Schimmel, *Mystical Dimensions of Islam* (1986) and *My Soul Is a Woman: The Feminine in Islam* (1997), and on Margaret Smith's *Muslim Women Mystics* (2001). See also Ernst 1992 and Hoffman 1995.

96. Bibi Jamal Khatun "was one of the outstanding saints of the Qadiriyya order during its formative period in the Punjab." She is the sister of Mian Mir (d. 1635), a Qadiri Sufi master who is buried in Lahore (Schimmel 1986, 433; see also Smith 2001, 183–84).

97. Jihanara was the eldest daughter of Shah Jahan, who had the Taj Mahal built as the resting place for his beloved wife, Mumtaz Mahal. Jihanara was "an outstanding mystic and a renowned author of mystical works" (Schimmel 1986, 363).

98. On Sassi and Sohni, see Schimmel 1997, 139–79, and Eglar 1957, 73.

ney to the United States, where she expressed her spiritual doubt through poetry, and the tragic death of her beloved son. I consider each event briefly
within a Sufi frame of reference before discussing Nilofar's role as a Sufi "female *khalifa*"[99] and her involvement with DOI.

Doubting Faith, Knowing Self

Nilofar's internal connection with her faith and her understanding of self in
the tradition of Sufis came about as a consequence of a journey when she left
her homeland to study in the United States. Her passage to the United States
and her coming into contact with different peoples, religions, and cultural traditions seem to have been watershed experiences. It was in the United
States—in a kind of exile—that she experienced the pangs of existential
doubts. Who was she? Where did she come from? What kind of spiritual and
religious anchor did she need to have in order to make her life meaningful and
purposeful? Articulating her doubts through poetry, a language best suited to
the expression of Sufi feelings and experiences (Troll 1986, 245), Nilofar connected intellectually and emotionally with Western and Eastern philosophers
and mystics.

Only subliminally aware in the beginning, as she put it, Nilofar expressed
her doubts, temporally and spatially, in terms of Sufi icons, places, and personalities. Her poem "Flying to Istanbul" and her references to dervishes ring
familiar with the work of the great mystic poet-philosopher Rumi. Rumi's con-
version to mysticism was facilitated by his "sudden encounter with a strange
wandering dervish," Shams al-Din of Tabriz,[100] which consequently led to his
finding "his true self" (Troll 1986, 245).

Nilofar's journey to the United States sharpened her awareness of her surroundings, cleared some of the dust in her heart, and set her on a quest that
eventually led to meeting her sheikh and converting to Sufism. Once she

99. In a subsequent reading of this chapter, Nilofar expressed hesitation with my choice of
the term *khalifa* in discussing her spiritual calling. She believed that becoming a *khalifa* meant oc-
cupying a highly exulted position and becoming an authorized successor of a Sufi master. Although she was authorized to start a Sufi order in the United States, she was not sure if she
qualified for the title and did not feel comfortable thinking of herself as a *khalifa*, so hereafter I
use the word *leader* instead to describe her.

100. See fn. 58, this chapter, for information on Rumi.

found her path, there was "no turning back," in her words. Sufism is what gives her life direction and meaning, and all her activities are guided by the spirit of Sufism.

Affliction: Death of a Beloved

Sufi literature and poetry are rich with numerous mystics' contemplation of *bala*, affliction, and what it means or ought to mean to the afflicted. For a Sufi, affliction is first and foremost a sign of divine love,[101] which "makes the seeker capable of bearing, even enjoying, all the pains and afflictions that God showers upon him in order to test him and to purify his soul" (Schimmel 1986, 4). Affliction is also necessary for a Sufi's spiritual development: it is the "salt of the faithful, and when the salt lacks, the faithful becomes rotten" (Schimmel 1986, 44–45). Affliction is the knowledge that, in Nilofar's words, "you are with God, even if you are suffering."

Throughout Sufi history, however, the death of a child generally was not perceived as an affliction among South Asian Sufis and early ascetics, and seemed to cause little stir (Schimmel 1986, 347–48). They often considered married life an affliction (Schimmel 1986, 428; Smith 2001, 196–97), although Islam specifically condemns celibacy (Smith 2001, 195). For that matter, perhaps, and for devotional and personal reasons, some Sufi women saints refrained from marrying and forming a family. In fact, several convents for women existed in Mecca "for women Sufis desiring to lead a celibate life . . . in the year AH 590" (Smith 2001, 201). Exemplary among them is Rabi'a, the most inspirational Muslim female mystic, who persistently rejected her numerous suitors (Smith 2001, 29–37). "By maintaining celibate lifestyles, [women] rejected the guardianship of men and the requirement of obedience to men, as well as the burdens and responsibilities of being wives and mothers" (Hoffman 1995, 229). Many, of course, did marry and care for their children. For these women, the death of a child would be taken as an affliction. It was certainly so for Nilofar.

Nilofar went through deep suffering and perhaps never completely recovered, though in the spirit of a true mystic she became resigned to the calamity that had afflicted her life. It was the tragic death of her beloved son, however,

---

101. "Who say, when afflicted with calamity: 'To God we belong, and to Him is our return' " (Qur'an 2:156).

that finally pushed her into crossing the threshold of her lingering doubt, brought her closer to God, and convinced her to become a Sufi disciple. The little boy's death was the most significant turning point in her life, one that, though very painful, put her squarely on the path of faith, emotionally and intellectually. Her suffering sensitized her to afflictions of other kinds and brought into focus the deep suffering of many Muslim women in her society.

A Female Sufi Leader

Women mystics are found throughout the Muslim world, according to Schimmel, "but the area in which women saints flourished most is probably Muslim India" (1986, 433; see also Ernst 1992, 144, 237, and Smith 2001, 183 ff.). This prevalence is in part owing to the fact that the cultural atmosphere of South Asia has been particularly conducive to the development of various Sufi orders, and Sufis have had a more tolerant attitude toward women. It can be said that "Sufism, more than stern orthodoxy, offered women a certain amount of possibilities to participate actively in the religious life in general" (Schimmel 1986, 432). Stern the orthodoxy has remained toward Sufism, if not in fact becoming more intolerant of it, as Nilofar suggests. Apprehensive of the orthodoxy's negative reaction, Nilofar often underplays her Sufi affiliation and spirituality in public. Her caution becomes understandable when one considers the double jeopardy in which she may find herself culturally and religiously: as a woman whose feminist interpretations of religion challenge the traditional religious ideas and hierarchy, and as a Sufi who is also clamoring for greater tolerance, equality, and social justice. This equality, which is closer to the original Islam in Nilofar Ahmed's view—and in others' views—is abhorrent to the orthodoxy, which has increasingly turned into "petrifying stratification" (Schimmel 1997, 180).

Nilofar's gender, however, was no barrier to her sheikh's recognition of her leadership quality and to the development of a warm and caring relationship between master and disciple, one imbued with mutual respect and devotion.[102] Hazrat Sahib openly expressed his affection for her and was confident of his disciple's ability to continue the teachings of the order. In that, the sheikh was

102. On the strong relationship between sheikh and devotee, see Schimmel 1986, 237, and Smith 2001, 184. Nilofar herself has written on the topic. See "Bai'at: The Formal Shaykh-Disciple Relationship and Its Need," *Jehangiri Link*, no. 6 (1997).

perhaps guided by the text as well as by precedence. The procedure for the initiation of women disciples was based on the Qur'anic injunction (60:12) "women could undertake initiation with a Sufi shaykk just as women had taken the oath of allegiance to Muhammad" (Ernst 1992, 128). The grand Sufi master Ibn-i Arabi writes therefore in his *Futuhat al-makkiyya* (Meccan revelations) that women can attain the highest mystical rank (Schimmel 1986, 431, and 1997, 23; Hoffman 1995, 235—41). Such keen trust by a sheikh and *khalifa* in his female disciple is also not without its precedence in South Asia. The Qadiri Sufi master Molla Shah Badakhshi (d. 1661) thought of Jihanara, the Mughal princess, as "worthy to be his successor." That succession did not actually materialize, however (Schimmel 1986, 363; Smith 2001, 183–84). In Nilofar's case, it was not Hazrat Sahib himself who gave her the permission to start a branch of their Sufi order in the United States, but his successor and brother, who also was disposed favorably toward Nilofar.

It is both significant and ironic to note here that for Nilofar to be a Sufi leader meant that she had to be outside her own society. Perhaps it was only in that transitional state, in the United States, that she actually could assume the role of a Sufi teacher, a role traditionally reserved for men back in her country. A further irony is the name Nilofar chose for her order: Jehangiri. Jehangiri was, of course, Hazrat Sahib's name, and she used it as a tribute to her sheikh, but *jehangir* also means "world conqueror," literally. The crosscutting connections and the multiplicity of coincidences and associations between a Muslim feminist's starting a Sufi order called the "world conqueror" perhaps can be explained only in mystical terms or be thought of as subliminally subversive.

Firmly positioning herself on the path of her faith and certain about the possibility, indeed the necessity, of a woman-friendly interpretation of the Qur'an, Nilofar moved cautiously to publicize her views and at the same time facilitated other women's access to religious knowledge and self-understanding. She also was caught between the political necessity to keep a low profile and her desire to profess and propagate Sufism. In her view, Sufism is not only a more genuine way to understand Islam, but also a way to foster a more tolerant attitude toward one's fellow citizens, women or men. Although there is historical justification for Sufis' fear and anxiety, Syed Vahiduddin, an Indian Muslim scholar, argues that in fact Sufism has brought about the rapprochement between Shi'ism and Sunnism on a deeper level of religious experience (Troll 1986, 255). There is no reason to believe that Sufism potentially cannot play a similarly mediatory role in contemporary Pakistan, given the influential role

Sufism and Sufi women have played historically in South Asia. That is to say, it can play a mediatory role not only between various religious denominations, but also between religion and the secular structures of power, one that ultimately may lead to greater equality and respect between the genders.

For the moment, religious revivalist discourse may dominate the social and political scenes in Pakistan. Voices of dissent, however, are heard from secular and spiritual corners. What may happen in this crosscutting cacophony of domineering and dissenting voices and conflicts of interests remains to be seen. Nilofar, however, may take heart in the determination that her spiritual sisters Sassi and Sohni, two of South Asia's favorite folk heroines, showed in setting out on a quest to reach their beloved. Their quest ended in their physical destruction in the Sufi context, in their spiritual unification with their Divine Beloved. Nilofar's quest, however, will lead to the rehabilitation of her contemporary sisters and to the raising of their consciousness, ultimately bringing about greater gender parity, which Nilofar, like many other Muslim women, believes to be closer to the original Islam.

Daughters of Islam

"[T]he strong and untiring role women played in Islam" is remarkable, according to Schimmel (1986, 429). In modern times, she writes, "Sufi teaching is, to a large extent, carried on by women again," and "some of the most genuine representatives of mystical tradition, directors of souls, in Istanbul and Delhi (and probably in other places as well) are women, who exert a remarkable influence upon smaller or larger groups of seekers who find consolation and spiritual help in their presence" (435; see also Smith 2001, 225–32).

Nilofar Ahmed is in good company. It was her Sufism that prompted her finally to join the DOI and to concentrate actively on the plight of women in Pakistan, who—in her view and in her DOI colleagues' view—are unaware of the legitimate rights given them in the Qur'an. Not everyone in DOI is as spiritual as Nilofar, although one may assume that just as Nilofar is apprehensive of the orthodoxy's reaction to her Sufi leanings, there might be others among her colleagues who share her anxieties and so keep *their* spirituality secret. The secrecy, however, has not prevented them from charging ahead to work for social justice and a more egalitarian and woman-friendly society.

For that matter, Nilofar believes Sufism is Islam, and she is not shy about positioning her knowledge firmly in the Qur'an and drawing legitimacy di-

rectly from the source, while challenging—for now discretely—the orthodoxy's long-held misogynist view of women and gender relations. With an untiring faith, she and her colleagues play an important role in changing their
community and believe that women ought to be perceived, as only men have
been seen all along, as citizens of the Muslim community and as *ashraful
makhluqat,* the noblest of creatures.

Conclusion

MY RESEARCH among middle-class and upper-middle-class professional Pakistani women led me to examine critically certain assumptions, theories, and methods for the study of religion and gender and for the study of self and society in the Muslim world. Following Laura Nader's (1974) exhortation to "study up," I conducted research among people who are more like myself, educated and professional women.

This book is an attempt to encourage greater reflexivity by expanding research among people with a similar or equal degree of power, position, and privilege to that of the anthropologist. Although there has been a move toward self-reflexivity and "a new form of ethnographic discourse" (Layton 1997, 191), the ethnographers' dominant "other" has continued to remain the downtrodden, the rural, the peasant, and the tribal. The lives of skilled, educated, and professional Muslim women, unlike those of their veiled sisters, have attracted little attention.

The six extensive narratives of educated and professional Pakistani women brought into focus aspects of women's lives that I think have not been explained sufficiently. The diversity of women's experiences and their interactions with power structures and institutional restrictions revealed the influential roles that working and educated women have played in their society. To understand the paradoxical changes in Muslim societies, particularly with regard to feminism and to the religious backlash that has engulfed the Muslim world—indeed much of the world—we need to understand the active roles independent, educated and working women have played in their society, Muslim or non-Muslim.

Fieldwork among Equals

In retelling the lives of these remarkable women, I adopted an experimental ethnographic approach: "shared ethnography." I actively sought their critical interventions and solicited their social analyses by engaging them in long discussions, debates, and disputes regarding various personal and social issues in their society. That I was an Iranian Muslim woman from a similar professional and cultural background greatly facilitated our discussions, creating mutual respect and friendship. My views of them came to be based on long-term association and continued friendship and contact as we shared stories, compared notes, and exchanged ideas. I tried not to fragment these women's life stories into pieces for purposes of analysis and devoted each life to a chapter. Although the women spoke for themselves, I included extensive footnotes to provide cultural and historical contexts for the purpose of clarity for the reader. At the end of each chapter, I interpreted that particular life by discussing it within anthropological and feminist theoretical frameworks.

The experience of conducting fieldwork among Pakistani professional women was different from the one I had earlier in Iran. In Iran, in the early 1980s, I was an Iranian American, a "halfie," researching the legal history, the legalities, and the practices of temporary marriage or *sigheh*, a marginal and stigmatized form of marriage among lower-class Iranian women who, for a variety of personal and social reasons, had made use of it. They could not relate to or were not interested in my research (beyond occasional curiosity) despite my effort to explain it. Some even believed I was an American spy. Why else would anyone go all the way to Iran and to places such as Qom and Kashan to research temporary marriage and to interview them!

In Pakistan, however, the educated, middle-class professional women were different. My interests overlapped with them in terms of career objectives and education, despite differences in our nationality. As educated citizens of a postcolonial society, the Pakistani professional women I met were familiar with social research, and some had conducted research of their own. They were forthcoming with their critiques and analyses of their culture, and articulated their experiences passionately and frankly within and despite Pakistani society's institutional boundaries and cultural and moral constraints. Like their sisters in other parts of the world, they negotiated, challenged, accommodated, and attempted to resolve religious, cultural, political, and personal conflicts while pursuing their professional objectives. Their narratives provide more complex frameworks for understanding women and culture in Pakistan and, by implication, in other parts of the Muslim world.

Recognizing Islam and Muslim Women

Last year at a Christmas party I was introduced to a professional woman, a clinical psychologist, as an Iranian Muslim feminist. Without a pause, she said, "Wow, that must be an oxymoron!" With no chance for comments on my part, she continued, "Well, there are always exceptions." She seemed to suggest that I, as a Muslim woman, presumably should be veiled or at least not be so similar to my Western counterpart. My imagined difference from other Muslim women was, in fact, less confounding than my perceived commonality with Western women.

The women's life stories presented in this book reveal the simplicity of stereotypes such as those indicated in my experience. They bring into focus multiple areas of tensions and conflicts, transgressions and aspirations, as women try to juggle professional requirements and family demands and to engage with religion and custom, law and politics, husbands and bosses, parents and siblings, in-laws and children. Like their counterparts in the West and elsewhere, Pakistani professional women have to reconcile their careers with their culture's demand regarding their duties as wives and mothers. Working women the world over, of course, are not unfamiliar with such tensely demanding juggling.

These women's struggles to reach their professional goals underscore the historic ambivalence the Pakistani state has shown toward the growing needs of its working female citizens. The state's ambivalence stems from the convergence of several contending forces: its national objectives; a growing religious intolerance and influence; and the dominant code of honor characteristic of a feudal and tribal society. Successive Pakistani regimes have given their women citizens conflicting signals. As a sovereign, the state has in theory promoted the rights of its women citizens to education, professional goals, and individual aspirations. However, because the state is made up of feudal aristocracy, religious parties, and particular lineages, it has tended to perceive women as objectifiable entities—in the same order as land, zamin, and gold, zar—whose conduct bears directly on the honor of their male kin. Conflicts and tensions consequently become endemic to professional women's relationships with their husbands, families, culture, religion, and politics.

The range of relationships and roles that emerge from these women's narratives highlights the inadequacy of characterizing Pakistani society exclusively in patriarchal terms. They expose the paucity of the assumption of a unitary patriarchal images of an ever-dominant and domineering man/husband/father and of an obedient and victimized woman/wife/mother. Kishwar and Qurat clearly drew a picture of their mothers as domineering and decisive disciplinarians, while portraying their fathers (more clearly Qurat's) as loving and giving, as followers (of their wives) rather than as decision makers.

Ayesha's parents' relationship, though resembling a traditional hierarchical conjugal union in the sense of the sexual division of authority and power within the household, also departed from the "norm": a highly educated, middle-class, and intellectual wife with a barely educated feudal husband. Ayesha's relationship with her parents raises questions about the hegemony of the conventional role models in Pakistan. Very interested in her daughter's welfare, Ayesha's mother was too emotionally aloof and opaque for Ayesha to be able to have a mutually satisfying relationship with her, to feel comfortable and comforting. Her father, the great patriarch and feudal lord, seemed freer in expressing his love and devotion to his daughter. Ayesha's strong relationship with her father took on a much greater significance. Not only did he provide solace in her life, but he also recognized her as the heir apparent and bestowed legitimacy on her as a feudal lord—with all its trappings of authority, power, and privilege. For a majority of women in this book, except for Sajida and possibly Kishwar, their relationship with their fathers was of particular significance.

Likewise, the dynamics of mother-daughter relations among these women—and among many more in similar situations—are more complex and unconventional than generally presumed in Pakistani society. The underlying tension between mother and daughter manifested itself more intensely and openly in the lives of Kishwar and Qurat. Personally independent, domineering, and even willful, these two women's mothers could not tolerate a reflection of their own persona in their daughters. They upheld the patriarchal tradition to suppress and subdue their daughters' individuality and autonomy. Kishwar, insecure in her relationship with her mother, did not develop a warm and satisfying relationship with her father either, though she found her relationship to her father less conflictual. Qurat also felt emotionally distanced from her mother, but she felt closer to her father than did Kishwar to her father. Rahila and Ayesha had a more intense, complex, and ongoing love-hate relationship with their mothers, though Ayesha felt deeply conflicted by her mother's strict morality.

Clearly the significance of father-daughter relationships in Pakistan and in other Muslim societies remains un(der)appreciated. To perceive the bond between father and daughter as negligible or solely as emotionally satisfying to them is inadequate and unrepresentative of the existing range of such relationships. The dynamics and significance of the cross-gender filial bond should be of much theoretical interest to anthropologists as well, as I argued in Ayesha's chapter. Many ethnographies are written on the patrilineal social structure, on the nature and the dynamics of the father-son relationship, and on the rivalries and tension between them, but hardly anything has been written on cross-gender relationships. As I pointed out, such countermodels, as that of the relationship between Ayesha and her father or that between Benazir Bhutto and her prime minister father—to give a more nationally prominent example—have generated little theoretical excitement or attention among anthropologists. It is with respect to such "paradox of patrilineay," as I have argued, that we can appreciate the significance of prominent powerful and politically prominent women leaders in South Asia, coexisting with many powerless and oppressed women.

Moreover, unwilling to relinquish the religious domain to men and drawing much comfort and satisfaction from it, women such as Nilofar reclaim religion by interpreting it from a feminist perspective as something more empowering to women than oppressive. Nilofar and others do not deny the misogyny that historically has shackled women in Pakistan, but they see that bondage more in terms of culture and traditional code of conduct rather than of religion, though of course much violence is committed in the name of religion. Nilofar happened to be the only practicing Muslim in my sample, but the other women I interviewed also identified with their religion in their own ways. Nilofar's Sufism, Rahila's spiritualism, Kishwar's materialism, Qurat's secularism, and Ayesha's local variation demand a reexamination of Islam as a religion that is multifaceted rather than singular, that is dynamic rather than all-determining, and that can be empowering to women rather than oppressive.

No Shame for the Sun attempts to situate the diverse life experiences of professional Pakistani women in their proper context, to highlight the women's discourse, and to underscore the womens uniqueness by making them visible outside their own society—like the sun that shines brilliantly and publicly.

Glossary

Works Cited

Index

Glossary

URDU IS CLOSELY ASSOCIATED with Hindi grammatically, yet distinguished from it by script and vocabulary. It borrows heavily from Persian and Arabic, although pronunciation and meaning may vary slightly or significantly from province to province in Pakistan. I have checked the Urdu spellings with Ferozsons' *Urdu-English Dictionary* (n.d.), as well as with a native speaker to account for variations in pronunciations. I also have included here the names of important places and languages in Pakistan as well as events in the Islamic calender and the names of various branches of Islam.

aaq: disown.
abba/abbu: father, lord or master.
achchhi: good, proper, fine.
alim (pl. *ulama*): scholar.
allaho akbar: God is great.
almari: cupboard.
amma/ammi: mother.
ana: ego, self.
arusi: wedding.
ashraful makhluqat: noblest of God's creatures.
atish fishan: volcano.
atta: flour.
awami: of common folk.
ayat/ayeh (pl. *ayaat*): verse of the Qur'an.
azan: call to the daily prayer.
azim qurbani: great sacrifice.
baba: father, an old man.
baba bhag gaien: father ran away.
baba e-qaum: father of the nation.
bachpan: childhood.
badal: revenge.

bad kirdar: bad character, corrupt.

bait bazi: poetry contest.

baizzat: honorable.

baji : elder sister.

bakhshish: gift, tip, donation, forgiveness.

bala: affliction, calamity.

barakat: spiritual power, blessing, abundance.

basirat: attributes of God and the Prophet.

bebasi: helplessness.

beghairat: shameless.

begum (pl. *begumaat*): rich lady, wife.

behaya: shameless.

behen/bahan: sister.

beizzati: dishonor.

besharam: shameless.

beti/bitya: daughter.

bewuquf: foolish.

bewuqufi: foolishness.

bhabi: sister-in-law (brother's wife).

bhai: brother.

bhai jan: dear brother, older brother.

bibi: lady, woman.

botkadah: temple for idols.

bradri/baradri: brotherhood, tribal fraternity.

buddha: old man.

buqchah: bundle.

burda: Prophet Muhammad's outer garment.

buri: bad.

burqa: an all-enveloping veil.

buzdil: coward.

chacha: father's younger brother, uncle.

chand: moon.

chappal: sandal, slipper.

char diwari: the four walls of the home.

chehlum: forty-day ritual of mourning after death.

chikh: scream.

chokidar: gatekeeper.

choti: small.

dacoit/daku (dacoity): thief, robbery.

dada: paternal grandfather.

dadi: paternal grandmother.

daff: tambourine.

dal: lentil.

dam: breath, life, vitality, energy.

dars: Islamic education, lesson.

darr: fear, dread.

desi: native, local.

devi: goddess.

dhoti/lungi: a piece of cloth wrapped around the hips, passed between the legs, and fastened at the back.

din: day.

diya: an earthen lamp.

doshman: enemy.

dupata: long, rectangular, thin scarf worn by Pakistani women.

durood/darud: salutations, benedictions.

faqah: starvation.

faqih: Islamic scholar.

faqir: mendicant, beggar.

faqr: poverty.

fatiha: Qur'anic prayer for the dead.

fatwa: a religious and judicial decree.

fiqh: jurisprudence.

fitnah: chaos, discord, temptation, enchantment.

fitrat: nature.

gand: filth, stink.

gandi: bad character (fem.), dirty.

ghaddar: disloyal, treacherous.

ghairat: protection of honor, care of what is scared and inviolable.

ghalat: wrong, untrue.

ghar: house, home.

gharara: a pleated, long skirt.

ghazal: lyrical poetry.

ghee: clarified butter, butter oil.

ghilaz/ghilazat: filth.

ghulel: slingshot, catapult.

ghundah: a bad man, a rogue, a bully.

giriftari: captivity, arrest, difficulty.

gunah: sin, crime.

haal: spiritual ecstasy.

haari: landless peasant.

hai na: isn't it?.

haji: a pilgrim who makes the *hajj*.

hajj: Muslims' annual pilgrimage to Mecca.

halal: permitted, lawful.

haram: forbidden, unlawful.

har dil aziz: popular, loved by all.

hazrat: honorific address.

hertal: strike.

hijab: covering, commonly associated with veiling, modest dress.

hookah: water pipe.

hudood (pl.): punishments.

ibrat: example, warning.

ilm: knowledge.

ilm-i ghaib: divination, foreknowledge.

imandar: honest.

imandari: honesty.

imtihan (pl. *imtihanon*): test.

inqilab: revolution.

inshallah: God willing.

Islamabad: capital city of Pakistan.

izzat: honor.

jagir: land given by the government as a reward for services rendered.

jagirdar: landowner, feudal lord.

jahiz/jihaz: dowry, from bride to groom.

jala dia: burned.

jallad: executioner, cruel.

jerga: assembly of elders.

Jum'a *khutba*: Friday sermons.

kachchi abadi: slum area.

kafir: infidel.

kahani: a story, a tale.

kalam: word, poetry.

Kalma: the Word, Qur'an.

kambakht: unlucky, wretched.

kamiz/qamiz: shirt, chemise.

kanal: standard unit of land measurement (in Lahore, 500 square yards; elsewhere in Pakistan, 604 square yards).

Karachi: capital city of Sindh Province.

Karbala: city in Iraq where the Shi'ites third imam, Hussain, was martyred (680 C.E.).

khab: dream.

khairat: charity.

khala: maternal aunt.

khalas: finished.

khalifa/caliph: the Prophet's successor, leader.

khanqah: abode of holy men, monastery.

kharab: bad, corrupt.

kharaj: tribute, duty.

khatam: finished, gone; also the recitation of the Qur'an for the mourning ritual.

khatarnak: dangerous.

khauf zadah: scared, frightened.

khazana: treasure.

kholi: dark, solitary cell.

khuda: God, Allah.

khud nivisht: autobiography.

khula: divorce initiated by a woman.

kurta: a loose outergarment.

laddu: sweetmeat rolled into balls.

ladli: a [female] child indulged with love.

Lahore: capital city of Punjab Province.

langar: food distributed to the poor.

lihaf: quilt.

lotta: water pitcher used in a toilet.

lungi/dhoti: a cloth worn around the hips and legs.

maas: flesh.

maasi: mother's sister.

madrasa: school, traditional school.

mahaul: environments, surroundings.

mahr/meher: dower, bride-price.

mahram: lawful, permitted, relative before whom veiling is not required.

majazi khuda: false gods.

makkar: cunning, deceitful.

maktab: traditional school.

mali: gardener.

mamu: maternal uncle.

manhus: inauspicious, unlucky.

mannat: vow, prayer for a wish.

mardana khana: men's quarters, public area.

marsiya: elegy.

masalla: several spices mixed together.

maulvi/mullah: a general term for low-ranking clergy.

mazar: shrine, tomb.

mehndi: part of the marriage ceremony in which the bride and other women decorate their hands and feet with henna..

melmastia: hospitality code among the Pathans.

mitha/meetha: sweets.

mitti: earth, soil.

mosahib: companion.

muhajir: Urdu-speaking immigrant from India, a refugee.

muharib (Qur'anic): warring.

Muharram: first month of the Arabic calendar, also commemorated by Shi'ites for the martyrdom of Imam Hussain in 680 C.E.

muhkamat: indisputable verses in the Qur'an.

mujeza: miracle.

munafiq (pl. *munafiqun*) (Qur'anic): hypocrite.

munshi: secretary, scribe.

murid: a devotee, a disciple.

murshid: a Sufi spiritual teacher.

mushaera: poetry contests, contending or excelling in poetry.

mutashabihat: similar, ambiguous passages in the Qur'an.

naat: ode.

na-aurat: not woman.

nafel: religious offering.

nafsiyati pagal: mentally disturbed (literally, psychologically crazy).

namahram: unlawful, forbidden, not permitted, unrelated men before whom women are required to veil.

namaz: daily prayers.

nanawatee: peacemaking code among the Pathans.

nani: maternal grandmother.

nawab/nabob: rich person, a governor of a district or town.

nawa-e: voice of.

nazm: free-verse poetry.

nikah: Muslim marriage contract.

nikah namah: marriage certificate.

nishana: target.

noton ka haar: money garland.

pagal: crazy.

pagal khana: madhouse, asylum.

pahna: to wear.

pak: pure.

Pakhtunwali: codes of honor among the Pathans.

palki: covered chair used to carry women.

paratha: fried bread.

pashiman: repentant, penitent.

patthar: grinding stone.

patwari: accountant, a keeper of records.

Peshawar: capital city of the North-West Frontier Province.

phuphi: father's sister.

pir: spiritual leader.

pir behen: spiritual sister.

Punjabi: resident of Punjab Province.

qabilah: tribe.

qana'at: contentment.

qasida: an ode, laudatory poem.

qaum (pl. *qaumoun*): tribe, race, people.

qawwali: devotional songs.

qawwamun: superior.

qazi: judge.

quaid: leader, the title used for Mohammad Ali Jinnah, the founder of Pakistan.

Quetta: capital city of Baluchistan Province.

rafiq: friend, supporter.

rahmat: God's blessing.

Ramazan/Ramadan: Muslim month of fasting.

rasul: messenger, the Prophet.

rij'at pasand: retrogressive, conservative.

rishteh dar: kinfolk.

roti: bread.

rozah: fasting.

sahib: master, lord, sir (a courtesy title).

sajjada nishin: a spiritual person attached to a mosque or religious endowment.

sama': hearing, listening, spiritual dance.

Saraiki: one of languages spoken in Pakistan.

sarkari: belonging to the state or government.

sarkari ghundah: bad people connected with the government.

savab: religiously meritorious.

sayyid: presumed descendent of the Prophet.

sahari: predawn meal for fasting.

shadi: wedding.

shahid: martyr.

shahinshahiyyat: imperial system.

shaitan: devil.

shalwar-kamiz: the two-piece suit worn by Pakistani women.

shamiyana: a canopy, a pavilion, a tent.

sharm/sharam: humility, honor.

sheikh: a spiritual leader.

Shi'a: a follower of Ali; the minority branch of Islam.

shighar: pre-Islamic marriage, where two women were exchanged between two families without the exchange of bride-price.

shihadat: martyrdom.

Shi'ite: a follower of Ali, the fourth caliph and first Shi'ite imam.

siday-i haq: voice of truth.

Sindhi: from Sindh Province, also the language of that area.

Sufi: a devotee of mysticism and spiritualism in Islam.

Sunna: body of Islamic custom and practice based on the Prophet Muhammad's words and deeds.

Sunni: a follower of the Sunna tradition, a follower of the majority branch of Islam.

sura: a chapter of the Qur'an.

suraj: sun.

tabla: a small tambourine, a drum.

tafsir: interpretation of Qur'an.

tahajjud: midnight prayers.

tahlil: legal procedure for reconciliation between husband and wife.

thanah: police station.

takbir: God is great.

talaq: divorce.

tamasha: show.

tarannum: sung poetry.

tarawi: recitation of the Qur'an.

tarbiyat: education, upbringing.

tasbih: worry beads, rosary.

tasvir: image, photo.

ta'wiz: amulet, protective charm.

thuk: spit.

tilawat: Qur'anic recitation.

tore: "darky."

tuhmat: false accusation.

umra: off-season pilgrimage to Mecca.

urs: a *pir*'s or sheikh's death anniversary.

viva: Ph.D. oral examination.

wa'da: promise, commitment.

walima: the marriage feast given by the groom's family, marking the marriage consummation.

waqf (pl. *auqaf*): endowment for public charity and piety.

watta-satta: exchange marriage, usually of a brother and a sister with another brother-sister pair.

wazifa khar: salaried personnel.

wedera/wadera: feudal lord.

zakat: the 2.5 percent of Muslims' income that is to be given to the poor.

zalim: cruel.

zamin: earth, property.

zamindar: landowner.

zamir: conscience.

zan: woman.

zar: gold, wealth.

zarur: definitely.

zehn: mind.

zibah: slaughter, sacrifice.

zidd: stubborn, persistent.

zina: adultery.

zindagi: life.

zindeh raho: stay alive.

Works Cited

Abouzeid, Leila. 1996. "Experiences in—among Other Places—Syria and Beijing." *Middle East Women's Studies Review* 11, no. 2 (June): 13.

Abu-Lughod, Lila. 1991. "Writing Against Culture." In *Recapturing Anthropology*, edited by Richard G. Fox, 137–62. Santa Fe, N.M.: School of American Research Press.

Afzal Khan, Fawzia. 1997. "Pakistani Street Theatre in the Punjab and the Women Question: The Cases of Ajoka and Lok Rehan." *Drama Review* 41, no. 3: 39–63.

Ahmad, Mumtaz. 1991. "Islamic Fundamentalism in South Asia: The Jama'at-i Islami and the Tablighi Jama'at." In *Fundamentalism Observed*, edited by Martin E. Marty and R. Scott Appleby, 457–530. Chicago: Univ. of Chicago Press.

Ahmad, Nausheen. 1992. "Criminal Abuse of Women by Law Enforcing Agencies." In *Criminal Abuses of Women and Children*, 4–16. Karachi: Pakistan Association for Mental Health.

Ahmad, Rukhsana. 1990. *Beyond Belief: Contemporary Urdu Feminist Poetry*. Lahore: ASR.

Ahmed, Akbar S. 1976. *Millennium and Charisma among Pathans: A Critical Essay in Social Anthropology*. London: Routledge and Kegan Paul.

———. 1977. *Pieces of Green: The Sociology of Change in Pakistan (1964–1974)*. Karachi: Royal Book Co.

———. 1980. *Pukhtun Economy and Society: Traditional Structure and Economic Development in a Tribal Society*. London: Routledge and Kegan Paul.

———. 1989. *Pakistan Society: Islam, Ethnicity, and Leadership in South Asia*. Karachi: Oxford Univ. Press.

Ahmed, Durre Sameen. 1994. *Masculinity, Rationality, and Religion: A Feminist Perspective*. Lahore: ASR.

———. 1997. "The Changing Face of Tradition." In *Women's Lifeworlds: Women's Narratives on Shaping Their Realities*, edited by Edith Sizoo, 39–53. London: Routledge.

Ahmed, Khalid. 1992. "The Sociology of Rape." *Slogan* (February): 36–37.

Ahmed, Leila. 1992. *Women and Gender and Islam*. New Haven, Conn.: Yale Univ. Press.

————. 1999. *A Border Passage: From Cairo to America—A Woman's Journey*. New York: Far-rar, Straus and Giroux.

Ahmed, Nilofar. 1992. *Islam: A Feminist Perspective*. Karachi: Daughters of Islam.

————. 2000. "When Mortals Act as Gods [Of *nikab* and *talaq*]." *Dawn* (April): 23.

Ahmed, S. Haroon, ed. 1991. *Contemporary Conflict*. Karachi: Pakistan Psychiatric Soci-ety, Sindh Chapter.

Alam, Talat. 1989. "The Year of Living Dangerously." *Herald* (Karachi) (December): 31–42.

Alavi, Hamza. 1987. "Ethnicity, Muslim Society, and the Pakistan Ideology." In *Islamic Reassertion in Pakistan: The Application of Islamic Law in a Modern State*, edited by Anita M. Weiss, 21–47. Lahore, Pakistan: Vanguard.

Altorki, Soraya. 1986. *Women in Saudi Arabia: Ideology and Behavior among the Elite*. New York: Columbia Univ. Press.

————. 1988. "At Home in the Field." In *Arab Women in the Field: Studying Your Own Soci-ety*, edited by Soraya Altorki and Camillia Fawzi El-Solh, 49–68. Syracuse, N.Y.: Syracuse Univ. Press.

Altorki, Soraya, and Camillia Fawzi El-Solh. 1988. *Arab Women in the Field: Studying Your Own Society*. Syracuse, N.Y.: Syracuse Univ. Press.

Ammerman, Nancy. 1991. "North American Protestant Fundamentalism." In *Funda-mentalism Observed*, edited by Martin E. Marty and R. Scott Appleby, 1–65. Chicago: Univ. of Chicago Press.

Arberry, A. J. 1967. *Classical Persian Literature*. London: George Allen and Unwin.

Armstrong, Nancy, and Leonard Tennenhouse. 1989. *The Violence of Representation*. Lon-don: Routledge.

Asad, Talal. 1986. "The Concept of Cultural Translation in British Social Anthropol-ogy." In *Writing Culture: The Poetics and Politics of Ethnography*, edited by James Clifford and George E. Marcus, 141–64. Berkeley and Los Angeles: Univ. of California Press.

————. 1993. *Genealogies of Religion: Discipline and Reasons of Power in Christianity and Islam*. Baltimore and London: Johns Hopkins Univ. Press.

Badawi, Jamal A. 1995. *Gender Equity in Islam*. Plainfield, Ind.: American Trust.

Bakhteari, Quratul Ain. 1988. "Building on Traditional Patterns for Women's Empow-erment at Grassroots Level." *Development* 4.

————. 1992. *From Sanitation to Development: Case Study of the Baldia Soakpit Project*. The Hague: International Water and Sanitation Center.

————. 1995. *Home School for Education*. Lahore, Pakistan: ASR.

Bakhtiar, Idrees. 1992. "The Politics of Rape." *Herald Annual* (Kararchi) (January): 36–42.

Balchin, Casandra, ed. 1994. *A Handbook on Family Law in Pakistan.* Lahore, Pakistan: Shirkat Gah.

———, ed. 1996. *Women, Law, and Society: An Action Manual.* Lahore, Pakistan: Shirkat Gah.

Bano, Nasim, and Thira Fahim. 1995. "Women Workers' Center." In *A Celebration of Women: Essays and Abstracts from the Women's Studies Conference, March 1994,* edited by N. Said Khan, R. Saigol, and A. S. Zia, 108–111. Lahore, Pakistan: ASR.

Bari, Farzana. 1995. "Historical Continuities and Discontinuities in the Women's Movement in Pakistan." In *A Celebration of Women: Essays and Abstracts from the Women's Studies Conference, March 1994,* edited by N. Said Khan, R. Saigol, and A. S. Zia, 135–137. Lahore, Pakistan: ASR.

Barth, Fredrick. 1970. *Political Leadership among Swat Pathans.* 1959. Reprint, London: Athlone.

———. 1981. *Features of Person and Society in Swat: Collected Essays on Pathans.* Vol. 2. London: Routledge and Kegan Paul.

Behar, Ruth. 1996. *The Vulnerable Observer: Anthropology That Breaks Your Heart.* Boston: Beacon.

Benard, Cheryl. 2002. *Veiled Courage: Inside the Afghan Women's Resistance.* New York: Broadway.

Bennett, Lynn. 1983. *Dangerous Wives and Sacred Sisters: Social and Symbolic Roles of High-Caste Women in Nepal.* New York: Columbia Univ. Press.

Bhatty, Zarina. 1975. "Women in Uttar Pradesh: Social Mobility and Directions of Change." In *Women in Contemporary India,* edited by A. DeSouza, 25–36. Delhi: Manohar.

Bhutto, Benazir. 1989. *Daughter of the East: An Autobiography.* London: Mandarin.

Bouhdiba, A. 1985. *Sexuality in Islam.* Translated from French by Alan Sheridan. London: Routledge.

Breckenridge, Carol A., and Peter van der Veer, eds. 1993. "Orientalism and the Postcolonial Predicament." In *Orientalism and the Postcolonial Predicament: Perspectives on South Asia,* 1–19. Philadelphia: Univ. of Pennsylvania Press.

Brown, M. F. 1988. "On Resistance." *American Anthropologist* 4: 729–35.

Bumiller, Elisabeth. 1990. *May You Be the Mother of a Hundred Sons: A Journey among the Women of India.* New York: Random House.

Burki, Shahid Javed. 1987. "Economic Management Within an Islamic Context." In *Islamic Reassertion in Pakistan: The Application of Islamic Law in a Modern State,* edited by Anita M. Weiss, 49–58. Lahore, Pakistan: Vanguard.

Caroe, Olaf. 1983. *The Pathans: 550 B.C.-A.D. 1957.* 1958. Reprint, Karachi: Oxford Univ. Press.

Chatty, Dawn. 2000. "Women Working in Oman: Individual Choice and Cultural Constraints." *International Journal of Middle East Studies* 32, no. 2: 241–54.

Chehabi, Houshang. 2000. "Voices Unveiled: Women Singers in Iran." In *Iran and Beyond: Essays in Middle Eastern History in Honor of Nikki R. Keddie*, edited by R. Matthee and Beth Baron, 151–66. California: Mazda.

Chhachhi, Amrita. 1991. "Forced Identities: The State, Communalism, Fundamentalism, and Women in India." In *Women, Islam, and the State*, edited by Deniz Kandiyoti, 144–75. Philadelphia: Temple Univ. Press.

Chodorow, Nancy J. 1989. *Feminism and Psychoanalytic Theory*. New Haven, Conn.: Yale Univ. Press.

Clark, Grace. 1987. "Pakistan's Zakat and 'Ushr as a Welfare System." In *Islamic Reassertion in Pakistan: The Application of Islamic Law in a Modern State*, edited by Anita M. Weiss, 79–95. Lahore, Pakistan: Vanguard.

Clifford, James, and George E. Marcus, eds. 1986. *Writing Culture: The Poetics and Politics of Ethnography*. Berkeley and Los Angeles: Univ. of California Press.

Corbin, Henry. 1971. *The Man of Light in Iranian Sufism*. Translated from French by Nancy Pearson. Boulder, Colo.: Shambhala.

Cornwall, Andrea, and Nancy Lindesfarne. 1994. *Dislocating Masculinity: Comparative Ethnographies*. London: Routledge.

Currie, P. M. 1989. *The Shrine and Cult of Mu'in Al-Din Chishti of Ajmer*. Delhi: Oxford Univ. Press.

Das, Veena. 1986. "Gender Studies, Cross-Cultural Comparisons, and the Colonial Organization of Knowledge." *Berkshire Review*:: 58–76.

De Tassy, Garcin. 1995. *Muslim Festivals in India and Other Essays*. Translated from Urdu and edited by M. Waseem. Delhi: Oxford Univ. Press.

Doniger, Wendy. 1999. *Splitting the Difference: Gender and Myth in Ancient Greece and India*. Chicago: Univ. of Chicago Press.

Dossa, Parin A. 1999. "Narrating Embodied Lives: Muslim Women on the Coast of Kenya." In *Feminist Fields: Ethnographic Insights*, edited by R. Bridgman, S. Cole, and H. Howard-Bobiwash, 157–72. Peterborough, Ontario: Broadview.

Douglas, Mary. 1966. "The Abomination of Leviticus." In *Purity and Danger: An Analysis of Concepts of Pollution and Taboo*. New York: Frederick A. Praeger.

Dumato, Eleanor Abdella. 1995. "Seclusion." In *The Oxford Encyclopedia of the Modern Islamic World*, edited by John L. Esposito, 4:19–20. New York: Oxford Univ. Press.

———. 1996. "Am I 'Part of the Problem'?" *Middle East Women's Studies Review* 11, no. 2: 11–13.

Durrani, Tehmina. 1997. *My Feudal Lord*. An autobiography, with William Hoffer and Marilyn Hoffer. 1994. Reprint, London: CORGI.

———. 1998. *Blasphemy*. Lahore, Pakistan: Ferozsons Ltd.

Eglar, Zakiye. 1957. "Panjani Village Life." In *Pakistan: Society and Culture*, edited by Stanley Maron, 62–80. New Haven, Conn.: HRAF.

Ehrenberg, Margaret. 1997. "The Role of Women in Human Evolution." In *Gender in Cross-Cultural Perspective*, edited by C. B. Brettell and C. F. Sargent, 15–20. Englewood Cliffs, N.J.: Prentice Hall.

Eickelman, Dale. 1989. *The Middle East: An Anthropological Approach.* 2d ed. Englewood Cliffs, N.J.: Prentice Hall.

El Guindi, Fadwa. 1999. *Veil: Modesty, Privacy, and Resistance.* Oxford: Berg.

El-Solh, Camillia Fawzi, and Judy Mabro, eds. 1994. *Muslim Women's Choices: Religious Belief and Social Reality.* Providence, R.I.: Berg.

Engineer, A. A. 1987. *Status of Women in Islam.* Delhi: Ajanta.

Ernst, Carl W. 1992. *Eternal Garden: Mysticism, History, and Politics at a South Asian Sufi Center.* New York: State Univ. of New York Press.

Esfandiari, Haleh. 1997. *Reconstructed Lives: Women and Iran's Islamic Revolution.* Washington, D.C.: Woodrow Wilson Center Press.

Esposito, John. 1982. *Women in Muslim Family Law.* Syracuse, N.Y.: Syracuse Univ. Press.

Fayzee, Asaf A. A. 1974. *Outlines of Muhammadan Law.* 4th ed. 1949. Delhi: Oxford Univ. Press.

Fernandes, Nora. 1995. "Women's Action Forum and the Women's Movement in Pakistan Today." In *A Celebration of Women: Essays and Abstracts from the Women's Studies Conference, March 1994*, edited by N. Said Khan, R. Saigol, and A. S. Zia, 87–94. Lahore, Pakistan: ASR.

Filali-Ansary, Abdou. 1999. "The Debate on Secularism in Contemporary Societies of Muslims." *International Institute for the Study of Islam in the Modern World (ISIM) Newsletter* 2 (March): 6.

Firdousi, Ishrat, ed. 1996. *The Year That Was.* Dhaka, Bangladesh: Bastu Prakashan.

Foucault, Michel. 1973. *The Order of Things.* New York: Vantage.

Fox, Richard G. 1991. *Recapturing Anthropology: Working in the Present.* Santa Fe, N.M.: School of American Research Press.

Freire, Paulo. 1970. *Pedagogy of the Oppressed.* New York: Continuum.

Ganesh, Kamala. 1997. "Etching on a Grain of Rice." In *Women's Lifeworlds: Women's Narratives on Shaping Their Realities*, edited by Edith Sizoo, 21–38. London: Routledge.

Garakani, Fazlollah. 1977. *Tuhmat-i shaeri* (Accused of being a poet). Tehran: Alborz.

Gardezi, Hassan. 1983. "Feudal and Capitalist Relations in Pakistan." In *Pakistan, the Roots of Dictatorship: The Political Economy of a Praetorian State*, edited by Hassan Gardezi and Jamil Rashid, 19–39. London: Zed.

Gardezi, Hassan, and Jamil Rashid, eds. 1983. *Pakistan, the Roots of Dictatorship: The Political Economy of a Praetorian State.* London: Zed.

Geertz, Clifford. 1973. "Religion as a Cultural System." In *The Interpretation of Cultures*, 87–125. New York: Basic.

———. 1986. "Making Experiences, Authoring Selves." In *The Anthropology of Experience*, edited by V. Truner and E. Bruner, 373–80. Urbana: Univ. of Illinois Press.

———. 1994. "Primordial and Civic Ties." In *Nationalism*, edited by John Hutchinson and Anthony D. Smith, 29–34. Oxford: Oxford Univ. Press.

Gerami, Shaheen. 1996. *Women and Fundamentalism: Islam and Christianity*. New York: Garland.

Gilmartin, David. 1998. "Partition, Pakistan, and South Asian History: In Search of a Narrative." *Journal of Asian Studies* 57, no. 4: 1068–95.

Gilmore, David. 1987. "Introduction: The Shame of Dishonor." In *Honor and Shame and the Unity of the Mediterranean*, edited by David Gilmore, 2–21. Washington, D.C.: American Anthropological Association.

Gilsenan, Michael. 1990. "Very Like a Camel: The Appearance of an Anthropologist's Middle East." In *Localizing Strategies: Regional Traditions of Ethnographic Writing*, edited by Richard Fardon, 222–39. Edinburgh: Scottish Academic Press and Smithsonian Institution Press.

Goodwin, Ian. 1994. *Price of Honor: Muslim Women Lift the Veil of Silence of the Islamic World*. New York: Plume.

Gujral, J. S. 1987. "Widowhood in India." In *Widows: The Middle East, Asia, and the Pacific*, edited by H. Z. Lopata, 43–55. Durham, N.C.: Duke Univ. Press.

Haeri, Shahla. 1993a. *Law of Desire: Temporary Marriage in Shi'i Iran*. 1989. Reprint, Syracuse, N.Y.: Syracuse Univ. Press.

———. 1993b. "Obedience versus Autonomy: Women and Fundamentalism in Iran and Pakistan." In *Fundamentalism and Society: Reclaiming the Sciences, the Family, and Education*, edited by M. E. Marty and R. S. Appleby, 181–213. Chicago: Univ. of Chicago Press.

———. 1995a. "Of Feminism and Fundamentalism in Iran and Pakistan." *Contention: Debates in Society, Culture, and Sciences* 4, no. 3 (spring): 129–49.

———. 1995b. "Politics of Dishonor: Rape and Power in Pakistan." In *Faith and Freedom: Women's Human Rights in the Muslim World*, edited by M. Afkhami, 161–74. London: I. B. Tauris.

Hale, Sandra. 1996. "Modernism and Middle East Women's Studies." *Middle East Women's Studies Review* 11, no. 2 (June): 1–3.

Haroon, Anis. 1995. "The Woman's Movement in Pakistan." In *Unveiling the Issues: Pakistani Women's Perspectives on Social, Political, and Ideological Issues*, edited by N. Said Khan and A. S. Zia, 178–86. Lahore, Pakistan: ASR.

Harris, W. H., and J. S. Levey, eds. 1975. *New Columbia Encyclopedia*. New York: Columbia Univ. Press.

Hashmi, Jamila. 1941. *Atash-i rafteh* (Extinguished fire, or Gone glory). Lahore, Pakistan: Dastangu.

———. 1987. *Rang bhum* (Spoiling a good time). Lahore, Pakistan: Writer's Club.

———. n.d. *Chehra be chehra ru be ru* (Face to face). Lahore, Pakistan: Writer's Club.

Hassan, Riffat. 1982. "On Human Rights and the Qur'an Perspective." In *Human Rights in Religious Traditions*, edited by Arlene Swidler, 51–65. New York: Pilgrim.

———. 1985. "Made from the Adam's Rib: The Woman's Creation Question," *Al-Mushir* 26, no. 3: 124–54.

Hefner, Robert. 1998. "Multi Modernities: Christianity, Islam, and Hinduism in a Globalizing Age." *Annual Review of Anthropology* 27: 83–104.

Heilbrun, Carolyn G. 1988. *Writing a Woman's Life*. New York: Norton.

Herzfeld, Michael. 1985. *The Poetic of Manhood*. Princeton: Princeton Univ. Press.

Hillman, James. 1996. *The Soul's Code: In Search of Character and Calling*. New York: Random House.

Hina, Zahida. 1994. "The Earth Is Ablaze and the Heavens Are Burning." In *In Her Own Write*, edited and translated from Urdu by Samina Rehman, 109–33. Lahore, Pakistan: ASR.

Hoffman, Valerie. 1995. *Sufism, Mystics, and Saints in Modern Egypt*. Columbia: Univ. of South Carolina Press.

Human Rights Watch. 1992. *Double Jeopardy: Police Abuse of Women in Pakistan*. New York: Human Rights Watch.

———. 1996. *All Too Familiar: Sexual Abuse of Women in the U.S. State Prisons*. New York: Human Rights Watch.

Hussain, Akmal. 1987. *Status of Women in Islam*. Lahore, Pakistan: Law.

———. 1990. "The Karachi Riots of December 1986: Crisis of State and Civil Society in Pakistan." In *Mirror of Violence: Communities, Riots, and Survivors in South Asia*, edited by Veena Das, 185–93. Delhi: Oxford Univ. Press.

Imam, Hina Faisal. 1991. "Women Poets: The Image and Reality in Pakistan." In *Finding Our Way: Reading on Women in Pakistan*, edited by Fareeha Zafar, 177–86. Lahore, Pakistan: ASR.

Inden, Ronald. 1990. *Imagining India*. Cambridge, Mass.: Blackwell.

Iqbal, Javid. 1988. "Crime Against Women in Pakistan." Paper presented at the Triennial Conference of the All Pakistan Women's Association (APWA), Karachi, April 9.

Jahangir, Asma. 1992. "The Many Faces of Rape." *Herald Annual* (Karachi) (January): 52A, 52B.

Jahangir, Asma, and Hina Jilani. 1992. *Hudood Ordinance: A Divine Sanction?* Lahore, Pakistan: Rhotas.

Jalal, Ayesha. 1985. *The Sole Spokesman: Jinnah, the Muslim League, and the Demand for Pakistan*. Cambridge: Cambridge Univ. Press.

———. 1991a. "The Convenience of Subservience: Women and the State of Pakistan." In *Women, Islam, and the State,* edited by Deniz Kandiyoti, 48–76. Philadelphia: Temple Univ. Press.

———. 1991b. *The State of Marshal Rule: The Origin of Pakistan's Political Economy of Defense.* Lahore, Pakistan: Vanguard.

———. 1995. *Democracy and Authoritarianism in South Asia: A Comparative and Historical Perspective.* Cambridge: Cambridge Univ. Press.

———. 2001. *Self and Sovereignty: Individual and Community in South Asian Islam Since 1850.* Lahore, Pakistan: Sang-e-Meel.

Jami, Maulana Abdulrahman. 1957 [1336]. *Nafahat al-Uns min hazarat al-Quds.* Edited by M. Tauhidi Pour. Tehran: Mahmoudi.

Jilani, Hina. 2000. Interview. *Amnesty Now* (spring): 15.

Kahf, Mohja. 1999. *Western Representations of the Muslim Woman: From Termagant to Odalisque.* Austin: Texas Univ. Press.

Kakar, Sudhir. 1989. *Intimate Relations: Exploring Indian Sexuality.* Chicago: Univ. of Chicago Press.

Kamal, Zainab. 1995. "Reflections on the Women's Movement in Pakistan." In *A Celebration of Women: Essays and Abstracts from the Women's Studies Conference, March 1994,* edited by N. Said Khan, R. Saigol, and A. S. Zia, 131–34. Lahore, Pakistan: ASR.

Kamran, Yousef. 1981. *Akaile safar ka akaila musafer* (Lonely traveler of a lonely journey). Lahore, Pakistan: Tariqu.

———. 1984. *Safar tamam hova* (The journey is over). Lahore, Pakistan: Sang-e-Meel.

Kanda, K. C. 1990. *Masterpieces of Urdu Ghazal from 17th to 20th Century.* Lahore, Pakistan: Vanguard.

Kandiyoti, Deniz, ed. 1991. *Women, Islam, and the State.* Philadelphia: Temple Univ. Press.

Kar, Mehrangiz. 1999 [1378]. *Sakhtar-i nizam-i khanivadeh dar Iran* (The legal structure of the family in Iran). Tehran: Roshangran and Women Studies.

Katz, Ruth, and Nitza Ben-Dor. 1987. "Widowhood in Israel." In *Widows: The Middle East, Asia, and the Pacific,* edited by H. Z. Lopata, 133–47. Durham, N.C.: Duke Univ. Press.

Kennedy, Charles H. 1987. "The Implementations of the Hudood Ordinance in Pakistan." *Islamic Studies* 26, no. 4 (winter): 307–19.

———. 1990. "Islamization and Legal Reform in Pakistan, 1979–89." *Public Affairs* 63, no. 1 (spring): 62–77.

Kiernan, Victor. 1971. *Poems by Faiz.* Translated from Urdu by V. Kiernan. Lahore, Pakistan: Vanguard.

Kritzeck, James. 1970. *Modern Islamic Literature from 1800 to the Present.* New York: Holt, Rinehart and Winston.

Kuper, Adam. 1999. *Culture: The Anthropologists' Account.* Cambridge, Mass.: Harvard Univ. Press.

Lane, Edward. 1973. *The Manners and Custom of the Egyptians.* 1836. Reprint, New York: Dover.

Lawrence, Bruce. 1989. *Defenders of God: The Fundamentalist Revolt Against the Modern Age.* New York: Harper and Row.

Layton, Robert. 1997. *An Introduction to Theory in Anthropology.* Cambridge: Cambridge Univ. Press.

Lindholm, Charles. 1982. *Generosity and Jealousy: The Swat Pukhtun of Northern Pakistan.* New York: Columbia Univ. Press.

Lindholm, Cherry. 1996. "The Swat Pukhtun Family as Political Timing." In *Frontier Perspective: Essays in Contemporary Anthropology,* edited by Charles Lindholm, 17–27. Karachi: Oxford Univ. Press.

Lokhandwala, S. T. 1987. "The Position of Women under Islam." In *The Status of Women in Islam,* edited by A. A. Engineer, 1–76. Delhi: Ajnata.

Lopata, H. Z. 1996. *Current Widowhood: Myths and Realities.* Thousand Oaks, Calif.: Sage.

Low, S. M. 1996. "The Anthropology of Cities: Imagining and Theorizing the City." *Annual Review of Anthropology* 25: 383–409.

Malik, Hafeez. 1980. *Sir Sayyid Ahmad Khan and Muslim Modernization in India and Pakistan.* New York: Columbia Univ. Press.

Malik, Iftikhar. 1997. *State and Civil Society in Pakistan: Politics of Authority, Ideology, and Ethnicity.* London: Macmillan.

Mandelbaum, David G. 1988. *Women's Seclusion and Men's Honor: Sex Roles in North India, Bangladesh, and Pakistan.* Tucson: Univ. of Arizona Press.

Mann, E. A., 1992. *Boundaries and Identities: Muslim Work and Status in Aligarh.* New Delhi: Sage.

Mannan, M. A. 1995. *D. F. Mulla's Principles of Mahomedan Law.* Lahore, Pakistan: PLD.

Mansfield, Peter. 1985. *The Arabs.* New ed. New York: Penguin.

Manto, Saadat Hasan. 2000. "Toba tek singh." In *Manto's World: A Representative Collection of Saadat Hasan Manto's Fiction and Non-Fiction,* translated from Urdu by Khalid Hasan, 9–16. Lahore, Pakistan: Sang-e-Meel.

Marty, Martin, and Scott Appleby. 1991–96. *Fundamentalism Project.* Chicago: Univ. of Chicago Press.

Maskiell, Michelle. 1984. *Women Between Cultures: The Lives of Kinnaird College Alumnae in British India.* Syracuse, N.Y.: Maxwell School of Citizenship and Public Affairs.

Mastoor, Khadija. 1981. "The Hand Pump." In *Pakistan: Modern Urdu Short Stories,* edited by S. Viqar Azim, translated from Urdu by S. Mahmud, 159–78. Islamabad: R.C.D. Cultural Institute.

———. 1994. "Disdain." In *In Her Own Write*, edited and translated from Urdu by Samina Rehman, 13–24. Lahore, Pakistan: ASR.

Maududi, Abul'ala. 1977. *Towards Understanding Islam*. Translated from Urdu and edited by Khurshid Ahmed. Indianapolis, Ind.: Islamic Teaching Center.

———. 1987. *Purdah and the Status of Women in Islam*. 9th ed. Translated from Urdu and edited by Al Ash'ari. Lahore, Pakistan: Islamic.

Mazari, Shirin. 1983. "Islamization and the Status of Women in Pakistan: A Note." *South Asian Bulletin* 3, no. 1 (spring): 79–82.

Mehdi, Baqer. 1984. *Izhar* (Expression). Bombay: n.p.

Mehdi, Rubya. 1997. "The Offence of Rape in the Islamic Law of Pakistan." *Dossier* 18 (July): 98–108.

Mernissi, Fatima. 1994. *Hidden from History: Forgotten Queens of Islam*. Pakistan ed. Lahore, Pakistan: ASR.

Messner, Michael A. 2001. "Becoming 100 Percent Straight." In *Men's Lives*, edited by Michael S. Kimmel and Michael A. Messner, 5th ed., 401–6. Boston: Allyn and Bacon.

Ministry of Information and Broadcasting. 1991. *Pakistan 1991: An Official Handbook*. Islamabad: Ministry of Information and Broadcasting, Government of Pakistan.

Monshipouri, M. 1995. *Democratization, Liberalization, and Human Rights in the Third World*. Boulder, Colo.: Lynne Rienner.

Moore, Erin P. 1998. *Gender, Law, and Resistance in India*. Tucson: Univ. of Arizona Press.

Moore, Henrietta. 1988. *Feminist Anthropology*. Minneapolis: Univ. of Minnesota Press.

Moorhouse, Geoffrey. 1984. *To the Frontier*. New York: Holt, Rinehart and Winston.

Morris, Brian. 1995. *Anthropological Studies of Religion: An Introductory Text*. Cambridge: Cambridge Univ. Press.

Morsy, Soheir. 1988. "Fieldwork in My Egyptian Homeland: Toward the Demise of Anthropology's Distinctive-Other Hegemonic Tradition." In *Arab Women in the Field: Studying Your Own Society*, edited by Soraya Altorki and Camillia Fawzi El-Solh, 69–90. Syracuse, N.Y.: Syracuse Univ. Press.

Mumtaz, Khavar. 1989. "Khawateen mahaz-e-amal and Sindhiani Tehrik: Two Responses to Political Development in Pakistan." Paper prepared for the 1989 Annual Meeting of the Association for Asian Studies, Washington, D.C.

Mumtaz, Khavar, and Fareeda Shaheed, eds. 1987. *Women of Pakistan: Two Steps Forward, One Step Back?* London: Zed.

Murphy, Richard. 1996. "Space, Class, and Rhetoric in Lahore." Ph.D. diss. Oxford Univ.

Mutahhari, Murtiza. 1974. *Nizam-i huquq-i zan dar Islam* (Women's legal rights in Islam). Qom, Iran: Sadra.

Naber, Nadine. 1996. "The Most Invisible of the Invisibles." *Middle East Women's Studies Review* 11, no. 2 (June): 6–8.

Nader, Laura. 1974. "Up the Anthropologist: Perspectives Gained from Studying Up." In *Reinventing Anthropology*, edited by D. Hymes, 284–311. New York: Vintage.

Naheed, Kishwar. 1971. *Galyan, dhoop, darwazey* (Lanes, sunshine, and doors). Lahore: Sang-e-Meel.

———. 1976. *Malamaton kay dar mian* (In the midst of humiliation). Lahore: Sang-e-Meel.

———. 1985. *Siah hashieh main gulabi rang* (Pink color in black margin). Lahore, Pakistan: Sang-e-Meel.

———. 1988. *Aurat: Khab or khak ke dar mian* (Woman: Between dream and dust). Lahore, Pakistan: Sang-e-Meel.

———. 1991a. *Benaam musafat* (Nameless distance). 1971. Reprint, Lahore, Pakistan: Sang-e-Meel.

———. 1991b. *Lab-i guya* (Speaking lips) 1969. Reprint, Lahore, Pakistan: Sang-e-Meel.

———. 1991c. *The Scream of an Illegitimate Voice: Selection of Poems of Kishwar Naheed.* Translated from Urdu by Baidar Bakht, Leslie Lavigne, and Derek M. Cohen. Lahore, Pakistan: Sang-e Meel.

———. 1992. *Khiyali shakhs se muqableh* (Face-to-face with an imaginary person). Lahore, Pakistan: Sang-e-Meel.

———. 1997. *Buri 'aurat ki katha* (The story of a bad woman). 1995. Reprint, Lahore, Pakistan: Sang-e-Meel.

Najmabadi, Afsaneh. 1997. "Teaching and Research in Unavailable Intersections." *Difference: A Journal of Feminist Studies* 9, no. 3: 65–78.

Nanada, Serena. 1996. *Neither Man nor Woman: The Hijras of India.* Belmont, Calif.: Wadsworth.

Narasimhan, Sakuntala. 1990. *Sati: Widow Burning in India.* New York: Anchor Books, Doubleday.

Nasr, S. Vali Reza. 1994. *The Vanguard of the Islamis Revolution: The Jama'at Islami of Pakistan.* Berkeley and Los Angeles: Univ. of California Press.

Nelson, Cynthia. 1996. *Doria Shafik, Egyptian Feminist: A Woman Apart.* Gainesville: Univ. Press of Florida.

Nicholson, Reynold A. 1950. *Rumi: Poet and Mystic.* Translated from Persian. London: Allen and Unwin.

Ortner, Sherry. 1996. "The Virgin and the State." In *Making Gender: The Politics and Erotics of Culture*, 43–58. Boston: Beacon.

Papanek, Hanna, and Gail Minault. 1982. *Separate Worlds: Studies of Purdah in South Asia*. Columbia, Mo.: South Asia.

Parveen, Farhat, and Karamat Ali. 1995. "Organizing Women Factory Workers in Pakistan." In *A Celebration of Women: Essays and Abstracts from the Women's Studies Conference, March 1994*, edited by N. Said Khan, R. Saigol, and A. S. Zia, 112–30. Lahore, Pakistan: ASR.

Personal Narratives Group, ed. 1989. *Interpreting Women's Lives: Feminist Theory and Personal Narratives*. Bloomington: Indiana Univ. Press.

Pickthall, Muhammad Marmaduke. 1977. *The Meaning of Glorious Qur'an: Text and Explanatory Translation*. New York: Muslim World League.

Ram Baveja, Malik. 1981. *Women in Islam*. New York: Advent.

Richter, William L. 1987. "The Political Meaning of Islamization in Pakistan: Prognosis, Implications, and Questions." In *Islamic Reassertion in Pakistan: The Application of Islamic Law in a Modern State*, edited by Anita M. Weiss, 129–40. Lahore, Pakistan: Vanguard.

Riesebrodt, Martin. 1993. *Pious Passion: The Emergence of Modern Fundamentalism in the United States and Iran*. Berkeley and Los Angeles: Univ. of California Press.

Rifaat, Alifa. 1987. "Distant View of a Minaret." In *Distant View of a Minaret*, 1–4. Translated from Arabic by Denys Johnson-Davis. Oxford: Heinemann.

Rosaldo, Renato. 1993. *Culture and Truth*. Boston: Beacon.

Rumi, Maulana Jalaluddin. 1925–40. *Mathnavi ma'navi*. 8 vols. Translated from Persian by Reynold A. Nicholson. Gibb Memorial Series, n.s. 4. London: Luzac.

Rushdie, Salman. 1983. *Shame*. New York: Alfred A. Knopf.

Said, Edward. 1991. "Foucault and the Imagination of Power." In *Foucault: A Critical Reader*, edited by David Couzens Hoy, 149–55. Cambridge, Mass.: Basil Blackwell.

Said Khan, Nighat. 1988. *Women in Pakistan: A New Era? A Publication of Change*. International Reports: Women and Society. Lahore, Pakistan: ASR.

———. 1992. *Voices Within: Dialogues with Women on Islam*. Lahore, Pakistan: ASR.

———. 1995. "Identity, Ideology, and Religion." In *Unveiling the Issues: Pakistani Women's Perspectives on Social, Political, and Ideological Issues*, edited by N. Said Khan and A. S. Zia, 117–25. Lahore, Pakistan: ASR.

Said Khan, Nighat, Rubina Saigol, and Afiya Shehabano Zia, eds. 1995. *A Celebration of Women: Essays and Abstracts from the Women's Studies Conference, March 1994*. Lahore, Pakistan: ASR.

Said Khan, Nighat, and Afiya Shehabano Zia, eds. 1995. *Unveiling the Issues: Pakistani Women's Perspectives on Social, Political, and Ideological Issues*. Lahore, Pakistan: ASR.

Saigol, Rubina. 1995. *Knowledge and Identity: Articulation of Gender in Educational Discourse in Pakistan.* Lahore, Pakistan: ASR.

Sardar Ali, Shaheen, and Kamran Arif, eds. 1994. *Blind Justice for All? Parallel Judicial Systems in Pakistan: Implications and Consequences for Human Rights.* Lahore, Pakistan: Shirkat Gah.

Schimmel, Annamarie. 1986. *Mystical Dimensions of Islam.* Chapel Hill: North Carolina Univ. Press.

———. 1997. *My Soul Is a Woman: The Feminine in Islam.* Translated from German by Susan H. Ray. New York: Continuum.

Scott, Joan. 1994. "The Evidence of Experience." In *Question of Evidence: Proof, Practice, and Persuasion Across Disciplines,* edited by J. Chandler, A. I. Davidson, and H. Harootunian, 363–88. Chicago: Univ. of Chicago Press.

Shaarawi, Huda. 1986. *Harem Years: The Memoirs of an Egyptian Feminist (1879–1924).* Edited, introduced, and translated from Arabic by Margot Badran. London: Virago.

Shah, Nafisa. 1994a. "Sexual Harrassment: The Working Women's Dilemma." *Newsline* (January): 28–45.

———. 1994b. "The Women's Room." *Newsline* (April): 82–83.

Shaheed, Farida. 1984. "Creating One's Own Media: WAF in Pakistan." In *Women and Media: Analysis, Alternatives, and Action,* edited by Kamla Bhasin and Bina Agarwal, 82–88. New Delhi: Kali for Women.

———. 1989. "Purdah and Poverty in Pakistan." In *Women, Poverty, and Ideology in Asia: Contradictory Pressures, Uneasy Resolutions,* edited by H. Afshar and B. Agarwal, 17–42. London: Macmillan.

———. 1990. *Pakistan's Women: An Analytical Description.* Islamabad: Royal Norwegian Embassy, NORAD, August.

———, ed. 1992. *The Women of Pakistan: A Selected Bibliography with Annotations.* Lahore, Pakistan: Shirkat Gad.

Shahnawaz, Jahan Ara. 1971. *Father and Daughter.* Lahore, Pakistan: Nigarishat.

Sheikh, Shehnaaz. 1989. "Divorce under Muslim Law." *Dossier* 7–8 (October): 42–45.

Shirazi, Faegheh. 2001. *The Veil Unveiled: The Hijab in Modern Culture.* Gainsville: Univ. Press of Florida.

Shweder, Richard A. 2000. "Rethinking the Object of Anthropology (and Ending Up Where Kroeber and Kluckhohn Began)." *Items and Issues: Social Science Research Council* 1, no. 2 (summer): 7–9.

Sidhwa, Bapsi. 1983. *Bride.* New York: St. Martin's.

———. 1991. *Cracking India.* Minneapolis: Milkweed.

Sizoo, Edith. 1997. *Women's Lifeworlds: Women's Narratives on Shaping Their Realities.* London: Routledge.

Smith, Margaret. 2001. *Muslim Women Mystics: The Life and Work of Rabiʻa and Other Women Mystics in Islam*. Oxford: Oneworld.

Spain, J. W. 1957. "Pathans of the Tribal Area." In *Pakistan: Society and Culture*, edited by S. Maron, 135–53. New Haven, Conn.: Human Relations Area Files.

Stewart, Frank. 1994. *Honor*. Chicago: Univ. of Chicago Press.

Stowasser, Barbara F. 1996. "Women and Citizenship in the Qurʼan." In *Women, the Family, and Divorce Laws in Islamic History*, edited by A. El Azhary Sonbol, 23–38. Syracuse, N.Y.: Syracuse Univ. Press.

Street, Brian. 1990. "Orientalist Discourse in the Anthropology of Iran, Afghanistan, and Pakistan." In *Localizing Strategies: Regional Traditions of Ethnographic Writing*, edited by Richard Fardon, 240–59. Edinburgh: Scottish Academic Press and Smithsonian Institution Press.

Stump, Roger W. 2000. *Boundaries of Faith: Geographical Perspectives on Religious Fundamentalism*. New York: Rowman and Littlefield.

Suleri, Sara. 1989. *Meatless Days*. Chicago: Univ. of Chicago Press.

Sunder Rajan, Rajeswari. 1993. *Real and Imagined Women: Gender, Culture, and Postcolonialism*. London: Routledge.

Tapper, Nancy. 1991. *Bartered Brides: Gender and Marriage in an Afghan Tribal Society*. Cambridge: Cambridge Univ. Press.

"Text of Shariat Bill." 1991a. *Dawn*, April 12, 1.

"Text of Shariat Bill." 1991b. *Pakistan Today*, April 14, 3.

Thanvi, Maulana Ashraf Ali. 1981. *Heavenly Ornaments*. Translated from Urdu by M. M. Khan Saroha. Lahore, Pakistan: Sh. Muhammad Ashraf.

Troll, Christian. 1986. *Islam in India: Studies and Commentaries*. Delhi: Bhanakya.

Trouillot, Michel-Rolph. 1991. "Anthropology and the Savage Slot: The Poetics and Politics of Otherness." In *Recapturing Anthropology: Working in the Present*, edited by Richard G. Fox, 17–44. Santa Fe, N.M.: School of American Research Press.

Turner, Victor. 1974. *Dramas, Fields, and Metaphors: Symbolic Action in Human Society*. Ithaca, N.Y.: Cornell Univ. Press.

———. 1976. *The Ritual Process: Structure and Anti Structure*. Chicago: Aldine.

Visram, Rozina. 1992. *Women in India and Pakistan: The Struggle for Independence from British Rule*. Cambridge: Cambridge Univ. Press.

Vreede-de Stuers, Cora. 1968. *Parda: A Study of Muslim Women's Life in Northern India*. Assen, Netherlands: Koninklijke Van Gorcum.

Wagner-Martin. Linda. 1994. *Telling Women's Lives: The New Biography*. New Brunswick, N.J.: Rutgers Univ. Press.

Ward, Martha. 1996. *A World Full of Women*. Boston: Allyn and Bacon.

Weaver, Mary Anne. 2000 "Gandhi's Daughters: India's Poorest Women Embark on an Epic Social Experiment." *The New Yorker* 52 (January 10): 52–54.

Weiss, Anita M., ed. 1987. *Islamic Reassertion in Pakistan: The Application of Islamic Laws in a Modern State.* Lahore, Pakistan: Vanguard.

————. 1992. *Walls Within Walls: Life Histories of Working Women in the Old City of Lahore.* Boulder, Co.: Westview.

————. 1994. "The Consequences of State Policies for Women in Pakistan." In *The Politics of Social Transformation in Afghanistan, Iran, and Pakistan,* edited by M. Weiner and A. Banuazizi, 412–44. Syracuse, N.Y.: Syracuse Univ. Press.

————. 1995. "Women's Action Forum." In *The Oxford Encyclopedia of the Modern Islamic World,* edited by John L. Esposito, 4:346–48. Oxford: Oxford Univ. Press.

Williams, John A. 1995. "Fitnah." In *The Oxford Encyclopedia of the Modern Islamic World,* edited by John L. Esposito, 2:26–28. New York: Oxford Univ. Press.

Williams, L. 1999. *Wives, Mistresses, and Matriarchs: Asian Women Today.* New York: Rowman and Littlefield.

Wolf, Margery. 1990. *A Thrice Told Tale: Feminism, Postmodernism, and Ethnographic Responsibility.* Stanford, Calif.: Stanford Univ. Press.

Wolpert, Stanley. 1993 *Zulfi Bhutto of Pakistan: His Life and Times.* New York: Oxford Univ. Press.

Women's Rights in Muslim Family Law in Pakistan: 45 Years of Recommendations vs. the FSC Judgement. 2000. Special Bulletin no. 29. Lahore, Pakistan: Shirkat Gah, February.

Yule, Henry, and A. C. Burnell. 1989. *Hobson-Jobson: A Glossary of Colloquial Anglo-Indian Words and Phrases, and of Kindred Terms, Etymological, Historical, Geographical, and Discursive.* 1886. New edition by William Crooke. Calcutta: Rupa and Co.

Yusuf, Zohra. 1992a. "A Rising Graph?" *Herald Annual* (Karachi) (January): 47–48.

————. 1992b. "Unsung Warriors." *Herald Annual* (Karachi) (January): 49.

Zafar, Fareeha, ed. 1991. *Finding Our Way: Reading on Women in Pakistan.* Lahore, Pakistan: ASR.

Zaidi, Farhanaz. 1994. "The Working Women's Dilemma." *Newsline* (January): 28–45.

Zia, Afiya Shehrbano. 1994. *Sex Crime in the Islamic Context: Rape, Class, and Gender in Pakistan.* Lahore, Pakistan: ASR.

Zonis, Marvin. 1991. "Autobiography and Biography in the Middle East: A Plea for Psychological Studies." In *Middle Eastern Lives: The Practice of Biography and Self-Narrative,* edited by Martin Kramer, 61–88. Syracuse, N.Y.: Syracuse Univ. Press.

Index